Lecture Notes in Computer Science

Lecture Notes in Artificial Intelligence 15922

Founding Editor

Jörg Siekmann

Series Editors

Randy Goebel, *University of Alberta, Edmonton, Canada*
Wolfgang Wahlster, *DFKI, Berlin, Germany*
Zhi-Hua Zhou, *Nanjing University, Nanjing, China*

The series Lecture Notes in Artificial Intelligence (LNAI) was established in 1988 as a topical subseries of LNCS devoted to artificial intelligence.

The series publishes state-of-the-art research results at a high level. As with the LNCS mother series, the mission of the series is to serve the international R & D community by providing an invaluable service, mainly focused on the publication of conference and workshop proceedings and postproceedings.

Tianqing Zhu · Wanlei Zhou · Congcong Zhu
Editors

Knowledge Science, Engineering and Management

18th International Conference, KSEM 2025
Macao, China, August 4–7, 2025
Proceedings, Part IV

Springer

Editors
Tianqing Zhu (iD)
City University of Macau
Macau, China

Wanlei Zhou (iD)
City University of Macau
Macau, China

Congcong Zhu (iD)
City University of Macau
Macau, China

ISSN 0302-9743   ISSN 1611-3349 (electronic)
Lecture Notes in Artificial Intelligence
ISBN 978-981-95-3057-1   ISBN 978-981-95-3058-8 (eBook)
https://doi.org/10.1007/978-981-95-3058-8

LNCS Sublibrary: SL7 – Artificial Intelligence

This Springer imprint is published by the registered company Springer Nature Singapore Pte Ltd.
The registered company address is: 152 Beach Road, #21-01/04 Gateway East, Singapore 189721, Singapore

If disposing of this product, please recycle the paper.

Preface

On behalf of the Conference Committee, we are pleased to present the proceedings of the 18th International Conference on Knowledge Science, Engineering and Management (**KSEM 2025**), held at the Wynn Palace, Macau Special Administrative Region, China, from August 4–7, 2025. KSEM 2025 was the eighteenth event in this well-established series of conferences, founded by Academician Ruqian Lu, which is recognized as a premier international forum for the exchange of research in artificial intelligence, data science, knowledge engineering, AI safety, large language models, and related frontier areas. Over the years, KSEM has provided an important venue for disseminating both theoretical advances and practical innovations, fostering interdisciplinary collaboration between academia and industry.

This year, KSEM 2025 received 354 submissions from authors around the world. Following a rigorous single-blind peer-review process, with an average of 2.82 reviews received per submission, involving 342 Program Committee members and external reviewers, 106 regular papers, 66 short papers, and 16 workshop papers were accepted for inclusion in these proceedings and will be submitted for EI indexing. In addition to the contributed papers, the program featured keynote lectures by distinguished scholars, as well as workshops and tutorials on emerging research topics, offering valuable opportunities for academic exchange and collaboration.

Among the accepted papers, the following were selected for the **Best Paper Awards**:

- *Masked Aggregation Learning for Enhancing Distributed Gradient Boosting Decision Trees* Yuting Zha, Chao Lin, Xinyi Huang, and Dugang Liu
- *Label Inference Attacks against Federated Unlearning* Wei Wang, Xiangyun Tang, Yajie Wang, Yijing Lin, Tao Zhang, Meng Shen, Dusit Niyato, and Liehuang Zhu

The **Best Student Paper Awards** went to:

- *LVLM-FDA: Protecting Large Vision-language Models via Fast Detection of Malicious Attempts* Boxu Chen, Chaoyi Wang, Le Yang, Ziwei Zheng, Cong Wang, Qian Wang, and Chao Shen
- *FATFI: A Framework to Generate Adversarial Traffic with Feature Interpretability* Yikang Wang, Weina Niu, Dujuan Gu, Qingjun Yuan, Jiacheng Gong, Shuangqi Gan, Xin Lin, and Xiaosong Zhang

We would like to express our sincere gratitude to all authors for their valuable contributions, and to the Program Committee members and reviewers for their professional and timely evaluations. We also warmly thank all the volunteers who supported the conference at various stages.

We further extend our appreciation to the following chairs for their invaluable contributions:

- **General Chairs:** Wanlei Zhou, Zhi Jin, Aniello Castiglione
- **Program Chairs:** Tianqing Zhu, Gang Li, Congcong Zhu, Lucia Cimmino

- **Local Chairs:** Wenjian Liu, Minghao Wang, Huajie Chen
- **Publication Chairs:** Lefeng Zhang, Youyang Qu
- **Workshop Chairs:** Jia Gu, Bo Liu, Chi Liu
- **Publicity Chairs:** Yu Huang, Minfeng Qi

We were so honored to have many renowned scholars be part of this conference. Finally, we would like to thank all speakers, authors, and participants for their great contribution to and support for the success of KSEM 2025.

August 2025

Tianqing Zhu
Wanlei Zhou
Congcong Zhu

Committees

General Chairs

Wanlei Zhou   City University of Macau, China
Zhi Jin   Peking University, China
Aniello Castiglione   University of Salerno, Italy

Program Chairs

Tianqing Zhu   City University of Macau, China
Gang Li   Deakin University, Australia
Congcong Zhu   City University of Macau, China
Lucia Cimmino   University of Salerno, Italy

Local Chairs

Wenjian Liu   City University of Macau, China
Minghao Wang   City University of Macau, China
Huajie Chen   City University of Macau, China

Publication Chairs

Lefeng Zhang   City University of Macau, China
Youyang Qu   Shandong Computer Science Center, China

Workshop Chairs

Jia Gu   City University of Macau, China
Bo Liu   University of Technology Sydney, Australia
Chi Liu   City University of Macau, China

Publicity Chairs

Yu Huang	Peking University, China
Minfeng Qi	City University of Macau, China

Contents – Part IV

INDRE: An Interpretable News Driven Risk Evaluation Model 1
Weihong Wang, Zuhao Jin, and Cheng Zhao

Efficient Transductive Few-Shot Learning with Active Learning
for Imbalanced Data 15
Yujun Li and Lei Yu

Parallel FHE-Based Neural Network Inference with Knowledge
Distillation for Efficient Privacy-Preserving Image Classification 28
*Dian Jiao, Junyu Lin, Jiageng Chen, Jichao Xiong, Weizhi Meng,
and Chunhua Su*

MatSciES: Automated Knowledge Extraction and Summarization
from Materials Science Literature with Large Language Models 40
*Jialin Xu, Jinguo You, Chuhan Zhang, Huaze Huang, Jingmei Tao,
and Jianhong Yi*

A Robust Video Steganography Method Based on Multi-scale
Decomposition and Invertible Networks 52
*Shiwei Li, Jianxiang Liao, Zhenyu Liu, Mengyuan Wei, Yuhang Wang,
and Jian Liu*

IR-SDTNet: An Infrared Small Target Detection Network Based
on Denoising Enhancement 65
Mengdi Sun, Xiao Yu, Linyi Hou, Huanhuan Li, and Xiaoyu Li

Blockchain-Enhanced Copyright Protection for Fashion Industry:
A DBAE-Net Based and Traceable Image Similarity Ranking Scheme 77
Zheng Dong, Huijie Yang, Jingang Li, and Jian Shen

Mixture of Experts Enhanced Heterogeneous Graph Transformer 92
Qiheng Mao and Jianling Sun

CertBA: A Decentralized Authentication Scheme via Blockchain
and Dynamic Cryptographic Accumulator 104
Huiying Zhang, Wenmao Liu, Wei Ren, and Xianchao Zhang

Adaptive Capsule Graph Neural Network with Attention Mechanism
for Parathyroid Glands Detection 116
  Wanling Liu, Wenhuan Lu, Fei Chen, Jianping Cai, Bo Wang,
  and Wenxin Zhao

HGC: A Hybrid Method Combining Gravity Model and Cycle Structure
for Identifying Influential Spreaders in Complex Networks 129
  Jiaxun Li, Yonghou He, Zhefan Dong, and Li Tao

Code Refactoring with ChatGPT: Analysis Based on Real and Synthetic
Extract Method Opportunities 138
  Ally S. Nyamawe and Estomii Edward

A Robust Data Watermarking Method Based on Secret Sharing and GAN
for Digital Elevation Model 150
  Jinge Ma, Jia Duan, Xi Liu, Xianghan Zheng, and Wei Ren

MOAT: A Multi-objective Approach to Federated IoT Botnet Detection 163
  Yangzong Zhang, Wenjian Liu, Bin Shi, and Tianqing Zhu

In-Context Contrastive Learning for Temporal Knowledge Graph
Reasoning 174
  Xingyi Li, Jiapeng Wang, Boyuan Jia, Yiheng Lyu, Xiang Cheng,
  and Sen Su

Emotion-Aware Knowledge Tracing: Enhancing Student Performance
Prediction with Multi-Head Emotional Attention and Dynamic Gating 186
  Lijing Tong, Xingjian Xu, Fanjun Meng, and Yan Gou

Mask-Guided Visual Text Transformer for Radiology Reports
Representation Learning 195
  Jiazheng Sun and Xiaoyan Cai

MCIGLE: Multimodal Exemplar-Free Class-Incremental Graph Learning 209
  Haochen You and Baojing Liu

MTCA-ViT: Multi-Modal Temporal Contrastive Vision Transformer
for Depression Detection 218
  Liangguo Wang, Yuxuan Wu, Jiaqian Wu, and Eziz Tursun

SGCoT: Self-generating Chain-Of-Thought for Discipline Classification 226
  Peng Yu, Faren Yan, and Xin Chen

Learning Interaction-Aware and Neighborhood Semantic-Enhanced
Embedding for Link Prediction 238
   Zhen Ren, Fei Pu, Siyuan Wang, Bailin Yang, and Lirong Cheng

PromptPilot: Autonomous Prompt Optimization via Genetic Particle
Filtering and Dynamic Exploration 248
   Jie Wang and Jiaye Wang

A Unified Computation Framework of Lattices in Hierarchical Data
Analysis 260
   Wen Shang, Jingwen Xu, Jinguo You, Kang Wu, Xingrui Huang,
   and Jialin Xu

Generating Event-Oriented Attribution for Movies via Two-Stage
Prefix-Enhanced Multimodal LLM 269
   Yuanjie Lyu, Tong Xu, Zihan Niu, Bo Peng, and Jing Ke

Multi-scale Masked Transformer for Robust Point Cloud Registration 278
   Taihao Zhang, Longxiang Gao, Youyang Qu, Zonghao Ji, and Rong Liu

Expert Data - Assisted Diagnosis: An INFO - iTransformer - XGBoost
Combined Discriminative System for Prenatal Diagnosis of Fetal
Congenital Heart Disease 291
   Runze Liu, Yingying Zhang, Hao Sheng, Jingyi Wang, Xiaoyan Gu,
   Jiancheng Han, Da Yang, Xuefei Huang, Yihua He, and Haogang Zhu

Temporal Knowledge Graph Reasoning Based on Historical Statistical
Reward Mechanism 299
   Changlong Wang, Jianlong Cao, Yaoyao Hu, Xiaopan Cao,
   Wenzheng Guo, Jie Hu, Yawei Li, and Yi Liu

Optimized DFA-Based URL Filtering for P4 Programmable Switches 308
   Hongfei Zhang, Jie Li, Yike Zhao, Shu Li, Zhongyi Zhang, Kedong Liu,
   and Qingyun Liu

Improving Mongolian-Chinese Translation Quality Using Noise-Enhanced
mBART 317
   Bailun Wang, Yatu Ji, and Nier Wu

RMNS: Robust Hyper-relational Link Prediction Model Based
on Multi-level Negative Sampling 325
   Xikai Ke, Fang Liu, Zhehao Hou, Min Jiang, Weike Xia, Tongliang Li,
   Hezhong Jiang, and Wei Hu

HG-GIN: Double Layer Attention Graph Isomorphism Network Based
on Hybrid Neighborhood 334
  Jiahao Gu, Fang Liu, Min Jiang, Jingyong Du, Weike Xia, Tongliang Li,
  Hezhong Jiang, and Wei Hu

Matching Ancient Dunhuang Manuscripts Based on Multi-dimensional
Feature Fusion 342
  Yanping Xiang, Jiaqi Dai, Mingkun Chen, Teer Song, Yutong Zheng,
  and Xuan Liu

NexaFusion: Integrating Multi-team Collaboration for High-Impact
Outcomes 354
  Lele Shen, Minghao Yu, Yulong Fan, Jie Ma, Han Wang, and Hui Wang

Comprehensive Evaluation of Large Language Model Responses:
A Multi-factor Scoring System 362
  Yiming Gai, Junde Lu, Xuefei Huang, and Ying Li

Service Area Vehicle Flow Prediction Model for Highway Service Areas
Based on Gravity Model Quadratic Assignment 373
  Feng Xu, Lai Meng, Yichu Dai, Zhengdong Fei, Canghong Jin,
  and Lina Wei

Multi-agent Collaborative Framework with Few-Shot CoT for Threat
Detection 384
  Tianxiang Xu, Chang Liu, Zihao Wang, and Kangsheng Wang

CombDE: Direct-Distillation Combined with Self-distillation
for Knowledge Graph Embeddings 393
  Yusi Chen, Hongtao Zhou, and Housheng Su

Rethinking Lightweight and Efficient Human Pose Estimation with Star
Operation Reconstruction 403
  Zhoujie Xu, Meng Dai, Qing Zhang, and Huawen Liu

Comparing Large Language Model-Based Prompt Engineering Strategies
with Feature Engineering Strategies for Complex Word Identification 415
  Tonghui Han, Yaxin Bi, Maurice Mulvenna, Xiaolu Liu, Zixian Meng,
  and Dongqiang Yang

DARIS: Dynamic Adaptive Refinement of Interaction Sequence
for Sequential Recommendation 424
  Wenxu Zhao, Yuheng Wu, Danhui Shi, Yongkang Li, Xingyu Zhu,
  and Xiaona Xia

PolyBERT: Fine-Tuned Poly Encoder BERT-Based Model for Word Sense
Disambiguation 433
    Linhan Xia, Mingzhan Yang, Guohui Yuan, Shengnan Tao, Yujing Qiu,
    Guo Yu, and Kai Lei

FedDYS: Federated Learning Based on Local Regularization Against Data
Heterogeneity 444
    Jiao Xue and Chundong Wang

Author Index 457

INDRE: An Interpretable News Driven Risk Evaluation Model

Weihong Wang, Zuhao Jin, and Cheng Zhao[✉]

College of Computer Science, Zhejiang University of Technology, Hangzhou 310000,
Zhejiang, China
{wwh,zhaoc}@zjut.edu.cn

Abstract. Financial news exerts a profound impact on market volatility, particularly during abrupt negative events. However, traditional risk management approaches relying on historical data face significant challenges in real-time analysis, due to the high velocity and unstructured nature of incoming news, as well as the difficulty in promptly identifying relevant information. In addition, they lack the ability to explicitly reveal which parts of the news contribute to risk predictions, limiting their interpretability and usefulness in decision-making. To address these issues, we propose INDRE, a novel framework that integrates real-time financial news with market data for dynamic risk assessment. Leveraging Rhetorical Structure Theory (RST), the model decomposes news texts into Elementary Discourse Units (EDUs) and constructs semantic graphs where EDUs serve as nodes and rhetorical relationships as edges. A Graph Attention Network (GAT) captures fine-grained semantic dependencies among events. Concurrently, a BiLSTM network extracts temporal market features, while a cross-modal attention mechanism fuses textual and market information to predict trends and assess risks. Experimental results confirm the superior performance of INDRE. Furthermore, INDRE enhances interpretability by visualizing the influence of specific EDUs and their semantic roles, making the reasoning behind risk assessments transparent. This study offers methodological advancements for real-time financial risk analysis and demonstrates the practical value of structured text representation in event-driven quantitative investment.

Keywords: Risk management · Event-driven analysis · Graph Attention Network · Rhetorical Structure Theory · Interpretability

1 Introduction

Risk management involves assessing and controlling risks to preserve and grow an investor's wealth. Market volatility and investment risks can significantly affect personal finances, but through effective financial risk management, investors can predict potential losses and better anticipate future conditions. This process helps identify, analyze, and control risks that may cause asset depreciation, thus avoiding significant financial losses. Hence, studying risk management is crucial.

T. Zhu et al. (Eds.): KSEM 2025, LNAI 15922, pp. 1–14, 2026.
https://doi.org/10.1007/978-981-95-3058-8_1

Positive financial news, such as company acquisitions or shareholder dividends, tends to follow predictable patterns and can be anticipated based on previous data. Conversely, negative news, such as pandemics or disasters, often comes suddenly and has widespread market impacts. For example, in 2007, Tetlock [21] constructed a Media Pessimism Index, showing it was negatively correlated with future stock returns. Many studies [1,2,4,6] have confirmed a strong link between negative news and stock price volatility. Companies may also release false positive news to maintain market expectations, while negative news is usually disclosed only when necessary. A notable case is the financial fraud at Zhuangzi Island, where the company inflated profits by 130 million yuan in its 2016 report, only disclosing the loss in the 2017 earnings forecast, severely harming investors. Therefore, understanding the impact of negative news on risk management is important. Most current risk management methods rely on historical data [3,7,9,18,19]. However, with the rapid development of the internet and social media, the speed of information flow has greatly increased, making the impact of news on markets almost instantaneous. Traditional methods require extensive data preprocessing steps, such as manual feature extraction, normalization, and cleaning, which are time-consuming and often not automated. This preprocessing bottleneck makes it difficult for these methods to keep up with the high velocity and continuous flow of real-time financial news. As a result, there are inevitable delays in incorporating new information, leading to failures in timely responding to unpredictable market events. And traditional explainability techniques, such as sentiment analysis, struggle to capture all aspects of the news and its implications. Therefore, creating an accurate, comprehensive, and explainable system for analyzing negative news is a significant technical challenge.

To address these challenges, we propose INDRE, an interpretable news-driven risk evaluation model based on Rhetorical Structure Theory (RST) and Graph Attention Networks (GAT). INDRE represents real-time financial news as semantic units (EDUs) linked by rhetorical relationships, forming a structural graph. This approach captures the impact of negative financial events on stock prices and quantifies their influence. By visualizing EDU weights and their connections, INDRE improves explainability and supports better investment decisions. The main contributions of this work are as follows:

- We propose a method to associate real-time news with stock prices, labeling stock prices for easier information fusion.
- We introduce RST to represent news events between sentence and word levels, using EDUs as nodes and their rhetorical relationships as graph edges, improving model explainability.
- We design a finance risk management model using GAT to analyze relationships in news graphs and predict market trends by integrating market data.

2 Related Work

Event-driven financial risk management is a crucial and proven approach in investment. It focuses on market changes caused by specific events affecting relevant sectors. By analyzing stock price movements around these events, investors can develop trading strategies, gain insights, and make more informed decisions.

In earlier studies, risk forecasting primarily relied on judging news sentiment through keyword statistics. For example, Schumaker [20] developed the AZFinText system, which combined linguistic, financial, and statistical methods to predict discrete stock prices. By applying text representation and machine learning to financial news grouped by industry, they found that industry-based stock categorization yielded the highest predictability, achieving a mean square error of 0.1954, 71.18% accuracy in predicting price direction, and an 8.50% simulated trading return. In recent years, new approaches and advanced technologies have been introduced. In 2023, Wang et al. [22] proposed a general tensor representation and fusion framework that captures multimodal and multitemporal stock market interactions using a tensor robust principal component analysis (TRPCA) model. Ma et al. [17] introduced a hybrid forecasting framework for enterprise financing risk, combining data preprocessing, feature selection, and an improved extreme learning machine model, achieving superior accuracy and robustness in predicting risks for SMEs and A-share enterprises. In 2024, Deng et al. [5] proposed a causal inference-based deep learning model for explainable stock trend prediction, integrating causal graphs from financial news and a novel keyword extraction method (DWF-KST). Liu et al. [13] presented Melody-GCN, a Multiscale Multimodal Dynamic Graph Convolution Network that integrates numerical and textual features, refines temporal information through a multiscale architecture, and captures dynamic spatio-temporal stock relationships.

3 Methodology

3.1 Overview of Model Architecture

The model includes three components: a text feature extractor, a market information module, and a fusion classifier. The text module encodes news semantics, while the market module captures historical trends. Their outputs are combined to predict risk. Figure 1 illustrates the INDRE workflow.

3.2 Real-Time News Event Labeling

To ensure real-time performance driven by financial events, we construct data samples based on financial events. For each financial news event E corresponding to a specific stock at time t the historical stock data from the previous T days is represented as $X_t = (X_{t-T+1}, X_{t-T+2}, \ldots, X_t) \in \mathbb{R}^{T \times F^1}$ where F^1 denotes the number of feature dimensions. Additionally, the label y for news event E is determined by the market trend. In this task, for each news event E, we

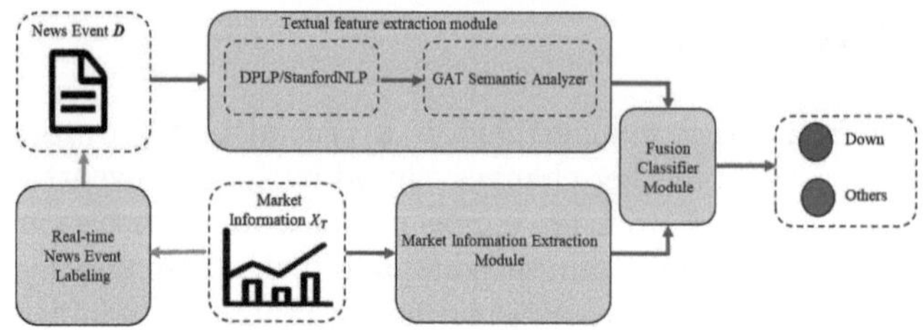

Fig. 1. The Architecture Overview Of INDRE

compute the target stock price change P_t after the event occurs. The calculation is as follows:

$$P_t = \frac{X_t - X_{t-1}}{X_t},\qquad(1)$$

$$y = \begin{cases} 0, & P_t \geq \tau \\ 1, & P_t < \tau \end{cases},\qquad(2)$$

where τ is the threshold used to exclude the influence of irrelevant news event. In this paper, τ is set to -0.035, and news associated with price changes below this threshold is discarded. Our objective is to predict market trends following news events, with a particular focus on negative news.

3.3   Text Feature Extraction Module

The text feature extraction module extracts key event details from news by dividing text into EDUs and analyzing their rhetorical relationships. It uses a news text encoder and a GAT-based semantic analyzer, which represents EDUs as word embeddings and aggregates them through GAT to generate meta-knowledge.

News Text Encoder. News is divided into $E = (w_1, w_2, \ldots, w_N) \in \mathbb{R}^N$ by the Stanford CoreNLP tokenization tool, where N is the total number of words in the text, and w_i represents the $i-th$ word. Unlike previous studies, we apply rhetorical theory to structurally represent text, using EDUs as the basic unit. To make the text segmentation more reasonaly, we employ the $DPLP$ [10] model. Then, we obtain news $U = (EDU_1, EDU_2, \ldots, EDU_n) \in \mathbb{R}^{n \times S}$ in the form of EDU and their relationship r.

$$R = \{(EDU_i, EDU_j, r) | EDU \in U, r \in \epsilon\},\qquad(3)$$

where n is the number of EDUs, S is the max division length and ϵ is the set of rhetorical relations. A total of 19 rhetorical relationships [23] are used to explain the text structure. To improve efficiency and robustness, we merge rare and similar relationships, retaining only 10 types in this paper.

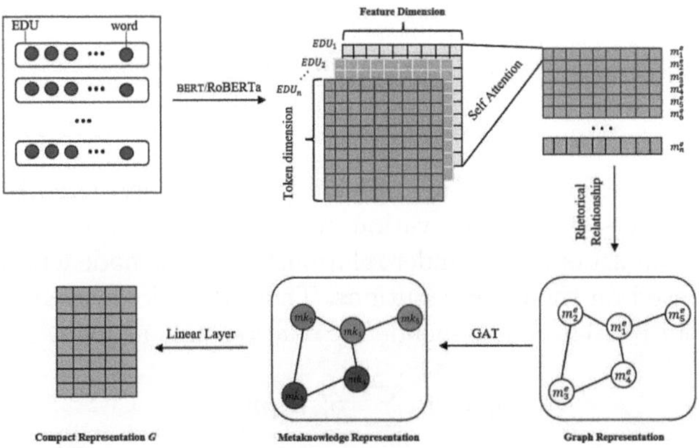

Fig. 2. GAT Semantic Analyzer

GAT Semantic Analyzer. In order to better utilize the relationship between EDU and rhetoric, we use graph neural networks to learn intrinsic information. Figure 2 illustrates the framework of GAT semantic analyzer. To handle tokens, we first transfer words to word embedding, i.e.,

$$m_{ij} = BERT(w_{ij}), \tag{4}$$

here, $m_{ij} \in \mathbb{R}^{F_2}$ represents the word encoding of the $j-th$ word in $j-th$ EDU, where F_2 is the feature dimension. The self-attentive span extractor [12] is used to learning the textual features m_i^e of $i-th$ EDU. The calculation is as follows:

$$\alpha_{ij} = W_2 \cdot Relu(W_1 m_{ij} + b_1) + b_2, \tag{5}$$

$$a_{ij} = \frac{exp(\alpha_{ij})}{\sum_{k=1}^{\phi_i} exp(\alpha_{ik})}, \tag{6}$$

$$m_i^e = \sum_{k=1}^{\phi_i} a_{ij} \cdot m_{ij}, \tag{7}$$

here, α_{ij} is the attention score for the i-th EDU at the j-th token, and W_1, W_2, b_1, and b_2 are learnable parameters. The EDUs are then represented as $G = \{m_1^e, m_2^e, \ldots, m_n^e\} \in \mathbb{R}^{n \times F_2}$. Finally, we treat EDUs as nodes and rhetorical relationships as edges to construct a graph representing the news event.

After converting the news event into a graph, we apply GAT for graph learning. GAT assigns weights to different relationships and aggregates node information via an attention mechanism. It consists of multiple Graph Attention Layers, where the attention score β_{ij}^r between node pair (i, j) under relation r is computed as follows:

$$\beta_{ij}^{r} = \frac{exp(\sigma(Q[W_3 m_i^e || W_3 m_j^e]))}{\sum_{k \in \mathcal{N}_i^r} exp(\sigma(Q[W_3 m_i^e || W_3 m_j^e]))}, \tag{8}$$

where $m_i^e \in \mathbb{R}^{F_2}$ is the input feature of node i in this layer, Q and W_3 are shared learnable parameters, σ is the activation function, $||$ denotes concatenation, and $\mathcal{N}_i^r$ is the neighbor set of node i under relationship r. The node features $h_i^r \in \mathbb{R}^{F_2}$ are updated based on these contributions. Then, meta-knowledge $mk_i \in \mathbb{R}^{F_3}$ is aggregated from related node dependency relationships as follows:

$$h_i^r = \sigma(\sum_{j \in \mathcal{N}_i^r} \beta_{ij}^r W_4 m_j^e), \tag{9}$$

$$mk_i = W_5 \cdot \sum_r W_r h_i^r + b_3, \tag{10}$$

where W_4, W_5, W_r and b_3 are the learnable parameters. Then, We obtain the compact representation G of news text D:

$$G = (mk_1, mk_2, \ldots, mk_n) \in \mathbb{R}^{n \times F_4}. \tag{11}$$

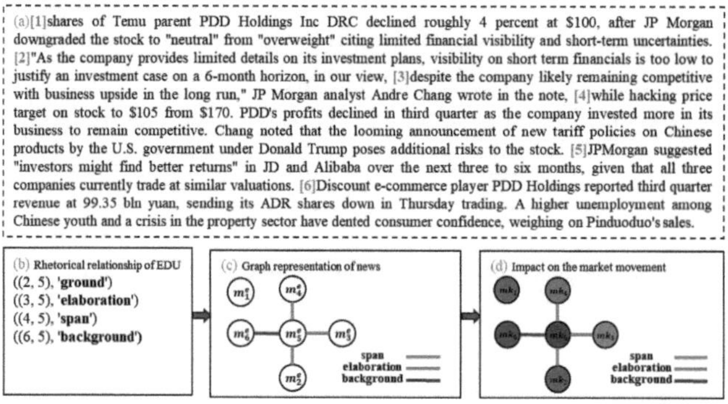
(a)[1]shares of Temu parent PDD Holdings Inc DRC declined roughly 4 percent at $100, after JP Morgan downgraded the stock to "neutral" from "overweight" citing limited financial visibility and short-term uncertainties. [2]"As the company provides limited details on its investment plans, visibility on short term financials is too low to justify an investment case on a 6-month horizon, in our view, [3]despite the company likely remaining competitive with business upside in the long run," JP Morgan analyst Andre Chang wrote in the note, [4]while hacking price target on stock to $105 from $170. PDD's profits declined in third quarter as the company invested more in its business to remain competitive. Chang noted that the looming announcement of new tariff policies on Chinese products by the U.S. government under Donald Trump poses additional risks to the stock. [5]JPMorgan suggested "investors might find better returns" in JD and Alibaba over the next three to six months, given that all three companies currently trade at similar valuations. [6]Discount e-commerce player PDD Holdings reported third quarter revenue at 99.35 bln yuan, sending its ADR shares down in Thursday trading. A higher unemployment among Chinese youth and a crisis in the property sector have dented consumer confidence, weighing on Pinduoduo's sales.
(b) Rhetorical relationship of EDU
((2, 5), 'ground')
((3, 5), 'elaboration')
((4, 5), 'span')
((6, 5), 'background')
(c) Graph representation of news
span
elaboration
background
(d) Impact on the market movement
span
elaboration
background

Fig. 3. The Process Of News Text Analysis

Notably, during this process, the model implicitly learns the influence of each EDU on the prediction results, providing a clear demonstration of interpretability. Figure 3 shows how a news event is transformed into a graph structure and how its components contribute to the outcome.

3.4 Market Information Extraction Module

The market information module captures historical trends as a supplement to news data. Technical indicators X_t are fed into a BiLSTM to extract features, producing a market representation $H \in \mathbb{R}^{F_4}$ as follows:

$$\overleftarrow{h} = \overleftarrow{LSTM}(X_t), \tag{12}$$

$$\overrightarrow{h} = \overrightarrow{LSTM}(X_t), \tag{13}$$

$$H = W_6[\overleftarrow{h} || \overrightarrow{h}] + b_4, \tag{14}$$

where $\overrightarrow{h}, \overleftarrow{h} \in \mathbb{R}^{F_3}$ is the forward and backward final step of BiLSTM model output respectively.

3.5 Fusion Classifier Module

From the text and digital features, we obtain the respective representations G and H. In order to obtain the connection between market information and news, we apply dot-product attention to G and H. The fusion representation F is calculate as follows:

$$F = softmax(\frac{GH^T}{\sqrt{F_4}})H, \tag{15}$$

through the above procedures, we ensure that the extracted features complement each other. We then utilize a MLP layer to predict market movements. Finally, the optimization and training process is guided by the following loss function:

$$L = -\sum_{i=1}^{K} y_i \log \hat{y}_i + (1 - y_i) \log(1 - \hat{y}_i), \tag{16}$$

where K is the size of training set, y_i is the true label of the $i - th$ sample, and $\hat{y}_i$ is the predicted probability.

4 Experiments

4.1 Datasets and Experiment Settings

We select stocks from the Nasdaq-100 index along with their corresponding news articles, covering the period from February 2022 to August 2023. To specifically study the impact of negative news, we filter the data, resulting in a final dataset of 8,762 entries.

In our implementation, we preprocess the news text by segmenting it into EDUs, with a maximum EDU length of 200. During training, we directly use EDUs as input data. We set the batch size to 16, the learning rate to 10^{-3}, and the dropout rate to 0.2. The Adam optimizer is employed for parameter optimization, and the model is trained for 10 epochs.

4.2   Evaluation Metrics

In this study, we select accuracy, precision, recall, F1 score, and Matthews Correlation Coefficient (MCC) as evaluation metrics. Here, to demonstrate the predictive ability of the model on negative news, stock price down is considered a positive label. These metrics are chosen to provide a comprehensive assessment of the model's performance, especially under class imbalance common in financial prediction tasks.

4.3   Baseline Model

To evaluate the effectiveness of the model, we compare it with the following state-of-the-art models on the aforementioned parameters as baselines:

VGC-GAN [16]: Predicting Stock Prices Using Generative Adversarial Networks as a Framework Combined with Variational Mode Decomposition.
SA-TrellisNet [14]: Integrating stock data and extracted news polarity with TrellisNet to predict market trends.
MagicNET [15]: Combining real-time updated news text representation with stock prices to apply Causal Interaction Graph to learn features and predict market trends.
FinBERT [11]: Using the FinBERT large language model for sentiment analysis of financial news data, and employing an LSTM-based model to predict financial market trends.
INDRE-TF: Using only the text feature extraction module to predict market trends.
INDRE-MI: Using only the market information extraction module to predict market trends.
INDRE-SC: Using a simple concatenation classification module instead of the fusion classification module.

Table 1. Comparison of accuracy between our method and other models

Models	Accuracy	Precision	Recall	F1	MCC
VGC-GAN	0.571	0.572	0.756	0.651	0.130
SA-TrellisNet	0.579	0.582	0.761	0.659	0.143
MagicNET	**0.661**	**0.710**	0.784	**0.745**	**0.243**
FinBERT	0.643	0.681	0.782	0.727	0.223
INDRE-TF	0.656	0.701	**0.785**	0.740	0.241
INDRE-MI	0.590	0.591	0.770	0.668	0.165
INDRE	**0.733**	**0.790**	**0.821**	**0.805**	**0.381**

5   Results and Discussions

5.1   Accuracy Analysis

Table 1 shows that our model outperforms all baselines across metrics, especially in precision. VGC-GAN and SA-TrellisNet perform worst—one relies solely on price data, the other on sentence-level sentiment. FinBERT performs better by leveraging pre-trained semantics, and MagicNET benefits from real-time updates.

INDRE integrates the strengths of these models while further improving text representation through RST. By using EDUs as semantic units and GAT to learn relationships between them, INDRE achieves more accurate predictions, especially for negative news, highlighting the advantages of graph-based over sentiment-based approaches.

Compared with INDRE-MI, the textual module significantly boosts performance. Against INDRE-GCN and INDRE-GAN, the GAT module proves more effective at capturing fine-grained graph features among EDUs.

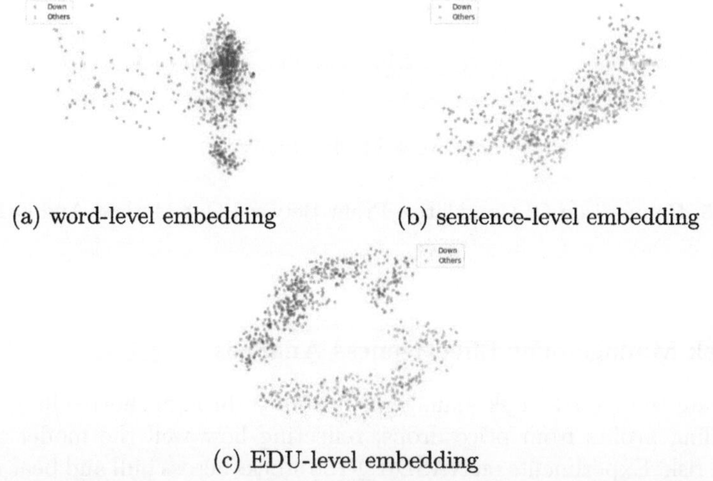

(a) word-level embedding   (b) sentence-level embedding

(c) EDU-level embedding

Fig. 4. visualization of text embedding on different granularities

5.2   Text Embedding Analysis

To demonstrate the performance advantages of EDU-level embeddings in financial news text, we visualize embeddings at different granularities, including word-level, sentence-level, and EDU-level. For embeddings at different granularities, we apply max-pooling and dimensionality reduction using UMAP, followed by classification based on labels, as shown in Fig. 4.

Upon observation, it is evident that word-level embeddings almost completely overlap, showing no distinguishable boundaries. Sentence-level embeddings, while showing some separation, lack clear boundaries between different categories and fail to precisely represent the text's semantics. In contrast, EDU-level embeddings clearly reveal boundaries between different categories. This result demonstrates that EDU-level embeddings are more effective in preserving the semantic quality of the text and enhancing embedding performance.

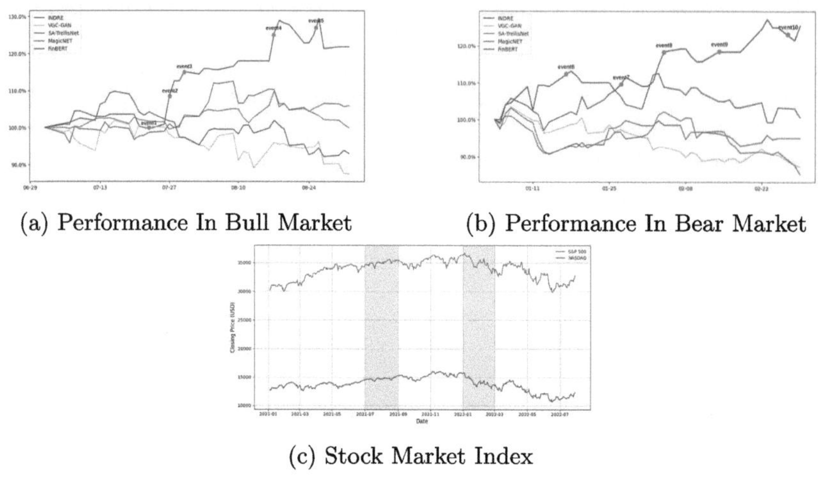

(a) Performance In Bull Market   (b) Performance In Bear Market

(c) Stock Market Index

Fig. 5. Comparison Of Cumulative Profit Between Our Method And Others

5.3   Risk Management Effectiveness Analysis

We evaluate the model's risk management ability through short-selling returns. Short selling profits from price drops, reflecting how well the model captures downside risk. Experiments on NASDAQ-100 stocks across bull and bear markets select the top two stocks with the highest predicted decline probability. If no stock exceeds 60%, no short is taken. Positions are opened at market open and closed the next day, excluding borrowing costs.

Figure 5(c) uses the S&P 500 and NASDQ Index as a benchmark to illustrate this macroeconomic backdrop. Figure 5(a) and Fig. 5(b) present the experimental results. The specific content of the news events mentioned in the figure can be found in Appendix. INDRE consistently achieved stable and positive returns throughout both bull and bear markets, outperforming all baseline models. And several representative news events are selected for analysis, such as event1, event2, event6, etc., which correctly predicted market trends based on news events. Prediction errors such as Event 10, Russia's invasion of Ukraine, and war generally lead to market panic, but due to Russia being a major energy exporting country causing energy shortages, related energy companies' stocks have actually risen, due to limited data.

Overall, INDRE effectively identified market trends, achieving cumulative returns exceeding 21% in both bear and bull markets. By strategically managing risk through short-selling overvalued stocks, borrowing, selling at high prices, and repurchasing at lower prices, the model demonstrates its ability to manage risks in complex market condition.

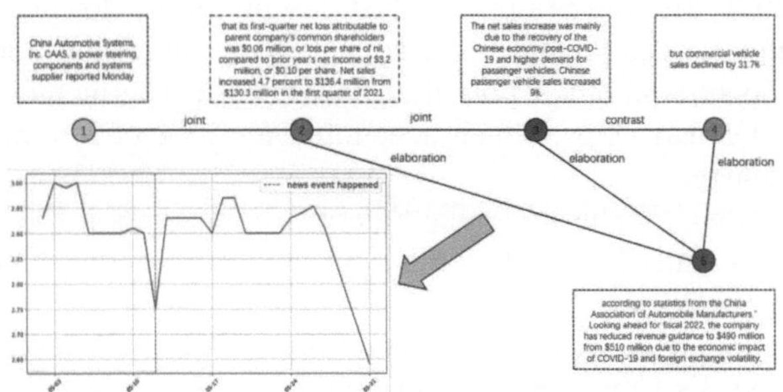

Fig. 6. Interpretable analysis of news events

5.4   Interpretability Analysis

To demonstrate INDRE's effectiveness, we analyze a news article about CAAS's 2021 revenue and 2022 expectations and their impact on stock prices. As shown in Fig. 6, the article is divided into five EDUs, with circle shading indicating relative weight. EDU_3 and EDU_5 have the greatest influence, while EDU_1 has little impact. EDU_3 and EDU_4 provide background: a recovering Chinese economy and rising passenger vehicle demand (positive), but declining commercial vehicle sales (negative). EDU_5 notes the company's lowered profit forecast. Considering this, INDRE predicts a stock price drop, which occurred 4.84% decline in closing price. This shows INDRE helps investors by analyzing EDU relationships and offering interpretable, visually structured news graphs.

6   Conclusion

This paper presents a novel event-driven model that predicts market trends and mitigates risks by representing news text as graphs and integrating historical market data. By labeling price fluctuations as targets, it enables real-time analysis and offers explainability through visualizing relational weights. Extensive experiments demonstrate superior performance over existing methods. Future work will focus on real-world testing and model refinement for practical use.

Appendix

News List

1. MicroStrategy announced its Q2 2021 financial results, reporting a revenue of $125.35 million, a 13.4% year-over-year increase. However, the company also reported a net loss of $299.3 million, primarily due to the impairment loss on digital assets.
2. Microsoft's cloud computing service Azure outage
3. In August 2021, Morgan Stanley analyst Joseph Moore downgraded Micron's stock to "equal weight" and reduced his price target by $30 to $75. He expressed concerns about a potential downturn in the memory chip sector, particularly DRAM chips, which accounted for 73% of Micron's revenue in the recent quarter.
4. The U.S. National Highway Traffic Safety Administration (NHTSA) opened an investigation into Tesla's Autopilot system after a series of crashes involving emergency vehicles.
5. A critical remote code execution vulnerability (CVE-2021-26084) was discovered in Atlassian's Confluence Server and Data Center products
6. Microsoft announced plans to acquire Activision Blizzard for $69 billion. This move drew attention from regulatory bodies concerned about potential antitrust issues, given Microsoft's substantial presence in the gaming industry
7. PayPal reported mixed fourth-quarter results and issued a weaker-than-expected revenue and profit forecast for 2022. The company cited factors such as higher inflation impacting consumer spending and the ongoing transition of eBay, a former parent company and significant client, to its own payments platform.
8. NVIDIA's planned $40 billion acquisition of Arm was canceled due to regulatory hurdles and opposition from major industry players concerned about competition and Arm's neutrality.
9. Texas Attorney General Ken Paxton sued Facebook for collecting biometric data of users without consent and sharing it with third parties, violating state privacy laws.
10. The invasion of Ukraine by Russia in February 2022 had profound effects on global energy supplies

References

1. Baker, M., Wurgler, J.: Investor sentiment and the cross-section of stock returns. J. Financ. **61**(4), 1645–1680 (2006)
2. Bollen, J., Mao, H., Zeng, X.: Twitter mood predicts the stock market. J. Comput. Sci. **2**(1), 1–8 (2011)
3. Chang, P.C., Fan, C.Y., Liu, C.H.: Integrating a piecewise linear representation method and a neural network model for stock trading points prediction. IEEE Trans. Syst. Man. Cybern. C (Appl. Rev.) **39**(1), 80–92 (2008)

4. Chen, H., De, P., Hu, Y., Hwang, B.H.: Wisdom of crowds: the value of stock opinions transmitted through social media. Rev. Financ. Stud. **27**(5), 1367–1403 (2014)
5. Deng, Y., Liang, Y., Yiu, S.M.: Towards interpretable stock trend prediction through causal inference. Expert Syst. Appl. **238**, 121654 (2024)
6. Engelberg, J.E., Parsons, C.A.: The causal impact of media in financial markets. J. Finance **66**(1), 67–97 (2011)
7. Gao, R., Cui, S., Xiao, H., Fan, W., Zhang, H., Wang, Y.: Integrating the sentiments of multiple news providers for stock market index movement prediction: a deep learning approach based on evidential reasoning rule. Inf. Sci. **615**, 529–556 (2022)
8. Gao, R., Cui, S., Xiao, H., Fan, W., Zhang, H., Wang, Y.: Integrating the sentiments of multiple news providers for stock market index movement prediction: a deep learning approach based on evidential reasoning rule. Inf. Sci. **615**, 529–556 (2022)
9. Hao, P.Y., Kung, C.F., Chang, C.Y., Ou, J.B.: Predicting stock price trends based on financial news articles and using a novel twin support vector machine with fuzzy hyperplane. Appl. Soft Comput. **98**, 106806 (2021)
10. Ji, Y., Eisenstein, J.: Representation learning for text-level discourse parsing. In: Proceedings of the 52nd Annual Meeting of the Association for Computational Linguistics (volume 1: Long Papers), pp. 13–24 (2014)
11. Jiang, T., Zeng, A.: Financial sentiment analysis using FinBERT with application in predicting stock movement. arXiv preprint arXiv:2306.02136 (2023)
12. Lee, K., He, L., Lewis, M., Zettlemoyer, L.: End-to-end neural coreference resolution. arXiv preprint arXiv:1707.07045 (2017)
13. Liu, R., Liu, H., Huang, H., Song, B., Wu, Q.: Multimodal multiscale dynamic graph convolution networks for stock price prediction. Pattern Recogn. **149**, 110211 (2024)
14. Liu, W.J., Ge, Y.B., Gu, Y.C.: News-driven stock market index prediction based on trellis network and sentiment attention mechanism. Expert Syst. Appl. **250**, 123966 (2024)
15. Luo, D., Li, S., Liao, W., Yan, R.: MagicNet: memory-aware graph interactive causal network for multivariate stock price movement prediction. IEEE Trans. Knowl. Data Eng. (2025)
16. Ma, D., Yuan, D., Huang, M., Dong, L.: VGC-GAN: a multi-graph convolution adversarial network for stock price prediction. Expert Syst. Appl. **236**, 121204 (2024)
17. Ma, Z., Wang, X., Hao, Y.: Development and application of a hybrid forecasting framework based on improved extreme learning machine for enterprise financing risk. Expert Syst. Appl. **215**, 119373 (2023)
18. Pagolu, V.S., Reddy, K.N., Panda, G., Majhi, B.: Sentiment analysis of twitter data for predicting stock market movements. In: 2016 International Conference on Signal Processing, Communication, Power and Embedded System (SCOPES), pp. 1345–1350. IEEE (2016)
19. Patel, J., Shah, S., Thakkar, P., Kotecha, K.: Predicting stock and stock price index movement using trend deterministic data preparation and machine learning techniques. Expert Syst. Appl. **42**(1), 259–268 (2015)
20. Schumaker, R.P., Chen, H.: A quantitative stock prediction system based on financial news. Inf. Process. Manage. **45**(5), 571–583 (2009)
21. Tetlock, P.C.: Giving content to investor sentiment: the role of media in the stock market. J. Financ. **62**(3), 1139–1168 (2007)

22. Wang, J., Hu, Y., Jiang, T.X., Tan, J., Li, Q.: Essential tensor learning for multimodal information-driven stock movement prediction. Knowl.-Based Syst. **262**, 110262 (2023)
23. Zhu, Y., Wu, O.: Elementary discourse units with sparse attention for multi-label emotion classification. Knowl.-Based Syst. **240**, 108114 (2022)

Efficient Transductive Few-Shot Learning with Active Learning for Imbalanced Data

Yujun Li and Lei Yu

University of Electronic Science and Technology of China, Chengdu, China
leiyu722@outlook.com

Abstract. Transductive few-shot learning (TFSL) is a promising approach to improve model performance in data scarcity scenarios. But the labeled samples are normally supposed to be uniformly distributed across classes, which is not only non-informative but also unrealistic. We propose an Active Learning-assisted Prototype Rectification method to address the challenges of TFSL by effectively leveraging unlabeled data and enhancing model generalization. Firstly, multi-round active learning based on the Class Distribution Difference criterion is proposed to obtain the representative and boundary-aware samples, resulting in optimal prototype initialization; Secondly, robust prototype rectification via parameter-free Laplacian smoothing enforces manifold-consistent label propagation. Our experiments demonstrate the method achieves state-of-the-art performance within the active TFSL framework while maintaining runtime efficiency close to inductive methods.

Keywords: transductive few-shot learning · active learning · Laplacian smoothing · imbalanced data

1 Introduction

Despite the success of deep learning models in visual recognition, dependence on large labeled datasets limits their applications in data scarcity scenarios, such as diagnosis of rare diseases with few CT images annotated by medical specialists. Few-shot learning (FSL) has emerged as a solution that enables models to generalize effectively to new classes using only a few labeled samples. The mainstream FSL tasks are formulated in an episodic training and testing paradigm under meta-learning protocols, such as ProtoNet [1], RelationNet [2], MatchingNet [3], MAML [4] and so on. Most of these methods primarily target inductive inference, where each unlabeled query sample is inferred individually only with knowledge learning from the labeled support set. Nevertheless, the collect of unlabeled query samples provides more useful information on class distribution than single query. By making predictions on all unlabeled query samples rather than one by one, TFSL [5] shows strong improvements over inductive FSL in classification accuracy, especially in scenarios with extremely limited data. As

T. Zhu et al. (Eds.): KSEM 2025, LNAI 15922, pp. 15–27, 2026.
https://doi.org/10.1007/978-981-95-3058-8_2

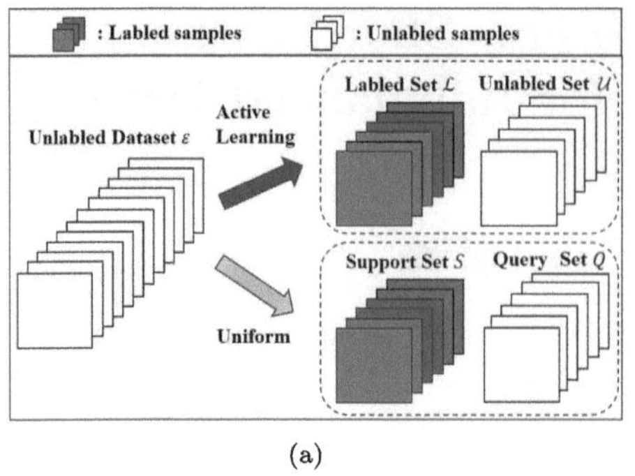

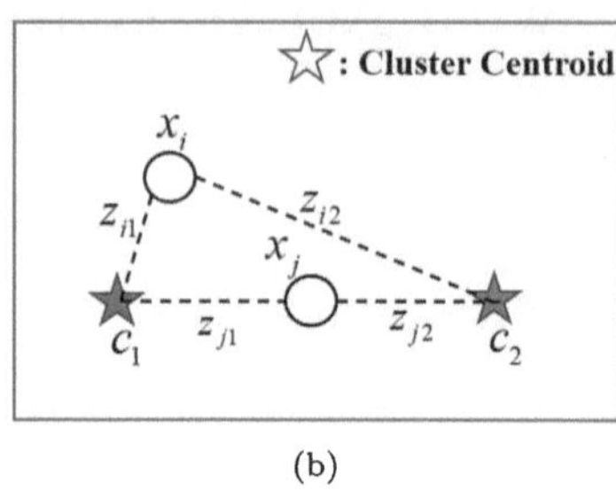

Fig. 1. (a) standard v.s. active TFSL. The active framework selects the most informative samples for labeling based on their CDD values while the standard one labels the support set uniformly. (b) An example of two samples with large(x_i) and small(x_j) CDD values.

illustrated in Fig. 1a, a standard transductive few shot classification [6–9] problem under meta-learning protocol contains a support set S and a query set Q in each episode. Labeled samples in S are uniform distributed (K-shot for each class) across N classes. And all unlabeled samples in Q are utilized to make inference contrary to their inductive counterpart.

Apparently, image samples don't have equal representativeness of a class. With a labeling quota in data scarcity scenarios, it's more efficient to label the most informative samples by active learning [10, 11]. To overcome the limitations of standard TFSL, we propose an Active Learning-assisted Prototype Rectification (ALPR) algorithm for extreme data scarcity and imbalanced classes. Specifically, we propose a multi-round active learning strategy to pick out the most informative unlabeled samples for labeling as the support set, which ensures better prototype initialization and provides more valuable information for prototype rectification. To avoid bias caused by data imbalance and data scarcity, the prototypes and contributions of samples to their prototypes are updated alternatively by imposing Laplacian smoothing on nearby samples analogous to fixed-point iteration, which is parameter-free and computationally efficient. Then we experiment on four commonly used FSL datasets with multiple backbones, achieving competitive performance but as efficient as inductive methods.

2   Related Work

In order to take advantage of deep neural networks and make accurate predictions by learning from very small number of labeled samples, a powerful base model can be trained on large scale dataset, then finetuning classifier layer with limited target task data [5]. Mainstream researches in this field formulate FSL problem in an episodic training and testing way under meta-learning protocol. Each episode contains a support set with limited labeled samples for meta-training and a query set for meta-testing. Inductive FSL approaches learn a model from the support set, and make predictions on each query sample independently. For example, data augmentation methods learn a hallucinator with GANs [12] or VAEs [13] to enlarge the support set. Metric-based methods, such as MatchingNet [3], ProtoNet [1], learn an embedding space or metric where classes in the support set are easily distinguishable. Optimization-based methods learn good initial parameters from support set so that they can be adapted quickly to new task with limited data, such as MAML [4]. Unlike these inductive approaches, our method adopts transductive inference and incorporates active learning to dynamically construct the support set from imbalanced data. With the same learning protocol, transductive methods make predictions on all query samples collectively, where data and class distribution serve as auxiliary information to learn a model from limited support set. Graph-based methods typically build a graph with kernel functions among all samples in support and query set. Then labels would be propagated from labeled samples to the unlabeled ones. EPNet [6] enhances performance by propagating both labels and embeddings, reducing intra-class variance. Since incorrect connections in a once-build static graph affects label propagation a lot. TPN [7] proposes to build the graph dynamically to make sure correct and robust label propagation. Prototype-based methods are more efficient by incorporating query samples to get representative prototypes. PT-MAP [8] uses power transformation to make the feature distribution Gaussian and combines iterative maximum a posteriori estimation based on optimal transmission to optimize the category center. BD-CSPN [9] rectify prototypes by minimizing both inter-class and intra-class variance. TIM [14] maximizes the mutual information between query features and label predictions for a few-shot task, incorporating a supervisory loss on the support set to enhance generalization to new classes. Hybrid methods integrate label propagation and prototype refinement to overcome the limitations inherent in both method. This combination results in a robust framework for TFSL. protoLP [5] utilizes label propagation to identify and update class centroids, enhancing prototype estimation through a prototype-based approach. AM [15] leverages manifold similarities for imbalanced TFSL, optimizing class centroids and manifold parameters. While sharing the prototype refinement paradigm, our prototype rectification distinguishes itself by introducing active sample selection and parameter-free Laplacian smoothing to handle severe class imbalance without complex optimization. Active learning (AL) aims to select the most informative samples to maximize model performance while minimizing annotation costs [16]. It works by uncertainty sampling [17], Query-by-Committee [18], Expected-model-change [19], Variance Reduction [20], Estimated Error Reduction [21] and so on. Active learning has been integrated into TFSL for extremely scarcity data scenarios. LSS [10] uses soft k-means to label high-confident samples and the most uncertain ones to learn a model improving classification accuracy. The S4M framework [11] selects representative samples from unlabeled data to construct a support set through clustering, and combines Gaussian modeling with probability maximization to optimize classification. Our approach advances beyond these methods by proposing a multi-round Class Distribution Difference (CDD)-based selection strategy

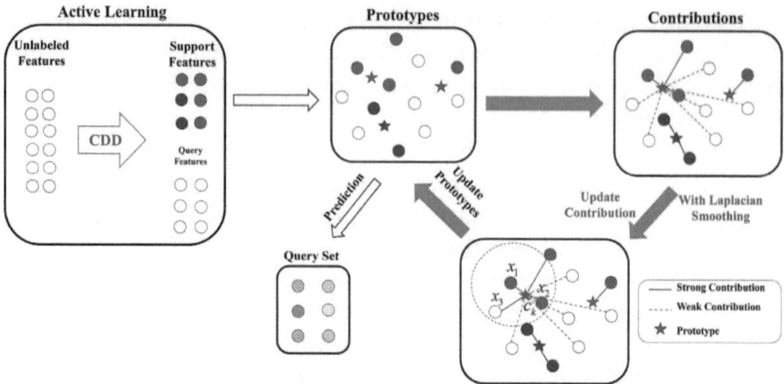

Fig. 2. Pipeline of our method. With unlabeled sample features extracted by pretrained model, multi-round active learning with CDD value is applied to select representative samples for labeling and initial prototypes. Then contributions of samples to their prototypes are updated with laplacian smoothing, before prototypes are rectified.

that adaptively balances representative and boundary-aware sampling, coupled with efficient prototype rectification specifically designed for imbalanced data.

3   Methodology

Following the prototype-refine few shot learning approaches [5,8,9,14], we propose active learning for good initial prototypes, and Laplacian smoothing for parameter-free prototype rectification. The framework is illustrated in Fig. 2.

3.1   Prototype Initialization with Active Learning

In order to pick out the most informative L samples, the unlabeled dataset $\mathcal{E} = \{x_i\}_{i=1}^{L+U}$ is firstly clustered with soft k-means++ [22], which results in more robust prototype initialization than standard soft k-means, and is more computationally efficient in episodic active learning than alternative methods such as spectral clustering. This results in N centroids $\{\mu'_k\}_{k=1}^{N}$ and soft assignments $Z = (z_{ij})_{(L+U)\times N}$, where z_{ij} indicates the probability of the i-th sample belonging to the j-th cluster. Then inspired by the CDD criterion [23], we redefine the CDD value of a sample as: $\text{CDD}(x_i) = z_{i,j_1} - z_{i,j_2}$,

Where z_{i,j_1} and z_{i,j_2} denote the largest two elements in the i-th row of assignment matrix Z. Large z_{ij} means sample x_i belongs to cluster j with high probability. So larger CDD value indicates a sample is more confident in its assignment than others. An example of two samples with different CDD values is illustrated in Fig. 1b. L samples are actively selected for labeling in $r = \lfloor L/N \rfloor$ rounds according to the CDD value in an exclusive way. Specifically, starting from an empty labeled set $\mathcal{L}$, in the first round, we select samples with the highest CDD values from each cluster. This ensures robust initial prototypes by labeling the most representative samples to establish a solid prototype foundation. Subsequent rounds focus on samples with the lowest CDD values. These boundary samples contribute to more effective prototype updates.

$$S_k = \begin{cases} \arg\max_{x_i \in \text{cls}_k} \text{CDD}(x_i), & \text{if } r = 1, \\ \arg\min_{x_i \in \text{cls}_k} \text{CDD}(x_i), & \text{if } r > 1; \end{cases} \quad \mathcal{L} = \mathcal{L} \cup S_k \ (k = 1, 2, \dots, N)$$

Then the remaining unlabeled samples in $\mathcal{E}$ would be our query samples. The labeled samples of each class might be very imbalanced or even not existing caused by the aforementioned active strategy, which is also consistent with real application scenarios. We make another soft k-means on data in this episode with cluster initialized by the labeled class means. The cluster centroids would be our initial prototypes $C^{(0)} = (c_1^{(0)}, c_2^{(0)}, \cdots, c_N^{(0)})$ of each class. Implementation details can be found in Algorithm 1.

3.2 Prototype Rectification with Laplacian Smoothing

Since each image sample doesn't have equal representativeness of a class, it's reasonable to carefully consider the contribution of each sample to its class prototype, especially in imbalanced data cases. We propose to update the prototypes C and contributions W alternatively by incorporating the intrinsic manifold structure of unlabeled data without additional parameter optimization.

Update Contribution. The contribution $W = (w_{ij})_{(L+U) \times N}$ of all samples in this episode is initialized in the following way: the rows for labeled samples are set as one-hot vector, and that for unlabeled samples setting as normalized cosine distance to their prototypes. In order to further mitigate bias caused by uneven class distribution, we propose to update the contribution analogous to fixed point iteration by considering the consistency of nearby samples:

$$W^{(t+1)} = (I - \beta L)W^{(t)} \tag{1}$$

where $L = D - A$ is the Laplacian matrix. A is adjacent matrix of all samples in this episode, with $A_{ij} = 1$ if sample x_j being in the B-nearest neighborhood of sample x_i(excluding itself), and $A_{ij} = 0$ otherwise. The diagonal matrix D with $D_{ii} = \sum_{j=1}^{L+U} A_{ij}$ is degree matrix. β is learning rate. By iteratively removing the sharp difference among nearby samples' contribution to their prototypes, the graph-based smoothing naturally adapts to local density variations, making it effective even under class imbalance.

Update Prototypes. The prototypes are firstly updated by considering the contributions of each sample: $c_k^{(t)} = \frac{\sum_{i=1}^{L+U} w_{ik}^{(t)} x_i}{\sum_{i=1}^{L+U} w_{ik}^{(t)}}$, then refined stably by:

$$C^{(t)} = (1 - \alpha)C^{(t-1)} + \alpha W^{(t)T} X, \tag{2}$$

where α controls the adaptation speed. Prototypes are updated to better represent their associated samples. This process minimizes intra-class variance and

---

Algorithm 1. Active Learning-assisted Prototype Rectificatio

Require: A task dataset $\mathcal{E} = \{x_i\}_{i=1}^{L+U}$, number of active learning rounds R, number of prototype rectification iterations T, hyperparameters: B, λ, α, β.

Ensure: Predicted labels $\tilde{\mathbf{y}} = \{\tilde{y}_i\}_{i=1}^{U}$ of all query samples

1: Initialize centroids: $\{\mu'_k\}_{i=1}^{N} \leftarrow$ **soft k-means++**$(\mathcal{E})$ // Active Learning Stage

2: Initialize $\mathcal{L} = \emptyset$ and $\mathcal{U} = \mathcal{E}$

3: **for** round $r = 1$ to R **do**

4:     **for** round $k = 1$ to N **do**

5:         Select informative samples S_k for each cluster

6:         Update labeled set $\mathcal{L}$

7:     **end for**

8: **end for**   // End of Active Learning Stage

9: Initialize prototypes: $C^{(0)} \leftarrow$ **soft k-means**$(\mathcal{L}, \mathcal{U})$

10: **for** $t = 1 : T$ steps **do**

11:     Compute Soft Labels: $W^{(t)} \leftarrow \mathrm{Cos}(x_i, c_k^{(t)})$

12:     Laplacian Smoothing using Eq.(1)

13:     Rectify Prototypes: $\boldsymbol{C}^{(t)} = (1 - \alpha)\boldsymbol{C}^{(t-1)} + \alpha W^{(t)^T} X$

14: **end for**

15: **return** $\tilde{y}_i = \arg\min_k \|x_i - c_k^{(*)}\|^2$ with respect to the optimized prototype $C^{(*)}$

---

ensures prototypes align closely with their respective classes. After iterative refinement, the optimized prototypes $\boldsymbol{C}^{(*)}$ are used to predict labels for query samples. Specifically, for each unlabeled sample $x_i \in \mathcal{U}$, its label $\tilde{y}_i$ is determined by the class of the nearest prototype. This iterative process utilizes both labeled and unlabeled data, overcoming challenges posed by label imbalance and limited supervision. By integrating active learning and iterative prototype rectification, our approach ensures improved label prediction accuracy and robust prototype alignment.

4   Experiment

We experiment on four public datasets on few shot classification task: mini-ImageNet [3], tiered-ImageNet [24], CUB-200 [25], and CIFAR-FS [26]. Two most related baselines are selected for comparison:

- **LSS** [10]: Implements soft k-means sampling with log-probability weighting, prioritizing central and boundary samples for classification. We compare our method with LSS to demonstrate the superiority of prototype rectification with laplacian smoothing in active TFSL.
- **protoLP** [5]: Combines prototype label propagation with optimal transport constraints for class distribution balancing. We include protoLP in our comparisons to highlight the simplicity and efficiency of our Laplacian smoothing mechanism in improving class distribution without the need for complex iterative graph optimization;

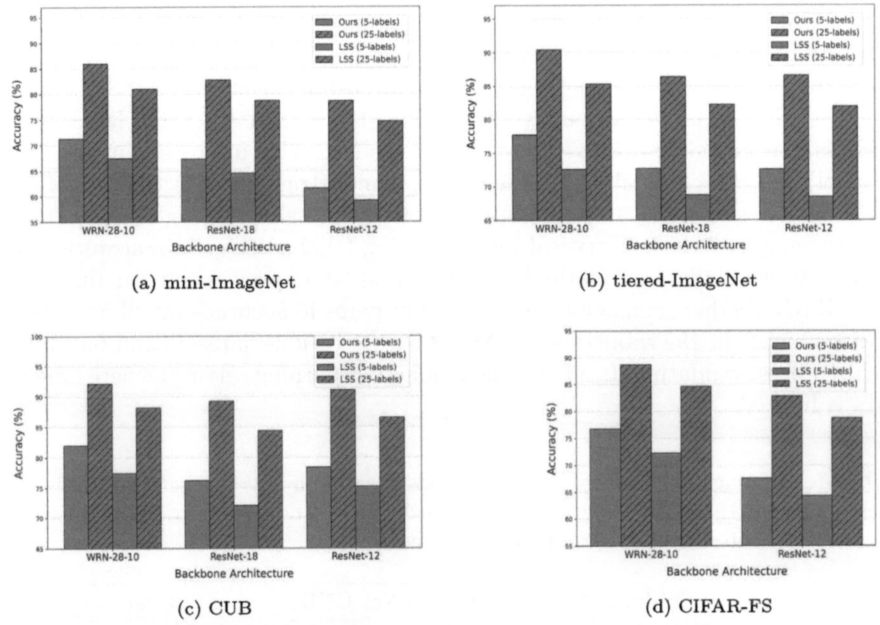

(a) mini-ImageNet

(b) tiered-ImageNet

(c) CUB

(d) CIFAR-FS

Fig. 3. Active TFSL performance comparison across different datasets and label configurations with different feature extractor backbones.

Our default episode setting is N-way, L-label, U-query, where $N = 5$, labeling budget $L = 5$ or 25, $U = 75$. To simulate the real class imbalance scenario, following [10], we sample imbalanced tasks by modeling the proportion of examples from each class as a vector $\pi = (\pi_1, \ldots, \pi_N)$ sampled from a symmetric Dirichlet distribution with parameter $\gamma = 2$. In order to broadly demonstrate the effectiveness of the method and the differences between different active strategies, we also conducted additional experiments in a balanced setting. We experiment with different image feature extractor ResNet-12, ResNet-18 [27], and WRN-28-10 [28], all of which are pretrained with S2M2-R framework [29]. To ensure fairness, feature preprocessing follows protoLP [5], such as $L2$ normalization and SVD decomposition. The performance numbers are given as accuracy %, and the results are based on the average performance (95% confidence interval) of 10,000 randomly drawn 5-ways episodes. For conciseness, we do not report the confidence intervals, but those are all close to 0.30. The hyperparameters are set as: $B = 3$, $\alpha = 0.2$, $\beta = 0.1$, $T = 10$, if active learning is not used, $T = 100$.

4.1   Overall Performance on Imbalanced Data

Compare to LSS. The purpose of this comparison to LSS [10] is to demonstrate the superiority of the CDD strategy under imbalanced data conditions and the importance of rectifying prototypes. Our method effectively addresses the challenges posed by imbalanced datasets. We present a comprehensive performance comparison of our proposed active learning framework with LSS across multiple datasets. As shown in Fig. 3, our method significantly outperforms LSS, especially under imbalanced label settings. On mini-ImageNet (WRN-28-10 backbone), ALPR improves accuracy by 3.9% (5-label) and 5.0% (25-label) over LSS. Similar gains are observed on tiered-ImageNet, with improvements of 4.4% (5-label) and 5.6% (25-label). These results demonstrate the effectiveness of our CDD-guided two-stage active learning strategy in selecting high-information-density samples, which is critical for mitigating label scarcity in real-world scenarios. Additionally, our method shows consistent improvements on the CUB and CIFAR-FS datasets, achieving significant gains in accuracy over LSS. These findings highlight the robustness of ALPR across various datasets and backbone architectures, validating its effectiveness in active learning settings where labeled data is limited.

Table 1. Comparison to protoLP and methods therein on four datasets with different backbones and the same experimental setup. '-' means no results provided in those papers. * indicates results reproduced by our code.

Method	mini-ImageNet		tiered-ImageNet		CUB		Cifar	
	5-labels	25-labels	5-labels	25-labels	5-labels	25-labels	5-labels	25-labels
WRN-28-10								
LaplacianShot [30]	68.1	83.2	73.5	86.8	-	-	-	-
TIM [14]	69.8	81.6	75.8	85.4	-	-	-	-
BD-SCPN [9]	70.4	82.3	75.4	85.9	-	-	-	-
α-TIM [31]	69.8	84.8	76.0	87.8	-	-	-	-
PT-MAP* [8]	64.4	69.4	68.9	74.0	70.2	69.9	67.5	69.1
protoLP* [5]	68.9	85.5	77.1	**89.5**	80.5	**90.0**	76.6	**87.00**
PR (ours)	**74.4**	**85.7**	80.4	89.3	**84.3**	86.3	**80.1**	85.4
ResNet-18								
PT-MAP* [8]	61.5	65.7	65.4	70.7	67.0	69.3	-	-
protoLP* [5]	64.69	**82.4**	71.1	**86.3**	72.6	**87.6**	-	-
PR (ours)	**69.6**	81.0	**74.3**	84.8	**77.2**	84.7	-	-
ResNet-12								
protoLP* [5]	59.2	77.4	69.7	86.1	74.8	**89.3**	65.0	82.1
PR (ours)	**62.5**	**78.5**	**74.0**	**86.8**	**81.7**	86.6	**69.1**	**82.4**

Compare to ProtoLP. Without the incorporation of active learning, our Laplacian graph smoothing strategy outperforms the SOTA label propagation method protoLP [5] in the imbalanced setting, highlighting the efficiency of our approach. As shown in Table 1, our method is more effective than Protolp on ResNet-12, and achieves competitive performance results on ResNet-18 and

Table 2. Performance comparison on the mini-ImageNet and tiered-ImageNet datasets with WRN-28-10 backbone. AL: Active Learning, LS: Laplacian Smoothing. If active learning is not used, random selection is used by default

AL	LS	mini-ImageNet		tiered-ImageNet	
		5-labels	25-labels	5-labels	25-labels
		53.70	82.64	56.92	81.76
✓		69.82	83.92	75.16	88.67
	✓	54.40	83.37	57.17	87.64
✓	✓	**74.44**	**85.66**	**80.36**	**89.30**

WRN-28-10. Specifically, our method performs better in the 5-labels setting, and achieves a lead of 3.2% to 6.9% in different settings. In the 25-labels setting, it also achieves competitive results, especially on lightweight networks such as ResNet12. This shows that PR improves performance by smoothing the labels of neighboring samples to refine the prototype and is more suitable for lightweight networks.

4.2   Ablation Study

As shown in Table 2, we performed an ablation study to evaluate the impact of Active Learning (AL) and Prototype Rectification with Laplacian smoothing (LS). The experiments were conducted with WRN-28-10 on mini-ImageNet and tiered-ImageNet with 5-label and 25-label settings. First, we compared the performance without using AL and LS, relying only on prototype rectification with Eq. (2) performs poorly in the 5-labels setting. Next, applying AL significantly improved the performance, reaching 1.3% to 18.0% improvements across two datasets. Under 5-labels, CDD selects samples with high confidence, which plays a key role in estimating a good prototype. Then, using LS alone also brought 0.2% to 5.9% performance gains across two datasets. Finally, combining AL and LS further improved the results, reaching the best performance. It also proves the mutual promotion effect of AL and LS. In summary, AL achieves a huge performance improvement by selecting samples with high confidence to get a good initialization prototype under the 5-labels setting, while LS helps rectifying a more robust prototype by aggregating the contribution of neighboring samples to the prototype.

4.3   Effectiveness of Sampling Strategies

Our proposed CDD criterion demonstrates significant advantages over conventional active learning strategies across various settings. As evidenced in Table 3, On mini-ImageNet, CDD outperforms random sampling by 24.3% (5-label) and 3.6% (25-label), while maintaining consistent improvements of 8.4% and 1.4% over margin sampling in respective settings. This dual-phase strategy – initial

Table 3. Comparison of active strategies in class-balanced setting with WRN-28-10.

Labels	Active Strategy	mini-ImageNet	tiered-ImageNet
5 labels	Random	60.76 ± 0.43	66.55 ± 0.43
	Margin	76.66 ± 0.38	84.76 ± 0.33
	K-medoids	85.08 ± 0.20	90.18 ± 0.19
	LSS	85.11 ± 0.20	90.18 ± 0.19
	CDD (ours)	85.09 ± 0.21	**90.23 ± 0.19**
25 labels	Random	87.46 ± 0.13	90.90 ± 0.13
	Margin	89.68 ± 0.15	92.82 ± 0.14
	K-medoids	87.97 ± 0.14	91.74 ± 0.14
	LSS	88.06 ± 0.14	91.83 ± 0.14
	CDD (ours)	**91.08 ± 0.13**	**94.03 ± 0.13**

representative sampling followed by boundary selection – effectively balances maximizing sample information and robustly rectifying prototypes under imbalanced data in active TFSL. While centroid-based methods (K-medoids/LSS) achieve comparable performance to CDD in 5-label scenarios on mini-ImageNet, their static selection patterns fail to adapt to high-label regimes. As shown in Fig. 4a, CDD's dynamic transition from centroid-focused to boundary-aware sampling enables 4.1% and 3.0% accuracy gains over K-medoids and LSS respectively in 25-label settings on mini-ImageNet. And the situation is similar on tiered-ImageNet. This adaptive behavior is particularly crucial for real-world scenarios where initial class distributions are often skewed.

4.4   Efficiency Analysis

We further evaluated the inference efficiency of our method compared to protoLP [5]. Figure 4b presents the average inference time and classification accuracy

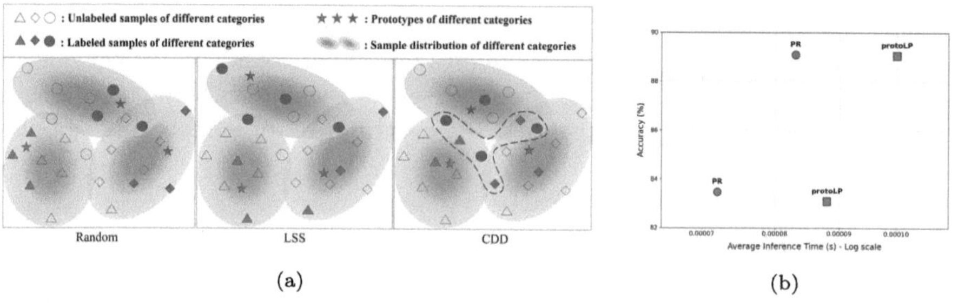

Fig. 4. (a) Active learning strategies tend to select different samples. LSS selects samples near and far from centroids; CDD prioritizes the boundary-adjacent samples. (b) Accuracy over Average inference time of protoLP and our method (PR) on 5-labels (red) and 25-labels (blue) tasks under class-balanced setting. (Color figure online)

for 5-label and 25-label tasks on mini-ImageNet with WRN-28-10 backbone. Our method outperforms protoLP, achieving much lower inference time while maintaining high classification accuracy.

5   Conclusion

We propose a novel framework for TFSL which incorporates active learning with graph-based prototype rectification. Firstly, multi-round active learning based on CDD value is proposed to obtain the representative and boundary-aware samples, resulting in optimal prototype initialization; Secondly, robust prototype rectification via parameter-free Laplacian smoothing enforces manifold-consistent label propagation. Cooperation of active learning and graph-based prototype evolution demonstrates strong adaptability to class-imbalanced scenarios, which is investigated by the overall improvement over most related baselines. Ablation study is conducted to explore the function of each module. Multi-round active learning based on CDD values builds a robust prototype by selecting high-confidence representative samples in the first round, and focuses on boundary samples in subsequent rounds to refine the decision boundary, which significantly improves the prototype optimization efficiency and classification performance in the class-imbalanced scenario. The parameter-free Laplacian smoothing not only controls the intra-class variations, but also computationally efficient, and can serve as a plug-and-play module for other graph-based methods.

Acknowledgments. This work is supported by the National Natural Science Foundation of China (Grant No. 12201101).

References

1. Snell, J., Swersky, K., Zemel, R.: Prototypical networks for few-shot learning. In: Advances in Neural Information Processing Systems, vol. 30, pp. 4077–4087 (2017)
2. Sung, F., Yang, Y., Zhang, L., Xiang, T., Torr, P.H., Hospedales, T.M.: Learning to compare: relation network for few-shot learning. In: Proceedings of the IEEE Conference on Computer Vision and Pattern Recognition (2018)
3. Vinyals, O., Blundell, C., Lillicrap, T., Kavukcuoglu, K., Wierstra, D.: Matching networks for one shot learning. In: Advances in Neural Information Processing Systems, vol. 29, pp. 3630–3638 (2016)
4. Finn, C., Abbeel, P., Levine, S.: Model-agnostic meta-learning for fast adaptation of deep networks. In: Proceedings of the 34th International Conference on Machine Learning (2017)
5. Zhu, H., Koniusz, P.: Transductive few-shot learning with prototype-based label propagation by iterative graph refinement. In: Proceedings of the IEEE/CVF Conference on Computer Vision and Pattern Recognition, pp. 23996–24006 (2023)
6. Rodríguez, P., Laradji, I., Drouin, A., Lacoste, A.: Embedding propagation: smoother manifold for few-shot classification. In: Vedaldi, A., Bischof, H., Brox, T., Frahm, J.-M. (eds.) ECCV 2020. LNCS, vol. 12371, pp. 121–138. Springer, Cham (2020). https://doi.org/10.1007/978-3-030-58574-7_8

7. Liu, Y., Lee, J., Park, M., Kim, S., Yang, E., Kweon, I.S.: Learning to propagate labels: transductive propagation network for few-shot learning. In: International Conference on Learning Representations (2019)

8. Hu, Y., Gripon, V., Pateux, S.: Leveraging the feature distribution in transfer-based few-shot learning. In: Farkaš, I., Masulli, P., Otte, S., Wermter, S. (eds.) ICANN 2021. LNCS, vol. 12892, pp. 487–499. Springer, Cham (2021). https://doi.org/10.1007/978-3-030-86340-1_39

9. Liu, J., Song, L., Qin, Y.: Prototype rectification for few-shot learning. In: Vedaldi, A., Bischof, H., Brox, T., Frahm, J.-M. (eds.) ECCV 2020. LNCS, vol. 12346, pp. 741–756. Springer, Cham (2020). https://doi.org/10.1007/978-3-030-58452-8_43

10. Abdali, A., Gripon, V., Drumetz, L., Boguslawski, B.: Active learning for efficient few-shot classification. In: IEEE International Conference on Acoustics, Speech and Signal Processing, pp. 1–5. IEEE (2023)

11. Ye, C., Wang, Q., Dong, L.: Single-step support set mining for realistic few-shot image classification. In: 2024 International Joint Conference on Neural Networks (2024)

12. Zhang, R., Che, T., Ghahramani, Z., Bengio, Y., Song, Y.: MetaGAN: an adversarial approach to few-shot learning. In: Neural Information Processing Systems (2018)

13. Luo, Q., Wang, L., Lv, J., Xiang, S., Pan, C.: Few-shot learning via feature hallucination with variational inference. In: Proceedings of the IEEE/CVF Winter Conference on Applications of Computer Vision, pp. 3963–3972 (2021)

14. Boudiaf, M., Ziko, I., Rony, J., Dolz, J., Piantanida, P., Ben Ayed, I.: Information maximization for few-shot learning. Adv. Neural. Inf. Process. Syst. **33**, 2445–2457 (2020)

15. Lazarou, M., Avrithis, Y., Stathaki, T.: Adaptive manifold for imbalanced transductive few-shot learning. In: Proceedings of the IEEE/CVF Winter Conference on Applications of Computer Vision (2024)

16. Ren, P., et al.: A survey of deep active learning. ACM Comput. Surv. **54**(9), 1–40 (2021)

17. Yang, Y., Loog, M.: A benchmark and comparison of active learning for logistic regression. Pattern Recogn. **83**, 401–415 (2018). https://doi.org/10.1016/j.patcog.2018.06.004

18. Hino, H., Eguchi, S.: Active learning by query by committee with robust divergences. Inf. Geom. **6**(1), 81–106 (2023)

19. Cai, W., Zhang, Y., Zhou, J.: Robust expected model change for active learning in regression. Neurocomputing (2019)

20. Sourati, J., Akcakaya, M., Erdogmus, D., Leen, T.K., Dy, J.G.: A probabilistic active learning algorithm based on fisher information ratio. IEEE Trans. Pattern Anal. Mach. Intell. **40**(8), 2023–2029 (2018). https://doi.org/10.1109/TPAMI.2017.2743707

21. Mussmann, S., Reisler, J., Tsai, D., Mousavi, E., O'Brien, S., Goldszmidt, M.: Active learning with expected error reduction. arXiv preprint arXiv:2211.09283 (2022)

22. Arthur, D., Vassilvitskii, S.: K-means++: the advantages of careful seeding. In: Proceedings of the Eighteenth Annual ACM-SIAM Symposium on Discrete Algorithms, pp. 1027–1035 (2007)

23. Li, J., Chen, P., Yu, S., Liu, S., Jia, J.: BAL: balancing diversity and novelty for active learning. IEEE Trans. Pattern Anal. Mach. Intell. **46**(5), 3653–3664 (2023)

24. Ren, M., et al.: Meta-learning for semi-supervised few-shot classification. In: International Conference on Learning Representations (2018)

25. Welinder, P., et al.: Caltech-UCSD birds 200 (2010)
26. Krizhevsky, A., Hinton, G., et al.: Learning multiple layers of features from tiny images (2009)
27. Oreshkin, B., Rodríguez López, P., Lacoste, A.: TADAM: task dependent adaptive metric for improved few-shot learning. Adv. Neural Inf. Process. Syst. **31** (2018)
28. Rusu, A.A., et al.: Meta-learning with latent embedding optimization. In: International Conference on Learning Representations (2019)
29. Mangla, P., Kumari, N., Sinha, A., Singh, M., Krishnamurthy, B., Balasubramanian, V.N.: Charting the right manifold: manifold mixup for few-shot learning. In: Proceedings of the IEEE/CVF Winter Conference on Applications of Computer Vision, pp. 2218–2227 (2020)
30. Ziko, I., Dolz, J., Granger, E., Ayed, I.B.: Laplacian regularized few-shot learning. In: III, H.D., Singh, A. (eds.) Proceedings of the 37th International Conference on Machine Learning. Proceedings of Machine Learning Research, vol. 119, pp. 11660–11670 (2020)
31. Veilleux, O., Boudiaf, M., Piantanida, P., Ben Ayed, I.: Realistic evaluation of transductive few-shot learning. In: Advances in Neural Information Processing Systems, vol. 34, pp. 9290–9302 (2021)

Parallel FHE-Based Neural Network Inference with Knowledge Distillation for Efficient Privacy-Preserving Image Classification

Dian Jiao[1], Junyu Lin[1], Jiageng Chen[1(✉)], Jichao Xiong[1], Weizhi Meng[2], and Chunhua Su[3]

[1] School of Computer, and Hubei Provincial Key Laboratory of Artificial Intelligence and Smart Learning, Central China Normal University, Wuhan, China
`jiageng.chen@ccnu.edu.cn`
[2] School of Computing and Communications, Lancaster University, Lancaster, UK
[3] Department of Computer Science and Engineering, The University of Aizu, Aizuwakamatsu, Japan

Abstract. We present a novel parallel FHE-based inference framework specifically designed for encrypted image classification, substantially improving computational efficiency while preserving high accuracy. Although Fully Homomorphic Encryption (FHE) provides strong privacy guarantees, its computational overhead typically hinders real-world applicability. To address this issue, we propose three key innovations: (1) a patch-level parallel inference architecture that partitions images for simultaneous encrypted computation, (2) an overlapping patch mechanism integrated with a dual-stage knowledge distillation pipeline to mitigate global feature loss while maintaining efficient encrypted inference, and (3) use of the CKKS scheme, which natively supports floating-point arithmetic and SIMD operations. Experiments on benchmark datasets highlight the effectiveness of our approach: on MNIST, it achieves 99.05% accuracy with a latency of only 1.09 s, while on CIFAR-10, it attains 82.74% accuracy in 47.3 s of encrypted inference. Compared with classical baselines such as CryptoNets and CryptoDL, our framework reduces latency by 35.9× ∼ 293.6×, and it outperforms cutting-edge solutions (LoLa, Falcon, bi-CryptoNets) by a 1.1× ∼ 2.3× speedup, while maintaining comparable or acceptable accuracy. Overall, this work advances practical Privacy-Preserving Machine Learning (PPML) by striking a favorable balance among accuracy, latency, and data privacy, paving the way for secure, real-world machine learning deployments.

Keywords: Privacy-Preserving Machine Learning (PPML) · Fully Homomorphic Encryption (FHE) · Parallelized Encrypted Inference · Knowledge Distillation (KD) · Information Security

---

D. Jiao, J. Lin and J. Chen—Contributed equally to this work.

1   Introduction

With the increasing adoption of Machine Learning as a Service (MLaaS), deep learning has become increasingly reliant on cloud computing. While centralizing data on cloud servers maximizes computational efficiency, the requisite offloading of raw data engenders critical security vulnerabilities and consequent legal and regulatory ramifications, Privacy-Preserving Machine Learning (PPML) using Fully Homomorphic Encryption (FHE) has emerged as a promising solution. FHE allows cloud servers to perform inference directly on encrypted data and return encrypted results, ensuring user data remains confidential throughout the entire process.

However, FHE-based secure inference incurs substantial computational overhead compared to plaintext operations. For instance, early works like CryptoNets [11] and CryptoDL [12] require 205 and 320 s, respectively, for a single MNIST image inference, whereas the plaintext counterpart takes merely 0.05 s. This stark performance gap has driven extensive research into optimizing and accelerating FHE-based inference while preserving strict privacy guarantees.

To mitigate these inefficiencies, initial research focused on improving inference efficiency. FCryptoNets [7] leveraged network sparsity to reduce homomorphic multiplications. LoLa [4] introduced an optimized ciphertext packing method to minimize homomorphic operations, and Falcon [20] employed Fourier transform-based convolutions to reduce dot-product overhead. Despite these advances, these methods are restricted to shallow networks (typically ≤ 5 layers), limiting their accuracy on complex datasets like CIFAR-10 to below 76.5%.

To overcome these limitations, recent State-of-the-Art (SOTA) approaches have focused on enabling deeper neural networks. For example, VDSCNN [17] proposed a multiplexed parallel convolution algorithm, enabling very deep CNNs (e.g., ResNet) with accuracy close to plaintext models. Other notable methods include optimized compilers (EVA [8]), TFHE-based boolean circuits (SHE [18]), and hybrid architectures (bi-CryptoNets [21]). While these techniques achieve over 90% accuracy on CIFAR-10, they still suffer from prohibitively high latency, often exceeding 2000 seconds, which poses a significant challenge for real-world deployment.

In this paper, we present a novel parallel FHE-based inference framework designed to enhance both efficiency and accuracy for secure image inference. Our key contributions are as follows:

1. **Efficiency Optimization:** We introduce a **patch-level parallel FHE-based inference architecture** that partitions input images into multiple patches for concurrent encrypted inference. This approach significantly accelerates inference, achieving at least **39.1×** and **247.1×** speedups over classical frameworks on MNIST and CIFAR-10, respectively. Compared to the fastest SOTA solution, Falcon, our method reduces latency by **1.1×** on MNIST and **2.3×** on CIFAR-10.

2. **High-Accuracy Retention:** Our framework integrates three key techniques to maintain performance:

- A **dual-layer knowledge distillation** pipeline. First, knowledge is distilled from a deep VGG-19 model to a compact, FHE-friendly CNN. Second, another distillation step compensates for global feature loss from patch-based parallelism by aligning patch-level representations with a global teacher.
- An **overlapping patch-based partitioning** scheme that preserves essential boundary features in local patches, helping to recover holistic semantic relationships from fragmented image regions.
- Adoption of the **CKKS FHE scheme**, which supports high-precision floating-point arithmetic and SIMD operations, preserving both accuracy and efficiency in encrypted inference.

Comprehensive ablation studies confirm the effectiveness of each component in our framework. Experimental results show our method achieves **99.05%** accuracy with a latency of just **1.09 s** on MNIST dataset. On CIFAR-10 dataset, it attains an acceptable accuracy of **82.74%** with an inference latency of **47.3 s**, representing a significant efficiency improvement over existing HE-based methods.

2 Preliminaries

2.1 Fully Homomorphic Encryption (FHE)

Fully Homomorphic Encryption (FHE) [10] enables computations directly on encrypted data, ensuring privacy without requiring decryption. It is a cornerstone of Privacy-Preserving Machine Learning (PPML) for secure inference in untrusted environments. Various schemes, including BFV, CKKS, and TFHE, are tailored for different computational tasks.

The BFV scheme [9] supports exact integer arithmetic, representing ciphertexts in the polynomial ring $\mathcal{R}_q = \mathbb{Z}_q[x]/(x^N+1)$. While precise, BFV's efficiency is limited by the need for frequent bootstrapping to manage noise accumulation. The CKKS scheme [5] is designed for approximate floating-point arithmetic, making it highly suitable for MLaaS. Ciphertexts in CKKS belong to the ring $\mathcal{R}_p^2$, where $\mathcal{R}_p = \mathbb{Z}_p[x]/(x^N + 1)$. CKKS supports Single Instruction Multiple Data (SIMD) operations, enabling multiple values to be packed into a single ciphertext, which substantially reduces latency. However, it lacks native support for nonlinear operations, requiring polynomial approximations that introduce computational overhead. In contrast, the TFHE scheme [6] is designed for Boolean operations, representing encrypted values on the torus $\mathbb{T} = \mathbb{R}/\mathbb{Z}$. TFHE features fast bootstrapping, allowing for unrestricted computational depth and native support for nonlinear functions via lookup tables, but it remains expensive for complex numerical tasks.

In FHE, fundamental operations like homomorphic addition ($\oplus$) and multiplication ($\otimes$) can be performed on encrypted data. Given an encryption function Enc and decryption function Dec, for any two plaintexts m_1, m_2:

$$Dec(Enc(m_1) \oplus Enc(m_2)) = m_1 + m_2, \tag{1}$$

$$Dec(Enc(m_1) \otimes Enc(m_2)) = m_1 \times m_2. \tag{2}$$

These properties allow computations on encrypted values, maintaining data confidentiality. To facilitate efficient inference, we leverage the CKKS scheme. We denote its encryption as $\mathcal{E}(\cdot)$ and represent encrypted inference with an FHE-friendly network f_S as: $\mathcal{E}(Y) = f_S(\mathcal{E}(X))$.

2.2 Knowledge Distillation (KD)

Knowledge Distillation (KD) [13] is a technique for transferring the capacity of a complex teacher model f_T to a lightweight student model f_S, achieving comparable performance under computational constraints. The teacher model produces soft probability distributions $p_T(y|x)$ that encapsulate rich inter-class relationships. The student learns to replicate these outputs by minimizing a distillation loss, typically using the KullbackâĂŞLeibler (KL) divergence:

$$\mathcal{L}_{KD} = \lambda_1 \mathcal{L}_{CE}(y, \hat{y}) + \lambda_2 \tau^2 D_{KL}(p_T(y|x; \tau) \| p_S(y|x; \tau)), \tag{3}$$

where $\mathcal{L}_{CE}$ is the cross-entropy loss, D_{KL} is the KL divergence, τ is a temperature scaling factor, and λ_1, λ_2 are weighting coefficients.

In PPML, KD facilitates compressing large, high-accuracy models into smaller, FHE-friendly ones. This process typically involves: (1) training a high-capacity teacher network to establish robust feature representations and (2) distilling these representations into a lightweight student model optimized for homomorphic computation, often by approximating activation functions with polynomials. The student learns from the teacher's softened predictions:

$$p_S(y|x) = \text{softmax}\left(\frac{z_S(x)}{\tau}\right), \tag{4}$$

where $z_S(x)$ represents the student's logits.

Moreover, KD integrates seamlessly with transfer learning. A pre-trained teacher model (e.g., VGG19 on ImageNet [16]) first extracts general features, which are then adapted to a target dataset (e.g., MNIST, CIFAR-10). These refined representations are subsequently distilled into an even more compact student model. This process preserves essential semantic features while discarding redundant parameters, enabling the FHE-optimized model to maintain high accuracy and reduced computational overhead.

2.3 Image Patch Partition

Inspired by Hou et al. [14], we adopt a patch-based partitioning strategy, in which input images are divided into independent patches for CNN inference. Formally, given an image $I \in \mathbb{R}^{H \times W \times C}$, where H, W, and C denote the height, width, and the number of channels respectively, we partition it into n patches:

$$I = \bigcup_{k=1}^{n} P_k, \quad P_k \in \mathbb{R}^{h \times w \times C}, \quad n = \frac{H}{h} \times \frac{W}{w}. \tag{5}$$

Each patch P_k is processed in parallel by the same neural network model, denoted as f_k^P to indicate that all n patches undergo simultaneous inference. The extracted feature representation for each patch is given by $v_k^P = f_k^P(P_k)$, where $v_k^P \in \mathbb{R}^d$ represents the feature map obtained from the k-th patch. The patch-level feature representations are then fused using a feature fusion mechanism $\mathcal{A}$, such as average pooling: $F_P = \mathcal{A}(\{v_k^P\}_{k=1}^n)$, where F_P denotes the final aggregated feature representation obtained by merging all patch-wise features.

To mitigate feature loss at patch boundaries, we employ an overlapping patching strategy, where adjacent patches share boundary regions: $\tilde{P}_k = P_k \cup \delta_k$, where δ_k represents the overlapping region. The overlapping region δ_k is introduced to mitigate boundary discontinuities and retain transitional features between adjacent patches, ensuring smoother transitions between patches and preserving global semantic coherence after aggregation.

By partitioning images into multiple independent patches, encrypted inference computations can be executed concurrently, distributing homomorphic workloads across multiple computational nodes or threads and significantly reducing latency.

2.4   Threat Model

Our threat model follows prior work in PPML [4,11,17,19]. We assume the server is untrusted and may attempt to glean private information but does not deviate from the prescribed protocol (i.e., an honest-but-curious or semi-honest model). The client first encrypts its sensitive data with a FHE scheme, then transmits the ciphertext to the server. Without ever decrypting the data or accessing the client's secret key, the server conducts inference computations directly on the encrypted inputs and returns the encrypted inference results. Finally, only the client—holding the decryption secret key—can recover the cleartext results, thereby protecting data confidentiality from the server.

3   Framework Design

In this section, we present our proposed framework, depicted in Fig. 1, designed to achieve an optimal balance between accuracy, latency, and privacy in encrypted inference. Our design leverages (1) a patch-level parallel inference strategy that reduces latency and computational overhead through partitioning and overlapping patches, and (2) a dual-layer knowledge distillation pipeline that compresses a deep pre-trained network into an FHE-friendly CNN while compensating for the loss of global context under patch-level processing. The resulting system ensures strong classification performance under the constraints of FHE.

3.1   Patch-Level Parallel Encrypted Inference

To address the computational burden of homomorphic operations on large input images, we introduce a patch-level parallel inference architecture. Specifically,

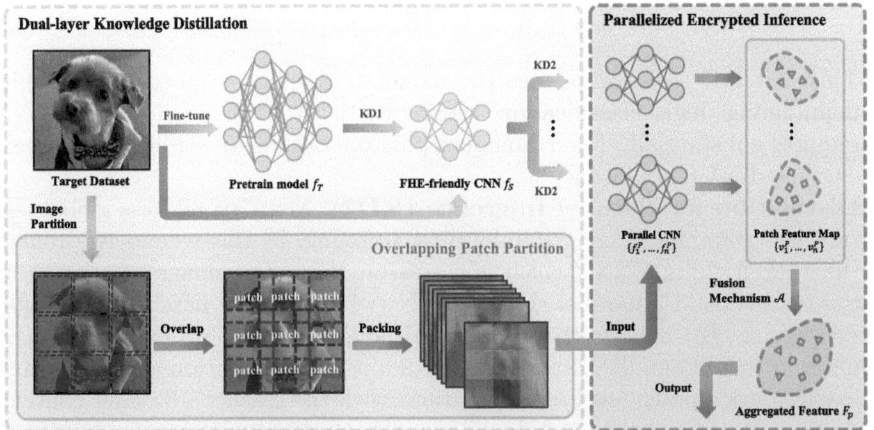

Fig. 1. Overview of the Proposed Framework for Parallel Privacy-Preserving Encrypted Inference.

we partition the input image into multiple smaller regions or patches, each of which is fed into a CNN for encrypted inference. These patches are processed in parallel—significantly reducing the end-to-end latency compared to running a single large-scale encrypted convolution on the entire image.

However, naive partitioning may introduce local feature loss at the patch boundaries, compromising global feature representation. To mitigate this effect, we adopt an overlapping patch mechanism, wherein adjacent regions share boundary pixels in a layered fashion. By overlapping patches, partial redundancy is preserved near the patch edges, allowing the CNN to better capture transitional or boundary features. Consequently, although each patch is evaluated separately in the encrypted domain, we minimize the degradation of global semantics while leveraging the inherent parallelism of patch-level processing.

3.2 Dual-Layer Knowledge Distillation with Transfer Learning

We further enhance our framework through a Dual-layer Knowledge Distillation (KD) Pipeline grounded in transfer learning. First, we initialize a powerful deep CNN (e.g., VGG19) pre-trained on ImageNet, which provides robust feature extraction capabilities. To adapt this model to the local task (e.g., MNIST or CIFAR-10), we freeze the convolutional layers—retaining their learned filters—and fine-tune the fully connected layers on the target dataset. Despite VGG19's strong accuracy, directly using it for homomorphic inference remains prohibitively expensive due to extensive parameters and deep architecture. To resolve this issue, we introduce two stages of knowledge distillation:

1. **Distillation for Model Compression (KD1)**. We transfer knowledge from the fine-tuned deep model f_T to a more compact FHE-friendly CNN f_S, using soft targets:

$$\mathcal{L}_{KD1} = \lambda_1 \mathcal{L}_{CE}(y, \hat{y}) + \lambda_2 \tau^2 D_{KL}(p_T(y|x;\tau)\|p_S(y|x;\tau)). \tag{6}$$

This first KD step compresses the model—reducing parameter size—while maintaining high classification accuracy. Because the compressed CNN requires substantially fewer homomorphic operations, it significantly lowers encrypted inference latency.

2. **Distillation for Parallel Inference (KD2)**. Next, we address global feature loss stemming from patch-level partitioning. In this second KD round, the FHE-friendly CNN (which operates on the entire image) f_S serves as the teacher, and a parallel shallow CNN (which accepts patch-sized inputs) $\{f_1^p, f_2^p, \ldots, f_n^p\}$ acts as the student. Although overlapping patches already mitigate local boundary omissions, this additional distillation aligns the shallow network's patch-level representations with the teacher's broader context. As a result, the parallel patch-based model better captures global semantics—thereby compensating for fragmentation—yet remains lightweight and efficient enough for practical homomorphic operations.

$$\mathcal{L}_{KD2} = \lambda_3 \mathcal{L}_{CE}(y, \hat{y}) + \lambda_4 \mathcal{L}_{MSE}(F_S, F_k^p) \tag{7}$$

By combining overlapping patch partitioning with a dual-layer knowledge distillation framework, we achieve encrypted inference that preserves accuracy while substantially reducing latency and upholding rigorous data privacy guarantees.

4 Experiments

All our experiments were performed on a Linux server equipped with two Intel Xeon Platinum 8352S CPUs (32 cores each, for a total of 128 threads) running at 2.20 GHz base frequency and up to 3.4 GHz turbo frequency. The system includes 251 GB of RAM and operates under Ubuntu 22.04.2 LTS with kernel version 6.5.0-18-generic. We implemented our methods in Python using PyTorch for deep learning. For FHE, we utilized the open-source TenSEAL library (developed by OpenMined), which supports privacy-preserving inference by enabling operations on encrypted data. We evaluated our approach on two standard image classification benchmarks:

- **MNIST**, which consists of 70,000 handwritten digit images (28×28, grayscale).
- **CIFAR-10**, containing 60,000 labeled images (32×32, RGB).

We configure our encryption parameters in accordance with the guidelines outlined in the Homomorphic Encryption Standard [2], guaranteeing a minimum security level of 128 bits. Specifically, we set the polynomial modulus degree to 16,384, the multiplication depth to 8, and the scaling bits to 26, with decimal precision aligned with the scaling bits. To accommodate nonlinear activation functions within the FHE framework, we approximate the ReLU function using a quadratic polynomial: $p(x) = 0.125x^2 + 0.5x + 0.25$ [7]. This approximation effectively balances computational efficiency and accuracy, ensuring the practicality of encrypted inference.

4.1 Ablation Study

To systematically clarify the impact of each framework component, we conducted ablation experiments under four progressively enhanced configurations, as detailed in Table 1. Each configuration incrementally incorporates overlapping patch partitioning and the two-stage knowledge distillation approaches. Throughout these experiments, we measured classification accuracy on both MNIST and CIFAR-10 datasets, clearly demonstrating the incremental contribution of each technique towards preserving accuracy in encrypted inference.

1. **FHE-friendly Parallel CNN (Baseline)**: A compressed CNN optimized for FHE operations, capable of parallel inference on independent input patches. This configuration serves as our baseline without further enhancements.
2. **Baseline + Overlapping**: Building upon the baseline, we introduce overlapping patches during input partitioning to reduce boundary-induced feature loss
3. **Baseline + Overlapping + KD2**: Building further upon overlapping patches, we incorporate the second stage of knowledge distillation (KD2), in which a global teacher network refines the patch-level student model.
4. **Baseline + Overlapping + KD2 + KD1 (Ours)**: Our complete approach, integrating overlapping patches and a dual-stage knowledge distillation framework to enhance parallel encrypted inference.

Table 1. Ablation Results on MNIST and CIFAR-10. Accuracy, Accuracy Gain, and F1-Score are Reported. Checkmarks (✓) Indicate the Inclusion of Each Component.

Overlap	KD2	KD1	MNIST			CIFAR-10		
			Acc (%)	Gain (%)	F1-Score	Acc (%)	Gain (%)	F1-Score
–	–	–	96.41	–	0.9636	59.93	–	0.5989
✓	–	–	97.68	+1.27	0.9765	67.38	+7.45	0.6727
✓	✓	–	98.35	+0.67	0.9832	73.67	+6.29	0.7359
✓	✓	✓	**99.05**	**+0.70**	**0.9896**	**82.74**	**+9.07**	**0.8271**

The baseline configuration (FHE-friendly Parallel CNN without overlapping patches or knowledge distillation) achieves an accuracy of 96.41% on MNIST and 59.93% on CIFAR-10, with corresponding F1-scores of 0.9636 and 0.5989, respectively. While this establishes a reasonable starting point, the limited CIFAR-10 accuracy highlights the challenges faced by compressed models on more complex datasets under encryption constraints. Introducing overlapping patch partitioning substantially improves performance, increasing MNIST accuracy to 97.68% (+1.27%) and CIFAR-10 accuracy to 67.38% (+7.45%), with F1-scores rising to 0.9765 and 0.6727, respectively. This improvement demonstrates the effectiveness of overlapping patches in alleviating boundary-induced feature loss and enhancing global semantic reconstruction, particularly beneficial for the more complex CIFAR-10 dataset.

Subsequently integrating the second-stage knowledge distillation (KD2) further elevates accuracy to 98.35% (+0.67%) on MNIST and 73.67% (+6.29%) on CIFAR-10, with improved F1-scores of 0.9832 and 0.7359, respectively. These enhancements underline KD2's capacity to align patch-level representations with global teacher models, significantly improving feature consistency across parallel computations.

Finally, incorporating the first-stage knowledge distillation (KD1) results in our complete framework (+ Overlapping + KD2 + KD1), achieving the highest accuracies: 99.05% (+0.70%) on MNIST and 82.74% (+9.07%) on CIFAR-10, with corresponding F1-scores of 0.9896 and 0.8271, respectively. This configuration demonstrates a clear synergistic benefit from dual-stage knowledge distillation: KD1 effectively transfers rich knowledge from a pre-trained deep model to compensate for compression-induced feature loss, while KD2 ensures feature robustness under patch-based parallelism. The notably higher gains on CIFAR-10 indicate that our proposed techniques are especially advantageous for complex datasets requiring richer feature representations.

These results underscore the critical contribution of each individual component toward achieving superior accuracy and robustness in encrypted inference, marking a substantial improvement over baseline FHE-friendly CNN.

4.2 Performance Comparison with Previous Works

We evaluate our complete approach (+ Overlapping + KD1 + KD2) against existing FHE-based inference methods on both MNIST and CIFAR-10 datasets. To ensure real-world applicability, we report key performance metrics, including classification accuracy, encrypted inference latency, network layer configuration—where C represents Convolutional layers, P denotes Pooling layers, and F signifies Fully Connected layers—and the specific HE scheme employed.

On the MNIST dataset, as shown in Table 2, our proposed framework achieves a 99.05% accuracy, matching SOTA performance for FHE-based inference. Crucially, by combining an optimized FHE-friendly CNN architecture with patch-level parallel inference, it reduces encrypted inference latency to 1.09 s—a 39.1× ∼ 293.6× improvement over classical baselines (e.g., CryptoDL, CryptoNets, FCryptoNets). Moreover, our method remains superior even compared to the latest, most efficient SOTA schemes, offering at least a 1.9× speedup over LoLa and bi-CryptoNets and a 1.1× speedup over Falcon.

Table 2. Comparison of SOTA Schemes for Encrypted Inference on MNIST in Terms of Latency, Accuracy, Number of Layers, and HE Method.

Scheme	Latency (s)	Speedup	Acc (%)	# Layer	HE Method
CryptoDL [12]	320	1×	99.52	10(C6P2F2)	CKKS
CryptoNets [11]	205	1.6×	98.95	6(C2P2F2)	YASHE
FCryptoNets [7]	39.1	8.2×	98.71	6(C2P2F2)	RNS-FV
nGraph-HE [3]	135	2.4×	98.95	6(C2P2F2)	CKKS
EVA [8]	121.5	2.6×	99.05	7(C2P2F3)	CKKS
VDSCNN [17]	105	3×	99.19	21(C19P1F1)	CKKS
SHE [18]	9.3	34.4×	99.54	6(C2P2F2)	TFHE
A*FV [1]	5.2	61.5×	99.00	3(C2F1)	BFV
LoLa [4]	2.2	145.5×	98.95	6(C2P2F2)	BFV
bi-CryptoNets [21]	2.1	152.4×	99.15	6(C2P2F2)	CKKS
Falcon [20]	1.2	266.7×	98.95	6(C2P2F2)	BFV
Ours	**1.09**	**293.6×**	99.05	4(C1F3)	CKKS

On the CIFAR-10 dataset, as illustrated in Table 3, our method achieves a competitive accuracy of 82.74%, requiring only 47.3 s for each encrypted image inference, representing approximately a 2.3× latency improvement compared to existing methods. In comparison, existing FHE-based methods such as CryptoNets, LoLa, and Falcon, which utilize the BFV scheme, exhibit lower accuracies (below 76.72%) due to constraints on network depth and integer arithmetic

Table 3. Comparison of SOTA Schemes for Encrypted Inference on CIFAR-10 in Terms of Latency, Accuracy, Number of Layers, and HE Method.

Scheme	Latency (s)	Speedup	Acc (%)	# Layer	HE Method
CryptoDL [12]	11686	1×	91.5	10(C8P1F1)	CKKS
FCryptoNets [7]	22372	0.5×	76.72	6(C2P2F2)	RNS-FV
nGraph-HE [3]	1628	7.2×	62.1	4(C2P1F1)	CKKS
EVA [8]	3062	3.8×	81.5	6(C2P4)	CKKS
VDSCNN [17]	2271	5.1×	91.31	21(C19P1F1)	CKKS
SHE [18]	2258	5.2×	92.54	11(C6P3F2)	TFHE
OptFHE-CNN [15]	398	29.4×	94.0	21(C19P1F1)	CKKS
A*FV [1]	304	38.5×	77.55	8(C3P3F2)	BFV
LoLa [4]	730	16.1×	76.5	7(C3P3F1)	BFV
bi-CryptoNets [21]	2962	3.9×	93.27	24(C16P5F3)	CKKS
Falcon [20]	107	109.2×	76.5	7(C3P3F1)	BFV
Ours	**47.3**	**247.1×**	82.74	7(C3P3F1)	CKKS

limitations. Meanwhile, recent high-precision CKKS-based approaches, including OptFHE-CNN and VDSCNN, achieve higher accuracies (over 91.31%) but incur substantially greater inference latencies (398 $\sim$ nearly 3000 s), making them approximately 8.4$\times$ $\sim$ 247.1$\times$ slower than our proposed solution.

Thus, the experimental results clearly illustrate that our parallel FHE-friendly inference architecture, combined with overlapping patch partitioning and a dual-stage knowledge distillation strategy, effectively achieves an optimal trade-off among accuracy, latency, and privacy guarantees. This makes our framework highly competitive and practical for real-world encrypted inference scenarios.

5 Conclusions

In this paper, we introduced a novel parallel FHE-based inference framework that combines patch-level parallelization, overlapping patch partitioning, and dual-layer knowledge distillation, effectively mitigating homomorphic overhead and striking a favorable balance among latency, accuracy, and privacy. Despite these advancements, two primary limitations remain. First, classification accuracy for more complex datasets (e.g., CIFAR-10) still lags behind plaintext inference, indicating potential for further improvement. Second, although our method significantly reduces encrypted inference latency, it remains considerably higher than plaintext inference. Future endeavors will concentrate on implementing deeper encrypted neural networks and refining homomorphic computation architectures, ciphertext packing methods, and parallelization strategies to push both accuracy and latency closer to plaintext levels, thus enhancing practical applicability.

Acknowledgements. This work is financially supported by National Natural Science Foundation of China under Grant No. 12441102 and self-determined research funds of CCNU from the colleges' basic research and operation of MOE under Grant No. CCNU24ai010.

References

1. Al Badawi, A., Jin, C., et al.: Towards the alexnet moment for homomorphic encryption: Hcnn, the first homomorphic cnn on encrypted data with gpus. IEEE Trans. Emerg. Top, Comput (2020)
2. Albrecht, M., Chase, M., et al.: Homomorphic encryption standard. Protecting privacy through homomorphic encryption (2021)
3. Boemer, F., Lao, Y., et al.: ngraph-he: a graph compiler for deep learning on homomorphically encrypted data. In: ACM Computing Frontiers (2019)
4. Brutzkus, A., Gilad-Bachrach, R., et al.: Low latency privacy preserving inference. In: ICML (2019)
5. Cheon, J.H., Kim, A., et al.: Homomorphic encryption for arithmetic of approximate numbers. In: ASIACRYPT (2017)

6. Chillotti, I., Gama, N., et al.: Tfhe: fast fully homomorphic encryption over the torus. J. Cryptology (2020)
7. Chou, E., Beal, J., et al.: Faster cryptonets: leveraging sparsity for real-world encrypted inference. arXiv preprint arXiv:1811.09953 (2018)
8. Dathathri, R., Kostova, B., et al.: Eva: an encrypted vector arithmetic language and compiler for efficient homomorphic computation. In: ACM SIGPLAN PLDI (2020)
9. Fan, J., Vercauteren, F.: Somewhat practical fully homomorphic encryption. Cryptology ePrint Archive (2012)
10. Gentry, C.: Fully homomorphic encryption using ideal lattices. In: ACM STOC (2009)
11. Gilad-Bachrach, R., Dowlin, N., et al.: Cryptonets: applying neural networks to encrypted data with high throughput and accuracy. In: ICML (2016)
12. Hesamifard, E., Takabi, H., et al.: Deep neural networks classification over encrypted data. In: ACM Conf. Data and App. Security and Privacy (2019)
13. Hinton, G., Vinyals, O., et al.: Distilling the knowledge in a neural network. arXiv preprint arXiv:1503.02531 (2015)
14. Hou, L., Samaras, D., et al.: Patch-based convolutional neural network for whole slide tissue image classification. In: CVPR (2016)
15. Kim, D., Guyot, C.: Optimized privacy-preserving cnn inference with fully homomorphic encryption. IEEE Trans. Inf. Forensics Secur. (2023)
16. Krizhevsky, A., Sutskever, I., et al.: Imagenet classification with deep convolutional neural networks. NeurIPS (2012)
17. Lee, E., Lee, J.W., et al.: Low-complexity deep convolutional neural networks on fully homomorphic encryption using multiplexed parallel convolutions. In: ICML (2022)
18. Lou, Q., Jiang, L.: She: a fast and accurate deep neural network for encrypted data. NeurIPS (2019)
19. Lou, Q., Jiang, L.: Hemet: A homomorphic-encryption-friendly privacy-preserving mobile neural network architecture. In: ICML (2021)
20. Lou, Q., Lu, W.j., et al.: Falcon: fast spectral inference on encrypted data. NeurIPS (2020)
21. Yuan, M.J., Zou, Z., et al.: Bi-cryptonets: leveraging different-level privacy for encrypted inference. In: PAKDD (2024)

MatSciES: Automated Knowledge Extraction and Summarization from Materials Science Literature with Large Language Models

Jialin Xu[1], Jinguo You[1,2]([envelope]), Chuhan Zhang[1], Huaze Huang[1], Jingmei Tao[3], and Jianhong Yi[3]

[1] Faculty of Information Engineering and Automation, Kunming University of Science and Technology, Kunming, China
`{jlxu,hzhuang,chzhang,hwliu}@stu.kust.edu.cn, jgyou@126.com`
[2] Yunnan Key Laboratory of Artificial Intelligence, Kunming, China
[3] Faculty of Material Science and Engineering, Kunming University of Science and Technology, Kunming, China

Abstract. Vast amounts of materials science literature accumulate rich knowledge resources, yet extracting valuable knowledge from this corpus poses significant challenges. Although large language models (LLMs) have demonstrated the capability in general domains, they have not performed well in the highly specialized field of materials science, primarily due to their insufficient knowledge base in this area. In this study, we propose an innovative multi-model automated approach called MatSciES (Materials Science Extraction and Summarization). Specifically, we first extract the texts with keywords filtering and the text context, followed by multi-models to assess the relevance of the texts to materials science knowledge and to summarize the relevant texts efficiently. Due to the absence of datasets in the field, we meticulously labeled multiple datasets combining public datasets for the assessment of relevance, text summarization and question answer. The experimental results demonstrate our approach achieves a high accuracy rate of 99.3% in relevance assessment tasks; in summarization task evaluations, the accuracy rate reaches 95.7% and the average text compression is 56%. Moreover, to validate the capability of integrating LLMs with the knowledge base, we conducted tests on manually annotated and public datasets, resulting in an accuracy improvement of up to 32.4%. Our method can assist materials science researchers with limited computer skills in rapidly constructing a substantial knowledge base. This provides a novel solution for developing LLMs knowledge base in the materials science field.

Keywords: Information extraction · Text summarization · Knowledge base construction · Multi-Model automation

1   Introduction

Recent decades have witnessed the exponential growth of publications in the field of materials science [11]. It encompasses a wealth of relevant knowledge and experimental data [13]. However, these valuable information resources are scattered throughout various paragraphs of literature and have not been effectively integrated. To address this challenge, knowledge mining from materials science literature has emerged as a main research focus, and automated data extraction technology is playing an increasingly important role in constructing knowledge databases in materials science and other fields. A variety of knowledge mining tools targeting materials science have been developed. For instance, ChemDataExtractor [14,17] focuses on extracting chemical entities and their attributes, measurement values, etc., from chemical literature, with its technical core including unsupervised word clustering, rule-based grammar, and dictionary matching. Subsequently, many researchers have further used and optimized this tool [6,7,22,26], they also attained outstanding accomplishments. He et al. [4], Weston et al. [21], and Korvigo et al. [12] have employed deep learning models, including LSTM networks and convolutional architectures, to identify chemical and material terminology within textual literature. Furthermore, they have utilized contextual information to ascertain the accuracy. Research based on the BERT architecture has demonstrated outstanding performance in materials science tasks such as named entity recognition, relation classification, and table extraction, including models like MatSciBERT [3], MaterialsBERT [18], alOpticBERT [27], and BatteryBERT [8].

With the emergence of LLMs like ChatGPT, the field of deep learning has experienced significant development. In just a few years, numerous general-purpose LLMs have emerged in the market, with their parameter counts increasing and their performance in natural language processing tasks, including dialogue question-answering, machine translation [10], named entity recognition [20,23], and text summarization [9], continually improving. Moreover, the development of LLMs has also had a positive impact on the field of materials science. This is because the large-scale training of these models on extensive texts endows them with excellent knowledge extraction capabilities even without fine-tuning. Recently, the popularity of DeepSeek and its open-source contributions have further enhanced the performance of general-purpose LLMs and reduced the cost of using these models.

In recent years, the research focus of data mining in materials science literature has gradually shifted from traditional machine learning models and pre-trained models to LLMs. For example, Dagdelen et al. [1] and Polak et al. [15] have effectively extracted structured data from texts using LLMs and achieved significant results. Venugopal et al. [19] have utilized LLMs to extract a dataset containing over 70,000 entities and 5.4 million unique triplets, thereby constructing a vast knowledge graph for materials science. Zheng et al. [28] have employed ChatGPT and prompt engineering techniques to extract synthesis conditions of metal-organic frameworks (MOFs) from literature. Additionally, Zhang et al. [25] have demonstrated the capabilities of GPT-3.5-turbo in five complex chemical text mining tasks, including compound entity recognition, reaction role labeling, and MOF synthesis information extraction, all achieving favorable research outcomes.

It can be observed from related studies that data extraction tasks in the field of materials science have often been designed with specific or a few tasks in mind, which, to some extent, limits the versatility of the models.

Currently, several large-scale datasets, such as DROP [2], HumanEval [16], HellaSwag [5], etc., have been developed for evaluating the professional capabilities of LLMs. However, in the field of materials science, datasets for assessing the performance of LLMs in specific knowledge domains are relatively scarce. The research work by Mohd et al. [24] annotated a dataset containing 650 multi-type question-answer pairs specifically for the materials science domain. On this dataset, the accuracy rate of ChatGPT4 is approximately 62%, revealing the insufficient reserves of LLMs in the materials science knowledge domain. To date, the research community has not yet developed an efficient and quality-assured method for constructing knowledge bases in the materials domain for LLMs.

In this study, we employed prompt engineering techniques to efficiently extract and summarize data from the literature. The main contributions of our paper are as follows:

1. We proposed a multi-model approach to assess the relevance of text to materials science, utilizing models including ChatGPT, DeepSeek, and LLaMA3, which can achieve up to 99.3% accuracy in relevance evaluation tasks.
2. We introduced a method using LLMs to summarize the content of materials science texts, reducing the average sentence length to 56% of the original text while retaining semantics, significantly decreasing the storage of irrelevant knowledge in the knowledge base. During the paper writing process, we have automatically extracted over 30,000 valid pieces of knowledge without any human intervention. Currently, the knowledge extraction work is ongoing.
3. We validated the capability of LLMs combined with a knowledge base using retrieval-augmented generation and tested it on both public datasets and manually annotated datasets. On the manually annotated dataset, the accuracy of the LLMs combined with the knowledge base can be increased by up to 32.4%. Using this method, a massive knowledge database can be constructed if time permits, and the difficulty and cost for non-computer professionals are greatly reduced due to the elimination of fine-tuning.

2 Methods

2.1 Data Preprocessing

Sentence Segmentation and Filtering. We initially conducted a systematic collection of literature in the field of materials science. The collected literature encompassed a variety of formats, such as PDF, DOC, and XML. Subsequently, we processed these documents by first extracting the abstract from each piece of literature and storing it as a separate entity for subsequent analysis. Following this, the remaining content of the literature was segmented into sentences as the basic unit of processing.

Building on this, we employed a keyword-based filtering method to further refine the data. These keywords were pre-established, and the current keyword library includes terms related to material entity names (e.g., Fe, Cu etc.), common performance descriptors, units of measurement, process flows, and experimental methods. Through this filtering step, we effectively removed a substantial amount of irrelevant data, thereby significantly reducing the time and cost associated with processing LLMs in subsequent stages.

Context Enrichment. During the course of our research, we observed that the outcomes of subsequent model processing based solely on individual sentences that had undergone keyword filtering were not satisfactory. This approach may have overlooked the ambiguity in the expression of certain sentences, or the content of these sentences may not have held significant referential value. Consequently, following the filtering step, we adopted a strategy that involved expanding the text by selecting the sentences immediately preceding and following each target sentence, thereby enhancing the clarity of semantic expression.

Furthermore, to more accurately reflect the significance and expression of the current sentence within the context of the entire article, we integrated the previously extracted article abstracts with the expanded text. Given that the abstracts typically encapsulate the primary information of the articles, this fusion method aids in achieving a more comprehensive and precise textual representation, thereby providing more efficient information input for subsequent model processing. Data preprocessing is shown flowchart in Fig. 1a.

2.2   Model Processing

Relevance Assessment. Following the completion of the aforementioned text processing pipeline, we systematically analyze extensive textual corpora, employing LLMs to conduct relevance assessments on material science literature segments. Specifically, this evaluation aims to determine whether a text segment contains domain-specific knowledge in materials science, such as chemical properties or experimental methodologies etc. Text segments identified as relevant by the model are retained for subsequent processing stages, while irrelevant ones are excluded.

During our investigation, we observed that reliance on a single LLM for relevance assessment may compromise accuracy due to inherent limitations in the model's reasoning and contextual comprehension capabilities, potentially leading to erroneous judgments. To enhance decision reliability, we implemented a multi-model fusion strategy: an odd number of independent LLMs concurrently evaluate the same text segment, the final result refers to the evaluation results of most LLMs. By adopting the majority consensus across models, we establish higher-confidence identification of potential knowledge candidates for downstream processing. Subsequent empirical validation confirmed the robust performance of LLMs in such relevance classification tasks.

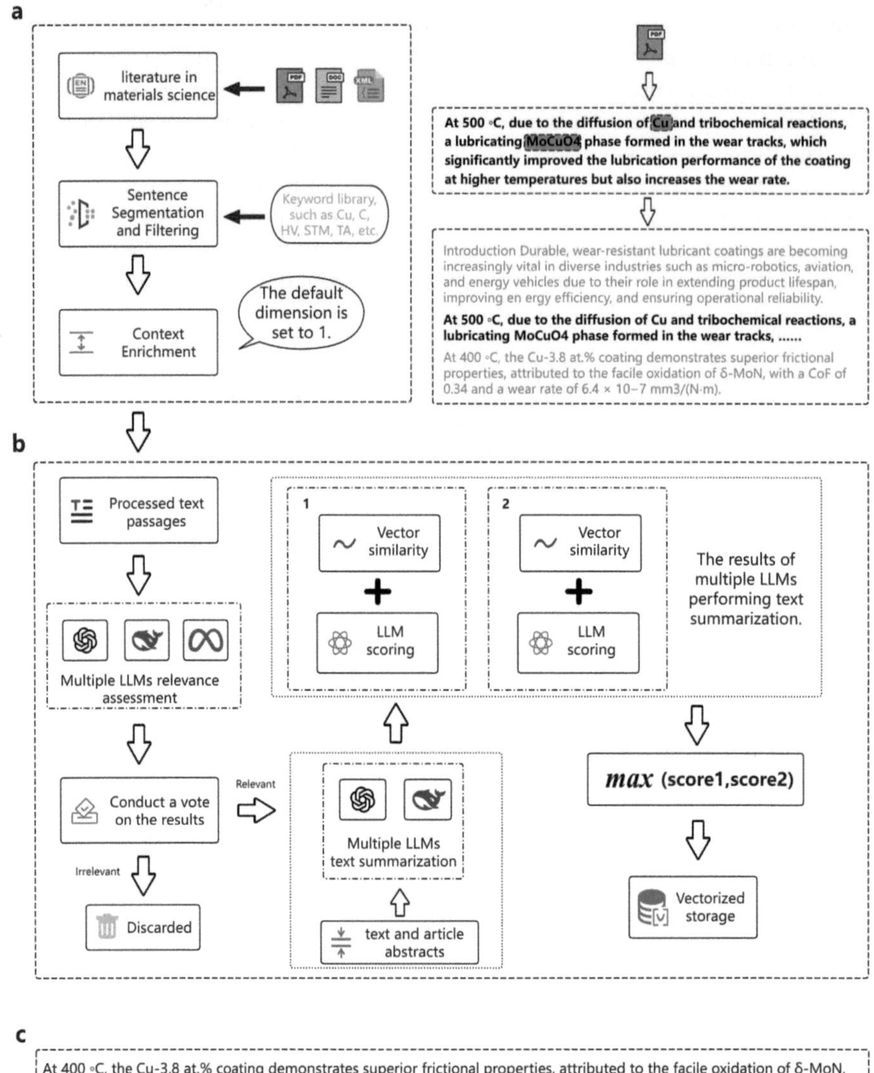

Fig. 1. (a) The Text Preprocessing Module, which encompasses Sentence Segmentation and Filtering, as well as Context Enrichment. (b) The Model Processing Module, incorporating procedures for Relevance Assessment and Text Summarization. (c) The output results corresponding to the example depicted in section (a).

Text Summarization. Text passages that have undergone relevance assessment, even after being filtered, cannot guarantee that every part of the passage is directly related to the professional knowledge in the field of materials science.

In fact, these passages may contain a substantial amount of information that is only loosely connected to the topic. Storing the full content in a knowledge base would inevitably compromise the overall quality of the knowledge base and increase the storage costs of the vector database. Therefore, at this stage, we select only those passages deemed relevant by the LLMs during the relevance assessment and use these LLMs to further process the text for summarization. This step aims to preserve the normal narrative content and meaning of the text while extracting the professionally relevant knowledge content related to materials science, in conjunction with the information from the article abstract.

Subsequently, we submit the summarization results produced by multiple LLMs to another LLM specialized in assessing the quality of summaries. This model evaluates and scores the Summarization results. Simultaneously, we measure the accuracy of the summaries by comparing the vector similarity of the original sentences with those of the summarized sentences. By combining the weights of these two evaluations, we calculate a comprehensive score for each summarization result and select the summarization with the highest score as the final outcome, among them, the optimal ratio of model weight to vector weight obtained through experiments is 3.54. Ultimately, convert the text results into vector data for storage. Model Processing flowchart in Fig. 1b.

Processing Results. In Fig. 1c, the results corresponding to the example presented in Fig. 1a are depicted. It is evident that the model exhibits a satisfactory level of text summarization. Notably, the model not only preserves the semantic content of the original text but also effectively reduces its length.

2.3 Dataset Preparation

In this study, to validate the performance of specific stages of the model, it is necessary to employ datasets for evaluation. Mohd et al. [24] have annotated a materials science knowledge quiz dataset for investigating materials science knowledge of LLMs, MaScQA, which we subsequently utilize to verify the capability of integrating LLMs with knowledge bases. However, for other aspects, there are currently no publicly available research datasets. Therefore, this study employs a dataset that has been manually annotated by the research team. The annotation task was collaboratively carried out by two graduate students specializing in materials science. Moreover, to ensure the quality of the annotations, we also involved two graduate students from the field of computer science in the review process of the data. This interdisciplinary collaborative approach aims to enhance the accuracy and reliability of the dataset.

MatSciRel. This dataset is designed to serve the relevance assessment module within the model. To this end, we have meticulously annotated a dataset comprising 1000 records for relevance assessment. In this dataset, the outcomes of the relevance assessments are categorized into two classes: relevant and irrelevant. This issue can be regarded as a typical binary classification task. A detailed representation of the data see Fig. 2a.

a
```
1 {
2    "text": "Most MoN-Cu coatings demonstrate excellent wear resistance at this
  temperature, except for MoN-Cu-19.3 at.%,  …… ",
3    "relevance": 1
4 }
```

b
```
1 {
2      "question": "By approximately what percentage does the coefficient of friction
  (COF) of a composite sample decrease when incorporating graphene, compared to the
  COF of a coarse-grained Cu counterpart?",
3      "options": " A) 40% B) 50%  C) 55%  D) 60%",
4      "correct_answer": "D"
5 }
```

c
```
1 {
2      "text": "……… underscoring the advantageous influence of increased Al2O3
  percentages on this progression. Among the selected samples, S5, with a 10% Al2O3
  content, exhibits better homogeneity and less agglomeration, ………",
3      "results": [{
4          "summary":"The synthesis of graphene nanosheets was achieved through
  mechanical co-milling, with increased Al2O3 percentages positively influencing the
  process, and sample S5, containing 10% Al2O3, exhibited better homogeneity, less
  agglomeration, and high-quality surface texture."
5      },{ "summary":"……" },{ "summary":"……"}, ]
6      "better_answer_index": "1"
7 }
```

Fig. 2. (a) Example of MatSciRele Dataset. (b) Example of MatSciQA Dataset. (c) Example of MatSciSummary-Eval Dataset.

MatSciQA. To accurately evaluate the effectiveness of integrating LLMs with a knowledge base, we have also annotated a dataset for testing purposes. This dataset is designed to validate the effectiveness of material science knowledge extracted from literature in enhancing the knowledge base of a LLMs using the Retrieval-Augmented Generation (RAG) approach. The dataset consists of 500 choice questions, encompassing various aspects such as knowledge application, numerical reasoning, and logical reasoning. Furthermore, the correctness of the questions has been verified by two master's researchers in the field of material science. Through the quantitative metric of accuracy, the multiple-choice questions provide an objective assessment of the LLMs proficiency in the domain of material science knowledge. Example data is see Fig. 2b.

MatSciSummary-Eval. The objective of this dataset is to evaluate the performance of the model's summarization module. To this end, we have annotated a dataset comprising 1000 entries, each entry featuring three distinct summary outputs from different models. From these outputs, we selected the most appropriate summary as the reference answer for each entry. Considering the subjective nature of model summarization, there may be discrepancies among annotators in terms of the effectiveness of compression and the selection of the optimal summary. Consequently, the annotation process for this dataset involved three professionals who scored the three model-generated summaries, with the highest overall scoring summary being chosen as the standard answer. Example data is see Fig. 2c.

3   Evaluation and Results

3.1   Relevance Assessment Result

In this experiment, we conducted tests using the manually annotated MatSciRel dataset, with partial results presented in Fig. 3. As our approach employs a multi-model fusion strategy for relevance assessment, the experimental design encompassed both combined model configurations and individual model testing. All models were tested in a zero-shot learning mode. The experimental outcomes indicate that across models, there is a remarkable performance in relevance judgment, which can be attributed to the models' robust reasoning capabilities. In the individual model tests, ChatGPT-4o demonstrated the best performance with an accuracy rate of 97.4%. The highest accuracy rate achieved by a model combination was 99.3%. We can conclude that LLMs possess the ability to efficiently evaluate the relevance of materials science literature.

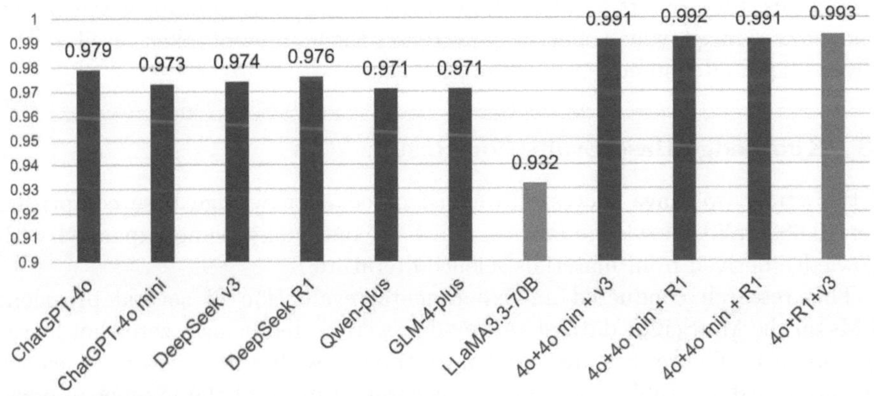

Fig. 3. Partial model correlation evaluation results. The orange bars represent the highest combination. (Color figure online)

3.2   Compression Evaluation Results

This experiment validates the accuracy of the model in selecting multi-model compression outcomes. We utilized the manually annotated MatSciSummary-Eval dataset to assess the accuracy of the compression results. As shown in Fig. 4, the data indicate that the model's compression effect evaluation can achieve a maximum accuracy rate of 95.7%, demonstrating superior performance in the selection of compression outcomes. Although the accuracy rate of the compression effect does not reach 100%, the negative impact of selecting other knowledge as the optimal knowledge is relatively minor, given that the goal of compression is to choose the best possible outcome.

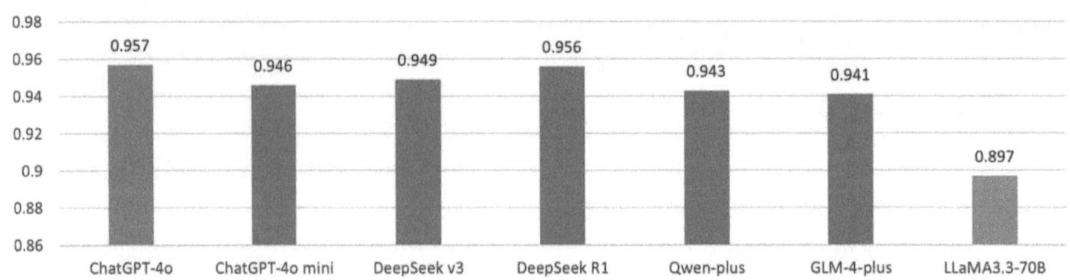

Fig. 4. Experimental results of the model on the MatSciComp dataset.

We also calculated the average compression ratio between the original text and the summarized text, with the results indicating an average compression rate of 56%. The compression performance is notable, enabling the knowledge base to accommodate a more substantial collection of knowledge within the same storage space. Furthermore, when utilizing RAG and LLMs for conversational interactions, the proportion of the knowledge base used as prompt words in the dialogue is reduced, which effectively decreases the number of tokens used during conversation and, consequently, lowers the cost.

3.3   Knowledge Base Evaluation Results

In this study, we have successfully constructed a knowledge base comprising over 10,000 valid knowledge entries, which is continually being expanded with knowledge derived from materials science literature.

This research conducted an experimental evaluation of several prevalent LLMs on the MatSciQA dataset. All models were tested using a zero-shot learning approach. The results are detailed in Table 1, with accuracy serving as the evaluation metric. Table 1 presents the accuracy rates and the number of questions correctly answered by each model. The observed results indicate that, without the use of a knowledge base, the performance of the models on the dataset was generally suboptimal. Among them, the DeepSeek R1 model exhibited a slightly superior knowledge reserve in the domain of materials science.

Table 1. Experimental results of the model on the MatSciQA dataset (own)

Models	Unused knowledge base	Use knowledge base	Improvement effect
ChatGPT-4o	56.2% (281)	86.8%(434)	30.6%(153)
ChatGPT-4o mini	54.4%(272)	85.4%(427)	31%(155)
DeepSeek v3	55.4%(277)	86.6%(433)	31.2%(156)
DeepSeek R1	56.2%(281)	87.2%(436)	31%(155)
Qwen-plus	53.0%(265)	84.6%(423)	31.6%(158)
GLM-4-plus	53.8%(261)	84.0%(420)	31.8%(159)
LLaMA3.3-70B	27.4%(137)	59.8%(299)	32.4%(162)

Upon integrating the knowledge base, the DeepSeek R1 model continued to demonstrate the best performance, with an increase in accuracy of 31%. Notably, although the LLaMA3.3-70B did not perform outstandingly without the knowledge base, its performance improvement was the most significant when combined with the knowledge base.

Table 2. Experimental results of the model on the MaScQA dataset

Models	Unused knowledge base	Use knowledge base	Improvement effect
ChatGPT-4o	66.30% (431)	67.53%(439)	1.23%(8)
ChatGPT-4o mini	61.38% (399)	62.46%(406)	1.07%(7)
DeepSeek v3	65.69%(427)	86.6%(434)	1.07%(7)
DeepSeek R1	66.00%(429)	66.76%(437)	1.23%(8)
Qwen-plus	59.38%(386)	60.76%(395)	1.38%(9)
GLM-4-plus	58.61%(381)	60.00%(390)	1.38%(9)
LLaMA3.3-70B	26.00%(169)	27.80%(181)	1.85%(12)

The validation results on the public MaScQA test set are presented in Table 2. The findings indicate that LLMs still lack sufficient knowledge in the field of materials science, with their performance merely reaching an acceptable level. Although integrating our constructed knowledge base led to a moderate improvement in performance, the extent of this enhancement was limited. This may be attributed to the fact that our knowledge base contains insufficient knowledge directly related to this dataset, which represents a limitation of our study. However, we anticipate that optimizing the knowledge base by continuously expanding its scale will lead to better outcomes. It is noteworthy that the extraction process of our materials knowledge can be fully automated. Therefore, with an appropriate investment of time, we aim to construct a knowledge base that is both extensive and of high quality.

4   Conclusion

In this study, we investigated the efficacy of LLMs in assessing the similarity of material science literature and in tasks related to text summarization. Utilizing a manually annotated dataset, we found that LLMs demonstrated exceptional performance even in a zero-shot learning setting, which not only reduced the application costs of the models but also significantly shortened the experimental duration. The research delved into the potential of LLMs in natural language processing and validated the effectiveness of the knowledge extracted through an enhanced retrieval generation approach, thereby enhancing the knowledge base of LLMs in the field of material science. Additionally, our method effectively reduces storage space requirements while preserving the original intent of the knowledge.

Our approach offers a convenient and efficient tool for building knowledge bases for material science researchers with limited computer skills. Furthermore, as models continue to evolve, we can dynamically replace the models within our method to pursue even better outcomes. This study is expected to advance the data-driven innovation process in the field of material science.

References

1. Dagdelen, J., et al.: Structured information extraction from scientific text with large language models. Nat. Commun. **15**(1), 1418 (2024)
2. Dua, D., Wang, Y., Dasigi, P., Stanovsky, G., Singh, S., Gardner, M.: Drop: a reading comprehension benchmark requiring discrete reasoning over paragraphs. arXiv preprint arXiv:1903.00161 (2019)
3. Gupta, T., Zaki, M., Krishnan, N.A., Mausam: Matscibert: a materials domain language model for text mining and information extraction. NPJ Comput. Mater. **8**(1), 102 (2022)
4. He, T., et al.: Similarity of precursors in solid-state synthesis as text-mined from scientific literature. Chem. Mater. **32**(18), 7861–7873 (2020)
5. Hendrycks, D., et al.: Aligning AI with shared human values. arXiv preprint arXiv:2008.02275 (2020)
6. Huang, D., Cole, J.M.: A database of thermally activated delayed fluorescent molecules auto-generated from scientific literature with chemdataextractor. Sci. Data **11**(1), 80 (2024)
7. Huang, S., Cole, J.M.: A database of battery materials auto-generated using Chem-DataExtractor. Sci. Data **7**(1), 260 (2020)
8. Huang, S., Cole, J.M.: Batterybert: a pretrained language model for battery database enhancement. J. Chem. Inf. Model. **62**(24), 6365–6377 (2022)
9. Jin, H., Zhang, Y., Meng, D., Wang, J., Tan, J.: A comprehensive survey on process-oriented automatic text summarization with exploration of LLM-based methods. arXiv preprint arXiv:2403.02901 (2024)
10. Kocmi, T., et al.: Findings of the 2023 conference on machine translation (WMT23): LLMs are here but not quite there yet. In: WMT23-Eighth Conference on Machine Translation, pp. 198–216 (2023)
11. Kononova, O., He, T., Huo, H., Trewartha, A., Olivetti, E.A., Ceder, G.: Opportunities and challenges of text mining in materials research. Iscience **24**(3) (2021)
12. Korvigo, I., Holmatov, M., Zaikovskii, A., Skoblov, M.: Putting hands to rest: efficient deep CNN-RNN architecture for chemical named entity recognition with no hand-crafted rules. J. Cheminform. **10**, 1–10 (2018)
13. Lei, G., Docherty, R., Cooper, S.J.: Materials science in the era of large language models: a perspective. Digit. Discov. **3**(7), 1257–1272 (2024)
14. Mavracic, J., Court, C.J., Isazawa, T., Elliott, S.R., Cole, J.M.: Chemdataextractor 2.0: autopopulated ontologies for materials science. J. Chem. Inf. Model. **61**(9), 4280–4289 (2021)
15. Polak, M.P., Morgan, D.: Extracting accurate materials data from research papers with conversational language models and prompt engineering. Nat. Commun. **15**(1), 1569 (2024)
16. Sakaguchi, K., Bras, R.L., Bhagavatula, C., Choi, Y.: Winogrande: an adversarial winograd schema challenge at scale. Commun. ACM **64**(9), 99–106 (2021)

17. Swain, M.C., Cole, J.M.: Chemdataextractor: a toolkit for automated extraction of chemical information from the scientific literature. J. Chem. Inf. Model. **56**(10), 1894–1904 (2016)
18. Trewartha, A., et al.: Quantifying the advantage of domain-specific pre-training on named entity recognition tasks in materials science. Patterns **3**(4) (2022)
19. Venugopal, V., Olivetti, E.: Matkg: an autonomously generated knowledge graph in material science. Sci. Data **11**(1), 217 (2024)
20. Wang, S., et al.: GPT-NER: named entity recognition via large language models. arXiv preprint arXiv:2304.10428 (2023)
21. Weston, L., et al.: Named entity recognition and normalization applied to large-scale information extraction from the materials science literature. J. Chem. Inf. Model. **59**(9), 3692–3702 (2019)
22. Wilary, D.M., Cole, J.M.: Reactiondataextractor 2.0: a deep learning approach for data extraction from chemical reaction schemes. J. Chem. Inf. Model. **63**(19), 6053–6067 (2023)
23. Ye, J., et al.: LLM-DA: data augmentation via large language models for few-shot named entity recognition. arXiv preprint arXiv:2402.14568 (2024)
24. Zaki, M., Krishnan, N.A., et al.: Mascqa: investigating materials science knowledge of large language models. Digit. Discov. **3**(2), 313–327 (2024)
25. Zhang, W., et al.: Fine-tuning large language models for chemical text mining. Chem. Sci. **15**(27), 10600–10611 (2024)
26. Zhao, J., Cole, J.M.: A database of refractive indices and dielectric constants auto-generated using ChemDataExtractor. Sci. Data **9**(1), 192 (2022)
27. Zhao, J., Huang, S., Cole, J.M.: Opticalbert and opticaltable-sqa: text-and table-based language models for the optical-materials domain. J. Chem. Inf. Model. **63**(7), 1961–1981 (2023)
28. Zheng, Z., Zhang, O., Borgs, C., Chayes, J.T., Yaghi, O.M.: Chatgpt chemistry assistant for text mining and the prediction of MOF synthesis. J. Am. Chem. Soc. **145**(32), 18048–18062 (2023)

A Robust Video Steganography Method Based on Multi-scale Decomposition and Invertible Networks

Shiwei Li⬭, Jianxiang Liao⬭, Zhenyu Liu⬭, Mengyuan Wei, Yuhang Wang⬭, and Jian Liu(✉)

Hefei University of Technology, Hefei, China
{2023217504,2023216521,2023217371,2023170724}@mail.hfut.edu.cn,
jianliu@hfut.edu.cn
https://www.hfut.edu.cn/

Abstract. To address the challenges of dynamic consistency, high capacity requirements, and resistance to distortion attacks in video steganography, this paper proposes a multi-scale robust video steganography framework, RMCIN. RMCIN consists of three key modules, each designed to tackle specific challenges in video steganography. The Dual-scale Attention (DSA) module extracts cross-frame features and integrates semantic information, while the Frequency-domain Multi-scale Decomposition (FMD) module constructs a time-frequency representation through reversible transformations. Finally, the Multi-scale Fusion (MSF) module enhances the robustness of information embedding by jointly refining spatial and frequency-domain features. A specially designed Multi-step Robust Training Strategy (MRTS) progressively injects mixed distortions, including Gaussian noise and JPEG compression, dynamically strengthening the model's resistance to attacks. Experimental results demonstrate that the proposed method achieves high-fidelity secret video reconstruction under various distortion conditions and attains state-of-the-art steganographic robustness in Gaussian noise and Joint Photographic Experts Group(JPEG) compression scenarios, offering valuable insights for real-world applications of video steganography.

Keywords: Video steganography · Frequency domain · Multi-scale fusion · Robustness · Frequency-domain decomposition · Deep learning · Anti-distortion attacks

1   Introduction

With the rapid development of multimedia technology and growing concerns over data security, steganography [1] has become an essential technique for secure communication by covertly embedding information into digital media such as

---

S. Li and J. Liao—These authors contributed equally to this work.

T. Zhu et al. (Eds.): KSEM 2025, LNAI 15922, pp. 52–64, 2026.
https://doi.org/10.1007/978-981-95-3058-8_5

images and videos [1,2]. While deep learning-based methods have made significant progress in image steganography [3,4], video steganography remains challenging due to temporal dependencies and higher data volume. Efficiently capturing long-range temporal dependencies and ensuring robustness against distortions like Gaussian noise and JPEG compression [5,6] are key obstacles.

Although Invertible Neural Networks (INN) [7,8] improve image steganography robustness via reversible transformations, they struggle with video's multiscale spatiotemporal and frequency characteristics. Existing approaches often neglect the complementary benefits of spatial details and frequency information, limiting robustness under compression and complex distortions.

To address these challenges, we propose a novel video steganography framework called RMCIN (Robust Multi-scale Coupled Invertible Network). This framework integrates spatial and frequency domain representations with advanced fusion strategies to enhance robustness. Our contributions include:

1. We perform dual-scale decomposition in both spatial and DCT frequency domains (FMD module) to enrich feature representations for robust embedding.
2. We design a Hierarchical Feature Network (HFN) composed of Multi-scale Fusion (MSF) and Dynamic Semantic Aggregation (DSA) modules. The DSANet extracts cross-frame semantic features, while MSF adaptively fuses spatial and frequency information to fully leverage multi-scale representations.
3. A progressive distortion simulation strategy is employed during training, introducing increasingly complex distortions such as Gaussian noise and JPEG compression to enhance model robustness under real-world conditions.

2 Related Work

2.1 Deep Learning-Based Steganography

Deep learning–based steganography enables high-capacity embedding through end-to-end training. HiDDeN [9] employ encoder–decoder architectures with adversarial training to enhance image quality. Baluja [10] was the first to embed full-size images, and Weng et al. [11] subsequently proposed a video steganography model leveraging temporal residuals to improve robustness, but its resistance to attacks remains limited. Recent studies incorporate noise layers during training to simulate various attacks [7,8], yet these methods depend on predefined attack types, limiting generalization.

2.2 Invertible Neural Networks (INN) for Steganography

INNs achieve lossless recovery via symmetric mappings, offering theoretical guarantees for steganography. ISN [12] and HiNet [13] embed secret images into same-resolution carriers, but strict reversibility reduces robustness. Xu et al.

[8] proposed RIIS, incorporating a denoising module and asymmetric inverse mapping to mitigate distortion, yet its performance degrades over time in video scenarios. Yamauchi et al. [7] designed quantized activation functions to simulate JPEG compression but did not address non-structured attacks such as Gaussian noise. These studies indicate that enhancing INN robustness requires modular, attack-aware design.

2.3 Challenges in Robust Video Steganography

Video steganography must balance spatial imperceptibility and temporal consistency. DVMark [14] enhances compression robustness via a multi-scale network but ignores frame-wise noise propagation. REVMark [15] employs temporal alignment to resist H.264 compression, yet struggles under non-uniform attacks. Most existing methods simply extend image-based frameworks to video without fully considering temporal attacks that affect information integrity.

3 Method

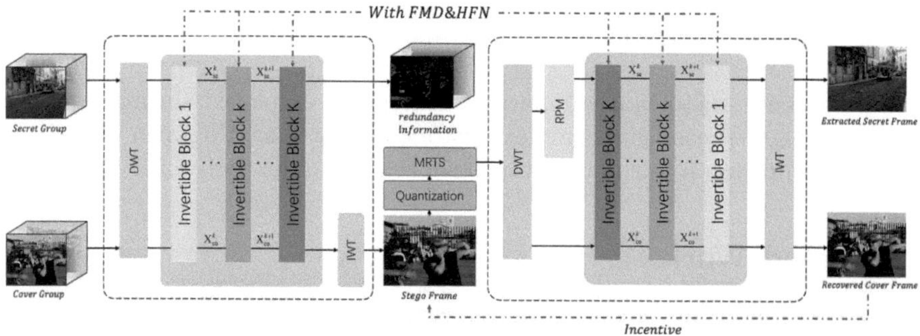

Fig. 1. We propose an overall framework for robust video steganography, where we modify the internal components of the reversible block to better handle distortion attacks. The RPM module is derived from LF-VSN [16].

3.1 Overview

The proposed robust video steganography framework is shown in Fig. 1. It takes the host video frame x_c and secret information x_s as input, generating a stego-video. After transmission or distortion attacks, the extracted information x_d is restored to x_e. The system consists of three key components: the Frequency-domain Multi-scale Decomposition (FMD) module captures local textures and global energy distribution using spatial-frequency dual-domain features; the DSANet refines features deeply, while the MSF module adaptively weights them;

and the Multi-scale Invertible Flow Network ensures bidirectional mapping for covert and reversible embedding $x_h \leftrightarrow x_s$. To enhance robustness, a multi-modal noise simulation layer is incorporated during training, along with a Multi-step Robust Training Strategy (MRTS) to progressively improve attack resistance. The entire framework is trained end-to-end and demonstrates superior performance in various distortion scenarios.

3.2   Multi-scale Invertible Flow Network

Overall Architecture. As shown in Fig. 2, the input feature $x \in \mathbb{R}^{C \times H \times W}$ is processed through two pathways:

- **High-frequency path**: $x_{high} = A_{DSA}(x)$, satisfying the Lipschitz constraint $\|A_{DSA}(x) - A_{DSA}(y)\| \leq L\|x - y\|$.
- **Low-frequency path**: $x'_{low} = A'_{DSA}(F_{DCT^{-1}}(P_\Omega(F_{DCT}(x))))$, where Ω represents low-frequency projection.

The fusion module G then combines the two paths as $x_{fused} = G(x_{high}, x'_{low})$.

Invertible Transformation Construction. Define an invertible mapping $T : \mathbb{R}^{C \times H \times W} \times \mathbb{R}^{C \times H \times W} \to \mathbb{R}^{C \times H \times W} \times \mathbb{R}^{C \times H \times W}$ as:

$$\text{Forward:} \begin{cases} h = x_{fused} + \Phi(y) \\ y' = y \odot \exp(\Psi(h)) + \Gamma(h) \end{cases}$$

$$\text{Inverse:} \begin{cases} y = (y' - \Gamma(h)) \oslash \exp(\Psi(h)) \\ x_{fused} = h - \Phi(y) \\ x = T^{-1}(x_{fused}, x_{low}) \end{cases} \tag{1}$$

where Φ, Ψ, Γ are learnable functions, and $\odot/\oslash$ denote element-wise multiplication and division. This construction strictly satisfies the invertibility requirement.

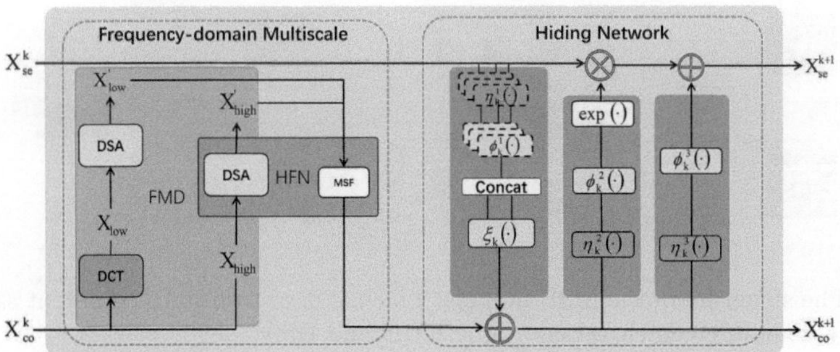

Fig. 2. The structure of the reversible block in the multi-scale invertible flow network, with the FDM module added on the left side, is shown.

3.3 Frequency-Domain Multi-scale Decomposition (FMD)

To improve robustness against frequency-domain attacks, we propose a Frequency-domain Multi-scale Decomposition (FMD) module combining spatial and frequency features. Its dual-branch design extracts spatial details and frequency-domain features separately, achieving adaptive fusion. High-frequency components prone to quantization noise are handled independently, while low-frequency components ensure stable representations.

In the spatial branch, global semantics and local textures are preserved for input video frames $V \in \mathbb{R}^{B \times C \times H \times W}$. In the frequency branch, block-wise DCT is applied: video frames are divided into 8×8 blocks, and low-frequency sub-bands (top-left 2×2 coefficients) are retained via masking to suppress high-frequency noise. An inverse DCT reconstructs frequency features V_{freq}, stabilizing low-frequency information while redistributing signal energy (Fig. 3).

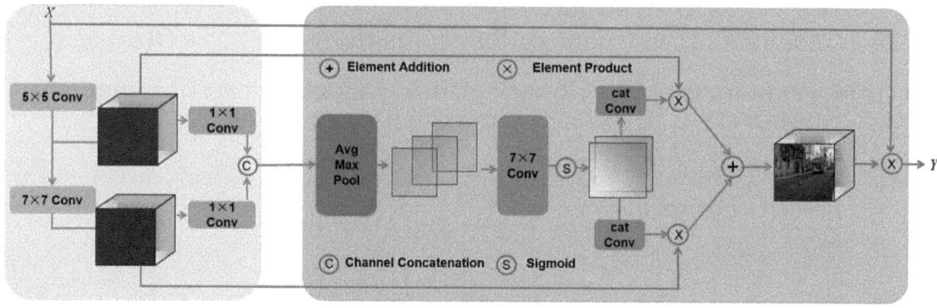

Fig. 3. The structure of the DSA module, where the input X is multiplied by the original weights after passing through the dual-channel attention.

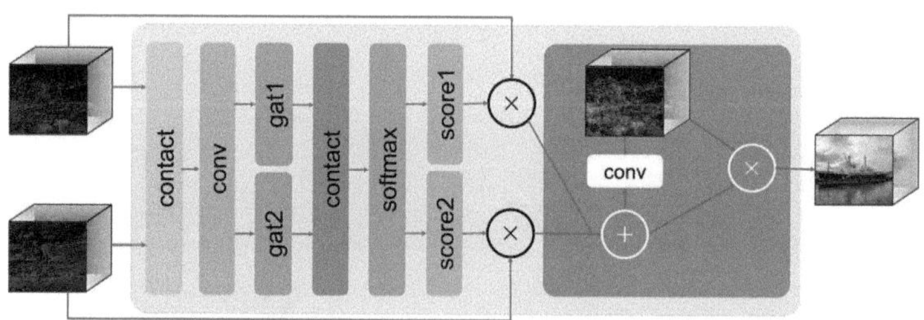

Fig. 4. The structure of the MSF module, which is used to fuse the different sampling frequency domain channels generated by FMD and DSA.

3.4 Hierarchical Fusion Network (HFN)

To address multi-scale fusion challenges, we design a Hierarchical Fusion Network (HFN) based on LSKNet [19]. It integrates spatial details and frequency anti-interference features through multi-resolution extraction and adaptive fusion.

Multi-resolution Feature Extraction. Spatial features are extracted using large receptive field convolutions (e.g., 7×7) and depthwise separable convolutions for global-local aggregation. The FMD module provides stable frequency features via band selection. This design preserves low-frequency contours under compression and noise attacks.

Given an input $\mathbf{X} \in \mathbb{R}^{B \times C \times H \times W}$, the extraction can be summarized as:

$$\Gamma_i(X) = \mathcal{C}_{1 \times 1}(DWConv_i(X))$$
$$\Phi(\cdot) = \mathcal{C}_{rec}(\sigma(\mathcal{C}_{sq}([\mu, \max]))) \tag{2}$$
$$Y = X \odot \Phi(\Gamma_5 \oplus \Gamma_{7_d})$$

Adaptive Dynamic Fusion. As shown in Fig. 4, HFN employs gated attention and residual connections for multi-source feature fusion, enhancing robustness under diverse distortions.

3.5 Loss Function Design

Three-level Joint Optimization Objective. This method constructs a joint loss function with multiple constraints:

$$\mathcal{L}_{\text{total}} = \underbrace{\lambda_1 \| G^{\text{stego}} - G^{\text{host}} \|_2}_{\text{Visual Fidelity}} + \underbrace{\lambda_2 \| \Psi(\hat{G}^{\text{stego}}) - S \|_1}_{\text{Information Integrity}} + \underbrace{\lambda_3 \| \Psi(\hat{G}^{\text{stego}}) - G^{\text{host}} \|_1}_{\text{Temporal Consistency}} \tag{3}$$

where the encoder Φ generates the stego-video $G^{\text{stego}} = \Phi(G^{\text{host}})$, and the decoder Ψ recovers the information from the noisy stego-video $\hat{G}^{\text{stego}}$.

Forward Constraint: The L2 norm enforces pixel-level alignment between the stego-video G^{stego} and the host video G^{host}, ensuring imperceptibility of the steganography.

Backward Constraint: The L1 norm optimizes the information reconstruction error $\| \Psi(\cdot) - S \|_1$ for the noisy stego-video $\hat{G}^{\text{stego}}$, improving robustness against interference.

Temporal Constraint: The L1 distance between the central frame features $\Psi(\hat{G}^{\text{stego}})$ and the host video ensures temporal stability across the video sequence.

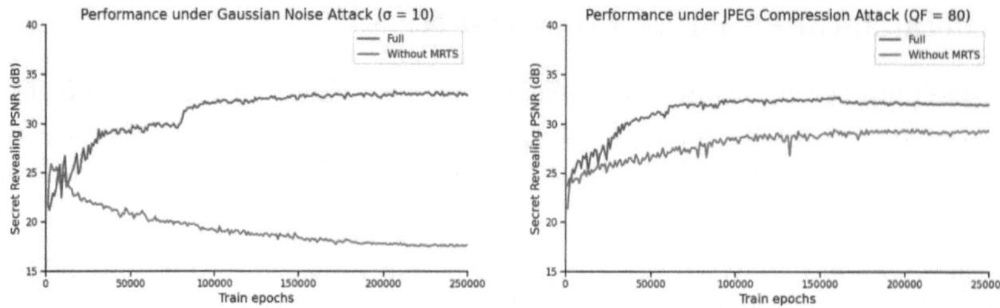

Fig. 5. The comparison of $PSNR_s$ curves with and without the MRTS training strategy under JPEG compression and Gaussian noise attacks shows that MRTS significantly improves the model's performance degradation under distortion conditions. The blue curve represents the results with the MRTS strategy, while the green curve represents the results without the MRTS strategy.

3.6   Multi-step Robust Training Strategy (MRTS)

To enhance the resilience of the steganography system against distortions in open environments, we propose a multi-stage progressive training framework called MRTS. This strategy introduces a hierarchical distortion simulation mechanism, guiding the network to develop robust representations against multi-modal attacks. The training process consists of three progressive stages:

Stage 1: Single-modal Feature Stabilization. During initial training, a single distortion type is applied while other augmentations are disabled. This phase establishes a fundamental mapping between distortion patterns and embedding, optimizing reconstruction loss to learn key feature associations. This clean setup accelerates parameter convergence under a single attack mode.

Stage 2: Multi-modal Coupled Training. After single-distortion training, a randomized multi-distortion mechanism is introduced, applying different distortions dynamically at moderate intensities. This enhances the network's ability to handle mixed distortions, improving robustness against cross-interference.

Stage 3: Full Parameter-space Reinforcement. In the final training phase, distortion intensity constraints are further relaxed, allowing multiple mixed attacks with varying intensities to occur simultaneously within the same batch. This strategy creates a more challenging adversarial environment, encouraging the network to adapt to extreme distortion scenarios.

As shown in Fig. 5, our training strategy demonstrates outstanding resistance to distortions and a significant improvement in robustness under various distortion conditions.

4   Experiments

4.1   Implementation Details

In this study, we use the Vimeo-90K dataset [17] as the primary training material, extracting video sequences for model learning. The training process employs the Adam optimizer [18] with momentum parameters set as ($\beta_1 = 0.9, \beta_2 = 0.5$). The initial learning rate is set to $1e - 4$ with a periodic decay mechanism (50% reduction every 30,000 iterations). The batch size is set to 8, and the regularization coefficient is $1e - 12$ to control model complexity. The entire training process consists of 250,000 iterations, requiring approximately 28 h for model convergence on an NVIDIA GEFORCE RTX 4090D GPU.

Table 1. Ablation experiment results ($PSNR_s$), including the ablation of FMD, HFN, and MRTS. The best-performing metrics are highlighted in bold.

FMD	HFN	MRTS	Gaussian	JPEG		
			$\sigma = 10$	$Q = 70$	$Q = 80$	$Q = 90$
X	✓	✓	18.2	26.72	27.50	27.16
✓	X	✓	14.76	28.80	30.47	32.39
✓	✓	X	17.71	28.02	29.37	30.79
✓	✓	✓	**30.59**	**29.33**	**30.98**	**33.04**

4.2 Ablation Study

Effect of Frequency-domain Multi-scale Decomposition (FMD). FMD uses block-wise DCT to separate low-frequency energy and high-frequency details, aligning steganographic embedding with visually sensitive regions. Removing FMD causes a PSNR drop of 2.61–5.88 dB under JPEG compression (Table 1), demonstrating its importance for robustness against quantization attacks.

Effect of Hierarchical Fusion Network (HFN). Table 2 shows that both the DSA and MSF modules are necessary for optimal performance. Without DSA, MSF's feature extraction weakens, reducing reconstruction quality under noise. Without MSF, DSA oversuppresses textures, causing detail loss under compression. Together, they balance noise suppression and texture preservation, ensuring stable reconstruction under severe degradation.

Table 2. Ablation results ($PSNR_s$) for removing DSA and MSF in HFN.

DSA	MSF	$\sigma = 20$	$\sigma = 10$	$\sigma = 5$	$Q = 80$
X	✓	11.53	19.54	28.03	**31.40**
✓	X	11.74	19.95	27.20	28.37
✓	✓	**24.77**	**30.59**	**29.33**	30.98

HFN employs DSANet for multi-scale feature extraction and MSF for dynamic fusion. DSANet alone suppresses high-frequency textures excessively;

MSF alone causes noisy fusion. Their synergy via "extraction-denoising-fusion" is essential for robust feature construction.

Effect of Multi-step Robust Training Strategy (MRTS). MRTS improves feature invariance through progressive training stages: (1) Single-distortion training on JPEG compression; (2) Mixed training combining Gaussian noise and compression to exploit spatial-frequency complementarity; (3) Multi-intensity reinforcement with dynamic distortion levels to distinguish minor and severe attacks.

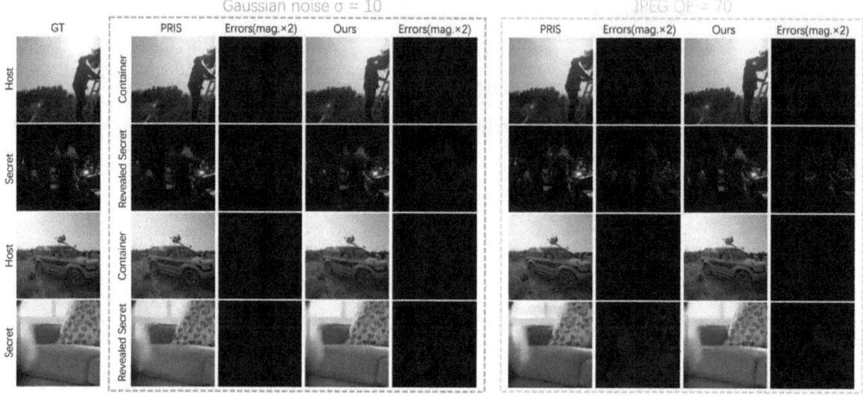

Fig. 6. Visual reconstruction comparison under attack. Our model shows better color fidelity under JPEG compression.

Table 3. Comparison of $PSNR_s/SSIM_s$ under JPEG compression.

Method	$QF = 90$	$QF = 80$	$QF = 70$
HiNet [13]	12.95/0.2571	12.13/0.2096	11.50/0.1894
LF-VSN [12]	10.60/0.3311	10.57/0.3309	10.56/0.3313
PRIS [7]	32.95/**0.9273**	29.05/0.8764	25.29/0.8059
Ours	**33.04**/0.9244	**30.98**/0.8956	**29.33**/0.8670

4.3   Comparative Experiments

Robustness to JPEG Compression. We use randomized quantization indices during training and adapt quantization parameters at test time. An adaptive DCT frequency band embedding strategy mitigates conflicts between embedding and compression. Table 3 shows our method achieves superior reconstruction under high compression compared to existing methods.

Robustness to Gaussian Noise. A noise-aware gating unit in the encoder suppresses high-frequency noise via adaptive thresholding. Table 4 demonstrates our method maintains better image quality under strong noise than prior approaches.

Visual and quantitative comparisons (Fig. 6) reveal our method better preserves structural details and yields lower reconstruction errors than PRIS under intense compression and noise. PSNR curves in Fig. 7 further confirm our method's stable performance and gradual degradation under increasing distortion.

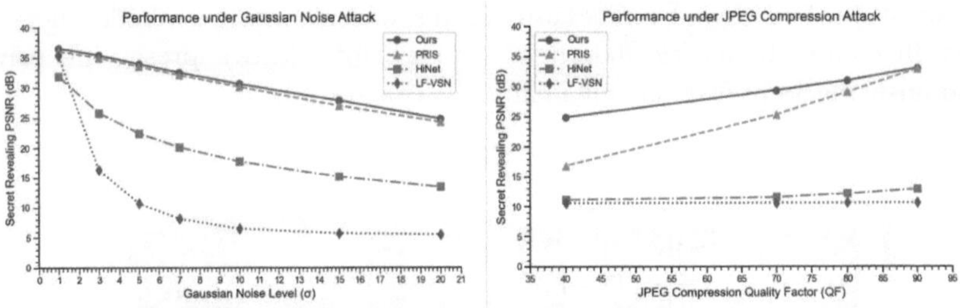

Fig. 7. Performance comparison under JPEG compression and Gaussian noise attacks.

Generalization Ability. Cross-domain tests on DIV2K and COCO datasets (Table 5) verify our method's robustness across diverse content and encoding parameters, confirming the adaptability of our joint spatiotemporal embedding.

Table 4. Comparison of $PSNR_s/SSIM_s$ under Gaussian noise.

Method	$\sigma = 1$	$\sigma = 10$	$\sigma = 15$
HiNet [13]	31.89/0.8924	17.71/0.2769	15.11/0.1908
LF-VSN [12]	35.26/0.9494	6.47/0.0300	5.69/0.0163
PRIS [7]	36.05/0.9580	30.12/0.8849	26.96/0.8113
Ours	**36.54/0.9625**	**30.59/0.9045**	**27.82/0.8551**

4.4 Applications

In real scenarios such as printing or screen capture, images often undergo severe distortions (e.g., geometric transformations, sensor noise, motion blur). Unlike conventional methods, our multi-scale spatial-frequency embedding enables successful secret recovery even after such attacks (Fig. 8).

This robustness supports various applications:

Table 5. PSNR under JPEG compression for different datasets.

Dataset	$QF = 90$	$QF = 80$	$QF = 70$
Vimeo-90K	34.90/33.04	34.35/30.98	33.88/29.33
udm10 [22]	37.38/35.75	36.90/33.70	36.37/32.17
RESD [21]	33.84/28.68	33.08/26.93	32.49/25.53

1. **Media Copyright Protection and Traceability**: Embedding invisible watermarks into digital content ensures copyright traceability across print, photography, and multiple conversions.
2. **Biometric Privacy Protection**: Blind watermarking embeds encrypted identifiers into biometric data (e.g., fingerprints, faces), preserving privacy and ensuring tamper-resistant identity verification [20].

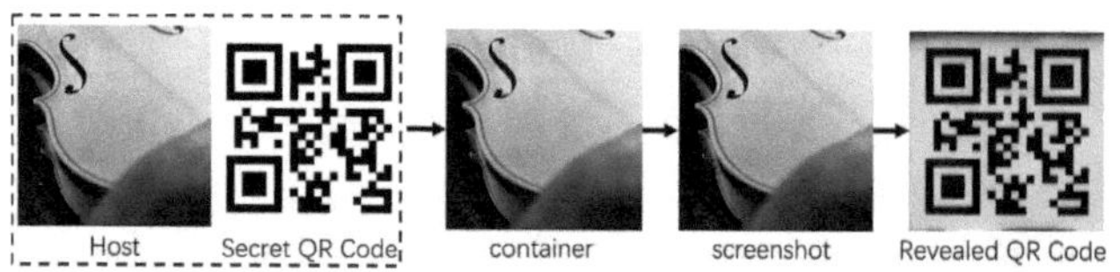

Fig. 8. Reconstruction results under real-world screenshot attacks. The container image captured via CMOS still enables QR code recovery.

5   Conclusion

This paper proposes a multi-scale robust method for video steganography that addresses the challenges of robustness and reconstruction quality in complex distortion scenarios. By leveraging Frequency-domain Multi-scale Decomposition (FMD), a Hierarchical Fusion Network (HFN), and a Multi-step Robust Training Strategy (MRTS), our method effectively enhances video steganography performance. Experimental results demonstrate that our approach significantly improves secret video reconstruction PSNR under Gaussian noise and JPEG compression attacks compared to existing state-of-the-art methods. By dynamically fusing spatial details with frequency-domain anti-interference features and employing a progressive adversarial training strategy, our model exhibits notable advantages in hybrid distortion scenarios. Furthermore, cross-domain testing validates the framework's strong adaptability to variations in video encoding parameters, laying a solid foundation for real-world applications.

Acknowledgments. This work was supported in part by the Hefei Municipal Natural Science Foundation under Grant (No. HZR2403), Natural Science Research Project of

Colleges and Universities in Anhui Province (No. 2022AH051889, No. 2308085QF227), General Project of Anhui Province Outstanding Young Teachers Cultivation Program in 2024 (No. YQYB2024096).

References

1. Liu, Y., Liu, S., Wang, Y., Zhao, H., Liu, S.: Video steganography: a review. Neurocomputing **335**, 238–250 (2019)
2. Setiadi, D.R.I.M.: PSNR Vs SSIM: imperceptibility quality assessment for image steganography. Multimedia Tools Appl. **80**(6), 8423–8444 (2020)
3. Subramanian, N., Elharrouss, O., Al-Maadeed, S., Bouridane, A.: Image steganography: a review of the recent advances. IEEE Access **9**, 23409–23423 (2021)
4. Tang, W., Li, B., Tan, S., Barni, M., Huang, J.: CNN-based adversarial embedding for image steganography. IEEE Trans. Inf. Forensics Secur. **14**(8), 2074–2087 (2019)
5. Tao, J., Li, S., Zhang, X., Wang, Z.: Towards robust image steganography. IEEE Trans. Circuits Syst. Video Technol. **29**(2), 594–600 (2019)
6. Lu, W., Zhang, J., Zhao, X., Zhang, W., Huang, J.: Secure robust JPEG steganography based on AutoEncoder with adaptive BCH encoding. Comput. Sci. **31**(7), 2909–2922 (2021)
7. Yang, H., Xu, Y., Liu, X., Ma, X.: PRIS: practical robust invertible network for mage steganography. Eng. Appl. Artif. Intell. **133** (2024)
8. Xu, Y., Mou, C., Hu, Y., Xie, J., Zhang, J.: Robust invertible image steganography. In: Conference on Computer Vision and Pattern Recognition Workshops. IEEE Computer Society Conference on Computer Vision and Pattern Recognition. Workshops (2022)
9. Zhu, J., Kaplan, R., Johnson, J., Fei-Fei, L.: HiDDeN: hiding data with deep networks. Lecture Notes in Computer Science, pp. 682–697 (2018)
10. Baluja, S.: Hiding images in plain sight: deep steganography. In: Conference on Neural Information Processing Systems, vol. 30, pp. 2066–2076 (2017)
11. Weng, X., Li, Y., Chi, L., Mu, Y.: High-Capacity Convolutional Video Steganography with Temporal Residual Modeling. arXiv Multimedia, pp. 87–95 (2019)
12. Lu, S.P., Wang, R., Zhong, T., Rosin, P.L.: Large-capacity image steganography based on invertible neural networks. In: 2021 IEEE/CVF Conference on Computer Vision and Pattern Recognition, CVPR 2021, pp. 10811–10820 (2021)
13. Jing, J., Deng, X., Xu, M., Wang, J., Guan, Z.: HiNet: deep image hiding by invertible network. In: International Conference on Computer Vision, pp. 4733–4742 (2021)
14. Luo, X., Li, Y., Chang, H., Liu, C., Milanfar, P., Yang, F.: DVMark: a deep multiscale framework for video watermarking. IEEE Trans. Image Process. (2024)
15. Zhang, Y., Ni, J., Su, W., Liao, X.: A novel deep video watermarking framework with enhanced robustness to H.264/AVC compression. In: Proceedings of the 31st ACM International Conference on Multimedia, MM 2023, pp. 8095–8104 (2023)
16. Mou, C., Xu, Y., Song, J., Zhao, C., Ghanem, B., Zhang, J.: Large-capacity and flexible video steganography via invertible neural network. Comput. Res. Repository 22606–22615 (2023)
17. Xue, T., Chen, B., Wu, J., Wei, D., Freeman, W.T.: Video enhancement with task-oriented flow. Int. J. Comput. Vision **127**(8), 1106–1125 (2019)

18. Kingma, D.P., Ba, J.: Adam: a method for stochastic optimization. In: International Conference on Learning Representations abs/1412.6980 (2014)
19. Li, Y., Hou, Q., Zheng, Z., Cheng, M.M., Yang, J., Li, X.: Large selective kernel network for remote sensing object detection. In: Proceedings of the IEEE/CVF International Conference on Computer Vision (ICCV), pp. 16794–16805 (2023)
20. Douglas, M., Bailey, K., Leeney, M., Curran, K.: An overview of steganography techniques applied to the protection of biometric data. Multimedia Tools Appl. **77**(13), 17333–17373 (2017)
21. Son, S., Lee, S., Nah, S., Timofte, R., Lee, K.M.: NTIRE 2021 challenge on video super-resolution. In: Proceedings of the CVPR Workshops, pp. 166–181 (2021)
22. Yi, P., Wang, Z., Jiang, K., Jiang, J., Ma, J.: Progressive fusion video super-resolution network via exploiting non-local spatio-temporal correlations. In: IEEE International Conference on Computer Vision, pp. 3106–3115 (2019)

IR-SDTNet: An Infrared Small Target Detection Network Based on Denoising Enhancement

Mengdi Sun, Xiao Yu[✉], Linyi Hou, Huanhuan Li, and Xiaoyu Li

School of Computer Science and Technology, Shandong University of Technology,
Zibo, China
yuxiao8907118@163.com

Abstract. Infrared small target images are usually interfered by thermal and speckle noise, and their detection accuracy and robustness face severe challenges. Under high-noise conditions, issues such as low signal-to-noise ratio, background clutter, and blurred target structures severely hinder detection accuracy.In this paper, we propose IR-SDTNet, a denoising detection framework for infrared small targets. It adopts a hierarchical framework and enhances feature representation through dual modeling of local and global features. A multiscale feature fusion mechanism combined with a jump connection integrates the encoder's multi-level features with the decoder's up-sampling features, which enables noise reduction and detail recovery. Experimental results show that IR-SDTNet not only eliminates most noise from infrared images but also helps restore fine details, and furthermore enhances the detectability of small targets, especially under high-noise backgrounds where its denoising and restoration capabilities are particularly strong.

Keywords: Infrared small target detection · U-Net · Transformer · Image denoising

1 Introduction

Infrared imaging is the process of generating images by capturing the infrared radiation emitted by an object through a thermal imaging camera, which is characterized by all-weather, non-contact passive imaging [1], and is widely used in military, aerospace, ocean monitoring, search and rescue and other scenarios. In recent years, infrared small target detection has become a key focus in infrared image processing.

Since infrared images themselves are often disturbed by noise (e.g., thermal noise and speckle noise), target detection, especially small target detection, becomes exceptionally difficult. Denoising methods based on traditional models suffer from the problem of easily losing target details or introducing pseudo-targets, while deep learning-based denoising methods, have the advantages of stronger adaptivity, multi-scale feature extraction capability, joint optimization of denoising and detection, and show better generalization ability under complex backgrounds and different noise conditions. Therefore the technique of combining denoising enhancement with target detection becomes an important means to improve detection accuracy.

To enhance target visibility and detection accuracy in low signal-to-noise ratio (SNR) environments, this paper introduces IR-SDTNet (Infrared Small Target Detection with Denoising Network), a deep learning model tailored for infrared small target detection. IR-SDTNet incorporates a denoising module that processes the original infrared image through three key steps: shallow feature capture, deep feature extraction with a residual Swin Transformer, and high-fidelity image restoration. These steps work together to suppress noise and restore image details. Then the denoised output is passed to an improved U-Net, which integrates multi-layer features via skip connections and leverages a multi-scale prediction mechanism to enhance detection accuracy. Experimental results demonstrate that IR-SDTNet significantly improves infrared image quality and small target detection performance, particularly in high-noise environments, where it exhibits strong robustness in both denoising and detail recovery. The main contributions of this work are summarized as follows.

(1) This paper presents IR-SDTNet, a deep learning model for infrared small target denoising detection. Leveraging its strong denoising ability, IR-SDTNet effectively enhances infrared image quality, significantly boosting the saliency and detectability of small targets, even in complex backgrounds with high noise interference.
(2) The target detection module of IR-SDTNet adopts the improved U-Net structure to conduct small target detection experiments using the IRSTD1K dataset, which verifies that the denoising process of IR-SDTNet leads to a substantial improvement in image quality, which in turn significantly enhances the accuracy of target detection and performs excellently in detail preservation and multiscale feature fusion.

2   Related Work

Image denoising approaches are generally classified into two groups: traditional model-based methods and deep learning techniques. Traditional denoising methods recover noise-contaminated images by modeling the image a priori [2]. These methods generally do not impose strict restrictions on the noise type, and thus are able to adapt to a wide range of noise conditions and exhibit strong generalization capabilities [4]. Nonetheless, such methods still have some limitations in the reconstruction of image content, and the results are often less than ideal.

In contrast, deep learning-based denoising methods significantly improve denoising performance through complex architectural designs, such as residual learning [5] and dense connectivity [12], which still suffer from the problem of partially convolving the layers, although the effectiveness has been considerably enhanced over conventional model-driven approaches, Transformer [1] substitutes CNNs with a self-attention mechanism that captures global relationships between contexts. We make improvements to the traditional Transformer to make it more suitable for infrared small goal detection tasks.

Regarding small target recognition, for the problem of denoising, the Asymmetric Contextual Modulation method proposed by Dai et al. improves the recognizability of small targets through contextual modulation denoising, especially in noisy scenes [3]. In addition, Zhang et al. introduced a technique utilizing Guided Hyperspectral Image Denoising, which retains the detail information of small targets while denoising and effectively reduces the impact of background noise on detection [11]. Although the existing methods have achieved good results in noisy environments and complex backgrounds, they still face challenges, especially in low-contrast and widely varying infrared images.

The fast advancement of deep neural networks has facilitated the research of IR small target detection methods, and convolutional neural networks (CNNs) and other advanced architectures are extensively applied in infrared small target detection. To illustrate, Wu et al. put forward UIU-Net, which enhances small target detectability in infrared images by leveraging multi-level feature fusion and contextual information extraction [9]. Similarly, ISNet proposed by Zhang et al. combines the target shape information and enhances the detectability by designing a special network structure that enhances the saliency of the goal at different scales [10]. Additionally, the attention mechanism is incorporated into infrared small target detection to improve goal saliency. For example, Li et al proposed Dense Nested Attention Network (DNAN), which employs a nested attention mechanism to strengthen small goal feature representation, enhancing their visibility in complex backgrounds [6].

Even though current approaches for infrared small target detection have shown some effectiveness in noisy environments, they still face greater challenges in high-noise and low-contrast conditions. Therefore, this paper proposes an improved framework for image denoising by introducing an improved Swin Transformer to enhance the quality of the image, and target detection by utilizing U-Net with multi-scale head, aiming to effectively boost the detection capabilities of small targets in high-noise conditions and low-contrast images.

3 Methodology

The framework of IR-SDTNet is composed of two principal components: image denoising and small target detection. The denoising module is architected around three core stages: shallow feature extraction, deep feature extraction leveraging the Residual Swin Transformer, and high-fidelity image reconstruction [7]. Initially, the shallow feature extraction module captures low-frequency information via a convolutional layer and forwards it directly to the reconstruction module, thereby preserving fundamental structural features of the image. Subsequently, the deep feature extraction module is constructed using Residual Swin Transformer Blocks (RSTBs), whose internal configuration is illustrated in Fig. 1(a). The operational logic of each Swin Transformer Layer (STL) within an RSTB is depicted in Fig. 1(b), wherein long-range dependencies are modeled through local window attention and cross-window interaction mechanisms. Feature representation is further enriched through the incorporation of terminal convolutional layers and residual connections. Ultimately, the reconstruction module integrates both shallow and deep features and restores high-fidelity imagery through sub-pixel convolution, thereby ensuring precise visual recovery.

For the small target detection module, an enhanced U-Net architecture is employed. The denoised image is input into the decoder, with skip connections established between encoder and decoder to retain fine-grained information. Moreover, a dedicated convolutional layer is appended after each upsampling operation within the decoder, enabling more effective utilization of multi-scale features and significantly improving the network's capacity to detect small targets of varying sizes.

3.1 IR-SDTNet

IR-SDTNet Denoising Module. The IR-SDTNet denoising module comprises three key components: Shallow feature capture, deep feature extraction with a residual Swin Transformer, and high-fidelity image restoration,the overall framework is shown in Fig. 1.

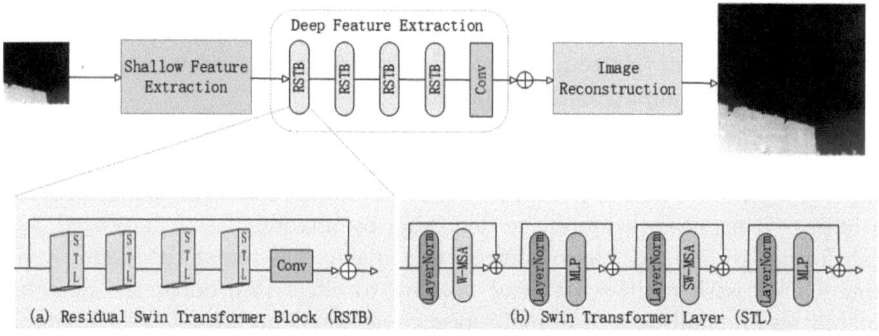

Fig. 1. IR-SDTNet Denoising Module Structure Diagram. Where (a) shows the internal framework of RSTB and (b) shows the internal framework of STL.

• *Shallow Feature Capture Module.* The shallow feature extraction module extracts preliminary image features from the input image by means of a convolutional layer (usually 3×3 convolution), which mainly captures low-frequency information about the image, such as general contour and structural information, and is crucial for tasks such as denoising. The input image I_{input} is subjected to the convolution operation Conv to get the feature map F_{shallow} as

$$F_{\text{shallow}} = \text{Conv}(I_{input}). \tag{1}$$

• *Deep Feature Capture Module.* This part of IR-SDTNet consists of multiple RSTBs, each of which includes STLs as shown in Fig. 1(b). The STLs are optimized by leveraging the original multi-attention transformer layer with two key enhancements: 1. local attention 2. shifted window mechanism.

The core idea of Swin Transformer is to reduce the computational complexity through a local attention mechanism. The traditional global self-attention mechanism needs to calculate the interactions of each image patch, which captures the global information, but the computation is very large, especially in high-resolution images. To enhance efficiency, Swin Transformer introduces a local attention mechanism, which divides the image into multiple windows, and performs the self-attention computation within each window, while the patches between the windows do not interact with each other. This approach significantly reduces the amount of computation while still maintaining good information extraction capability. In each Swin Transformer block, the Window Attention Mechanism (W-MSA) is specifically used to perform local self-attention computation, i.e., self-attention operations are performed only within each window, thus reducing computational overhead while ensuring that the model can effectively model local features.

In the specific implementation, Swin Transformer first divides the image into multiple patches, then extracts features for each patch and further divides these features into windows for computation. In IR-SDTNet, a patch size of 1×1 is used, which means that each patch corresponds to the features of one pixel, thus avoiding the step of dividing larger patches in the traditional Swin Transformer. For a given patch feature X_{patch}, each patch will participate in the attention computation as Query, Key, and Value, such as

$$Attention(Q, K, V) = Soft\max(\frac{QK^T}{\sqrt{d}})V, \tag{2}$$

where d is the feature dimension. With this self-attentive computation, all patches within the window are weighted and averaged over the features according to the similarity weights, capturing the local information within the window. This approach enables IR-SDTNet to process image details more finely, and is particularly suitable for denoising tasks because it can capture detail information more accurately during image restoration without the need for large computational resources.

Shifted Window Mechanism (SWM) is an improved solution proposed by Swin Transformer to address the limitations of traditional window self-attention (W-MSA), which only calculates self-attention within each fixed window, which restricts the model from capturing long-distance dependencies across windows. To solve this problem, Swin Transformer realizes cross-window information interaction by displacing windows in each layer, resulting in intersections between otherwise non-overlapping windows, i.e., the Moving Window Multiattention Mechanism (SW-MSA). For each layer, the window division is calculated as:

$$ShiftedAttention = Soft\max(\frac{(Q + \Delta)(K + \Delta)^T}{\sqrt{d}})V, \tag{3}$$

where Δ denotes the amount of window displacement (e.g., offsetting the window size by half to the right and down). With this displacement, overlap is created between windows that originally have no intersection, which in turn leads to self-attention computation across windows and enhances the modeling capabilities of the model.

After the SW-MSA results are concatenated, the features are normalized by LayerNorm (layer normalization) to ensure that they have a consistent distribution. Next, the features are further transformed by a Multilayer Perceptron (MLP), it consists of two dense layers followed by GELU activation function applied between the two layers to enhance nonlinearity. In order to maintain the stability of the features, residual connectivity is added between the MSA and the MLP, which helps in the transfer of information.

In order to avoid an increase in computation due to an excessive number of windows after displacement, Swin Transformer adopts a cyclic displacement mechanism. The cyclic displacement ensures that the number of windows after displacement remains relatively stable and the window size remains consistent, thus improving computational efficiency and parallelism. This mechanism not only effectively expands the sensory field of the model, enabling it to simultaneously capture Local-level details and model global dependencies at a distance, but also strengthens the model's capability to manage sophisticated visual tasks.

Infrared Small Target Detection Module for IR-SDTNet. U-Net is a widely recognized convolutional network architecture frequently applied in image segmentation. In this paper, the enhanced U-Net is employed for infrared small target detection, with the architecture shown in Fig. 2. The denoised infrared image serves as the input to the U-Net encoder, which focuses on feature extraction. The image passes through several convolutional layers and downsampling operations to progressively capture features from low to high levels.

Symmetrically with the encoder, each layer of the decoder contains upsampling operations and convolution operations to progressively reconstruct the spatial resolution of the image, and ultimately outputs a feature map of identical dimensions as the input image. At each decoding stage, Skip Connections integrate the decoder with corresponding encoder features, retaining more details and aiding in the recovery of high-resolution features, especially the fine structure of small targets. A separate convolutional layer (i.e., prediction header) is also added after each upsampling layer of the decoder, and these prediction heads are responsible for predicting the target directly from the feature maps at various scales are combined to generate the detection results at multiple scales. Let x_i be the feature map of the decoder at level i and use 3×3 convolutional layers $Conv(x_i)$ for prediction as in the following equation:

$$p_i = Sigmoid(Conv(x_i)), \tag{4}$$

where p_i is the prediction result of i level scale and $Sigmoid$ serves to normalize the output. The final prediction obtained based on the four predictions p is obtained by up-sampling all scales of p_i uniformly to the original image size :

$$p = Sigmoid(Conv([\uparrow (p_{1,8}), \uparrow (p_{2,4}), \uparrow (p_{3,2}), p_4])), \tag{5}$$

$\uparrow (\cdot, \cdot)$ is a process that resamples the first parameter spatially using the second parameter as a scaling factor, and $[\cdot, \ldots, \cdot]$ Merges all given parameters along the channel axis.

In the output layer of U-Net, after multi-layer feature extraction and image recovery, the feature map output from the model will be used for small target detection. Through the convolutional layer and Bounding Box Regression (BBR), U-Net is not only able to determine whether the target exists or not, but also to predict the location of the target.

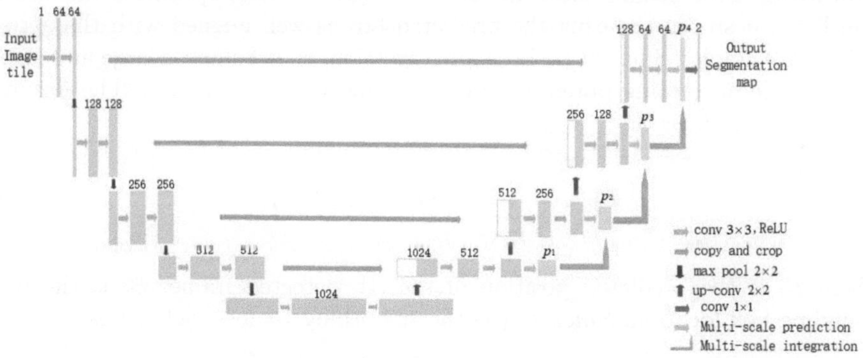

Fig. 2. Improved U-Net module main architecture. A separate convolutional layer is added after each upsampling layer of the decoder to make predictions from feature maps at multiple scales, fusing information from different scales.

3.2 Loss Function

Overall Loss Function Design. As the task of this paper involves target detection and image denoising, the total loss function comprises three components, target classification, bounding box regression and denoising, which are formulated as follows:

$$L_{total} = \lambda_{cls}L_{cls} + \lambda_{bbox}L_{bbox} + \lambda_{denoise}L_{denoise}, \tag{6}$$

where L_{cls} is the target categorization loss; L_{bbox} is the bounding box regression loss; $L_{denoise}$ is the denoising loss; λ_{cls}, λ_{bbox}, $\lambda_{denoise}$ represent the weights assigned to each part of the loss.

Target Categorization Loss. The target categorization loss is computed for the category prediction of each candidate region, and in this paper, Cross-Entropy Loss is used to measure the difference between the predicted categories and the true categories. Specifically, assume that for the ith detection frame, the predicted category is

$$L_{cls} = - \sum_{i=1}^{N} y_i \log(\hat{y}_i) + (1 - y_i) \log(1 - \hat{y}_i), \tag{7}$$

where y_i is the true category label of the ith frame, and $\hat{y}_i$ is the probability value predicted by the model.

Bounding Box Regression Loss. This loss function optimizes the detection box's position, ensuring the predicted box is well aligned with the actual object. We employ Smooth L1 Loss for regression, as it balances large and small errors while preventing potential gradient explosion from L2 loss. The formula for Smooth L1 Loss is:

$$L_{bbox} = \sum_{i=1}^{N} Smooth_{L1}(\hat{B}_i - B_i), \tag{8}$$

where $\hat{B}_i$ is the predicted position of the ith detected frame, B_i is the true bounding box location, $Smooth_{L1}$ is the smoothing L1 loss, defined as:

$$Smooth_{L1}(x) = \begin{cases} 0.5x^2 & \text{if} |x| < 1 \\ |x| - 0.5 & \text{if} |x| \geq 1 \end{cases} \tag{9}$$

Denoising Loss. The denoising loss enhances IR-SDTNet's image restoration ability by minimizing the discrepancy between the reconstructed and actual images. Mean Squared Error (MSE) serves as the loss function for assessing pixel-wise variations between the recovered and target images. The formula is as follows:

$$L_{denoise} = \frac{1}{N} \sum_{i=1}^{N} | F_{output}(i) - F_{\text{target}}(i) |^2, \tag{10}$$

Where $F_{output}(i)$ is the recovered image of the ith pixel, $F_{\text{target}}(i)$ represents the corresponding pixel of the target image, with N denoting the entire number of pixels within the image.

4 Experimentation

4.1 Datasets, Experimental Settings and Evaluation Criteria

Datasets. This paper examines two publicly obtainable infrared small target detection datasets, IRSTD1K [10] and SIRST [4]. Of the two, there are 1,000 real images within the IRSTD1K dataset with rich target shapes, scales, and complex backgrounds, and the targets in the IRSTD1K dataset are generally small and sparse, with about 75% of the target area less than 0.02% of the image. At 256 × 256 resolution, most of the targets have a pixel count of less than 13 (i.e., the size of the target is about 3.6 × 3.6), which has an accurate pixel-level annotation and is well-suited for small target detection. In contrast, SIRST only takes hundreds of sequences and extracts the most representative images in the sequence. There are five labeling forms for image targets, adapting to the forms of different detection models. The specific data pairs are shown in Fig. 3.

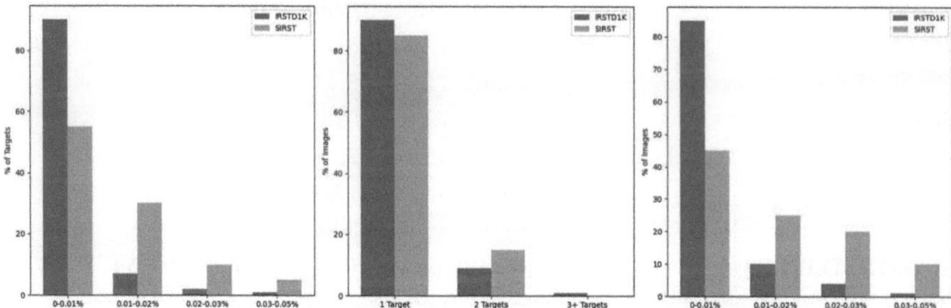

Fig. 3. Schematic of the target area distribution, target number distribution, and high response pixel comparison between the two datasets IRSTD1K and SIRST.

Experimental Details. All experiments were performed on a system powered by an NVIDIA RTX 3080 GPU. For the image denoising task, the input image resolution was set to 256×256, with an initial learning rate of 1e-4 and a batch size of 64. In the small target detection task, the input size remained 256×256, while the learning rate was adjusted to 0.05, and the batch size was set to 4.

Evaluation Criteria. In this paper, we evaluate the model's performance using intersection over Union, false alarm rate, and target detection accuracy.

4.2   Comparison with Existing Methods

For a complete evaluation of the proposed method's effectiveness, we compare it with a number of benchmark approaches. Among deep learning-based methods, DNANet [6], ALCNet [4], and HINTU [8] are selected as the main baselines. Their performance, along with that of our proposed method, is presented in Table 1. In addition, several classical traditional methods based on low-rank approximation, including IPI, NRAM, RIPT, PSTNN, and MSLSTIPT, are also included for comparison. To ensure fairness, all methods are re-implemented and tested under the same experimental conditions. Evaluations are conducted on two publicly available datasets, IRSTD1K and SIRST, using three widely adopted metrics: Intersection over Union (IoU), detection probability (P_d) and false alarm rate (F_a).

Table 1. Quantitative comparison of traditional and deep learning methods on IRSTD1K and SIRST datasets

Method	Category	IRSTD1K			SIRST		
		IoU/%	P_d /%	$F_a/10^{-6}$	IoU/%	P_d /%	$F_a/10^{-6}$
IPI	Low-Rank Approx.	26.82	81.44	16.23	15.76	72.39	41.23
NRAM		15.34	71.68	16.96	7.14	56.42	19.27
RIPT		14.11	77.55	28.31	29.44	91.85	344.30
PSTNN		24.37	71.99	35.44	15.36	66.07	44.17
MSLSTIPT		12.43	79.15	1522	8.23	46.40	888.10
DNANet	Deep Learning	63.15	91.67	32.41	74.13	97.34	20.21
ALCNet		60.21	87.18	21.56	72.89	96.19	30.40
HINTU		61.01	88.56	13.58	78.82	96.27	15.41
Ours (IR-SDTNet)		**63.42**	**90.48**	**20.19**	**79.98**	**97.54**	**12.77**

This paper presents a novel infrared small target detection framework that integrates a denoising-enhanced Swin Transformer backbone with a multi-scale head based on an improved U-Net architecture. The proposed method shows better results than several state-of-the-art approaches. For the IRSTD1K dataset, the IoU of this paper's method is 63.42%, which is 0.27% higher than that of the best method, DNANet; P_d is slightly lower than DNANet but still higher than the other two models; F_a is slightly higher than HINTU but still much lower than DNANet. For the SIRST dataset, the IoU of this paper's model is 79.98%, which is 1.16% higher than the best method, HINTU; and are slightly higher than other representative methods. HINTU, which is 1.16% higher than the best method; P_d and F_a are both improved compared with other models. These results indicate that our model exhibits enhanced localization accuracy and robustness, particularly in challenging scenarios with small targets and complex backgrounds. The improvements stem from our architecture's ability to effectively suppress noise and capture rich contextual information across scales. The visualization results are shown in Fig. 4.

Figure 4 presents a comprehensive visual comparison between the proposed method and several representative approaches on both the IRSTD1K and SIRST datasets. As illustrated in the figure, the proposed model shows a distinct advantage in accurately localizing and delineating small targets, even in the presence of complex backgrounds and high levels of noise. The predicted targets are closely aligned with the ground truth annotations, exhibiting precise boundary adherence and high target completeness. In contrast, competing methods such as DNANet and HINTU exhibit notable shortcomings. Specifically, these models often produce false positives by mistakenly highlighting background regions with similar intensity distributions, or fail to detect dim and small-scale targets due to their limited ability to suppress noise and capture fine-grained features. Overall, the visualization results clearly validate the robustness and effectiveness of our model in challenging infrared scenarios. The proposed IR-SDTNet model, not only enhances target saliency but also improves discrimination against background clutter, leading to more accurate and reliable target detection outcomes.

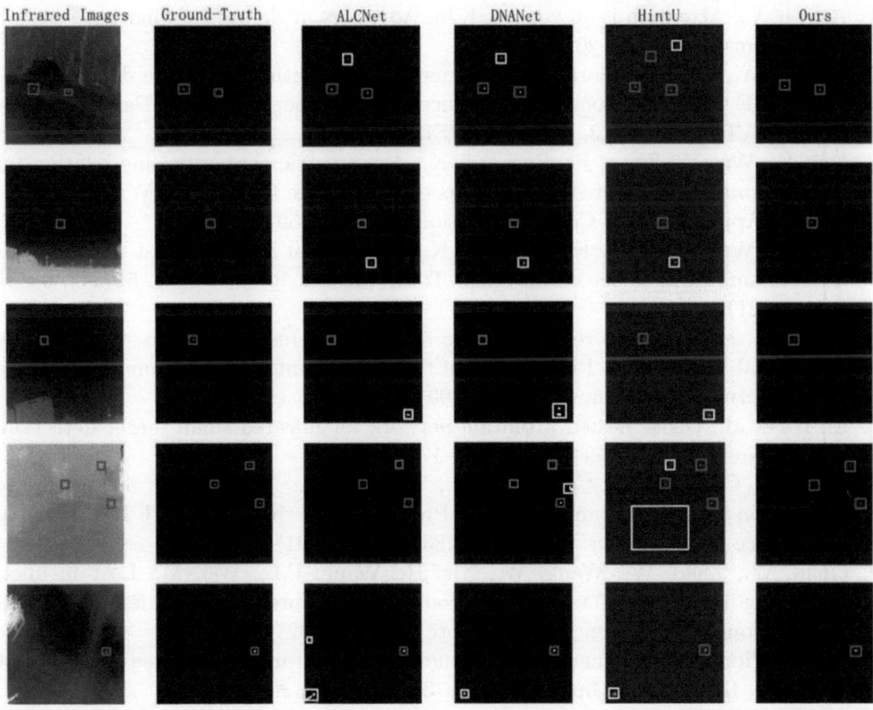

Fig. 4. Results of the visualization comparison of several IR images. Where the red boxes are correct detections, the yellow boxes are false alarms, and the blue boxes are missed targets. (Color figure online)

5 Conclusion

This paper addresses noise interference and localization accuracy issues in infrared small target detection by proposing IR-SDTNet. The model integrates a residual Swin Transformer block (RSTB) for denoising and feature enhancement, effectively suppressing noise while preserving high-frequency target details. For detection, IR-SDTNet employs an improved U-Net, merging multi-level encoder features with upsampled decoder features via skip connections. Additionally, a multi-scale prediction mechanism strengthens small target representation. Experimental results on the IRSTD1K and SIRST datasets demonstrate significant performance gains, surpassing existing methods in IoU, false alarm rate, and detection accuracy. Future research will investigate more sophisticated denoising networks to improve detection accuracy.

References

1. Ashish, V.: Attention is all you need. In: Advances in Neural Information Processing Systems, vol. 30, I (2017)
2. Buades, A., Coll, B., Morel, J.M.: A non-local algorithm for image denoising. In: 2005 IEEE Computer Society Conference on Computer Vision and Pattern Recognition (CVPR'05), vol. 2, pp. 60–65. IEEE (2005)
3. Dai, Y., Wu, Y., Zhou, F., Barnard, K.: Asymmetric contextual modulation for infrared small target detection. In: Proceedings of the IEEE/CVF Winter Conference on Applications of Computer Vision, pp. 950–959 (2021)
4. Dai, Y., Wu, Y., Zhou, F., Barnard, K.: Attentional local contrast networks for infrared small target detection. IEEE Trans. Geosci. Remote Sens. **59**(11), 9813–9824 (2021)
5. Ledig, C., et al.: Photo-realistic single image super-resolution using a generative adversarial network. In: Proceedings of the IEEE Conference on Computer Vision and Pattern Recognition, pp. 4681–4690 (2017)
6. Li, B., et al.: Dense nested attention network for infrared small target detection. IEEE Trans. Image Process. **32**, 1745–1758 (2022)
7. Liang, J., Cao, J., Sun, G., Zhang, K., Van Gool, L., Timofte, R.: Swinir: image restoration using swin transformer. In: Proceedings of the IEEE/CVF International Conference on Computer Vision, pp. 1833–1844 (2021)
8. Quan, W., Zhao, W., Wang, W., Xie, H., Wang, F.L., Wei, M.: Lost in unet: Improving infrared small target detection by underappreciated local features. IEEE Transactions on Geoscience and Remote Sensing (2024)
9. Wu, X., Hong, D., Chanussot, J.: Uiu-net: U-net in u-net for infrared small object detection. IEEE Trans. Image Process. **32**, 364–376 (2022)
10. Zhang, M., Zhang, R., Yang, Y., Bai, H., Zhang, J., Guo, J.: Isnet: shape matters for infrared small target detection. In: Proceedings of the IEEE/CVF Conference on Computer Vision and Pattern Recognition, pp. 877–886 (2022)
11. Zhang, T., Fu, Y., Zhang, J.: Guided hyperspectral image denoising with realistic data. Int. J. Comput. Vision **130**(11), 2885–2901 (2022)
12. Zhang, Y., Tian, Y., Kong, Y., Zhong, B., Fu, Y.: Residual dense network for image super-resolution. In: Proceedings of the IEEE Conference on Computer Vision and Pattern Recognition, pp. 2472–2481 (2018)

Blockchain-Enhanced Copyright Protection for Fashion Industry: A DBAE-Net Based and Traceable Image Similarity Ranking Scheme

Zheng Dong[1] , Huijie Yang[1,2,3(✉)] , Jingang Li[1] , and Jian Shen[1,2,3]

[1] School of Information Science and Engineering (School of Cyber Science and Technology), Zhejiang Sci-Tech University, Hangzhou 310018, China
[2] Zhejiang Key Laboratory of Digital Fashion and Data Governance, Zhejiang Sci-Tech University, Hangzhou 310018, China
[3] Zhejiang Provincial International Cooperation Base for Science and Technology on Cloud Computing Security and Data Aggregation, Zhejiang Sci-Tech University, Hangzhou 310018, China
hjyang3086@gmail.com

Abstract. To address design plagiarism and insecure copyright management in the fashion industry, this paper proposes a unified framework that synergizes deep learning with blockchain cryptography. Our framework utilizes neural networks to provide AI-assisted evidence ranking for expert review. We introduce two core components. First, a Dual-Branch Attribute Embedding Network (DBAE-Net) enables precise similarity ranking of prior works by capturing both global style and fine-grained local details. This ranking assists human experts in identifying potential plagiarism. Second, we design a Traceable Verifiable Scheme (TVS) using bilinear pairings that provides an unforgeable on-chain proof of ownership. The TVS balances signer anonymity against external parties with robust, authority-led traceability. We formally prove the TVS's security and empirically validate the framework's effectiveness, offering a novel, pragmatic solution for streamlining copyright verification in the digital fashion ecosystem.

Keywords: Blockchain · Copyright Protection · Image Similarity Ranking · Neural Network · Signature

1 Introduction

The fashion industry has long faced challenges in intellectual property protection, particularly in verifying the originality of garment designs and combating counterfeiting. Traditional copyright management systems rely on centralized authorities for registration and dispute resolution, often leading to inefficiencies, high costs, and vulnerability to tampering. With the rapid growth of digital

© The Author(s), under exclusive license to Springer Nature Singapore Pte Ltd. 2026
T. Zhu et al. (Eds.): KSEM 2025, LNAI 15922, pp. 77–91, 2026.
https://doi.org/10.1007/978-981-95-3058-8_7

design tools and e-commerce platforms, the risk of unauthorized replication and distribution of creative works has escalated, necessitating a more robust solution to safeguard designers' rights.

With its decentralized, immutable, and traceable characteristics, blockchain technology has emerged as a promising tool for digital copyright protection. By anchoring copyright information such as design sketches, patterns, and product images onto a distributed ledger, blockchain provides an unforgeable timestamp and ownership certificate. However, existing blockchain-based solutions primarily focus on data storage and verification, but lack proactive mechanisms to detect potential infringements during the content upload phase. This limitation allows plagiarized works to persist on the chain, undermining the integrity of copyright ecosystems.

Recent advances in artificial intelligence, particularly deep neural networks, offer opportunities to address this gap. Convolutional Neural Networks (CNNs) have demonstrated exceptional performance in Image Similarity Ranking, enabling automated comparison between newly uploaded designs and existing copyrighted works. Integrating such models with blockchain could establish a dynamic screening layer, preventing infringing content from entering the system while ensuring traceability of legitimate creations. However, current research remains fragmented, with isolated blockchain implementations for copyright storage or AI-based plagiarism detection systems, lacking a unified framework that synergizes real-time infringement identification with preservation of decentralized evidence. This paper bridges the divide by integrating a DBAE-Net (Dual-Branch Attention-Enhanced Network) for image similarity analysis with a Traceable Verifiable Scheme (TVS) based on bilinear pairings.

1.1 Related Work

Signature Schemes. Kiayias et al. [1] proposed traceable group signatures using zero-knowledge proofs (ZKP) and quadratic residues, relying on strong RSA/DDH assumptions. Shao et al. [2] designed threshold-based tracing through multisecret sharing and bilinear pairings with overhead trade-offs. Kuchta et al. [3] combined designated verifier and group signatures for anonymity and manager-led tracing, but incurred high computational costs based on DBDH. Ding et al. [4] balanced privacy and traceability in TABS using dual-trusted parties and LSSS. Gu et al. [5] employed monotonic span programs for attribute authority tracing, excluding nonmonotonic structures. Kang et al. [6] achieved constant-size TFS-ABS with complex key updates. Scafuro et al. [7] built post-quantum one-time ring signatures with Naor commitments. Tang et al. [8] enabled threshold-audited tracing in smart grids. Li et al. [9] implemented permissioned blockchain-based aggregate tracing with centralized trust. Xie et al. [10] proposed accountability tagged with events k times via pseudorandom functions, suffering linear verification costs. Feng et al. [11] combined lattice/symmetric primitives for logarithmic-sized signatures but faced lattice inefficiency. Liang et al. [12] improved quantum resistance by rejection sampling and lattice cryptography. Zhao et al. [13] introduced a traceable ring signature scheme that employs a trusted third party (TTP) for tracing, while using zero-knowledge proofs (ZKP) to protect the privacy of the entity requesting the trace.

Clothing Image Similarity Ranking. Liu et al. [14] used landmark-guided pooling for cross-scene matching but struggled under occlusion. Lang et al. [15] detected localized plagiarism via adaptive weighting, limited to dual region edits. Ak et al. [16] learned attribute-agnostic similarity via part-based attention but required pose assumptions. Ma et al. [17] optimized metrics via spatial/channel attention (ASA/ACA); Dong et al. [18] enhanced accuracy with dual-branch structures at higher complexity. Wang et al. [19] increased Recall@1 using multi-similarity loss with hyperparameter tuning. Kinli et al. [20] reduced parameters via capsule networks but ignored texture details. While existing methods are effective for general retrieval, they often overlook the nuanced requirements of copyright detection, such as identifying subtle, multi-scale similarities, and are rarely designed for blockchain integration. Our work bridges this gap with DBAE-Net, an architecture featuring an innovative Attribute-Aware Feature Pyramid Network. This design is specially geared towards identifying fine-grained similarities indicative of plagiarism and supporting our end-to-end blockchain copyright protection scheme.

1.2 Motivation and Contributions

While blockchain offers immutable storage and AI provides similarity detection, a critical gap exists in their integration for copyright protection. Current blockchain solutions often lack proactive infringement screening, passively recording potentially plagiarized content. In contrast, existing image similarity models are not architecturally designed to meet the evidentiary and traceability demands of an on-chain system. Motivated by these challenges, this paper proposes an integrated framework to provide a scalable and secure end-to-end solution. Our primary contributions are threefold:

(1) **A Novel AI-Powered Evidence Ranking System for Copyright Assessment.** We propose the Dual-Branch Attribute Embedding Network (DBAE-Net), architecturally designed for the nuanced task of copyright protection. Its core function is to generate a highly accurate, similarity-ranked list of prior works for any new design. By presenting human reviewers with the most relevant evidence first, this AI-powered ranking mechanism drastically reduces manual workload and enhances the efficiency and accuracy of the copyright verification workflow.

(2) **An Efficient Traceable Verifiable Scheme (TVS).** We design and implement a computationally efficient TVS that provides an unforgeable proof of ownership on the blockchain. The scheme balances signer anonymity against external parties with robust, multi-authority traceability, and its verification algorithm requires only a single pairing operation, ensuring system scalability.

(3) **Formal Security and Performance Analysis.** We provide a formal security analysis for the TVS, proving its existential unforgeability under the q-Strong Diffie-Hellman (q-SDH) assumption in the random oracle model. We also conduct a comprehensive theoretical and empirical evaluation to demonstrate the scheme's practical efficiency and performance advantages.

2 Preliminaries

Definition 1 (q-SDH Problem). *Let G_1 be a multiplicative cyclic group of prime order p, and let g be a generator of G_1. Given a tuple $(g, g^\alpha, g^{\alpha^2}, \ldots, g^{\alpha^q})$ as input, where $\alpha \in \mathbb{Z}_p$, the q-SDH problem is to output a pair $(c, g^{1/(\alpha+c)})$ for some $c \in \mathbb{Z}_p^*$.*

Definition 2 (q-SDH Assumption). *The q-SDH problem is said to be (t, ϵ)-computationally infeasible in $\mathbb{G}_1$ if, for any probabilistic polynomial-time (PPT) adversary $\mathcal{A}$ running in time at most t, the advantage satisfies:*

$$\Pr\left[(c, g^{1/(\alpha+c)}) \leftarrow \mathcal{A}(g, g^\alpha, g^{\alpha^2}, \ldots, g^{\alpha^q})\right] \leq \epsilon,$$

where ϵ is negligible in the security parameter λ.

3 Traceable Verifiable Signature

3.1 Syntax of TVS Scheme

A TVS scheme involves five algorithms: *Setup, KeyGen, Sign, Verify*, and *Trace*. Our model comprises two authoritative parties: the Identity Authority (IA) and the Traceability Authority (TA). The traceability process is jointly completed by IA and TA. The formal definition of the TVS scheme is as follows.

Setup$(\lambda) \rightarrow (mpk, msk_{IA}, msk_{TA})$: This probabilistic algorithm takes a security parameter λ. It outputs the system public parameters mpk, a master secret key for the Identity Authority (IA) msk_{IA}, and a master secret key for the Tracing Authority (TA) msk_{TA}.

KeyGen$(msk_{IA}, ID_i) \rightarrow sk_i$: This deterministic algorithm is run by the IA. It takes the IA's master secret key msk_{IA} and a user identity ID_i. It outputs the user's secret signing key sk_i.

Sign$(mpk, sk_i, ID_i, m) \rightarrow \sigma$: This probabilistic algorithm takes the public parameters mpk, a user's secret key sk_i and identity ID_i, and a message m. It outputs a signature σ.

Verify$(mpk, \sigma, m) \rightarrow \{0, 1\}$: This deterministic algorithm takes the public parameters mpk, a signature σ, and a message m. It outputs 1 if the signature is valid, and 0 otherwise.

Trace$(mpk, msk_{IA}, msk_{TA}, \sigma) \rightarrow ID_i \cup \{\bot\}$: This deterministic algorithm takes the public parameters mpk, the secret keys msk_{IA} and msk_{TA}, and a signature σ. It outputs the signer's identity ID_i or an error symbol $\bot$.

Correctness. A TVS scheme is correct if for any $(mpk, msk_{IA}, msk_{TA}) \leftarrow$ Setup(λ), $sk_i \leftarrow$ KeyGen(msk_{IA}, ID_i), and $\sigma \leftarrow$ Sign(mpk, sk_i, ID_i, m), it holds that Verify$(mpk, \sigma, m) = 1$.

3.2   Security Model

Our security model is designed to address three primary threats: 1) Signature Forgery, where an unauthorized adversary generates a valid signature for a copyright they do not own; 2) Anonymity Breach, where an external party links a public signature to its anonymous signer; and 3) Traceability Abuse, where a single authority unilaterally performs tracing or a legitimate signature fails to be traced. The following formal definitions are constructed to prove the scheme's resilience against these threats.

A TVS scheme needs to fulfill the fundamental security requirements for existential unforgeability, anonymity and traceability.

Existential Unforgeability. We define the existential unforgeability of the TVS scheme under an adaptive chosen-message attack (EUF-CMA). The security goal is to demonstrate that no probabilistic polynomial time (PPT) adversary $\mathcal{A}$ can generate a valid signature on a new message for any identity, since the Identity Authority (IA) is honest.

Honest IA Assumption: In this security model, the Identity Authority (IA) is assumed to be a trusted entity that correctly executes the KeyGen algorithm according to the protocol. The adversary $\mathcal{A}$ cannot corrupt the IA or gain access to its master secret key msk_{IA}. The security guarantee holds against an external adversary.

The formal definition of EUF-CMA is provided through the following game between a challenger $\mathcal{C}$ and an adversary $\mathcal{A}$.

Initialization Phase. The challenger $\mathcal{C}$ executes the Setup(λ) algorithm to generate the system public parameters mpk, the IA's secret key msk_{IA}, and the TA's secret key msk_{TA}. $\mathcal{C}$ provides mpk to the adversary $\mathcal{A}$ and keeps msk_{IA} and msk_{TA} private.

Query Phase. The adversary $\mathcal{A}$ is permitted to adaptively make a polynomially bounded number of queries to the following oracles, which are simulated by the challenger $\mathcal{C}$:

- Key Generation Oracle($\mathcal{O}_{KeyGen}$): $\mathcal{A}$ submits an identity ID_i. $\mathcal{C}$ runs KeyGen(msk_{IA}, ID_i) to obtain sk_i and returns sk_i to $\mathcal{A}$. Let $\mathcal{Q}_{KeyGen}$ be the set of all identities queried to this oracle.
- Signing Oracle ($\mathcal{O}_{Sign}$): $\mathcal{A}$ submits a pair (ID_i, m). $\mathcal{C}$ first obtains sk_i by running KeyGen(msk_{IA}, ID_i), then computes $\sigma \leftarrow Sign(mpk, sk_i, ID_i, m)$ and returns the signature σ to $\mathcal{A}$. Let $\mathcal{Q}_{Sign}$ be the set of all pairs (ID_i, m) queried to this oracle.

Forgery Phase. After the query phase, the adversary $\mathcal{A}$ outputs a tuple (ID^*, m^*, σ^*). The adversary $\mathcal{A}$ wins the game if the following two conditions are met:

- Validity: Verify(mpk, σ^*, m^*) = 1.
- Non-triviality: The pair (ID^*, m^*) was not previously submitted to the Signing Oracle, $(ID^*, m^*) \notin \mathcal{Q}_{Sign}$.

Note that the adversary is permitted to forge a signature for an identity ID^* for which it has previously requested the secret key via $\mathcal{O}_{KeyGen}$ (i.e., $ID^* \in \mathcal{Q}_{KeyGen}$), as long as it has not asked the oracle to sign the specific message m^* with that identity.

Adversarial Advantage. The advantage of an adversary $\mathcal{A}$ in breaking the EUF-CMA security of the TVS scheme is defined as the probability that it wins the game:

$$\mathrm{Adv}_{\mathrm{TVS},\mathcal{A}}^{\mathrm{EUF\text{-}CMA}}(\lambda) = \Pr\left[\mathrm{Verify}(mpk, \sigma^*, m^*) = 1\right]$$

$$\wedge\ (ID^*, m^*) \notin \mathcal{Q}_{Sign}$$

Definition 3 (Existential Unforgeability). *A TVS scheme is existentially unforgeable under an adaptive chosen-message attack (EUF-CMA) if, for any probabilistic polynomial-time (PPT) adversary $\mathcal{A}$, the advantage $Adv_{TVS,\mathcal{A}}^{EUF\text{-}CMA}(\lambda)$ is a negligible function in the security parameter λ.*

Definition 4 (Anonymity). *A TVS scheme provides anonymity if for any PPT adversary $\mathcal{A}$, its advantage in the following game is negligible in the security parameter λ.*

The challenger $\mathcal{C}$ generates $(mpk, msk_{IA}, msk_{TA}) \leftarrow \mathrm{Setup}(\lambda)$ and gives mpk to $\mathcal{A}$. $\mathcal{A}$ is given access to Key Generation and Signing oracles. $\mathcal{A}$ outputs two distinct identities, ID_0 and ID_1, for which it has not queried the secret keys, and a challenge message m^*. $\mathcal{C}$ selects a random bit $\zeta \in \{0, 1\}$, computes the challenge signature $\sigma^* \leftarrow \mathrm{Sign}(mpk, sk_\zeta, ID_\zeta, m^*)$, and sends σ^* to $\mathcal{A}$. $\mathcal{A}$ outputs a guess $\zeta' \in \{0, 1\}$ and wins if $\zeta' = \zeta$. The adversary's advantage is defined as:

$$\mathrm{Adv}_{\mathrm{TVS},\mathcal{A}}^{\mathrm{Anon}}(\lambda) = \left| \Pr[\zeta' = \zeta] - \frac{1}{2} \right|.$$

Definition 5 (Traceability). *Let TVS = (Setup, KeyGen, Sign, Verify, Trace) be a signature scheme above. The TVS scheme provides traceability if for any security parameter λ, for any $(mpk, msk_{IA}, msk_{TA}) \leftarrow Setup(\lambda)$, for any user identity ID_i and its corresponding secret key $sk_i \leftarrow KeyGen(msk_{IA}, ID_i)$, and for any message m, the following holds: if $\sigma \leftarrow Sign(mpk, sk_i, ID_i, m)$ is a valid signature, then the algorithm $Trace(mpk, msk_{IA}, msk_{TA}, \sigma)$, when honestly executed by the IA and TA, outputs the identity ID_i.*

4   Dual-Branch Attribute Embedding Network

To address the challenges of multi-scale feature correlation and local detail sensitivity in fashion copyright detection, we design a Dual-Branch Attribute Embedding Network (DBAE-Net). It comprises a semantic fusion branch and a detail perception branch to model clothing images from global style to local details. While building on concepts from prior works (e.g., [15, 18, 20]), DBAE-Net introduces key architectural enhancements tailored for our blockchain protection scheme. A core innovation is the Attribute-Aware Feature Pyramid Network (Attribute-Aware FPN) within the semantic fusion branch, which dynamically integrates multi-level semantics to identify nuanced similarities. Concurrently, the detail perception branch uses a lightweight backbone to focus on fine-grained features in key regions. This dual-pronged approach is designed to generate discriminative features that effectively support the subsequent on-chain verification and traceability, as shown in Fig. 1.

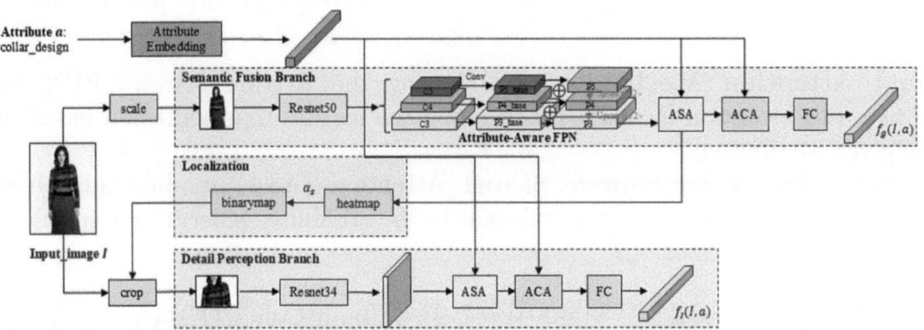

Fig. 1. The architecture of DBAE-Net

4.1   Semantic Fusion Branch

Attribute-Aware Feature Pyramid Networks (Attribute-Aware FPN). To address the distribution differences of fashion clothing attributes across spatial and semantic levels, an Attribute-Aware Feature Pyramid Networks (Attribute-Aware FPN) is introduced within the semantic fusion branch. This module operates on multi-level features (C_3, C_4, C_5) extracted by the ResNet backbone network, employing a dynamic fusion strategy to resolve multi-scale association issues between global attributes, such as clothing contours and styles, and detailed attributes, like buttons and textures. Specifically,

$$P_i = Conv_{lat}(C_i) + UpSampling(P_{i+1}) \tag{1}$$

where P_i represents the feature map of the ith layer, $UpSampling$ refers to the upsampling operation that enlarges the feature map from a higher level to match the size of the current level. The fusion weights across each level are dynamically adjusted based on the attribute embedding vector, allowing for adaptive contribution adjustments of each pyramid level according to varying attribute requirements of the input image. Specifically, after the attribute embedding undergoes nonlinear mapping through two fully connected layers,

$$[w_3, w_4, w_5] = Softmax(FC_2(ReLU(FC_1(a)))) \tag{2}$$

three-channel normalized weights are generated to control the contribution ratio of P_3 (high resolution), P_4 (medium resolution), and P_5 (low resolution). This attribute-driven dynamic fusion strategy results in the final feature map F being represented as $F = w_3 \times P_3 + w_4 \times P_4 + w_5 \times P_5$, where w_3, w_4, w_5 are weight coefficients; FC_1, FC_2 are fully connected layers; F is the final feature map. This attribute-driven dynamic fusion is a key differentiator from models like ASEN++ ([18]) that lack such explicit, attribute-guided level-wise weighting. By allowing the attribute embedding to modulate the contribution of each pyramid level, DBAE-Net adaptively focuses on the most relevant feature scales (e.g., fine textures from P_3 or broader styles from P_5 for the attribute under analysis. This adaptive multi-scale analysis is crucial for detecting subtle plagiarisms.

Dual Attention Mechanisms. Following the Attribute-Aware FPN, we employ two attention mechanisms to refine the feature representation based on the given attribute a.

First, the Attribute-Aware Spatial Attention (ASA) module adaptively focuses on specific image regions relevant to the attribute, generating a spatially-attended feature vector x_s:

$$x_s = \sum_{j=1}^{h \times w} \left(\mathrm{softmax} \left(\frac{\sum_{i=1}^{c_1}[\tanh(W_s a) \cdot 1]_i \odot [\tanh(\mathrm{Conv}_{c_1}(F))]_i}{\sqrt{c_1}} \right)_j \cdot F_j \right) \quad (3)$$

where F is the feature map from the FPN and F_j is its j-th feature vector.

Subsequently, the Attribute-Aware Channel Attention (ACA) module functions as an element-wise gate to select the most relevant feature dimensions from x_s, producing the final feature vector x_c for this branch:$x_c = x_s \odot \sigma\left(W_2 \delta\left(W_1[q(a), x_s]\right)\right)$, where $q(a)$ is a projected feature vector from attribute a, W_s, W_1, W_2 are transformation matrices, σ denotes the sigmoid function, and δ denotes the ReLU function.

Global Attribute Feature Generation. Finally, the feature vector x_c, which encapsulates the attribute-aware multi-scale spatial and channel information, is processed by a fully connected (FC) layer to produce the final global attribute-specific feature embedding $f_g(I, a)$:$f_g(I, a) = W x_c + b$, where W is the transformation matrix, b is the bias term, and c_o is the output dimensionality.

4.2   Detail Perception Branch

The detail perception branch complements the semantic fusion branch by focusing on fine-grained local details. It takes a Region of Interest (RoI) as input, which is generated via a weakly supervised localization method that leverages the attention map from the ASA module of the semantic fusion branch. This process involves upsampling the attention map, binarizing it to find the most salient region, and cropping this RoI from the original image. The cropped RoI is then processed by a similar pipeline of feature extraction (using a lightweight backbone), ASA, and ACA modules to produce the local feature vector $f_l(I, a)$. Both branches share the same attribute embedding.

The synergy between the semantic fusion branch (with its dynamically weighted multi-scale features) and the detail perception branch (with its high-resolution local focus) allows DBAE-Net to form a comprehensive understanding of both global style and fine-grained elements. This dual-pronged analysis, guided by shared attribute embeddings, provides a robust feature representation critical for detecting nuanced design similarities in copyright disputes.

5   Our Construction of TVS Scheme

This section details the concrete construction of our proposed TVS scheme. The scheme operates in an asymmetric bilinear pairing environment, involves two distinct authorities: Identity Authority (IA) and Tracing Authority (TA), and uses two cryptographic hash functions, $H_1 : \{0,1\}^* \to \mathbb{Z}_p^*$ and $H_2 : \{0,1\}^* \to \mathbb{Z}_p^*$, which are modeled as random oracles in our security analysis.

Setup(λ). The algorithm takes a security parameter λ as input. It generates bilinear group parameters (G_1, G_2, G_T) of prime order p with respective generators $g_1 \in G_1$ and $g_2 \in G_2$. IA randomly chooses a master secret key $\alpha \in \mathbb{Z}_p^*$ and its tracing key share $\beta_1 \in \mathbb{Z}_p^*$, then computes the public components $P_1 = g_2^\alpha$ and $P_2 = g_1^{\beta_1}$. Concurrently, TA randomly chooses its tracing key share $\beta_2 \in \mathbb{Z}_p^*$ and computes its public component $P_3 = g_1^{\beta_2}$. A combined public tracing key is then established as $P_4 = P_2 \cdot P_3$. Finally, the algorithm outputs the system public parameters $mpk = (g_1, g_2, P_1, P_4)$, the IA's secret key $msk_{IA} = (\alpha, \beta_1)$, and the TA's secret key $msk_{TA} = (\beta_2)$.

KeyGen(msk_{IA}, ID_i). This algorithm is executed by the IA and takes as input its master secret key $msk_{IA} = (\alpha, \beta_1)$ and a user identity ID_i. It first computes the identity hash $h_i = H_1(ID_i)$. It then uses the master secret α to compute the user's secret key as $sk_i = g_1^{1/(\alpha+h_i)}$. The algorithm outputs the secret key $sk_i \in G_1$.

Sign(mpk, sk_i, ID_i, m). This algorithm is executed by a signer possessing the secret key sk_i for identity ID_i. It takes as input the public parameters mpk, the secret key sk_i, the identity ID_i, and a message m. First, the signer computes the identity hash $h_i = H_1(ID_i)$ and selects two independent random numbers $r, x \in \mathbb{Z}_p^*$. It then computes a commitment $R = g_1^r$, the randomized identity components $V_1 = g_2^{h_i+x}$ and $V_2 = g_2^x$, and a traceable ciphertext $C_{trace} = g_1^{h_i} \cdot P_4^r$. Next, a challenge hash is computed over the message and these components as $c = H_2(m, R, V_1, V_2, C_{trace})$. Finally, the algorithm computes the signature core $S = sk_i \cdot R^c$. The algorithm outputs the final signature $\sigma = (c, S, R, V_1, V_2, C_{trace})$.

Verify(mpk, σ, m). This deterministic algorithm is executed by any verifier. It takes as input the public parameters mpk, a signature $\sigma = (c, S, R, V_1, V_2, C_{trace})$, and a message m. The algorithm first performs an integrity check by computing $c' = H_2(m, R, V_1, V_2, C_{trace})$; it outputs 0 if

$c' \neq c$. If the check passes, it then computes the temporary identity component $V_{tmp} = V_1 \cdot V_2^{-1}$ and the temporary secret key component $X = S \cdot R^{-c}$. Finally, it verifies the core signature validity by checking if the following equation holds: $e(X, P_1 \cdot V_{tmp}) = e(g_1, g_2)$. The algorithm outputs 1 if the equation holds, and 0 otherwise.

Trace$(mpk, msk_{IA}, msk_{TA}, \sigma)$. This algorithm is executed jointly by the IA and TA to recover a signer's identity. It takes as input the public parameters mpk, the IA's secret key $msk_{IA} = (\alpha, \beta_1)$, the TA's secret key $msk_{TA} = (\beta_2)$, and a signature $\sigma = (c, S, R, V_1, V_2, C_{trace})$. First, the TA parses the signature to obtain R and computes its partial decryption key $K_{TA} = R^{\beta_2}$, which it then transmits to the IA. Upon receiving K_{TA}, the IA computes its own partial decryption key $K_{IA} = R^{\beta_1}$. The IA then recovers the identity-as-group-element $M_i = C_{trace} \cdot (K_{IA} \cdot K_{TA})^{-1}$. Finally, the IA performs a lookup in its pre-computed IdentityMap to resolve M_i to the corresponding identity string ID_i. The protocol outputs the identity ID_i, or $\perp$ if the process fails.

6   Security Analysis

Our proposed TVS scheme is designed to achieve correctness, existential unforgeability against adaptive chosen-message attacks (EUF-CMA), signer anonymity, and traceability. The security of the scheme is formally proven in the random oracle model. The EUF-CMA property is based on the computational hardness of the q-Strong Diffie-Hellman (q-SDH) assumption. Anonymity is guaranteed against external adversaries due to the randomization of each signature with fresh ephemeral values. Finally, traceability is ensured by the correct design of the tracing protocol between the Identity Authority (IA) and the Tracing Authority (TA).

Due to page limitations, the full formal proofs for these properties are deferred to the extended version of this paper.

7   Performance Analysis

7.1   TVS Scheme Performance Experiments

We evaluate the performance of our proposed Traceable Signature (TVS) scheme through theoretical analysis and Experimental measurement.

Experimental Setup. Experiments were conducted on a system running Linux kernel 5.15.0 with GCC 9.4.0. The implementation uses the GMP (v6.3.0) and PBC libraries. We employed a Type A symmetric pairing with a 160-bit group order and a 512-bit base field size. All Experimental timings are the average of 10 executions.

Theoretical Analysis. The dominant computational costs are summarized in Table 1. We denote a pairing by P and a group exponentiation by E. The analysis reveals that our verification algorithm is highly efficient, requiring only a single pairing.

Table 1. Theoretical Computational Costs.

Algorithm	Dominant Computational Cost
Setup	$1P + 3E$
KeyGen	$1E$
Sign	$6E$
Verify	$1P + 1E$
Trace	$2E$

Experimental Analysis. To demonstrate the practical advantage of our optimized verification, we compared its performance against a naive implementation that performs two pairing operations per verification. We measured the total time required for a central verifier to process a batch of N signatures, where $N \in \{1, 10, 50, 100, 500\}$.

The results, presented in Fig. 2, show that our optimized verification method consistently outperforms the naive approach. The performance gap scales linearly with the number of signatures, resulting in a stable time saving of approximately 24%. This confirms the significant real-world benefit of the pre-computation strategy, making the scheme highly suitable for applications with frequent public verifications, such as blockchain systems or large-scale authenticated networks.

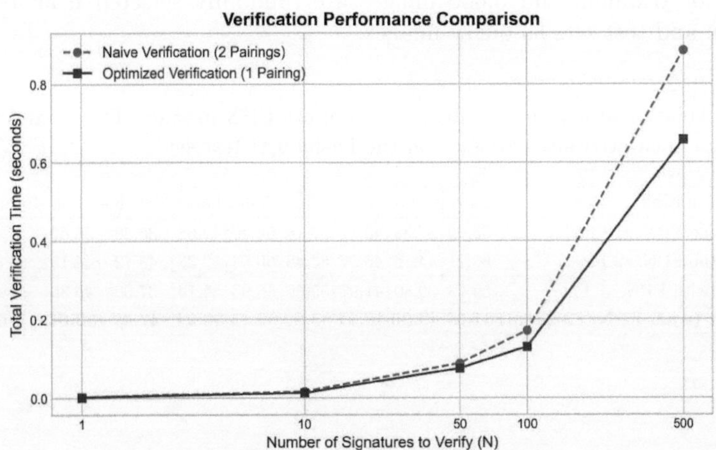

Fig. 2. Total time to verify a batch of N signatures, comparing the naive (2 pairings) and optimized (1 pairing) methods.

7.2   Image Similarity Ranking Experiments

Our models were implemented using PyTorch and trained on a single NVIDIA RTX 4060 GPU. We employed the Adam optimizer for all training processes. The training was conducted in two stages for a total of 25 epochs. For the first stage (10 epochs), the initial learning rate was set to 1e-4 for the main model layers and 1e-5 for the pretrained backbone layers. We then resumed training for a second stage (15 epochs) from the best-performing checkpoint of the first stage, continuing with the same learning rates. A step-wise learning rate scheduler was applied, which decayed the learning rate by a factor of 0.9 after each epoch. All experiments were conducted with a batch size of 16. The composite loss function was a weighted sum of the global branch loss, local branch loss, and a feature alignment loss, with weights set to 1.0, 0.1, and 0.1, respectively. A margin of 0.2 was used for the metric learning loss component. During dual-branch feature extraction, the global and local features were combined with a weighting factor β of 0.6.

To verify the effectiveness of DBAE-Net in fine-grained fashion similarity prediction, we evaluated it on an attribute-specific fashion retrieval task. The objective of this task is to retrieve fashion images that share the same attribute value as a given fashion image and a specified attribute. Based on the literature [17,18], we use the modified FashionAI dataset, which consists of 180,335 fashion images annotated with eight attributes. The dataset is split into a training set (144,000 images), a validation set (18,000 images), and a test set (18,000 images) in an 8:1:1 ratio. In each training epoch, 100,000 triplets are randomly sampled for training, and 3,600 images are randomly selected from both the validation and test sets as query images.

Table 2. Ablation study on the effectiveness of the FPN module. The MeanAP (%) is reported for each attribute category on the FashionAI test set.

Model Configuration	Skirt	Sleeve	Coat	Pant	Collar	Lapel	Neckline	Neck	Total MeanAP
DBAE-Net (no FPN, s1 Final)	56.99	37.38	40.12	57.18	54.40	42.68	36.30	36.62	44.18
DBAE-Net (no FPN, s2 Final)	60.71	44.16	45.87	63.48	60.53	52.33	43.72	44.15	50.74
DBAE-Net (with FPN, s1 Final)	56.73	39.80	41.97	55.96	56.93	45.13	37.00	46.35	45.99
DBAE-Net (with FPN, s2 Final)	**61.37**	**49.00**	**48.31**	**63.89**	**66.71**	**53.21**	**47.07**	**52.61**	**54.00**

Table 3. Overall Recall@K (%) performance comparison. The FPN-enhanced model shows a clear advantage in top-1 retrieval accuracy (Recall@1).

Model Configuration	Recall@1	Recall@10	Recall@100
DBAE-Net (no FPN, Final)	59.39	92.06	**99.17**
DBAE-Net (with FPN, Final)	**60.50**	**93.31**	99.14

Table 4. Comparison of model complexity and efficiency.

Model Configuration	Parameters (M)	FLOPs (G)	Latency (ms)
DBAE-Net (no FPN)	**19.04**	6.67	**2.97**
DBAE-Net (with FPN)	20.85	**8.29**	3.93

Our experimental evaluation is designed to validate the effectiveness of DBAE-Net in its primary role within our framework: an AI-powered ranking engine to assist expert review. For a real-world copyright protection task where the cost of a false accusation is high, our system is built to provide a ranked list of evidence rather than making an automated binary decision. Consequently, we evaluate our model's performance using standard ranking-based metrics: MeanAP and Recall@K ($K = 1, 10, 100$).

Ablation Study. We conducted a comprehensive ablation study to quantify the contribution of our proposed FPN module. The detailed results on the FashionAI test set are presented in Table 2, and Table 3.

As shown in Table 2, the full DBAE-Net architecture (with FPN) achieves a superior Total MeanAP of 54.00%, a significant improvement over the 50.74% from the baseline model without FPN. This performance gain is consistently observed across all 8 attribute categories. Furthermore, Table 3 demonstrates that the FPN-enhanced model improves the critical Recall@1 metric from 59.39% to 60.50%. These results confirm that the FPN is a valuable component that systematically enhances the model's ability to rank the most relevant items at the top.

Efficiency Analysis. The practical efficiency of our proposed model is detailed in Table 4. The results show that the significant accuracy gains from the FPN architecture are achieved with only a moderate increase in computational cost. Specifically, on an NVIDIA RTX 4060 GPU, the average inference latency increases slightly from 2.97 ms for the baseline model to 3.93 ms for the FPN-enhanced model, confirming its suitability for deployment within our AI-assisted workflow.

8 Conclusion

This paper introduced a unified framework that synergizes deep learning and blockchain cryptography to address critical copyright protection challenges in the fashion industry. Our proposed DBAE-Net provides an effective mechanism for AI-powered evidence ranking, enabling human experts to efficiently assess potential plagiarism with high accuracy. Concurrently, our computationally efficient TVS guarantees the integrity and provenance of on-chain evidence. We have formally proven its security under the q-SDH assumption and, critically, demonstrated its practical advantage in verification speed, which is essential for scalable, decentralized applications.

For future work, we will explore adversarial training to enhance the DBAE-Net's robustness against sophisticated image manipulations. Furthermore, the integration of batch verification techniques for the TVS could further improve throughput for large-scale transaction processing on the blockchain.

Acknowledgements. This work is supported by the Zhejiang Provincial Natural Science Foundation of China No. LQN25F020002, the Fundamental Research Funds of Zhejiang Sci-Tech University under Grants No. 24222238-Y, the National Natural Science Foundation of China (62402109, 62372108) and NSFC-FDCT under its Joint Scientific Research Project Fund, China & Macau (0051/2022/AFJ).

References

1. Kiayias, A., Tsiounis, Y., Yung, M.: Traceable signatures. In: International Conference on the Theory and Applications of Cryptographic Techniques, pp. 571–589. Springer, Heidelberg (2004)
2. Shao, J., Cao, Z.: A traceable threshold signature scheme with multiple signing policies. Comput. Secur. **25**(3), 201–206 (2006)
3. Kuchta, V., Sahu, R. A., Saraswat, V., et al.: Anonymous yet traceable strong designated verifier signature. In: Information Security: 21st International Conference, ISC 2018, Guildford, UK, September 9–12, 2018, Proceedings 21. Springer International Publishing (2018), pp. 403–421 (2018)
4. Ding, S., Zhao, Y., Liu, Y.: Efficient traceable attribute-based signature. In: 2014 IEEE 13th International Conference on Trust, Security and Privacy in Computing and Communications. IEEE (2014), pp. 582–589 (2014)
5. Gu, K., Wang, K., Yang, L.: Traceable attribute-based signature. J. Inform. Secur. Appl. **49**, 102400 (2019)
6. Kang, Z., Li, J., Shen, J., et al.: TFS-ABS: traceable and forward-secure attribute-based signature scheme with constant-size. IEEE Trans. Knowl. Data Eng. **35**(9), 9514–9530 (2023)
7. Scafuro, A., Zhang, B.: One-time traceable ring signatures. In: Computer Security–ESORICS 2021: 26th European Symposium on Research in Computer Security, Darmstadt, Germany, October 4–8, 2021, Proceedings, Part II 26. Springer International Publishing (2021), pp. 481–500 (2021)
8. Tang, F., Pang, J., Cheng, K., et al.: Multiauthority traceable ring signature scheme for smart grid based on blockchain. Wirel. Commun. Mob. Comput. **2021**(1), 5566430 (2021)
9. Li, T., Wang, H., He, D., et al.: Permissioned blockchain-based anonymous and traceable aggregate signature scheme for industrial internet of things. IEEE Internet Things J. **8**(10), 8387–8398 (2020)
10. Xie, J., Zhou, J., Cao, Z., et al.: Linkable, k-times traceable and revocable ring signature for fine-grained accountability in blockchain transactions. IEEE Internet Things J. (2024)
11. Feng, H., Liu, J., Li, D., et al.: Traceable ring signatures: general framework and post-quantum security. Des. Codes Crypt. **89**, 1111–1145 (2021)

12. Liang, J., Huang, Q., Huang, J., et al.: An identity-based traceable ring signatures based on lattice. Peer-to-peer networking and applications **16**(2), 1270–1285 (2023)
13. Zhao, X., Cao, S., Wang, Z., et al.: A Traceable and anonymous authentication ring signature scheme with privacy protection. In: 2024 27th International Conference on Computer Supported Cooperative Work in Design (CSCWD). IEEE (2024), pp. 570–575 (2024)
14. Liu, Z., Luo, P., Qiu, S., et al.: Deepfashion: powering robust clothes recognition and retrieval with rich annotations. In: Proceedings of the IEEE Conference on Computer Vision and Pattern Recognition. IEEE (2016), pp. 1096–1104 (2016)
15. Lang, Y., He, Y., Yang, F., et al.: Which is plagiarism: fashion image retrieval based on regional representation for design protection. In: Proceedings of the IEEE/CVF Conference on Computer Vision and Pattern Recognition. IEEE (2020), pp. 2595–2604 (2020)
16. Ak, K. E., Lim, J. H., Tham, J. Y., et al.: Efficient multi-attribute similarity learning towards attribute-based fashion search. In: 2018 IEEE Winter Conference on Applications of Computer Vision (WACV). IEEE (2018), pp. 1671–1679 (2018)
17. Ma, Z., Dong, J., Long, Z., et al.: Fine-grained fashion similarity learning by attribute-specific embedding network. In: Proceedings of the AAAI Conference on Artificial Intelligence, vol. 34(07), 11741–11748 (2020)
18. Dong, J., Ma, Z., Mao, X., et al.: Fine-grained fashion similarity prediction by attribute-specific embedding learning. IEEE Trans. Image Process. **30**, 8410–8425 (2021)
19. Wang, X., Han, X., Huang, W., et al.: Multi-similarity loss with general pair weighting for deep metric learning. In: Proceedings of the IEEE/CVF Conference on Computer Vision and Pattern Recognition. IEEE (2019), pp. 5022–5030 (2019)
20. Kinli, F., Ozcan, B., Kirac, F.: Fashion image retrieval with capsule networks. In: Proceedings of the IEEE/CVF International Conference on Computer Vision Workshops. IEEE (2019)

Mixture of Experts Enhanced Heterogeneous Graph Transformer

Qiheng Mao[✉][ID] and Jianling Sun[ID]

Zhejiang University, Hangzhou, China
{maoqiheng,sunjl}@zju.edu.cn

Abstract. Effectively modeling Heterogeneous Information Networks (HINs) is hindered by a dual challenge: the need for both scalable global attention and adaptive, parameter-efficient feature transformation. Existing methods like HGNNs and standard Graph Transformers fail to address both issues simultaneously. To resolve this, we propose MoE-HGT, a Mixture-of-Experts-enhanced Heterogeneous Graph Transformer. Our framework uses sparsely-activated MoE layers to provide specialized, adaptive processing for diverse node types while maintaining parameter efficiency. To achieve scalability, it constructs efficient token sequences from local and metapath-derived contexts, enabling global attention without prohibitive cost. Experiments on four HIN benchmarks show that MoE-HGT consistently outperforms state-of-the-art models.

Keywords: Heterogeneous Information Network · Graph Neural Network · Heterogeneous Graph Transformer · Mixture of Experts

1 Introduction

Graph representation learning has become essential for analyzing complex systems modeled as networks. Heterogeneous Information Networks (HINs) [15], encompassing multi-typed entities and diverse relations, provide a powerful and expressive framework for such systems. Leveraging the rich semantic diversity inherent in HINs is crucial for downstream tasks like node classification, recommendation, and knowledge graph completion.

Heterogeneous graph neural networks (HGNNs) [10,18], typically built on message-passing frameworks, have demonstrated success in learning representations for HINs. However, their effectiveness is fundamentally constrained by inherent limitations. Primarily, HGNNs rely on localized neighborhood aggregation [19], which struggles to capture intricate long-range dependencies that span diverse node and edge types. Furthermore, the prevalent design strategy of employing distinct, type-specific modules [6,24] introduces significant parameter redundancy and computational inefficiency, particularly as the number of types increases, which not only escalates resource demands but also risks impairing model generalization.

© The Author(s), under exclusive license to Springer Nature Singapore Pte Ltd. 2026
T. Zhu et al. (Eds.): KSEM 2025, LNAI 15922, pp. 92–103, 2026.
https://doi.org/10.1007/978-981-95-3058-8_8

Graph Transformers, leveraging global self-attention mechanisms [16], present a promising alternative to overcome the structural limitations of localized aggregation. However, directly applying standard Graph Transformers to HINs introduces two fundamental and interconnected challenges. First, the quadratic computational complexity associated with full pairwise attention renders it prohibitively expensive for large-scale HINs [9], necessitating more efficient strategies for capturing global context. Second, and more critically, the standard Transformer architecture, particularly its homogeneous feed-forward networks (FFNs), is inherently ill-equipped to model the diverse semantic patterns manifested across different node and edge types. This architectural homogeneity forces a single set of parameters to handle all semantic variations, leading to suboptimal representations [12,23].

Addressing these dual challenges—achieving scalable global attention while enabling adaptive, specialized feature transformations without succumbing to parameter explosion—forms the core motivation for our work. Effectively reconciling the need for expressive modeling of complex heterogeneous patterns with the imperative of computational and parametric efficiency requires a fundamentally new architectural approach.

To this end, we propose **MoE-HGT**, a Mixture-of-Experts Enhanced Heterogeneous Graph Transformer. **MoE-HGT** is specifically designed to tackle these issues head-on. To address the challenge of scalable global attention, it employs a strategy of constructing context-rich token sequences by strategically combining local neighborhoods with meta-path derived nodes. This approach preserves long-range semantics while drastically reducing the attention scope. To combat the problem of architectural homogeneity, its core innovation lies in an MoE-Enhanced Transformer Layer, which replaces the standard homogeneous FFNs with a dynamically routed set of experts. This mechanism directly enables type-adaptive feature transformation with high parameter efficiency through sparse activation. These components are unified by a gated heterogeneous fusion mechanism that explicitly incorporates type semantics into a unified feature space. By synergistically combining these elements—MoE-driven adaptive computation, efficient sequence-based global modeling, and explicit heterogeneity encoding—**MoE-HGT** provides a cohesive solution to the identified challenges.

Extensive experiments on multiple benchmark HIN datasets demonstrate that **MoE-HGT** consistently outperforms state-of-the-art HGNNs and homogeneous Graph Transformers. Ablation studies confirm the critical contribution of the MoE mechanism in enhancing model capacity efficiently and validate the effectiveness of the sequence construction and fusion components. The consistent performance gains underscore **MoE-HGT**'s ability to effectively capture and utilize complex heterogeneous graph semantics.

The primary contributions of this work are: (1) The introduction of **MoE-HGT**, the first framework integrating the Mixture-of-Experts paradigm with a Heterogeneous Graph Transformer, specifically designed to achieve parameter-efficient, adaptive modeling of diverse heterogeneous patterns. (2) The development of a scalable token sequence construction method unifying local neighborhoods and meta-path context, enabling efficient global attention computation crucial for large-scale HINs. (3) Comprehensive empirical validation demonstrating **MoE-HGT**'s superior performance and the efficacy of its core innovations across diverse HIN datasets.

2   Related Work

Recent years have seen a surge in Heterogeneous Graph Neural Networks (HGNNs), which typically fall into two categories. Meta-path-based methods [3,18] leverage predefined schemas to capture high-order semantics, while meta-path-free approaches [6,24] use type-aware message passing. Despite their success, these methods, being fundamentally based on localized message-passing, are inherently limited in capturing complex long-range dependencies. Furthermore, to handle heterogeneity, they often employ numerous type-specific parameters, which can lead to significant parameter redundancy and scalability challenges.

The limitations of message-passing have naturally shifted attention toward Graph Transformers [21], which use global attention to enhance expressive power. However, their direct application to HINs presents a difficult trade-off. On one hand, full-graph attention is computationally prohibitive for large-scale graphs. On the other, the standard Transformer's homogeneous architecture is ill-equipped to model diverse heterogeneous semantics. While models like HINormer [12] attempt to improve efficiency, they do so by restricting the model's receptive field, failing to fully resolve the fundamental tension between scalability and expressive, heterogeneity-aware modeling.

The Mixture-of-Experts (MoE) framework [7,14] offers a powerful paradigm for increasing model capacity through sparsely activated, specialized networks. While a few studies have explored MoE for homogeneous GNNs [11,20], they do not address the unique challenges within a Heterogeneous Graph Transformer. Our work is the first to integrate a sparse MoE framework into the feed-forward layers of an HGT which allows **MoE-HGT** to perform adaptive, specialized feature transformations for different node types and simultaneously ensures parameter efficiency.

3   Preliminaries

3.1   Heterogeneous Information Network

A heterogeneous information network (HIN) is characterized by diverse node and edge types, formally represented as $G = (V, E, \mathbf{X}, \phi, \psi)$. Here, V and E denote node and edge sets respectively, with $\mathbf{X} \in \mathbb{R}^{|V| \times d_x}$ being the feature matrix where $\mathbf{x}_v \in \mathbb{R}^{d_x}$ corresponds to node v. Type mapping functions $\phi : V \rightarrow T_v$ and $\psi : E \rightarrow T_e$ assign categorical types to nodes and edges, where T_v and T_e represent distinct type sets. Typically, a HIN is with $|T_v| + |T_e| > 2$, and the network becomes homogeneous when $|T_v| = |T_e| = 1$.

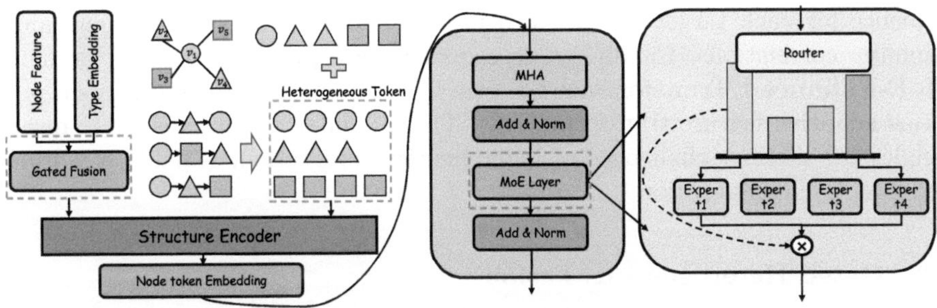

Fig. 1. Overall framework of **MoE-HGT**.

3.2 Transformer Architecture

The standard Transformer layer is composed of two major components, a multi-head self-attention (MSA) module and a feed-forward network (FFN). In the following part, we will briefly introduce MSA without multi-head for simplicity.

Given an input sequence $\mathbf{H} = [\mathbf{h}_1, \mathbf{h}_2, ..., \mathbf{h}_n]^\top \in \mathbb{R}^{n \times d}$, where d is the hidden dimension and $\mathbf{h}_i \in \mathbb{R}^d$ is the hidden representation at position i, the MSA firstly projects the input $\mathbf{H}$ to the query-, key-, value-spaces, denoted as $\mathbf{Q}, \mathbf{K}, \mathbf{V}$, by resorting to three parameter matrices $\mathbf{W_Q} \in \mathbb{R}^{d \times d_K}$, $\mathbf{W_K} \in \mathbb{R}^{d \times d_K}$ and $\mathbf{W_V} \in \mathbb{R}^{d \times d_V}$, as

$$\mathbf{Q} = \mathbf{H}\mathbf{W_Q}, \quad \mathbf{K} = \mathbf{H}\mathbf{W_K}, \quad \mathbf{V} = \mathbf{H}\mathbf{W_V}. \tag{1}$$

Then, the scaled dot-product attention mechanism is applied to the corresponding $< \mathbf{Q}, \mathbf{K}, \mathbf{V} >$ as

$$\mathrm{MSA}(\mathbf{H}) = \mathrm{SOFTMAX}\frac{\mathbf{Q}\mathbf{K}^\top}{\sqrt{d_K}}\mathbf{V}. \tag{2}$$

Thereafter, the output of MSA will be connected to the FFN with two layers of Layer Normalization (LN) [1] and the residual connection [4] to obtain the output of the l-th Transformer layer. By stacking with L layers, Transformers could learn the feature-based proximities between different positions for the input sequences, then the final output $\mathbf{H}^L \in \mathbb{R}^{n \times d}$ can be used as the representation of the input sequence for downstream tasks.

4 The Proposed Model: MoE-HGT

4.1 Overall Framework

The architecture of **MoE-HGT** (Fig. 1) is a novel graph Transformer designed to address the key challenges of scalability and adaptive modeling in HINs. The framework processes heterogeneous graph data through three core stages. It begins by enriching node features with the **Gated Heterogeneous Fusion** module to explicitly encode type semantics. Subsequently, the **Metapath-Augmented Sequence Construction** module generates a context-rich input sequence for each target node, capturing both local structure and long-range semantic correlations. Finally, these sequences are processed by one or more **MoE-Enhanced Transformer Layers**, where a sparse MoE mechanism performs adaptive feature transformations. This modular design effectively disentangles the distinct challenges of heterogeneity integration, scalable attention, and adaptive computation.

4.2   Gated Heterogeneous Fusion

The semantic weight of a node's type is critical in HINs, yet integrating it is nontrivial. Simply concatenating features with type embeddings can cause dimensional inconsistency, while direct addition may disrupt the original feature distribution. We introduce a gated fusion mechanism to integrate type information in a more nuanced and adaptive manner.

First, each node type is assigned a unique, learnable type embedding $t \in \mathbb{R}^D$. This embedding is then fused with the node's projected features $h \in \mathbb{R}^D$ via a learnable gate, α, which adaptively controls the influence of the type information:

$$\begin{aligned}
\alpha &= \sigma(W_{\alpha,2}(\text{ELU}(W_{\alpha,1}[h;t]))), \\
h' &= h + \alpha \cdot t
\end{aligned} \tag{3}$$

where h' is the resulting fused representation, $[h;t]$ denotes concatenation, and $W_{\alpha,1}, W_{\alpha,2}$ are weight matrices. The explicit incorporation of type embedding significantly enhances the Transformer's capability to recognize and analyze heterogeneous relationships among nodes, thereby providing essential heterogeneity reference for the training of individual experts. Following feature fusion, similar to HINormer [12], the integrated features are processed through a message-passing architecture-based structural encoder to initialize token embeddings. We adopt GATv2 [2] due to its superior expressive power in capturing complex graph relationships.

4.3   Metapath-Augmented Sequence Construction

Applying Transformers to graphs requires defining a meaningful input sequence, a challenge given their non-sequential nature. Standard neighborhood sampling (e.g., BFS) is often biased towards topological proximity, failing to include semantically related but distant nodes. To overcome this, we propose a hybrid sequence construction strategy that leverages the semantic richness of metapaths, which facilitates more effective heterogeneous modeling by expert networks.

For each target node v, its input sequence $S(v)$ is constructed from the union of two distinct node sets:

1. **Local Neighborhood** $(N_K(v))$: This set comprises nodes sampled from the K-hop neighborhood of v, ensuring the model retains fine-grained information about the node's immediate surroundings.

2. **Metapath-based Neighbors** $(N_M(v))$: This set captures high-order, long-range semantic relationships. we employ widely-used metapath structures, such as "A–P–A" representing collaborative relationships and "A-P-C-P-A" indicating potential competitive relationships, to sample corresponding neighborhood nodes.

In practice, to maintain computational efficiency, we select three common metapaths for each dataset in our experiments, with each metapath contributing an equal number of sampled nodes to the sequence. The final token sequence is defined as $S(v) = N_K(v) \cup N_M(v)$. This hybrid approach allows the self-attention mechanism to operate over a much richer context, balancing local structural fidelity with global semantic reach, which directly addresses the scalability challenge.

4.4   MoE-Enhanced Transformer Layer

The inherent structural complexity of heterogeneous graphs, where nodes of different types exhibit distinct feature distributions and structural relationships, poses a significant challenge. Conventional HGNNs address this by allocating dedicated parameters for each node/edge type, leading to parameter redundancy and limited adaptability to high-order interactive patterns. The MoE mechanism, with its expert groups and dynamic routing, naturally models heterogeneity by assigning distinct computational paths for nodes with varying features and structural characteristics. Integrating MoE into the Transformer architecture for heterogeneous graphs addresses two key limitations of conventional approaches: (1) the inability of homogeneous FFN layers to handle diverse node/edge types with distinct semantic patterns, and (2) the parameter redundancy caused by applying identical transformations to all nodes.

The MoE Transformer Layer retains the core Multi-Head Self-Attention (MHSA) mechanism for feature fusion across different tokens in the sequence, while replacing the standard FFN with a MoE Layer composed of multiple expert networks and a routing network. The MoE layer itself consists of a set of N independent expert networks and a gating network (router). To further promote expert diversity and computational efficiency, our experts are designed with heterogeneous hidden dimensions. For instance, out of N experts, a subset may have a hidden dimension of $D/2$, another $D/4$, and so on, alongside full-dimension experts. Each expert Expert_i is a simple two-layer FFN:

$$\text{Expert}_i(x) = W_{i,2}(\text{GELU}(W_{i,1}x)) \tag{4}$$

The gating network, typically a simple linear layer, takes an input x and produces routing scores $g(x) \in \mathbb{R}^N$. We employ a sparse top-k gating strategy, activating only the k experts with the highest scores for each token ($k \ll N$). This sparse activation is key to MoE's parameter efficiency. The final output $Y(x)$ is the weighted sum of the outputs from the activated experts:

$$Y(x) = \sum_{i \in \text{TopK}(g(x))} w_i \cdot \text{Expert}_i(x), \quad \text{where} \quad w = \text{Softmax}(g(x)_{\text{TopK}}) \tag{5}$$

To ensure balanced utilization of expert networks and prevent MoE mode collapse, we introduce an auxiliary sequential load-balancing loss. This loss penalizes imbalanced expert utilization and encourages an even distribution of tokens across experts by computing the variance of each expert's activation scores for each heterogeneous token sequence, defined as:

$$\mathcal{L}_{\text{balance}} = \frac{1}{B} \sum_{b=1}^{B} \frac{\text{Var}(g_b)}{\text{Mean}(g_b)^2 + \epsilon} \tag{6}$$

where B is the batch size, g_b represents the routing scores for the b-th sequence, and ϵ is a small constant for numerical stability.

4.5 Model Training and Optimization

The entire **MoE-HGT** framework is trained end-to-end. The optimization objective is a linear combination of the primary task loss and the auxiliary load-balancing loss:

$$\mathcal{L} = \mathcal{L}_{\text{classification}} + \lambda \cdot \mathcal{L}_{\text{balance}} \tag{7}$$

Here, $\mathcal{L}_{\text{classification}}$ is the standard cross-entropy loss, computed on the output representations of the central nodes in each input sequence. The hyperparameter λ serves as a regularization coefficient balancing classification accuracy and expert utilization. We use the AdamW optimizer with a learning rate scheduler for stable and efficient convergence.

4.6 Complexity Analysis

The time complexity of a single **MoE-HGT** layer is primarily determined by the sequence length L, hidden dimension D, the total number of experts N, and active experts k. The MHSA component has a complexity of $O(L^2 \cdot D)$. As our sequence length L is a fixed hyperparameter where $L \ll |V|$, this avoids the prohibitive $O(|V|^2 \cdot D)$ cost of full-graph attention. The subsequent MoE-enhanced FFN has a complexity of $O(L \cdot (D \cdot N + k \cdot D_{avg}^2))$, where the first term is for the gating network and the second is for the sparse expert computations. Note that to enhance expert differentiation and efficiency, our experts operate at varying dimensions (e.g., from D down to $D/4$); thus, D_{avg}^2 represents the average complexity of an expert, and the overall cost is lower than if all experts had dimension D. This design decouples model capacity (related to N) from computational cost (related to k). In essence, **MoE-HGT** achieves scalability through sampling ($L \ll |V|$) and high parameter-to-computation efficiency through sparse, dimension-varied expert activation.

5 Experiments

In this section, we conduct extensive experiments on node classification to evaluate the performance of the proposed **MoE-HGT**, and further give detailed model analysis from several aspects.

Table 1. Summary of datasets.

	# Nodes	# Node Types	# Edges	# Edges Types	Target	# Classes
DBLP	26,128	4	239,566	6	author	4
IMDB	21,420	4	86,642	6	movie	5
ACM	10,942	4	547,872	8	paper	4
Freebase	43,854	4	15,1034	6	movie	3

5.1 Experimental Setups

Datasets. We employ four widely used HIN benchmark datasets, including two academic citation datasets (*DBLP* and *ACM*), a movie rating dataset (*IMDB*), and a knowledge graph dataset (*Freebase*. Among these datasets, DBLP, ACM, and IMDB are sourced from a standardized benchmark called the Heterogeneous Graph Benchmark (HGB) [10]. The preprocessing and data-splitting procedures follow the guidelines established by HGB. For Freebase, we have employed the version provided by **HINormer**. Table 1 summarizes the statistics of the datasets.

Baselines. To comprehensively evaluate the proposed **MoE-HGT** against the state-of-the-art approaches, we consider a series of baselines from three main categories, *basic models* (including **GCN** [8], **GAT** [17], **Transformer** [16]), *Meta-path based HGNNs* (including **RGCN** [13], **HetGNN** [22], **HAN** [18], **MAGNN** [3]) and *Meta-path free HGNNs* (including **RSHN** [24], **HetSANN** [5], **HGT** [6], **SimpleHGN** [10]), **HINormer** [12].

Settings and Parameters. We conduct multi-class node classification on *DBLP*, *ACM*, and *Freebase*, while multi-label node classification on *IMDB*. For DBLP, IMDB and ACM, we used the same data split from HGB for training, validation, and testing on each dataset. For the Freebase dataset, we use the split provided by HINormer. Micro-F1 and Macro-F1 are employed as metrics to evaluate the classification performance. All experiments are repeated for five times, and we report the averaged results with standard deviations.

5.2 Performance Evaluation

We conduct node classification on the four benchmark datasets. We report the performance comparison in Table 2 and observe that **MoE-HGT** can outperform all the baselines. In particular, we make the following observations. Firstly, **MoE-HGT** achieves consistent performance gains over the state-of-the-art graph Transformers like HINormer on datasets with complex type interactions. This advantage stems from its MoE architecture's dynamic routing mechanism towards heterogeneity, which automatically allocates diverse semantic patterns to specialized experts. The integration of type embeddings and meta-path-based

Table 2. Performance evaluation on four benchmarks(%). The best result is **bolded** and the runner-up is underlined. The error bar ($\pm$) denotes the standard deviation of the results over five runs.

Methods	DBLP		IMDB		ACM		Freebase	
	Mi-F1	Ma-F1	Mi-F1	Ma-F1	Mi-F1	Ma-F1	Mi-F1	Ma-F1
GCN	91.5 ± 0.3	90.8 ± 0.3	64.8 ± 0.6	57.9 ± 1.2	92.1 ± 0.2	92.2 ± 0.2	65.2 ± 0.9	60.2 ± 1.1
GAT	93.4 ± 0.3	93.8 ± 0.3	64.9 ± 0.4	58.9 ± 1.4	92.2 ± 0.9	92.3 ± 0.9	66.7 ± 0.7	62.0 ± 1.2
Transformer	94.0 ± 0.1	93.5 ± 0.1	66.3 ± 0.7	62.8 ± 0.7	92.3 ± 0.4	92.6 ± 0.3	67.4 ± 0.5	62.0 ± 0.6
RGCN	92.1 ± 0.5	91.5 ± 0.5	62.1 ± 0.2	58.9 ± 0.3	91.4 ± 0.8	91.6 ± 0.7	60.8 ± 1.2	59.1 ± 1.4
HAN	92.1 ± 0.6	91.7 ± 0.5	64.6 ± 0.6	57.7 ± 1.0	90.8 ± 0.4	90.9 ± 0.4	61.4 ± 3.6	57.1 ± 2.1
HetGNN	92.3 ± 0.4	91.8 ± 0.4	51.2 ± 0.7	48.3 ± 0.7	86.1 ± 0.3	85.9 ± 0.3	63.0 ± 2.3	58.4 ± 2.0
MAGNN	93.8 ± 0.5	93.3 ± 0.5	64.7 ± 1.7	56.5 ± 3.2	90.8 ± 0.7	90.9 ± 0.6	64.4 ± 0.7	58.2 ± 3.9
HGT	93.5 ± 0.3	93.0 ± 0.2	67.2 ± 0.6	63.0 ± 1.2	91.0 ± 0.8	91.1 ± 0.8	66.4 ± 1.9	60.0 ± 2.2
Simple-HGN	94.5 ± 0.2	94.0 ± 0.2	67.4 ± 0.6	63.5 ± 1.4	$\underline{93.4} \pm 0.5$	$\underline{93.4} \pm 0.4$	67.5 ± 1.0	62.5 ± 1.7
HINormer	$\underline{94.9} \pm 0.2$	$\underline{94.6} \pm 0.2$	$\underline{67.8} \pm 0.3$	$\underline{64.7} \pm 0.5$	92.1 ± 0.3	92.2 ± 0.3	$\underline{67.6} \pm 1.3$	$\underline{63.1} \pm 1.1$
MoE-HGT	$\mathbf{95.3} \pm 0.2$	$\mathbf{94.9} \pm 0.2$	$\mathbf{68.0} \pm 0.5$	$\mathbf{65.4} \pm 0.4$	$\mathbf{94.1} \pm 0.3$	$\mathbf{94.0} \pm 0.3$	$\mathbf{68.8} \pm 0.7$	$\mathbf{63.8} \pm 0.6$

high-order semantic tokens further enables explicit modeling of type-specific feature distributions, allowing experts to develop complementary specialization profiles. Even on the ACM where local structure-focused models excel, MoE-HGT maintains competitive performance through adaptive fusion of local structural signals (via structural encoder) and global heterogeneous semantics (via MoE-Transformer). Secondly, **MoE-HGT** outperforms both meta-path-based and meta-path-free HGNNs, which shows the potential of applying graph transformers on HIN representation learning. **MoE-HGT** integrates the strengths of two HGNN approaches into the graph Transformer architecture for heterogeneous modeling. By leveraging the MoE structure, it achieves an adaptive fusion of diverse heterogeneous patterns. Through meta-path sampling, it constructs node sequences with high-order semantic relationships, while utilizing a load-balancing loss to equilibrate different heterogeneous experts. This design effectively overcomes the inherent weakness of Transformer architectures in modeling heterogeneous information. Thirdly, The continuous performance improvements from Transformer to HINormer and then to **MoE-HGT** not only highlight the critical importance of heterogeneous modeling capabilities for the performance of graph Transformers but also demonstrate the superiority of our MoE-based architecture for enhancing heterogeneity representation.

5.3   Ablation Study

To evaluate the contribution of each component in **MoE-HGT**, we conduct an ablation study by comparing with several degenerate variants: (1) *w/o MoE*: we replace the MoE-enhanced Transformer layers with standard Transformer layers, removing the expert mixture mechanism; (2) *w/o Heterogeneous Token*: we remove the meta-path-based heterogeneous token and only use the original local structural token as node input sequences; (3) *w/o Type-aware Fusion*: we remove

Table 3. Micro-F1 (%) for ablation studies.

	DBLP	IMDB	ACM	Freebase
w/o MoE	94.2	67.4	92.6	67.9
w/o Heterogeneous Token	94.9	67.6	93.4	68.0
w/o Type-aware Fusion	95.1	67.8	93.8	68.5
w/o Sequential Balance	94.8	67.4	93.5	68.4
MoE-HGT	95.3	68.0	94.1	68.8

the type-aware fusion mechanism and directly use the original node features as input; (4) *w/o Sequential Balance*: we remove the sequential-level load-balancing loss, allowing the MoE routing mechanism to operate without balancing expert utilization.

We show the results of the ablation study in Table 3 and make the following observations. Firstly, without the MoE mechanism, **MoE-HGT** experiences the most significant performance degradation. Its success stems from two synergistic effects: 1) Experts implicitly learn type-specific feature transformation patterns, acting as "soft" semantic filters; 2) The routing gate serves as a lightweight heterogeneity detector, dynamically aligning node features with expert competencies. Secondly, without heterogeneous token embeddings, the model loses the ability to explicitly encode high-order heterogeneous semantics, leading to a noticeable drop in performance. This highlights the importance of incorporating heterogeneous relationships into the node sequences for better generalization. Thirdly, without the type-aware fusion mechanism, the performance degradation is the least significant among the variants. This suggests that while the type-aware fusion contributes to the model's effectiveness, other components such as MoE and heterogeneous token embeddings play a more critical role. However, the slight drop in performance still indicates the utility of integrating node type embeddings with node features. Finally, without the sequential balance mechanism, the model suffers from imbalanced expert utilization, leading to suboptimal performance. This underscores the importance of the load-balancing loss in ensuring fair and efficient utilization of expert networks towards complex heterogeneity. Overall, the complete **MoE-HGT** achieves the best performance, demonstrating the effectiveness of its components in handling heterogeneous graph data and learning effectiveness node representations.

5.4 Parameters Sensitivity

We evaluate the sensitivity of several important hyperparameters in **MoE-HGT**, and show their impact in Fig. 2. For the number of Transformer layers L, Shallow architectures (L=2-3) achieve optimal performance, particularly for node classification tasks with limited labeled data. For the number of experts n, performance peaks at n=4 experts across datasets, beyond which excessive specialization leads to under-trained experts. This suggests the expert quantity

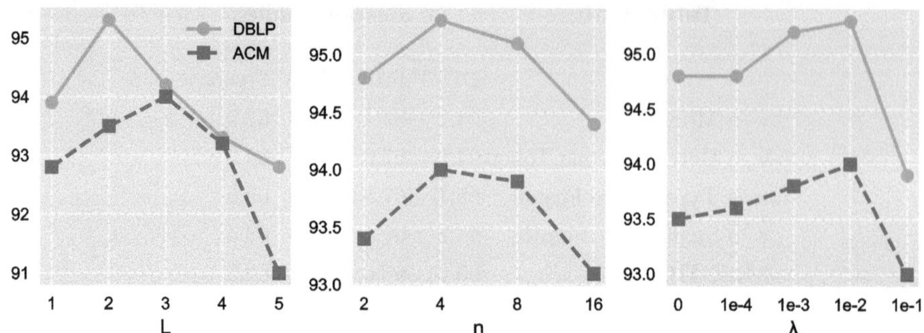

Fig. 2. Hyper-parameters sensitivity studies.

should align with the intrinsic heterogeneity complexity of the target HIN. For sequential balance loss weight λ, $\lambda=0.01$ achieves optimal trade-off between expert diversity and task focus. Deviations cause either compromised specialization or optimization interference.

6 Conclusion

MoE-HGT effectively addresses the limitations of existing heterogeneous graph models through its MoE-enhanced architecture. By dynamically routing node representations to specialized experts, the model achieves parameter-efficient and type-aware processing. The integration of metapath-augmented token sequences ensures comprehensive semantic capture, while gated heterogeneous fusion maintains feature fidelity. Extensive experiments on four benchmark datasets demonstrate the effectiveness of our proposed **MoE-HGT**.

References

1. Ba, J.L., Kiros, J.R., Hinton, G.E.: Layer normalization. arXiv preprint arXiv:1607.06450 (2016)
2. Brody, S., Alon, U., Yahav, E.: How attentive are graph attention networks? arXiv preprint arXiv:2105.14491 (2021)
3. Fu, X., Zhang, J., Meng, Z., King, I.: MAGNN: Metapath aggregated graph neural network for heterogeneous graph embedding. In: Proceedings of The Web Conference 2020, pp. 2331–2341 (2020)
4. He, K., Zhang, X., Ren, S., Sun, J.: Deep residual learning for image recognition. In: Proceedings of the IEEE conference on computer vision and pattern recognition, pp. 770–778 (2016)
5. Hong, H., et al.: An attention-based graph neural network for heterogeneous structural learning. In: Proceedings of the AAAI conference on artificial intelligence, vol. 34, pp. 4132–4139 (2020)
6. Hu, Z., Dong, Y., Wang, K., Sun, Y.: Heterogeneous graph transformer. In: Proceedings of The Web Conference 2020, pp. 2704–2710 (2020)

7. Jacobs, R.A., Jordan, M.I., Nowlan, S.J., Hinton, G.E.: Adaptive mixtures of local experts. Neural Comput. **3**(1), 79–87 (1991)
8. Kipf, T.N., Welling, M.: Semi-supervised classification with graph convolutional networks. In: ICLR (2017)
9. Lu, Z., Fang, Y., Yang, C., Shi, C.: Heterogeneous graph transformer with poly-tokenization. International Joint Conferences on Artificial Intelligence (2024)
10. Lv, Q., et al.: Are we really making much progress? revisiting, benchmarking and refining heterogeneous graph neural networks. In: Proceedings of the 27th ACM SIGKDD Conference on Knowledge Discovery and Data Mining, pp. 1150–1160 (2021)
11. Ma, L., Han, H., Li, J., Shomer, H., Liu, H., Gao, X., Tang, J.: Mixture of link predictors on graphs. arXiv preprint arXiv:2402.08583 (2024)
12. Mao, Q., Liu, Z., Liu, C., Sun, J.: Hinormer: representation learning on heterogeneous information networks with graph transformer. In: Proceedings of the ACM Web Conference 2023, pp. 599–610 (2023)
13. Schlichtkrull, M., et al.: Modeling relational data with graph convolutional networks. In: European semantic web conference, pp. 593–607. Springer (2018)
14. Shazeer, N., et al.: Outrageously large neural networks: the sparsely-gated mixture-of-experts layer. arXiv preprint arXiv:1701.06538 (2017)
15. Shi, C., Li, Y., Zhang, J., Sun, Y., Philip, S.Y.: A survey of heterogeneous information network analysis. IEEE Trans. Knowl. Data Eng. **29**(1), 17–37 (2016)
16. Vaswani, A., et al.: Attention is all you need. Adv. Neural Inf. Process. Syst. **30** (2017)
17. Veličković, P., et al.: Graph attention networks. In: ICLR (2018)
18. Wang, X., et al.: Heterogeneous graph attention network. In: The world wide web conference, pp. 2022–2032 (2019)
19. Xu, K., Hu, W., Leskovec, J., Jegelka, S.: How powerful are graph neural networks? In: ICLR (2019)
20. Yao, Z., et al.: DA-MoE: addressing depth-sensitivity in graph-level analysis through mixture of experts. arXiv preprint arXiv:2411.03025 (2024)
21. Ying, C.: Do transformers really perform badly for graph representation? Adv. Neural. Inf. Process. Syst. **34**, 28877–28888 (2021)
22. Zhang, C., Song, D., Huang, C., Swami, A., Chawla, N.V.: Heterogeneous graph neural network. In: Proceedings of the 25th ACM SIGKDD international conference on knowledge discovery and data mining, pp. 793–803 (2019)
23. Zhao, Z., et al.: Hetcan: a heterogeneous graph cascade attention network with dual-level awareness. In: Joint European Conference on Machine Learning and Knowledge Discovery in Databases, pp. 57–73. Springer (2024)
24. Zhu, S., Zhou, C., Pan, S., Zhu, X., Wang, B.: Relation structure-aware heterogeneous graph neural network. In: 2019 IEEE international conference on data mining (ICDM), pp. 1534–1539. IEEE (2019)

CertBA: A Decentralized Authentication Scheme via Blockchain and Dynamic Cryptographic Accumulator

Huiying Zhang[1,2], Wenmao Liu[3], Wei Ren[1,4]($\boxtimes$) (iD), and Xianchao Zhang[4]

[1] School of Computer Science, China University of Geosciences, Wuhan, China
2735986723@qq.com, weirencs@cug.edu.cn
[2] Key Laboratory of Data Intelligence and Advanced Computing in Provincial Universities, Soochow University, Soochow, China
[3] NSFOCUS Technologies Group Company Ltd., Beijing, China
liuwenmao@nsfocus.com
[4] Provincial Key Laboratory of Multimodal Perceiving and Intelligent Systems, Jiaxing University, Jiaxing, China
zhangxianchao@zjxu.edu.cn

Abstract. With the rapid advancement of blockchain technology, numerous studies have explored its application in Public Key Infrastructure. However, existing blockchain-based PKI systems predominantly utilize blockchain for storing certificate information, relying on traversing the blockchain for certificate queries. Given that blockchain data can only be appended, the efficiency of identity authentication tends to degrade over time. To tackle these challenges, we propose CertBA, a novel certificate management scheme that integrates blockchain with dynamic cryptographic accumulators. In this framework, blockchain serves as a distributed and immutable ledger to record essential data for certificate verification. Distributed Certificate Authority nodes function as miners within the blockchain network, processing certificate operation requests, thereby enhancing the system's scalability and robustness. Specifically, CertBA extends the certificate structure by introducing a witness field W_i and a smart contract account within the certificate extensions, both populated by the CA during certificate issuance. Upon certificate revocation, the CA employs the dynamic cryptographic accumulator to remove the user's value, invalidating the witness W_i and signaling the certificate's revocation. When a user needs to verify a certificate's status, the CA computes the result based on the witness W_i and the current accumulator value on the blockchain, then returns the result to the user. Experimental results demonstrate that CertBA effectively addresses the misjudgment issues prevalent in existing blockchain-based certificate revocation schemes and significantly enhances the efficiency of querying certificate revocation information.

Keywords: Blockchain · PKI · Dynamic Cryptographic Accumulator · Decentralization · Certificate

1   Introduction

Since the advent of the Internet, it has continuously transformed the way people live, communicate, and conduct business. Today, the World Wide Web has become an indispensable part of our daily work and life, involving the transmission of vast amounts of data every day. Notably, a significant portion of this transmitted data is sensitive, making the protection of user privacy particularly crucial. At the same time, modern communication systems require strict authentication for most service requests to ensure system security and reliability.

The certificate revocation mechanism, as one of the core functions of the Public Key Infrastructure (PKI) security framework, plays a crucial role in maintaining the overall security of the system [1]. This mechanism ensures that the validity of a certificate can be promptly terminated during its lifecycle in cases such as private key leakage, changes in certificate subject information, or fraudulent activities by the certificate holder. The importance of the certificate revocation mechanism has been fully demonstrated in real-world cybersecurity incidents. Research indicates that the use of expired or compromised certificates in certificate-based authentication and authorization systems can lead to severe security risks [2]. A notable example is the "Heartbleed" SSL/TLS vulnerability exposed in 2014 [3]. This vulnerability not only allowed attackers to steal sensitive information, such as private keys, from vulnerable servers but also made it difficult to detect security threats in a timely manner, as web server access logs typically do not record such intrusions.

To address the technical challenges of certificate revocation, both academia and industry have proposed various solutions. Currently, mainstream certificate revocation methods include the Certificate Revocation List (CRL) [4] and the Online Certificate Status Protocol (OCSP) [5]. However, these traditional methods still face several limitations in practical applications. First, in terms of scalability, the exponential growth in the number of certificates poses significant challenges to the storage and transmission efficiency of CRLs. Second, in terms of operational costs, real-time verification protocols like OCSP require additional computational resources and network bandwidth, increasing system operating costs.

In response to the aforementioned issues, this paper proposes an efficient scheme. We have designed a lightweight certificate structure, used blockchain technology to build a decentralized PKI system with distributed CA nodes, and designed a complete set of certificate operation algorithms, including certificate registration, and certificate revocation. We also used a dynamic cryptographic accumulator to improve the efficiency of certificate status queries. Finally, through analysis, we have demonstrated the security and applicability of this scheme.

The main contributions of this paper are listed as follows:

- We propose a blockchain-based architecture for CA management over consortium blockchain, by replacing layered CA verification to chain checking. The consortium blockchain ensures that authorized CA nodes can join the consortium blockchain and improve the overall robustness and scalability of the CA system.

- We use a dynamic cryptographic accumulator to revoke certificates, which further shortens the time for certificate status queries in the blockchain. During identity authentication, devices only need to verify whether the certificate has been revoked through the accumulated value of the dynamic cryptographic accumulator, significantly improving the efficiency of certificate status queries.

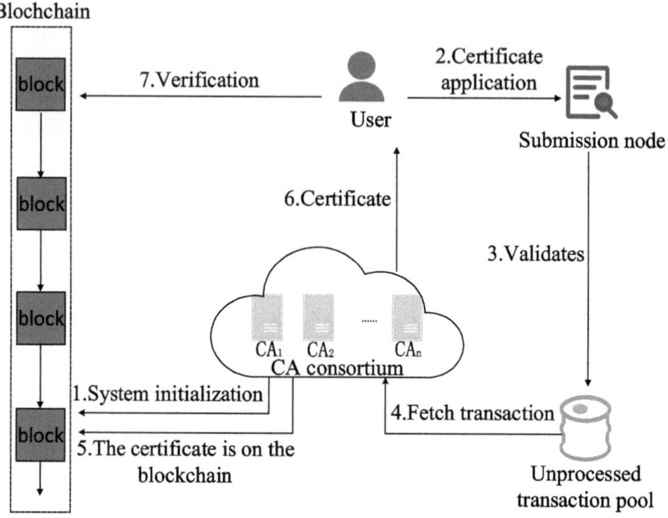

Fig. 1. System Model

2 Problem Formulation

2.1 System Model

The system model of the proposed scheme is illustrated in Fig. 1. The entire system consists of four entities: the Certificate Authority (CA), the blockchain, submission nodes, and users. The data structure of CertBA is illustrated in Fig. 2. The certificate structure of CertBA is an improvement based on the X.509 certificate, introducing a new certificate design. A comparison between the X.509 certificate and the CertBA certificate structure is shown in Fig. 2. Compared to the traditional X.509 certificate, the main improvements of CertBA are as follows:

- CertBA introduces a new witness field W_i in the extension field of the X.509 certificate. When the CA generates a certificate for a user, the authorized

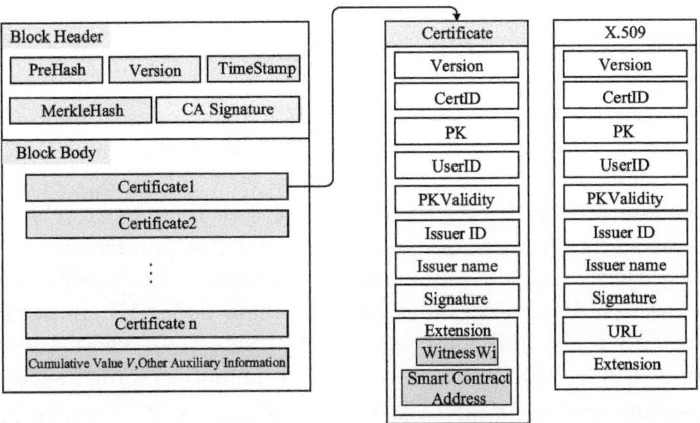

Fig. 2. Data Structure

blockchain smart contract uses a dynamic cryptographic accumulator to generate the witness W_i and the accumulator value. The witness W_i is returned to the CA, which inserts it into the extension field of the certificate and writes the accumulator value and the certificate to the blockchain. When a user verifies the certificate status, the CA uses the witness W_i to verify whether the certificate is included in the accumulator, thereby determining the validity of the certificate.

- CertBA replaces the URL of the certificate revocation checking service with a smart contract address. In traditional PKI systems, checking whether a certificate is revoked requires locating the CRL distribution point based on the URL of the certificate revocation checking service, downloading the CRL list, and checking the certificate serial number to determine the certificate status. The CertBA scheme replaces the URL module with the address of a smart contract. When a user needs to query the certificate status, they only need to verify whether the unique value contained in the certificate is included in the accumulator value based on the witness W_i provided by the user, thereby quickly determining the certificate status.

3   Proposed Scheme

1) System initialization:

1. Main Node Selection and System Parameter Generation. The CA consortium system employs a decentralized consensus mechanism, such as Delegated Proof of Stake (DPOS), to select the Main Node (MN). After selecting the main node MN, the system generates the following key parameters: (1) Security Parameter: The main node MN generates a security parameter n of length k *bit*, which is used to ensure the cryptographic strength and security of the system. (2) Empty Set Initialization: An empty set Au is initialized to

store auxiliary information for the dynamic accumulator in subsequent steps. (3) Definition of Initial Participant List: The public key set of the initial participants is defined as $L = \{PK_1, PK_2, ..., PK_m\}$, where m is the current number of participants. The number of participants m must be at least 1 and at most the threshold value M. The public key of the main node MN, PK_{MN}, must be included in the set L. Additionally, let $CPK = Z_{n^2}^* \setminus \{1\}$ represent the candidate set for the system public key. Let $T' = \{3, ..., n^2\}$ be used to restrict the selection range of dynamic accumulator parameters.

2. Dynamic Cryptographic Accumulator Construction. Its construction process is as follows: (1) Parameter Selection: The main node MN adaptively selects a parameter $\sigma \in Z_{n^2}$ and computes $\beta = \sigma\lambda \bmod \varphi(n^2)$, where λ is a function evaluation process that ultimately yields a numerical value, such that $\beta \in T'$. Uniformly and randomly select $\gamma \xleftarrow{R} Z_{\varphi(n^2)}$, $\gamma \notin (\beta, \sigma)$, to ensure the independence and security of the parameters. (2) Key Generation: Denote the public key of the dynamic accumulator as $PK = (n, \beta)$ and the private key as $SK = (\sigma, \lambda, \gamma)$. Let $P = (PK, SK)$. (3) Initial Accumulator Value Calculation: Select $PK_{(m+1)} \xleftarrow{R} CPK$ from CPK and compute:

$$x_i = F(PK_i^{\gamma\sigma^{-1}} \bmod n^2) \bmod n \ (i = 1, ..., m + 1) \tag{1}$$

$$V_0 = \sigma \sum_{i=1}^{m+1} x_i \bmod n \tag{2}$$

$$y_i = PK_i^{\gamma\beta^{-1}} \bmod n^2 \ (i = 1, ..., m + 1) \tag{3}$$

$$a_c = \prod_{i=1}^{m+1} y_i \bmod n^2 \tag{4}$$

Output initial cumulative value V_0, auxiliary information a_c, $Al = (y_1, ..., y_m)$, where $F(x) = (x - 1)/n$.

3. Consensus Mechanism and Blockchain Storage. The CA consortium nodes validate the data block based on a consensus mechanism such as Delegated Proof of Stake (DPOS). If the validation is successful, the data block is appended to the blockchain; if the validation fails, the block generation authority is passed to the next candidate node until consensus is reached. Once the data block is successfully written to the blockchain, the system initialization process is completed, and the CA consortium system officially enters its operational state.

2) certificate application: (1) Parameter Preparation: The CA node first queries the existing auxiliary information a_c and the auxiliary list $Al = (y_1, ..., y_m)$ in the system, and retrieves the system parameters $P = (PK, SK)$, where $PK = (n, \beta)$ is the public key of the dynamic accumulator, and $SK = (\sigma, \lambda, \gamma)$ is the private key of the dynamic accumulator. (2) Random Set Selection: The CA node randomly selects a set $T = \{t_1, ..., t_m\}$ containing m elements, satisfying $T \subset T' \backslash \{\beta, \gamma\}$ (3) Witness Calculation: For each user $i(i = 1, 2, ..., m)$, the CA node computes their witness:

$$w_i = a_c y_i^{\frac{-t_i}{\gamma}} \bmod n^2 \ (i = 1, ..., m) \tag{5}$$

Here, a_c represents the auxiliary information generated during the system initialization phase. y_i is the auxiliary information for user i, stored in the auxiliary list $Al = (y_1, ..., y_m)$, t_i is a random element from the set T, and γ is part of the private key of the dynamic accumulator. The witness W_i can be expressed as $W_i = (w_i, t_i)$, where w_i is the computed result and t_i is the corresponding random element. (4) Certificate Generation and Issuance: The CA node writes the user's witness information $W_i = (w_i, t_i)$ into the extension field of the certificate, generating the user's digital certificate. Finally, the CA node issues the generated certificate to the user and records the certificate on the blockchain.

3) New user certificate registration: This section details the steps involved in the certificate registration process for new users, including user key generation, the challenge-response mechanism, dynamic accumulator updates, and blockchain storage.

User Key Generation and Registration Request: Before applying for a digital certificate, a new user must first generate their own public-private key pair. The user employs a secure key generation algorithm, such as RSA or ECC, to generate a public-private key pair, denoted as (PK_{user}, SK_{user}). The user then submits a registration request to the submission node, which includes the following: user identity identifier ID, user public key PK_{user}, certificate validity period, and other necessary information.

Challenge-Response Mechanism: To ensure the legitimacy of the registration request and the authenticity of the certificate applicant's identity, the submission node initiates a challenge to verify whether the user indeed possesses the private key PK_{user} corresponding to the public key SK_{user}. The specific process is as follows: (1) Challenge Generation: The submission node generates a random number r and sends it to the user. (2) Response Calculation: The user signs the random number r using the private key SK_{user}, generating a response $Sign(r)$, and returns it to the submission node. (3) Response Verification: The submission node verifies the validity of the signature using the user's public key PK_{user}. If the verification passes, it confirms that the user possesses the corresponding private key, and the registration request is legitimate.

Dynamic Accumulator Update: The main node MN selects a certain number of user certificate application transactions from the unprocessed transaction pool and performs the dynamic accumulator update operation. The specific steps are as follows: (1) Public Key Set Recording: Record the public key set of users applying for certificates as $L^+ = \{PK_1^+, ..., PK_m^+\}$. (2) Random Parameter Selection: Randomly select an auxiliary public key PK_{k+1} from CPK, and randomly select a set $T^+ = \{t_1^+, ..., t_k^+\}$ satisfying $T^+ \xleftarrow{R} T' \backslash \{T \cup \{\beta, \gamma\}\}$, where $T' = \{3, ..., n^2\}$. (3) Compute New Accumulator Value and Auxiliary

Information:

$$x_i^+ = F((PK_i^+)^{\gamma\sigma^{-1}} \bmod n^2) \bmod n \ (i = 1, ..., k+1) \tag{6}$$

$$V' = V + \sigma \sum_{i=1}^{K+1} x_i^+ \bmod n \tag{7}$$

$$y_i^+ = (PK_i^+)^{\gamma\beta^{-1}} \bmod n^2 \ (i = 1, ..., k+1) \tag{8}$$

$$a_u = \prod_{i=1}^{k+1} y_i^+ \bmod n^2 \tag{9}$$

$$w_i^+ = a_u a_c (y_i^+)^{\frac{-t_i^+}{\gamma}} \bmod n^2 \ (i = 1, ..., k+1) \tag{10}$$

Let $T = T \cup T^+$, $Au = Au \cup \{a_u\}$, $a_c = a_c a_u \bmod n^2$. The main node MN will invoke the smart contract to package the updated accumulator value V', auxiliary information a_u, a_c and related parameters into a data block. This block is then broadcast to the entire CA consortium network. The CA consortium nodes validate the data block based on the consensus mechanism. If the validation passes, the data block is appended to the blockchain. The block body hash value is computed, the hash value of the previous block's header is calculated, and the main node's private key is used to sign the block header. The block header is then generated and written to the blockchain. The main node MN writes the new user's witness $W_i = (w_i^+, t_i^+)$ into the extension field of the certificate, generates the digital certificate, sends it to the user, and records the certificate on the blockchain.

4) Certificate revocation: (1)When a user discovers that their private key has been compromised or encounters other security issues, they must immediately submit a certificate revocation request to the submission node. The user provides the submission node with their identity identifier ID, the information of the certificate to be revoked, the reason for revocation, and other relevant details. The submission node verifies the user's identity to ensure the legitimacy of the revocation request. After verifying the user's identity, the submission node sends the certificate revocation information to the unprocessed transaction pool, where it awaits further processing by the main node MN. (2) The main node MN selects a certain number of certificate revocation transactions from the unprocessed transaction pool and performs the dynamic accumulator update operation. The set of public keys to be revoked is recorded as $L^- = \{PK_1^-, ..., PK_k^-\}$, where $L^- \subset L$ and $1 \leq k < m$. An auxiliary public key PK_{k+1}^- is randomly selected from CPK, and the following computation is performed:

$$x_i^- = F((PK_i^-)^{\gamma\sigma^{-1}} \bmod n^2) \bmod n \ (i = 1, ..., k+1) \tag{11}$$

$$V' = V - \sigma \sum_{i=1}^{K} x_i^- + \sigma x_{k+1}^- \bmod n \tag{12}$$

$$y_i^- = (PK_i^-)^{\gamma\beta^{-1}} \bmod n^2 \ (i = 1, ..., k+1) \tag{13}$$

$$a_u = y_{k+1}^- \prod_{i=1}^{k} (y_i^-)^{-1} \bmod n^2 \tag{14}$$

Let $Au = Au \cup \{a_u\}$, $a_c = a_c a_u \bmod n^2$. The new accumulator value and new auxiliary information are computed. The main node MN packages the updated accumulator value V', auxiliary information a_c, a_u, and related parameters into a data block, which is then broadcast to the entire CA consortium network. If the validation passes, the data block is appended to the blockchain.

5) Certificate update: When a user needs to use a new public-private key pair, they must submit a certificate renewal request to the CA consortium system. The user generates a new public-private key pair (PK', SK') and submits the following information to the submission node: user identity identifier ID, the old digital certificate, the new public key PK', and the reason for the certificate renewal. Upon receiving the user's certificate renewal request, the submission node performs multiple verifications to ensure the legitimacy and security of the request. The specific verification steps are as follows: (1) User Registration Verification: Verify whether the user is already registered in the system. (2) Private Key Ownership Verification: The submission node generates a random number r and sends it to the user. The user signs the random number r using the private key SK', generating a response $Sign(r)$, and returns it to the submission node. The submission node verifies the validity of the signature using the user's public key PK'. If the verification passes, it confirms that the user indeed possesses the corresponding private key, and the renewal request is legitimate. (3) Public Key Consistency Verification: Verify that the user's new public key PK' is different from the old public key PK to prevent adversaries from maliciously renewing the certificate using the compromised old public key.

MN packages the updated accumulator value, auxiliary information, and related parameters into a data block, which is then broadcast to the entire CA consortium network. If the validation passes, the data block is appended to the blockchain.

6) Certificate status verification: When a user needs to verify whether a certificate has been revoked, they provide the user certificate and the witness W_i. The verification process checks whether $(\{PK, w_i\} \subset CPK)$, $t_i \in \mathbf{T}'$, and $F(w_i^\beta PK_i^{t_i} \bmod n^2) \equiv V \bmod n$. If all conditions are satisfied, the output is "Yes," indicating that the user has indeed been accumulated in V and the certificate is valid. Otherwise, the certificate is invalid.

4   Analysis

4.1   Security Analysis

(1) Data Security Analysis: In this scheme, certificate data is stored on the blockchain, and any modifications to certificates require consensus from multiple CA nodes before the updated status can be recorded on-chain. The

protocol employed in this study is the PBFT (Practical Byzantine Fault Tolerance) algorithm, which demonstrates superior performance in consortium blockchain environments, particularly when no malicious nodes interfere, enabling rapid consensus. Furthermore, to ensure system security, this model enforces a strict admission review mechanism for nodes joining the consortium blockchain, effectively reducing the likelihood of malicious nodes and further safeguarding the integrity and reliability of certificate data on the blockchain.

(2) Single-Point Failure Analysis: The PBFT consensus mechanism remains functional even if nearly one-third of the nodes fail. As long as at least two-thirds of the nodes remain honest, the system can continue operating normally.

(3) Preemptive Registration: Preemptive registration refers to the act of individuals or organizations, driven by self-interest, registering potentially valuable names, identifiers, digital assets, or resources before others can do so. To address this issue, the CertBA model initiates an identity challenge-response mechanism upon receiving a certificate registration request. Regulatory nodes verify the true ownership of the claimed identity, ensuring the security and legitimacy of the certificate registration process.

(4) Malicious CA: If a CA node attempts to insert a forged certificate into the blockchain, it is engaging in malicious behavior and is thus classified as a malicious CA. However, since certificate submission requires consensus from the CA consortium, the malicious operation will be rejected during the consensus process, preventing the fraudulent certificate from being recorded on the blockchain.

(5) Sybil Attack: In this scheme, new nodes must undergo rigorous authentication by regulatory nodes to ensure each node possesses only one legitimate identity. Consequently, adversaries cannot execute Sybil attacks by creating multiple fake identities, effectively mitigating such threats.

4.2   Scheme Comparison

A comparative analysis of the proposed scheme and related PKI schemes is shown in Table 1. Specifically: Certcoin [6]: This scheme builds a PKI model based on blockchain, using offline keys to protect online keys. It also leverages RSA accumulators and distributed hash tables to achieve efficient certificate management. Aucoin [7]: This is a decentralized PKI scheme. It employs a flexible challenge-response mechanism for verification and identity authentication when publishing public keys, effectively reducing illegal occupancy and Sybil attacks. IKP [8]: This scheme uses smart contracts to incentivize and regulate CA behavior: rewarding CAs for correctly issuing digital certificates, penalizing malicious CAs, and rewarding reporters of unauthorized certificates. These measures effectively ensure the trustworthiness of certificates issued by CAs.

This scheme does not produce false positive results. The verification algorithm will always return 1 for all honestly generated keys, all honestly computed accumulator values, and their corresponding witnesses. Generating membership

Table 1. Scheme Comparison

Scheme	Attributes					
	PKI [9]	Ref. [6]	Ref. [7]	Ref. [8]	Ref. [10]	CertBA
Certificate Registration	✓	✓	✓	✓	✓	✓
Certificate Revocation	✓	✓	✗	✗	✓	✓
Single Point of Failure	✗	✓	✗	✓	✓	✓
Preemptive Registration	✗	✗	✓	✗	✓	✓
Certificate Transparency	✗	✓	✓	✓	✓	✓
Malicious CA	✗	✓	✗	✓	✓	✓
Batch Updates	✗	✗	✗	✗	✗	✓
Sybil Attack Resistance	✗	✓	✓	✗	✗	✓
Replay Attack Resistance	✗	✗	✓	✓	✗	✓

proofs for elements not belonging to the set is computationally difficult; similarly, generating non-membership proofs is also challenging due to the collision resistance of the accumulator. Furthermore, the accumulator possesses undeniability, meaning that generating two conflicting proofs for the same element x simultaneously proving $x \in x$ or $x \notin x$ is computationally infeasible.

4.3 Experiments

CertBA is implemented on the Hyperledger Fabric blockchain network. The smart contracts are written in Python. CertBA operates in an environment with an AMD R7 6800H CPU @3.20 GHz $\times$ 2, 16 GB RAM, Ubuntu 22.04, and WSL2 LTS 64-bit operating system.

Before conducting the experimental tests, 9,000 digital certificates were created in bulk. To avoid randomness in the experimental results, the tests were repeated five times to calculate the average values. Figure 3 shows the average time required to query the status of revoked certificates. The average revocation certificate query time for CertBA is 35.01ms, and querying 10,000 certificates takes approximately 1 s. RSI [11] requires more time than IABC [12] and CertBA because additional verification is needed when querying the status of revoked certificates. As the number of certificates increases, the required additional verification also increases. IABC has the most efficient query but suffers from false positives (providing a positive response when the certificate is not yet revoked). Our method has no false positives, and the response time is within a reasonable range.

From the performance tests described above, it can be observed that the certificate query time for RSI increases linearly with the size of the test set. In contrast, the time consumption for CertBA fluctuates very little as the number of certificates increases, although it lags behind the query speed of IABC. However,

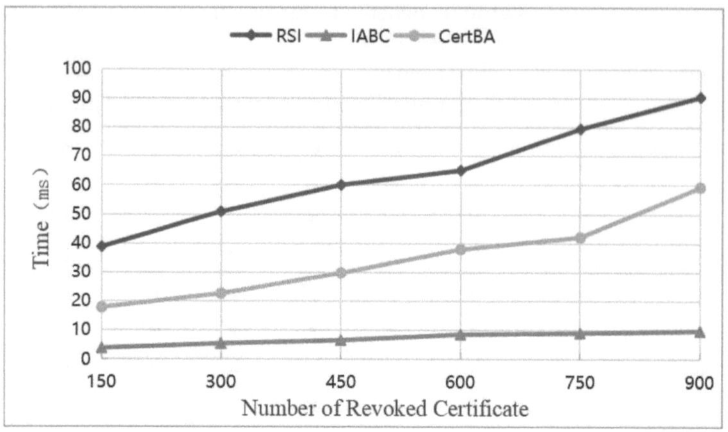

Fig. 3. Query time of the revoked certificate.

IABC has the potential for false positives, whereas CertBA does not suffer from this issue.

5   Conclusion

The certificate management scheme designed in this paper integrates dynamic cryptographic accumulators, blockchain technology, and consensus mechanisms to construct an efficient, secure, and scalable certificate management system. The core advantages of the scheme are as follows:

Real-time verification of certificate status is achieved through accumulator values and witness information, eliminating the storage and query overhead associated with traditional certificate revocation lists. Blockchain is utilized to store certificate registration, revocation, and update information, ensuring data transparency and security. During certificate registration and updates, the challenge-response mechanism and public key consistency verification effectively prevent forgery and malicious operations. Functional modules such as system initialization, certificate registration, revocation, updates, and status verification are modularized, facilitating scalability and maintenance.

This scheme is suitable for scenarios such as blockchain identity authentication, IoT device management, and financial transaction systems, effectively addressing some of the pain points in traditional certificate management systems.

Acknowledgement. The research was financially supported by the Key Laboratory of Data Intelligence and Advanced Computing in Provincial Universities, Soochow University (No. KJS2409), Provincial Key Laboratory of Multimodal Perceiving and Intelligent Systems, Jiaxing University (No. MPIS202416), the Key Laboratory of Data Protection and Intelligent Management, Ministry of Education, Sichuan University and also the Fundamental Research Funds for the Central Universities (No.

SCU2023D008), and the CCF-NSFOCUS Kun-Peng Scientific Research Fund (No. CCFNSFOCUS2023009).

References

1. Liu, Y., et al.: An end-to-end measurement of certificate revocation in the web's pki. In: Proceedings of the 2015 Internet Measurement Conference, pp. 183–196 (2015)
2. Zhang, L., et al.: Analysis of ssl certificate reissues and revocations in the wake of heartbleed. In: Proceedings of the 2014 Conference on Internet Measurement Conference, pp. 489–502 (2014)
3. Durumeric, Z., et al.: The matter of heartbleed. In: Proceedings of the 2014 Conference on Internet Measurement Conference, pp. 475–488 (2014)
4. Cooper, D., Santesson, S., Farrell, S., Boeyen, S., Housley, R., Polk, W.: Internet x. 509 public key infrastructure certificate and certificate revocation list (crl) profile. Technical report (2008)
5. Myers, M., Ankney, R., Malpani, A., Galperin, S., Adams, C.: X. 509 internet public key infrastructure online certificate status protocol-ocsp. Technical report (1999)
6. Fromknecht, C., Velicanu, D., Yakoubov, S.:. A decentralized public key infrastructure with identity retention. Cryptology ePrint Archive (2014)
7. Leiding, B., Cap, C.H., Mundt, T., Rashidibajgan, S.: Authcoin: validation and authentication in decentralized networks. arXiv preprintarXiv:1609.04955 (2016)
8. Matsumoto, S., Reischuk, R.M.: Ikp: Turning a pki around with decentralized automated incentives. In: 2017 IEEE Symposium on Security and Privacy (SP), pp. 410–426. IEEE (2017)
9. Weise, J.: Public key infrastructure overview. Sun BluePrints OnLine, August, pp. 1–27 (2001)
10. Qin, B., Huang, J., Wang, Q., Chen, X., Zhang, L., Wang, Yu.: Cecoin: a decentralized pki mitigating mitm attacks. Futur. Gener. Comput. Syst. **107**, 805–815 (2020)
11. Adja, Y.C.E., Hammi, B., Serhrouchni, A., Zeadally, S.: A blockchain-based certificate revocation management and status verification system. Comput. Secur. **104**, 102209 (2021)
12. Sui, H., Jian, L., Fan, B.: Iabc: a cross-domain authentication method based on blockchain and cuckoo filter. J. Chinese Comput. Syst. **41**(12), 2620–2625 (2020)

Adaptive Capsule Graph Neural Network with Attention Mechanism for Parathyroid Glands Detection

Wanling Liu[1,2], Wenhuan Lu[1], Fei Chen[2], Jianping Cai[3], Bo Wang[4,5], and Wenxin Zhao[4,5(✉)]

[1] College of Intelligence and Computing, Tianjin University, Tianjin 300072, China
[2] College of Computer and Data Science, Fuzhou University, Fuzhou 350116, China
[3] The Faculty of Data Science, City University of Macau, Macau 999078, China
[4] Department of Thyroid Surgery, Fujian Medical University Union Hospital, Fuzhou, FJ, China
zhaowx@fjmu.edu.cn
[5] Clinical Research Center for Precision Management of Thyroid Cancer of Fujian Province, Fuzhou, FJ, China

Abstract. Developing a precise parathyroid identification model is difficult due to the intricacies of thyroid surgical environments, including obstruction of surgical instruments, light variations, extrusion, and deformation. Given that traditional detectors (such as Faster R-CNN) rely on limited receptive fields, they cannot effectively solve the problems of occlusion, deformation, and data scarcity in PG detection. This research presents an adaptive capsule graph neural network (ALCapsule-GNN) for parathyroid gland (PG) detection, a new model that integrates capsule networks with graph convolutional networks (GNN) to improve the efficacy of PG object detection tasks in medical images. The model employs a capsule network-based Backbone to extract multi-scale features and constructs an adaptive graph using a dynamic graph generator, where nodes represent capsules and edges encode spatial-semantic relationships. The hierarchical graph capsule network incorporates an attention mechanism to refine the graph structure while leveraging a shared weight mechanism to minimize redundant computations. Iterative message passing enhances target detection performance and improves the robustness to occlusion and deformation. ALCapsuleGNN efficiently captures spatial relationships and contextual information among objects while preserving the model's computational efficiency and adaptability. Comprehensive trials in a proprietary parathyroid data set demonstrate that our method achieves exceptional results in automated parathyroid detection.

Keywords: Parathyroid gland · Object detection · Neural Capsule Graph · Medical Image

1   Introduction

Endoscopic thyroidectomy offers excellent cosmetic outcomes by avoiding neck scars for patients with thyroid cancer [1]. However, it has a higher risk of complications, with hypoparathyroidism common after total thyroidectomy. Improving the identification of parathyroid glands (PG) during surgery is crucial [2].

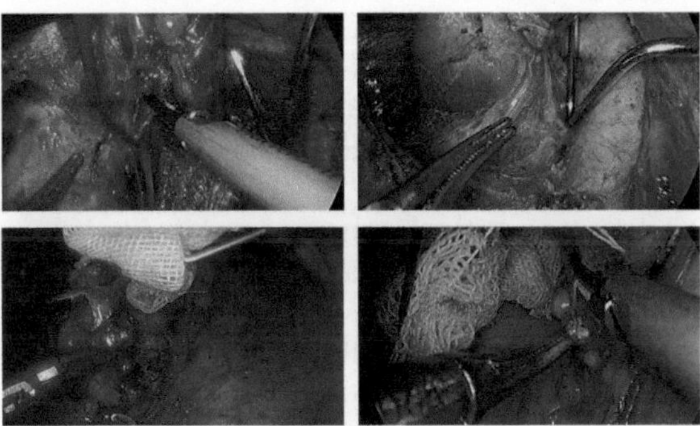

Fig. 1. Surgical instruments such as blades and cotton balls obstruct the view of PG.

This paper addresses the automatic detection of PG, a task complicated by occlusion, tissue deformation, and limited annotated data. The primary challenge lies in effectively capturing discriminative features under complex surgical conditions.

Existing approaches predominantly adopt convolutional neural networks (CNNs) and graph neural networks (GNNs) to extract relevant features. CNN-based methods [2] leverage multiscale convolutional kernels and global average pooling to capture local details and global context. GNN-based approaches [2] aggregate node and neighbor information to model local spatial dependencies, aiding in contextual understanding. Additionally, some studies [1] further enhance CNN performance through variable-sized kernels to adapt to diverse contextual environments.

Despite these advances, excessive reliance on global context often introduces irrelevant information, increasing model complexity and degrading detection speed and accuracy. As shown in Fig. 1, surgical instruments such as blades and cotton swabs frequently obscure the PG, and visually similar structures like adipose granules further complicate recognition. Moreover, PGs are spatially sparse—rarely appearing close to each other—which makes accurate spatial modeling essential.

To address these issues, we propose a lightweight and adaptive detection framework named ALCapsGNN-PGD. The model integrates capsule networks and GNNs to capture meaningful contextual information while maintaining efficiency selectively. A capsule-based backbone is used to extract multiscale features, followed by a dynamic graph constructor that builds an adaptive graph, where capsules serve as nodes and edges encode spatial-semantic relationships. The hierarchical graph capsule network enhances feature representation via iterative message passing. Additionally, matrix capsules are used instead of scalar neurons, applying view-invariant linear transformations to generate predictions across layers, thereby improving spatial variation and occlusion robustness.

2   Related Work

Accidental excision of the PGs during endoscopic thyroid surgery can lead to severe hormonal imbalances and, in extreme cases, life-threatening complications [1]. Therefore, accurate intraoperative identification and preservation of PGs is of critical clinical importance.

Traditional PG detection methods rely on visual inspection, positive parathyroid imaging, or nanocarbon-based negative imaging [2]. However, these techniques struggle with occlusion, surgical artifacts, and tissue deformation [3]. With the advent of deep learning, computer vision techniques have been increasingly applied to assist surgeons in PG localization [4]. However, practical difficulties remain: PGs are small, often obscured by instruments, and undergo significant shape and color changes during surgery, making detection difficult [5]. Early PG detection studies employed CNNs to model image features [1], leveraging multiscale kernels, data augmentation, and attention mechanisms [6]. While effective at local feature extraction, CNNs struggle to capture spatial relationships and contextual dependencies—both critical in complex surgical scenes.

To address these shortcomings, recent works have explored capsule networks [7] and GNNs [8] for structured representation learning. Capsule networks model part-whole relationships through routing mechanisms, while GNNs encode spatial and topological dependencies between regions of interest. GraphCaps [9] enhances PG detection by constructing graph representations of visual features, integrating local and global spatial context using features such as FGSD [10]. Extensions like CapsGNNEM [11] incorporate matrix capsules and EM-routing to capture hierarchical relationships better while reducing network complexity. Nevertheless, existing models still face two significant limitations: (1) limited ballot generation strategies and (2) high temporal and spatial complexity, which restrict their applicability to large-scale medical datasets.

Our work proposes an improved architecture that integrates a fast voting mechanism and an optimized routing strategy to overcome these issues. These enhancements significantly reduce training time while improving detection accuracy. We also introduce an attention-based capsule backbone to strengthen feature representation at a lower computational cost. Furthermore, we build an adaptive sparse graph guided by attention and apply a shared-weight mechanism to reduce redundancy and enhance scalability.

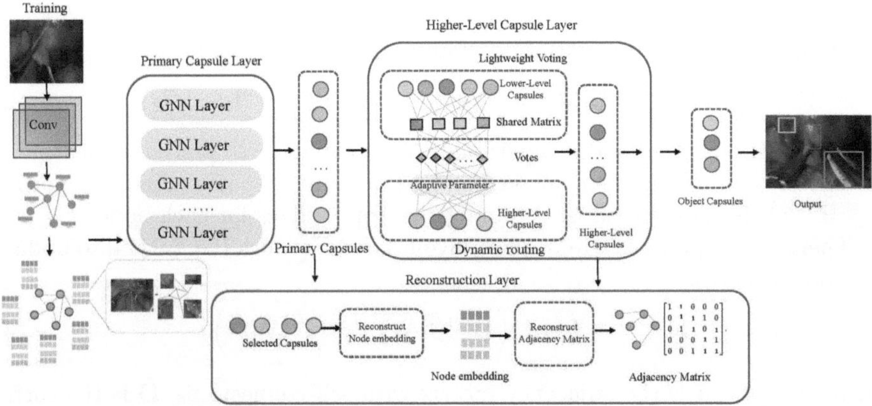

Fig. 2. The framework of ALCapsGNN-PGD for PG detection

3 Methodology

3.1 ALCapsGNN Network

The framework of ALCapsGNN-PGD for PG detection is illustrated in Fig. 2. Adaptive capsule graph neural network framework based on the attention mechanism: the front end generates the primary feature representation of the image through CNN [12] and capsule laye [13]r; the middle end uses the capsule output as a graph node, combines spatial distance and semantic similarity to build an adaptive sparse graph, and dynamically optimizes the weight of the edge through the attention mechanism; the back end uses GCN to aggregate neighborhood information to complete the detection and classification of the target. The algorithm realizes end-to-end learning of feature encoding, relational reasoning, and detection tasks by jointly optimizing capsule reconstruction, node classification, and edge prediction loss. The dynamic routing and shared weight mechanism significantly improve the model's adaptability to complex scenes while reducing computational redundancy.

Given an input image $\mathbf{I} \in \mathbb{R}^{H \times W \times 3}$, we extract a set of multi-scale feature maps $\{\mathbf{F}_i\}_{i=1}^{N}$ using a ResNet-50 backbone, where each feature map $\mathbf{F}_i \in \mathbb{R}^{H_i \times W_i \times C_i}$. Then, for each spatial location (x, y), a feature vector $\mathbf{f}_{x,y} \in \mathbb{R}^{C_i}$ is extracted and passed through two fully connected layers:

$$\mathbf{u}_{x,y} = \text{ReLU}(W_1 \mathbf{f}_{x,y} + \mathbf{b}_1), \quad \mathbf{v}_{x,y} = \text{Squash}(W_2 \mathbf{u}_{x,y} + \mathbf{b}_2), \qquad (1)$$

where $\mathbf{v}_{x,y} \in \mathbb{R}^{d_c}$ denotes the capsule activation vector, and the squash function is defined as:

$$\text{Squash}(\mathbf{z}) = \frac{\|\mathbf{z}\|^2}{1 + \|\mathbf{z}\|^2} \cdot \frac{\mathbf{z}}{\|\mathbf{z}\|}.$$

To construct a sparse graph, the set of capsule outputs $\{\mathbf{v}_i\}_{i=1}^{M}$ (where $M = H_i \times W_i$) is treated as graph nodes. The corresponding node feature matrix is $\mathbf{X} \in \mathbb{R}^{M \times d_c}$. Edges are adaptively constructed, and the edge weight A_{ij} is computed based on both spatial proximity and semantic similarity:

$$A_{ij} = \sigma\left(\alpha \cdot \mathrm{MLP}([\mathbf{v}_i; \mathbf{v}_j]) + (1 - \alpha) \cdot \exp\left(-\gamma\|\mathbf{l}_i - \mathbf{l}_j\|_2\right)\right), \tag{2}$$

where $\mathbf{l}_i$ denotes the spatial coordinate of node i, $\alpha \in [0, 1]$ is a learnable parameter, and $\sigma(\cdot)$ is the sigmoid function. Finally, a sparse adjacency matrix $\mathbf{A} \in \mathbb{R}^{M \times M}$ is constructed by retaining the Top-k edges for each node.

Then, we adopt a 2-layer Graph Convolutional Network (GCN) [14] to update the node features:

$$\mathbf{H}^{(l+1)} = \mathrm{ReLU}\left(\tilde{\mathbf{D}}^{-1/2}\tilde{\mathbf{A}}\tilde{\mathbf{D}}^{-1/2}\mathbf{H}^{(l)}\mathbf{W}^{(l)}\right), \tag{3}$$

where $\tilde{\mathbf{A}} = \mathbf{A} + \mathbf{I}$ is the adjacency matrix with self-connections, $\tilde{\mathbf{D}}$ is the corresponding degree matrix, and the initial feature matrix is $\mathbf{H}^{(0)} = \mathbf{X}$.

For the detection head, an MLP is applied to each node feature to produce the final predictions:

$$\hat{\mathbf{y}}_i = \mathrm{Softmax}(\mathbf{W}_c\mathbf{h}_i), \quad \hat{\mathbf{b}}_i = \mathbf{W}_r\mathbf{h}_i, \tag{4}$$

where $\mathbf{h}_i \in \mathbf{H}^{(2)}$ is the final feature of node i, $\hat{\mathbf{y}}_i \in \mathbb{R}^C$ denotes the category probability vector, and $\hat{\mathbf{b}}_i \in \mathbb{R}^4$ represents the predicted bounding box coordinates.

3.2 Dynamic Graph Learning

3.2.1 Dynamic Routing

The routing mechanism in capsule networks is used to determine the connection weights between capsules at adjacent layers dynamically. The adaptive routing adjusts the assignment coefficients based on the input graph structure and the specific task requirements [7].

The routing process aims to compute a high-level capsule representation by aggregating lower-level capsule votes through a weighted sum. Let $\mathbf{v}_{ij} \in \mathbb{R}^{d'}$ denote the vote from capsule i to higher-level capsule j, and $\mathbf{s}_j \in \mathbb{R}^{d'}$ be the aggregated output (i.e., the center of cluster j). The initial logits b_{ij}, representing the similarity between $\mathbf{v}_{ij}$ and $\mathbf{s}_j$, are usually initialized as zeros. The assignment coefficients $c_{ij} \in [0, 1]$ are then computed via a softmax function:

$$c_{ij} = \frac{\exp(b_{ij})}{\sum_k \exp(b_{ik})}, \quad \mathbf{s}_j = \sum_i c_{ij} \cdot \mathbf{v}_{ij}. \tag{5}$$

Next, we apply the nonlinear squash function, as in [7], to normalize the output capsule vector:

$$\mathbf{s}'_j = \mathrm{squash}(\mathbf{s}_j) = \frac{\|\mathbf{s}_j\|^2}{1 + \|\mathbf{s}_j\|^2} \cdot \frac{\mathbf{s}_j}{\|\mathbf{s}_j\|}. \tag{6}$$

The logits $b_{ij} \in \mathbb{R}$ are then updated by measuring the agreement between $\mathbf{v}_{ij}$ and the normalized capsule $\mathbf{s}'_j$:

$$b_{ij} \leftarrow b_{ij} + \mathbf{v}_{ij} \cdot \mathbf{s}'_j. \tag{7}$$

This routing procedure can be iterated multiple times to refine the capsule assignments. However, we explore a variant to improve computational efficiency where the logits b_{ij} are learned directly via backpropagation.

3.2.2 Multi-head Attention in Dynamic Graph Learning

To enhance the robustness and expressiveness of dynamic graph learning, we introduce a multi-head attention mechanism. By parallelizing the computations across multiple attention heads, the model can reduce the sensitivity of a single attention weight to noise or outlier edges. In addition, feature splitting and weight sharing reduce the parameter count while maintaining sufficient modeling capacity. The attention-based edge weights are computed using multi-head dot-product attention:

$$A_{ij} = \frac{1}{K} \sum_{k=1}^{K} \sigma \left(\left(\mathbf{W}_k^Q \mathbf{h}_i \right)^\top \left(\mathbf{W}_k^K \mathbf{h}_j \right) \right), \tag{8}$$

where $\mathbf{W}_k^Q, \mathbf{W}_k^K \in \mathbb{R}^{\frac{d_c}{K} \times d_c}$ are the learnable projection matrices for the k-th head, shared across layers for efficiency.

For each node feature $\mathbf{h}_i \in \mathbb{R}^{d_c}$, we compute query and key vectors through K sets of independent linear transformations:

$$\mathbf{q}_i^k = \mathbf{W}_k^Q \mathbf{h}_i, \quad \mathbf{k}_j^k = \mathbf{W}_k^K \mathbf{h}_j, \quad k = 1, \dots, K. \tag{9}$$

The attention score between nodes i and j for the k-th head is calculated as:

$$e_{ij}^k = \frac{\left(\mathbf{q}_i^k \right)^\top \mathbf{k}_j^k}{\sqrt{d_c/K}}, \quad \alpha_{ij}^k = \text{Softmax}_j \left(e_{ij}^k \right), \tag{10}$$

where the softmax is computed over all neighbors $j \in \mathcal{N}(i)$.

To preserve spatial structure, we incorporate spatial distance prior into the attention score:

$$e_{ij}^k \leftarrow e_{ij}^k + \beta \cdot \exp \left(-\gamma \| \mathbf{l}_i - \mathbf{l}_j \|_2 \right), \tag{11}$$

where $\mathbf{l}_i$ denotes the spatial coordinate of node i, and β is a learnable coefficient controlling the influence of the distance prior.

Each head aggregates the transformed neighbor features independently. The output of the k-th attention head is:

$$\mathbf{h}_i^k = \sum_{j \in \mathcal{N}(i)} \alpha_{ij}^k \cdot \left(\mathbf{W}_k^V \mathbf{h}_j \right), \tag{12}$$

where $\mathbf{W}_k^V \in \mathbb{R}^{\frac{d_c}{K} \times d_c}$ is the value projection matrix. The final node representation is obtained by concatenating the outputs from all heads: $\mathbf{h}_i' = \big\|_{k=1}^{K} \mathbf{h}_i^k$.

To avoid information degradation in deep GCN layers, we add a residual connection followed by layer normalization:

$$\mathbf{h}_i^{\text{out}} = \text{LayerNorm} \left(\mathbf{h}_i + \mathbf{W}_O \mathbf{h}_i' \right), \tag{13}$$

where $\mathbf{W}_O \in \mathbb{R}^{d_c \times d_c}$ is the output projection matrix.

3.3 Loss Function

The overall loss function consists of three components: capsule reconstruction loss, node detection loss (including classification and bounding box regression), and edge prediction loss [15].

To encourage the capsule layer to retain meaningful latent features, we apply an L_2 reconstruction loss between the input image I and its reconstructed version from the capsule features V:

$$\mathcal{L}_{\text{recon}} = \|I - \text{Decoder}(V)\|_2^2. \tag{14}$$

To address class imbalance, we use Focal Loss [2] for binary classification:

$$\mathcal{L}_{\text{cls}} = -\frac{1}{M} \sum_{i=1}^{M} \left[y_i (1 - \hat{y}_i)^\gamma \log(\hat{y}_i) + (1 - y_i) \hat{y}_i^\gamma \log(1 - \hat{y}_i) \right], \tag{15}$$

where $\gamma = 2$ is the focusing parameter, $\hat{y}_i$ is the predicted probability, and $y_i \in \{0, 1\}$ is the ground truth label.

For localization, we adopt the Complete IoU (CIoU) loss [2] which considers overlap, center distance, and aspect ratio:

$$\mathcal{L}_{\text{box}} = 1 - \text{IoU}(\hat{b}_i, b_i^{gt}) + \frac{\rho^2(\hat{b}_i, b_i^{gt})}{c^2} + \alpha v, \tag{16}$$

where ρ denotes the Euclidean distance between box centers, c is the diagonal length of the smallest enclosing box, v measures aspect ratio consistency, and α is a balancing factor.

The total detection loss is:

$$\mathcal{L}_{\text{det}} = \lambda_{\text{cls}} \mathcal{L}_{\text{cls}} + \lambda_{\text{box}} \mathcal{L}_{\text{box}}, \tag{17}$$

with hyperparameters $\lambda_{\text{cls}} = 1.0$, $\lambda_{\text{box}} = 0.5$.

To ensure the semantic rationality of the dynamically learned graph, we supervise the edge weights using binary cross-entropy:

$$\mathcal{L}_{\text{edge}} = -\sum_{i,j} \left[A_{ij}^{gt} \log A_{ij} + (1 - A_{ij}^{gt}) \log(1 - A_{ij}) \right], \tag{18}$$

where A^{gt} is constructed based on whether the IoU between ground-truth object boxes b_i^{gt}, b_j^{gt} exceeds a threshold (e.g., IoU > 0.5).

The total loss is a weighted combination of the three terms:

$$\mathcal{L}_{\text{total}} = \lambda_1 \mathcal{L}_{\text{recon}} + \lambda_2 \mathcal{L}_{\text{det}} + \lambda_3 \mathcal{L}_{\text{edge}}, \tag{19}$$

where the default weights are set as $\lambda_1 = 0.5$, $\lambda_2 = 1.0$, and $\lambda_3 = 0.2$.

4   Experiments

4.1   Dataset

We conducted experiments on a parathyroid dataset approved by the institutional review board of the Union Hospital of Fujian Medical University. We agreed to use video data and medical records [2]. The Thyroid Surgery Treatment Group of the Union Hospital of Fujian Medical University calibrated the dataset [1,2], The dataset contains 1,3740 images. These images were randomly divided into training sets 70%, validation sets 15%, and test sets 15%.

The laparoscopic parathyroid dataset differs significantly from standard public datasets. The PG often share similar colors and shapes with surrounding fat tissues, making them difficult to distinguish—even by experts—under direct visual inspection. Moreover, intraoperative lighting conditions can vary greatly, leading to inconsistent image brightness.

4.2   Implementation Details

The proposed model was implemented using PyTorch and optimized with the Adam optimizer [16]. All experiments were conducted on a Ubuntu 20.04 workstation equipped with an Intel(R) Core i7-5930K CPU (6 cores) and a GeForce GTX 1080 GPU with 8 GB of memory.

Regarding the hyperparameter settings, the number of GCN layers was fixed at $L = 3$, the number of dynamic routing iterations at $T = 3$, and the number of advanced capsule layers at 2. Other parameter settings were as follows: batch_size $= 16$, weight_decay $= 1 \times 10^{-5}$, learning_rate $= 0.001$, learning rate decay step size $\text{lr}_{\text{decay\_step\_size}} = 150$, capsule_dimensions $= 6$, number of capsules capsule_num $= 5$, number of shared parameter matrices $k = 5$, number of capsules selected in the middle layer of the reconstruction module $k_2 = 3$, dropout rate dropout $= 0.5$, and reconstruction loss coefficient $\theta = 0.1$.

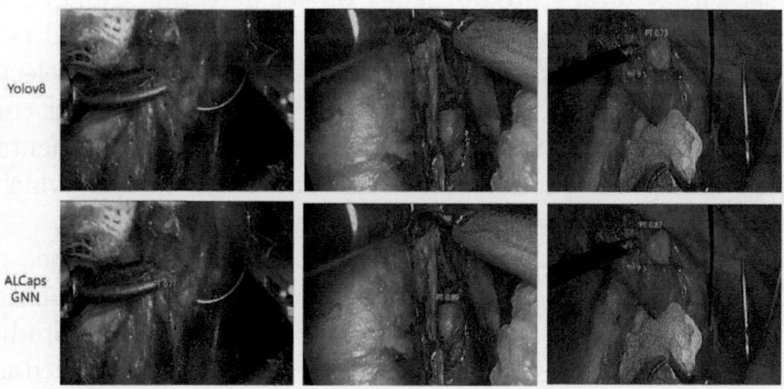

Fig. 3. Visualized results of Yolov8 and ALCapsGNN-PGD.

4.3   Evaluation Metrics

We evaluate the model's performance using Frames Per Second (FPS) and Average Precision (AP). FPS measures the number of images processed per second and reflects the detection speed of the model [17,18]. A high FPS is critical to meet real-time requirements in laparoscopic surgery.

Average Precision (AP) assesses detection accuracy. A prediction is considered correct if the Intersection over Union (IoU) between the predicted and ground truth bounding boxes exceeds 0.5. AP combines precision and recall, calculated as:

$$\text{Precision} = \frac{TP}{TP + FP}, \quad \text{Recall} = \frac{TP}{TP + FN}, \tag{20}$$

where: TP (True Positive): correctly predicted PG, FP (False Positive): background regions incorrectly predicted as glands, FN (False Negative): missed detections of actual glands.

AP is computed as the area under the precision–recall curve:

$$AP = \int_0^1 \text{Precision}(\text{Recall}), d(\text{Recall}). \tag{21}$$

Higher AP values indicate better model accuracy [19]. The confidence score of each predicted box affects AP, as high-confidence false positives or false negatives can lower it significantly.

We report several standard AP metrics: $AP@0.5$: IoU threshold $= 0.5$, $AP@0.75$: IoU threshold $= 0.75$, $AP@[0.5 : 0.95]$: average AP across IoU thresholds from 0.5 to 0.95 in steps of 0.05.

4.4   Comparison Results

To evaluate the effectiveness of our proposed method, we conducted a comparative analysis with several state-of-the-art object detection frameworks, noting that no prior studies have specifically addressed parathyroid gland (PG) detection. Given the real-time performance demands of this task, we selected Faster R-CNN, YOLOv3, YOLOv5, YOLOX, YOLOv7, and YOLOv8 for comparison. For fairness, all models were implemented under the same experimental settings and initialized with pre-trained weights from the COCO dataset, which provides strong feature extraction capabilities for natural images.

Quantitative Comparison: Table 1 summarizes the performance of various methods. Our proposed approach significantly outperforms all compared models on the parathyroid dataset. Results for baseline methods are reproduced from existing studies, with the best values highlighted in bold. A detailed analysis of the Average Precision (AP) scores reveals that our method achieves an outstanding AP_{50} of 95.2%, surpassing the second-best model by 1.5%. This demonstrates the superior detection capability of our approach for parathyroid gland identification. In addition to the substantial accuracy gains, our model achieves an

Table 1. Comparative Results of Different Parathyroid Detection Methods.

Methods	AP_{50}	AP_{75}	$AP_{50:95}$	FPS
Faster-RCNN	81.9%	43.8%	44.5%	16.8
Yolov3	78.2%	31.2%	39.9%	20.18
Yolov5	85.7%	47.3%	47.9%	21.2
YoloX	89.2%	49.7%	46.4%	20.18
Yolov7	90.3%	51.6%	50.0%	26.14
Yolov8	91.3%	56.5%	53.2%	25.58
ALCapsGNN-PGD	**95.2%**	**55.6%**	**54.83%**	**27.8**

inference speed of 27.8 FPS, fully meeting the requirements for real-time laparoscopic detection.

To validate the visual quality of our detection results, we conducted comprehensive comparisons with two representative models: YOLOv8 and ALCapsGNN-PGD. As shown in Fig. 3, YOLOv8 tends to miss parathyroid gland (PG) targets in complex surgical scenarios due to limited robustness. In contrast, ALCapsGNN-PGD leverages the dynamic routing mechanism of capsule networks to capture intricate spatial and structural features. This enables it to maintain computational efficiency while accurately detecting PG targets in challenging surgical environments.

To further assess performance under difficult conditions, we present examples in Fig. 4, including: (1) a PG target being pulled by surgical instruments, and (2) a squeezed target susceptible to misdetection.

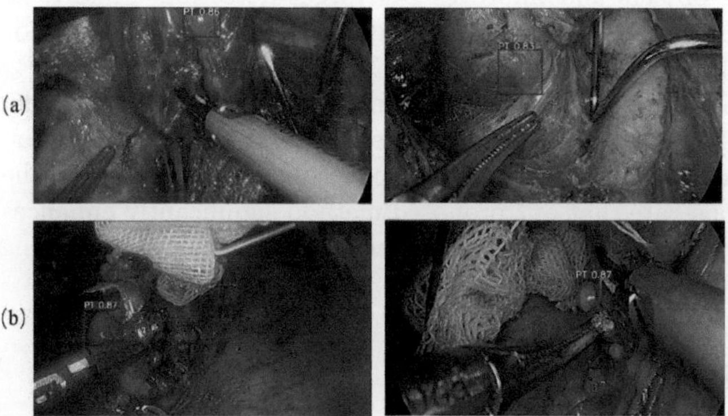

Fig. 4. Performance of ALCapsGNN-PGD under Challenging Conditions

4.5   Ablation Study

In this section, we conduct ablation studies on the parathyroid (PG) dataset to evaluate the individual contributions of the proposed modules. The experimental results are summarized in Table 2. **ALCapsule+**: This variant removes the GNN component from the full ALCapsule-GNN model and instead uses a traditional CNN for feature extraction. **GNN+**: This variant excludes the adaptive capsule network component, retaining only the GNN module alongside basic convolutional or fully connected layers.

Table 2. Ablation studies on the PG test set.

Method	Adaptive Capsule	GNN	AP_{50}
Baseline	×	×	91.1%
+ALCapsule	✓	×	92.7%
+GNN	×	✓	92.3%
ALCapsule-GNN	✓	✓	**95.2%**

Table 2 presents the results in terms of AP_{50} under different module configurations. When comparing the baseline model with the GNN+ variant, we observe an improvement in AP_{50} from 91.1% to 92.3%, confirming that the introduction of the GNN module contributes a 1.2% performance gain. The effect of the Adaptive Capsule Network is further demonstrated by comparing the baseline and ALCapsule+ models, where AP_{50} improves from 91.1% to 92.7%. This suggests that the adaptive capsule network effectively captures spatial relationships among objects and improves PG target detection. Finally, our complete model, **ALCapsule-GNN**, which integrates both the GNN and Adaptive Capsule Network modules, achieves the best performance with an AP_{50} of 95.2%, yielding a significant 4.1% improvement over the baseline. This confirms that the integration of both modules results in superior performance for PG detection, especially in scenarios involving occlusion and deformation. These ablation results demonstrate that our proposed method significantly enhances PG target detection by effectively capturing spatial dependencies and addressing challenges such as occlusion and deformation.

5   Conclusion

In laparoscopic thyroidectomy, inadvertent damage to the PG can lead to permanent hypocalcemia. To address this risk, we propose ALCapsuleGNN, an adaptive and lightweight capsule graph neural network for automatic PG detection in medical images. The proposed model effectively captures spatial relationships and contextual information while maintaining computational efficiency and adaptability. By integrating capsule networks with GNNs, ALCapsuleGNN robustly handles challenges such as instrument occlusion and target deformation. An adaptive mechanism dynamically adjusts the model's structure and parameters, enhancing accuracy and generalization. Experimental results on a dedicated parathyroid dataset demonstrate that ALCapsuleGNN significantly outperforms existing methods in detection performance.

Funding Information. This research was funded by Clinical Research Center for Precision Management of Thyroid Cancer of Fujian Province (Grant No.: 2022Y2006; 2024YGPT003) and Joint Funds for the Innovation of Science and Technology, Fujian Province (Grant No.: 2023Y9190; 2023Y9135); Fujian Province Young and Middle-aged Teacher Education Research Project(Grant No.: JAT231010).

References

1. Wang, B., Zheng, J., Yu, J.F., et al.: Development of artificial intelligence for parathyroid recognition during endoscopic thyroid surgery. Laryngoscope **132**(12), 2516–2523 (2022)
2. Liu, W., Cai, Z., Chen, F., et al.: Ellipse shape prior based anti-noise network for parathyroid detection. In: Fourteenth International Conference on Graphics and Image Processing (ICGIP 2022), vol. 12705, pp. 897–909. SPIE (2023)
3. Uslu, A., Okut, G., Tercan, I.C., et al.: Anatomical distribution and number of parathyroid glands, and parathyroid function, after total parathyroidectomy and bilateral cervical thymectomy. Medicine **98**(23) (2019)
4. Lin, S.Y., Li, M.Y., Yu, J.F., et al.: Power of PTAIR 2.0 in prediction, identification, and ischemia assessment of the parathyroid gland under endoscopic thyroid surgery. VideoEndocrinology **10**(1), 7–8 (2023)
5. Wang, B., Yu, J.F., Lin, S.Y., et al.: Intraoperative AI-assisted early prediction of parathyroid and ischemia alert in endoscopic thyroid surgery. Head Neck **46**(8), 1975–1987 (2024)
6. Dhillon, A., Verma, G.K.: Convolutional neural network: a review of models, methodologies and applications to object detection. Progr. Artif. Intell. **9**(2), 85–112 (2020)
7. Yan, Y., Li, J., Xu, S., et al.: LightCapsGNN: light capsule graph neural network for graph classification. Knowl. Inf. Syst. **66**(10), 6363–6386 (2024)
8. Tang, J., Qu, M., Wang, M., et al.: Line: large-scale information network embedding. In: Proceedings of the 24th International Conference on World Wide Web, 1067–1077 (2015)
9. Hamilton, W., Ying, Z., Leskovec, J.: Inductive representation learning on large graphs. Adv. Neural Inf. Process. Syst. **30** (2017)
10. Grover, A., Leskovec, J.: Node2vec: scalable feature learning for networks. In: Proceedings of the 22nd ACM SIGKDD International Conference on Knowledge Discovery and Data Mining, pp. 855–864 (2016)
11. Velikovi, P., Cucurull, G., Casanova, A., et al.: Graph attention networks. Stat **1050**(20), 10–48550 (2017)
12. Sadeghnezhad, E., Salem, S.: InceptionCapsule: inception-Resnet and CapsuleNet with self-attention for medical image Classification. arXiv preprint arXiv:2402.02274 (2024)
13. Noor, K.T., Robles-Kelly, A.: H-CapsNet: a capsule network for hierarchical image classification. Pattern Recogn. **147**, 110135 (2024)

14. Andrushia, A.D., Neebha, T.M., Patricia, A.T., et al.: Capsule network-based disease classification for Vitis Vinifera leaves. Neural Comput. Appl. **36**(2), 757–772 (2024)
15. Janocha, K., Czarnecki, W.M.: On loss functions for deep neural networks in classification. arXiv preprint arXiv:1702.05659 (2017)
16. Kingma, D.P.: Adam: a method for stochastic optimization. arXiv preprint arXiv:1412.6980 (2014)
17. Zou, Z., Chen, K., Shi, Z., Guo, Y., Ye, J.: Object detection in 20 years: a survey. Proc. IEEE **111**(3), 257–276 (2023)
18. Liu, W., Lu, W., Li, Y., et al.: Parathyroid gland detection based on multi-scale weighted fusion attention mechanism. Electronics **14**(6), 1092 (2025). https://doi.org/10.3390/electronics14061092
19. Liu, W., Lu, W., Sun, Q., et al.: Real-time double-layer graph attention networks for parathyroid detection. In: 2024 IEEE International Conference on Bioinformatics and Biomedicine (BIBM). IEEE, pp. 1606–1610 (2024)

HGC: A Hybrid Method Combining Gravity Model and Cycle Structure for Identifying Influential Spreaders in Complex Networks

Jiaxun Li, Yonghou He, Zhefan Dong, and Li Tao[(⊠)]

College of Computer and Information Science, Southwest University,
Chongqing, China
{lijiaxun,holder523,dongzhefan}@email.swu.edu.cn, tli@swu.edu.cn

Abstract. Identifying influential spreaders in complex networks is crucial for applications in disease control, information dissemination, and social network analysis. The gravity model, a distinctive approach for identifying influential spreaders, has attracted significant attention due to its ability to integrate node influence and the distance between nodes. However, the law of gravity is symmetric, whereas the influence between different nodes is asymmetric. Existing gravity model-based methods commonly rely on the topological distance as a metric to measure the distance between nodes. Such reliance neglects the strength or frequency of connections between nodes, resulting in symmetric influence values between node pairs, which ultimately leads to an inaccurate assessment of node influence. Moreover, these methods often overlook cycle structures within networks, which provide redundant pathways for nodes and contribute significantly to the overall connectivity and stability of the network. In this paper, we propose a hybrid method called HGC, which integrates the gravity model with effective distance and incorporates cycle structure to address the issues above. Effective distance, derived from probabilities, measures the distance between a source node and others by considering its connectivity, providing a more accurate reflection of actual relationships between nodes. Experiments on eight real-world networks using the Susceptible-Infected-Recovered model show that HGC outperforms seven other methods in identifying influential nodes.

Keywords: Complex Networks · Influential Spreaders · Effective Distance · Gravity Model · Susceptible-Infected-Recovered Model

1 Introduction

One of the most significant challenges in network science is identifying influential spreaders, commonly referred to as important nodes. These nodes play a critical role in the propagation of information [1] and diseases [2] across the network. For example, during an infectious disease outbreak, immunizing key individuals

© The Author(s), under exclusive license to Springer Nature Singapore Pte Ltd. 2026
T. Zhu et al. (Eds.): KSEM 2025, LNAI 15922, pp. 129–137, 2026.
https://doi.org/10.1007/978-981-95-3058-8_11

can help prevent a large-scale epidemic [3]. Effectively identifying these nodes can lead to better strategies for controlling epidemics, enhancing information dissemination, and maximizing influence in social networks.

Methods for identifying important nodes in complex networks can be categorized into global and local approaches. Global methods, such as betweenness centrality (BC) [4] and closeness centrality (CC) [5], analyze the overall network structure. BC measures how often a node appears on shortest paths, while CC quantifies a node's proximity to others. Despite their effectiveness, these methods have high computational costs, making them unsuitable for large-scale networks. Additionally, cycles play a key role in network structure. Fan et al. [6] introduced the cycle number matrix and cycle ratio to assess node importance, but this approach struggles in sparse networks. Local methods, such as degree centrality (DC) [7] and the H-index [8], are more computationally efficient than global approaches, making them suitable for large-scale networks. DC assumes that a node's influence increases with the number of its neighbors but overlooks their attributes. To address this, Li et al. [9] proposed RDP, which captures higher-order neighborhood information with minimal iterations and low complexity. However, these methods focus only on local structures, potentially leading to suboptimal results.

The gravity model, combining local and global information, has gained attention for integrating node influence and distance. Inspired by gravity law, Ma et al. [10] proposed models G and G+, using the K-shell value as mass and shortest path as distance. Li et al. [11] introduced the gravity model (GM) with degree as mass and later proposed the local gravity model (LGM) with a truncation radius. Further, Li et al. [12] developed DKGM by incorporating the K-shell iteration factor and later introduced MCGM [13] by considering multiple node characteristics. Zhu et al. [14] proposed HVGC, a gravity centrality method based on the H-index. However, gravity-based methods assume symmetric influence between nodes, assigning equal distances while ignoring interaction strength, which contradicts real-world information propagation. In practice, node connectivity affects information flow, making distances asymmetric.

To overcome these limitations, we propose HGC, a hybrid method integrating the gravity model, cycle structure, and structural hole theory [15] to identify influential nodes. HGC considers neighboring influence, effective distance, and cycle structure. We evaluated HGC using the SIR model [16] on eight real-world networks, comparing it with seven methods. Kendall's Tau [17], Jaccard similarity [18], and Monotonicity [19] were used for evaluation. Results showed that HGC achieved more accurate rankings, identified strong spreaders, and reduced ranking redundancies.

The remaining sections of this paper are organized as follows. Section 2 presents the proposed HGC method. Section 3 presents the specific experimental setup, including datasets and compared methods. Section 4 presents the experimental results, analysis, and discussion. We conclude our study in Sect. 5.

2   Methods

In the previous section, we discussed the merits and limitations of various methods for identifying important nodes in networks. To address these limitations, we propose the HGC method. The overall framework of our proposed method HGC is presented in Fig. 1.

2.1   Proposed Method

The proposed method HGC consists of three components: interaction effects, information propagation effects, and weighted fusion. Firstly, the node degree and effective distance between nodes are incorporated into the gravity model to calculate the interaction effects, while the network constraint coefficient is used to evaluate the importance of a node's position within the network. Then, the cycle ratio is employed to quantify the significance of cycle structures in the network, with higher-order neighbour information being obtained through several iterations. Finally, a balancing factor is introduced to integrate the above two scores. HGC of node i is defined as follows.

$$HGC(i) = GM(i) + \gamma RCP(i) \tag{1}$$

where $GM(i)$ represents the interaction score of node i calculated by gravity model, $RCP(i)$ represents the information propagation score of node i, and γ is a balancing factor.

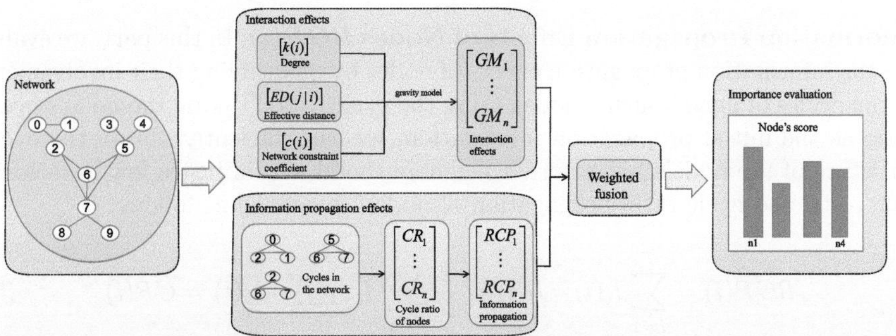

Fig. 1. HGC Overall Framework Diagram. The overall framework of HGC comprises three parts: (1) interaction effects between nodes based on the gravity model; (2) information propagation effects based on the cycle structure; and (3) weighted fusion. The framework can compute the influence scores of all nodes in the network through the three parts outlined above.

Interaction Effects $GM(i)$ Between Nodes. In this part, we calculate the interaction effects between nodes, which are evaluated based on the local properties of the nodes, the effective distance between them, and their positions within the network. The interaction effects between nodes can be calculated as follows.

$$GM(i) = \sum_{ED_{(j|i)} \leq R, j \neq i} e^{-c(i)} \frac{k_i \times k_j}{ED_{j|i}^2} \tag{2}$$

where R is the truncation radius, $c(i)$ is the network constraint coefficient, $ED_{j|i}$ is the effective distance from node i to node j, and k_i represents the degree of node i.

Effective distance [20] (ED) is a distance abstracted from probabilities, and it provides a more detailed distance metric based on the interaction strength between nodes and their neighbours. Effective distance from node i to node j is defined as

$$ED_{j|i} = 1 - log_2(P_{j|i}) \quad P_{j|i} = \frac{a_{ij}}{k_i} \tag{3}$$

where k_i is the degree of node i, a_{ij} is the element in the adjacent matrix of graph G.

Structural holes [15] refer to gaps in a network where two individuals are not directly connected but are indirectly connected through a third node, represented as follows.

$$c_i = \sum_j (\mu_{ij} + \sum_{q \neq i,j} \mu_{iq}\mu_{qj})^2 \quad \mu_{ij} = \frac{z_{ij}}{\sum_{j \in \Gamma(i)} z_{ij}} \tag{4}$$

where node q represents the common neighbors between nodes i and j. μ_{ij} denotes the proportion of effort that node i invests to maintain its relationship with node j out of its total effort. $\Gamma(i)$ denotes the set of neighbors of node i, and $z_{ij} = 1$ if there exists an edge between nodes i and j, otherwise $z_{ij} = 0$.

Information Propagation Effects of Nodes $RCP(i)$. In this part, we evaluate the information propagation effects of nodes by quantifying their involvement in the cycles of neighbouring nodes using the cycle ratio. Taking the node's cycle ratio as the initial propagation information, we can efficiently obtain the cycle structure of the node's higher-order neighbourhood within just a few iterations. The restricted cycle ratio propagation of node i is defined as follows.

$$RCP(i) = \sum_{l=1}^{T} I_l(i) \quad I_l(i) = \frac{1}{l^2} \sum_{j \in \Lambda_i} I_{l-1}(j) \quad I_0(i) = CR(i) \tag{5}$$

where T is the number of iterations, and Λ_i is the set of neighbors of the node i.

The value of the cycle ratio for each node can be obtained through Eq. 6.

$$CR(i) = \left\{ \begin{matrix} 0, & c_{ii} = 0 \\ \sum_{j,c_{ij}>0} \frac{c_{ij}}{c_{jj}}, & c_{ii} > 0 \end{matrix} \right\} \tag{6}$$

where c_{ii} represents the number of cycles associated with node i, and c_{ij} represents the number of cycles that pass through i and j.

Weighted Fusion. We introduce a balancing factor γ, defined as the ratio of GM to RCP. This adjustment is necessary because of the disparity in scales between GM and RCP, they cannot be integrated directly.

$$\gamma = \frac{\langle GM \rangle}{\langle RCP \rangle} \tag{7}$$

where $\langle GM \rangle$ and $\langle RCP \rangle$ denote the average values of GM and RCP, respectively.

3 Experiments Setup

This section outlines the experimental setup to validate HGC. We first introduce the datasets (Sect. 3.1), then discuss the methods for comparison (Sect. 3.2).

3.1 Datasets

The effectiveness of the proposed method is evaluated using eight real-world networks from six categories: USAir (transportation), Email (communication), Yeast (biology), Power (infrastructure), Jazz and NS (collaborative), and Facebook and PB (social). Table 1 provides the basic topological information, including the number of nodes (N), edges (M), average degree ($< k >$), average distance ($< d >$), and clustering coefficient (C). All data is available for download at https://github.com/MLIF/Network-Data.

Table 1. The topological features of eight real-world networks.

Networks	N	M	$< k >$	$< d >$	C
Jazz	198	2742	27.6970	2.2350	0.6334
USAir	332	2126	12.8072	2.7381	0.7494
NS	379	914	4.8232	6.0419	0.7981
Email	1133	5451	9.6222	3.6060	0.2540
PB	1222	16714	27.3552	2.7375	0.3600
Yeast	2361	7182	5.6289	3.8832	0.1301
Facebook	4039	88234	43.6910	3.6925	0.6170
Power	4941	6594	2.6691	18.9892	0.1065

3.2 Methods to Compare

We selected several traditional and relevant methods to compare the proposed HGC method's performance comprehensively. Including Degree Centrality [7]

(DC), Betweenness Centrality [4] (BC), Closeness Centrality [5] (CC), the K-Shell decomposition method [21] (KS), Cycle Ratio [6] (CR), the Local Gravity Model [11] (LGM), and the Restricted Degree Information Propagation [9] (RDP). In this paper, we set $R = 2$ and $T = 2$ due to the small-world property [22] in most real-world networks.

4   Results and Discussion

In this section, we conducted several experiments on eight datasets of different sizes, evaluating them from accuracy, spreading ability, and distinguishing ability.

4.1   The Comparison of Accuracy

Table 2 shows the Kendall's Tau results for eight networks. HGC outperformed other methods in Jazz, NS, Email, PB, and Facebook, thanks to its use of cycle structure and effective distance in dense networks. In USAir and Yeast, it performed similarly to the top method. In the sparse Power network, HGC still ranked second despite limited cycle structure impact.

Table 2. The methods' accuracies for $\beta = \beta_c$, measured by the Kendall's Tau. The top-ranked value in each row of the table is marked in bold, while the second-ranked value is underlined.

Networks	DC	BC	CC	KS	CR	LGM	RDP	HGC
Jazz	0.8145	0.5008	0.7113	0.7465	0.6327	<u>0.855</u>	0.8326	**0.865**
NS	0.63	0.3559	0.3248	0.5606	0.3699	<u>0.8003</u>	0.764	**0.8107**
USAir	0.7378	0.5577	0.7098	0.7324	0.4505	**0.7758**	0.7256	<u>0.766</u>
Email	0.7933	0.6786	0.7631	0.8035	0.5867	<u>0.8485</u>	0.8221	**0.8609**
Yeast	0.6655	0.6259	0.723	0.7356	0.6017	**0.8099**	0.7656	<u>0.8085</u>
Power	0.6066	0.4697	0.2295	0.4098	0.3462	**0.7383**	0.7007	<u>0.7145</u>
PB	0.8223	0.6776	0.7298	0.8087	0.6399	<u>0.8277</u>	0.8145	**0.8388**
Facebook	0.6798	0.5156	0.3338	0.7075	0.4022	<u>0.7473</u>	0.6876	**0.7575**

4.2   The Comparison of Spreading Ability

Figure 2 shows the propagation influence of the top 10 nodes across eight networks. HGC achieved superior infection performance in Jazz, USAir, NS, and Facebook. In PB, dense connections narrowed performance gaps among methods. HGC performed comparably to RDP and LGM in Yeast and Email, and improved over time in the sparse Power network due to its use of cycle structure. Overall, HGC's identified nodes exhibited excellent propagation ability.

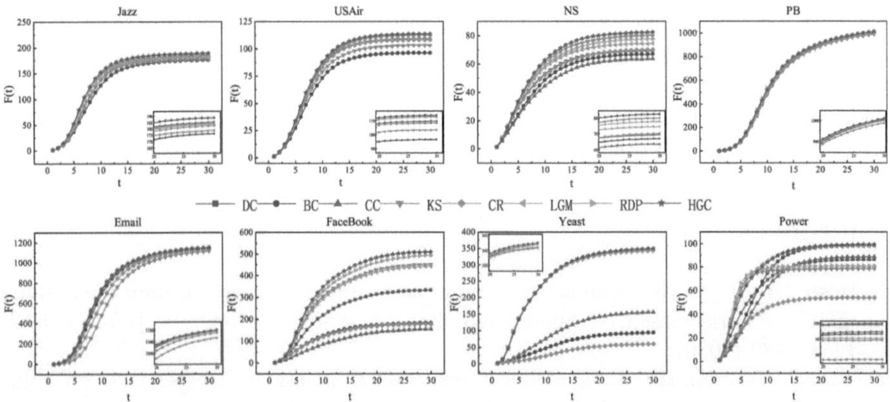

Fig. 2. The propagation influence of the top-10 ranking nodes of various methods simulated by SIR (under $\beta = \beta_c$). The X-axis represents the time step, and the Y-axis represents the number of infected and recovered nodes at time t.

Table 3. Monotonicity of node-ranked sequences derived by the eight methods. The top-ranked value in each row of the table is marked in bold, while the second-ranked value is underlined.

Networks	DC	BC	CC	KS	CR	LGM	RDP	HGC
Jazz	0.9659	0.9885	0.9878	0.7944	0.9985	<u>0.9993</u>	0.9992	**0.9994**
NS	0.7642	0.339	0.9928	0.6421	0.983	<u>0.9949</u>	0.9933	**0.9952**
USAir	0.8586	0.697	0.9892	0.8114	0.9451	**0.9951**	<u>0.995</u>	**0.9951**
Email	0.8874	0.94	0.9988	0.8088	0.9631	**0.9999**	<u>0.9998</u>	**0.9999**
Yeast	0.8314	0.8293	0.9988	0.7737	0.8831	<u>0.9991</u>	0.9986	**0.9992**
Power	0.5927	0.8319	<u>0.9998</u>	0.246	0.7653	0.9984	0.9903	**0.9999**
PB	0.9328	0.9489	<u>0.998</u>	0.9064	0.9748	**0.9993**	**0.9993**	**0.9993**
Facebook	0.9739	0.9855	0.9967	0.9419	<u>0.9993</u>	**0.9999**	**0.9999**	**0.9999**

4.3   The Comparison of Distinguishing Ability

Table 3 shows monotonicity results across eight networks. HGC achieves the highest values in all networks, demonstrating strong ability to identify important nodes. RDP performed best in Email, while RDP and LGM excelled in PB and Facebook. Overall, HGC outperforms all compared methods in distinguishing node importance.

5   Conclusion

This paper proposed a hybrid method combining the gravity model, structural holes, and cycle structure to identify influential spreaders in networks. Experimental results on eight real-world datasets confirmed its superior performance over seven baseline methods in accuracy, spreading capability, and node differentiation. However, given the small-world property of most real-world networks, HGC is currently limited to considering neighbouring nodes up to the second order. Determining the appropriate truncation radius for networks with varying structures remains an open challenge.

References

1. Hosni, A.I.E., Li, K., Ahmad, S.: Minimizing rumor influence in multiplex online social networks based on human individual and social behaviors. Inf. Sci. **512**, 1458–1480 (2020)
2. Yao, S., Fan, N., Hu, J.: Modeling the spread of infectious diseases through influence maximization. Optim. Lett. **16**, 1563–1586 (2022)
3. Chaharborj, S.S., Nabi, K.N., Feng, K.L., Chaharborj, S.S., Phang, P.S.: Controlling COVID-19 transmission with isolation of influential nodes. Chaos Solit. Fract. **159**, 112035 (2022)
4. Freeman, L.C.: A set of measures of centrality based on betweenness. Sociometry, 35–41 (1977)
5. Freeman, L.C., et al.: Centrality in social networks: conceptual clarification. In: Social Network: Critical Concepts in Sociology, vol. 1, pp. 238–263. Londres: Routledge (2002)
6. Fan, T., Lü, L., Shi, D., Zhou, T.: Characterizing cycle structure in complex networks. Commun. Phys. **4**, 272 (2021)
7. Bonacich, P.: Factoring and weighting approaches to status scores and clique identification. J. Math. Sociol. **2**, 113–120 (1972)
8. Lü, L., Zhou, T., Zhang, Q.M., Stanley, H.E.: The H-index of a network node and its relation to degree and coreness. Nat. Commun. **7**, 10168 (2016)
9. Li, Z., Huang, X.: Identifying influential spreaders using local information. Mathematics **11**, 1302 (2023)
10. Ma, L.l., Ma, C., Zhang, H.F., Wang, B.H.: Identifying influential spreaders in complex networks based on gravity formula. Physica A: Stat. Mech. Appl. **451**, 205–212 (2016)
11. Li, Z., Ren, T., Ma, X., Liu, S., Zhang, Y., Zhou, T.: Identifying influential spreaders by gravity model. Sci. Rep. **9**, 8387 (2019)
12. Li, Z., Huang, X.: Identifying influential spreaders in complex networks by an improved gravity model. Sci. Rep. **11**, 22194 (2021)
13. Li, Z., Huang, X.: Identifying influential spreaders by gravity model considering multi-characteristics of nodes. Sci. Rep. **12**, 9879 (2022)
14. Zhu, S., Zhan, J., Li, X.: Identifying influential nodes in complex networks using a gravity model based on the H-index method. Sci. Rep. **13**, 16404 (2023)
15. Burt, R.S.: Structural holes and good ideas. Am. J. Sociol. **110**, 349–399 (2004)
16. Hethcote, H.W.: The mathematics of infectious diseases. SIAM Rev. **42**, 599–653 (2000)
17. Kendall, M.G.: A new measure of rank correlation. Biometrika **30**, 81–93 (1938)
18. Zareie, A., Sheikhahmadi, A., Jalili, M., Fasaei, M.S.K.: Finding influential nodes in social networks based on neighborhood correlation coefficient. Knowl.-Based Syst. **194**, 105580 (2020)
19. Bae, J., Kim, S.: Identifying and ranking influential spreaders in complex networks by neighborhood coreness. XXPhys. A **395**, 549–559 (2014)

20. Brockmann, D., Helbing, D.: The hidden geometry of complex, network-driven contagion phenomena. Science **342**, 1337–1342 (2013)
21. Kitsak, M., et al.: Identification of influential spreaders in complex networks. Nat. Phys. **6**, 888–893 (2010)
22. Watts, D.J., Strogatz, S.H.: Collective dynamics of 'small-world' networks. Nature **393**, 440–442 (1998)

Code Refactoring with ChatGPT: Analysis Based on Real and Synthetic Extract Method Opportunities

Ally S. Nyamawe[1,2](✉) ⓘ and Estomii Edward[3]

[1] United Nations University Institute in Macau, Macau SAR, China
nyamawe@unu.edu
[2] Department of Computer Science and Engineering, The University of Dodoma, Dodoma, Tanzania
[3] Tanzania Commission for Universities, Dodoma, Tanzania

Abstract. Recently, Large Language Models (LLMs) like OpenAI's ChatGPT have shown potential in various aspects of software engineering. As a result, practitioners are increasingly exploring their use in code refactoring. While prior research has investigated ChatGPT's capabilities in areas such as requirements engineering, code generation, code review, and unit test generation, its strengths and limitations in code refactoring remain insufficiently explored. This paper evaluates ChatGPT's capability to identify extract method opportunities (EMOs). Our study leverages two widely used benchmark datasets containing synthetic and real EMOs, previously employed to assess extract method refactoring techniques. The results indicate that while ChatGPT successfully identifies EMOs, its low overlap with benchmark-defined refactorings raises concerns about the practicality of its recommendations. Additionally, while the model excels in generating descriptive method names for the extracted methods, its overall effectiveness requires further validation against multiple refactoring tools.

Keywords: Code refactoring · ChatGPT · Extract method · Large Language Models · Method naming

1 Introduction

In recent years, Large Language Models (LLMs), such as GPT (Generative Pre-trained Transformer) models, have increasingly received attention in software engineering (SE) [1]. Within the broader field of SE, LLMs have begun to play a pivotal role in automating tasks previously considered challenging for human developers. These models, trained on massive corpora of text and code, can generate human-like responses and assist in SE tasks such as program repair, code generation, and code summarization [1, 2]. Integrating LLMs in development environments (e.g., through plugins like GitHub Copilot) has allowed developers to benefit from real-time code insights and automated suggestions, reducing the cognitive load and accelerating the software development lifecycle. However, LLMs still have some limitations, as reported in the recent studies by Du et al. [3] and Tian et al. [1].

In software refactoring, machine learning (ML) and deep learning (DL) advancements are increasingly transforming the field. Notably, ML and DL models can analyze vast code datasets, identify patterns, and enhance the performance of automated refactoring. For example, neural networks, particularly deep learning models such as Long Short-Term Memory (LSTM) and Transformer architectures, have shown promise in tasks like code smell detection, mining of refactorings, and recommending refactorings [4]. Combining ML-driven analysis tools with human expertise has significantly advanced refactoring automation, making the process more reliable and efficient. As LLMs like OpenAI's ChatGPT gain popularity, software engineering practitioners increasingly utilize their capabilities to assist code refactoring [5, 6], including extract method refactoring [7]. Notably, among the various refactoring techniques, extract method refactoring stands out as one of the most frequently employed strategies [8] and is often used to address code smells such as long method and duplicated code [9]. Extract method refactoring entails isolating a portion of a method into a separate, smaller method to reduce complexity and improve modularity. By breaking down lengthy and convoluted methods, this technique improves code clarity, simplifies debugging, and promotes code reuse [9]. However, manually identifying opportunities for extract method refactoring can be time-consuming and prone to errors. As a result, various tools based on different heuristic approaches [7] and LLM-based [10] have been developed to automate the extraction process.

Understanding ChatGPT's capabilities and limitations in delivering SE tasks is essential to effectively harnessing its strengths and mitigating potential drawbacks. For example, Tian et al. [1] explored the feasibility of using LLMs as assistant bots to support programmers. The study assessed the performance of ChatGPT in program repair, code generation, and code summarization. Among its findings, the study shows that while ChatGPT is effective at solving common programming problems, it struggles when faced with new and unseen problems. Another recent study [11] evaluated ChatGPT's ability to understand code syntax and semantics, revealing that the tool excels in comprehending syntax but performs less effectively in grasping code semantics. ChatGPT was also found to be vulnerable to hallucination and fabricating non-existence facts when interpreting code semantics structures [11]. Champa et al. [12] suggest that ChatGPT has varied performance across different software development tasks. An evaluation that involved 180 coding questions from LeetCode found that the tool is highly effective at solving easy to medium coding problems, but its reliability decreases with more complex problems [13]. Moreover, ChatGPT has also been evaluated in other aspects of software engineering, including requirements engineering [14], coding algorithms [15], unit test generation [16], and code review [17]. However, studies evaluating the limitations and abilities of ChatGPT in refactoring code are still scarce [6]. To shrink the gap, this paper evaluates the capabilities of ChatGPT in suggesting extract method opportunities (EMOs). We use two common and publicly available benchmarks containing synthetic [18] and real EMOs [10]. This study contributes to understanding the feasibility of using LLMs as code refactoring assistants.

2　Related Works

The advent of machine learning and deep learning has advanced the automation of refactoring, transforming how code maintenance and improvements are managed [4]. Recently, various approaches have been proposed to leverage the capabilities of LLMs in software engineering [19]. However, the black-box nature of LLMs necessitates multi-faceted evaluation to discern their feasibility [3]. DePalma et al. [6] conducted an evaluation of ChatGPT's refactoring capabilities using a dataset of 40 Java code segments. The study aimed to determine whether ChatGPT could effectively refactor code, maintain the original code's behavior, and provide adequate documentation for the refactored code. The authors tasked ChatGPT with refactoring code to improve performance and address eight other quality attributes. While ChatGPT often suggested valuable code enhancements, some recommendations were impractical or introduced violations, necessitating the programmer's review and decision. Additionally, ChatGPT largely succeeded in preserving the original code behavior and offering basic documentation for the refactored code. In contrast to the study by DePalma et al. [6], which focused on broader code improvements, our research takes a more specific approach. We aim to assess how effectively ChatGPT can identify extract method refactoring opportunities.

AlOmar et al. [5] investigated how developers interact with ChatGPT to receive assistance on code refactoring tasks. The paper highlighted key patterns in developers' prompts and ChatGPT's responses during refactoring discussions. It was revealed that developers often ask for guidance using general refactoring terms like "extract", "rename", or "move". Whereas, ChatGPT responds by focusing on internal and external quality attributes and code smells. The analysis emphasized the importance of prompt engineering in maximizing the effectiveness of refactoring suggestions, noting that developers' prompts vary in precision, which can influence the quality of ChatGPT's responses. Moreover, the study suggests that ChatGPT provides valuable refactoring suggestions, particularly for non-critical tasks such as improving code style and adding comments. However, ChatGPT may also suggest refactoring, which could lead to compiler errors and test failures contrary to the refactoring principle of preserving system behaviour. This is attributed to the ChatGPT's limited understanding of the broader context of the codebase. Pomian et al. [10] proposed EM-Assist, a tool that leverages the capabilities of LLMs to perform extract method refactoring. The study assessed the abilities of three different LLMs (i.e., GPT-3.5, GPT-4, and PaLM), showing that GPT-3.5 performs better than the rest. However, findings suggest that the majority (76.3%) of the refactoring suggestions recommended by GPT-3.5 were hallucinations. These include suggestions containing code segments that are invalid to extract and those that are unlikely to be applied by developers. The authors emphasized the need for caution and advised against entirely relying on LLM-generated suggestions when performing refactoring with the assistance of LLMs. Building on the work of Pomian et al. [10], our study specifically targets the evaluation of ChatGPT's ability to identify extract method refactoring opportunities.

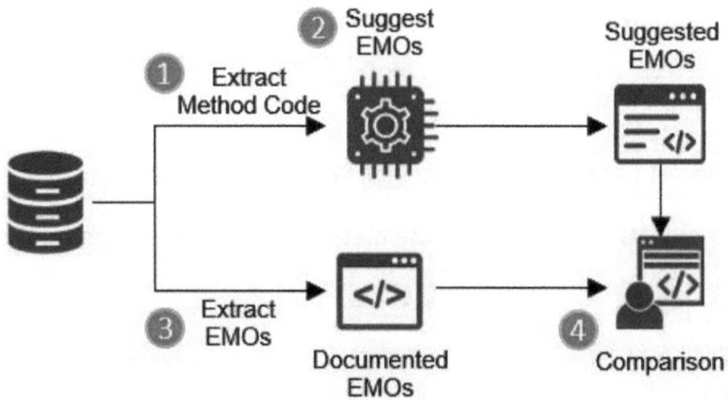

Fig. 1. Research Methodology Steps

Table 1. Summary of the datasets.

Category	Tool	Number of EMOs	Total EMOs
Synthetic [18]	JavaPoet-1.12.1	20	90
	Mockito-3.3.8	45	
	EventBus-3.2.0	25	
Real [10]	DataSketches	30	110
	JavaParser	30	
	Spring Boot	50	
Total			**200**

3 Methodology

The core of our methodology involves a comparative analysis between ChatGPT's suggested refactorings and pre-established EMOs in existing benchmarks. As depicted in Fig. 1, we begin by extracting code segments of the methods known to contain EMOs from publicly available benchmark datasets. Next, these code segments are fed into ChatGPT with specific prompts requesting the identification of EMOs. Then, we extract pre-defined EMOs of the methods in question from the benchmark. Consequently, ChatGPT's responses are compared to the EMOs documented in the benchmarks to determine the model's effectiveness.

3.1 Dataset

As summarized in Table 1, two publicly available benchmark datasets are used in this study. The first dataset contains synthetic EMOs that were introduced by inline refactoring [20]. This dataset was previously used to evaluate different approaches for identifying extract method refactoring. The goal was to establish key parameters affecting their performance to help users select the most appropriate tool and assist researchers in designing better approaches [20]. The second dataset contains the actual refactorings that developers applied. The dataset was generated by mining refactorings from commit histories across 12 open-source repositories using the RefactoringMiner tool [10].

ALGORITHM 1: Iterative EMOs Generation Process

Input: Target system S, Code segment of the method M_c , Code segment of EMO EMO_c, Prompt p

Output: Suggested EMOs

1: $new\_emo \leftarrow \emptyset$

2: $sim\_emo \leftarrow \emptyset$

3: **for all** methods $M_c \in S$ **do**

4:     Let $i = 1$, initialize iterations counter

5:     **while** $i < 6$ **do**

6: $suggestedEMOs \leftarrow \emptyset$

7: $suggestedEMOs = generateEMOs(M_c, p)$

8: **for all** $emo_j \in suggestedEMOs$ **do**

9:     **if** $(emo_j$ contains $EMO_c)$ **then**

10:         $sim\_emo_i \leftarrow emo_j$

11:     **else**

12:         $new\_emo_i \leftarrow emo_j$

13:         **end if**

14:   **end for**

15:   **end while**

16: **end for**

17: compute EMO_n using Equation (1)

18: compute EMO_p using Equation (2)

19: **End**

This dataset was used to evaluate the EM-Assist tool, which leverages LLMs and static analysis to recommend extract method refactoring. In our experiment, we selected three Java applications from each dataset, focusing on a few extract method opportunities (i.e., 200 EMOs).

3.2 EMOs Generation

Algorithm 1 outlines the key steps of our approach to generate EMOs with ChatGPT and compare them with the predefined EMOs. We take as input a target system S from the benchmark dataset, a code segment of a method M_c, a code segment of an existing EMO EMO_c and a prompt p. The target is to use ChatGPT to suggest EMOs for a given method M_c. Each target system is represented by a collection of methods known to contain EMOs. The existing EMOs are pre-identified for each method, marking specific segments of the method that should be extracted as a new method. A prompt p contains a set of instructions that tell what ChatGPT should do with the code segment of a method

M_c. The model is instructed to suggest parts of the method that can be extracted to form a new method. The instructions outline the task's context, which involved addressing the Long Method code smell and identifying opportunities for extract method refactoring. Defining context is among the best practices of prompt engineering and helps enhance the model's performance and minimizes the risks of hallucination [21]. Next, we initialize two empty sets: *new_emo* to store newly suggested EMOs and *sim_emo* to store EMOs that are similar to or contain code segments given EMO_c. The algorithm then iterates over all methods in the target system S. For each method, we perform five iterations of prompting ChatGPT. During each iteration, the model generates a set of suggested EMOs for the method M_c. The goal is to identify possible EMOs that the model can suggest—noting that ChatGPT can generate different results for the same prompt. Then, we analyze each suggested EMO to identify if it is similar or contains the code segment of a known EMO given by EMO_c. If the suggested EMO is not similar or does not contain EMO_c, then such EMO is stored in *new_emo*, as a newly identified EMO, else is stored in *sim_emo*. The loop continues until all five iterations are completed, and the same process is repeated for every method in the system S. Consequently, after processing all methods of a system S, we compute EMO_n and EMO_p of a system for each iteration using predefined equations (Eqs. 1 and 2, respectively). EMO_n and EMO_p denote the percentage of new and similar suggested EMOs, respectively. It is worth noting that, EMO_p includes both EMOs that exactly match those suggested in the benchmark and those that include additional lines of code proposed for extraction alongside the benchmark suggestions.

$$EMO_n(S) = \frac{\sum_{i=1}^{m} |new\_emo_i|}{\sum_{i=1}^{m} |new\_emo_i| + \sum_{i=1}^{m} |sim\_emo_i|} \tag{1}$$

$$EMO_p(S) = \frac{\sum_{i=1}^{m} |sim_{emoi}|}{\sum_{i=1}^{m} |sim_{emoi}| + \sum_{i=1}^{m} |new_{emoi}|} \tag{2}$$

where m is the total number of methods in a given system S, and for a given iteration, $|new\_emo_i|$ and $|sim\_emo_i|$ are the total number of new and similar suggested EMOs of a method i respectively, such that i ranges from 1 to m.

3.3 Suggested Method Names Analysis

In this stage, we aim to assess the method names suggested by ChatGPT after performing the extract method refactoring. Since the benchmark datasets do not provide method names for the extracted methods, we used JDeodorant, a state-of-the-art refactoring tool, to identify EMOs and apply refactoring. The goal was to ensure that the method segment extracted was consistent, making a fair comparison possible between the method names suggested by JDeodorant and those proposed by ChatGPT. The process involves selecting a method, denoted as m, of a target system S. JDeodorant was employed to identify potential EMOs within the method m and apply the extract method refactoring. Notably, after refactoring, JDeodorant also suggests appropriate names for the newly created methods based on the extracted segments, reflecting the functionality of the extracted code. ChatGPT was prompted with the code segment of the same method *m* and tasked with identifying potential EMOs and suggesting names for the extracted methods. To ensure the validity and fairness of our comparison, we only compared the names proposed by JDeodorant and ChatGPT when the suggested EMOs were identical. Furthermore, a detailed analysis was conducted on the suggested names and the corresponding responsibilities of the newly created methods to evaluate whether the names accurately reflect the functionality of the extracted code.

4   Results and Discussion

4.1   Research Questions

Our research is focused on addressing the following research questions.

- **RQ1**: How effective is ChatGPT in suggesting extract method opportunities?
- **RQ2**: How effective is ChatGPT in suggesting method names after extract method refactoring?
- **RQ3**: What are the common benefits of the extract method refactoring suggested by ChatGPT?

4.2   Results

Effectiveness of ChatGPT in Suggesting EMOs

To address the first research question: *How effective is ChatGPT in identifying extract method opportunities (EMOs)?* we evaluated ChatGPT's performance over five iterations, focusing on Synthetic and Real EMOs. The goal was to assess the model's accuracy and reliability in identifying and suggesting viable extract method opportunities. Tables 2 and 3 summarize ChatGPT's performance on Synthetic EMOs and Real EMOs across the analyzed projects, respectively. In the following subsections, we provide a detailed analysis of our results.

Synthetic EMOs

Table 2 summarizes the results of ChatGPT's performance on Synthetic EMOs across three distinct projects, namely JavaPoet-1.12.1, EventBus-3.2.0, and Mockito-3.3.8. As shown in the table (based on EMO_n), it was noted that, on average, 63.5% of the EMOs suggested by ChatGPT were new. In other words, these EMOs were not suggested in the analyzed benchmark. The results further highlight that, across all five iterations, ChatGPT suggested multiple new EMOs. We observed that, in some instances, ChatGPT extracts every part of the original method into newly created methods, leaving the original method to function solely as a caller for these newly generated methods. Conversely, the number of EMOs suggested by ChatGPT, similar to those defined in the benchmark, was notably low, an average of 36.5% based on EMO_p. Additionally, as mentioned earlier, EMO_p encompasses both EMOs that exactly match those outlined in the benchmark and those that include additional lines of code proposed for extraction alongside the benchmark suggestions. When considering only the exact matches of the suggested EMOs for the JavaPoet application, we observed that only an average of 11% of the EMOs suggested by ChatGPT matched exactly with the benchmark suggestions. This indicates that up to 89% of the EMOs recommended by ChatGPT were new. Similarly, in some cases, ChatGPT suggested extracting portions of the method that consist of lines of code, forming a subset of the predefined EMOs.

Table 2. Performance of ChatGPT on Synthetic EMOs.

Iterations	JavaPoet-1.12.1		EventBus-3.2.0		Mockito-3.3.8	
	EMO_n (%)	EMO_p (%)	EMO_n (%)	EMO_p (%)	EMO_n (%)	EMO_p (%)
1	65.38	34.62	61.11	38.89	62.86	37.14
2	64.29	35.71	62.16	37.84	62.86	37.14
3	65.52	34.48	62.16	37.84	63.89	36.11
4	65.52	34.48	62.16	37.84	63.89	36.11
5	64.29	35.71	62.16	37.84	63.89	36.11
Average	**65.00**	**35.00**	**61.95**	**38.05**	**63.48**	**36.52**

Table 3. Performance of ChatGPT on Real EMOs.

Iterations	DataSketches		JavaParser		Spring Boot	
	EMO_n (%)	EMO_p (%)	EMO_n (%)	EMO_p (%)	EMO_n (%)	EMO_p (%)
1	69.00	31.00	69.70	30.30	64.54	35.46
2	69.90	30.10	70.59	29.41	66.22	33.78
3	71.30	28.70	71.43	28.57	66.23	33.77
4	72.07	27.93	69.70	30.30	65.77	34.23
5	72.07	27.93	69.70	30.30	65.77	34.23
Average	**70.87**	**29.13**	**70.22**	**29.78**	**65.71**	**34.29**

Real EMOs

Table 3 presents ChatGPT's performance on real EMOs across three projects: DataSketches, JavaParser, and Spring Boot. On average, ChatGPT suggested 70.87% new EMOs for DataSketches, 70.22% for JavaParser, and 65.71% for Spring Boot, resulting in an overall average of 68.93% new refactoring opportunities across these codebases. The data indicates that ChatGPT consistently generated several new EMOs across all five iterations. Moreover, its performance in suggesting EMOs closely aligned with benchmark data (EMO_p) was comparatively low, with alignment rates of 29.13%, 29.78%, and 34.29% for the three projects. That is equivalent to an average of 31.1% of all suggested EMOs. Notably, a deeper analysis revealed that only 24.6% of ChatGPT's suggested EMOs for the DataSketches application matched exactly with the benchmark suggestions, indicating that 75.4% of its recommendations were new. Overall, the results reported for real EMOs and synthetic EMOs show no significant difference, indicating that ChatGPT frequently suggests a large number of EMOs, many of which may be irrelevant or impractical for immediate application. However, further analysis is crucial to determine whether some of these newly suggested EMOs, although not aligned with the current benchmark suggestions, could prove valuable as software evolves. This potential foresight underscores the need to assess the long-term utility of ChatGPT's recommendations in evolving codebases.

Table 4. Summary of the number of methods analyzed.

Tool	Number of Methods Analyzed	Number of Similar method names
JavaPoet-1.12.1	12	0
Mockito-3.3.8	22	2
EventBus-3.2.0	18	1
JavaParser	63	4
TOTAL	**115**	**7**

Effectiveness of ChatGPT in Suggesting Method Names

To address RQ2, we conducted a comparative analysis of the method names suggested by JDeodorant [9] and ChatGPT after applying extract method refactoring. Table 4 presents the number of methods where both tools identified identical EMOs. Our findings indicate that, in most cases, ChatGPT's suggested method names differed from those generated by JDeodorant. Specifically, out of the 115 analyzed methods, only seven extracted methods had identical names in both tools. This suggests that ChatGPT and JDeodorant employ distinct naming strategies when proposing extracted method names. A key observation from our analysis is that ChatGPT's suggested names tended to be more descriptive and context-aware than those provided by JDeodorant. For instance, in an extraction involving the *writeToPath* method from JavaPoet, JDeodorant suggested *getPath*, whereas ChatGPT proposed *constructOutputDirectory* as the new method's name. The latter conveys a broader semantic understanding of the method's functionality. The analysis suggests that ChatGPT's naming approach somehow reflects contextual awareness than its counterpart. By generating method names that better capture the intent and functionality of the extracted code, ChatGPT demonstrates a potential advantage over traditional refactoring tools like JDeodorant in method naming. However, a more comprehensive analysis involving a larger set of methods and a detailed comparison with well-established extract method refactoring tools is necessary to assess further ChatGPT's effectiveness in recommending method names.

Extract Method Refactoring Benefits

To address RQ3, we summarized the most frequently occurring benefits identified by ChatGPT in each iteration of EMO suggestions. This research question examines the advantages of the extract method refactoring proposed by ChatGPT and validates them against existing literature findings. According to Silva et al. [22], Extract Method is the most frequently applied refactoring and has the highest number of motivations. Extract Reusable Method is one of the leading motivations that aim at extracting reusable code that can be called in multiple places, whereas Improve Testability is among the least common motivations [22]. Reduced Method Length is a core advantage, as shorter methods minimize cognitive load and make the code easier to navigate. Moreover, Valente [23] suggests that the extract method refactoring enhances the comprehensibility and clarity of the original method and facilitates code reuse. A recent study by AlOmar et al. [24] underscores the intent of the extract method refactoring, revealing that existing studies frequently employ this technique to address code clones, mitigate long methods, and enhance the separation of concerns. The study involving 25 developers also found that the major motivations for applying the extract method refactoring include clone resolution, code reuse, and decomposing long methods [8]. The latter helps in improving software maintainability and readability. A large-scale study on the commit of 325 open-source Java repositories found that the major motivations of extract method refactorings include removing duplications, creating reusable methods, and decomposing long methods to enhance their readability [25]. Some of the suggested benefits by ChatGPT are also reported in the study by Kim et al. [26]. Accordingly, the benefits of the extract method refactoring suggested by ChatGPT align closely with those documented in the literature. However, balancing potentially conflicting benefits when determining EMOs is a key challenge. According to Fowler [27], the first step in decomposing a method is to identify a logical block of code that can be extracted into its own method. If this step is executed incorrectly, it may introduce errors in the code and compromise the system's behaviour. Therefore, overemphasizing certain benefits could lead to impractical suggestions. For instance, in certain cases, ChatGPT recommended extracting the entire method body and leaving the original method as a simple caller function of several other methods. Future research may explore whether the proposed EMOs by ChatGPT are effective in delivering the suggested benefits.

5   Conclusion

This study provides an in-depth evaluation of ChatGPT's capabilities in extract method refactoring, highlighting its strengths and limitations. While ChatGPT successfully identifies EMOs, the low overlap with benchmark-defined refactorings suggests that its recommendations may not always be practical. Additionally, although the tool excels in generating descriptive method names that enhance code comprehensibility, its overall effectiveness requires further validation against multiple refactoring tools. The analysis also reveals that ChatGPT's suggested refactoring benefits align with existing literature but may lead to unintended consequences such as excessive code fragmentation. Given these findings, we advocate for a hybrid approach integrating LLMs with established refactoring tools and post-processing techniques to enhance refactoring outcomes. Future work should improve GPT's models' contextual understanding of refactoring decisions and develop methodologies that leverage AI-assisted refactoring alongside traditional techniques to achieve more reliable and practical refactoring suggestions.

References

1. Tian, H., et al.: Is ChatGPT the Ultimate Programming Assistant--How Far is it? (2023). arXiv Prepr. arXiv2304.11938
2. Ahmed, T.: Few-Shot Training LLMs for project-Specific Code-Summarization (2022). https://doi.org/10.1145/3551349.3559555
3. Du, X., et al.: Evaluating large language models in class-level code generation. In: Proceedings of the IEEE/ACM 46th International Conference on Software Engineering. Association for Computing Machinery, New York, NY, USA (2024). https://doi.org/10.1145/3597503.363 9219

4. Nyirongo, B., Jiang, Y., Jiang, H., Liu, H.: A Survey of Deep Learning Based Software Refactoring (2024)

5. AlOmar, E.A., Venkatakrishnan, A., Mkaouer, M.W., Newman, C., Ouni, A.: How to refactor this code? An exploratory study on developer-ChatGPT refactoring conversations. In: Proceedings of the 21st International Conference on Mining Software Repositories, pp. 202–206 (2024). Association for Computing Machinery, New York, NY, USA. https://doi.org/10.1145/3643991.3645081

6. Depalma, K., Miminoshvili, I., Henselder, C., Moss, K., Alomar, E.A.: Exploring ChatGPT's code refactoring capabilities : an empirical study. Expert Syst. Appl. **249**, 123602 (2024). https://doi.org/10.1016/j.eswa.2024.123602

7. Imazato, A., Higo, Y., Hotta, K., Kusumoto, S.: Finding extract method refactoring opportunities by analyzing development history. In: Proceedings - International Computer Software and Applications Conference, pp. 190–195 (2017). https://doi.org/10.1109/COMPSAC.2017.129

8. Liu, W., Liu, H.: Major motivations for extract method refactorings: analysis based on interviews and change histories. Front. Comput. Sci. **10**, 644–656 (2016). https://doi.org/10.1007/s11704-016-5131-4

9. Tsantalis, N., Chatzigeorgiou, A.: Identification of extract method refactoring opportunities for the decomposition of methods. J. Syst. Softw. **84**, 1757–1782 (2011). https://doi.org/10.1016/j.jss.2011.05.016

10. Pomian, D., et al.: Together We Go Further: LLMs and IDE Static Analysis for Extract Method Refactoring (2024)

11. Ma, W., et al.: The Scope of ChatGPT in Software Engineering: A Thorough Investigation (2023)

12. Champa, A.I., Rabbi, M.F., Nachuma, C., Zibran, M.F.: ChatGPT in action: analyzing its use in software development. Proc. - 2024 IEEE/ACM 21st Int. Conf. Min. Softw. Repos. MSR 2024, pp. 182–186 (2024). https://doi.org/10.1145/3643991.3645077

13. Kuhail, M.A., Mathew, S.S., Khalil, A., Berengueres, J., Shah, S.J.H.: "Will I be replaced?" Assessing ChatGPT's effect on software development and programmer perceptions of AI tools. Sci. Comput. Program. **235**, 103111 (2024). https://doi.org/10.1016/j.scico.2024.103111

14. Marques, N., Silva, R.R., Bernardino, J.: Using ChatGPT in software requirements engineering: a comprehensive review. Futur. Internet. **16**, 1–21 (2024). https://doi.org/10.3390/fi16060180

15. Arefin, S.E., Heya, T.A., Al-Qudah, H., Ineza, Y., Serwadda, A.: Unmasking the giant: a comprehensive evaluation of ChatGPT's proficiency in coding algorithms and data structures. Int. Conf. Agents Artif. Intell. **1**, 412–419 (2024). https://doi.org/10.5220/0012467100003636

16. Yuan, Z., et al.: Evaluating and improving ChatGPT for unit test generation. In: Proceedings of the ACM on Software Engineering, pp. 1703–1726 (2024). https://doi.org/10.1145/3660783

17. Watanabe, M., Kashiwa, Y., Lin, B., Hirao, T., Yamaguchi, K., Iida, H.: On the use of ChatGPT for code review: do developers like reviews by ChatGPT? ACM Int. Conf. Proceeding Ser., pp. 375–380 (2024). https://doi.org/10.1145/3661167.3661183

18. Tiwari, O.: Pluto-A Synthetic Benchmark for Extract Method Refactoring. https://doi.org/10.6084/m9.figshare.20206382.v1

19. Fan, A., et al.: Large language models for software engineering: survey and open problems. In: Proceedings - 2023 IEEE/ACM International Conference on Software Engineering: Future of Software Engineering, ICSE-FoSE 2023, pp. 31–53 (2023). https://doi.org/10.1109/ICSE-FoSE59343.2023.00008

20. Tiwari, O., Yadav, V.: A review of methods for identifying extract method refactoring. Proc. Int. Conf. Softw. Eng. Knowl. Eng. SEKE, pp. 203–208 (2023). https://doi.org/10.18293/SEKE2023-199

21. Huang, Z., Zhou, J., Xiao, G., Cheng, G.: Enhancing in-context learning with answer feedback for multi-span question answering. In: Liu, F., Duan, N., Xu, Q., Hong, Y. (eds.) Natural Language Processing and Chinese Computing, pp. 744–756 (2023). Springer Nature Switzerland, Cham

22. Silva, D., Tsantalis, N., Valente, M.T.: Why we Refactor? Confessions of Github contributors. In: Proceedings of the ACM SIGSOFT Symposium on the Foundations of Software Engineering, pp. 858–870 (2016). Association for Computing Machinery. https://doi.org/10.1145/2950290.2950305

23. Valente, M.T.: Software Engineering: A Modern Approach (2024)

24. Alomar, E.A., Mkaouer, M.W., Ouni, A.: Behind the intent of extract method refactoring: a systematic literature review. IEEE Trans. Softw. Eng. **50**, 668–694 (2024). https://doi.org/10.1109/TSE.2023.3345800

25. Aalizadeh, M.S.: Automatic Motivation Detection for Extract Method Refactoring Operations, (2021)

26. Kim, M., Zimmermann, T., Nagappan, N.: An empirical study of refactoringchallenges and benefits at microsoft. IEEE Trans. Softw. Eng. **40**, 633–649 (2014). https://doi.org/10.1109/TSE.2014.2318734

27. Fowler, M.: Refactoring: Improving the Design of Existing Code. Addison-Wesley Professional (2018)

A Robust Data Watermarking Method Based on Secret Sharing and GAN for Digital Elevation Model

Jinge Ma[1,2,3], Jia Duan[4], Xi Liu[4], Xianghan Zheng[5], and Wei Ren[1,6(✉)]

[1] School of Computer Science, China University of Geosciences, Wuhan, China
{20211003691mjg,weirencs}@cug.edu.cn
[2] Key Laboratory of Data Intelligence and Advanced Computing in Provincial Universities, Soochow University, Soochow, China
[3] Key Laboratory of Data Protection and Intelligent Management (Sichuan University), Ministry of Education, Chengdu, China
[4] Hunan Engineering Research Center of Geographic Information Security and Application, Changsha, China
[5] Fuzhou University, Fuzhou, China
xianghan.zheng@fzu.edu.cn
[6] Provincial Key Laboratory of Multimodal Perceiving and Intelligent Systems, Jiaxing University, Jiaxing, China

Abstract. This study proposes an advanced watermarking technique for Digital Elevation Model (DEM) data, combining the cryptographic resilience via Shamir's Secret Sharing and the integrity enhancement via Generative Adversarial Network (GAN). This method embeds a watermark into binary image carriers that are converted from DEM data, and the watermark can be reconstructed if the number of loss is no more than a threshold value. The usage of GAN ensures the seamless integration of the watermark, preserving the integrity of the original DEM data. Our experimental results and analysis demonstrate the exceptional performance of the proposed method, particularly its high resistance to a range of simulated attacks and its ability to maintain the fidelity of the DEM data, which justified that our method can be applied for data provenance of typical geospatial data.

Keywords: Watermarking · Secret Sharing · Generative Adversarial Network (GAN) · Digital Elevation Model (DEM)

1 Introduction

With the growing importance of data across industries, Geographic Information Systems (GIS) have become a critical resource, providing rich spatial and environmental information for fields such as urban planning, environmental protection, and disaster management. Data sharing enhances efficiency and promotes interdisciplinary collaboration but also raises risks of sensitive information leakage, including personal data and national security content. Thus, ensuring secure data sharing and tracing data provenance are vital.

Digital watermarking plays a key role in protecting GIS data by enabling source tracing, copyright protection, and integrity verification. Among GIS data, Digital Elevation Models (DEM), which capture surface elevation with high spatial resolution, are widely used in 3D modeling, geographic analysis, flood simulation, and disaster assessment. However, conventional watermarking techniques face challenges when applied to DEM data, struggling to maintain robustness due to its unique structure and high precision.

Table 1 compares representative DEM watermarking schemes. Methods based on Discrete Cosine Transform (DCT), Discrete Wavelet Transform (DWT), and one-way hash functions exhibit limited resistance to manual attacks [2–4], highlighting the need for stronger approaches.

Table 1. Comparison of different DEM watermarking schemes.

Scheme	Basic Method	Manual Attacks
Mina Al-Saad [2]	DCT-DWT	Weak
Fahmi Amhar [3]	2D DCT-DWT and 2D DFT	Moderate
LUO Yong [4]	WT and One-way Hash	Moderate
Our Scheme	Secret Sharing and GAN	Strong

To address these challenges, we propose combining Generative Adversarial Networks (GAN) with secret sharing for DEM watermarking. GAN-generated watermarks enhance resilience against adversarial attacks due to their complexity and diversity, improving concealment and integrity. Since DEM data differ from standard images, preprocessing into lower-resolution binary images is necessary, posing additional technical challenges.

Recent research has demonstrated the effectiveness of secret sharing and deep learning in watermarking. Secret sharing splits watermark information into multiple parts, mitigating single-point failures [5,6]. Deep learning models, particularly CNN- and GAN-based methods, have improved robustness and invisibility [7–10]. Hybrid techniques combining DWT with GANs further enhance security [11]. In the GIS field, spatial topology-based watermarking improves resistance to geometric transformations [12], and blockchain-assisted zero-watermarking has been introduced to strengthen copyright protection [13]. Robust watermarking methods have also been extended to point cloud and raster data. These advances highlight the evolving role of deep learning and secret sharing in securing geospatial data and digital media watermarking.

This paper presents a novel watermarking method for digital elevation data based on GAN and secret sharing. Compared to previous works, the key innovations are as follows:

1. A watermarking framework is developed by transforming DEM data into binary images and applying Shamir's secret sharing and GAN techniques. The watermark is split and embedded across multiple carriers, enhancing both robustness and concealment.
2. A combination and block arrangement strategy is introduced to generate diverse binary image carriers, increasing embedding flexibility and improving the covert capacity of the watermark.
3. The use of GAN and binary carriers improves resistance against various attacks while reducing storage requirements and enhancing processing efficiency due to the simplified binary format.

2 Proposed Method

In this article, we propose a watermarking method applied to digital elevation model. In this section, the general structure of watermark embedding and extraction is first introduced, and then each part is described in detail.

2.1 Notations

We list the notations used throughout this paper in Table 2.

Table 2. Commonly used notations and their meanings in this book.

Notation	Meaning
I	The digital elevation model (DEM) data
I_W	The DEM data I with embedded watermark
W	The watermark information
W_i'	The ith sub-watermark information generated by W
(t, n)	The threshold parameters of the Shamir Secret Sharing Scheme
w_{i_j}	The jth share of the ith sub-watermark
k	The number of binary image carriers used for each w_{i_j}
η_c	The capacity of a binary image carrier for the watermark
η	The bit length of the watermark information W
ρ	The bit accuracy rate of watermark extraction

Other notations: Gen(.), S(.), G(.), L(.), C(.) represent the functions for generating carriers, partitioning watermark, splitting and reconstructing secrets, and combining watermarks, respectively.

2.2   Overview

Digital Elevation Models (DEMs) differ from ordinary images in three key aspects: (1) they capture surface elevation data, (2) have much higher resolution, and (3) require significantly more memory.

The high resolution of DEMs results in large transformation matrices, making conventional image watermarking impractical. To address this, elevation data are converted into binary contour images and divided into blocks, with each block serving as a watermark carrier; additional carriers are formed by merging blocks.

Watermark embedding involves three steps: (1) splitting and merging binary carriers, (2) dividing watermark information, and (3) embedding the watermark.

Figure 1 illustrates the watermark embedding process. First, the DEM data I is transformed into $k \times n \times d$ binary image carriers using the function $Gen(\cdot)$:

$$c_{i_j} = Gen(I) \quad (i = 1, \cdots, d \ \ j = 1, \cdots, n)$$

Next, the watermark information W is divided into d sub-watermark information pieces W_i', and $n \times d$ shared watermarks w_{i_j} are generated using the secret information splitting function of Shamir's Secret Sharing, denoted as $G(\cdot)$:

$$w_{i_j} = G(W_i') = G(S(W)) \quad (i = 1, \cdots, d \ \ j = 1, \cdots, n)$$

Finally, by using a GAN (Generative Adversarial Network) neural network, the shared watermark w_{i_j} is embedded into the binary image carrier c_{i_j}. The carrier with embedded information, denoted as c_{i_j}', is added as a new layer to the DEM data I, resulting in the DEM data with watermark information, denoted as I_W:

$$\begin{aligned} I_W &= I + c_{1_1}' + \cdots + c_{d_n}' \\ &= I + \text{GAN}(w_{i_j}, c_{i_j}) \\ &\quad (i = 1, \ldots, d; \quad j = 1, \ldots, n) \end{aligned}$$

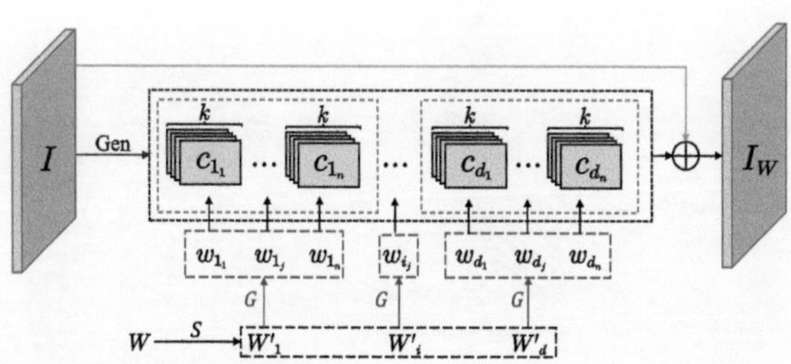

Fig. 1. The process of watermark embedding.

Figure 2 illustrates the watermark extraction process. After extracting the carrier c_{i_j}' containing the embedded information from the DEM data I_W with watermark information, blind extraction is performed using a GAN (Generative Adversarial Network) neural network to recover the shared watermark w_{i_j}:

$$w_{i_j} = GAN(c'_{i_j}) \quad (i = 1, \cdots, d \;\; j = 1, \cdots, n)$$

Finally, using the Shamir secret reconstruction function $L(\cdot)$, the extracted shared watermark w_{i_j} is reconstructed into sub-watermark information W'_{i_j}, and then combined to obtain the extracted watermark information W^*:

$$W^* = C(W'_{i_j}) = C(L(w_{i_j})) \quad (i = 1, \cdots, d \;\; j = 1, \cdots, n)$$

By comparing whether W^* and W are equal, we can determine whether the extracted watermark is correct.

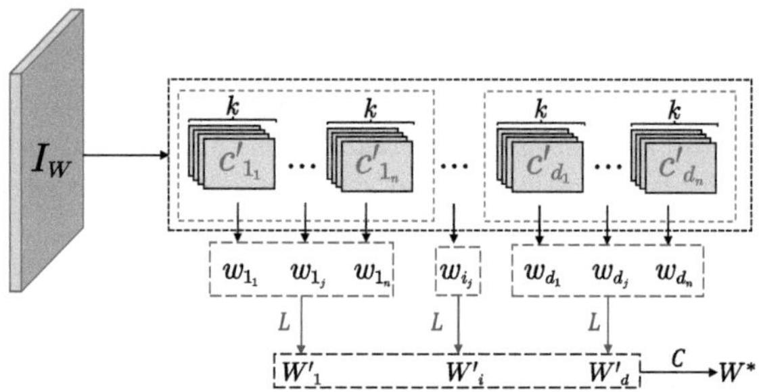

Fig. 2. The process of watermark extraction.

2.3   Division and Merging of Binary Carriers

As shown in Fig. 3, by converting the elevation data into a binary image of contour lines, and then segmenting this binary image, a series of binary blocks can be obtained.

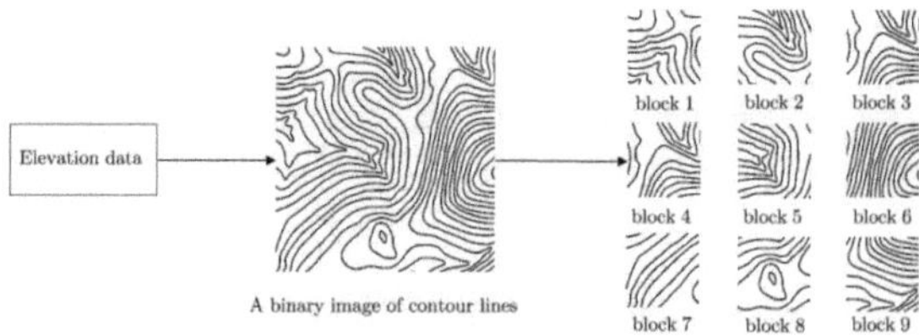

Fig. 3. The process of dividing binary image blocks.

Assuming that there are m binary image blocks, the contents of the $i(i = 1, 2, \cdots, m)$ layer are generated by permutation and combination methods using

XOR operations. Using this method, $2^n - 1$ binary image carriers can be generated as shown in Eq. (1).

$$C_m^1 + C_m^2 + \cdots + C_m^{m-1} + C_m^m = (1+1)^m - 1 = 2^m - 1 \tag{1}$$

The binary image carrier is created by blockwise XOR. As shown in Fig. 4, two binary image blocks of size 3×3 are XORed by taking the XOR of pixel values at corresponding positions, resulting in a binary image carrier.

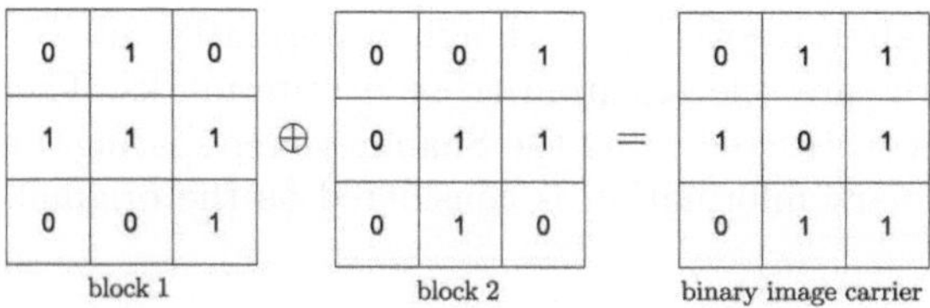

Fig. 4. The process of producing binary image carriers.

This means that as the number of blocks in the digital elevation model I increases, the number of binary image carriers will increase exponentially. The robustness of the watermark in the watermarked data I_W will also improve significantly.

2.4   Watermark Division and Recovery

Suppose there is an image watermarking model for binary images, where the watermark capacity that can be embedded is η_c bits, under the condition of ensuring a watermark extraction bit accuracy rate of ρ. For a watermark information W with a bit length of η, $d = \frac{\eta}{\eta_c}$ sub-watermark information W' will be generated, where $W = W_1' \parallel W_2' \parallel \cdots \parallel W_d'$. If η is not an integer multiple of η_c, then 0 bits will be padded at the beginning of W until η becomes an integer multiple of η_c.

The n shared watermarks are created using Shamir secret sharing with a threshold of t. Each shared watermark is embedded in k different binary image carriers, ensuring that $dnk \leq 2^m - 1$.

During watermark recovery, the corresponding shared watermarks are extracted from the binary image layers of I_w that contain embedded watermarks. This means that for each shared watermark, k results are extracted.

The bit values at each position of the shared watermark w_{i_j} are determined by taking the bit that occurs most frequently at that position among the k extracted bit strings.

Therefore, to correctly recover a bit at a position in w_{i_j} requires no less than $\lceil k/2 \rceil$ bits. Thus, the probability of correctly recovering a single bit is

$P_b = \sum_{i=\lceil k/2 \rceil}^{k} C_k^i \rho^i (1-\rho)^{k-i}$. The probability of correctly recovering the shared watermark w_{i_j} is

$$P_w = P_b^{\eta_c} = \left(\sum_{i=\lceil \frac{k}{2} \rceil}^{k} C_k^i \rho^i (1-\rho)^{k-i} \right)^{\eta_c} \tag{2}$$

Thus, if $\rho > 0.5$, the larger k, the greater the probability of correctly recovering w_{i_j}. This indicates that as k increases, the robustness of the watermark also increases.

In addition, after recovering n shared watermarks, all combinations of t shared watermarks are selected from these n watermarks. The sub-watermark information is reconstructed using the Shamir secret sharing, and the most frequent sub-watermark information is considered as the original sub-watermark information W'.

Theorem 1. *There is a binary image watermarking model where the watermark capacity that can be embedded is η_c bits, under the condition of ensuring a watermark extraction bit accuracy rate of ρ. It is known that a sub-watermark information, when processed by the Shamir secret sharing, generates n shared watermarks, and the bit length of the watermark information W is η. If $\frac{\eta}{\eta_c} \times n \times (k+1) \leq 2^m - 1$, the robustness of the watermark increases as k increases, and the embeddable watermark capacity is not affected. If $\frac{\eta}{\eta_c} \times n \times (k+1) > 2^m - 1$, the robustness of the watermark still increases as k increases, but the embeddable watermark capacity decreases.*

Proof. First, it is known from Eq. (1) that when $\rho > 0.5$, the robustness of the watermark increases with k.

Second, since each shared watermark requires k binary image carries, the values of d, n, and k must satisfy the condition: $dnk = \frac{\eta}{\eta_c} \times n \times k \leq 2^m - 1$.

So if $\frac{\eta}{\eta_c} \times n \times (k+1) \leq 2^m - 1$, increasing k does not change the value of η, and the embeddable watermark capacity remains unchanged. However, if $\frac{\eta}{\eta_c} \times n \times (k+1) > 2^m - 1$, then increasing k means that the value of η must decrease to satisfy $\frac{\eta}{\eta_c} \times n \times (k+1) \leq 2^m - 1$, resulting in a reduction of the embeddable watermark capacity. $\square$

2.5 GAN-Based Watermark Embedding Model

This study adopts an attention-guided robust image watermarking model (ARW-GAN) based on a generative adversarial network (GAN) framework. To better suit our objectives, we made the following key modifications:

1. We changed the model's input and output from color to binary images by adjusting the number of channels from 3 to 1 in the first and last convolutional layers of the encoder and decoder. As binary images contain only two pixel values (0 and 255), a single channel is sufficient, improving efficiency and embedding accuracy.

2. The noise subnetwork was removed. In our method, watermark robustness is ensured by parameters k, n, and threshold t, making the noise network unnecessary. This simplifies the model and reduces computational complexity.

The modified ARWGAN embeds a watermark into the input image via an encoder and extracts it using a decoder. A discriminator evaluates the similarity between the original and watermarked images to ensure concealment. The model is optimized using encoder loss, decoder loss, and adversarial loss.

3   Experimental Results and Analysis

3.1   Basic Settings

The watermarking model was implemented in PyTorch and trained on a system with Intel Xeon Platinum processors.

As shown in Table 3, 5000 training and 1000 test images were selected from both MNIST and Fashion-MNIST datasets. MNIST contains grayscale hand-written digits, and Fashion-MNIST includes images from 10 fashion categories. All images were binarized before training.

Table 3. Training and test set sizes.

	MNIST	Fashion-MNIST
Training	5000	5000
Test	1000	1000

For elevation data, we used the ASTGTMV003_N30E114 [1] dataset from ASTER GDEM V003, based on the GEODETIC coordinate system, covering latitudes 29.9998611–31.0001389 and longitudes 113.9998611–115.0001389. The elevation data was converted into a binary contour image with 50 m intervals and divided into 9 blocks (3×3 grid), as shown in Fig. 5.

Using these 9 blocks, a total of $2^9 - 1 = 511$ binary image carriers were generated. Subsequent experiments evaluate the watermarking scheme in terms of invisibility, robustness, runtime, and storage based on these carriers.

3.2   Invisibility of Watermarks

Since our watermarking scheme uses binary image carriers based on blocks, invisibility is evaluated from four aspects: subjective visual assessment, Peak Signal-to-Noise Ratio (PSNR), Structural Similarity Index (SSIM), and Mean Squared Error (MSE).

For subjective evaluation, two binary carriers and their watermarked versions are compared. The first carrier uses Block 1 alone, as shown in Fig. 6.

The second carrier merges Blocks 1–3, with results shown in Fig. 7.

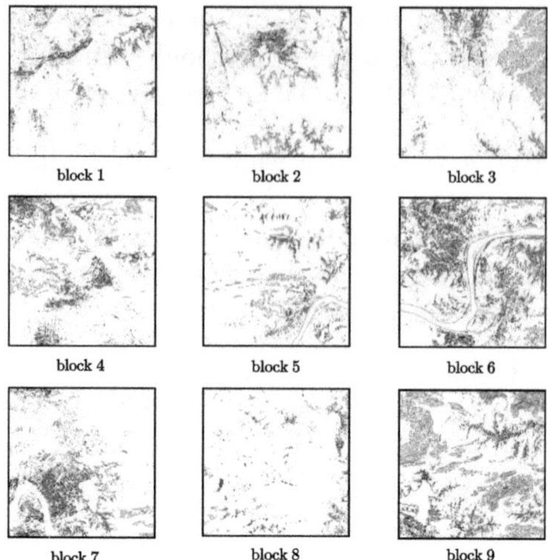

Fig. 5. Contour map divided into 9 blocks.

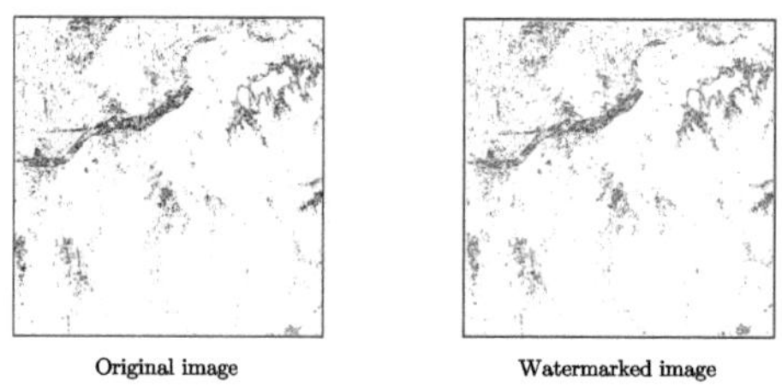

Fig. 6. Comparison before and after watermark embedding in Carrier 1.

From Figs. 6 and 7, the watermarked images show minimal visual differences from the originals, maintaining high structural similarity.

Further, we evaluated 511 binary carriers under natural conditions and various attacks (Gaussian noise, JPEG compression, cropout, and mixed attacks), calculating average MSE, PSNR, and SSIM. Results are shown in Table 4.
Table 4 shows consistently low MSE, high PSNR, and high SSIM values under both normal and attack conditions, demonstrating strong invisibility performance.

3.3   Robustness of Watermarks

Watermark robustness was evaluated under varying parameters: embedded image count $k \in \{10, 20, 30, 40, 50\}$, Shamir thresholds $(t, n) \in \{(4,5), (5,7), (6,9), (7,11), (8,13)\}$, and divisions $d \in \{1, 2, 3, 4, 5\}$, subject to $d \times n \times k \leq 511$.

Table 5 presents the average accuracy under different parameter settings.

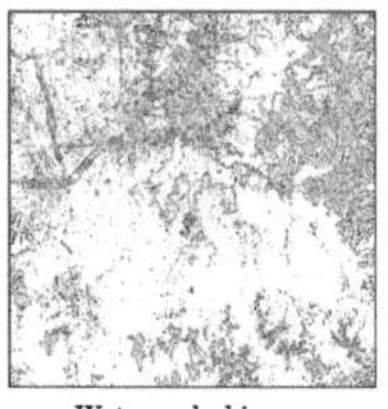

Fig. 7. Comparison before and after watermark embedding in Carrier 2.

Table 4. Invisibility under natural and attack conditions.

Condition	MSE	PSNR	SSIM	Condition	MSE	PSNR	SSIM
Noiseless	0.478	51.498	0.705	Gaussian Noise (0.06)	0.480	50.521	0.693
Gaussian Noise (0.08)	0.479	49.818	0.686	Gaussian Noise (0.1)	0.479	50.215	0.681
JPEG (0.8)	0.484	51.541	0.688	JPEG (0.65)	0.479	51.669	0.686
JPEG (0.5)	0.484	51.466	0.687	Cropout (10%)	0.478	51.476	0.693
Cropout (20%)	0.472	51.555	0.689	Cropout (30%)	0.471	51.498	0.705
Cropout+Noise	0.475	51.566	0.690	Cropout+JPEG	0.475	51.508	0.685
JPEG+Noise	0.482	51.477	0.687	**Average**	**0.478**	**51.216**	**0.690**

Rows 1–2 show the accuracy for different k values. Higher k improves accuracy, indicating enhanced robustness with more embedded images.

Rows 3–4 show the accuracy for different Shamir thresholds (t, n). Increasing n increases reconstruction options and improves robustness.

Rows 5–6 show the effect of varying d values. Larger d leads to reduced accuracy, indicating a trade-off between robustness and sparsity.

Table 5. Average accuracy under different parameter settings.

Parameter	Setting 1	Setting 2	Setting 3	Setting 4	Setting 5
k	10	20	30	40	50
Accuracy	0.8512	0.9135	0.9457	0.9624	0.9711
(t, n)	(4,5)	(5,7)	(6,9)	(7,11)	(8,13)
C_n^t	5	21	84	330	1287
Accuracy	0.7426	0.8988	0.9359	0.9527	0.9717
d	1	2	3	4	5
Accuracy	0.9439	0.9093	0.8780	0.8593	0.8193

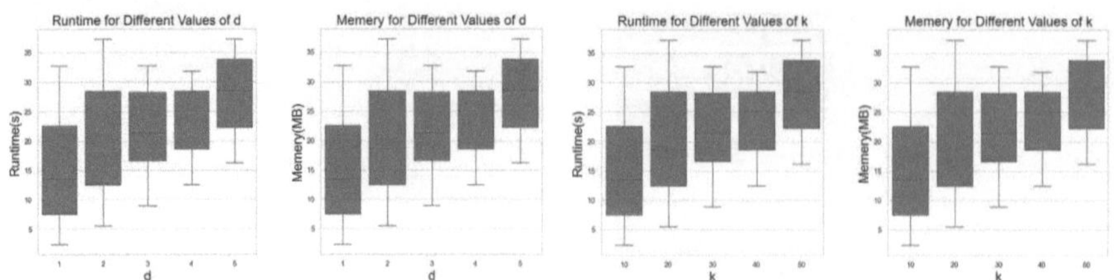

(a) Boxplot of watermarking cost for different d values.

(b) Boxplot of watermarking cost for different k values.

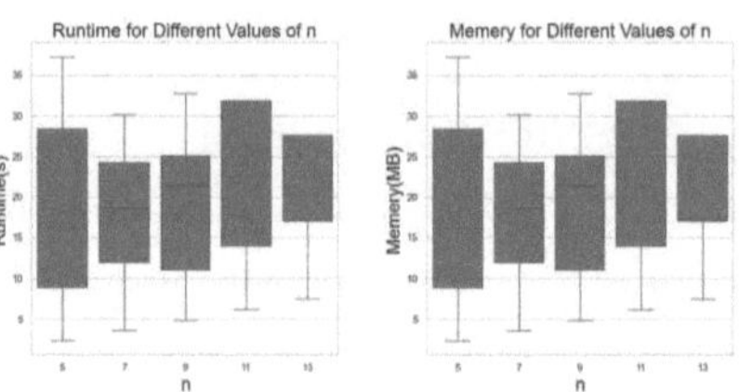

(c) Boxplot of watermarking cost for different n values.

Fig. 8. Boxplots of watermarking cost under different parameter settings.

3.4 Cost of Watermarks

When analyzing the cost of watermarking, we consider two aspects: memory usage and runtime for all binary image carriers after embedding.

First, we evaluated memory and runtime under varying k, d, and n values. Boxplots in Figs. 8a–8c show the distribution of overhead for different parameters.

Average runtime and memory usage for each parameter are summarized in Table 6.

Table 6. Average runtime and memory usage.

d	1	2	3	4	5
Runtime (s)	214.419	274.129	295.614	315.700	364.737
Memory (MB)	15.081	19.988	21.656	23.302	27.621
k	10	20	30	40	50
Runtime (s)	214.458	274.518	295.757	315.159	363.644
Memory (MB)	15.081	19.988	21.656	23.302	27.621
n	5	7	9	11	13
Runtime (s)	248.343	246.379	278.721	296.818	268.626
Memory (MB)	17.981	17.588	20.331	21.877	19.360

As shown in Figs. 8a–8c and Table 6, runtime and memory usage increase with d and k, while n has a lesser impact. Greater d values lead to more dispersed but overall increasing costs, indicating that larger watermark volumes escalate resource consumption.

Since the number of binary carriers is $d \times n \times k$, we also analyzed its relationship with overhead. Figure 9 presents the scatterplot with fitted trend lines.

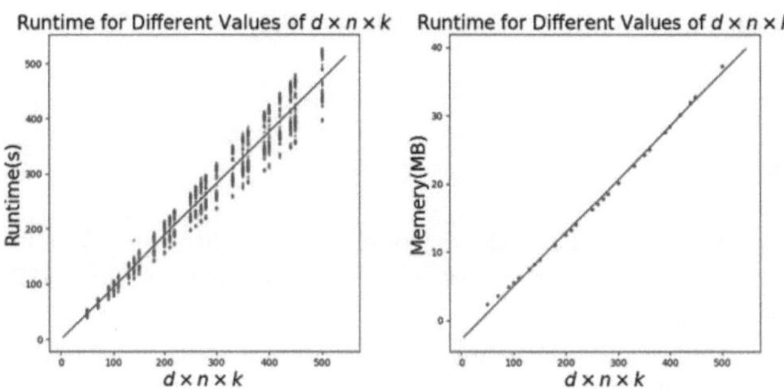

Fig. 9. Fitting curve of watermarking cost vs. $d \times n \times k$.

Figure 9 shows a positive correlation between $d \times n \times k$ and both runtime and memory usage. Memory consumption exhibits a clear linear trend, while runtime shows greater variance.

4   Conclusion

This paper presents a novel digital watermarking scheme for Digital Elevation Model (DEM) data by combining Shamir's secret sharing with Generative Adversarial Networks (GAN). Unlike traditional methods, our approach embeds shared watermarks in binary image carriers derived from DEM data, enhancing security and data integrity.

Experimental results show an average MSE of 0.478, PSNR of 51.216, and SSIM of 0.690, indicating high fidelity and imperceptibility. The highest accuracy of 0.97727 was achieved with $k = 30$, $d = 1$, and $(t, n) = (8, 13)$, demonstrating strong robustness. Moreover, runtime and memory usage increased linearly with $d \times n \times k$, ensuring practicality.

The key advantage of this method lies in its enhanced security, leveraging the strength of secret sharing and the adaptability of GANs. This dual-layer approach balances imperceptibility and robustness without compromising data usability.

This work offers a new perspective on DEM watermarking. Future research may focus on optimizing algorithms for real-time applications, improving scalability for large datasets, and integrating advanced deep learning techniques. Extending this method to fields such as medical imaging or sensitive document protection could further broaden its impact on digital security.

Acknowledgement. The research was financially supported by the Key Laboratory of Data Intelligence and Advanced Computing in Provincial Universities, Soochow University (No. KJS2409), Provincial Key Laboratory of Multimodal Perceiving and Intelligent Systems, Jiaxing University (No. MPIS202416), the Key Laboratory of Data Protection and Intelligent Management, Ministry of Education, Sichuan University and also the Fundamental Research Funds for the Central Universities (No. SCU2023D008), the Open Topic of Hunan Engineering Research Center of Geographic Information Security and Application (No. HNGISA2023001), and the CCF-NSFOCUS Kun-Peng Scientific Research Fund (No. CCFNSFOCUS2023009).

References

1. ASTER Global Digital Elevation Model V003: Astgtmv003_n30e114 (2019). https://lpcloud.measurementlab.net/echo10.jsp?acquisition_id=G1726778405-LPCLOUD. lPCLOUD
2. Al-Saad, M., Aburaed, N., Panthakkan, A., Al Mansoori, S., Al Ahmad, H.: Protection and authentication of Dubai digital elevation model using hybrid watermarking technique. In: 2021 4th International Conference on Signal Processing and Information Security (ICSPIS), pp. 13–16. IEEE (2021)
3. Amhar, F., et al.: Ownership protection on digital elevation model (DEM) using transform-based watermarking. ISPRS Int. J. Geo-Inf. **11**(3), 200 (2022)
4. Yong, L., Lizhi, C., Bo, C., Yi, W.: Study on digital elevation model data watermark via integer wavelets [in Chinese]. J. Softw. **16**(6), 1096–1103 (2005)
5. Guo, H., Georganas, N.D.: A novel approach to digital image watermarking based on a generalized secret sharing scheme. Multimedia Syst. **9**(3), 249–260 (2003)
6. Liu, X., Zhu, Y., Sun, Z., Diao, M., Zhang, L.: A novel robust video fingerprinting-watermarking hybrid scheme based on visual secret sharing. Multimedia Tools Appl. **74**, 9157–9174 (2015)
7. Li, D., Deng, L., Gupta, B.B., Wang, H., Choi, C.: A novel CNN based security guaranteed image watermarking generation scenario for smart city applications. Inf. Sci. **479**, 432–447 (2019)
8. Abuadbba, A., Kim, H., Nepal, S.: Deepisign: invisible fragile watermark to protect the integrity and authenticity of CNN. In: Proceedings of the 36th Annual ACM Symposium on Applied Computing, pp. 952–959 (2021)
9. Huang, J., Luo, T., Li, L., Yang, G., Xu, H., Chang, C.C.: Arwgan: attention-guided robust image watermarking model based on GAN. IEEE Trans. Instrum. Meas. (2023)
10. Mun, S.M., Nam, S.H., Jang, H.U., Kim, D., Lee, H.K.: A robust blind watermarking using convolutional neural network. arXiv preprint arXiv:1704.03248 (2017)
11. Sharma, H., Chaurasia, S., Pradhan, N., Singh, A.: DWT-GAN watermarking: discrete wavelet transform domain-based generative adversarial network for digital image watermarking. Int. J. Adv. Soft Comput. Appl. **15**(3) (2023)
12. Zhou, Q., Ren, N., Zhu, C., Zhu, A.X.: Blind digital watermarking algorithm against projection transformation for vector geographic data. ISPRS Int. J. Geo Inf. **9**(11), 692 (2020)
13. Ren, N., Zhao, Y., Zhu, C., Zhou, Q., Xu, D.: Copyright protection based on zero watermarking and blockchain for vector maps. ISPRS Int. J. Geo Inf. **10**(5), 294 (2021)

MOAT: A Multi-objective Approach to Federated IoT Botnet Detection

Yangzong Zhang[1], Wenjian Liu[1(⊠)], Bin Shi[2], and Tianqing Zhu[1]

[1] Faculty of Data Science, City University of Macau, Macau, China
`andylau@cityu.edu.mo`
[2] School of Computer Science and Technology, Xi'an Jiaotong University,
Xi'an, China

Abstract. This study presents an innovative intrusion detection approach focused on analyzing network traffic generated by Internet of Things (IoT) devices. Owing to their limited processing capabilities, IoT devices are generally more susceptible to cyber threats than conventional computing platforms. Botnets, which frequently exploit large numbers of IoT devices to launch distributed denial-of-service (DDoS) attacks, represent a major security concern. As a result, it is essential to design robust mechanisms for the identification and mitigation of botnet-related risks within IoT ecosystems. In this work, we propose an IP- and port-based classification framework that can detect novel forms of intrusions after deployment. By continuously observing variations in device activity patterns, the system is able to accurately differentiate between benign and suspicious behaviors. The proposed solution is validated on two widely known IoT botnets, namely Mirai and Bashlite. Furthermore, we investigate the impact of combining bootstrapping with averaging methods during data preprocessing, and observe that this approach substantially improves the model's ability to generalize. The MOAT architecture delivers superior results in both standalone and federated intrusion detection environments, achieving a mean accuracy of 96.25% across different nodes, even when evaluated on attack categories included in the training set.

Keywords: Network intrusion detection · Federated learning · Anomaly detection · Internet of Things

1 Introduction

The rapid expansion of Internet of Things (IoT) devices is poised to introduce a diverse range of innovative applications and services, fundamentally enhancing modern quality of life [4,7,11]. These devices, which encompass everything from simple sensors to sophisticated equipment, are predicted to reach a global count of nearly 25 billion in the foreseeable future [3]. However, the limited computational power and frequent configuration errors characteristic of many IoT devices make them particularly attractive targets for cyberattacks. This underscores the urgent demand for comprehensive security solutions [5,6,12].

© The Author(s), under exclusive license to Springer Nature Singapore Pte Ltd. 2026
T. Zhu et al. (Eds.): KSEM 2025, LNAI 15922, pp. 163–173, 2026.
https://doi.org/10.1007/978-981-95-3058-8_14

One major challenge associated with IoT systems is their proneness to bot infections, which often serve as the foundation for a multitude of cyber threats. Bots refer to malicious programs that allow adversaries, commonly termed botmasters, to exert remote control over compromised devices. When numerous devices fall under such control, they form what is known as a botnet [5]. The primary concern in these scenarios is that a single compromise can grant attackers extensive control, facilitating activities such as data theft, password cracking, keylogging, as well as orchestrating large-scale cyber offensives like spam dissemination and distributed denial-of-service (DDoS) campaigns [5,12].

Although an individual IoT device may possess minimal processing capabilities, the collective impact of many compromised devices can be immense, as highlighted by Kolias et al. [12]. For instance, during March and April 2019, a vast botnet of over 400,000 IoT devices was identified, generating more than 292,000 requests per minute aimed at exhausting the resources of a remote server. The magnitude of such coordinated attacks amplifies the effectiveness of DDoS incidents, posing serious challenges even to highly resilient infrastructures.

Building on the threat analysis presented by Abbas et al. [1], and considering the substantial dangers posed by DDoS attacks launched through botnets comprising billions of infected IoT nodes [3], it becomes imperative to formulate robust methods for their timely identification and counteraction. Defending against DDoS threats remains inherently complex due to their constantly changing tactics and diverse attack surfaces [18]. Therefore, prompt detection—achieved by monitoring deviations from established patterns of IoT device activity—offers a practical mitigation strategy. By establishing normative behavioral profiles for IoT devices, any significant departures can be promptly flagged as suspicious [10]. As Meidan et al. observe [14], this method proves especially suitable for IoT environments, where devices typically perform well-defined tasks and abrupt behavioral changes may indicate compromise [5].

The present work aims to address the following research questions:

- How do modifications in the operational patterns of IoT devices affect their IP address usage and distribution?
- If such effects are observable, can variations in IP address dynamics serve as reliable markers for detecting anomalous activity and, by extension, possible attacks?

IP address dynamics reflect the evolution of system behaviors and are instrumental for recognizing data instances that exhibit behavioral deviations linked to their network identifiers [7,16,17]. We hypothesize that the interactions between regular and irregular behaviors in IoT networks can be effectively monitored through analysis of these IP address transitions. Consequently, our detection strategy for IoT botnets centers on evaluating anomalies in the evolving network traffic profiles of devices, with the goal of distinguishing normal operations from malicious activities during both standard and attack conditions.

2   Related Work

Network traffic data constitutes a fundamental asset for tracking and assessing device activities across various domains. Analytical techniques range from remotely fingerprinting operating systems [13] to diagnosing device malfunctions by detecting irregularities in communication behavior [8,9]. As a result, leveraging insights drawn from network traffic is vital for comprehending how devices operate.

In the context of networked device security, deviations from expected communication patterns can indicate that a device has been compromised and is performing malicious actions. Consequently, the identification of anomalous traffic plays a crucial role in uncovering potential security issues. Chandola et al. [9] surveyed a wide array of anomaly detection methodologies and their practical utility, noting that infected devices generally produce more atypical traffic compared to normal device operation. Likewise, García-Teodoro et al. [10] reviewed multiple techniques for spotting irregularities in network data and emphasized their importance in the context of intrusion detection systems.

Numerous strategies have emerged for uncovering anomalies in network communications. For instance, Agarwal and Mittal [2] introduced an approach that evaluates the entropy of network features. After extracting these characteristics, normalized entropy values are computed and subsequently used as input to Support Vector Machines (SVMs) for distinguishing between legitimate and attack traffic. In a related effort, Yu et al. [19] focused on detecting flooding attacks by analyzing metrics gathered through Simple Network Management Protocol (SNMP) queries, such as counts of received, sent, and faulty packets, and utilized the C4.5 decision tree algorithm to recognize malicious behavior.

For the detection of botnet-driven attacks, Wang et al. [18] analyzed over 50,000 distinctive Internet-based DDoS incidents observed within a seven-month timeframe. Their findings highlight the importance of characterizing DDoS event patterns to build effective protection mechanisms. Among their observations, the periodic recurrence of time intervals separating consecutive DDoS attacks emerged as a promising feature for detection systems.

Mirsky et al. [15] introduced Kitsune, a Network Intrusion Detection System (NIDS) that leverages an ensemble of autoencoders to identify malicious activity within local networks. At the core of Kitsune is a feature extraction module, which collects a variety of network traffic statistics that are then processed by the autoencoders. This architecture has become foundational for subsequent research in the field.

Blaise et al. [6] put forward a Collaborative Intrusion Detection System (CIDS) designed to spot anomalies by monitoring cumulative network flows targeting specific ports. The authors argue that a sudden increase in traffic directed at a given port may serve as an early indicator of device compromise. They suggest that prioritizing port-based detection mechanisms enhances the prompt recognition of botnet-related threats.

2.1 MOAT System Architecture

Figure 1 illustrates a high-level representation of the MOAT system architecture. In this section, we thoroughly examine the system's constituent modules and their interactions, emphasizing the role each part plays in detecting and countering IoT-based botnet DDoS attacks.

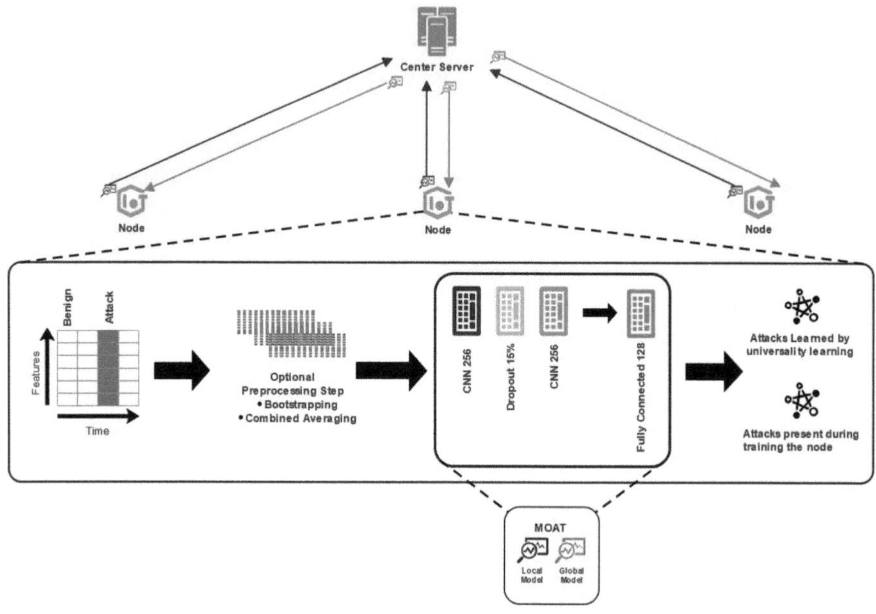

Fig. 1. Architecture of the proposed MOAT intrusion detection model

The MOAT platform consists of multiple integrated components, with each module dedicated to distinct tasks that together facilitate robust intrusion detection and timely response.

2.2 MOAT System Overview

Before deployment, each node in the MOAT framework is initially trained on pre-labeled datasets containing both normal and malicious network packets. This training phase is coordinated by a central server, which supports two operational paradigms:

– **Centralized Learning**: In this configuration, all nodes transfer their complete training data to the central server. The server then constructs a single deep learning model—identical in structure to the local models shown in Fig. 1—and distributes this unified model back to the nodes. In this case, nodes utilize the centrally-trained model as-is, without any further local adaptation.

– **Federated Learning**: Alternatively, each node independently trains a MOAT model on its own local dataset. Rather than sharing raw data, nodes communicate only the model parameters and updates with the central server. This approach preserves data privacy by keeping sensitive training samples onsite.

To combine the knowledge from different nodes in the federated setting, the central server applies the FedAvg aggregation algorithm [?]. This process merges the parameters from all participating local models, producing a global model that is subsequently distributed to every node. Each node then continues to refine this global model using its local data. This cycle of local training and global aggregation is performed over multiple iterative rounds. Although the underlying architectures of both the global and local models remain the same, as indicated in Fig. 1, their weights may diverge due to the variations in data across nodes.

The calculation of the global model parameters from local updates is formalized as follows:

$$\forall d,\ w_{t+1}^{d} \leftarrow w_t - \eta g_d \quad ; \quad w_{t+1} \leftarrow \sum_{d=1}^{D} \frac{n_d}{n} w_{t+1}^{d} \tag{1}$$

Here, the local update for each node is expressed as $\forall d,\ w_{t+1}^{d} \leftarrow w_t - \eta g_d$, where d indexes the node, w_t denotes the weight at iteration t, η is the learning rate, and g_d represents the gradient computed at node d. Each node individually adjusts its model weights based on its own data.

The subsequent aggregation step is given by $w_{t+1} \leftarrow \sum_{d=1}^{D} \frac{n_d}{n} w_{t+1}^{d}$, where D is the total number of nodes, n_d is the sample count at node d, and $n = \sum_{d=1}^{D} n_d$ is the total sample count across all nodes. This weighted averaging ensures that the global model incorporates contributions from all nodes in proportion to their dataset sizes, yielding a robust model that effectively represents the union of distributed data.

2.3   Nodes

Within the MOAT system architecture, every device on the network is modeled as an individual **node**. These nodes enable device-to-device communication and represent potential entry points for adversarial threats. Each node is outfitted with a deep learning-based Intrusion Detection System (IDS), which analyzes network traffic to detect and classify potentially harmful packets.

Nodes in the MOAT framework are integral to forming a robust and adaptive defense against IoT-based botnet DDoS attacks. By incorporating sophisticated detection mechanisms, secure communication schemes, and collaborative sharing of threat intelligence, each node enhances both the protection and resilience of the entire network.

2.4   Deep Learning Model

The deep learning architecture proposed in this work was constructed through rigorous experimentation to maximize classification accuracy for various types of attack data. Leveraging flow-based features, the model demonstrates strong deep feature extraction capabilities and is effective in managing both frequently occurring and rare attack types. The overall design is illustrated in Fig. 1.

Input to the model consists of a one-dimensional (1D) feature vector derived from individual data packets. This vector is sequentially processed by four convolutional layers, which are responsible for capturing multi-level feature representations from the input. To address overfitting, a dropout layer is included after the convolutional stages, randomly disabling certain neurons during training. The extracted features are then passed through two fully connected layers, which facilitate further integration and high-level abstraction.

At the final stage, the model uses an output layer with one-hot encoding to categorize each data sample as benign or malicious. This approach ensures the output reflects a probability distribution across the target classes, supporting accurate identification and classification of anomalous network traffic.

Bootstrapping. A major obstacle in developing network intrusion detection systems is the pronounced imbalance between the large number of benign packets and the relatively scarce intrusion instances. This disproportion poses difficulties for deep learning-based IDS, which generally rely on ample and representative training data to achieve optimal performance. To mitigate this issue, bootstrapping is frequently employed. By repeatedly re-sampling the minority class— namely, the attack samples—bootstrapping helps construct a training dataset with improved class balance. This adjustment enhances the model's capacity to recognize intrusions, thereby reducing the negative impact of class imbalance, increasing detection accuracy, and minimizing false positive rates.

IP Address Averaging. Within our framework, ip_t represents the mean value of IP addresses observed at time t. This metric is designed to smooth short-term fluctuations in network traffic, thereby offering a steadier basis for anomaly detection. The formula for computing the average IP address is given by:

$$ip_t = \frac{1}{r} \sum_{i=0}^{r-1} x(t - i), \quad r = \text{window size} \tag{2}$$

In this expression, $x(t - i)$ denotes the IP address data point at time $t - i$, and r specifies the window size used for averaging. The choice of r is essential, as it determines how many past data points contribute to the computed mean.

Averaging IP addresses serves to filter out random noise and highlight persistent trends within the data. For instance, when IP address values exhibit notable short-term variability, applying a moving average attenuates abrupt changes, allowing the underlying trend to become more apparent.

In the context of network monitoring, this smoothing technique increases the accuracy of anomaly detection mechanisms. By focusing on averaged IP address values, deviations from established behavioral patterns—such as those signaling botnet involvement or unauthorized access—are more easily identified.

Consider collecting IP address information at fixed intervals: if the window size r is chosen as 10, the mean IP address at time t is calculated by averaging the values from $t - 9$ through t. This approach reduces the impact of erratic changes and offers a clearer perspective on longer-term patterns.

The effectiveness of this method is highly dependent on the selection of the window size r. A window that is too small may fail to sufficiently suppress noise, while an overly large window could mask important short-term anomalies. Thus, determining an appropriate value for r requires consideration of the specific traffic characteristics and the intended objectives of the anomaly detection process.

Port Averaging. In our proposed framework, $port_t$ signifies the mean port activity observed at time t. This measure is designed to reduce the impact of short-term irregularities in network traffic, thereby yielding a more consistent and interpretable signal for anomaly detection purposes. The computation for average port activity is defined as:

$$port_t = \frac{1}{r} \sum_{i=0}^{r-1} x(t - i), \quad r = \text{window size} \tag{3}$$

Where $x(t - i)$ indicates the level of port activity at time $t - i$, and r specifies the number of previous time steps included in the averaging window. The selection of r is crucial, as it governs the temporal extent over which the data is aggregated.

The main objective of applying port activity averaging is to attenuate transient spikes and random noise, thereby accentuating persistent patterns and significant deviations. For instance, during periods of high variability in port usage, this approach helps to smooth abrupt changes and better expose the underlying behavioral trends of the network.

In the context of monitoring network traffic, employing an averaged port activity metric enhances the dependability of anomaly detection algorithms. By examining these smoothed values, it becomes easier to identify deviations from typical port usage, such as abnormal port scans or unauthorized access attempts.

As an illustrative example, suppose port activity is logged at uniform time intervals and the window size r is set to 10. The averaged port activity at time t is then determined by computing the mean of values from $t - 9$ through t. This method diminishes the influence of short-lived fluctuations, offering a clearer view of sustained trends.

The effectiveness of this averaging strategy hinges on the appropriate choice of window size r. A smaller window may leave residual noise, increasing the risk of false positives, whereas a larger window could mask meaningful short-term anomalies, potentially delaying critical alerts. Thus, the determination of

r should be informed by the specific attributes of the monitored traffic and the operational goals of the detection system.

In summary, port activity averaging is a key element of our anomaly detection methodology. By minimizing transient variations and highlighting long-term shifts in port behavior, this technique supports more accurate and reliable identification of emerging security threats, thereby strengthening proactive network defense mechanisms.

Combined Averaging. Within our detection framework, $feature_t$ denotes the joint average of IP address values and port activities at a given time t. This combined metric utilizes the smoothing benefits of averaging both variables, resulting in a more reliable indicator for detecting irregular network patterns. The calculation of this composite feature is as follows:

$$feature_t = \left(\frac{1}{r} \sum_{i=0}^{r-1} x(t-i), \frac{1}{r} \sum_{i=0}^{r-1} y(t-i) \right), \quad r = \text{window size} \tag{4}$$

In this formulation, $x(t-i)$ corresponds to the IP address observed at time $t-i$, while $y(t-i)$ captures the port activity for the same timestamp. The parameter r defines the number of time steps included in the averaging window, specifying the temporal scope for feature computation.

As an example, suppose network traffic is sampled at fixed intervals, and the window size r is set to 10. The combined feature at time t is then determined by calculating the mean of the IP address and port activity values across the most recent 10 time steps. This process reduces the influence of transient changes, enabling clearer identification of sustained trends.

The chief advantage of this Combined Averaging technique lies in its ability to suppress noise present in raw network data streams. By simultaneously averaging both IP address and port metrics, the resulting feature vector offers a more faithful representation of actual network conditions. This is essential for identifying deviations from expected behavior, which may signal emerging security issues, such as distributed denial-of-service (DDoS) attacks or unauthorized access events.

3   Experimental Results

The ROC analyses depicted in Fig. 2 and Fig. 3 provide further evidence of MOAT's enhanced performance. Figure 2 illustrates scenarios in which MOAT increases the accuracy of universality intrusion detection, as measured by recall. For instance, in the (5,3) attack pair, MOAT successfully identifies universality where alternative federated approaches do not, demonstrating its superior resilience across a variety of attack patterns. Correspondingly, Fig. 3 showcases examples such as PortScan attacks—specifically, the (9,8), (10,8), and (11,8) pairs—where MOAT is able to reveal universality that is not detected by competing methods. Utilizing recall as a key evaluation metric in these analyses

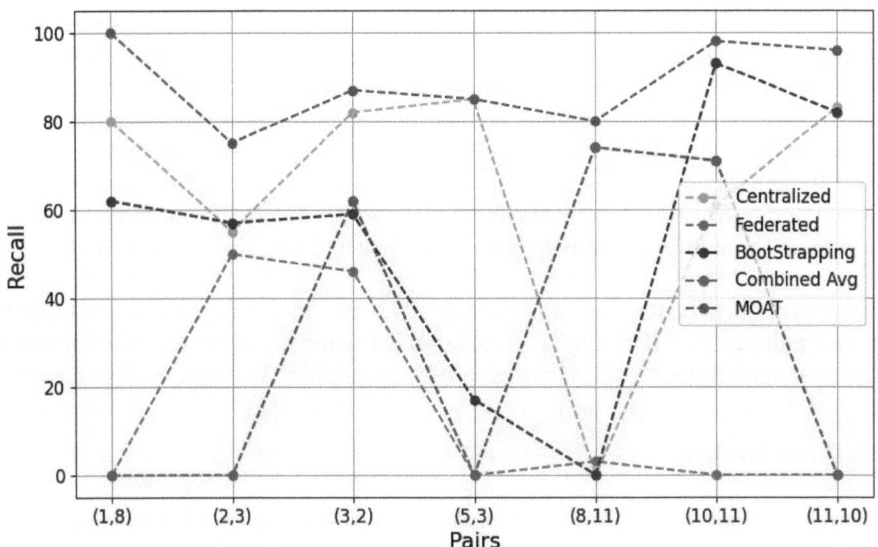

Fig. 2. Selected cases where MOAT improves universality.

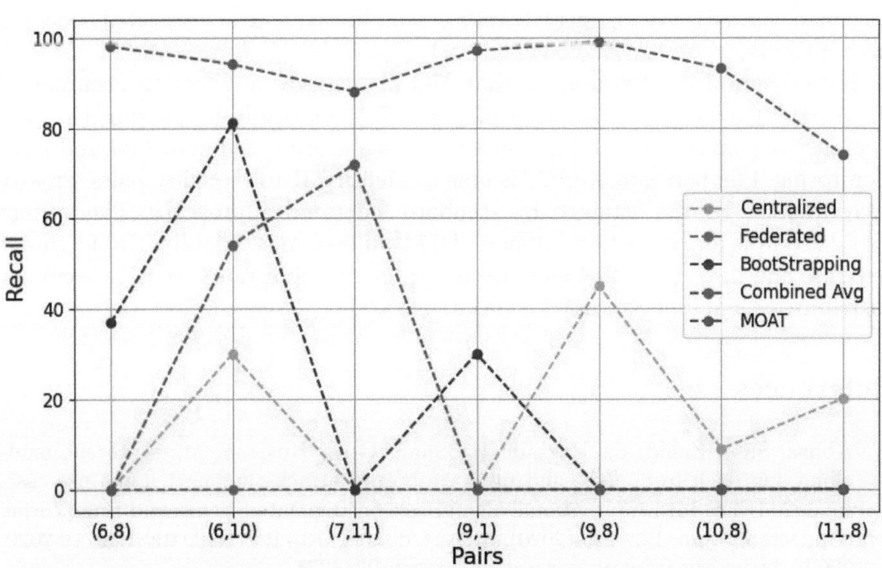

Fig. 3. Selected cases where MOAT uncovers universality.

highlights MOAT's ability to effectively recognize true attack cases, thereby overcoming the limitations of other approaches that struggle to classify certain attack data samples accurately.

The findings in this section emphasize the vital importance of dataset balancing and robust data aggregation for improving the universality of intrusion detection systems in federated learning settings. While the centralized training strategy sets a strong baseline with a considerable number of universality pairs, federated models initially show restricted generalization due to uneven datasets and limited local training samples. The implementation of bootstrapping and combined averaging techniques significantly addresses these obstacles, enabling federated models to reach performance levels similar to those of centralized solutions. By integrating both methods, the proposed MOAT framework not only maximizes the number of universality pairs detected but also sustains high accuracy across a broad spectrum of attack types. These results support the use of advanced preprocessing and aggregation strategies to strengthen the universality and reliability of IDS models in federated learning, paving the way for more adaptive and robust cybersecurity defenses in complex network environments.

4   Conclusion

This research presents MOAT, a federated deep learning-based intrusion detection framework that acts as a defensive barrier for IoT devices, enhancing universality in botnet detection. Through the integration of bootstrapping and combined averaging, MOAT effectively mitigates challenges related to data imbalance and the scarcity of local training samples typical of federated learning environments.

Experimental results indicate that MOAT achieves a detection accuracy of 96.25% with a false positive rate of just 0.7%, markedly surpassing the performance of conventional techniques such as signature-based detection and DNS monitoring. Furthermore, MOAT is able to identify 31 universality pairs, greatly exceeding the results attained by standard federated approaches. The system also delivers a low detection latency of 174 milliseconds, enabling rapid threat response and preventing incidents from escalating into serious security events or Distributed Denial of Service (DDoS) attacks.

References

1. Abbas, S.G., Zahid, S., Hussain, F., Shah, G.A., Husnain, M.: A threat modelling approach to analyze and mitigate botnet attacks in smart home use case. In: 2020 IEEE 14th International Conference on Big Data Science and Engineering (BigDataSE), pp. 122–129 (2020). https://doi.org/10.1109/BigDataSE50710.2020. 00024. https://ieeexplore.ieee.org/document/9343375
2. Agarwal, B., Mittal, N.: Hybrid approach for detection of anomaly network traffic using data mining techniques. Procedia Technol. **6**, 996–1003 (2012). https://doi. org/10.1016/j.protcy.2012.10.121. https://www.sciencedirect.com/science/article/pii/S2212017312006664
3. Al-Garadi, M.A., Mohamed, A., Al-Ali, A.K., Du, X., Ali, I., Guizani, M.: A Survey of Machine and Deep Learning Methods for Internet of Things (IoT) Security. IEEE Communi. Surv. Tutorials **22**(3), 1646–1685 (2020)
4. Atzori, L., Iera, A., Morabito, G.: The internet of things: a survey. Comput. Netw. **54**(15), 2787–2805 (2010)

5. Bertino, E., Islam, N.: Botnets and internet of things security. Computer **50**(2), 76–79 (2017)
6. Blaise, A., Bouet, M., Conan, V., Secci, S.: Detection of zero-day attacks: an unsupervised port-based approach. Comput. Networks **180**, 107391 (2020). https://doi.org/10.1016/j.comnet.2020.107391. https://www.sciencedirect. com/science/article/pii/S1389128620300761
7. Borges, J.B., Ramos, H.S., Mini, R.A.F., Viana, A.C., Loureiro, A.A.F.: The Quest for Sense: physical phenomena classification in the internet of things. In: 2019 15th International Conference on Distributed Computing in Sensor Systems (DCOSS), pp. 701–708 (2019). https://doi.org/10.1109/DCOSS.2019.00125. https://ieeexplore.ieee.org/abstract/document/8804789. iSSN: 2325-2944
8. Boukerche, A., Zheng, L., Alfandi, O.: Outlier detection: methods, models, and classification. ACM Comput. Surv. **53**(3), 55:1–55:37 (2020). https://doi.org/10. 1145/3381028
9. Chandola, V., Banerjee, A., Kumar, V.: Anomaly detection: a survey. ACM Comput. Surv. **41**(3), 15:1–15:58 (2009). https://doi.org/10.1145/1541880.1541882
10. García-Teodoro, P., Díaz-Verdejo, J., Maciá-Fernández, G., Vázquez, E.: Anomaly-based network intrusion detection: techniques, systems and challenges. Comput. Secur. **28**(1), 18–28 (2009)
11. Gubbi, J., Buyya, R., Marusic, S., Palaniswami, M.: Internet of things (IoT): a vision, architectural elements, and future directions. Futur. Gener. Comput. Syst. **29**(7), 1645–1660 (2013)
12. Kolias, C., Kambourakis, G., Stavrou, A., Voas, J.: DDoS in the IoT: mirai and other botnets. Computer **50**(7), 80–84 (2017)
13. Medeiros, J.P.S., Brito, A.M., Motta Pires, P.S.: An effective TCP/IP fingerprinting technique based on strange attractors classification. In: Garcia-Alfaro, J., Navarro-Arribas, G., Cuppens-Boulahia, N., Roudier, Y. (eds.) Data Privacy Management and Autonomous Spontaneous Security, pp. 208–221. Springer, Berlin, Heidelberg (2010). https://doi.org/10.1007/978-3-642-11207-2_16
14. Meidan, Y., et al.: N-BaIoT—network-based detection of IoT botnet attacks using deep autoencoders. IEEE Pervasive Comput. **17**(3), 12–22 (2018). https://doi.org/10.1109/MPRV.2018.03367731. https://ieeexplore.ieee. org/document/8490192. Conference Name: IEEE Pervasive Computing
15. Mirsky, Y., Doitshman, T., Elovici, Y., Shabtai, A.: Kitsune: an ensemble of autoencoders for online network intrusion detection (2018).https://doi.org/10. 48550/arXiv.1802.09089. http://arxiv.org/abs/1802.09089. arXiv:1802.09089
16. Rosso, O.A., Larrondo, H.A., Martin, M.T., Plastino, A., Fuentes, M.A.: Distinguishing Noise from Chaos. Phys. Rev. Lett. **99**(15), 154102 (2007)
17. Rosso, O.A., Olivares, F., Plastino, A.: Noise versus chaos in a causal Fisher-Shannon plane. Papers Physics **7**, 070006–070006 (2015). https://doi.org/10.4279/ pip.070006. https://www.papersinphysics.org/papersinphysics/article/view/228
18. Wang, A., Mohaisen, A., Chang, W., Chen, S.: Delving into internet DDoS attacks by botnets: characterization and analysis. In: 2015 45th Annual IEEE/IFIP International Conference on Dependable Systems and Networks, pp. 379–390 (2015). https://doi.org/10.1109/DSN.2015.47. https://ieeexplore.ieee. org/document/7266866. iSSN: 2158-3927
19. Yu, J., Kang, H., Park, D., Bang, H.C., Kang, D.W.: An in-depth analysis on traffic flooding attacks detection and system using data mining techniques. J. Syst. Archit. **59**(10, Part B), 1005–1012 (2013). https://doi.org/10.1016/j.sysarc.2013. 08.008. https://www.sciencedirect.com/science/article/pii/S1383762113001562

In-Context Contrastive Learning for Temporal Knowledge Graph Reasoning

Xingyi Li[(✉)], Jiapeng Wang, Boyuan Jia, Yiheng Lyu, Xiang Cheng, and Sen Su

State Key Laboratory of Networking and Switching Technology, Beijing University of Posts and Telecommunications, Beijing, China
{lixingyi2016,2025140768,jby222,lyhkk,chengxiang,susen}@bupt.edu.cn

Abstract. Temporal Knowledge Graph (TKG) reasoning aims at predicting future facts based on occurred facts. With the development of large language models (LLMs), it has shown that in-context learning based approaches can provide state-of-the-art performance. However, they tend to use historically relevant examples (i.e., historical information) as demonstrations, which brings challenges in predicting facts that have no historical interaction. In reality, the current fact is often the result of historical information combined with underlying factors (i.e., non-historical information). In this paper, we present CALENDAR (i.e., in-context **C**ontr**A**stive **L**earning t**E**mporal k**N**owle**D**ge gr**A**ph **R**easoning), an approach that leverages both histories and non-histories to create contrastive demonstrations, thereby reducing the bias toward predicting only historically occurred facts. In CALENDAR, we propose a demonstration candidate generation with high-order information method, which leverages high-order information from histories and non-histories to generate demonstration candidates. Moreover, we devise a contrastive importance based demonstration selection method which selects demonstrations by the sum frequency of entities in histories and non-histories of demonstration candidates. Furthermore, we design a contrastive chain-of-history based demonstration format which generates the negative principle for guiding the LLMs on why they should not rely only on the recurrence and periodicity histories. Experimental results on three benchmark datasets confirm the effectiveness of our approach.

Keywords: Temporal knowledge graph reasoning · In-context learning · Large language models · Contrastive learning · Knowledge graph

1 Introduction

Knowledge Graphs (KGs) [1,2,15,16], consisting of enormous relational triples, are valuable resources for many downstream natural language processing applications including question answering and recommender systems. Recently, temporal KGs (TKGs) have gained popularity to preserve the complex temporal

T. Zhu et al. (Eds.): KSEM 2025, LNAI 15922, pp. 174–185, 2026.
https://doi.org/10.1007/978-981-95-3058-8_15

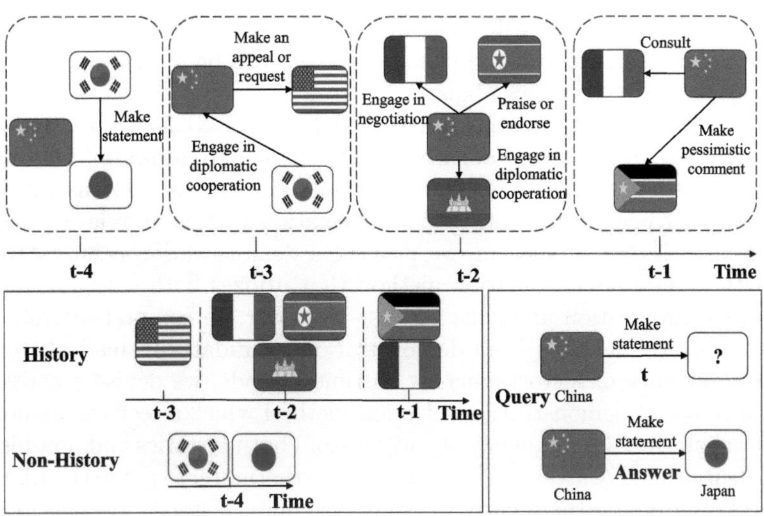

Fig. 1. An example of in-context learning for temporal knowledge graph reasoning.

dynamics of knowledge [5,8]. Most advanced research on TKGs mainly focuses on predicting future facts occur at time t_n based on historical facts occurring at time t, where $t < t_n$.

Most existing TKG reasoning approaches rely on large annotated samples for training [6,14]. However, acquiring high-quality labeled data is challenging. With the development of LLMs, model can be finetuned based on a small amount of labeled data from the downstream task. Prompt learning aims to reformulate downstream tasks to look more like those solved during the LLM training by prompt function with few or no labeled data [11]. In-context learning (ICL) is regarded as a kind of prompt learning with three major phases that are demonstration selection, demonstration ordering, and demonstration format. Recently, various ICL based TKG reasoning approaches have been proposed, such as WK-ICL [9], SA-CoH [13] and HO-CoH [18]. However, they fail to fully unlock the potential of LLMs, as they rely heavily on historical information while neglecting the underlying (i.e., non-historical) factors, which leads to inaccuracies in the TKG reasoning task.

Taking Fig. 1 as an example, the test instance is (China, Make statement, ?, t), which can be interpreted as "China will make statement with whom at t?". The histories are the quadruples involving entities that have a direct connection with China. In contrast, the non-histories refer to entities that do not have a direct connection. In this case, the histories are from t-3, t-2, and t-1, while the non-history occurs at t-4. LLMs tend to focus more on contextual information from the demonstrations during prediction. This means that if the demonstrations consist entirely of histories, LLMs are more likely to predict results based on them, potentially overlooking non-histories. However, if we add several highly relevant non-histories as demonstrations to the test instance such as "Japan" and "South Korea", LLMs will focus more on these rather than those that are not selected as demonstrations. In this way, there will be a higher probability of predicting the correct answer "Japan".

In this paper, we present an approach CALENDAR (i.e., in-context ContrAstive Learning tEmporal kNowleDge grAph Reasoning), which leverages both histories and non-histories to create contrastive demonstrations. In CALENDAR, to enrich the contextual information with more relevant histories and non-histories for prediction, we propose a demonstration candidate generation with high-order information method that utilizes both entity-related and pair-related information at higher orders. Moreover, to comprehensively select histories and non-histories from demonstration candidates instead of considering the occurrence of histories across all time periods, we devise a contrastive importance based demonstration selection method which select the demonstrations based on the sum frequency of entities from both histories and non-histories by a measure called contrastive importance. Furthermore, to guide the LLMs not excessively relying on the recurrence and periodicity histories, we design a contrastive chain-of-history based demonstration format. In this method, we mine the recurrence principle and the periodicity principle as two negative principles and format them as natural languages to construct the contrastive chain.

In summary, our contributions are fourfold:

- We present CALENDAR, a temporal knowledge graph reasoning approach via in-context contrastive learning, which considers both histories and non-histories as contrastive demonstrations.
- We design a demonstration candidate generation with high-order information method, which leverages high-order information from histories and non-histories to generate demonstration candidates.
- We propose a contrastive importance based demonstration selection method which selects demonstrations based on the sum frequency of entities in demonstration candidates by introducing a measure called contrastive importance. We further devise a contrastive chain-of-history based demonstration format which generates negative principles for guiding LLMs not excessively relying on the recurrence and periodicity histories.
- We conduct comprehensive experiments on three public datasets. The experimental results confirm the effectiveness of our approach.

2   Methodology

2.1   Overview

As shown in Fig. 2, our approach CALENDAR consists of three phases, namely demonstration candidate generation, demonstration selection and demonstration format. In the first phase, a demonstration candidate generation with high-order information method is proposed, which leverages high-order information from histories and non-histories to generate demonstration candidates. In the second

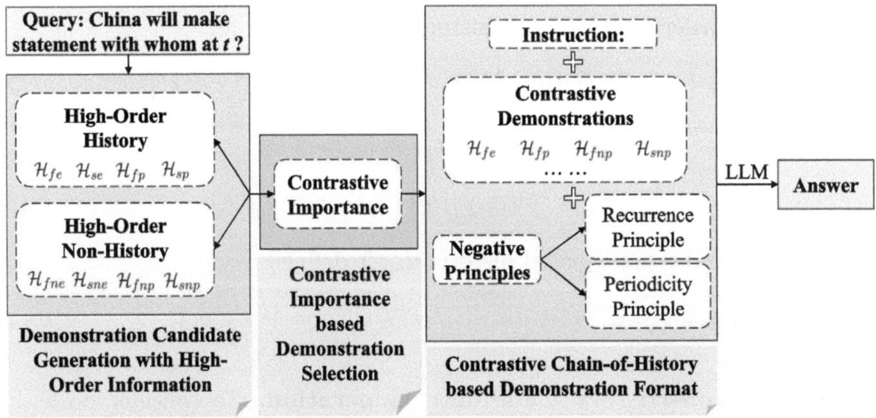

Fig. 2. Overview of our approach CALENDAR.

phase, a contrastive importance based demonstration selection method is proposed, which selects demonstrations based on the sum frequency of entities in demonstration candidates by introducing a measure called contrastive importance. In the third phase, a contrastive chain-of-history based demonstration format is proposed, which generates negative principles for guiding the LLMs on why they should not rely only on the recurrence and periodicity histories.

2.2 Demonstration Candidate Generation with High-Order Information

Existing works explore to use first-order histories as demonstrations, which leads to LLMs being constrained to infer incorrect answers to a large extent, as these limited first-order histories fail to encompass the correct answer [9,13]. When provided with high-order histories, LLMs can leverage the history chain to more effectively reason towards the correct answer [18]. However, these approaches overlook the potential of using non-historical information as demonstration candidates. To achieve this, we propose a demonstration candidate generation with high-order information method, which leverages high-order information to generate demonstration candidates from both histories and non-histories.

Given the query quadruple $q = (s_i, p_j, ?, t_q)$ for a test instance, we aim to generate the high-order histories and non-histories associated with this query.

High-Order History Candidate Generation. To consider both the entity and pair histories in high-order, we introduce two types of histories in first-order and second-order, which are entity-related history and pair-related history.

The first-order entity-related history $\mathcal{H}_{fe}$ is defined as:

$$\mathcal{H}_{fe} = \{(s_i, p, o, t) \,|\, (s_i, p, o, t) \in \mathcal{G}_t, p \in \mathcal{R}, o \in \mathcal{V}, t < t_q\}. \tag{1}$$

The second-order entity-related history $\mathcal{H}_{se}$ is defined as:

$$\mathcal{H}_{se} = \{(o, p, o', t) \,|\, (o, p, o', t) \in \mathcal{G}_t, p \in \mathcal{R}, o' \in \mathcal{V}, t < t_q\}. \tag{2}$$

The first-order pair-related history $\mathcal{H}_{fp}$ is defined as:

$$\mathcal{H}_{fp} = \{(s_i, p_j, o, t) \,|\, (s_i, p_j, o, t) \in \mathcal{G}_t, o \in \mathcal{V}, t < t_q\}. \tag{3}$$

The second-order pair-related history $\mathcal{H}_{sp}$ is defined as:

$$\mathcal{H}_{sp} = \{(o, p_j, o', t) \,|\, (o, p_j, o', t) \in \mathcal{G}_t, o' \in \mathcal{V}, t < t_q\}. \tag{4}$$

High-Order Non-History Candidate Generation. To consider both the entity and pair non-histories in high-order, we introduce two types of non-histories in first-order and second-order, which are entity-related non-history and pair-related non-history.

The first-order entity-related non-history $\mathcal{H}_{fne}$ is defined as:

$$\mathcal{H}_{fne} = \{(s, p, o, t) \,|\, s \in \mathcal{V} \setminus \{s_i\}, (s, p, o, t) \in \mathcal{G}_t, p \in \mathcal{R}, o \in \mathcal{V}, t < t_q\}, \tag{5}$$

where $\mathcal{O} = \{o_1, o_2, \ldots, o_n \,|\, o \in \mathcal{V}\}$.

The second-order entity-related non-history $\mathcal{H}_{sne}$ is defined as:

$$\mathcal{H}_{sne} = \{(s, p, o, t) \,|\, s \in \mathcal{V} \setminus \mathcal{O}, (s, p, o, t) \in \mathcal{G}_t, p \in \mathcal{R}, o \in \mathcal{V}, t < t_q\}. \tag{6}$$

The first-order pair-related non-history $\mathcal{H}_{fnp}$ is defined as:

$$\mathcal{H}_{fnp} = \{(s, p, o, t) \,|\, s \in \mathcal{V} \setminus \{s_i\}, p \in \mathcal{R} \setminus \{p_j\}, (s, p, o, t) \in \mathcal{G}_t, o \in \mathcal{V}, t < t_q\}, \tag{7}$$

where $\mathcal{P} = \{p_1, p_2, \ldots, p_n \,|\, p \in \mathcal{R}\}$.

The second-order pair-related non-history $\mathcal{H}_{snp}$ is defined as:

$$\mathcal{H}_{snp} = \{(s, p, o, t) \,|\, s \in \mathcal{V} \setminus \mathcal{O}, p \in \mathcal{R} \setminus \mathcal{P}, (s, p, o, t) \in \mathcal{G}_t, o \in \mathcal{V}, t < t_q\}. \tag{8}$$

For instance, Table 1 shows a subset of high-order histories and non-histories for $q = $ (Mexico, Host a visit, ?, 2014-12-01).

2.3   Contrastive Importance Based Demonstration Selection

Due to the large amount of high-order historical and non-historical demonstration candidates, it is necessary to select representative examples as demonstrations. Existing work [18] asks LLMs to infer the most important histories, potentially selecting demonstrations based on the frequency of occurrence of those histories across all time periods. In this way, the probability of selecting non-histories is extremely low, as the frequency of non-histories is small, which results in not fully leveraging non-historical information. To this end, we introduce a measure called contrastive importance CI, which selects demonstrations based

Table 1. An example of high-order histories and non-histories in ICEWS14 dataset.

Query	q	(Mexico, Host a visit, ?, 2014-12-01)	CI
High-Order Histories	$\mathcal{H}_{fe}$	(Mexico, Express intent to cooperate on intelligence, Colombia, 2014-02-09)	8
	$\mathcal{H}_{se}$	(Colombia, Accuse, Lawyer/Attorney (Colombia), 2014-01-08)	6
	$\mathcal{H}_{fp}$	(Mexico, Host a visit, City Mayor (United States), 2014-02-08)	8
	$\mathcal{H}_{sp}$	(City Mayor (United States), Host a visit, Nadezhda Tolokonnikova, 2014-02-08)	6
High-Order Non-Histories	$\mathcal{H}_{fne}$	(Ethiopia, Host a visit, South Sudan, 2014-01-03)	6
	$\mathcal{H}_{sne}$	(African Union, Make a visit, Ethiopia, 2014-01-05)	5
	$\mathcal{H}_{fnp}$	(Colombia, Sign formal agreement, Mexico, 2014-02-10)	8
	$\mathcal{H}_{snp}$	(Iran, Make a visit, Colombia, 2014-06-07)	7

on the sum frequency of entities from both histories and non-histories in the demonstration candidates.

Specifically, CI denotes the frequency of s, p, o in the above histories and non-histories. We select k-shot contrastive demonstrations, where k means the number of non-historical demonstrations. We use p to denote the proportion of historical and non-historical demonstrations. The total number of demonstrations is $k * p$. For instance from Table 1, since $\mathcal{H}_{fnp}$ and $\mathcal{H}_{snp}$ have the top two CI value among non-histories, if $k{=}2$, we will select them as non-historical demonstrations.

2.4   Contrastive Chain-of-History Based Demonstration Format

To enhance the demonstration format for guiding LLMs in generating more accurate results, Chain-of-Thought (CoT) [17] is proposed to mimic a step-by-step thought process for each demonstration before giving the final answer. Although we select demonstrations considering both the histories and non-histories, there is still a high probability of choosing recurrence or periodicity histories as demonstrations. If a particular history (i.e., recurrence or periodicity history) serves as a demonstration for several test instances, LLMs tend to focus on this recurrence or periodicity history to make predictions. However, the prediction of one test instance might be the subject entity s in other test instance $(s, p, ?, t)$ at the same time, resulting in a conflict as s can only be in one quadruple at the same time. Therefore, we propose a contrastive chain-of-history based demonstration format, which generates the negative principle for guiding the LLMs not excessively relying on the recurrence and periodicity histories, and uses contrastive chains to consider both histories and non-histories.

Negative Principle Mining. To prevent LLMs from highly depending on the recurrence and periodicity histories, we mine two types of negative principles that are recurrence principle and periodicity principle, aiming at avoiding these two errors in prediction.

Table 2. The examples of recurrence and periodicity principles in ICEWS14 dataset.

Principle	Query	Demonstration Candidates	Prediction	Correct Answer
Recurrence Principle	(Colombia, Host a visit, ? , 2014-12-07)	(Colombia, Host a visit, Joseph Robinette Biden, 2014-06-17) (Colombia, Host a visit, Joseph Robinette Biden, 2014-06-18) (Colombia, Host a visit, Joseph Robinette Biden, 2014-06-19) (Colombia, Host a visit, Joseph Robinette Biden, 2014-06-23) (Colombia, Host a visit, Foreign Affairs (Italy), 2014-08-08)	Joseph Robinette Biden	Ted Poe
Periodicity Principle	(Barack Obama, Make a visit, ? , 2014-12-25)	(Barack Obama, Make a visit, Japan, 2014-02-26) (Barack Obama, Make a visit, Japan, 2014-03-08) (Barack Obama, Make a visit, Japan, 2014-03-14) (Barack Obama, Make a visit, Japan, 2014-03-20) (Barack Obama, Make a visit, China, 2014-03-17)	Japan	Chine

Recurrence Principle. If we make predictions based on the recurrence events, there is a high likelihood of contradictions. From Table 2, the predicted object entity o is Joseph Robinette Biden. The prediction is wrong as another query is (Joseph Robinette Biden, Make statement, ? , 2014-12-07), which means at the same time, Joseph Robinette Biden is making statement with others. Thus, we introduce the recurrence principle by natural language "Even if an event is a recurrence event, we cannot directly use it as the prediction, because there could be other events at the same time or around the same time".

Periodicity Principle. If we make predictions based on the periodicity events, there is a high likelihood of contradictions. From Table 2, the predicted object entity o is Japan since (Barack Obama, Make a visit, Japan, t) is a periodicity event. However, the correct answer of o is China, and (Barack Obama, Make a visit, China, t) is not a periodicity event. Thus, we introduce the periodicity principle by natural language "Even if an event is a periodicity event, we cannot directly use it as the prediction, because some events do not occur exactly according to the periodicity".

Contrastive Chain Construction. The contrastive chain contains the instruction, contrastive demonstrations and the negative principles. Specifically, the instruction illustrates the task definition. The contrastive demonstrations are high-order histories and non-histories, which are selected by Contrastive Importance. The negative principles contain the recurrence principle and the periodicity principle.

3   Experiments

3.1   Datasets and Evaluation Metrics

To verify the effectiveness of our approach on TKG reasoning, we conduct experiments on three public datasets: ICEWS14 [5], ICEWS18 [3] and ICEWS0515 [5]. We evaluate on well-known metrics mean reciprocal rank (MRR) and Hits@k for $k \in \{1, 3, 10\}$.

3.2   Baselines

We mainly compare CALENDAR with the state-of-the-art TKG reasoning baselines. The baselines selected for comparative analysis fall into two categories: rule-based and supervised methods, as well as PLM-based and LLM-based methods.

- **Rule-based and Supervised Methods:** HyTE [4], TTransE [6], TA-DistMult [5], RGCRN [14], CyGNet [21], RE-NET [7], RE-GCN [10], and the rule-based TKG reasoning method TLogic [12].
- **PLM-based and LLM-based Methods:** PPT [19] is the previous SOTA TKG reasoning method based on PLMs. SALMON [20], WK-ICL [9], SA-CoH [13] and HO-CoH [18] are the LLM-based TKG reasoning methods.

3.3   Implementation Details

We use Llama-2-7B as our backbone. We evaluate the proposed approach CALENDAR under few-shot settings, in which the number of demonstrations is eight, with six histories and two non-histories as demonstrations for each test instance.

3.4   Results

Table 3 presents the results of the TKG reasoning task. We can observe that our approach CALENDAR outperforms the baselines on the ICEWS14, and ICEWS18 datasets. For example, in terms of Hits@10, CALENDAR outperforms the SA-CoH baseline by 1.08% and 0.98% on the ICEWS14 and ICEWS18 datasets. This shows our approach effectively exploits the in-context contrastive learning potential of LLMs. More surprisingly, CALENDAR even surpasses the SALMON baseline by 5.34% on the ICEWS14 dataset regarding MRR. Compared to the baseline SA-CoH on the ICEWS05-15 dataset, our approach performs slightly worse in terms of Hits@k. This suggests that our approach performs better on datasets with a shorter time span than on those with a longer span. However, it also shows that CALENDAR achieves the second best scores in Hits@1 and Hits@10, indicating that the approach has the capability to enhance the reasoning performance.

3.5   Further Analysis

Ablation Study. To analyze the effectiveness of high-order information, demonstration selection and demonstration format on the performance of our approach, we conduct ablation study and report detailed results in Fig. 3 (a). We setup our approach by ablating certain methods:

- W/O high-order information, where no demonstration candidate generation with high-order information is performed. Instead, we only adopt the first-order histories and non-histories as the demonstration candidates.

Table 3. Performance comparison of CALENDAR on TKG reasoning on three datasets in terms of MRR (%), Hits@1 (%), Hits@3 (%), and Hits@10 (%). The best scores are highlighted in bold, second best scores are underlined.

Method	ICEWS14				ICEWS05-15				ICEWS18			
	MRR	Hits@1	Hits@3	Hits@10	MRR	Hits@1	Hits@3	Hits@10	MRR	Hits@1	Hits@3	Hits@10
HyTE	16.78	2.13	24.84	43.94	16.05	6.53	20.20	34.72	7.41	3.10	7.33	16.01
TTransE	12.86	3.14	15.72	33.65	16.53	5.51	20.77	39.26	8.44	1.85	8.95	22.38
TA-DistMult	26.22	16.83	29.72	45.23	27.51	17.57	31.46	47.32	16.42	8.60	18.13	32.51
RGCRN	33.31	24.08	36.55	51.54	35.93	26.23	40.02	54.63	23.46	14.24	26.62	41.96
CyGNet	35.45	26.05	39.91	53.20	35.46	25.44	40.20	54.47	26.46	16.62	30.57	45.58
RE-NET	35.77	25.99	40.10	54.87	36.86	26.24	41.85	57.60	26.17	16.43	29.89	44.37
RE-GCN	37.78	27.17	42.50	58.84	38.27	27.43	43.06	59.93	27.51	17.82	31.17	46.55
Tlogic	-	26.50	39.50	53.10	-	-	-	-	-	15.50	27.20	41.20
PPT	38.42	28.94	42.50	57.01	38.85	28.57	43.35	58.63	26.63	16.94	30.64	45.43
SALMON	<u>38.78</u>	28.92	43.29	57.83	<u>39.38</u>	29.10	43.95	59.37	<u>28.57</u>	18.75	32.66	47.70
WK-ICL	31.79	22.38	37.67	47.70	35.34	25.18	43.92	56.24	21.51	14.77	26.08	40.57
SA-CoH	-	<u>33.80</u>	<u>46.20</u>	<u>58.70</u>	-	**37.00**	**53.10**	**69.90**	-	<u>21.90</u>	<u>36.10</u>	<u>52.00</u>
HO-CoH	34.51	24.20	39.67	51.21	37.51	27.72	<u>47.17</u>	59.58	23.94	16.81	28.15	42.68
CALENDAR	**44.12**	**34.21**	**47.56**	**59.78**	**39.85**	<u>30.05</u>	45.12	<u>60.50</u>	**28.97**	**22.21**	**36.45**	**52.98**

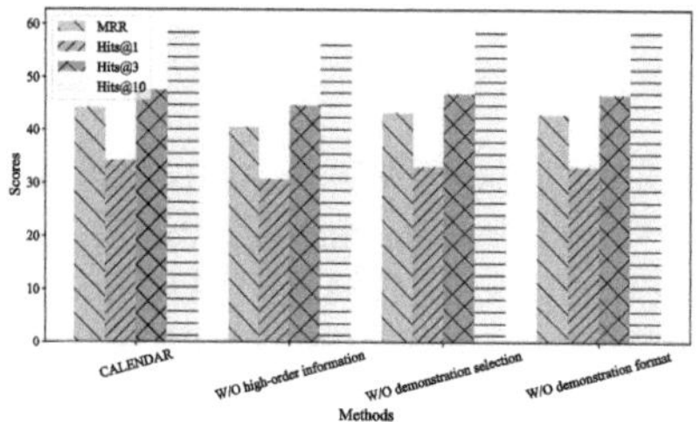

(a) Ablation study on ICEWS14 dataset

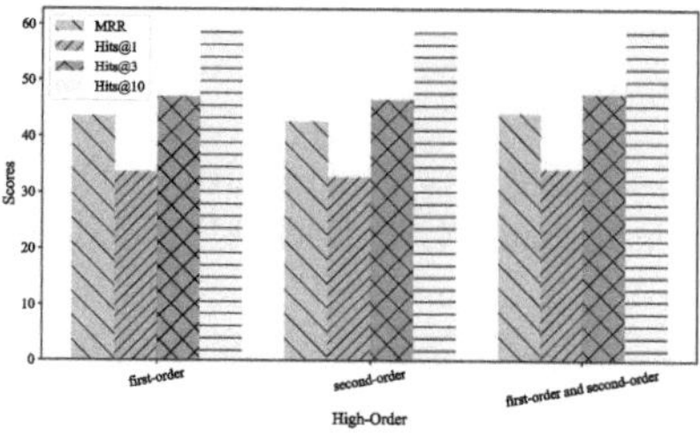

(b) Impact of the order on ICEWS14 dataset

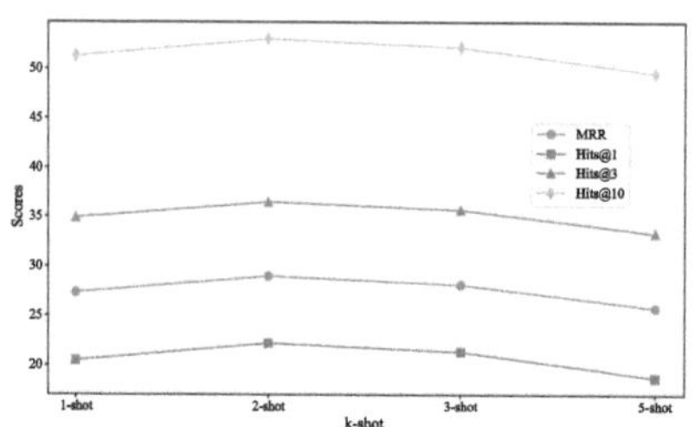

(c) Impact of k on ICEWS18 dataset

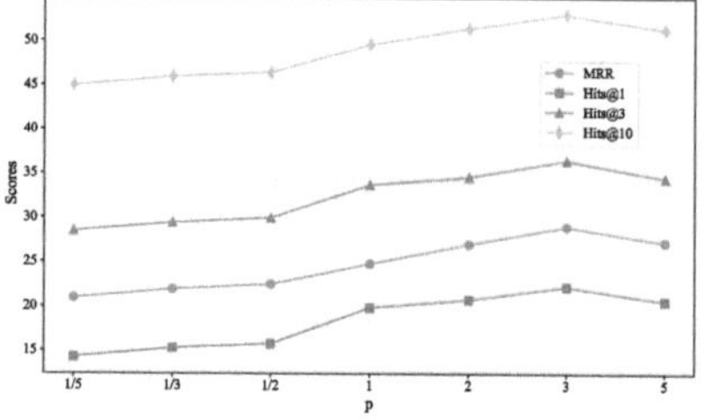

(d) Impact of p on ICEWS18 dataset

Fig. 3. Further Analysis on ablation study, impact of the order, k and p.

- W/O demonstration selection, where no contrastive importance based demonstration selection is performed. Instead, we randomly select the demonstration candidates as demonstrations.
- W/O demonstration format, where no contrastive chain-of-history based demonstration format is performed. In other words, we directly leverage the high-order histories and non-histories to form the demonstrations without mining the negative principles.

We use MRR, Hits@1, Hits@3 and Hits@10 to evaluate the TKG reasoning performance on ICEWS14 in Fig. 3 (a). From the results, we can observe that: (1) Demonstration candidate generation with high-order information is essential because the performance of our approach improves when a broader high-order histories and non-histories are selected as demonstration candidates. (2) Contrastive importance based demonstration selection plays an important role in our approach. The performance is poor when randomly select demonstrations. (3) Contrastive chain-of-history based demonstration format is significant because the performance of our approach is degraded when negative principles are not employed.

Impact of the Order. To verify the effectiveness of the high-order information for TKG reasoning, we use first-order, second-order, and both of them to predict answers, respectively. From the results in Fig. 3 (b), we can observe that the predicted results of LLMs based on both the first-order and second-order demonstrations are notably superior to the results derived from first-order or second-order demonstrations. This indicates the effectiveness of using both first-order and second-order demonstrations.

Impact of k. To illustrate the impact of different number of demonstrations k, we conduct further experiments on the ICEWS18 dataset with k-shot, in which k=1, 2, 3 and 5. The shot is defined as the number of non-historical demonstrations. From Fig. 3 (c), we can observe that the performance of our approach improves first and then declines as the shot increases. This means a relatively smaller number of demonstrations provide sufficient guidance for the test instance. In this work, we set $k = 2$, which means selecting the top six histories and top two non-histories based on the maximum sum of frequencies for s, p, o, respectively.

Impact of p. We conduct experiments to analyze the proportion p of histories and non-histories in demonstrations on the ICEWS18 dataset. We set the total number of demonstrations to a particular value twelve, and the number of histories and non-histories are changing. Specifically, $p = 2$ means the number of demonstrations of histories is twice as many as that of non-histories, i.e., the number of histories and non-histories are eight and four, respectively. From Fig. 3 (d), the effectiveness of our approach initially increases and then fluctuates as the number of non-historical demonstrations decreases. When histories provide adequate contextual information, adding more non-histories into demonstrations might increase noise and mislead the LLMs to generate wrong predictions. In this work, we set $p = 3$, that is to say, the number of histories is three times that of non-histories in demonstrations.

4   Conclusion

In this paper, we propose CALENDAR, a temporal knowledge graph reasoning approach via in-context contrastive learning, which considers both histories and non-histories as contrastive demonstrations. We design a demonstration candidate generation with high-order information method, which leverages high-order information from histories and non-histories to generate demonstration candidates. Moreover, we present a contrastive importance based demonstration selection method which select demonstrations based on the sum frequency of entities in demonstration candidates, and devise a contrastive chain-of-history based demonstration format which generates the negative principle for guiding the LLMs on why they should not rely only on the recurrence and periodicity histories. The experimental results confirm the effectiveness of our approach. In the future, we will investigate how to transfer our approach to continuously updated TKG, enabling more accurate and dynamic reasoning over time.

Acknowledgments. This work was supported by the National Natural Science Foundation of China (Grant No. 62372051).

Disclosure of Interests. The authors have no competing interests to declare that are relevant to the content of this article.

References

1. Auer, S., Bizer, C., Kobilarov, G., Lehmann, J., Cyganiak, R., Ives, Z.: Dbpedia: a nucleus for a web of open data. In: Proceedings of ISWC, pp. 722–735 (2007)
2. Bollacker, K., Evans, C., Paritosh, P., Sturge, T., Taylor, J.: Freebase: a collaboratively created graph database for structuring human knowledge. In: Proceedings of SIGMOD, pp. 1247–1250 (2008)
3. Boschee, E., Lautenschlager, J., O'Brien, S., Shellman, S., Starz, J., Ward, M.: ICEWS Coded Event Data (2015)
4. Dasgupta, S.S., Ray, S.N., Talukdar, P.P.: Hyte: hyperplane-based temporally aware knowledge graph embedding. In: Proceedings of EMNLP, pp. 2001–2011 (2018)
5. García-Durán, A., Dumancic, S., Niepert, M.: Learning sequence encoders for temporal knowledge graph completion. In: Proceedings of EMNLP, pp. 4816–4821 (2018)
6. Jiang, T., et al.: Encoding temporal information for time-aware link prediction. In: Proceedings of EMNLP, pp. 2350–2354 (2016)
7. Jin, W., Zhang, C., Szekely, P.A., Ren, X.: Recurrent event network for reasoning over temporal knowledge graphs. CoRR (2019)

8. Leblay, J., Chekol, M.W.: Deriving validity time in knowledge graph. In: Companion of the The Web Conference 2018 on The Web Conference 2018, WWW, pp. 1771–1776 (2018)

9. Lee, D.H., Ahrabian, K., Jin, W., Morstatter, F., Pujara, J.: Temporal knowledge graph forecasting without knowledge using in-context learning. arXiv preprint arXiv:2305.10613 (2023)

10. Li, Z., et al.: Temporal knowledge graph reasoning based on evolutional representation learning. In: Proceedings of SIGIR, pp. 408–417 (2021)

11. Liu, P., Yuan, W., Fu, J., Jiang, Z., Hayashi, H., Neubig, G.: Pre-train, prompt, and predict: a systematic survey of prompting methods in natural language processing. ACM Comput. Surv. (2023)

12. Liu, Y., Ma, Y., Hildebrandt, M., Joblin, M., Tresp, V.: Tlogic: Temporal logical rules for explainable link forecasting on temporal knowledge graphs. In: Proceedings of AAAI, pp. 4120–4127 (2022)

13. Luo, R., et al.: Chain of history: learning and forecasting with LLMs for temporal knowledge graph completion. arXiv preprint arXiv:2401.06072 (2024)

14. Seo, Y., Defferrard, M., Vandergheynst, P., Bresson, X.: Structured sequence modeling with graph convolutional recurrent networks. In: Proceedings of ICONIP, pp. 362–373 (2018)

15. Suchanek, F.M., Kasneci, G., Weikum, G.: Yago: a core of semantic knowledge. In: Proceedings of WWW, pp. 697–706 (2007)

16. Vrandečić, D., Krötzsch, M.: Wikidata: a free collaborative knowledgebase. Communications of the ACM (2014)

17. Wei, J., et al.: Chain-of-thought prompting elicits reasoning in large language models. In: Proceedings of NIPS, pp. 24824–24837 (2022)

18. Xia, Y., Wang, D., Liu, Q., Wang, L., Wu, S., Zhang, X.: Chain-of-history reasoning for temporal knowledge graph forecasting. In: Proceedings of ACL, pp. 16144–16159 (2024)

19. Xu, W., Liu, B., Peng, M., Jia, X., Peng, M.: Pre-trained language model with prompts for temporal knowledge graph completion. In: Proceedings of ACL, pp. 7790–7803 (2023)

20. Zhang, F., Lin, J., Cheng, J.: SALMON: A structure-aware language model with logicality and densification strategy for temporal knowledge graph reasoning. In: Proceedings of EMNLP, pp. 8761–8774 (2024)

21. Zhu, C., Chen, M., Fan, C., Cheng, G., Zhang, Y.: Learning from history: Modeling temporal knowledge graphs with sequential copy-generation networks. In: Proceedings of AAAI, pp. 4732–4740 (2021)

Emotion-Aware Knowledge Tracing: Enhancing Student Performance Prediction with Multi-Head Emotional Attention and Dynamic Gating

Lijing Tong, Xingjian Xu, Fanjun Meng, and Yan Gou[✉]

College of Computer Science and Technology, Inner Mongolia Normal University,
Hohhot Inner Mongolia Autonomous Region 010022, China
`ciecgy@imnu.edu.cn`

Abstract. Traditional cognitive diagnosis models primarily focus on students' knowledge states while neglecting the impact of emotional factors on learning performance. In recent years, deep learning methods have made progress in dynamic knowledge tracing, yet they have not fully considered the role of emotions. This study proposes the Emotion-Aware Knowledge Tracing (EAKT) model, which integrates multi-head emotional attention and dynamic emotional gating mechanisms to enhance student performance prediction. EAKT independently models the influence of different emotions on knowledge states through the emotional attention mechanism and adjusts knowledge representations via dynamic emotional gating to accommodate emotional fluctuations. Experimental results on the ASSISTments2012 and ASSISTments2017 datasets demonstrate that EAKT outperforms baseline models in ACC, AUC, and RMSE. The findings suggest that incorporating emotional factors improves the accuracy of knowledge tracing and provides a novel theoretical framework for personalized educational interventions.

Keywords: Knowledge Tracing · Emotion-Aware · Multi-Head Attention · Dynamic Emotional Gating · Personalized Learning

1 Introduction

Cognitive diagnosis models include classical probabilistic methods and modern deep learning approaches. The AKT model enhances this field with context-aware attention, tracking knowledge retention and forgetting patterns to improve prediction accuracy through dynamic modeling [1].

However, traditional cognitive diagnostic models focus primarily on cognitive abilities while overlooking emotional factors' impact. Emotions critically influence learning: positive emotions enhance motivation and cognition, while negative emotions impair attention and comprehension. Ignoring emotional factors limits the model's ability to differentiate between knowledge gaps and emotional barriers, reducing prediction accuracy and intervention effectiveness.

T. Zhu et al. (Eds.): KSEM 2025, LNAI 15922, pp. 186–194, 2026.
https://doi.org/10.1007/978-981-95-3058-8_16

This study proposes the Emotion-Aware Knowledge Tracing (EAKT) model, which innovatively incorporates emotional factors through a multi-head emotional attention mechanism and dynamic emotional gating. As shown in Fig. 1, EAKT effectively models the relationships between response patterns, emotional states, and knowledge mastery, demonstrating its value for personalized learning applications.

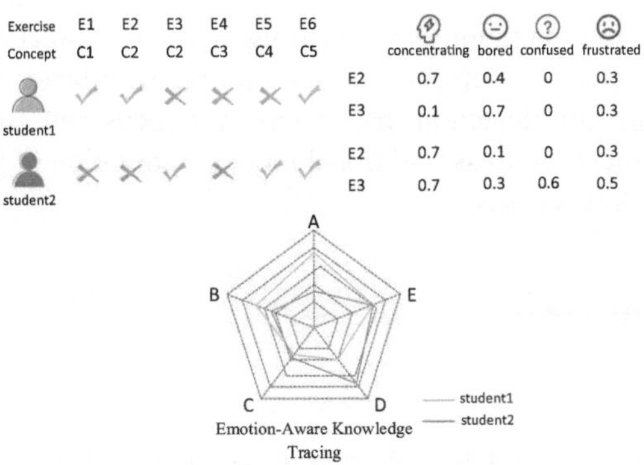

Fig. 1. EAKT demonstration using ASSIST2017 data, showing how responses, emotions, and knowledge mastery interact.

The EAKT model introduces a novel framework for personalized learning through four integrated components: The first module is the fundamental representation module, which encodes students' learning sequences and emotional states into a vector space; The second module is the multi-head emotional attention module, which captures emotion-specific influences on knowledge states; The third module is the dynamic emotional gating module, which adjusts knowledge representations based on emotional fluctuations; The fourth module is the response prediction module, which integrates knowledge states with question features to predict student performance.

2 Related Works

2.1 Cognitive Diagnosis

Cognitive diagnosis evaluates fine-grained knowledge mastery to enable personalized learning. Recent advances in intelligent education have expanded its application in tutoring systems and online platforms, evolving from early probabilistic models to modern deep learning approaches [19].

Cognitive diagnosis has evolved from early probabilistic models to modern deep learning approaches. Initial methods like DINA [4], DINO [5], and GDINA [6] relied on expert-constructed Q-matrices but faced generalization limitations. Deep learning introduced sequence modeling through DKT [7], enhanced by memory networks (DKVMN) [8] and attention mechanisms (SAKT) [9, 14]. Recent advances incorporate exercise texts (EKT) [10], forgetting effects (DGMN) [11], learning consistency (LPKT) [12], and difficulty adaptation (DMKT) [13], progressively improving diagnostic precision and personalization.

2.2 Emotional Factors in Cognitive Diagnosis

Recent studies highlight emotion's critical role in cognitive diagnosis, showing how states like focus, confusion, and frustration directly impact learning outcomes [15]. This has spurred emotion-aware models like the Dual-State Personalized Knowledge Tracing Model, which integrates emotional and cognitive states to enhance prediction accuracy [16]. Advanced approaches now incorporate emotion perception modules, demonstrating improved diagnostic interpretability by modeling emotions' direct effects on response performance [17]. Further refinements analyze missing skill labels and classroom features to optimize emotion detection, particularly for focus and confusion prediction [18]. These developments address traditional models' limitation of ignoring emotional influences on learning processes.

3 Modeling Approach

3.1 Problem Definition

In an intelligent tutoring system, consider a group of students denoted as $S = \{s_1, s_2, ..., s_n\}$. Each student $\(s\_i \)$ has a learning sequence represented as $S_i = \{(q_1, r_1, a_1), (q_2, r_2, a_2), ..., (q_T, r_T, a_T)\}$, where q_t is the question, $r_t \in \{0,1\}$ is the binary response (correct/incorrect), and a_t is an emotional state vector (e.g. concentration, boredom, confusion, frustration). The EAKT model employs a function $f(S)$ to predict the probability $P(r_{T+1} = 1|S)$ of a student answering a future question q_{T+1} correctly. By integrating emotional features and question difficulty d_t, the model dynamically updates the knowledge state $K_t = f(K_{t-1}, q_t, r_t, a_t, d_t)$, enabling more precise modeling of cognitive and affective states in knowledge tracing.

3.2 Model Architecture

In this chapter, the EAKT method is formally introduced based on the AKT framework. As shown in Fig. 2.

Fundamental Representation

The fundamental representation module transforms discrete inputs into continuous vector embeddings for neural processing.

At timestep t, we first define the exercise embedding matrix $W_Q \in R^{N_Q \times D}$ and the exercise-response joint embedding matrix $W_{QR} \in R^{N_Q \times D}$, The exercise q_t is transformed into an embedding vector through Eq. 1, while the student response pair (q_t, r_t) is mapped to a joint embedding representation via Eq. 2. To enhance model expressiveness, we introduce an affective embedding matrix $W_A \in R^{4 \times D}$ that encodes the emotional state a_t into an affective embedding vector following Eq. 3. The final knowledge state representation h_T is computed through the aggregation function in Eq. 4.

$$Q_t^{emb} = W_Q[q_t] \in R^D \tag{1}$$

$$Qr_t^{emb} = W_{QR}[q_t, r_t] \in R^D \tag{2}$$

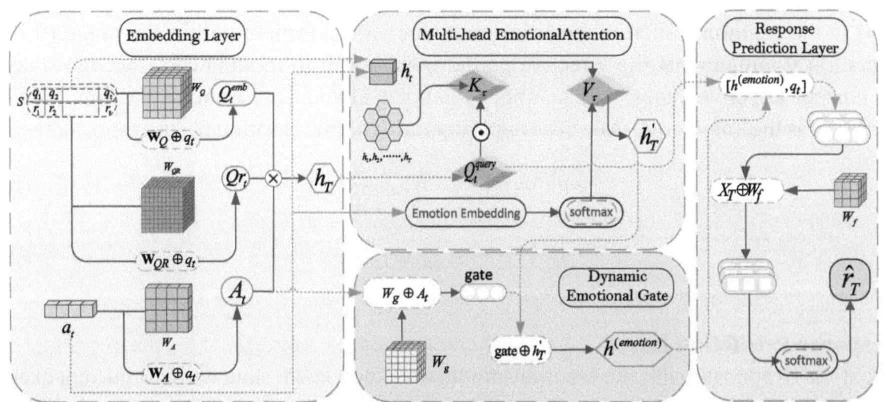

Fig. 2. The overall framework of the Emotion-Aware Knowledge Tracing (EAKT) model.

$$A_t = W_A[a_t] \in R^D \tag{3}$$

$$h_T = Q_t^{emb} + Qr_t^{emb} + A_t \tag{4}$$

Multi-Head Emotional Attention

For each affective state, we implement dedicated attention heads through Eq. 5 to capture emotion-specific influences on memory retention. Where Q_t^{query}, K_τ and V_τ represent the query, key and value vectors, respectively, learned from students' historical learning data. $d(t, \tau)$ is a context-aware temporal distance function used to attenuate the influence of different time steps. θ_e is the decay rate independently learned for each emotion, controlling the impact of different emotions across the time dimension. Crucially, these affective states - recognized as key determinants of learning behaviors - are incorporated into multi-head attention computation via Eq. 6 to modulate cognitive processing. Where $\sigma(\bullet)$ represents the Sigmoid activation function, ensuring that the embedding values remain within the range of (0,1). The final attention representation is obtained by integrating the computed affective attention scores through Eq. 7 using an adaptive fusion mechanism. Where $w_e(E_{emo})$ is a learnable parameter that represents the weighted influence of the emotion embedding on different emotional attention heads.

$$s_{t,\tau}^{(e)} = \frac{(Q_t^{query})^\top k_\tau}{\sqrt{D_k}} \cdot e^{-\theta_e \cdot d(t,\tau)} \tag{5}$$

$$E_{emo} = \sigma \left(W_a \cdot [a_{conc}, a_{bor}, a_{conf}, a_{fru}]^T + b_a \right) \tag{6}$$

$$\alpha_{t,\tau} = \sum_e w_e(E_{emo}) \cdot \text{softmax}\left(s_{t,\tau}^{(e)}\right) \tag{7}$$

Dynamic Emotional Gate

The gating vector is computed through Eq. 8 to modulate the knowledge state. Where

$\sigma(\bullet)$ is the Sigmoid function, ensuring that gate values remain within the range (0,1). Equation 9 implements the affective gating mechanism to modulate knowledge states by current affective states. The symbol $\odot$ denotes element-wise multiplication. While $h^{(emotion)}$ is the knowledge state after applying the dynamic emotional gating mechanism.

$$gate = \sigma\left(W_g \cdot E_{emo} + b_g\right) \tag{8}$$

$$h^{(emotion)} = gate \odot h'_T \tag{9}$$

Response Prediction Layer

Equation 10 concatenates the emotion-modulated knowledge state with the current exercise embedding, and a feedforward network predicts the final response probability. Where $\sigma(\bullet)$ is the Sigmoid activation function, ensuring that the predicted probability remains within the range (0,1).

$$r_t = \sigma\left(W_p\left[h^{(emotion)}; q_t\right] + b_p\right) \tag{10}$$

4 Experiment

4.1 Datasets and Evaluation Metrics

Datasets

To verify the generalization ability of the model, two datasets with emotion labels are used Table 1 presents the statistical details of all datasets, and a brief overview of the datasets is provided below. The ASSIST2012 dataset (2012–2013) contains learning records with four emotion features [20], while ASSIST2017 (2004–2007) provides longer-term behavioral data with seven emotion features. Both datasets enable research on emotion-learning interactions after data cleaning.

Table 1. Statistics of experimental datasets.

Statistics	Datasets	
	ASSIST2012	ASSIST2017
Students	29018	1709
Exercises	53091	3162
Concepts	265	102
Answer Time	26747	1326
Interval Time	29748	2839
Avg. Length	93.45	551.68

Baseline Methods

To evaluate the effectiveness of the EAKT model, we compared it with several baseline methods implemented under consistent experimental conditions. The compared models include DKT [7] which pioneered deep learning-based knowledge tracing using RNNs/LSTMs to track knowledge state evolution, AKT [1] that improves interpretability through attention mechanisms and Rasch model-regularized embeddings, ACD [17] incorporating emotional states to adjust cognitive diagnosis via the DINA model, LPKT [12] explicitly modeling learning and forgetting processes, and EKT [10] integrating practice records and exercise text for enhanced prediction. All models were implemented in PyTorch and tested in the same Linux server environment to ensure fair comparison.

4.2 Comparison Experiments and Result Analysis

The model parameters are initialized uniformly, with five-fold cross-validation applied across all datasets (80% training/validation, 20% testing). As shown in EAKT outperforms DEKT by integrating emotional modeling with cognitive diagnosis through its multi-head emotional attention and dynamic gating mechanisms. This dual-perspective approach (cognitive + emotional) enables more accurate knowledge state modeling, adaptive learning path adjustment, and superior generalization - yielding consistently higher prediction accuracy across metrics.

Table 2, EAKT consistently outperforms baseline models on both ASSIST2017 and ASSIST2012 datasets, achieving significant gains in accuracy (ACC), AUC, and RMSE. Compared to DEKT, EAKT shows notable improvements: on ASSIST2017, it boosts ACC by 4.88%, AUC by 1.89%, and reduces RMSE by 3.7%; while on ASSIST2012, it maintains comparable ACC but superior AUC and RMSE performance. These results demonstrate EAKT's enhanced capability in long-term knowledge tracing and emotional state modeling through its attention and gating mechanisms.

EAKT outperforms DEKT by integrating emotional modeling with cognitive diagnosis through its multi-head emotional attention and dynamic gating mechanisms. This dual-perspective approach (cognitive + emotional) enables more accurate knowledge state modeling, adaptive learning path adjustment, and superior generalization - yielding consistently higher prediction accuracy across metrics.

Table 2. Comparative performance of six KT methods on ASSIST2012/2017 datasets, with top models highlighted (bold for best, italics for second-best).

Method	ASSIST2017			ASSIST2012		
	ACC	AUC	RMSE	ACC	AUC	RMSE
DKT	0.7023	0.7425	O.4328	0.7412	0.7295	0.4211
AKT	0.7281	0.76623	0.4215	0.7656	0.7852	0.4096
DEKT	0.7724	0.8426	0.3921	**0.7793**	0.8274	0.3851
EKT	0.7098	0.7515	0.4323	0.7479	0.7652	0.4113
LPKT	0.7423	0.7943	0.4012	0.7512	0.7745	0.4067

(continued)

Table 2. (*continued*)

Method	ASSIST2017			ASSIST2012		
	ACC	AUC	RMSE	ACC	AUC	RMSE
EAKT	**0.8212**	**0.8615**	**0.3776**	<u>0.7789</u>	**0.8300**	**0.3824**

4.3 Ablation Experiments

This chapter conducts ablation Experiments to validate the contributions of each module in EAKT, evaluating three variant models: the model without multi-head emotional attention mechanism (w/o Emb), the model excluding dynamic emotional gating (w/o DEG), and the model with complete removal of emotional features (w/o Emo).

Table 3. The table presents ablation results for EAKT variants, comparing their ACC, AUC and RMSE performance.

Methods	Embedding	Emo-Gate	Emotion	ACC	AUC	RMSE
w/o Emb		✓	✓	0.8194	0.8583	0.3795
w/o DEG	✓		✓	0.8198	0.8602	0.3781
w/o Emo	✓	✓		0.7634	0.7825	0.4175
EAKT	✓	✓	✓	0.8212	0.8615	0.3776

Table 3 results show the complete EAKT model outperforms all variants. Removing emotional attention significantly reduces accuracy and AUC while increasing error, confirming its critical role. Eliminating emotional embeddings causes the most severe performance drop, proving their fundamental importance. Though dynamic gating shows milder effects, the full model's superiority validates emotion-enhanced knowledge tracing.

5 Conclusion

The EAKT model advances knowledge tracing by integrating emotional factors through multi-head emotional attention that captures emotion-specific learning influences and dynamic emotional gating that adjusts knowledge states based on affective fluctuations along with enhanced response prediction. Experimental results demonstrate its superior performance while current limitations involve potentially noisy predefined emotion labels that could benefit from unsupervised approaches oversimplified emotion modeling requiring more nuanced representations and the need to extend beyond prediction to personalized interventions highlighting both the value of emotional integration and important future research directions.

Acknowledgement. This work was supported by grants from the Natural Science Foundation of Inner Mongolia (2025MS06033), Hohhot Basic Research and Applied Basic Research Science and Technology Program Projects (2025-GUI-JI-44).

References

1. Ghosh, A., Heffernan, N., Lan, A.S.: Context-aware attentive knowledge tracing. In: Proceedings of the 26th ACM SIGKDD International Conference on Knowledge Discovery & Data Mining, pp. 2330–2339 (2020)
2. San Pedro, M.O. Z., Baker, R.S.J., Gowda, S.M., et al.: Towards an understanding of affect and knowledge from student interaction with an intelligent tutoring system. In: Artificial Intelligence in Education: 16th International Conference, AIED 2013, Memphis, TN, USA, July 9–13, 2013. Proceedings 16, pp. 41–50. Springer, Berlin Heidelberg (2013)
3. Botelho, A.F., Baker, R.S., Heffernan, N.T.: Improving sensor-free affect detection using deep learning. In: Artificial Intelligence in Education: 18th International Conference, AIED 2017, Wuhan, China, June 28–July 1, 2017. Proceedings 18, pp. 40–51 (2017). Springer, International Publishing
4. De La Torre, J.: DINA model and parameter estimation: a didactic. Journal of Educational and Behavioral Statistics 34(1), 115–130 (2009)
5. Junker, B.W., Sijtsma, K.: Cognitive assessment models with few assumptions, and connections with nonparametric item response theory. Appl. Psychol. Meas. 25(3), 258–272 (2001)
6. De La Torre, J.: The generalized DINA model framework. Psychometrika 76(2), 179–199 (2011)
7. Piech, C., Bassen, J., Huang, J., et al.: Deep knowledge tracing. Advances in Neural Information Processing Systems 28 (2015)
8. Zhang, J., Shi, X., King, I., et al.: Dynamic key-value memory networks for knowledge tracing. In: Proceedings of the 26th International Conference on World Wide Web, pp. 765–774 (2017)
9. Pandey, S., Karypis, G.: A Self-Attentive Model for Knowledge Tracing. arXiv preprint arXiv: 1907.06837 (2019)
10. Liu, Q., Huang, Z., Yin, Y., et al.: EKT: exercise-aware knowledge tracing for student performance prediction. IEEE Trans. Knowl. Data Eng. 33(1), 100–115 (2019)
11. Abdelrahman, G., Wang, Q.: Deep graph memory networks for forgetting-robust knowledge tracing. IEEE Trans. Knowl. Data Eng. 35(8), 7844–7855 (2022)
12. Shen, S., Liu, Q., Chen, E., et al.: Learning process-consistent knowledge tracing. In: Proceedings of the 27th ACM SIGKDD Conference on Knowledge Discovery & Data Mining, pp. 1452–1460 (2021)
13. Shen, S., Huang, Z., Liu, Q., et al.: Assessing student's dynamic knowledge state by exploring the question difficulty effect. In: Proceedings of the 45th International ACM SIGIR Conference on Research and Development in Information Retrieval, pp. 427–437 (2022)
14. Vaswani, A., Shazeer, N., Parmar, N., et al.: Attention is all you need. Advances in Neural Information Processing Systems 30 (2017)
15. Pardos, Z.A., Baker, R.S.J.D., San Pedro, M.O.C.Z., et al.: Affective states and state tests: investigating how affect and engagement during the school year predict end-of-year learning outcomes. Journal of Learning Analytics 1(1), 107–128 (2014)
16. Wang, S., Yuan, F., Wang, K., et al.: Dual-state personalized knowledge tracing with emotional incorporation. IEEE Transactions on Knowledge and Data Engineering 37(1) (2025)
17. Wang, S., Zeng, Z., Yang, X., et al.: Boosting neural cognitive diagnosis with student's affective state modeling. In: Proceedings of the AAAI Conference on Artificial Intelligence 38(1), 620–627 (2024)
18. Wang, Y., Heffernan, N.T., Heffernan, C.: Towards better affect detectors: Effect of missing skills, class features and common wrong answers. In: Proceedings of the Fifth International Conference on Learning Analytics and Knowledge, pp. 31–35 (2015)

19. Abdelrahman, G., Wang, Q., Nunes, B.: Knowledge tracing: a survey. ACM Comput. Surv. **55**(11), 1–37 (2023)
20. Feng, M., Heffernan, N., Koedinger, K.: Addressing the assessment challenge with an online system that tutors as it assesses. User Model. User-Adap. Inter. **19**, 243–266 (2009)

Mask-Guided Visual Text Transformer for Radiology Reports Representation Learning

Jiazheng Sun[1(✉)] and Xiaoyan Cai[2]

[1] School of Computer Science and Technology, Huazhong University of Science and Technology, Wuhan, China
u202315493@hust.edu.cn
[2] School of Automation, Northwestern Polytechnical University, Xi'an, China
xiaoyanc@nwpu.edu.cn

Abstract. Inspired by robustness and efficiency of human language processing, we present Mask-guided Visual Text Transformer (Mg-VTT), which incorporates the use of visual text representations and a mask mechanism into Vision Transformer, creating continuous vocabularies by processing visually rendered text using sliding windows, obtaining task-relevant embedding with mask operation and finally producing robust, word level, and open-vocabulary representations for classification task. We evaluate the proposed Mg-VTT on Chinese radiology reports dataset Xiangya radiology reports and English radiology reports datasets MIMIC-CXR with gradient-weighted class activation mapping (Grad-CAM) as the mask. Experimental results prove that Mg-VTT model significantly improves performance and efficiency when compared with vanilla Transformer and Vision Transformer. Furthermore, radiologists tend to use their native language to write, which hinders the comprehensive use of radiology reports in different languages. Although the previous studies respectively provide effective solutions to the problems of Chinese and English radiology reports, they are all modeled for a single language, lacking of research on text representation unified modeling of Chinese and English reports. Finally, Mg-VTT provides a novel view and a concrete method towards generalizing data-intensive and large-scale vision models (https://github.com/jzw1234/Mg-VTT).

1 Introduction

BERT (Devlin et al., 2018) has obtained great performance in many natural language processing tasks. Subword tokenization system of BERT which is depends on a predefined and finite set of wordpieces, is adopted by most of the recent language representation models, achieving a great balance between efficiency and flexibility. However, as a general-domain model, BERT is not suitable for specific domains, due to their domain-specific nouns and terms. Current researches tend to build suitable word embeddings for specialized domains using predefined vocabulary (Elwany et al., 2019). Nevertheless, with the development of

T. Zhu et al. (Eds.): KSEM 2025, LNAI 15922, pp. 195–208, 2026.
https://doi.org/10.1007/978-981-95-3058-8_17

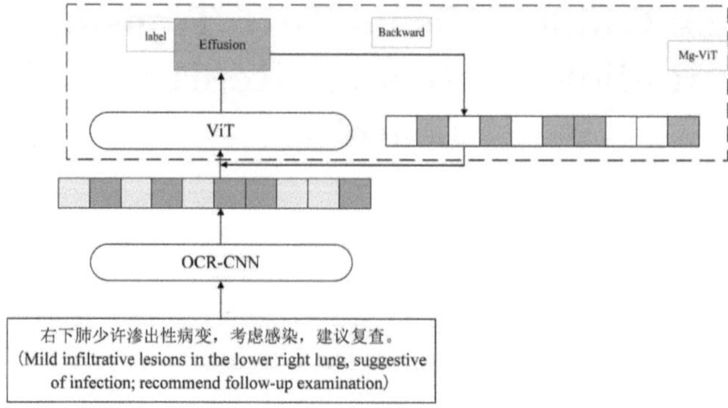

Fig. 1. Operation of obtaining visual text embedding and feeding it into Mg-ViT.

representation models, current trend favors fine-tuning general-domain models on downstream tasks using specialized corpora, instead of training models from scratch using a specialized vocabulary, such as BioBERT (Lee et al., 2020), ChestXRayBERT (Cai et al., 2021) and BioGPT (Luo et al., 2022). Although these methods produce good models, there still remains a problem: Predefined subword units may result in poor embeddings when new words out of vocabulary (OOV) appear. To tackle the above problem, in this paper, we present a novel vision model based representation approach, named Mask-guided Visual Text Transformer (Mg-VTT), which is a possible solution to adopt open vocabulary for reducing any biases caused by the employment of a predefined wordpiece vocabulary, and an attempt to recover to essentially simpler word-level models. This vision model based representation approach consults the rendered images from words to build visual text representations, instead of relying on wordpieces. Specifically, we replace conventional wordpiece (e.g. BERT'wordpiece) embedding layer with OCR-CNN (Salesky et al., 2021) module, and feed visual text embedding obtained from OCR-CNN to vision model (e.g. Mg-ViT (Chen et al., 2022)), as shown in Fig. 1. The key idea of Mg-ViT is to apply a mask on rendered image slices to screen out the task-irrelevant ones and guide ViT focusing on task-relevant and discriminative slices. The most task-relevant and discriminative slices are identified from the salience map by calculating gradient-weighted class activation mapping (Grad-CAM)(Selvaraju et al., 2017a). Moreover, since the visible slices that are not masked retain task-relevant information but lose global information, we add a residual connection between the first and last encoder layer to retain global information.

Our proposed Mg-VTT model is able to produce contextualized representations discriminatively using vision model and does not require a wordpiece vocabulary. When evaluated on classification tasks, Mg-VTT performs better than vanilla Transformer. To the best of our knowledge, Mg-VTT is the first work which directly applies vision model to text data. Our contributions are listed as follows:

(1) A novel vision model based representation approach is proposed, called Mg-VTT, that produces word-level contextual representations by consulting the rendered images from words.

(2) An elegant mask operation on visual text slices is introduced to guide ViT focusing on task-relevant and discriminative slices. The mask operation improves effectiveness of the model.

(3) Thorough experimental studies are designed and conducted to verify effectiveness of Mg-VTT.

2   Related Work

2.1   Visual Representations of Text

There exists many researches about visual representations of text on NLP tasks in recent years, mostly for Chinese language, with good and bad results. Selvaraju et al. (2017b) utilized visual representations from CNNs over rendered text in three language (i.e. Chinese, Korean and Japanese) for text classification with convolutional networks. Similarly, Dai and Cai (2017) used results from CNNs over character-level images for Chinese on two NLP tasks. Hybrid convolutional networks are introduced by Meng et al. (2019) to enhance several NLP tasks for Chinese language, utilizing historical scripts for additional visual representation information. Dense fixed-size square text renderings are created by Sun et al. (2018) in Chinese and English for convolutions to enhance sentiment analysis. Visual similarity is used by Ryskina et al. (2020) for Russian romanization. However, these researches mostly adopt classical convolutional networks (e.g. CNN, RNN), instead of excellent transformer. Salesky et al. (2021) used vanilla Transformer (Vaswani et al., 2017) based on visual representations of text for neural machine translation task. Although this neural network based visual text approach has shown outstanding performance, it pays equal attention to "noun", its modifier words and other words, which may hinder model focusing on important object quickly, such as "noun".

2.2   Vision Transformer

Vision Transformer (ViT; Dosovitskiy et al., 2020) is transferred from the structure of transformer (Vaswani et al., 2017) in natural language processing (NLP) tasks. Recently, several refined ViT models are proposed. Touvron et al. (2021) proposed ImageNet based transformer model, which is only trained on a single device in less than three days with a specific distillation strategy. Yuan et al. (2021) incorporated strengths of CNNs in extracting low-level features to enhance long-range dependencies, and proposed a Convolution-enhanced image Transformer (CeiT). Inspired by comparison between inverted residual blocks and feed-forward networks (FFNs), Li et al. (2021) introduced depth-wise convolution into FFN of vision transformers to add its locality. Zhang et al. (2021) nested basic local transformers over non-overlapping image blocks and aggregated these blocks in a hierarchical manner. These models are introduced with useful strategies including knowledge distillation, depth-wise convolution and tree-like structure, and achieve improved model performance and efficiency in image classification task. Moreover, Mg-ViT (Chen et al., 2022) is proposed to guide ViT pay more attention to task-relevant and discriminative patches for image classification. Although Mg-ViT has shown outstanding performance by allocating attention reasonably, it is not applicable to text classification task in NLP.

3   Mask-Guided Visual Text Transformer (Mg-VTT)

Mg-VTT mainly consists of an Ocr-CNN and the mask guided vision Transformer (Mg-ViT), as shown in Fig. 2. Specifically, Mg-VTT leverages advantage of visual text representation, to feed the representations into mask guided vision Transformer. In the following, we first illustate Ocr-CNN, which produces robust, word-level visual text representations. With visual text representations, we can fully avoid OOV problem that often occurs in classical text processing procedure. Secondly, we develop a Mask-guided Vision Transformer and knowledge distillation, which can focus on the key words via a mask mechanism.

3.1   Ocr-CNN

The first step of Ocr-CNN is transforming text into an image. The original text of each sentence is rendered into grayscale (one color channel) image. The image height h is a maximum value of the characters height based on the font and font size, and the image width w is variable according to the font and sentence length. Secondly, like feature extraction at intervals s according to a stride set, sliding windows are used to extract slices. Slices output from the rendering stage are similar to subword text tokens. The third step produces "embeddings" over the slices output. Generally, embedding refers to entries in a fixed size weight matrix, using the vocabulary 1D as its index. We do not draw image slices from a predetermined set, thus we could not adopt typical embeddings. Instead, we employ the outputs from 2D convolutional blocks running over the image slices, then we project the outputs to the model dimension, as a continuous vocabulary. In practice, we use a single convolutional block ($c = 1$) followed by a linear layer for producing flattened 1D representations, which is adopted by vanilla Transformer, but here the representations are drawn from a continuous space, instead of a predetermined size of embeddings. A convolutional block consists of three parts: a 2D convolution followed by a 2D batch normalization and a ReLU layer. Since this embedding process does not split words into wordpieces, each word is assigned a single final context-independent representation by Ocr-CNN, which is helpful for the following mask operation (Fig. 3).

3.2   Mask-Guided Vision Transformer

After obtaining visual text representations, we feed it into Mask-guided Vision Transformer. Like original Mg-ViT (Chen et al., 2022), a slice mask is added to

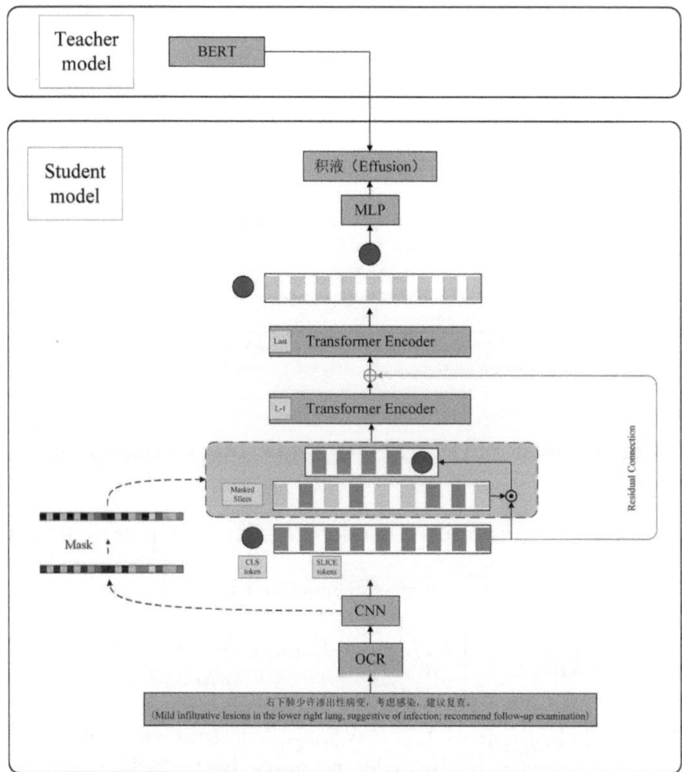

Fig. 2. Architecture of proposed Mask-guided Visual Text Transformer (Mg-VTT) model. During training, Ocr-CNN can extract visual text representation from input sample, Mask-guided ViT distinguishes and obtains important representation, and the predict module (MLP header) is supervised with a pre-trained BERT (teacher model) through a local alignment loss (e.g. KL-div). During testing, BERT is fully removed and the remaining part can predict accurate categories.

the slice embeddings before the first encoder layer of Transformer, selecting the task-relevant and discriminative ones. Note that the mask operation masks task-irrelevant ones, which helps ViT pay attention to task-relevant object quickly. Thus, the input of the first transformer encoder layer $\tilde{z}_0$ is:

$$z_0^{masked} = [x_{SLICE} \odot Mask; x_{CLS}]$$
$$+ [P_{SLICE} \odot Mask; P_{CLS}] \tag{1}$$

where P_{SLICE} and P_{CLS} are slice position embedding and class position embedding, respectively. $\odot$ is the element-wise production. Like original MG-ViT, we also adopt residual connection. Specifically, we add the embeddings of all original visual text slices to the input of the last encoder layer, as shown in Fig. 2.

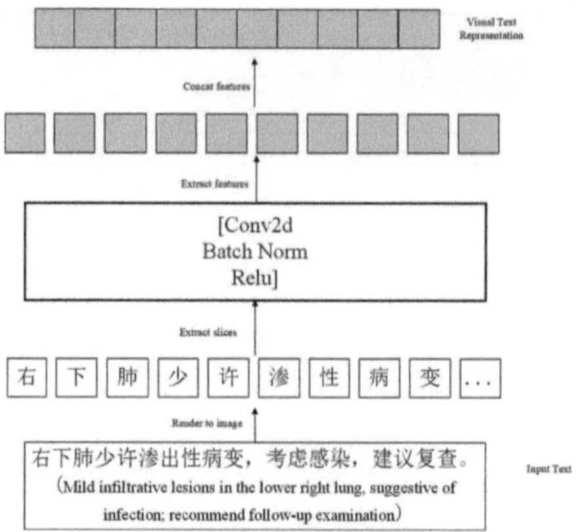

Fig. 3. Detials of Ocr-CNN for Visual Text representation.

The input of the last Transformer encoder layer $\tilde{z}_{L-1}$ is represented as:

$$\tilde{z}_{L-1} = [\tilde{x}_{SLICE}^{L-1}; x_{CLS}^{L-1}] \tag{2}$$

$$\tilde{x}_{SLICE}^{L-1} = \begin{cases} x_{SLICE}^{L-1} + x_{SLICE}^{0^i} & Mask_i = 1 \\ x_{SLICE}^{0^i} & otherwise \end{cases} \tag{3}$$

where $\tilde{x}_{SLICE}^{L-1} = \{x_{SLICE}^{L-1^i}|i = 1,\ldots,N\}, x_{CLS}^{L-1}$ is text slice token, class token of the last layer, respectively. In order to make better advantage of the prior knowledge and reduce noise of the input, we generate text slice masks, based on the most task-relevant slices from the salience map calculated by Grad-CAM (Selvaraju et al., 2017a). In practice, we first calculate salience map of the input sentence. Then we record gradient values of text slice feature after slice embedding, get top k salient slices with largest absolute values, and take them as the most task-relevant and discriminative ones. The next step produces a binary mask by labeling the top k salient slices as **1** and the remaining ones as **0**. Generation of text slice mask is represented as:

$$g_i = Sum|\frac{\partial L(f(x),y)}{\partial x_{SLICE}^i}|, i = 1,...,N \tag{4}$$

$$Mask_i = \begin{cases} 1, if \ g_i \ in \ topkG \\ 0, otherwise \end{cases} \tag{5}$$

where $G \in R^N = \{g_1, g_2, ..., g_N\}$ is the salience map of slices $x_{SLICE} = x_{SLICE}^1, ..., x_{SLICE}^N$, topk G is the set of selected salient slices and $Mask = \{Mask_1, ..., Mask_N\}$ is the binary mask.

3.3   Knowledge Distillation

Based on masked slices, we feed them into vision Transformer and take the attended [CLS] of the output for classification. To improve classification ability and generalization ability of the model, Knowledge distillation strategy is adopted for having the model supervised by a teacher model. Knowledge distillation (KD) (Ba and Caruana, 2014) is an effective model-agnostic method to model compression, where a student model obtains knowledge, which is learnt by great but cumbersome teacher model(s). Specifically, KD forces the student to mimic the soft target probabilities of the teacher to achieve knowledge transfer. Hinton et al. (2015) highlighted that it is in favor of the generalizability of the student model to learn exact class probabilities from a better model. In practice, the student model is trained using a classification objective in combination with distillation objective:

$$\mathcal{L} = \mathcal{L}_{classification} + \lambda \mathcal{L}_{distill} \tag{6}$$

where λ is a hyperparameter used for weighing the two optimization objectives. $\mathcal{L}_{classification}$ term denotes the task-specific classification loss. $\mathcal{L}_{distill}$ term denotes knowledge distill loss. $\mathcal{L}_{classification}$ is cross-entropy loss between the target labels and the logits of the student model, while $\mathcal{L}_{distill}$ quantifies difference between the predictions of student model and the output of teacher model. In practice, we use a fine-tuned BERT model on classification task as the teacher model, and experiment with various baseline approaches for the student models. Like Hinton et al. (2015), we utilize $\mathcal{L}_{distill}$ as the Kullback-Leibler divergence between the output logits by the student model and the teacher BERT model. After knowledge transfer (training) and entering the inference (test) stage, BERT is fully removed, and the remaining part of Mg-VTT model can predict categories.

4   Experiments

4.1   Datasets

Open vocabulary make Mg-VTT compatible with different languages. So we conduct experiment in two data scenarios, an English one (MIMIC-CXR[1]) and a Chinese one (finding-impression pairs from Department of Radiology at the Second Xiangya Hospital (XiangYa Radiology Reports)).

MIMIC-CXR. The MIMIC Chest X-ray JPG (MIMIC-CXR-JPG) database v2.0.0 is a large publicly available dataset of chest X-rays in JPG format with structured tags derived from the source text radiology report MIMIC-CXR-JPG data The set is fully derived from MIMIC-CXR and provides JPG format files derived from Digital Imaging and Communications in Medicine (DICOM) images and structured tags derived from free text reports. The purpose of MIMIC-CXR-JPG is to provide a conveniently processed version of MIMIC-CXR and provide a standard reference for data segmentation and image labeling. The dataset contains 377,110 JPGs Format images and structured tags derived from 227,827 free-text radiology reports associated with these images. This chapter only covers text reports in which it is applied. This dataset was de-identified to meet

---

[1] https://physionet.org/content/mimic-cxr-jpg/2.0.0/.

the U.S. Health Insurance Portability and Accountability Act of 1996 (HIPAA) safe harbor requirements. Protected health information (PHI) has been deleted. The dataset is designed to support a wide range of medical research, including image understanding, natural language processing, and decision support. Contains 14 categories, they are: No Finding, Enlarged Cardiomediastinum, Cardiomegaly, Lung Opacity, Lung Lesion, Edema, Consolidation, Pneumonia, Atelectasis, Pneumothorax, Pleural Effusion, Pleural Other, Fracture, Support Devices. The data sets are labeled with 1 as having the disease, 0 as not having the disease, and -1 as not sure whether they have the disease. Note that there are uncertain labels in this data set. This chapter treats the existing uncertain labels as suffering from the disease. More importantly, 20,000 pieces of data were randomly selected to construct a noisy version through the "addition, deletion, and replacement" strategy to test the robustness of the model.

Xiangya Radiology Reports. The Xiangya Radiology Report Dataset is a radiology report collected by the Xiangya Medical Radiology Department in the past ten years. It consists of reported imaging findings and reported diagnostic opinions. In order to learn a more effective and robust language indicates that, combined with Hexiangya Medical Professional Dictionary[2] and English-Chinese Medical Dictionary[3] the entity nouns extracted from the report are mapped to English diseases (Smit et al., 2020) to construct a 14-category classification Data set (Irvin et al., 2019), the corresponding relationship is shown in Table 1, and the label annotation of disease or not also follows the method of CheXpert (Irvin et al., 2019). Following the training set/test set/evaluation set division of the data set in (i.e. 8:1:1) to conduct experiments.

4.2   Model Settings

Our proposed Mg-VTT model is based on vanilla ViT-Base (Dosovitskiy et al., 2020), which utilizes 12 Transformer layers with 12 attention heads to produce 768-dimensional representations from visual texts. Based on vanilla ViT-Base, we perform mask operation to guide ViT focusing on task-relevant and discriminative words. Our Mg-VTT model has 88.57M parameters, which is smaller than 109.5M parameters of BERT-base-uncased (Salesky et al., 2021). We conduct all the experiments using Tesla V100 GPU and run 60 training epochs with nearly the same batch size (≤ 4). Note that, in rendering text to visual text, we don't adopt padding, so the data cannot be packaged, which means the batch size is limited to 1. Our Mg-VTTs are optimized using SGD optimizer with a learning rate 1e−6. At each epoch, the model is evaluated on validation set. Based on validation performance, the best model is saved. After all training epochs, the best model is loaded and evaluated on the test set. The above process is repeated many times to compute mean scores as final performance of Mg-VTT models.

---

[2] http://www.mcd8.com/.

[3] 5 https://esaurus.org/.

Table 1. A tabular representation delineating the correspondence between 14 distinct disease categories and their corresponding Chinese entities.

Disease Category	Medical Explanation in Chinese	Medical Entity in Chinese
Atelectasis	1. Underinflation: The lung or part of the lung does not fully inflate. It can occur congenitally (primary or secondary), or it can be an acquired disease; 2. Atelectasis: the once-expanded lung becomes airless; 3. Lung collapse	Atelectasis
Consolidation	Consolidation: The process or state of forming a solid, such as in pneumonia, when the alveoli are filled with exudate and the lungs consolidate.	Exudative lesions, consolidation, bilateral pulmonary congestion, increased pulmonary blood
Lung Opacity	Infiltration: the diffusion or accumulation of some components that are not normally present (or exceed the normal amount) in tissues or cells	Diffusion Disease
Pneumothorax	Pneumothorax: an accumulation of air or other gas in the chest cavity, which may occur spontaneously, as a result of trauma or some pathological change, or as a result of intentional introduction	Pneumothorax, Emphysema, Pneumothorax
Edema	Edema: The accumulation of abnormally large amounts of fluid in the interstitial spaces, usually in the subcutaneous tissue. Edema may be localized, such as due to venous or lymphatic obstruction or increased vascular permeability	Edema
Lung Lesion	fibrosis, fibrosis: the formation of fibrous tissue; fibrosis or fibrosis	fibrosis
Pleural Effusion	1. Exudation; 2. Exudate: divided into exudation and leakage according to protein content	Effusion
Pneumonia	Pneumonia: Inflammation of the lungs with consolidation	Pneumonia, patchy density increased shadow
Pleural Other	pleural hypertrophy, pleural thickening	pleural thickening
Cardiomegaly	cardiac hypertrophy	Increased heart shadow
Fracture	Fractures in the chest	Fractures
Enlarge Cardiomediastinum	mediastinal enlargement	mediastinal enlargement
No Finding	No disease	No obvious main lesions were found, no obvious exudative lesions were found in both lungs, and no obvious main lesions were found.
Support Devices	PICC	PICC.

4.3   Comparison with Other Vision Models and Text Models

Mg-VTT achieves a mode using vision models to process text data. To demonstrate effectiveness of Mg-VTT, we compare Mg-VTT model with classic vision models and traditional text models in this subsection.

4.3.1   Baseline Vision Models

Since our proposed Mg-VTT model provides a mode to directly apply CV model to text data without modification, we replace MG-ViT with classic vision models, such as ViT, for experiments to test feasibility of the mode. Except for replacing the visual model, other original parameter settings are retained, so that the comparison experiment can test effectiveness of the mask mechanism for attention distribution on slices. As reported in Table 2, Mg-VTT outperforms vanilla ViT-Base by 0.03 from 0.84 to 0.87. We attribute it to that Mg-VTT can locate key words more accurately by performing mask operation.

Table 2. Averaged Precision, Recall and F1 values in text classification task for Xiangya radiology reports subset. (Number of convolutional blocks is denoted by c. PT denotes pre-trained. KD denotes knowledge-distill)

Model	PT	KD	Precision	Recall	F1
ViT	✗	✓	0.84	0.83	0.84
Mg-ViT($c=1$)			0.91	0.88	0.90

Table 3. Averaged Precision, Recall and F1 values in text classification task based on Xiangya Radiology Reports subset. (Number of convolutional blocks is denoted by c. PT denotes pre-trained. KD denotes knowledge-distill)

Model	PT	KD	Precision	Recall	F1
TextCNN	✗	✗	0.82	0.80	0.81
TextRNN			0.83	0.81	0.82
Transformer			0.85	0.85	0.85
BERT	✓		0.96	0.93	0.95
Mg-ViT($c=0$)	✗	✓	0.52	0.51	0.52
Mg-ViT($c=1$)			0.91	0.88	0.90
Mg-ViT($c=0$)			0.85	0.83	0.84

4.3.2   Baseline Text Models

We use TextCNN (Chen, 2015), TextRNN (Liu et al., 2016), Transformer (Vaswani et al., 2017) and BERT (Devlin et al., 2018) as baseline text models. Note, TextCNN, TextRNN and Transformer are one-stage models, while BERT is two-stage model. All the above text models are trained using transformers[4]. For baseline text models, we follow the recommended architecture and

---

[4] https://github.com/huggingface/transformers.

optimization parameters with slight modifications to batch size and vocabulary. Our Mg-VTT($c = 1$) model achieves best performance among all one-stage models, while performs slightly worse than BERT, which is pre-trained on large-scale corpora. Experimental results can be found in Table 3 and detailed analysis of the results is presented in Subsect. 4.4 (Table 5).

Table 4. Averaged Precision, Recall and F1 values in text classification task for Xiangya Radiology Reports subset. (Number of convolutional blocks is denoted by c. PT denotes pre-trained. KD denotes knowledge-distill)

Model	PT	KD	Precision	Recall	F1
Mg-ViT($c=0$)	✗	✓	0.52	0.52	0.52
Mg-ViT($c=7$)			0.40	0.40	0.40

Table 5. Averaged F1 values in text classification and computational time cost for Mg-VTT and Transformer on the two datasets. (Number of convolutional blocks is denoted by c. PT denotes pre-trained. KD denotes knowledge-distill. XY denotes Xiangya Radiology Reports. CX denotes MIMIC-CXR)

Model	PT	KD	F1		Time	
			XY	CX	XY	CX
Transformer	✗	✓	0.85	0.85	×1.3	×1.2
Mg-VTT($c=1$)			0.90	0.87	×1.0	×1.0

4.4 Chasing Classification Parity

Mg-VTT replaces classical text embedding process with the visual text embedding. Pygame Python package[5] with Google Noto font family[6] is used for rendering text. For Chinese text, we use NotoSansCJK JP in pygame Python package, and for English text, we use NotoSans in the package. No preprocessing is applied before rendering except adding spaces to avoid overlapping. Mg-VTT avoids predetermining a fixed model vocabulary, but an optimized finite vocabulary may have good contribution to classification performance. Thus, the first concern is whether visual text can recover performance produced by baseline models with predetermined and optimized sub-word vocabularies. For radiology reports subset, we can obtain best results among the one stage models (i.e.,

---

[5] https://www.pygame.org.
[6] https://www.google.com/get/noto.

TextCNN, TextRNN and Transformer). Table 3 lists experimental results of our proposed Mg-VTT($c = 0/1/2$) model and baseline text models. From the table, we found that TextRNN performs better than TextCNN. Since neurons of TextRNN are sequentially associated, TextRNN is more suitable than TextCNN to process text sequences. Performance of Transformer is better than that of TextRNN, because Transformer overcomes TextRNN's reliance on past hidden states to learn current words representations, which is more helpful for learning text representations on concise data, like news. Mask-guided mechanism and knowledge distillation help Mg-VTT perform better than Transformer, because mask-guided mechanism can help Mg-VTT model learn to focus on key words according to its importance, while knowledge distillation lets Mg-VTT model learn semantically rich representations. BERT, as a two-stages model, benefits from pre-training data in the pre-training stage, and is fine-tuned on news data during classification stage, which naturally results in better classification performance than one-stage models. Table 2 also shows classification performance of our proposed Mg-VTT model varies with c. We set $c = 0$, $c = 1$ and $c = 2$ for experiment. The result shows that the best visual text results are obtained when using $c = 1$ convolutional block. The convolutional block ($c = 1$) could add some useful structural biases from convolutions without too much visual depth. In the following, we compare $c = 0$ and $c = 7$, which mean no convolutional blocks and the depth of state-of the-art OCR models (Rawls et al., 2017), respectively. Table 4 shows no signs of improvement of classification performance with greater visual capacity via a larger number of convolutional blocks.

5   Conclusion

We propose a novel Mask-guided Visual Text Transformer (Mg-VTT) by incorporating the use of visual text representations and a mask mechanism into Vision Transformer. Our main contribution is the combination between visual text representation and vision model, which drops the wordpiece system and classical text models altogether. The model consults the visually rendered texts, producing robust, word-level, open-vocabulary representations. Another contribution is our proposed mask mechanism, which produces guidance for effectively focusing on task-relevant words by performing a simple slice mask operation on visually rendered text. Experimental results show that our proposed Mg-VTT globally outperforms vanilla Transformer and Vision Transformer.

Acknowledgement. This work was supported in part by the National Natural Science Foundation of China under Grants 62372380 and U22B2036.

References

Ba, J., Caruana, R.: Do deep nets really need to be deep? In: Advances in Neural Information Processing Systems, vol. 27 (2014)

Cai, X., Liu, S., Han, J., Yang, L., Liu, Z., Liu, T.: Chestxraybert: a pretrained language model for chest radiology report summarization. IEEE Trans. Multimedia (2021)

Chen, Y.: Convolutional neural network for sentence classification. Master's thesis, University of Waterloo (2015)

Chen, Y., et al.: Mask-guided vision transformer (MG-VIT) for few-shot learning. arXiv preprint arXiv:2205.09995 (2022)

Dai, F.Z., Cai, Z.: Glyph-aware embedding of Chinese characters. arXiv preprint arXiv:1709.00028 (2017)

Devlin, J., Chang, M.-W., Lee, K., Toutanova, K.:. Bert: pre-training of deep bidirectional transformers for language understanding. arXiv preprint arXiv:1810.04805 (2018)

Dosovitskiy, A., et al.: An image is worth 16x16 words: transformers for image recognition at scale. arXiv preprint arXiv:2010.11929 (2020)

Elwany, E., Moore, D., Oberoi, G.: Bert goes to law school: quantifying the competitive advantage of access to large legal corpora in contract understanding. arXiv preprint arXiv:1911.00473 (2019)

Hinton, G., Vinyals, O., Dean, J., et al.: Distilling the knowledge in a neural network. arXiv preprint arXiv:1503.02531 $\mathbf{2}$(7) (2015)

Irvin, J., et al.: Chexpert: a large chest radiograph dataset with uncertainty labels and expert comparison. In: Proceedings of the AAAI Conference on Artificial Intelligence, vol. 33, pp. 590–597 (2019)

Lee, J., et al.: Biobert: a pre-trained biomedical language representation model for biomedical text mining. Bioinformatics $\mathbf{36}$(4), 1234–1240 (2020)

Li, Y., Zhang, K., Cao, J., Timofte, R., Van Gool, L.: LocalViT: bringing locality to vision transformers. arXiv preprint arXiv:2104.05707 (2021)

Liu, P., Qiu, X., Huang, X.:. Recurrent neural network for text classification with multi-task learning. arXiv preprint arXiv:1605.05101 (2016)

Luo, R., et al.: BioGPT: generative pre-trained transformer for biomedical text generation and mining. arXiv preprint arXiv:2210.10341 (2022)

Meng, Y., et al.: Glyph-vectors for Chinese character representations. arXiv preprint arXiv:1901.10125 (2019)

Rawls, S., Cao, H., Kumar, S., Natarajan, P.: Combining convolutional neural networks and LSTMs for segmentation-free OCR. In: 2017 14th IAPR International Conference on Document Analysis and Recognition (ICDAR), vol. 1, pp. 155–160. IEEE (2017)

Ryskina, M., Gormley, M.R., Berg-Kirkpatrick, T.: Phonetic and visual priors for decipherment of informal romanization. arXiv preprint arXiv:2005.02517 (2020)

Salesky, E., Etter, D., Post, M.: Robust open-vocabulary translation from visual text representations. arXiv preprint arXiv:2104.08211 (2021)

Selvaraju, R.R., Cogswell, M., Das, A., Vedantam, R., Parikh, D., Batra, D.: Gradcam: visual explanations from deep networks via gradient-based localization. In: Proceedings of the IEEE International Conference on Computer Vision, pp. 618–626 (2017a)

Selvaraju, R.R., Cogswell, M., Das, A., Vedantam, R., Parikh, D., Batra, D.: Gradcam: visual explanations from deep networks via gradient-based localization. In: Proceedings of the IEEE International Conference on Computer Vision, pp. 618–626 (2017b)

Smit, A., Jain, S., Rajpurkar, P., Pareek, A., Ng, A.Y., Lungren, M.P.: ChexBert: combining automatic labelers and expert annotations for accurate radiology report labeling using Bert. arXiv preprint arXiv:2004.09167 (2020)

Sun, B., Yang, L., Dong, P., Zhang, W., Dong, J., Young, C.: Super characters: a conversion from sentiment classification to image classification. arXiv preprint arXiv:1810.07653 (2018)

Touvron, H., Cord, M., Douze, M., Massa, F., Sablayrolles, A., Jégou, H.: Training data-efficient image transformers & distillation through attention. In: International Conference on Machine Learning, pp. 10347–10357. PMLR (2021)

Vaswani, A., et al.: Attention is all you need. In: Advances in Neural Information Processing Systems, vol. 30 (2017)

Yuan, K., Guo, S., Liu, Z., Zhou, A., Yu, F., Wu, W.: Incorporating convolution designs into visual transformers. In: Proceedings of the IEEE/CVF International Conference on Computer Vision, pp. 579–588 (2021)

Zhang, Z., Zhang, H., Zhao, L., Chen, T., Pfister, T.: Aggregating nested transformers. arXiv preprint arXiv:2105.12723 (2021)

MCIGLE: Multimodal Exemplar-Free Class-Incremental Graph Learning

Haochen You[1][(✉)] and Baojing Liu[2]

[1] Graduate School of Arts and Sciences, Columbia University, New York, USA
`hy2854@columbia.edu`
[2] School of Artificial Intelligence, Hebei Institute of Communications, Shijiazhuang,
People's Republic of China
`liubj@hebic.edu.cn`

Abstract. Exemplar-free class-incremental learning enables models to learn new classes over time without storing data from old ones. As multimodal graph-structured data becomes increasingly prevalent, existing methods struggle with challenges like catastrophic forgetting, distribution bias, memory limits, and weak generalization. We propose **MCIGLE**, a novel framework that addresses these issues by extracting and aligning multimodal graph features and applying Concatenated Recursive Least Squares for effective knowledge retention. Through multi-channel processing, MCIGLE balances accuracy and memory preservation. Experiments on public datasets validate its effectiveness and generalizability.

Keywords: Knowledge Representation · Multimodal · Continual Learning · Class-Incremental Learning · Graph Structure

1 Introduction

Class-Incremental Learning (CIL) addresses the challenge of incrementally learning new classes without forgetting previously learned ones, especially without access to historical data [13,25]. It has broad applications, including dynamic classification, continual learning, and privacy-sensitive scenarios [12]. Among CIL variants, exemplar-free learning is particularly challenging due to its strict constraint of not retaining any old class samples [15].

Without historical samples, exemplar-free CIL cannot rely on replay mechanisms and becomes more susceptible to catastrophic forgetting [14]. Parameter updates for new classes may interfere with learned representations, degrading performance on old classes [20]. As a result, the model must rely on parameter regularization, knowledge distillation, or generated features-requiring strong generalization.

With the growth of large-scale multimodal data, CIL has increasingly focused on learning from diverse modalities (e.g., text, images, audio) while retaining prior knowledge [6,16]. In many real-world scenarios, such data form structured

T. Zhu et al. (Eds.): KSEM 2025, LNAI 15922, pp. 209–217, 2026.
https://doi.org/10.1007/978-981-95-3058-8_18

relationships-like user interactions or item co-occurrence—that are naturally represented as graphs [22]. Graphs support dynamic topology, making them well-suited for continual learning. However, integrating graph-structured multimodal data remains underexplored. Existing approaches often rely on fixed GNN architectures, which lack scalability and adaptability, exacerbating forgetting in evolving tasks [2, 10].

To address the existing challenges, we integrate multiple key modules in this paper and propose a novel framework. Our main contributions are given:

(i) We propose a novel multimodal exemplar-free class-incremental graph learning framework, **MCIGLE**, illustrated in Fig. 1.
(ii) To capture and align multimodal graph-structured features, we design a Multimodal Feature Processing Module and a Periodic Feature Extraction Module. Additionally, a Non-Forgetting Mainstream Module, based on Concatenated Recursive Least Squares, and a Residual Fitting Enhancement Module help mitigate forgetting and compensate for historical knowledge.
(iii) Extensive comparative and ablation experiments on four public datasets validate the effectiveness, robustness, and generalization capability of MCIGLE.

2   Multimodal Class-Incremental Learning

2.1   Multimodal Feature Processing Module

This module processes sequential multimodal graph structures with textual and visual modalities [3], aligning information across modalities to support node classification in evolving graphs under continual learning.

Each modality $m \in \{v, t\}$ is represented as a graph $G_m = (V_m, E)$, where $V_m = \{X^m \mid X^m \in I_m\}$ and $E = \{(i, j)\}$. For the l-th layer, the feature update for node u in modality m is:

$$h_{u,m}^{(l)} = \sigma \left(W_m^{(l)} \cdot \Phi_{l,m} \left(\left\{ h_{v,m}^{(l-1)} : v \in N(u) \right\} \right) \right), \tag{1}$$

Here, $\Phi_{l,m}$ aggregates neighbor features using correlation-based weighting:

$$\Phi_{l,m} \left(\left\{ h_{v,m}^{(l-1)} \right\} \right) = \text{Agg} \left(\left\{ e_{u,v,m}^{(l)} h_{v,m}^{(l-1)} \right\} \right), \tag{2}$$

where $e_{u,v,m}^{(l)}$ is the correlation coefficient.

We align and fuse features via optimal transport. Specifically, visual features $h_{u,v}$ are projected to the textual feature space using the transport plan P^*:

$$h_u' = h_{u,v \to t} \| h_{u,t}, \quad \text{where } h_{u,v \to t} = P^* h_{u,v}, \tag{3}$$

and

$$P^* = \arg \min_{\mathbf{P} \in \mathcal{P}} \sum_{i,i',j,j'} \mathbf{P}_{ij} \left(\lambda_1 \mathbf{C}(x_i, y_j) + (1 - \lambda_1) \mathbf{L}(x_i, y_j, x_{i'}, y_{j'}) \mathbf{P}_{i'j'} \right) + \epsilon W(\mathbf{P}). \tag{4}$$

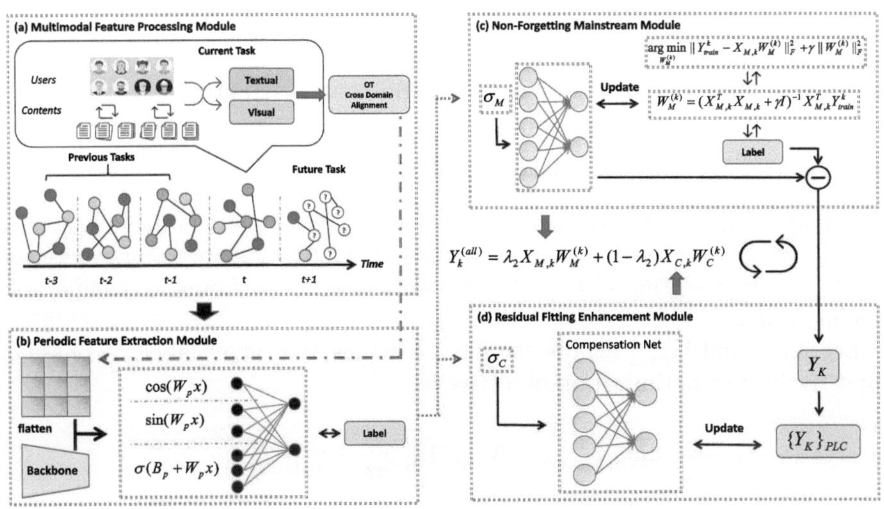

Fig. 1. Framework of **MCIGLE**.

where $\mathbf{C}$ is cost matrix, $\mathbf{L}$ the node similarity, and W the regularization term. Finally, node labels are predicted by:

$$\hat{y}_u = \mathrm{softmax}\left(\tanh\left(Wh_u^{(l)} + b\right)\right),\tag{5}$$

with W and b being trainable parameters.

2.2 Periodic Feature Extraction Module

After obtaining node-level embeddings, we flatten them into a global feature matrix and normalize the input. The data is then passed through neural layers based on Fourier analysis [7], with each layer defined as:

$$\phi^{(l)}(x) = \left[\cos\left(W_p^{(l)}x\right)\,\Big\|\,\sin\left(W_p^{(l)}x\right)\,\Big\|\,\sigma\left(B_{\bar{p}}^{(l)} + W_{\bar{p}}^{(l)}x\right)\right],$$

where x is the input, σ is a nonlinear activation (e.g., GELU or ReLU), and W_p, $W_{\bar{p}}$, $B_{\bar{p}}$ are trainable parameters. The full output is:

$$X_{\mathrm{FAN}} = \phi^{(L)} \circ \cdots \circ \phi^{(1)}(X_{\mathrm{norm}}).\tag{6}$$

We train the network using backpropagation with cross-entropy loss and optimizers such as AdamW. The output X_{FAN} is passed to a classifier head for final predictions:

$$\hat{Y} = \mathrm{softmax}(X_{\mathrm{FAN}} \cdot W_{FCN}),\tag{7}$$

with W_{FCN} optimized jointly. After training, all parameters are frozen for later incremental phases.

Fourier-based layers effectively capture periodic patterns with fewer parameters than CNNs or MLPs, improving efficiency and representation quality. This enhances inputs for both the mainstream and compensation stages.

2.3 Non-Forgetting Mainstream Module

This module addresses class-incremental learning via analytical linear mapping using Concatenated Recursive Least Squares (C-RLS), enabling recursive weight updates without storing historical data and achieving performance comparable to joint training.

Let $X_{M,k}$ and Y_{train}^k denote the input features and target labels at phase k, respectively. The optimization objective is:

$$\underset{W_M^{(k)}}{\arg\min} \left\| Y_{train}^k - X_{M,k}W_M^{(k)} \right\|_F^2 + \gamma \left\| W_M^{(k)} \right\|_F^2, \tag{8}$$

where γ is a regularization parameter. The closed-form ridge regression solution is omitted for brevity.

To support efficient updates, we define an autocorrelation matrix Φ_k and a cross-correlation matrix Z_k, both updated recursively with forgetting factor β. The inverse Φ_k^{-1} is maintained using the Sherman–Morrison formula without direct matrix inversion [8].

The final recursive weight update is given by:

$$\hat{W}_M^{(k)} = \hat{W}_M^{(k-1)} + k_k \left(Y_{train}^k - X_{M,k}\hat{W}_M^{(k-1)} \right), \tag{9}$$

where the gain coefficient is:

$$k_k = \frac{\Phi_{k-1}^{-1}X_{M,k}^T}{\beta + X_{M,k}\Phi_{k-1}^{-1}X_{M,k}^T}. \tag{10}$$

2.4 Residual Fitting Enhancement Module

Due to the linear nature of the Non-Forgetting Mainstream Module, it may underfit complex samples [23]. To address this, we introduce a Residual Fitting Enhancement Module that captures the residual information missed by the main stream via independent feature projection and nonlinear transformations.

After training, the residual matrix is defined as:

$$\widetilde{Y}_k = \left[0_{N_{0:k-1} \times d_{y,k-1}}, Y_k^{train} \right] - X_{M,k}W_M^{(k)}, \tag{11}$$

representing prediction errors, where the zero matrix enforces phase-wise label exclusivity [27].

The compensation stream generates embeddings via:

$$X_{C,k} = \sigma_C \left(B \left(\text{flat} \left(\text{CNN} \left(X_k^{train}, W_{CNN} \right) \right) \right) \right), \tag{12}$$

with σ_C (e.g., Tanh or Mish) different from the main stream's activation to capture complementary features [9].

To avoid error propagation from earlier phases, only the current-phase component of $\widetilde{Y}_k$ is retained:

$$\left\{\widetilde{Y}_k\right\}_{\mathrm{PLC}} = \left[0_{N_{0:k-1} \times d_{y,k-1}}, \left(\widetilde{Y}_k\right)_{\mathrm{new}}\right]. \tag{13}$$

The compensation weights are updated using C-RLS:

$$W_C^{(k)} = W_C^{(k-1)'} + R_{C,k} X_{C,k}^T \left(\left\{\widetilde{Y}_k\right\}_{\mathrm{PLC}} - X_{C,k} W_C^{(k-1)'}\right),$$

where $R_{C,k}$ is the inverse correlation matrix of the compensation stream.

The final prediction combines both streams:

$$\hat{Y}_k^{(\mathrm{all})} = \lambda_2 X_{M,k} W_M^{(k)} + (1 - \lambda_2) X_{C,k} W_C^{(k)}, \tag{14}$$

with λ_2 controlling the compensation contribution.

3 Experiments

We evaluate **MCIGLE** on four public datasets-**COCO-QA**[1], **VoxCeleb**[2], **SNLI-VE**[3], and **AudioSet-MI**[4] compare it with state-of-the-art methods including **CavRL** [26], **TAM-CL** [4], **GMM** [5], **DS-AL** [27], and **MedCoSS** [24]. As shown in Table 1, **MCIGLE** consistently outperforms baselines across most metrics and datasets, achieving high accuracy and low forgetting. The only exception is the Acc metric on AudioSet-MI, where CavRL performs better, which is expected given its specialization in audio-visual incremental learning. Figures 2 aand 2 bfurther illustrate the accuracy trends over cumulative classes on AudioSet-MI and VoxCeleb.

To verify component effectiveness, we conducted ablation studies by replacing key modules with representative alternatives. For Periodic Feature Extraction Module, we compared our Fourier-based network with **KAN** [11], **FNN** [19], and **SIREN** [17], as shown in Fig. 3 a. Results demonstrate superior accuracy and lower forgetting, validating our design for modeling temporal evolution.

We also replaced the C-RLS-based mechanism with classical forgetting mitigation approaches, including knowledge distillation [21], parameter regularization [1], and memory replay [18]. As shown in Fig. 3 b, our model consistently achieves a lower forgetting rate, confirming the robustness of the C-RLS design.

---

[1] https://www.cs.toronto.edu/~mren/research/imageqa/data/cocoqa/.
[2] https://www.robots.ox.ac.uk/~vgg/data/voxceleb/.
[3] https://github.com/necla-ml/SNLI-VE.
[4] https://research.google.com/audioset/index.html.

Table 1. Overall Performance of our model MCIGLE and the baselines.

Method	COCO-QA				VoxCeleb			
	Acc ↑	F ↓	BwF ↓	$\mathbb{T}_{\mathbf{F}}(j \leftarrow i)$ ↓	Acc ↑	F ↓	BwF ↓	$\mathbb{T}_{\mathbf{F}}(j \leftarrow i)$ ↓
CavRL	0.739	0.175	0.297	0.250	0.915	0.237	0.249	0.273
TAM-CL	0.741	0.199	0.363	0.267	0.860	0.213	0.291	0.204
GMM	0.698	0.154	0.413	0.312	0.832	0.305	0.314	0.357
DS-AL	0.749	0.269	0.321	0.288	0.904	0.246	0.285	0.190
MedCoSS	0.721	0.188	0.306	0.274	0.892	0.317	0.247	0.185
MCIGLE	**0.782**	**0.094**	**0.273**	**0.148**	**0.927**	**0.193**	**0.235**	**0.164**

Method	SNLI-VE				AudioSet-MI			
CavRL	0.740	0.258	0.302	0.204	0.685	0.194	0.455	0.211
TAM-CL	0.697	0.192	0.247	0.305	0.644	0.154	0.409	0.182
GMM	0.725	0.190	0.387	0.196	0.599	0.216	0.398	0.208
DS-AL	0.752	0.183	0.395	0.251	0.637	0.165	0.493	0.167
MedCoSS	0.641	0.140	0.372	0.209	0.671	0.251	0.413	0.253
MCIGLE	**0.767**	**0.131**	**0.195**	**0.182**	**0.683**	**0.095**	**0.352**	**0.149**

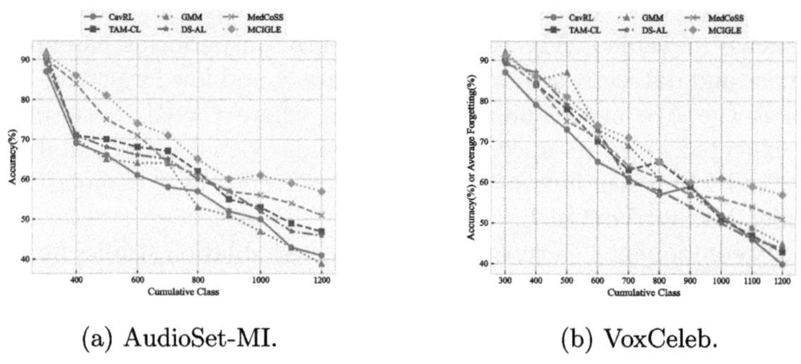

(a) AudioSet-MI.   (b) VoxCeleb.

Fig. 2. Changes in Prediction Accuracy of Various Models with Cumulative Class.

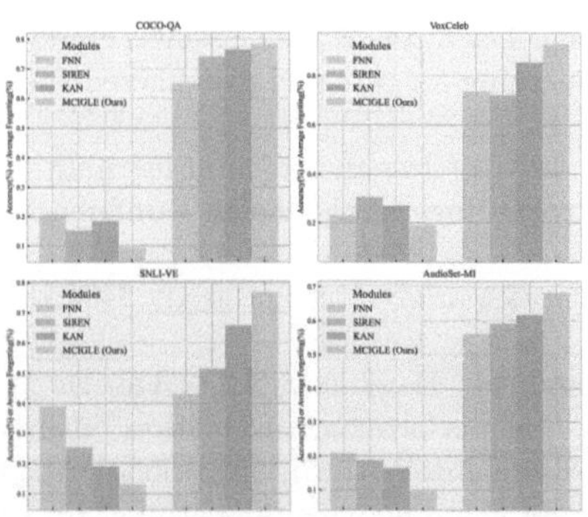

(a) Ablation study replacing Fourier network with FNN, SIREN, and KAN.

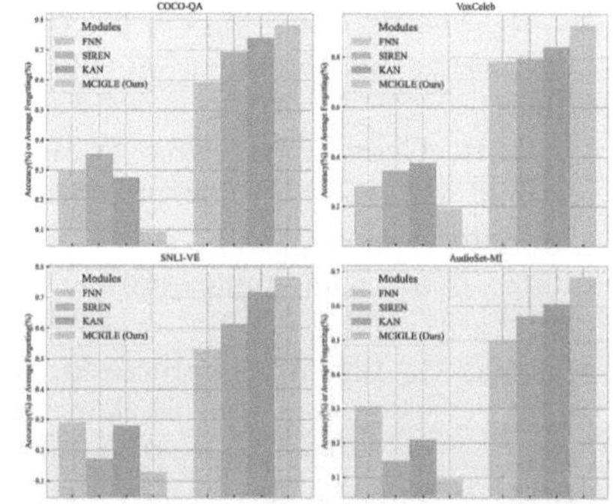

(b) Ablation study replacing C-RLS with TA, UCL, and DGR.

Fig. 3. Ablation results on accuracy and forgetting across model variants.

4   Conclusion

This paper integrates multiple key modules to propose **MCIGLE**, an exemplar-free multimodal class-incremental graph learning framework. It addresses several critical challenges in continual learning and achieves promising results on public datasets, laying a solid foundation for broader applications in this field.

References

1. Ahn, H., Cha, S., Lee, D., Moon, T.: Uncertainty-based continual learning with adaptive regularization. Adv. Neural Inf. Process. Syst. **32** (2019)
2. Belouadah, E., Popescu, A.: Il2m: class incremental learning with dual memory. In: Proceedings of the IEEE/CVF International Conference On Computer Vision, pp. 583–592 (2019)
3. Cai, J., et al.: Multimodal continual graph learning with neural architecture search. In: Proceedings of the ACM Web Conference 2022, pp. 1292–1300 (2022)
4. Cai, Y., Rostami, M.: Dynamic transformer architecture for continual learning of multimodal tasks. arXiv preprint arXiv:2401.15275 (2024)
5. Cao, X., Lu, H., Huang, L., Liu, X., Cheng, M.M.: Generative multi-modal models are good class incremental learners. In: Proceedings of the IEEE/CVF Conference on Computer Vision and Pattern Recognition, pp. 28706–28717 (2024)
6. D'Alessandro, M., Alonso, A., Calabrés, E., Galar, M.: Multimodal parameter-efficient few-shot class incremental learning. In: Proceedings of the IEEE/CVF International Conference on Computer Vision, pp. 3393–3403 (2023)
7. Dong, Y., et al.: Fan: fourier analysis networks. arXiv preprint arXiv:2410.02675 (2024)
8. Gao, J., Hu, W., Lu, Y.: Recursive least-squares estimator-aided online learning for visual tracking. In: Proceedings of the IEEE/CVF Conference on Computer Vision and Pattern Recognition, pp. 7386–7395 (2020)

9. He, H., Xie, H., Shen, G., Fu, B., You, H., Sanchez Silva, V.: 4s-classifier: empowering conservation through semi-supervised learning for rare and endangered species (2025)
10. Lei, C.H., Chen, Y.H., Peng, W.H., Chiu, W.C.: Class-incremental learning with rectified feature-graph preservation. In: Proceedings of the Asian Conference on Computer Vision (2020)
11. Liu, Z., et al.: Kan: kolmogorov-arnold networks. arXiv preprint arXiv:2404.19756 (2024)
12. Masana, M., Liu, X., Twardowski, B., Menta, M., Bagdanov, A.D., Van De Weijer, J.: Class-incremental learning: survey and performance evaluation on image classification. IEEE Trans. Pattern Anal. Mach. Intell. **45**(5), 5513–5533 (2022)
13. Mittal, S., Galesso, S., Brox, T.: Essentials for class incremental learning. In: Proceedings of the IEEE/CVF Conference on Computer Vision and Pattern Recognition, pp. 3513–3522 (2021)
14. Petit, G., Popescu, A., Schindler, H., Picard, D., Delezoide, B.: Fetril: feature translation for exemplar-free class-incremental learning. In: Proceedings of the IEEE/CVF Winter Conference on Applications of Computer Vision, pp. 3911–3920 (2023)
15. Petit, G., et al.: An analysis of initial training strategies for exemplar-free class-incremental learning. In: Proceedings of the IEEE/CVF Winter Conference on Applications of Computer Vision, pp. 1837–1847 (2024)
16. Pian, W., Mo, S., Guo, Y., Tian, Y.: Audio-visual class-incremental learning. In: Proceedings of the IEEE/CVF International Conference on Computer Vision, pp. 7799–7811 (2023)
17. Rußwurm, M., Klemmer, K., Rolf, E., Zbinden, R., Tuia, D.: Geographic location encoding with spherical harmonics and sinusoidal representation networks. arXiv preprint arXiv:2310.06743 (2023)
18. Shin, H., Lee, J.K., Kim, J., Kim, J.: Continual learning with deep generative replay. Adv. Neural Inf. Process. Syst. **30** (2017)
19. Silvescu, A.: Fourier neural networks. In: IJCNN'99. International Joint Conference on Neural Networks. Proceedings (Cat. No. 99CH36339). vol. 1, pp. 488–491. IEEE (1999)
20. Sun, W., Li, Q., Zhang, J., Wang, D., Wang, W., Geng, Y.a.: Exemplar-free class incremental learning via discriminative and comparable parallel one-class classifiers. Patt. Recogn. **140**, 109561 (2023)
21. Szatkowski, F., Pyla, M., Przewilikowski, M., Cygert, S., Twardowski, B., Trzciński, T.: Adapt your teacher: improving knowledge distillation for exemplar-free continual learning. In: Proceedings of the IEEE/CVF Winter Conference on Applications of Computer Vision, pp. 1977–1987 (2024)
22. Wang, S., Shi, W., Dong, S., Gao, X., Song, X., Gong, Y.: Semantic knowledge guided class-incremental learning. IEEE Trans. Circuits Syst. Video Technol. **33**(10), 5921–5931 (2023)
23. Xu, S., Ye, Y., Li, M., You, H., Wang, K., Zhang, W.: Drco: a toolkit for intelligently curbing illegal wildlife trade (2025)
24. Ye, Y., Xie, Y., Zhang, J., Chen, Z., Wu, Q., Xia, Y.: Continual self-supervised learning: Towards universal multi-modal medical data representation learning. In: Proceedings of the IEEE/CVF Conference on Computer Vision and Pattern Recognition, pp. 11114–11124 (2024)
25. Zhou, D.W., Wang, Q.W., Qi, Z.H., Ye, H.J., Zhan, D.C., Liu, Z.: Class-incremental learning: a survey. IEEE Trans. Patt. Anal. Mach. Intell. (2024)

26. Zhu, B., Wang, C., Xu, K., Feng, D., Zhou, Z., Zhu, X.: Learning incremental audio-visual representation for continual multimodal understanding. Knowl.-Based Syst. **304**, 112513 (2024)
27. Zhuang, H., He, R., Tong, K., Zeng, Z., Chen, C., Lin, Z.: Ds-al: A dual-stream analytic learning for exemplar-free class-incremental learning. In: Proceedings of the AAAI Conference on Artificial Intelligence. vol. 38, pp. 17237–17244 (2024)

MTCA-ViT: Multi-Modal Temporal Contrastive Vision Transformer for Depression Detection

Liangguo Wang[1,2], Yuxuan Wu[2], Jiaqian Wu[3(✉)], and Eziz Tursun[1]

[1] Xinjiang Hetian College, No. 169, West Beijing Road, Hetian City, Xinjiang 848000, People's Republic of China
lgwang@bistu.edu.cn

[2] Beijing Information Science and Technology University, No. 55, Taihang Road, Beijing 102206, People's Republic of China

[3] Beijing Anding Hospital, Capital Medical University, No. 5 An Kang Hutong, Beijing 100088, People's Republic of China
1310908555@qq.com

Abstract. Detecting depression poses a significant challenge in mental health assessment due to the complexity and subtlety inherent in behavioral manifestations. While traditional diagnostic methods rely on clinical interviews and questionnaires, they are often subjective, time-consuming, and may miss subtle behavioral indicators. The development of automated depression detection systems faces two critical challenges: effectively modeling the complex temporal patterns in behavioral manifestations, and capturing the intricate relationships between audio and visual modalities. To address these challenges, we propose MTCA-ViT, a novel multi-modal temporal contrastive vision transformer framework for automated depression detection. Our approach introduces two key innovations: a Cross-modal Contrastive Learning (CCL) strategy that effectively aligns representations while preserving modality-specific characteristics, and a Temporal Adaptive Attention (TAA) mechanism that dynamically captures depression-relevant temporal patterns in both modalities. Extensive experiments on the LMVD dataset demonstrate that our model outperforms existing methods across multiple evaluation metrics. This work represents a significant advancement in automated depression detection, offering both theoretical contributions to deep learning and practical value for mental health assessment.

Keywords: Depression Detection · Multi-modal · Vision Transformer · Temporal Attention · Contrastive Learning

1 Introduction

Depression is a severe mental health disorder affecting hundreds of millions of people worldwide [1], causing significant personal suffering and socioeconomic

T. Zhu et al. (Eds.): KSEM 2025, LNAI 15922, pp. 218–225, 2026.
https://doi.org/10.1007/978-981-95-3058-8_19

burden. Traditional diagnosis relies on clinical interviews and self-report questionnaires, which are time-consuming and subject to bias [2]. With the advancement of AI technologies, automated depression detection through audio-visual analysis has emerged as a promising approach to assist clinical diagnosis [3].

Developing effective automated depression detection systems faces several critical challenges. While existing studies have made progress using multimodal data [3,4], significant limitations remain. Depression manifests through subtle temporal patterns across multiple modalities, including visual features (facial expressions, body movements) and acoustic characteristics (speech prosody, voice quality) [4,5]. Current approaches often treat these patterns as simple sequential data, failing to model the varying significance of different temporal segments and their intricate relationships.

To address these limitations, we propose two key innovations. First, we introduce a cross-modal contrastive learning (CCL) strategy that aligns representations between audio and visual modalities while preserving their unique characteristics. Unlike conventional fusion approaches that simply concatenate features [8], our CCL framework learns a shared semantic space where complementary depression indicators are brought into alignment through contrastive objectives, maintaining modality-specific discriminative features crucial for depression detection [9].

Second, we develop a temporal adaptive attention (TAA) mechanism that dynamically adjusts attention weights to focus on depression-relevant temporal patterns. Traditional approaches often treat temporal information uniformly [6], potentially missing critical behavioral indicators. Our TAA mechanism identifies and emphasizes diagnostically significant temporal segments while suppressing irrelevant information, incorporating both local and global temporal contexts to capture fine-grained behavioral changes and long-term emotional patterns [7].

The main contributions of this work are threefold:

- We propose a novel cross-modal contrastive learning strategy that effectively aligns audio-visual representations while preserving modality-specific characteristics, enabling robust capture of complementary depression indicators across modalities.
- We develop an adaptive temporal attention mechanism that dynamically identifies and emphasizes depression-relevant temporal patterns, significantly improving the model's ability to detect subtle behavioral manifestations of depression.
- We conduct comprehensive experiments on the LMVD dataset demonstrating substantial improvements over state-of-the-art methods, and provide interpretable visualizations that offer insights into the model's decision-making process.

To validate our approach, we conduct extensive experiments on the LMVD dataset. Our model achieves substantial improvements over existing methods across multiple evaluation metrics. Through ablation studies, we demonstrate that both components contribute significantly to the model's performance.

2   Related Work

Depression detection research has evolved from single-modality approaches using hand-crafted features [3,10] to multimodal methods [4,11]. Early work extracted specific audio features and visual cues, but often employed simple fusion strategies. Recent deep learning approaches [4,11] have improved performance but typically rely on basic feature concatenation, failing to capture complex inter-modal relationships crucial for depression detection.

Contrastive learning has emerged as an effective paradigm for robust feature learning [12], though its application to audio-visual depression detection remains limited. Existing methods typically focus on image-text pairs rather than preserving modality-specific characteristics while learning aligned cross-modal representations [13].

Temporal modeling has progressed from RNN-based approaches [15] to transformer architectures with self-attention mechanisms [16]. However, current temporal attention techniques [17,18] may not be optimal for depression detection, which requires capturing subtle temporal patterns that vary significantly across modalities. Our work addresses these limitations through a novel temporal attention mechanism specifically designed for depression detection.

3   Methodology

3.1   Problem Formulation and Base Architecture

Given multimodal data with features $\mathcal{X}_i \in \mathbb{R}^{T_i \times D_i}$ from each modality i, our goal is to learn a mapping function $f : (\mathcal{X}_1, \mathcal{X}_2, ...) \to y \in \{0, 1\}$ for depression detection. Our model builds on the Vision Transformer architecture [14], where input features are embedded as:

$$E_i = \mathrm{Embed}(\mathcal{X}_i) + \mathrm{PosEmbed} + \mathrm{CLS}_i \tag{1}$$

These embeddings are processed through transformer layers

$$Z_l = \mathrm{TransformerLayer}(Z_{l-1}) \tag{2}$$

where Z_0 represents the concatenated embeddings from all modalities.

3.2   Cross-Modal Contrastive Learning

To enhance alignment between modalities while preserving modality-specific information, we propose a dual-path contrastive learning strategy, as illustrated in Fig. 1. The total contrastive loss combines intra-modal and inter-modal components:

$$\mathcal{L}_{\mathrm{contrast}} = \mathcal{L}_{\mathrm{intra}} + \lambda \mathcal{L}_{\mathrm{inter}} \tag{3}$$

The intra-modal loss $\mathcal{L}_{\mathrm{intra}}$ encourages consistency within each modality by contrasting positive pairs against negative pairs in a normalized feature space:

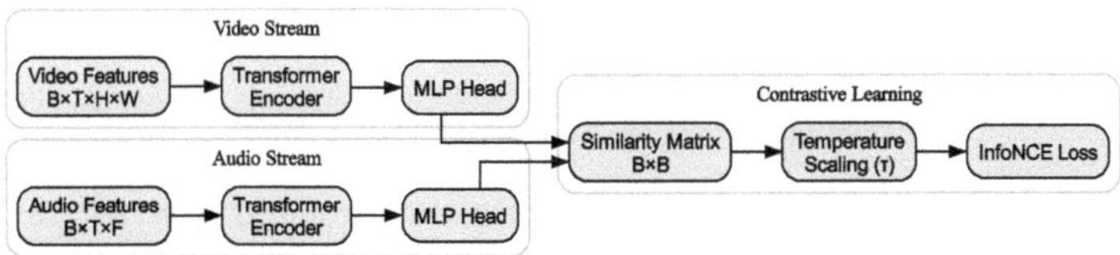

Fig. 1. Cross-modal contrastive learning framework: Parallel streams process video and audio inputs through transformer encoders and projection heads, with InfoNCE loss guiding cross-modal alignment.

$$\mathcal{L}_{\text{intra}} = - \sum_{m \in \{v,a\}} \log \frac{\exp(z_m^i \cdot z_m^j / \tau)}{\sum_{k=1}^{2N} \mathbb{1}_{[k \neq i]} \exp(z_m^i \cdot z_m^k / \tau)} \tag{4}$$

The inter-modal loss $\mathcal{L}_{\text{inter}}$ promotes alignment between modalities by maximizing agreement between corresponding audio-visual representations:

$$\mathcal{L}_{\text{inter}} = - \log \frac{\exp(z_v \cdot z_a / \tau)}{\sum_{k=1}^{N} \exp(z_v \cdot z_a^k / \tau)} \tag{5}$$

Here, τ is a temperature parameter that controls the sharpness of the distribution. This design enables the model to capture both modality-specific characteristics and cross-modal relationships critical for depression detection.

3.3 Temporal Adaptive Attention

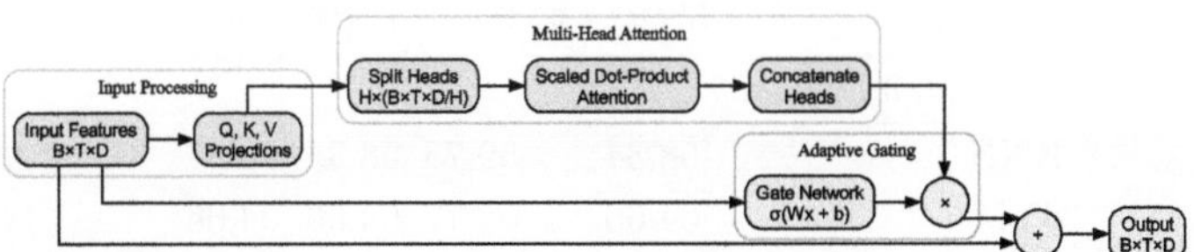

Fig. 2. Temporal adaptive attention mechanism with input processing, multi-head attention, and adaptive gating network to focus on depression-relevant temporal patterns.

To capture complex temporal patterns in depression manifestation, we introduce a temporal adaptive attention mechanism that extends standard multi-head self-attention with a learnable gating component, as shown in Fig. 2:

$$\text{TAA}(x) = \text{Gate}(x) \odot \text{MultiHead}(Q, K, V) + (1 - \text{Gate}(x)) \odot x \tag{6}$$

The gating mechanism $\text{Gate}(x) = \sigma(W_g x + b_g)$ learns to modulate attention output, dynamically focusing on depression-relevant temporal segments while suppressing irrelevant information.

The final prediction combines modality-specific representations:

$$y = \text{softmax}(W_c[\text{CLS}_v\|\text{CLS}_a] + b_c) \tag{7}$$

The overall training objective balances classification and contrastive learning:

$$\mathcal{L}_{\text{total}} = \mathcal{L}_{\text{cls}} + \alpha\mathcal{L}_{\text{contrast}} \tag{8}$$

This approach effectively addresses the two key challenges in depression detection: capturing temporal dynamics and learning aligned cross-modal representations.

4   Experiments

4.1   Experimental Settings

We conduct experiments on the LMVD dataset [19], containing vlog recordings with balanced depression/non-depression samples. We compare MTCA-ViT with traditional methods (KNN, SVM, LR, RF) and deep learning approaches (Xception [20], ViT [14], BiLSTM [6], SEResnet [21], MDDformer [19]). For evaluation, we employ 10-fold cross-validation with standard metrics (Accuracy, Precision, Recall, F1-score).

4.2   Results and Discussion

Table 1. Performance comparison with baseline methods on the LMVD dataset. Best results are highlighted in bold.

Method	ACC (%)	P (%)	R (%)	F1 (%)
Traditional Methods				
KNN	58.34	59.75	58.34	56.87
SVM	64.66	65.77	64.66	64.06
LR	64.88	65.19	64.88	64.73
RF	69.23	69.34	69.23	69.17
Deep Learning Methods				
Xception	71.38	71.94	71.38	71.19
BiLSTM	72.59	73.02	72.59	72.47
ViT	73.03	73.52	73.03	72.90
MDDformer	76.88	**77.02**	76.88	76.85
MTCA-ViT (Ours)	**77.19**	76.20	**79.82**	**77.76**

The experimental results presented in Table 1 demonstrate the effectiveness of MTCA-ViT across multiple evaluation metrics. Through comprehensive analysis, we identify several significant findings:

- **Superiority over Traditional Methods**: MTCA-ViT significantly outperforms conventional ML approaches (KNN, SVM, LR, Random Forest), highlighting the limitations of hand-crafted features in capturing complex depression-related behavioral patterns.
- **Competitive Deep Learning Performance**: MTCA-ViT shows consistent improvements over state-of-the-art deep learning approaches, particularly outperforming transformer-based models like MDDformer in recall and F1-score.

The superior performance of MTCA-ViT stems from two key innovations:

- **Enhanced Temporal Modeling**: Our temporal adaptive attention mechanism effectively captures depression-relevant dynamics across modalities, better modeling the evolution of behavioral patterns.
- **Effective Cross-modal Learning**: The contrastive framework enables robust alignment between modalities while preserving their distinctive characteristics, leading to more reliable depression detection.

These results demonstrate that MTCA-ViT effectively addresses the challenges in automated depression detection through its innovative architectural design. The consistent performance improvements across evaluation metrics validate the effectiveness of our approach.

4.3   Ablation Studies

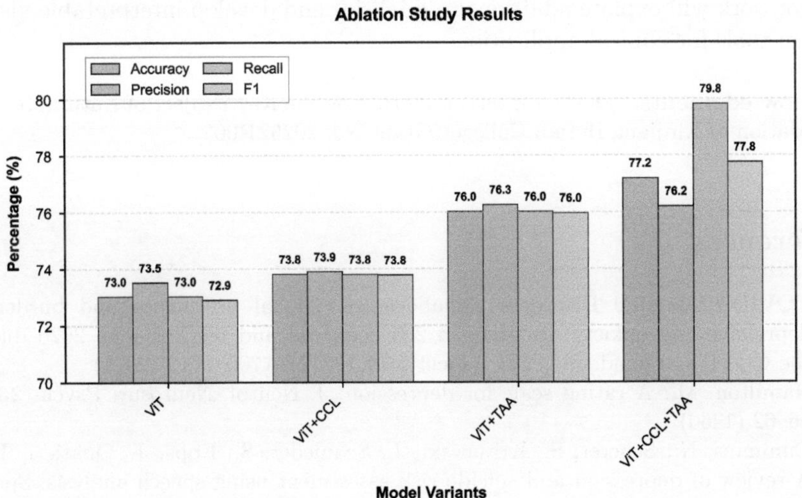

Fig. 3. Ablation analysis showing performance for four model variants: base ViT, ViT with CCL, ViT with TAA, and full MTCA-ViT.

To evaluate each component's contribution, we conduct ablation experiments with four model variants: (1) **Base-ViT**: standard transformer with basic multimodal fusion; (2) **ViT+CCL**: adding cross-modal contrastive learning; (3) **ViT+TAA**: adding temporal adaptive attention; and (4) **MTCA-ViT**: incorporating both CCL and TAA.

Results shown in Fig. 3 demonstrate that CCL improves performance by enabling better aligned multimodal representations, while TAA brings more substantial improvements through adaptive temporal modeling. The full MTCA-ViT model achieves the best overall performance, with particularly strong recall - crucial for clinical applications where missing depression cases has serious consequences. These results confirm that both components address complementary challenges in multimodal depression detection: CCL improves cross-modal alignment while preserving modality-specific characteristics, and TAA effectively captures temporal patterns essential for identifying subtle behavioral manifestations of depression.

5   Conclusion

We propose MTCA-ViT, a multi-modal temporal contrastive vision transformer framework for depression detection that introduces two key innovations: a Cross-modal Contrastive Learning strategy for aligning multi-modal representations while preserving modality-specific features, and a Temporal Adaptive Attention mechanism for capturing depression-relevant temporal patterns. Experiments on the LMVD dataset demonstrate that our model outperforms existing methods, with ablation studies confirming both components' significant contributions. Future work will explore additional modalities and develop interpretable visualization tools for clinical applications.

Acknowledgments. This work was supported by the Key Project of Natural Science Foundation of Xinjiang Hetian College (Grant No. 2025ZR002).

References

1. COVID-19 Mental Disorders Collaborators. Global prevalence and burden of depressive and anxiety disorders in 204 countries and territories in 2020 due to the COVID-19 pandemic. The Lancet **398**(10312), 1700–1712 (2021)
2. Hamilton, M.: A rating scale for depression. J. Neurol. Neurosur. Psych. **23**(1), 56–62 (1960)
3. Cummins, N., Scherer, S., Krajewski, J., Schnieder, S., Epps, J., Quatieri, T.F.: A review of depression and suicide risk assessment using speech analysis. Speech Commun. **71**, 10–49 (2015)
4. Yang, L., Jiang, D., He, L., Pei, E., Oveneke, M.C., Sahli, H.: Multimodal measurement of depression using deep learning models. In: Proceedings of the 7th Annual Workshop on Audio/Visual Emotion Challenge, pp. 53–59 (2017)

5. Fang, M., Peng, S., Liang, Y., Gong, Y., Lyu, X., Li, S.: A multimodal fusion model with multi-level attention mechanism for depression detection. Biomed. Signal Process. Control **82**, 104561 (2023)
6. Ma, X., Yang, H., Chen, Q., Huang, D., Wang, Y.: DepAudioNet: an efficient deep model for audio based depression classification. In: Proceedings of the 6th International Workshop on Audio/Visual Emotion Challenge, pp. 35–42 (2016)
7. Avola, D., Cinque, L., Fagioli, A., Foresti, G.L., Massaroni, C.: Deep temporal analysis for non-acted body affect recognition. IEEE Trans. Affect. Comput. **13**(3), 1366–1377 (2020)
8. Baltrušaitis, T., Ahuja, C., Morency, L.-P.: Multimodal machine learning: a survey and taxonomy. IEEE Trans. Patt. Anal. Mach. Intell. **41**(2), 423–443 (2018)
9. Pan, W., et al.: Exploring the ability of vocal biomarkers in distinguishing depression from bipolar disorder, schizophrenia, and healthy controls. Front. Psych. **14**, 1079448 (2023)
10. Zhu, Y., Shang, Y., Shao, Z., Guo, G.: Automated depression diagnosis based on deep networks to encode facial appearance and dynamics. IEEE Trans. Affect. Comput. **9**(4), 578–584 (2017)
11. Alghowinem, S., et al.: Multimodal depression detection: Fusion analysis of paralinguistic, head pose and eye gaze behaviors. IEEE Trans. Affect. Comput. **9**(4), 478–490 (2016)
12. Chen, T., Kornblith, S., Norouzi, M., Hinton, G.: A simple framework for contrastive learning of visual representations. In: International Conference on Machine Learning, pp. 1597–1607 (2020)
13. Wang, X., Wu, Y., Zhu, L., Yang, Y. : Symbiotic attention with privileged information for egocentric action recognition. In: Proceedings of the AAAI Conference on Artificial Intelligence, vol. 34, no. 07, pp. 12249–12256 (2020)
14. Dosovitskiy, A., et al.: An image is worth 16x16 words: Transformers for image recognition at scale. In: International Conference on Learning Representations (2021)
15. Choi, E., et al.: Retain: An interpretable predictive model for healthcare using reverse time attention mechanism. Adv. Neural Inf. Process. Syst. **29** (2016)
16. Vaswani, A., et al.: Attention is all you need. Adv. Neural Inf. Process. Syst. **30** (2017)
17. Golovanevsky, M., Eickhoff, C., Singh, R.: Multimodal attention-based deep learning for Alzheimer's disease diagnosis. J. Am. Med. Inf. Assoc. **29**(12), 2014–2022 (2022)
18. Cui, D., Xin, C., Wu, L., Wang, Y., Zhang, J.: ConvTransformer Attention Network for temporal action detection. Knowledge-Based Syst. **300**, 112264 (2024)
19. Zhang, Y., Wang, X., Li, H., Yang, Y., Li, X.: LMVD: a large-scale multimodal vlog dataset for depression detection in the wild. In: Proceedings of the IEEE/CVF Conference on Computer Vision and Pattern Recognition (CVPR), pp. 20961–20971 (2023)
20. Chollet, F.: Xception: Deep learning with depthwise separable convolutions. In: Proceedings of the IEEE Conference on Computer Vision and Pattern Recognition, pp. 1251–1258 (2017)
21. Hu, J., Shen, L., Sun, G.: Squeeze-and-excitation networks. In: Proceedings of the IEEE Conference on Computer Vision and Pattern Recognition, pp. 7132–7141 (2018)

SGCoT: Self-generating Chain-Of-Thought for Discipline Classification

Peng Yu[1,2] , Faren Yan[1,2] , and Xin Chen[1,2]

[1] Computer Network Information Center, Chinese Academy of Sciences, Beijing, China
{pyu,fryan,chx}@cnic.cn
[2] University of Chinese Academy of Sciences, Beijing, China

Abstract. This paper proposes SGCoT, an innovative framework for scientific data discipline classification that addresses critical challenges in multilingual support and cross-domain adaptability. Unlike traditional methods constrained by structured data requirements or annotation dependency, SGCoT integrates two key points: (1) A self-generated Chain-of-Thought mechanism that autonomously constructs reasoning processes through few-shot prompting, eliminating manual annotation; (2) Knowledge distillation that reduces inference costs by a factor of 10 while maintaining 66.4% accuracy comparable to supervised models. Experimental results on the CSLDCP dataset demonstrate superior performance over existing approaches, achieving 62.12% accuracy with GPT-4o-mini and 66.41% with GPT-4o, while significantly lowering annotation costs for 36M scientific records in practical deployments.

Keywords: Natural Language Processing · Large Language Models · Prompt Engineering · Scientific Data Management · Retrieval-Augmented Generation

1 Introduction

In scientific data preprocessing, the completion of discipline classification information plays a critical role in enhancing search efficiency. Our research on over thirty major global scientific data platforms reveals that approximately 42% lack systematic disciplinary classification information. Current systems commonly suffer from problems such as classification inaccuracies and inconsistent standards, leading to increased user search time and difficulties in accessing interdisciplinary data. Existing classification frameworks demonstrate varying characteristics: The National Institute of Standards and Technology (NIST) classification standard is widely adopted in engineering technology and natural science domains, characterized by detailed hierarchical classifications and clear definitions; the International Standard Classification (ISC) covers broader disciplinary scopes, suitable for global multidisciplinary data management; the Chinese National Standard for Discipline Classification and Codes (GB/T 13745–2009) has been extensively implemented in domestic academic and research institutions, particularly effective for natural sciences, engineering technologies, and social sciences. While these standards differ, they retain partial compatibility in classification hierarchies and definitions, providing valuable guidance for completing disciplinary classification information in scientific data platforms.

T. Zhu et al. (Eds.): KSEM 2025, LNAI 15922, pp. 226–237, 2026.
https://doi.org/10.1007/978-981-95-3058-8_20

Current automated methodologies face challenges in multilingual support and cross-disciplinary adaptability. Traditional rule-based approaches are constrained by structured data requirements, while statistical learning methods depend heavily on annotated datasets. Although deep learning techniques can process unstructured data, they still demand substantial annotation efforts. Large language models (LLMs), despite their cross-domain processing capabilities, are susceptible to hallucination-generated classification errors. These limitations underscore the necessity for developing novel disciplinary classification completion methods. The subsequent section will elaborate on an innovative solution based on self-generated Chain-of-Thought (CoT) mechanisms.

2 Definition of Discipline Classification Task

2.1 Scientific Data

Scientific data refers to various forms of data generated during the process of scientific research, including but not limited to experimental data, observational data, and computational data. Scientific data can be represented by the symbol D, and its formal definition is as follows:

$$D = \{d_1, d_2, \ldots, d_n\}$$

Here, d_i represents the i-th scientific data unit, and each data unit contains the following information:

- **Title:** Describes the primary content and research topic of the data.
- **Description:** Provides detailed information about the background, methodology, and results of the data.
- **Institution:** The research institution or laboratory where the data was generated.
- **Author:** The creator or researcher associated with the data.
- **Time:** The specific time or time period when the data was produced.
- **Type:** The type of data, such as experimental data, observational data, etc.

2.2 Single-discipline Classification

The single-discipline classification refers to the task of classifying scientific data into a single discipline category. Given a scientific dataset D and a set of disciplines C, the objective of the single-discipline classification problem is to assign each scientific data d_i to a discipline category c_j, ensuring high accuracy and consistency in the classification results. Its formal definition is as follows:

$$\Omega_{\text{Single-Discipline}}(D, C) = \{(d_i, c_j) | d_i \in D, c_j \in C\}$$

Here, (d_i, c_j) indicates that the scientific data d_i is assigned to the discipline category c_j.

2.3 Multi-discipline Classification

The multi-discipline classification refers to the task of classifying scientific data into multiple discipline categories while considering the cross-disciplinary influences and weight allocation among these disciplines. Given a scientific dataset D and a set of disciplines C, the objective of the multi-discipline classification problem is to assign each scientific data d_i to multiple discipline categories $\{c_{j_1}, c_{j_2}, \ldots, c_{j_k}\}$ and allocate an influence weight w_{ij} to each discipline category, ensuring that the classification results accurately reflect the multi-disciplinary attributes of the data and their significance across different disciplines. Its formal definition is as follows:

$$\Omega_{\text{multi-discipline}}(D, C)$$
$$= \{(d_i, (c_{j_1}, w_{ij_1}), (c_{j_2}, w_{ij_2}), \ldots, (c_{j_k}, w_{ij_k})\})|$$
$$d_i \in D, c_{j_l} \in C, w_{ij_l} \in$$
$$[0, 1], l = 1, 2, \ldots, k\}$$

Here, $(d_i, \{(c_{j_1}, w_{ij_1}), (c_{j_2}, w_{ij_2}), \ldots, (c_{j_k}, w_{ij_k})\})$ indicates that the scientific data d_i is assigned to multiple discipline categories $\{c_{j_1}, c_{j_2}, \ldots, c_{j_k}\}$, and each discipline category c_{j_l} is associated with an influence weight w_{ij_l}, where the weight value ranges between 0 and 1, representing the importance of the discipline in the data.

In multi-discipline classification, the determination of weights is critical as it directly impacts the accuracy and reliability of the classification results. Weights can be determined through various methods, such as the frequency of discipline-specific features in the data, evaluations by domain experts, or automatic learning via machine learning models. By reasonably allocating weights, the cross-disciplinary characteristics of scientific data can be better reflected, improving the precision and practicality of the classification.

3 Self-generating Chain-of-Thought Discipline Classification

This framework is designed to excavate the potential of LLMs in disciplinary field completion scenarios, where the input consists of basic scientific data information (title, description, etc.) and the output produces standardized disciplinary labels (e.g., Chinese National Standard GB/T13745). The approach addresses model hallucination through Self-Generated CoT mechanisms while reducing inference costs by over an order of magnitude via model distillation.

The framework comprises two core modules, as shown in Fig. 1:

Self-generated CoT Annotation A few-shot CoT technique generates disciplinary annotations, where LLMs autonomously produce quality-monitored reasoning processes stored in a vector database for similarity retrieval. For multi-level disciplinary labeling (e.g., GB/T13745's three-tier classification), a multi-stage reasoning mechanism enables hierarchical labeling with early stopping to reduce randomness. Cross-disciplinary scenarios are addressed through multiple sampling to obtain weighted distributions.

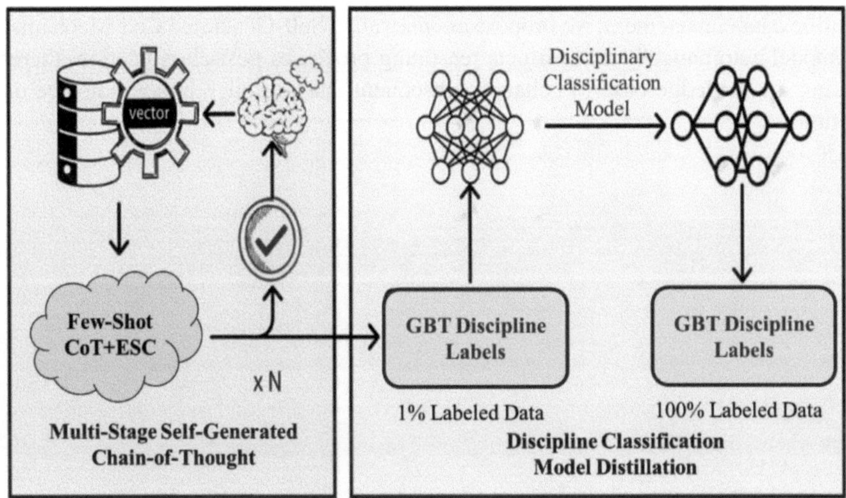

Fig. 1. Framework for Self-Generating Chain-of-Thought Discipline Classification

Model Distillation An end-to-end compact model is trained using LLM-annotated results. For the Findata platform containing over 36 million scientific data records, input-output formats are optimized into < scientific data information, disciplinary classification > pairs to minimize token consumption and enhance inference performance. This solution significantly reduces large-scale data annotation costs while maintaining accuracy.

3.1 Multi-stage Self-generated Chain-of-Thought

Recent advancements in LLMs have driven paradigm shifts in natural language processing[1]. Compared with traditional deep learning methods requiring task-specific training, the zero-training paradigm based on prompt engineering demonstrates significant advantages [2]. LLMs are increasingly being applied to text classification tasks [3]. This paper investigates how to enhance LLM performance for disciplinary classification through strategic prompt design.

The baseline strategy employs zero-shot learning by directly providing the model with task requirements, data descriptions, and discipline categories [4]. However, this approach underperforms supervised learning methods. To address this limitation, our framework proposes two optimization strategies:

Few-shot CoT. Injects reasoning exemplars through historical dialogues to guide the model in generating decision rationales [5-6].

Retrieval-Augmented Generation(RAG). Improves response accuracy by retrieving the most relevant CoT samples from knowledge bases via vector similarity search [7-8].

As shown in Fig. 2, the prompt structure comprises task description, CoT exemplars, and current data input. To overcome the challenge of insufficient annotated data in scientific data management, we propose an innovative Self-Generated CoT Mechanism: The model automatically reconstructs reasoning processes post-classification, thereby building a knowledge base to enhance subsequent tasks through annotation-free data iteration.

```
[
    {
        "role": "system",
        "content": "You are a scientific data manager. You need to classify the
literature based on its content into one of the following disciplines: [Materials
Science and Engineering, Crop Science,...]. You can only output one of these X
disciplines. If unsure, output the closest discipline. The output structure should be a
JSON containing two fields: Reason: Reflections on the content of the current
literature, from which characteristics can one analyze to determine the academic
discipline it belongs to. subject: the discipline name, one of the 67 listed above."
    },
    {
        "role": "user",
        "content": "Laser Scanning Confocal Microscopy (LSCM) is one of the most
advanced molecular and cellular biology analysis instruments in the world today. ..."
    },
    {
        "role": "assistant",
        "content": "{\"reason\": \"The content of the literature mainly involves the
application of laser scanning confocal microscopy in cell biology, particularly in the
localization, quantification, distribution of gap junction proteins, and intercellular
molecular migration and communication. These topics fall under the field of biology.\",
\"subject\": \"Biology/Biological Sciences and Engineering\"}"
    },
    ......,
    {
        "role": "user",
        "content": "Scanning Tunneling Microscope (STM) and Atomic Force Microscope
(AFM) have atomic-level ultra-high resolution, capable of obtaining real-space surface
micro three-dimensional morphology at the nanoscale and quantitatively characterizing
it. Therefore, they can be used to study the microscopic mechanisms of material
fracture and fatigue. This brief introduction covers the applications and some progress
made in this field using STM and AFM."
    }
]
```

Fig. 2. Examples of discipline classification prompt words

Figure 3 is a CoT generation prompt, which includes the task description, scientific data information, and the classified discipline, while requiring the output of a reasoning process. This approach enables autonomous CoT generation without the need for any human annotation.

3.2 Discipline Classification Model Distillation

In the task of disciplinary classification for scientific data, although the few-shot CoT method demonstrates superior performance on small-scale datasets, it suffers from excessively high token consumption and prohibitive annotation costs when processing large-scale data. For million-scale scientific data, directly employing LLMs for annotation proves impractical. Consequently, training specialized compact models through knowledge distillation has emerged as an effective solution.

Let the large model be T, the small model be S, the input data be x, and the corresponding ground truth label be y. The output of the large model for input x is a probability distribution $T(x)$, and the output of the small model is a probability distribution $S(x)$. The

```
[
    {
        "role": "user",
        "content": "You are a scientific data manager tasked with classifying
scientific data into their respective disciplines based on the dataset information.
Here is a dataset information: \"{\\\"introduction\\\": \\\"Surface reflectance
products are surface ...\\\"}\". It is classified as: Earth Sciences. Please analyze
why this dataset information can be classified into this discipline. Output structure
as a JSON containing one field: - reason: The reasoning process, identifying which
characteristics indicate which features, and how they align with the content of this
discipline, thus inferring this discipline. No more than 200 words."
    }
]
```

Fig. 3. Thoughts generate prompt

objective of knowledge distillation is to minimize the discrepancy between the outputs
of the small model and the large model while considering the ground truth label y. The
loss function can be expressed as:

$$L_{\text{distill}} = \alpha L_{\text{CE}}(S(x), y) + (1 - \alpha)L_{\text{KL}}(S(x), T(x))$$

- L_{CE} denotes the cross-entropy loss function, measuring the discrepancy between the small model's output and the ground truth label.
- L_{KL} denotes the Kullback-Leibler divergence, measuring the discrepancy between the small model's output and the large model's output.
- α is a hyperparameter that balances the cross-entropy loss and the Kullback-Leibler divergence.

In our framework, the knowledge distillation data originates from Self-Generated
CoT annotations. During the first phase, only minimal data annotation is required to
construct training data for the compact model, where the input comprises scientific data
information and the output corresponds to disciplinary labels. To reduce inference costs,
the distillation process explicitly avoids guiding the student model to output reasoning
processes, instead directly predicting disciplinary categories.

4 Experiment

4.1 Dataset

The CSLDCP (Chinese Science Literature Discipline Classification) dataset[9] comprises abstracts from Chinese scientific papers across multiple disciplines. This dataset
covers 13 major scientific domains, each further subdivided into specific categories, total-
ing 67 distinct discipline labels such as "Stomatology", "Sociology", and "Mechanical
Engineering". These categories span a broad spectrum from social sciences to natural
sciences, enabling comprehensive evaluation of classification capabilities across diverse
disciplinary contexts. Sourced from the CNKI academic literature database, the dataset
ensures authenticity and authority. To meet experimental requirements, the dataset is
partitioned into:

- **Training set**: 536 samples
- **Validation set**: 536 samples
- **Test set**: 1784 samples

Additionally, the dataset provides 2999 public test samples, 2 private test samples, and 18111 unlabeled samples, offering substantial data support for model training and evaluation.

4.2 Experimental Setup

Experimental Environment. The first stage of Self-Generated CoT was coded and executed on a MacBook Pro M3 Pro with 32GB of RAM, using Python 3.12 and the PyCharm 2024.1.2 IDE.The second stage of model distillation was conducted on a Windows 11 desktop with an Intel Core i9-14900K CPU and an Nvidia RTX 4090 GPU.

Models Used. LLMs:For cost-effectiveness, the primary model used in this experiment was gpt-4o-mini-2024–07-18. Additionally, comparative experiments employed several OpenAI models: gpt-3.5-turbo, gpt-4–0613, gpt-4-turbo-2024–04-09, gpt-4o-2024–05-13, and o1. For model distillation, ERNIE-Tiny-8K, ERNIE-Lite-8K, and LLAMA3.1-8B[11] were utilized.

Encoding Model: All vector encodings in the framework were generated using the text-embedding-ada-002 model.

Cloud Services. To ensure stable experimental conditions, some components relied on mature cloud service technologies. The vector database used Zilliz-hosted Milvus, with its ServerLess service model supporting pay-per-request billing to minimize unnecessary resource waste.

For model distillation, two approaches were employed:

- **Local Deployment:**Training of open-source small models was conducted on a local machine using the AI Tools framework.
- **Cloud-Based Deployment:** Model fine-tuning and inference services were provided by the Baidu Qianfan large model platform. Cloud-based training offered significant computational advantages over local deployment, enabling higher efficiency during simultaneous comparative experiments.

5 Experimental Results and Analysis

5.1 Main Results

Experimental results in Table 1 demonstrate that the SGCoT method achieves 62.12% accuracy on the GPT4o-mini model, outperforming supervised training by 2%. When deployed on GPT4o, the accuracy further improves to 66.4%, approaching the performance level of mainstream open-source fine-tuned models. The human baseline, representing trained annotators' average accuracy on CSLDCP classification tasks, serves as the performance upper bound. Comparative analysis reveals three key findings: First, LLAMA3.1-8B surpasses ERNIE1.0 by a significant 7.36% margin. Second, Pattern-Exploiting Training (PET) exhibits suboptimal effectiveness. Third, our framework trails supervised fine-tuning by merely 0.9%, thereby validating its practical efficacy.

Table 1. CSLDCP discipline classification task main results

Method	Model	P(%)	R(%)	F1(%)	Acc(%)
Human	-	-	-	-	68.00
FineTuning	ernie1.0	-	-	-	59.90
PET	ernie1.0	-	-	-	56.60
SGCOT	gpt4o-mini	67.01	62.13	62.01	62.12
SGCOT	gpt4o	69.02	66.42	65.48	66.41
FineTuning	llama3.1 8b	68.94	67.35	66.93	67.35

5.2 Ablation Experiments

Component importance analysis in Table 2 shows the full configuration (20 exemplars with vector retrieval and JSON formatting) achieves 62.12% accuracy. Removing CoT reasoning causes a 3% performance drop (59.12%), while substituting vector retrieval with random sampling further reduces accuracy by 3% (56.09%). Interestingly, reducing exemplars to 5 yields a marginal 0.19% improvement (56.28%), suggesting diminishing returns with excessive samples. Although Self-Consistency (SC)[10] provides a 0.5% accuracy gain, it introduces computational overhead. Conversely, Double-Checking (DC) negatively impacts performance. The JSON format demonstrates a 1.3% advantage over text output, while zero-shot learning underperforms few-shot approaches by 5%.

Table 2. Results of ablation experiments for CSLDCP discipline classification

Shots	Sample	COT	SC	DC	Format	P(%)	R(%)	F1(%)	Acc(%)
20	Vector	Yes	-	-	Json	67.01	62.13	62.01	62.12
20	Vector	-	-	-	Json	61.07	58.21	57.60	58.20
20	Random	-	-	-	Json	57.18	55.04	53.40	55.03
5	Vector	-	-	-	Json	62.31	58.40	58.04	58.39
5	Vector	-	Yes	-	Json	61.43	58.96	57.94	58.95
5	Vector	-	-	Yes	Json	58.26	56.72	55.46	56.71
5	Vector	-	-	-	Text	61.51	57.09	56.81	57.08
0	-	-	-	-	Json	56.54	53.17	51.81	53.17

5.3 Analysis of Influencing Factors

Impact of Few-Shot Sample Quantity on Results. As illustrated in Fig. 4, accuracy exhibits an inverted-U relationship with sample size, peaking at 20 exemplars. Vector retrieval consistently outperforms random sampling across all sample sizes, with performance degradation beyond the optimal threshold attributed to context forgetting. This pattern indicates that while limited exemplars enhance model focus, excessive samples overwhelm the context window.

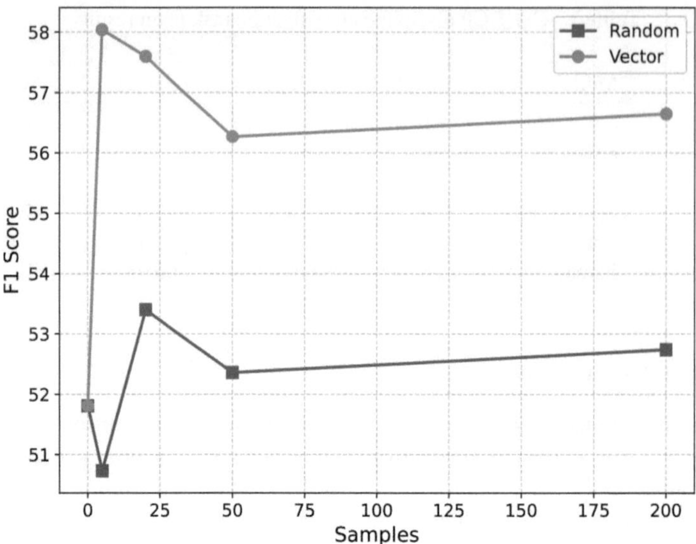

Fig. 4. The relationship between the number of samples and the accuracy

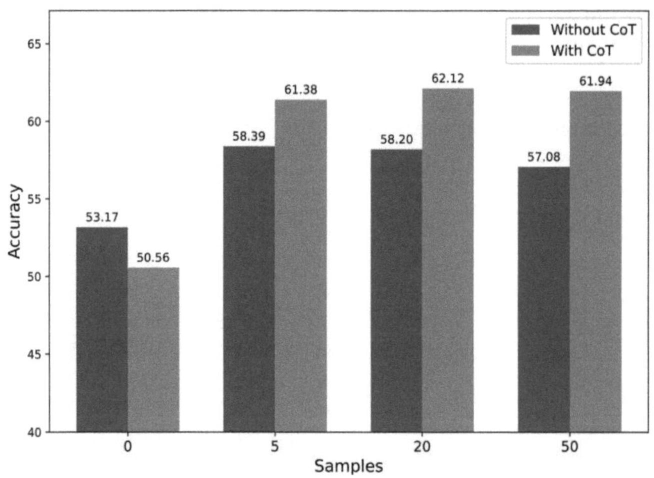

Fig. 5. The chain of thought affects the result

Impact of CoT on Results Figure 5 highlights CoT's contextual enhancement capabilities: In few-shot settings (20 samples), CoT delivers 4.2% higher accuracy than non-CoT approaches. However, it demonstrates negative impacts in zero-shot scenarios. Non-CoT methods achieve peak performance with only 5 samples, where as CoT enables better utilization of contextual information while mitigating context forgetting effects. Where as CoT enables better utilization of contextual information while mitigating context forgetting effects.

Impact of Different Base Models on Results As detailed in Table 3, the GPT-4o-2024–05-13 model demonstrates superior performance across all key metrics: precision (69.02%), recall (66.42%), F1-score (65.48%), and accuracy (66.41%). However, this excellence comes at a higher computational cost of 2.5 per million tokens.In contrast, GPT-4o-mini-2024–07-18 achieves a balanced cost-performance ratio with precision 62.3 and 12.5 per million tokens. In contrast, GPT-4o-mini-2024–07-18 achieves a balanced cost-performance ratio with precision 62.3 and 10.6 per million tokens. Although free lightweight models like ERNIE-Tiny-8K and ERNIE-Lite-8K have lower costs, their significantly inferior performance (34.17% accuracy) confirms the limitations of small models in prompt-based disciplinary classification tasks. For precision-critical applications, GPT-4o-2024–05-13 is the optimal choice, while GPT-4o-mini-2024–07-18 provides better cost-effectiveness for practical deployments.

Impact of Different Models on Fine-Tuning Results This section compares the accuracy differences of various models during the second-phase fine-tuning. Comparative analysis of pre-fine-tuning and post-fine-tuning performance metrics clearly demonstrates that fine-tuned models significantly outperform their non-fine-tuned counterparts across key indicators including precision, recall, F1-score, and accuracy. Full-parameter update methods (e.g., ERNIE and LLAMA) surpass models updated solely with Lora parameters across all evaluation metrics. This indicates that comprehensive parameter updates can more effectively enhance model performance, thereby achieving superior results under supervised training. Furthermore, fine-tuned compact models occasionally exceed the performance of non-fine-tuned large models, further validating the effectiveness of fine-tuning strategies (Table 4).

Table 3. Comparison of different models

Model	P(%)	R(%)	F1(%)	Acc(%)	1M Cost
LLAMA3-8B	46.50	34.70	33.92	34.70	0.7
ERNIE-Tiny-8K	32.19	17.54	16.65	17.53	0
ERNIE-Lite-8K	53.84	39.93	41.07	39.92	0
gpt-35-turbo	61.98	54.29	55.24	54.29	2
gpt-4	64.39	61.19	60.39	61.19	60
gpt-4-turbo	60.07	57.09	56.26	57.08	30
gpt-4o-mini	62.31	58.40	58.04	58.39	0.6
gpt-4o	69.02	66.42	65.48	66.41	10

Table 4. Fine-tuning comparison of different models

Model	Method	P(%)	R(%)	F1(%)	Acc(%)
ERNIE-Tiny-8K	-	32.19	17.54	16.65	17.53
ERNIE-Tiny-8K	Lora	50.17	45.71	45.85	45.70
ERNIE-Tiny-8K	Full	67.30	62.87	62.15	62.87
ERNIE-Lite-8K	-	53.84	39.93	41.07	39.92
ERNIE-Lite-8K	Lora	66.52	64.74	63.81	64.73
ERNIE-Lite-8K	Full	70.91	68.10	67.69	68.09
LLAMA3-8B	-	46.50	34.70	33.92	34.70
LLAMA-3.1-8B	Full	68.94	67.35	66.93	67.35

6 Conclusion

This chapter elaborates on a scientific information completion method based on self-generated CoT, aiming to address the issue of missing discipline classification information in scientific data retrieval systems. By constructing a self-generated CoT discipline classification framework and leveraging the potential of large language models, combined with few-shot CoT techniques and model distillation, the method achieves efficient and accurate completion of discipline classification information. Experimental results demonstrate that this method performs exceptionally well on the CSLDCP dataset, achieving an accuracy of 66.4%, which is comparable to current mainstream fine-tuning approaches for open-source models. Furthermore, ablation studies and factor analysis further validate the significant contributions of components such as few-shot learning, vector retrieval, and CoT to the framework's performance. In practical applications, this method has been successfully implemented for discipline information completion in the Findata platform, significantly enhancing data retrieval efficiency and user experience while demonstrating notable advantages in cost control. Future work will focus on exploring the application of CoT methods in other metadata completion tasks and further optimizing generation strategies to adapt to broader requirements. Through these efforts, the completion of scientific data information will become more intelligent and efficient.

Acknowledgements. This work was supported by the Informatization Plan of Chinese Academy of Sciences, Grant No.CAS-WX2022GC-02.

References

1. Zhao, W.X., Zhou, K., Li, J., et al.: A Survey of Large Language Models. arXiv preprint arXiv:2303.18223 (2023)
2. Brown, T., Mann, B., Ryder, N., et al.: Language models are few-shot learners. Adv. Neural. Inf. Process. Syst. **33**, 1877–1901 (2020)
3. Wang, Z., Pang, Y., Lin, Y.: Large Language Models are Zero-Shot Text Classifiers. arXiv preprint arXiv:2312.01044 (2023)

4. Radford, A., Wu, J., Child, R., et al.: Language models are unsupervised multitask learners. OpenAI blog **1**(8), 9 (2019)
5. Wei, J., Wang, X., Schuurmans, D., et al.: Chain-of-thought prompting elicits reasoning in large language models. Adv. Neural. Inf. Process. Syst. **35**, 24824–24837 (2022)
6. Kojima, T., Gu, S.S., Reid, M., et al.: Large language models are zero-shot reasoners. Adv. Neural. Inf. Process. Syst. **35**, 22199–22213 (2022)
7. Lyu, Y., Niu, Z., Xie, Z., et al.: Retrieve-Plan-Generation: An Iterative Planning and Answering Framework for Knowledge-Intensive LLM Generation. arXiv preprint arXiv:2406.14979 (2024)
8. Jia, P., Liu, Y., Zhao, X., et al.: MILL: Mutual Verification with Large Language Models for Zero-Shot Query Expansion. arXiv preprint arXiv:2310.19056 (2023)
9. Li, Y., Zhang, Y., Zhao, Z., et al.: CSL: a large-scale chinese scientific literature dataset. In: Proceedings of the 29th International Conference on Computational Linguistics, pp. 3917–3923 (2022)
10. Wang, X., Wei, J., Schuurmans, D., et al.: Self-Consistency Improves Chain of Thought Reasoning in Language Models. arXiv preprint arXiv:2203.11171 (2022)
11. Dubey, A., Jauhri, A., Pandey, A., et al.: The Llama 3 Herd of Models. arXiv preprint arXiv: 2407.21783 (2024)

Learning Interaction-Aware and Neighborhood Semantic-Enhanced Embedding for Link Prediction

Zhen Ren[1,2], Fei Pu[1,2(✉)], Siyuan Wang[1], Bailin Yang[1], and Lirong Cheng[3]

[1] School of Computer Science and Technology, Zhejiang Gongshang University, Hangzhou, China
{23020100045,pufei,ybl,22020100024}@zjgsu.edu.cn
[2] Economic Forecasting and Policy Simulation Laboratory, Zhejiang Gongshang University, Hangzhou, China
[3] School of Humanities and Communications, Zhejiang Gongshang University, Hangzhou, China

Abstract. Knowledge Graph Embedding (KGE) is crucial for representing entities and relations in vector space to support downstream tasks. Although neural network-based models, especially CNNs, have shown promise, they still struggle to capture complex interactions and semantic information from neighborhood structures. This paper introduces **InsE**, a novel KGE model that integrates an Adaptive **I**nteraction-Aware Learning Module and a **N**eighbourhood **S**emantic **E**xtraction Module to enhance entity-relation interaction and neighborhood semantic extraction. InsE adopts a cascading architecture comprising channel attention and normalization layers, coupled with a Glocal Triple Scoring mechanism, to enhance embedding learning. Extensive experiments on benchmark datasets demonstrate that InsE achieves competitive performance with high parameter efficiency, especially excelling on dense KGs.

Keywords: Knowledge graph embedding · Link prediction · Convolutional neural network

1 Introduction

Knowledge Graphs (KGs) represent a formalized way to structure human knowledge. KGs have found extensive applications in various domains [3]. However, with the information explosion nowadays, KGs face the issue of incompleteness. To efficiently and accurately complete the missing parts of KGs, Knowledge Graph Embedding (KGE) maps entities and relations into low-dimensional vector spaces to learn their distributed representations, thereby performing link prediction to achieve the completion of existing KGs.

T. Zhu et al. (Eds.): KSEM 2025, LNAI 15922, pp. 238–247, 2026.
https://doi.org/10.1007/978-981-95-3058-8_21

KGE models are commonly categorized into geometric translation, semantic matching, and neural network-based approaches. Though promising, geometric and semantic matching models are limited by constrained representation spaces and shallow architectures [2], hindering deep semantic modeling. Neural network-based approaches can be further divided into traditional CNN-based models and GCN-based models. However, Zhang et al. [11] note that GCN-based models are resource-intensive yet not notably superior.

Although CNNs excel at feature extraction, their application to KGE faces challenges. Traditional convolution struggles to model entity-relation interactions. To address this, models like AcrE [5] and InteractE [8] expand receptive fields and reshape inputs, improving performance but significantly increasing parameters. Moreover, most CNN-based models overlook the graph structure of KGs, missing rich semantic information in entity neighborhoods and LTE [11] shows that distinguishing entities with different semantics enhances performance.

In response to these challenges, we aspire to develop a model that retains convolution's efficiency and low parameter count, enhances entity-relation interaction, and capturing similar semantic information within the neighborhood to enhance embedding learnings. Accordingly, we propose InsE, comprising two core modules: Adaptive Interaction-Aware Learning (AIAL) and Neighborhood Semantic Extraction (NSE). Our main contributions are summarized as follows:

1. We propose the **AIAL Module**, which adaptively fuses head entities and relations through an addition-based mechanism to enhance interaction modeling.
2. We design the **NSE Module** with traditional convolution to extract semantic similarities from local graph neighborhoods.
3. We refine the joint use of channel attention and normalization layers and introduce the **Glocal Triple Scoring** strategy inspired by global-local matching and dropout techniques to improve embedding quality.
4. Extensive experiments demonstrate that InsE achieves competitive performance and high parameter efficiency, particularly on dense KGs.

2   Methodology

This section introduces InsE, which employs an AIAL module to capture entity-relation interactions and an NSE module to extract neighborhood semantics from the graph. For feature extraction, we parallelly use the same convolutional module as ConvE [2] and apply channel attention across regularization layers to adaptively select features. Finally, link prediction is performed using the Glocal Triple Scoring. The overall framework is shown in Fig. 1.

For a knowledge graph $\mathcal{G} = \{\varepsilon, \mathcal{R}, \mathcal{F}\}$, where ε, $\mathcal{R}$, and $\mathcal{F}$ denote entities, relations, and fact triples (h, r, t), we map h, r, and t into d-dimensional vectors $\mathbf{h}, \mathbf{r}, \mathbf{t} \in \mathbb{R}^d$. These are then reshaped into 2D matrices $\mathbf{M^h}, \mathbf{M^r} \in \mathbb{R}^{d_h \times d_w}$, with $d_h \times d_w = d$, and serve as input to the subsequent modules.

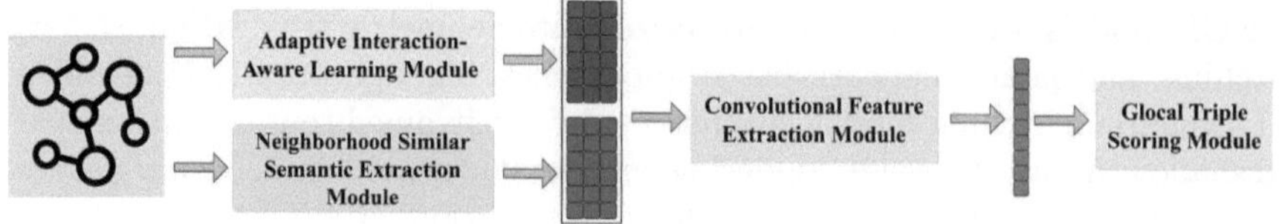

Fig. 1. Overview of InsE. (1) Features and neighborhood semantics are generated by Adaptive Interaction-Aware Learning and Neighborhood Semantic Extraction Modules; (2) Feature representations are learned by 2D convolutions and cross-regularization channel attention; (3) Link prediction is performed via Glocal Triple Scoring.

2.1 Input Feature Encoding

The Input Feature Encoding stage aims to efficiently capture interactions between entities and relations, as well as similar semantic information in the graph. To this end, we propose the AIAL and NSE modules. As shown in Fig. 2, the AIAL module adaptively adds head and tail entities element-wise using attention weights from a Vertically Spatial Attention Mechanism (VSAM) that integrates channel and spatial attention. The NSE module extracts adjacent entity information via convolution. Next, we will introduce these two modules in detail.

Adaptive Interaction-Aware Learning Module. For input matrix $\mathbf{M^h}, \mathbf{M^r}$, concatenate them twice horizontally and once vertically:

$$X_{11} = \mathbf{M^h} \oplus \mathbf{M^r}$$
$$X_{12} = \mathbf{M^r} \oplus \mathbf{M^h} \tag{1}$$
$$X_{13} = \mathbf{M^h} \otimes \mathbf{M^r}$$

Specifically, we use $\oplus$ to denote horizontal concatenation and $\otimes$ to vertical concatenation. Given $\mathbf{M^h}, \mathbf{M^r} \in \mathbb{R}^{d_h \times d_w}$, then $X_{11}, X_{12} \in \mathbb{R}^{2d_h \times d_w}$ and $X_{13} \in \mathbb{R}^{2 \times d_h \times d_w}$. Next, we design a Vertically Spatial Attention Mechanism to adaptively generate weights for guided summation. Briefly, we combine channel attention and spatial attention, performing pooling in the vertical direction:

$$X_{avg}(j,k) = F_{VAP}(X_{13}) = \frac{1}{2}\sum_{i=0}^{1} X_{13}(i,j,k)$$
$$X_{max}(j,k) = F_{VMP}(X_{13}) = MAX(X_{13}(0,j,k), X_{13}(1,j,k)) \tag{2}$$

Specifically, we refer to these two pooling operations as Vertically Average Pooling (VAP) and Vertically Max Pooling (VMP). Subsequently, we obtain the weights $F_\alpha \in \mathbb{R}^{H \times W}$ using convolution:

$$F_\alpha = (X_{13} * w_n) + I_1 \tag{3}$$

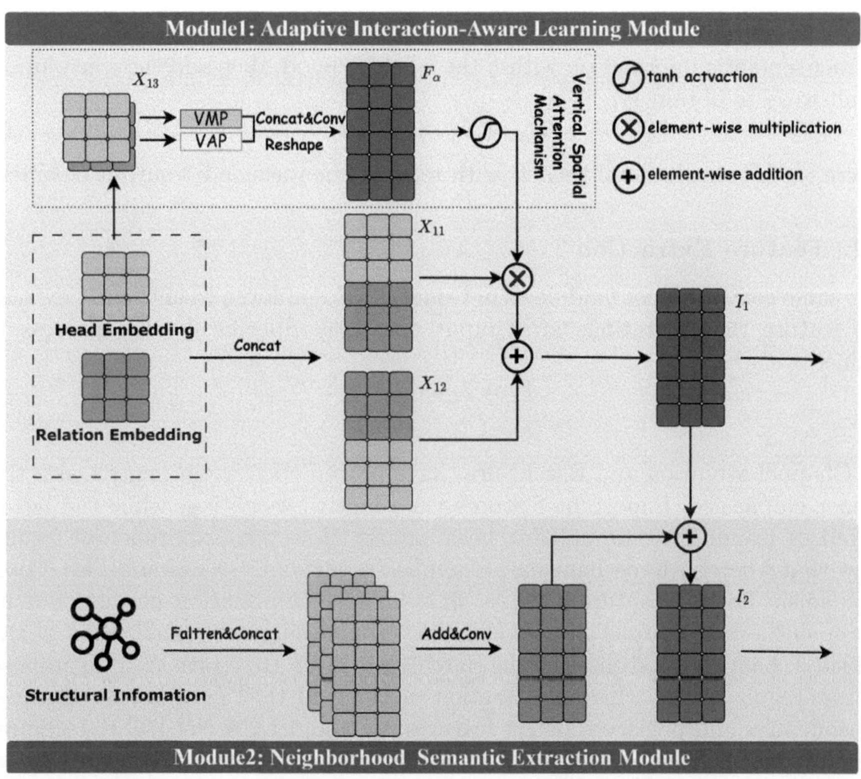

Fig. 2. Schematic diagram of the input encoding stage. Here, VMP denotes Vertically Max Pooling, and VAP denotes Vertically Average Pooling.

where $*$ denotes convolution operation, $w_\alpha \in \mathbb{R}^{2\times2\times w_{\alpha h}\times w_{\alpha w}}$ denotes filters with 2 inputs channel and 2 outputs channel, $f(\cdot)$ denotes tanh activation.

Thus, we perform a weighted summation of X_{11} and X_{12} to obtain $I_1 \in \mathbb{R}^{H\times W}$;

$$I_1 = (X_{11} \times F_\alpha) + X_{12} \tag{4}$$

Neighborhood Semantic Extraction Module. To aggregate neighborhood information for the central entity h, we extract n adjacent relations $\mathbf{r}_n$ and tail entities $\mathbf{t}_n$ from the training set, and obtain their 2D embedding matrices $\mathbf{M}^{\mathbf{h}_n}, \mathbf{M}^{\mathbf{r}_n} \in \mathbb{R}^{n\times d_h\times d_w}$. If h lacks neighbors, self-padding is applied. We then perform two-step vertical concatenation and summation to obtain $X_3 \in \mathbb{R}^{n\times H\times W}$.

$$\begin{aligned}
X_{21} &= \mathbf{M}^{\mathbf{h}_n} \oplus \mathbf{M}^{\mathbf{r}_n} \\
X_{22} &= \mathbf{M}^{\mathbf{r}_n} \oplus \mathbf{M}^{\mathbf{h}_n} \\
X_3 &= X_{21} + X_{22}
\end{aligned} \tag{5}$$

As mentioned earlier, we employ a straightforward convolution operation to extract semantic information within the neighborhood, then add the convolution result to I_1 to obtain I_2:

$$I_2 = (X_3 * w_n) + I_1 \tag{6}$$

where w_n is convolutional kernels with n input channels and 1 output channel.

2.2 Feature Extraction

The same convolutional module as in ConvE [2] is employed to efficiently extract the feature representations after input encoding. Specifically, the process is defined with Eq. 7.

$$F_1 = I_1 * w_1 + b_1$$
$$F_2 = I_2 * w_2 + b_2 \tag{7}$$

Channel attention and BatchNorm have proven effective in many tasks: the former emphasizes important features via adaptive weighting, while the latter stabilizes training by normalizing layer inputs. However, Experimental results show that when both mechanisms are applied sequentially, the channel attention mechanism fails to capture effective inter-channel information because Batch-Norm shifts each channel's mean close to zero, causing re-normalization of the adjusted channels upon entering the BatchNorm layer.To resolve this, we propose a cross-regularization channel attention mechanism that models inter-channel dependencies and preserves salient features. we adopt ECA-Net [10] to compute attention scores from the original feature map and apply them to the normalized output, enabling effective collaboration between attention and normalization:

$$F_1' = BN(F_1) \times ECA(F_1)$$
$$F_2' = BN(F_2) \times ECA(F_2) \tag{8}$$

where BN refers to 2D batch-normalization, and ECA refers to computing channel attention scores using ECA-Net.

We vertically concatenate and flatten F_1' and F_2', then project them to the embedding space using a fully connected layer to obtain the feature vector $\varrho \in \mathbb{R}$:

$$\varrho = Flatten(F_1' \odot F_2')W + b_w \tag{9}$$

where W is a transformation matrix and b_w is a bias vector.

2.3 Triple Scoring

The integration of global matching and local matching has been effectively utilized across a variety of tasks. Furthermore, it has been observed that Zhang et al.[11] enhanced model performance by incorporating an additional dropout strategy prior to triple scoring. By comprehensively considering these approaches and leveraging their respective strengths, we propose the **Glocal Triple Scoring mechanism**. First, we apply dropout to the tail entity **t** to obtain **t'**:

$$\mathbf{t'} = Dropout(\mathbf{t}) \tag{10}$$

The scoring function of InsE is defined with Eq. 11.

$$\psi(\mathbf{h}, \mathbf{r}, \mathbf{t}) = \eta \mathbf{t}\varrho + (1 - \eta)\mathbf{t}'\varrho \tag{11}$$

here η is a learnable parameter. Specifically, when $\eta = 1$, the Glocal Triple Scoring reduces to the triplet scoring function employed in ConvE [2]; conversely, when $\eta = 0$, it reduces to the triplet scoring function utilized in LTE [11].

2.4 Parameter Training

This paper employs the same binary cross-entropy loss as ConvE. Additionally, to enhance the model's generalization ability and training stability, we adopt Dropout, BatchNorm, and L2 regularization. Ultimately, the model is trained by minimizing the following cross-entropy loss function:

$$\mathcal{L} = -\frac{1}{N} \sum_{i=1}^{N} [t_i \log p\left(t_i \mid h, r\right) + (1 - t_i) \log\left(1 - p\left(t_i \mid h, r\right)\right)] \tag{12}$$

where t is a label vector whose elements are ones for relationships that exist and zero otherwise, and N is the number of entities in a KG.

3 Experiments

3.1 Datasets

To evaluate model performance, we use three key benchmark datasets: FB15k-237, WN18RR, and YAGO3-10. FB15k-237 and WN18RR are medium-scale datasets derived from Freebase and WordNet, respectively. YAGO3-10 is used for large-scale evaluation.

3.2 Main Results

We compared a series of influential KGE models with InsE, including ConvE [2], RotatE [7], InteractE [8], AcrE [5], JointE [12] MSHE [4], DTAE [1]. Table 1 presents the results for FB15k-237 and WN18RR, and Table 2 presents for YAGO3-10. The comparative data were extracted verbatim from the cited studies. The best results are shown in bold and the second-best results are underlined.

As shown in Table 1, InsE achieves state-of-the-art performance on FB15k-237, leading in both MRR and Hits@3. Compared to AcrE, the most efficient prior CNN-based model, InsE improves MRR, Hits@10, Hits@3, and Hits@1 by 1.1%, 0.2%, 1.8%, and 0.8%, respectively. Against the latest CNN model DTAE, it further gains 0.6% in MRR and 1.3% in Hits@3. On WN18RR, InsE surpasses AcrE by 0.7%, 3.8%, and 0.5% in MRR, Hits@10, and Hits@1. Notably, it sets a new Hits@10 benchmark, outperforming DTAE by a significant 4.0%.Table 2 shows InsE performs competitively on YAGO3-10, similar to FB15k-237. Compared to AcrE, InsE improves MRR by 1.5%, Hits@10 by 1.8%, Hits@3 by 2.6%,

Table 1. Link prediction results on FB15k-237 and WN18RR.

Method	FB15k-237				WN18RR			
	MRR	Hits@10	Hits@3	Hits@1	MRR	Hits@10	Hits@3	Hits@1
ConvE [2]	.325	.501	.356	.237	.430	.520	.440	.400
RotatE [7]	.338	.533	.375	.241	.476	**.571**	.492	.428
CompGCN [9]	.355	.535	.390	.264	**.479**	.546	**.494**	.443
InteractE [8]	.354	.535	–	.263	.463	.528	–	.430
AcrE [5]	.358	.545	.393	.266	.459	.532	.473	.422
JointE [12]	.356	.543	.393	.262	.471	.537	.483	.438
MSHE [4]	.356	.544	.392	.264	.461	.530	.473	.429
DTAE [1]	.360	**.547**	.395	**.269**	.472	.531	.486	**.440**
InsE(ours)	**.362**	.546	**.400**	.268	.462	.552	.472	.424

Table 2. Link prediction results on YAGO3âĂŞ10.

Method	YAGO3-10			
	MRR	Hits@10	Hits@3	Hits@1
ConvE [2]	.440	.620	.490	.350
RotatE [7]	.495	.670	.550	.402
InteractE [8]	.541	.687	–	.462
AcrE [5]	.546	.683	.585	.463
JointE [12]	**.556**	**.695**	**.605**	.481
MSHE [4]	.537	.682	.582	.460
DTAE [1]	.555	.684	.597	**.485**
InsE(ours)	.554	**.695**	.600	.477

and Hits@1 by 3.7%. Notably, InsE achieves the highest Hits@10 among all compared models on YAGO.

Compared to WN18RR, InsE performs better on FB15k-237 and YAGO3-10, where entities have significantly denser neighborhoods. This suggests that the effectiveness of the NSE module benefits from higher neighborhood density, highlighting its strength in handling large-scale, densely connected KGs.

3.3 Component Analysis

We conduct a series of experiments to evaluate the effectiveness of key components in InsE. Table 3 compares our additive fusion mechanism in the AIAL module with conventional approaches. Unlike concatenation (ConvE [2]) or checkerboard reshaping (InteractE [8]), our addition-based method achieves better performance with no increase in parameters.

Table 3. Comparison of Entity-Relation Fusion Methods

Method	FB15k-237	
	MRR	#Parameters
Concat (ConvE [2])	.325	≈ 5.05M
Checkerboard (InteractE [8])	.328	≈ 6.21M
Add (ours)	.334	≈ 5.05M

Table 4. Results of ablation study

Methods	FB15k-237			
	MRR	Hits@10	Hits@3	Hits@1
Proposed whole model	**.362**	**.546**	**.400**	**.268**
w/o AIAL	.343	.529	.378	.250
w/o NSE	.333	.507	.366	.246
w/o CRCA	.359	.542	.395	.266
w/o Global Triple Scoring	.359	.543	.394	.266
w/o Local Triple Scoring	.354	.537	.390	.263

To further validate the contribution of each module, we perform ablation studies, as shown in Table 4. Removing the AIAL or NSE modules leads to substantial performance drops up to 5.5% and 8.5% in MRR, respectively. Excluding CRCA slightly reduces performance, confirming its role in enhancing feature regularization. Additionally, removing either Global or Local scoring degrades performance, with the local scoring being more impactful.

Table 5. Parameter efficiency on FB15k-237.

Method	FB15k-237		
	MRR	Hits@10	#Parameters
RotatE [7]	.338	.533	≈ 17.96M
SACN [6]	.328	.535	≈ 6.21M
Acre [5]	.358	.545	≈ 5.93M
InteractE [8]	.354	.535	≈ 10.20M
DTAE [1]	.360	**.547**	≈ 7.89 M
InsE(ours)	**.362**	.546	≈ **5.90 M**

3.4 Parameters' Efficiency

As shown in Table 5, we evaluate InsE's parameter efficiency on FB15k-237. InsE achieves a notably low parameter count while maintaining competitive performance which confirms our design goal. Moreover, convolution-based KGE models benefit from lower embedding dimensions, further reducing computational cost.

4   Conclusion

This paper proposes the InsE model to address key limitations in CNN-based KGE methods. The AIAL module enhances the fusion of entity and relation embeddings to better capture interactive information, while the NSE module extracts similar semantic patterns from neighborhoods. The framework also enhances the cascading utilization of channel attention and regularization layers while designing a global-local triple scoring mechanism to improve the quality of feature learning. Experiments show that each module contributes effectively, with InsE achieving strong performance on dense KGs and maintaining high parameter efficiency.

Acknowledgments. This research is supported by Zhejiang Gongshang University "Digital+" Disciplinary Construction Management Project(No.SZJ2022A009), "Jianbing Lingyan+X" Research and Development Plan of Zhejiang Province(No.2 025C01130) and the project of Economic Forecasting and Policy Simulation Laboratory, Zhejiang Gongshang University(No.2024SYS006).

References

1. Deng, W., Zhang, Y., Yu, H., Li, H.: Knowledge graph embedding based on dynamic adaptive atrous convolution and attention mechanism for link prediction. Inf. Process. Manag. **61**(3), 103642 (2024)
2. Dettmers, T., Minervini, P., Stenetorp, P., Riedel, S.: Convolutional 2d knowledge graph embeddings. In: Proceedings of the AAAI Conference On Artificial Intelligence. vol. 32, pp. 1811–1818. AAI Publications (2018)
3. Ji, S., Pan, S., Cambria, E., Marttinen, P., Philip, S.Y.: A survey on knowledge graphs: representation, acquisition, and applications. IEEE Trans. Neural Netw. Learn. Syst. **33**(2), 494–514 (2021)
4. Jiang, D., Wang, R., Xue, L., Yang, J.: Multisource hierarchical neural network for knowledge graph embedding. Expert Syst. Appl. **237**, 121446 (2024)
5. Ren, F., Li, J., Zhang, H., Liu, S., Li, B., Ming, R., Bai, Y.: Knowledge graph embedding with atrous convolution and residual learning. In: Proceedings of the 28th International Conference on Computational Linguistics, pp. 1532–1543 (2020)
6. Shang, C., Tang, Y., Huang, J., Bi, J., He, X., Zhou, B.: End-to-end structure-aware convolutional networks for knowledge base completion. In: Proceedings of the AAAI Conference on Artificial Intelligence. vol. 33, pp. 3060–3067 (2019)
7. Sun, Z., Deng, Z.H., Nie, J.Y., Tang, J.: Rotate: knowledge graph embedding by relational rotation in complex space. arXiv preprint arXiv:1902.10197 (2019)
8. Vashishth, S., Sanyal, S., Nitin, V., Agrawal, N., Talukdar, P.: Interacte: improving convolution-based knowledge graph embeddings by increasing feature interactions. In: Proceedings of the AAAI Conference on Artificial Intelligence. vol. 34, pp. 3009–3016 (2020)

9. Vashishth, S., Sanyal, S., Nitin, V., Talukdar, P.: Composition-based multi-relational graph convolutional networks. In: International Conference on Learning Representations, pp. 1–15 (2019)
10. Wang, Q., Wu, B., Zhu, P., Li, P., Zuo, W., Hu, Q.: Eca-net: Efficient channel attention for deep convolutional neural networks. In: Proceedings of the IEEE/CVF Conference on Computer Vision and Pattern Recognition, pp. 11534–11542 (2020)
11. Zhang, Z., Wang, J., Ye, J., Wu, F.: Rethinking graph convolutional networks in knowledge graph completion. In: Proceedings of the ACM Web Conference 2022, pp. 798–807 (2022)
12. Zhou, Z., Wang, C., Feng, Y., Chen, D.: Jointe: jointly utilizing 1d and 2d convolution for knowledge graph embedding. Knowl.-Based Syst. **240**, 108100 (2022)

PromptPilot: Autonomous Prompt Optimization via Genetic Particle Filtering and Dynamic Exploration

Jie Wang[1,2]([✉]) and Jiaye Wang[3]

[1] Shenzhen Institute of Advanced Technology, CAS, Shenzhen, China
11832018@zju.edu.cn
[2] Sangfor Technologies Inc., Shenzhen, China
[3] College of Control Science and Engineering, Zhejiang University, Hangzhou, China

Abstract. Large Language Models (LLMs) have become pivotal in advancing the frontiers of versatile agents, yet their effectiveness is still largely reliant on the process of manually crafting prompts, which often remains a complex and resource-intensive challenge. In this study, we present PromptPilot, an innovative framework that addresses the critical challenge of automating the generation of high-quality, task-specific prompts through a novel application of advanced optimization techniques. PromptPilot deploys a fleet of optimizers that independently traverse the vast prompt landscape. Each optimizer refines prompts based on domain-specific feedback and a heuristic evaluation mechanism. Prompt tuning is viewed as a process of state optimization, with transitions between states facilitated by actions that involve sampling and trial-and-error. Consequently, the feedback from error samples facilitates detailed cause analysis and the distillation of experience, leading to deeper domain insights and a better understanding of the task. PromptPilot not only encourages a diverse exploration of the prompt space but also strategically converges on high-quality prompts through a dynamic resampling and branching methodology. Notably, PromptPilot achieves enhanced computational efficiency, with reduced dependency on value function calls. Experimental results across 6 benchmark tasks demonstrate the superiority of PromptPilot over methods like Chain-of-Thought and PromptAgent. By enabling the autonomous generation of precise and optimized prompts, PromptPilot democratizes the utilization of LLMs, paving the way for their broader application across various domains.

Keywords: large language model · prompt engineering · genetic particle filtering

1 Introduction

Prompt engineering focuses on optimizing input queries ("prompts") to elicit precise responses from large language models (LLMs). This process requires domain expertise, task comprehension, and the ability to construct contextually precise instructions that steer LLM outputs toward desired results. The impetus for automated prompt engineering, or prompt optimization, stems from the need to streamline this process, enhancing efficiency and scalability while maintaining, or even improving the quality of the results.

Current methodologies in prompt engineering heavily rely on human-computer interaction, necessitating a fusion of domain expertise and experiential knowledge. This symbiosis, though effective, presents significant challenges, particularly as the complexity of prompts increases. Experts in the field are tasked with navigating a vast landscape of potential variations, where each alteration can profoundly impact the model's performance. The inherent intricacies of this task make automated expert-level prompt engineering a formidable endeavor.

The limitations of existing prompt optimization techniques are pronounced. Predominantly heuristic in nature, these methods often lack a strategic framework, resulting in optimizations that are incremental at best. Such approaches typically yield local enhancements, falling short of achieving the finesse and high quality that are increasingly demanded in sophisticated applications.

To address these challenges, we propose PromptPilot, an approach that integrates human-inspired iterative refinement with machine-driven exploration. PromptPilot employs a Genetic Particle Filtering (GPF) strategy for prompt optimization, framing it as a strategic optimization problem. The method iteratively analyzes model errors, leveraging self-reflective capabilities of LLMs to generate diagnostic feedback. This methodology advances prompt engineering standards and fosters a more effective human-AI collaboration for optimized language model interaction.

- We propose PromptPilot, the first automated prompt optimization framework that integrates GPF with self-reflective LLM feedback, enabling systematic navigation of the prompt space through trial-and-error exploration and state-based optimization.
- PromptPilot alleviates the dependency on value function evaluations through dynamic resampling and branch pruning, lowering computational costs while maintaining high-quality prompt generation.
- Extensive experiments on six benchmark tasks demonstrate the superiority of our method over state-of-the-art methods, with statistical improvements in task accuracy.

2   Related Work

2.1   Prompt Optimization

Prompt engineering enhances large language and vision-language models through task-specific instructions (prompts) without modifying model parameters. Prompts include natural language instructions for context steering or learned representations for knowledge activation [2,13].

Several methods have been developed in prompt optimization, including gradient-based approaches, black-box methods, and model-adaptive techniques. Prompt Optimization with Textual Gradients (ProTeGi) [12] is the typical gradient-based approach, which generates natural language descriptions of the flaws in a given prompt based on its performance on a small batch of data. These gradients indicate the semantic direction in which the prompt needs to be improved. The advantages of gradient-based methods are that they are efficient and directed. However, they are hardly feasible for closed-sourced LLMs. Thus, the gradient-free methods begin to emerge. For example, Black-box Prompt Optimization (BPO) [4] optimizes prompts based solely on output performance without requiring model internals. Additionally, Model Adaptive Prompt Optimization (MAPO) [3] tailors the optimization to the specific characteristics of the LLM, potentially offering superior results.

2.2 Self-reflection and Planning

LLMs exhibit emergent reasoning capabilities at scale [25], defined as systematic logical inference using evidence [5,20]. However, practical deployment faces hallucination challenges—generating plausible but unfaithful outputs, especially in specialized domains like medicine [8,10,16].

Self-reflection addresses this by enabling LLMs to critique outputs and iteratively refine solutions [11,14,21]. Complementarily, LLM planning decomposes complex intents but suffers from plan diversity and suboptimality due to task complexity and model uncertainty. Multi-plan selection (generation + optimal selection) thus becomes essential [7].

In terms of multi-plan generation, self-consistency [19] obtains multiple distinct reasoning paths via sampling strategies embodied in the decoding process, such as temperature sampling, and top-k sampling. Tree-of-Thought (ToT) [23] proposes to explicitly instruct the LLM to generate various plans via few-shot examples in prompts. Similarly, Graph-of-Thought (GoT) [1] extends ToT by adding transformations of thoughts, which supports arbitrary thought aggregation. In terms of optimal plan selection, self-consistency applies the naive majority vote strategy, where the plan with the most votes is deemed the optimal choice. Due to tree architecture, ToT, LLM-MCTS [24], and RAP [6] apply tree search algorithms, such as Breadth First Search (BFS), Depth First Search (DFS), and Monte Carlo Tree Search (MCTS). When selecting a node for expansion, LLM is used to evaluate multiple actions and choose the optimal one. Additionally, the classic A* algorithm can also be used for optimal plan search [22].

3   Methodology

Given a base LLM $\mathcal{B}$ for a target task $\mathcal{T}$, the objective of prompt engineering is to discover an optimal prompt $\mathcal{P}^*$ that maximizes $\mathcal{B}$'s performance on $\mathcal{T}$. However, designing effective prompts, particularly for tasks requiring specialized domain expertise, remains challenging. Current approaches often rely on manual crafting, a process that is complex and resource-intensive. To address

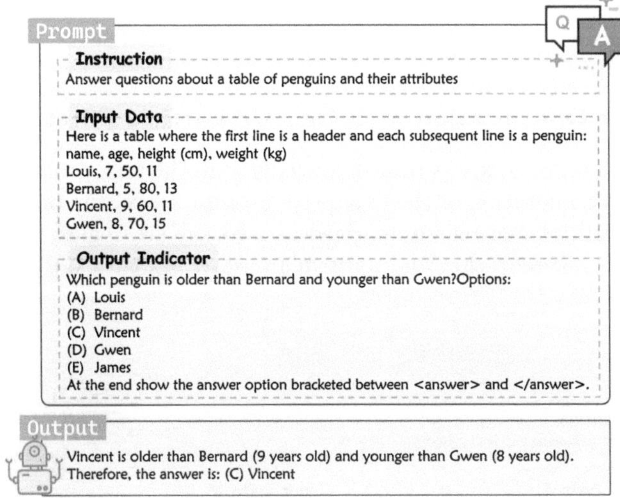

Fig. 1. The illustration of the prompt for a numerical comparison case.

these limitations, we propose PromptPilot, a framework for the automated generation of high-quality, task-specific prompts. While prior work, such as [18], utilizes MCTS for expert-level prompting, PromptPilot adopts a more efficient and effective optimization strategy. Specifically, we formulate prompt optimization as a strategic search problem and introduce GPF to navigate the prompt space. The subsequent sections detail the PromptPilot framework and the application of GPF for optimal prompt discovery.

3.1   The Framework of PromptPilot

Assuming that the initial natural language task prompt is P_0 and the question/answer pair samples are (q_i, a_i) where $i \in [1, N]$. Figure 1 shows a simple example of the initial prompt and the corresponding output from LLM, which obviously makes a mistake. The goal of our PromptPilot is to maximize the performance of $\mathcal{B}$ with the optimal natural language prompt P^*. Thus, the optimization problem can be formulated as $P^* = \arg\max_{P \in \mathcal{P}} \sum_i \mathcal{R}\left(p_{\mathcal{B}}(a_i|q_i, P)\right)$, where $\mathcal{P}$ represents the space for the natural language prompt. According to the previous findings on the self-reflection capabilities of LLMs [11,14,21], we propose to optimize the prompts iteratively in an efficient way to help LLMs reflect and progress from their own mistakes.

We use $s_{t,m}$ to denote the state of m-th agent ($m \in M$) at time t, where the number of agents is M. For each agent, the state represents the updating of prompts, thus $s_{0,m} = P_0$. The state transition of the agent is performed by the action choosing, which is sampled from the agent's policy $c_{t,m} \in \pi_c(c|s_{t,m})$. We use a value function $v(s)$ to evaluate each state. For each s, the value function represents the potential utility or performance, which can guide the search for the optimal state.

3.2   Prompt Optimization with Genetic Particle Filtering

To effectively integrate expert prior knowledge into the task prompt while ensuring an efficient exploration of the expansive prompt space, the prompt optimization of PromptPilot can be summarized as two key strategies, which are state transition with self-reflection and multi-plan searching with GPF.

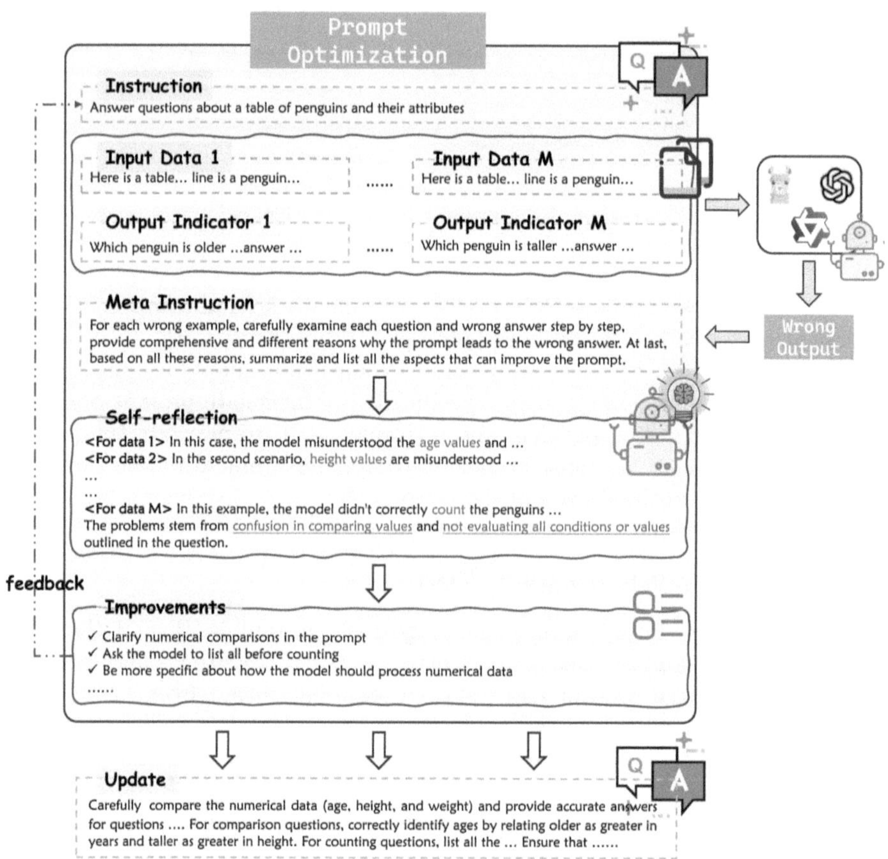

Fig. 2. The process of self-reflection of the base model.

State Transition with Self-reflection. The state in this context represents the current prompt, and the state transition is conducted through actions. These actions are modifications of current prompts based on error feedback, such as paraphrasing and word replacements. The error feedback from the base model is obtained through self-reflection and then can be used to refine the prompt.

For example, as shown in Fig. 2, we can instruct the base model to provide comprehensive and different reasons why the prompt leads to the wrong answer. Then the base model can find out the reason for the error in each case, summarize the common problems in a large number of similar cases (such as the numerical comparison problems), and finally list the direction that can be improved to answer such cases more accurately. Based on the improvements reflected by the base model itself, we can obtain an updated prompt for better instruction.

A key point in the state transition procedure lies in the value function, which evaluates the performance of each state and then instructs the potential optimization direction. Here we use the task performance of the base model as the value function, which means that $v(s)$ equals the task-specific metrics. For example, if the task is to make multiple-choice questions, then $v(s)$ is equal to the correct choice rate of the model belonging to the current state (or current prompt).

Multi-plan Searching with Genetic Particle Filtering. To efficiently search for the best prompt or best state, we propose to use the tree structure with GPF, which can be seen in Fig. 3. The ToT method allows LLMs to perform deliberate decision-making by considering multiple different reasoning paths and self-evaluating choices to decide the next course of action, as well as looking ahead or backtracking when necessary to make global choices [23]. Similarly, in our method, we allow several agents to autonomously take action to update and evaluate each prompt and finally lead to an optimal path. The basis of our multi-plan searching algorithm is performed by progressively constructing a tree structure with each node as a state and each edge as the action for transiting states. To expand the search tree, the GPF algorithm includes four operations, which are mutation, evaluation, resampling, and backtracking.

Mutation: In the t-th step, each agent independently samples action $c_{t,m} \in \pi(c|s_{t,m})$. The state actions are modifications performed on current prompts, which specifically can be paraphrasing or synonymous substitution. With the sampled action, each agent's state $s_{t,m}$ can be updated into $s_{t+1,m}$, which is detailed in the aforementioned state transition part.

Evaluation: For each updated state, the value function $v(s_{t,m})$ is used to evaluate the potential performance of each state. When the value function of a node after transition is less than the value function before transition, the search for this node is terminated.

Resampling: Based on the evaluation step, we can obtain the value of each current agent. Then, we can determine which can be further updated and which should be terminated to improve the search efficiency. The resampling weight $p(s_{t,m})$ denotes the sampling probability of m-th agent in the t-th step. The

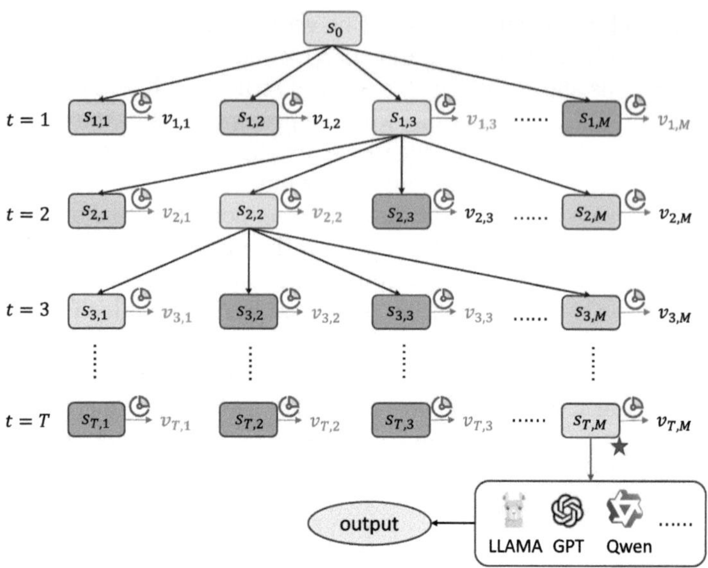

Fig. 3. The framework of the proposed multi-plan particle-filtering-based prompt optimization procedure.

corresponding formulation is shown below:

$$p(s_{t,m}) = \begin{cases} 1, & \text{if } s_{t,m} = \underset{s_{t,j}, j=1,\cdots,M}{\arg\max} v(s_{t,j}) \\ 0, & \text{otherwise} \end{cases} \tag{1}$$

To select a new set of agent states, we use the following resampling strategy based on the resampling weight.

$$s_{t+1,m} = \sum_{j=1}^{M} p(s_{t,j}) s_{t,j}, \, m = 1, 2, \ldots, M \tag{2}$$

Actually, the resampling equals using the agent with the best performance (highest value). Therefore, in each step, only the best agent is reserved and resampled for all M agents.

4   Experiments

In this section, the datasets, baselines, implementation details, and corresponding results are presented.

Datasets. To systematically assess the impact of methods across diverse applications, we conduct rigorous experimentation using challenging BIG-Bench Hard

(BBH) benchmarks. The BBH dataset [17] comprises complex problems that consistently challenge state-of-the-art language models. Our experimental design incorporates six BBH tasks specifically chosen to evaluate complementary capabilities: two domain-specific datasets requiring expertise (Geometric Shapes interpretation and Causal Judgment analysis) with four datasets requiring reasoning skills. The reasoning tasks are tabular reasoning in Penguins in a Table, quantitative analysis in Object Counting, logical deduction through Epistemic Reasoning, and temporal understanding in Temporal Sequences.

Baselines. Three categories of baselines are compared to reveal the superiority of our approach, which are standard human-crafted prompts, Chain-of-Thought (CoT) prompts, and state-of-the-art prompt optimization techniques.

- *Human prompts:* manually designed instructions derived from the original datasets. For BBH tasks, we utilize a few-shot (FS) variant of these prompts, incorporating teaching examples from [15], while for other tasks, we randomly select examples from the training set.
- *CoT prompts:* By encouraging step-by-step reasoning, CoT prompts are particularly beneficial for BBH tasks [15]. We adopt the CoT prompts for BBH tasks and develop our own for other tasks. Additionally, we implement a zero-shot (ZS) version of CoT, employing the phrase "Let's think step by step" to initiate CoT reasoning without the need for few-shot examples [9].
- *Prompt optimization methods:* GPT Agent and Automatic Prompt Engineer (APE) [26]. GPT Agent (AI Agents[1]) exemplifies the growing trend of LLM-driven autonomous agents, which are designed to independently plan and reflect to fulfill human tasks, including prompt refinement. APE, a cutting-edge prompt optimization technique, employs a Monte Carlo search-based strategy to iteratively generate and choose prompts. Similarly, PromptAgent [18] induces precise expert-level insights and in-depth instructions by reflecting on model errors and generating constructive error feedback.

Implementation Details. We now present the key implementation details of the proposed method.

Data Splitting. For datasets with predefined test or validation sets, we adhere to their original splits to construct our test set. In cases lacking official training/testing partitions, we extract a reasonably sized subset for stable evaluation. For datasets without predefined test splits, we shuffle the data and allocate approximately half for testing. From the remaining data, we derive a training subset and further reserve a validation subset for the reward computation. Detailed data partition statistics, consistent with those generated by PrompAgent, are shown in Table 1.

---

[1] https://aiagentslab.com/.

Initialization. Our algorithm initiates with a root node containing an initial prompt. For BBH tasks, we directly adopt the original dataset's task descriptions as initial prompts, except for object counting where the default description is reformatted to follow instruction-style templates. For other tasks, we craft initial prompts aligned with task objectives or QA formats. The root node undergoes reward evaluation prior to the first expansion.

Model Configuration. Unless specified otherwise, GPT-3.5 serves as the default base LLM for optimization. Given the requirement for enhanced self-reflective capabilities in the optimizer LLM, we employ GPT-4 as the default optimizer. Temperature settings are configured at 0.0 for base model predictions to ensure deterministic outputs, and 1.0 for other generative processes to encourage diversity.

Other Hyperparameters. In our implementation, the optimization process executes 5 iterations with 3 agent clusters generated per step. Each agent performs 2 exploration steps. During expansion phases, we batch-sample 5 error-prone training instances to guide action generation based on model failures. The remaining hyperparameters were optimized through empirical feedback analysis.

Table 1. Data Splitting Configuration

Task name	Train size	Test size
Penguins	150	200
Geometry	500	500
Epistemic	300	500
Object counting	300	500
Temporal	90	100
Causal judgement	90	100

Results. The experimental results on the BBH (Breadth of Human-like Reasoning) benchmark tasks, as summarized in Table II, demonstrate the effectiveness of PromptPilot across diverse reasoning scenarios. We evaluate PromptPilot against baseline methods, including human-designed prompts (zero-shot and few-shot), CoT, GPT Agent, APE, and PromptAgent, with accuracy as the primary metric.

– In Penguins (commonsense reasoning), PromptPilot achieves the highest accuracy of 0.886, outperforming the closest competitor, PromptAgent (0.873), by 1.5
– For Geometry (spatial reasoning), PromptPilot attains 0.710, a significant improvement over PromptAgent (0.670) and CoT (0.540), highlighting its ability to handle abstract and structured problems.

- While PromptAgent leads in Epistemic Reasoning (0.806 vs. PromptPilot's 0.748), PromptPilot dominates in Temporal Reasoning (0.952) and Causal Judgment (0.730), showcasing its versatility in temporal and cause-effect analyses.
- Notably, PromptPilot achieves 0.934 in Object Counting, nearly matching CoT's peak performance (0.960), which relies on handcrafted step-by-step instructions.

PromptPilot achieves 0.827 SOTA accuracy, outperforming PromptAgent (0.802) and APE (0.690). It reduces reliance on human prompts (0.505–0.581 zero/few-shot) by 41.8

These results validate reframing prompt engineering as state optimization guided by heuristic exploration and self-reflective feedback. Superiority over automated (APE) and human (CoT) baselines highlights the efficacy of integrating trial-and-error with systematic error analysis. Task-specific variance underscores the need for adaptive strategies—e.g., excelling in Temporal Reasoning where error feedback directly refines prompts, while Epistemic Reasoning requires deeper semantic parsing.

PromptPilot demonstrates that strategic optimization (vs. incremental heuristics) unlocks LLMs' potential, offering generalizable and computationally efficient solutions for real-world deployment (Table 2).

Table 2. Prompting performance on BBH tasks. ZS: Zero-Shot, FS: Few-Shot.

	Penguins	Geometry	Epistemic	Object Count	Temporal	Causal Judge	Avg.
Human (ZS)	0.595	0.227	0.452	0.612	0.720	0.470	0.513
Human (FS)	0.595	0.315	0.556	0.534	0.408	0.620	0.505
CoT (ZS)	0.747	0.320	0.532	0.542	0.734	0.610	0.581
CoT	0.747	0.540	0.720	**0.960**	0.626	0.650	0.707
GPT Agent	0.696	0.445	0.406	0.502	0.794	0.520	0.561
APE	0.797	0.490	0.708	0.716	0.856	0.570	0.690
Prompt Agent	0.873	0.670	**0.806**	0.860	0.934	0.670	0.802
Prompt Pilot	**0.886**	**0.710**	0.748	0.934	**0.952**	**0.730**	**0.827**

5   Conclusion

In this paper, we address the challenge of automating high-quality prompt generation for LLMs. By conceptualizing prompt engineering as a state optimization process, PromptPilot proposes a integration of heuristic-guided exploration and LLM-driven self-reflection to iteratively refine prompts. The framework's ability to learn from error analysis and distill domain insights enables it to outperform existing methods in both precision and adaptability. Our experiments validate

PromptPilot's efficacy, highlighting its capacity to reduce human intervention. The dynamic resampling strategy and feedback-driven optimization not only enhance computational efficiency but also ensure scalability.

Future directions include extending PromptPilot to multi-modal tasks and investigating its integration with reinforcement learning for even broader applicability. By lowering barriers to LLM utilization, PromptPilot represents a significant step toward democratizing advanced AI capabilities across industries.

Acknowledgments. This work is supported by Guangdong Provincial Key Laboratory of Cloud Security Key Technology (2022B1212020006). We also gratefully acknowledge the editor and all reviewers for their valuable suggestions.

References

1. Besta, M., et al.: Graph of thoughts: solving elaborate problems with large language models. In: Proceedings of the AAAI Conference on Artificial Intelligence, vol. 38, pp. 17682–17690 (2024)
2. Chen, B., Zhang, Z., Langrené, N., Zhu, S.: Unleashing the potential of prompt engineering in large language models: a comprehensive review. arXiv preprint arXiv:2310.14735 (2023)
3. Chen, Y., et al.: Mapo: boosting large language model performance with model-adaptive prompt optimization. arXiv preprint arXiv:2407.04118 (2024)
4. Cheng, J., et al.: Black-box prompt optimization: aligning large language models without model training. arXiv preprint arXiv:2311.04155 (2023)
5. Fagin, R., Halpern, J.Y., Moses, Y., Vardi, M.: Reasoning About Knowledge. MIT Press, Cambridge (2004)
6. Hao, S., et al.: Reasoning with language model is planning with world model. arXiv preprint arXiv:2305.14992 (2023)
7. Huang, X., et al.: Understanding the planning of LLM agents: a survey. arXiv preprint arXiv:2402.02716 (2024)
8. Ji, Z., Yu, T., Xu, Y., Lee, N., Ishii, E., Fung, P.: Towards mitigating LLM hallucination via self reflection. In: Findings of the Association for Computational Linguistics: EMNLP 2023, pp. 1827–1843 (2023)
9. Kojima, T., Gu, S.S., Reid, M., Matsuo, Y., Iwasawa, Y.: Large language models are zero-shot reasoners. In: Advances in Neural Information Processing Systems, vol. 35, pp. 22199–22213 (2022)
10. Lin, S., Hilton, J., Evans, O.: Truthfulqa: measuring how models mimic human falsehoods. arXiv preprint arXiv:2109.07958 (2021)
11. Paul, D., et al.: Refiner: reasoning feedback on intermediate representations. arXiv preprint arXiv:2304.01904 (2023)
12. Pryzant, R., Iter, D., Li, J., Lee, Y.T., Zhu, C., Zeng, M.: Automatic prompt optimization with "gradient descent" and beam search. arXiv preprint arXiv:2305.03495 (2023)
13. Sahoo, P., Singh, A.K., Saha, S., Jain, V., Mondal, S., Chadha, A.: A systematic survey of prompt engineering in large language models: techniques and applications. arXiv preprint arXiv:2402.07927 (2024)

14. Shin, T., Razeghi, Y., Logan IV, R.L., Wallace, E., Singh, S.: Autoprompt: eliciting knowledge from language models with automatically generated prompts. arXiv preprint arXiv:2010.15980 (2020)
15. Shinn, N., Cassano, F., Gopinath, A., Narasimhan, K., Yao, S.: Reflexion: language agents with verbal reinforcement learning. In: Advances in Neural Information Processing Systems, vol. 36 (2024)
16. Su, D., et al.: Read before generate! faithful long form question answering with machine reading. arXiv preprint arXiv:2203.00343 (2022)
17. Suzgun, M., et al.: Challenging big-bench tasks and whether chain-of-thought can solve them. arXiv preprint arXiv:2210.09261 (2022)
18. Wang, X., et al.: Promptagent: strategic planning with language models enables expert-level prompt optimization. arXiv preprint arXiv:2310.16427 (2023)
19. Wang, X., et al.: Self-consistency improves chain of thought reasoning in language models. arXiv preprint arXiv:2203.11171 (2022)
20. Wason, P.C.: Reasoning about a rule. Q. J. Exp. Psychol. **20**(3), 273–281 (1968)
21. Welleck, S., et al.: Generating sequences by learning to self-correct. arXiv preprint arXiv:2211.00053 (2022)
22. Xiao, H., Wang, P.: LLM a*: human in the loop large language models enabled a* search for robotics. arXiv preprint arXiv:2312.01797 (2023)
23. Yao, S., et al.: Tree of thoughts: deliberate problem solving with large language models. In: Advances in Neural Information Processing Systems, vol. 36 (2024)
24. Zhao, Z., Lee, W.S., Hsu, D.: Large language models as commonsense knowledge for large-scale task planning. In: Advances in Neural Information Processing Systems, vol. 36 (2024)
25. Zhou, D., et al.: Least-to-most prompting enables complex reasoning in large language models. arXiv preprint arXiv:2205.10625 (2022)
26. Zhou, Y., et al.: Large language models are human-level prompt engineers. arXiv preprint arXiv:2211.01910 (2022)

A Unified Computation Framework of Lattices in Hierarchical Data Analysis

Wen Shang, Jingwen Xu, Jinguo You$^{(\boxtimes)}$, Kang Wu, Xingrui Huang, and Jialin Xu

Faculty of Information Engineering and Automation, Kunming University of Science and Technology, Kunming, China
jgyou@kust.edu.cn, {shangwen,inweun,wk,xrhuang,jlxu}@stu.kust.edu.cn

Abstract. Data cubes, frequent itemsets, and concept lattices are the core data models in the fields of data warehouse, data mining, and formal concept analysis, respectively. Although they are applied to different fields of data analysis or mining, they all essentially establish similar partial-order structures in the form of lattices. However, previous work does not systematically and thoroughly study their correlation that will be greatly beneficial, say enhancing each other. To address this main concern, this paper deeply studies the lattice structure construction process of data cubes, frequent itemsets and concept lattices, and then generalizes them as a unified model by finding mapping among them. Further, we explore the wide spectrum application scenarios by exemplifying their fusion algorithms which means we may compute one using another with more efficient complexity by leveraging the mapping between them. Experiments on real datasets demonstrate the efficiency of the fusion algorithm, where the fusion algorithm achieves the highest improvement rate of 51.9%.

Keywords: Lattice · Data mapping · Lattice structure mapping · Unified framework · Hierarchical data analysis

1 Introduction

Data cubes, frequent itemsets and concept lattices are in different domains, but their core model is a lattice structure and they have a lot in common in essence. As an example, the basic table R, which has three-dimensional attributes Store (S), Product (P), Season (T) and a metric attribute Sales, with data records as {(1, 1, 1, 6), (1, 2, 1, 12), (2, 1, 2, 9)}, can be computed as a quotient cube [1] according to the equivalence class relationship shown in Fig. 1(a). After mapping the base table to the transaction set, the transaction set R' of the base table is obtained as {$(A, B, C), (A, D, C), (E, B, F)$}, and its closed itemset mining process can generate the subset-hyperset relationship between itemsets is shown in Fig. 1(b). Similarly, for the formal context R'' obtained from the mapping

T. Zhu et al. (Eds.): KSEM 2025, LNAI 15922, pp. 260–268, 2026.
https://doi.org/10.1007/978-981-95-3058-8_23

as $\{(A, B, C, 0, 0, 0), (A, 0, C, D, 0, 0), (0, B, 0, 0, E, F)\}$, the concept lattice structure shown in Fig. 1(c) is computationally generated based on the generalization-norm relation between concepts. It is evident that quotient cube, closed itemset lattice and concept lattice have similar partial order structures and the same computational results on the same dataset.

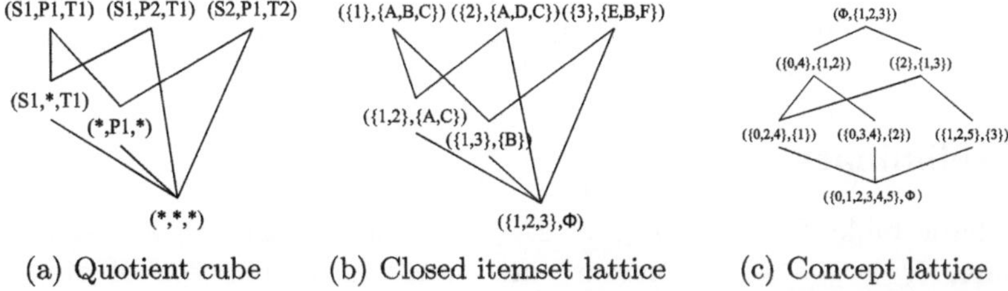

(a) Quotient cube   (b) Closed itemset lattice   (c) Concept lattice

Fig. 1. Quotient cubes, closed itemsets, and concept lattices

Existing data analysis models and methods often target specific types of data and are difficult to respond flexibly when facing diverse data. In this paper, from the perspective of algebraic lattice, we conduct a detailed study and demonstration on the fusion calculation of three lattice structures, construct a unified lattice structure model and calculation framework, and realize the efficient conversion and analysis of different data formats. Our main contributions are as follows:

- We propose a unified computing model for lattice structures based on the mapping rules between the three lattice structures.
- We give the fusion algorithm UCL (Unified Computation of Lattices) for three lattice structures and propose a unified computational framework for lattice structures.

2   Related Work

Data cube, as a core multidimensional data model, is the basis of online analytical processing (OLAP) [10,11]. In order to achieve fast response to OLAP and compress storage space, scholars have conducted extensive research on materialization of data cubes [12,13]. In addition, utilizing hardware acceleration [14] and improving storage efficiency (such as Quotient Cube [1,15] and QC-Tree [1]) are also ideas to enhance the computational efficiency of cubes.

The frequent itemset is the set of items that occur frequently and simultaneously in a transactional dataset.Agrawal proposed Apriori algorithm to realize frequent itemset mining [16]. Subsequently, some scholars improved the Apriori algorithm, such as LCM [3,4], FP-Growth [17]. In addition, other scholars have combined machine learning to improve data mining efficiency [18,19].

Concept lattice [20] formally represents solid objects or abstract concepts and establishes corresponding hierarchical relationships to describe the generalization and specialization relationships between concepts [21]. In recent years, scholars have investigated many algorithms for concept lattice computation, such as the In-close family of algorithms [5–9].

Existing research [3] only focuses on a single domain, while this paper systematically proves the isomorphism of the three lattice structures for the first time, and based on this, integrates the advantages of the three and constructs a unified lattice structure computation algorithm.

3   Preliminary

Given basic table $R = (D_1, D_2, \ldots, D_n, M)$, among them, D_i is a dimension attribute, M is the set of measure attributes. A combination of dimension attribute values forms data cells, $(d_1, d_2, \ldots, d_n)$, $(d_1, d_2, \ldots, d_{n-1}, ALL)$, ..., $(ALL, \ldots, ALL)$, where ALL is briefly described as *.

Definition 1 (basic tuple set(BTS)). *If there is an upward path from the basic tuple t to cell a, that is, if $a \preceq t$ holds in the cubic lattice, then cell a is said to cover the basic tuple t, and BTS (a) is the set of basic tuples covered by a.*

Theorem 1 (equivalence class relationship). *If $BTS(c1)$ contained in the equivalence class upper bound c1 contains $BTS(c2)$ and $BTS(c3)$ of the equivalence class upper bounds c2 and c3, and the tuples in $BTS(c1)$ are found to be present in either $BTS(c2)$ or $BTS(c3)$, then the equivalence class measure m1 of c1 can be computed from the equivalence class measures m2 and m3 of c2 and c3.*

Definition 2 (partial order relationship). *If $<A_1, B_1>$ and $<A_2, B_2>$ are two concepts, then $<A_1, B_1> \preceq <A_2, B_2>$ holds if and only if $A_1 \subseteq A_2(B_2 \subseteq B_1)$.. At this point, $<A_1, B_1>$ is a sub-concept of $<A_2, B_2>$, and $<A_2, B_2>$ is a super-concept of $<A_1, B_1>$.*

Let $\mathcal{J} = \{i_1, i_2, \ldots, i_n\}$ be the full set of items, and let the transaction sets in the database be $TD = (Tid, \mathcal{J})$. Each transaction I is a non-empty itemset, and $I \subseteq \mathcal{J}$, each transaction has an identifier $tid \subseteq Tid$.

4   Unified Framework

Through the discussion in the previous section, we proved the mapping relationship between the three lattice structure constructs and built a unified lattice structure framework based on it, as shown in Fig. 2. From Fig. 2, we know that the user can choose one of the three data input formats, convert the basic table, transaction set and formal context to the form of the bit array through the unified model, and then the UCL algorithm performs the computational operation to get the concept lattice structure, and then finally the user selects the desired output results from the quotient cube, frequent closed itemset and the concept lattice to generate the target lattice structure.

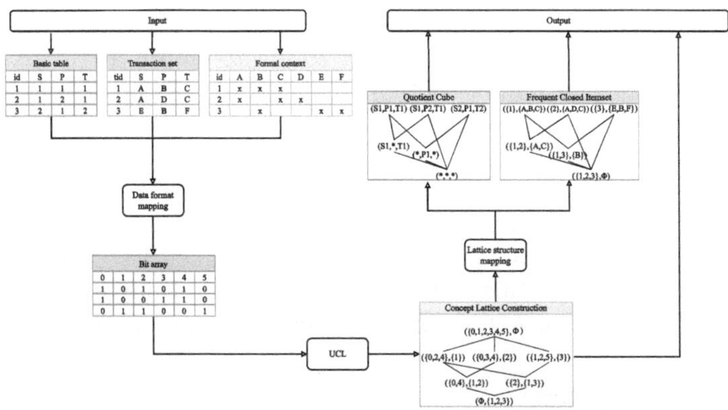

Fig. 2. Unified computation framework

4.1   Unified Model

Using the basic notions of set and partial order relations, we formalize the mapping relations between basic tables, transaction sets, and formal contexts, and prove isomorphisms between lattice structures.

Definition 3 (mapping of basic table to transaction set). *Let the basic table $R = (D, M)$, where D is the set of dimension attributes of the basic table R, M is the set of measure attributes of the basic table R. Define the mapping function between the basic table and the transaction set: $g_1(t) = \{d'_1, d'_2, ..., d'_n | d'_1 = d_1 - 1, d'_i = \sum_{j=1}^{i-1} |D_j|, i = 2, ..., n\}$.*

Definition 4 (mapping of basic table to formal context). *Given any data cell $(d_1, d_2, ..., d_n, m)$ on the basic table R, initialize the object of the formal context as $(a_1, a_2, ..., a_s) = \{0, 0, ..., 0\}$, where $s = |D| = \sum_{i=1}^{n} |D_i|$, defines the mapping function between the basic table and the formal context:$g_2(\{d'_1, d'_2, ..., d'_n\}) = \{a_1, a_2, ..., a_s | a_i = 1, i = d'_1, d'_2 ..., d'_n\}$*

Theorem 2. *Quotient cube, concept lattice, and closed itemset lattice are pairwise isomorphism.*

The introductory part of this paper can serve as an example of the theorem, and the detailed description will not be developed here to avoid repetition.

4.2   Our Optimization Methods

We migrate the idea of equivalence classes in the quotient cube (Theorem 1) to the computation of extents and connotations. Details can be found in Theorem 3.

Theorem 3 (the reverse relationship of concept node). *If the extent C of a concept $<C, D>$ is the intersection of the extents A_i of the other concepts $<A_i, B_i>$, then the intent D of that concept is the union of the connotations B_i of the other concepts. The reverse still holds true.*

According to the basic property [2] of the concept lattice, we introduce the idea of the conditional database in LCM to delete empty attribute columns, remove object rows that do not contain A (the extent of parent concepts), and merge the attribute columns of the same objects to form the internal intersection of the initial formal context.

In addition, frequency computation of attributes has been added to reduce the computational consumption of interval comparisons by converting interval comparisons that are to be represented using frequencies. The judgment of $F(C) = m - 1$ is added in this section to reduce invalid computation by storing the concept directly when $F(C) = m - 1$ is found in the concept computation.

4.3   Fusion Algorithm

To better understand the details of the unified computational method, we give a portion of the code for the UCL algorithm, as shown in Algorithm 1.

Algorithm 1: UCL (Unified Computation of Lattices)

---

1 **Function** `ComputeConceptsFrom`$((A, B),\ y,\ P,\ K,\ N)$:
    Input:
2   A - extent, B - intent, y - added attribute, P - the set of empty set intents
3   K - formal context / conditional database, N - empty attribute columns
    Output: concept lattice
4   **Procedure:**
5   **for** $j \leftarrow y$ *upto n-1* **do**
6   **if** $Frequency(A) = m - 1$ **then**
7   break;
8   **if** $j \notin B$ *and* $j \notin P$ *and* $j \notin N$ **then**
9   **if** $IsEmpty(K, A, j)$ **then**
10                $N \leftarrow N \cup \{j\}$
11             $C \leftarrow A \cap \{j\}^{\downarrow}$
12   **if** $Frequency(C) = 0$ **then**
13                $P \leftarrow P \cup \{j\}$
14   **else**
15   **if** $Frequency(C) = Frequency(A)$ **then**
16                   $B \leftarrow B \cup \{j\}$
17   **else**
18   **if** $B \cap Y_j = C^{\uparrow j}$ **then**
19   PutInQueue(C, j)
20   ProcessConcept$((A, B))$
21   Update ComputeConceptsFrom$((C, D'), j + 1, P, K', N)$

For the QC algorithm, we integrate the conditional database with UCL to reduce the traversal space of target data and shorten the scanning time. For the

LCM algorithm, The UCL algorithm retains the attribute inheritance in the In-close4 algorithm, which can make more efficient use of memory in the calculation process and reduce the space complexity at runtime. For the In-close4 algorithm, the UCL algorithm increases the conditional judgment of the child concept, so that when calculating the intents of the child concept, more pruning operations are added to the call tree to reduce repeated calculations.

5   Experiments

5.1   Experiment Conditions

All experiments in this paper were implemented on Windows 11 operating system using Visual Studio 2022 and gcc 9.2.0.

To evaluate the computational efficiency of UCL algorithms, we test the effectiveness of various lattice-structured algorithms using commonly used real datasets Mushroom[1], kddcup99[1], PowerC[1], SUSY[1] and Adult[2]

5.2   Experiment Results

In order to evaluate the computational efficiency of the fusion algorithm UCL, this section calculates the running time of the four algorithms on different datasets to evaluate the computational efficiency of the UCL algorithm.

The experiments were conducted on the Mushroom dataset, the Adult dataset and the SUSY dataset, respectively, and we calculated the running time of the four algorithms with different numbers of tuples, and the results are shown in Fig. 3. It can be noticed that the running time of the four algorithms continues to climb as the number of tuples increases. However, compared to the other three algorithms, the UCL algorithm has the smoothest growth trend, and its growth rate is significantly lower than that of the other three algorithms. This is because the UCL algorithm adds conditional judgments on the sub-concepts, performs more pruning operations on the call tree when calculating the intent of the sub-concepts, and reduces a large number of invalid calculations, meanwhile, the child node inherits the parent attributes and reduces the calculation of the memory,. thus making the overall performance of the algorithm more stable.

Next, we evaluated the improvement rate of the UCL algorithm, which is calculated as shown in Table 1. From the table, it can be found that on all five datasets, the UCL algorithm has a large improvement compared to the other algorithms. Therefore, the UCL algorithm is more efficient than the other algorithms in computing both small and large datasets.

---

¹ SPMF: A Java Open-Source Data Mining Library, https://www.philippe-fournier-viger.com/spmf/index.php.
² UC Irvine Machine Learning Repository, https://archive.ics.uci.edu/dataset/2/adult

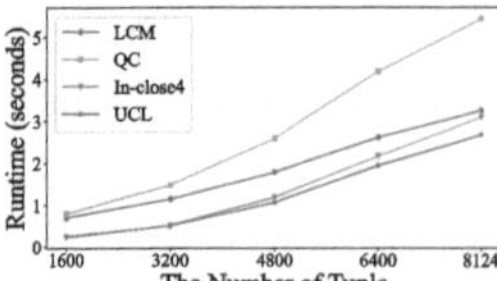 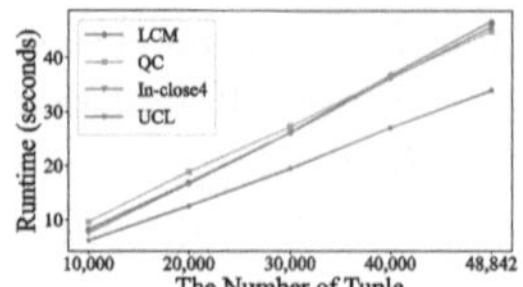 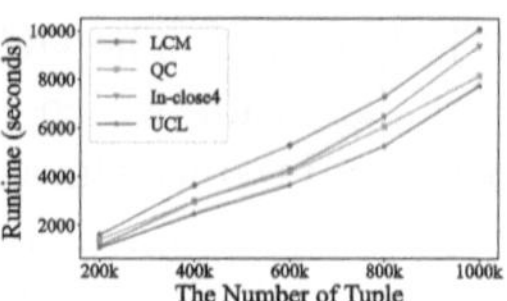

(a) The runtime compari- (b) The runtime compari- (c) The runtime comparison on Mushroom dataset   son on Adult dataset   son on SUSY dataset

Fig. 3. Running time comparison with different tuple numbers

Table 1. Algorithm runtime comparison (seconds)

Lattice structure	Algorithm	Dataset				
		Mushroom	Adult	POWERC	kddcup99	SUSY
Data Cube	QC	5.453	44.873	40.428	1665.177	8929.511
	UCL	2.623	34.019	29.409	1428.82	7728.42
	Improvement Rate	**51.9%**	**24.19%**	**27.26%**	**14.19%**	**13.42%**
Frequent Itemset	LCM	3.297	46.666	38.722	1906.475	10063.584
	UCL	2.623	34.019	29.409	1428.82	7728.42
	Improvement Rate	**20.44%**	**27.1%**	**24.05%**	**25.05%**	**23.2%**
Concept Lattice	In-close4	3.13	45.675	36.097	1726.972	9367.23
	UCL	2.623	34.019	29.409	1428.82	7728.42
	Improvement Rate	**16.2%**	**25.52%**	**18.53%**	**17.26%**	**17.5%**

Improvement Rate = (Original algorithm runtime - Fusion algorithm runtime)/Original algorithm runtime

6   Conclusion

Data cube, frequent itemset and concept lattice are three important data models in on-line analytical processing, data mining and formal conceptual analysis, respectively. In this paper, we take the algebraic lattice as the research basis, and combine the three in a systematic study from the perspective of lattice theory. A unified model of lattice structure is proposed, a fusion algorithm UCL and a unified computational framework of lattice structure are given, and experiments are conducted on real datasets to verify the effectiveness of the UCL algorithm.

In the future, we will deepen the related concepts and computational methods, establish a more unified lattice structure model relationship, synthesize the advantages of the data cube, frequent itemset lattice, and concept lattice in combinatorial computation, and further reduce the time overhead and space overhead in lattice structure computation.

References

1. Lakshmanan, L.V.S., Pei, J., Han, J.: Quotient cube: how to summarize the semantics of a data cube, pp. 778–789 (2002)
2. Wolff, K.E.: The first lesson in formal concept analysis. In: SoftStat 1993, pp. 89–96 (1993)
3. Janostik, R., Konecny, J., Krajca, P.: Lcm is well implemented CBO: study of lcm from FCA point of view. In: CLA, pp. 47–58 (2020)
4. Janostik, R., Konecny, J., Krajča, P.: Lcm from FCA point of view: a CBO-style algorithm with speed-up features. Int. J. Approximate Reasoning **142**, 64–80 (2022)
5. Andrews, S.: In-close, a fast algorithm for computing formal concepts (2009)
6. Andrews, S.: In-close2, a high performance formal concept miner. In: Andrews, S., Polovina, S., Hill, R., Akhgar, B. (eds.) ICCS 2011. LNCS (LNAI), vol. 6828, pp. 50–62. Springer, Heidelberg (2011). https://doi.org/10.1007/978-3-642-22688-5_4
7. Andrews, S.: A 'best-of-breed' approach for designing a fast algorithm for computing fixpoints of galois connections. Inf. Sci. **295**, 633–649 (2015)
8. Andrews, S.: Making use of empty intersections to improve the performance of CbO-type algorithms. In: Bertet, K., Borchmann, D., Cellier, P., Ferré, S. (eds.) ICFCA 2017. LNCS (LNAI), vol. 10308, pp. 56–71. Springer, Cham (2017). https://doi.org/10.1007/978-3-319-59271-8_4
9. Andrews, S.: A new method for inheriting canonicity test failures in close-by-one type algorithms (2018)
10. Gray, J., et al.: Data cube: a relational aggregation operator generalizing group-by, cross-tab, and sub-totals. Data Min. Knowl. Disc. **1**, 29–53 (1997)
11. Zhang, Y., Ordonez, C., García-García, J., Bellatreche, L., Carrillo, H.: The percentage cube. Inf. Syst. **79**, 20–31 (2019)
12. Basil John, S., Lindner, P., Jiang, Z., Koch, C.: Aggregation and exploration of high-dimensional data using the sudokube data cube engine. SIGMOD **4**, 175–178 (2023)
13. John, S.B., Koch, C.: High-dimensional data cubes. Proc. VLDB Endow. **15**(13), 3828–3840 (2022)
14. Silva, R.R., Hirata, C.M., de Castro Lima, J.: Big high-dimension data cube designs for hybrid memory systems. Knowl. Inf. Syst. **62**(12), 4717–4746 (2020). https://doi.org/10.1007/s10115-020-01505-9
15. Mining, W.I.D.: Data Mining: Concepts and Techniques, vol. 10, no. 559–569, p. 4. Morgan Kaufmann (2006)
16. Agrawal, R., Srikant, R., et al.: Fast algorithms for mining association rules. In: Proceedings of the 20th International Conference on Very Large Data Bases, VLDB, Santiago, Chile, vol. 1215, pp. 487–499 (1994)
17. Han, J., Pei, J., Yin, Y.: Mining frequent patterns without candidate generation. ACM SIGMOD Rec. **29**(2), 1–12 (2000)
18. Hong, T.-P., Hung, W.-T., Huang, W.-M., Tsai, Y.-C.: Incremental high fuzzy utility itemset mining. In: Proceedings of the 9th Multidisciplinary International Social Networks Conference, pp. 66–69 (2022)
19. Preti, G., De Francisci Morales, G., Bonchi, F.: Fresco: mining frequent patterns in simplicial complexes. In: Proceedings of the ACM Web Conference 2022, pp. 1444–1454 (2022)

20. Wille, R.: Restructuring lattice theory: an approach based on hierarchies of concepts. In: Ferré, S., Rudolph, S. (eds.) ICFCA 2009. LNCS (LNAI), vol. 5548, pp. 314–339. Springer, Heidelberg (2009). https://doi.org/10.1007/978-3-642-01815-2_23
21. Li, J., Wei Lin, Z.Z.: Conceptual lattice theory and methodology and its research perspectives. Pattern Recogn. Artif. Intell. **33**(7), 619–642 (2020)

Generating Event-Oriented Attribution for Movies via Two-Stage Prefix-Enhanced Multimodal LLM

Yuanjie Lyu, Tong Xu[✉], Zihan Niu, Bo Peng, and Jing Ke

University of Science and Technology of China, Hefei, China
{lyuyuanjie,niuzihan,pb1150300625,kejing}@mail.ustc.edu.cn,
tongxu@ustc.edu.cn

Abstract. The rise of social media platforms has increased the demand for semantic-rich services, such as event and storyline attribution. However, most existing research focuses on clip-level event understanding, mainly through basic captioning tasks, without addressing the causal relationships between events across an entire movie. This presents a significant challenge, as even advanced multimodal large language models (MLLMs) struggle with extensive multimodal information due to limited context length. To tackle this, we propose a Two-Stage Prefix-Enhanced MLLM (TSPE) approach for event attribution, which connects events through their causal semantics in movie videos. In the local stage, we introduce an interaction-aware prefix to guide the model's focus on relevant multimodal cues within a single clip, briefly summarizing each event. In the global stage, we enhance event connections using an inferential knowledge graph and design an event-aware prefix to focus on relevant events, not all preceding clips, leading to accurate event attribution. Extensive evaluations on two real-world datasets demonstrate that our framework outperforms state-of-the-art methods.

Keywords: Movie Understanding · Multi-modal Analysis · Natural Language Processing

1 Introduction

Online media consumption has driven demand for intelligent event-oriented services like **event attribution**, which connects video clips by their causal semantics to explain *why* events occur throughout a full-length movie. This task is crucial for storyline comprehension but remains challenging for current Multimodal Large Language Models (MLLMs) [2, 4] due to their limited context length and the complexity of analyzing numerous, often overlapping, events.

To generate event reasons from a whole-movie perspective despite MLLM limitations, we propose segmenting movies into clips and analyzing them in two

T. Xu—This work was supported in part by the grants from National Natural Science Foundation of China (No.62222213, U22B2059).

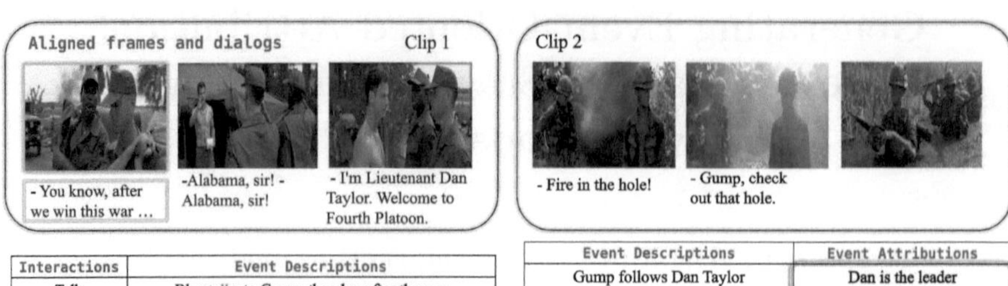

Interactions	Event Descriptions
Talk	Blue talks to Gump the plan after the war
Salute	Gump salutes Dan Taylor to welcome the leader
Welcome	Dan Taylor welcomes Gump to Fourth Platoon.

Event Descriptions	Event Attributions
Gump follows Dan Taylor on a mission	Dan is the leader
Taylor orders Gump check out that hole	An enemy could potentially exist

Fig. 1. A toy example selected from the MovieGraph dataset, which contains two clips from the movie *Forrest Gump*. Specifically, Clip 1 contains three events, and Clip 2 contains two events. The reason behind the event "Gump follows Dan Taylor on a mission" in Clip 2 is derived from the event "Gump salutes Dan Taylor" in Clip 1.

stages: a **local stage** for individual events within clips, and a **global stage** for identifying causal relationships between events across different clips by selecting relevant prior clips. This strategy faces two main challenges:

- **Local Event Ambiguity:** Clips often contain multiple events (For example, Clip 1 in Fig. 1), making it hard to align multimodal cues with a specific target event.
- **Global Causal Linking:** Identifying truly relevant prior clips from many candidates is difficult, as superficial sentence similarity may not capture deeper causal connections (e.g., between Clip 1 and Clip 2 in Fig. 1).

To address these issues, we introduce the **Two-Stage Prefix-Enhanced MLLM (TSPE)** framework. For the local stage, an **interaction-aware prefix** helps the MLLM focus on relevant multimodal cues for a specific event, mitigating interference from overlapping events in the same clip. For the global stage, an **event-aware prefix** and the ATOMIC knowledge graph enhance semantic understanding between events, enabling the MLLM to capture long-range causal relationships using pertinent prior events and commonsense predictions from ATOMIC.

We validate TSPE on the MovieGraph dataset and our new CHAR (Character Behavior Analysis and Reasoning) dataset. Comparative and ablation experiments demonstrate TSPE's effectiveness against state-of-the-art methods.

2   Related Work

Video Semantic Understanding. Video understanding encompasses various semantic levels, from identifying basic actions and objects to more complex, increasingly studied higher-level interpretations like events [9]. Datasets such as MovieGraphs [11] offer rich annotations that support these advanced video understanding tasks. However, most research concentrates on short clips, often

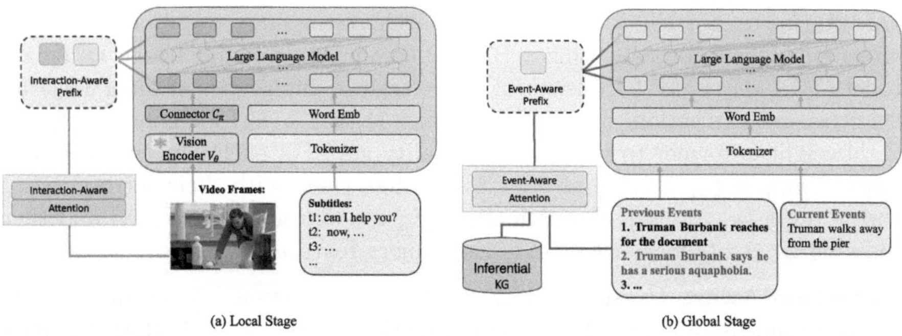

Fig. 2. Illustration of the Two-Stage Prefix-Enhanced MLLM (TSPE) for event attribution in movie videos: Stage 1 extracts multimodal cues for event summarization, while Stage 2 infers underlying causes from these summaries.

neglecting long-term dependencies and logical relationships. While some works delve into long-form video, for instance, by segmenting movies by storyline [12], our work distinctively targets semantic-level event description and attribution within extended video narratives.

Vision-Language Pre-trained Models. Vision language pre-training (VLP) has led to multimodal foundation models for both understanding (e.g., image-text retrieval) and generation (e.g., image captioning), utilizing architectures like encoder-decoders [6]. LLM-based vision-language models, such as Instruct-BLIP [4], integrate a visual encoder with a pre-trained LLM. Although effective for tasks like visual question answering, these models often struggle with long, complex videos, particularly in filtering pertinent multimodal cues. Nevertheless, VLPs provide a robust foundation for specialized adaptations, with recent efforts [8] showing significant improvements across various domains. Drawing inspiration from this, we employ BLIP-2 as our backbone, capitalizing on its flexibility for comprehensive vision-language understanding and generation.

3   Method

We propose a Two-Stage Prefix-Enhanced MLLM (TSPE) approach for event attribution in movie videos, as illustrated in Fig. 2. The method comprises two stages: local and global.

3.1   Local Stage

The local stage aims to extract multimodal cues from video clips and generate high-level event summaries, which subsequently aid in event attribution.

Preprocessing. Since narrative videos are lengthy, they are typically segmented into shorter scene-based clips, each containing one or more complete events. As segmentation is not the focus of our research, we assume these clips are pre-segmented. Our approach utilizes BLIP-2 as the Multimodal Large Language Model (MLLM). BLIP-2 consists of a pre-trained image transformer (F_v) for visual feature extraction, a text transformer (FlanT5, F_s) for generation, and a lightweight Q-former to bridge the modality gap. For each clip, we uniformly sample t frames $\{v_1, \ldots, v_t\}$ at 1 FPS and align them with their corresponding subtitle texts $\{s_1, \ldots, s_t\}$. Frame features f_{v_i} are extracted via $F_v(v_i)$ and then processed by the Q-former to yield visual query features.

Interaction-Aware Prefix. A naive approach to summarizing events involves feeding all multimodal cues from a clip directly into the MLLM. However, clips often contain dense yet irrelevant visual and textual information. To distill the most pertinent details, we introduce an **Interaction-Aware Prefix**. This prefix is an embedding formed by weighting short-term subtitles and frames based on their relevance to detected social interactions.

Social interactions are pivotal for event understanding. We leverage existing methods [5] to detect these interactions and then assess the relevance of multimodal cues to them. Subtitles s_i highly similar to a detected interaction I receive greater weight. Specifically, we use the frozen encoder of FlanT5 (F_s) [3] to extract features H_{s_i} from subtitle s_i and H_{I_s} from the textual description of interaction I_s. The [CLS] token's hidden state from the encoder serves as the global representation for both.

Using the sequence of subtitle representations $\{h_{s_1}, \ldots, h_{s_t}\}$ as keys and the interaction representation h_{I_s} as the query, a dot-product attention mechanism calculates the association scores A_s for subtitles:

$$A_s = \text{Softmax}\left(\frac{\mathbf{W_q}h_{I_s}(\mathbf{W_k}\{h_{s_1}, \ldots, h_{s_t}\})^T}{\sqrt{d}}\right), \tag{1}$$

where d is the feature dimension, and $\mathbf{W_q}, \mathbf{W_k}$ are learnable parameters. Similarly, to filter irrelevant visual data, visual features of the interaction f_{I_v} (extracted via an image transformer) and frame features $\{f_{v_1}, \ldots, f_{v_t}\}$ are used to compute visual attention scores A_v:

$$A_v = \text{Softmax}\left(\frac{\mathbf{W_q}f_{I_v}(\mathbf{W_k}\{f_{v_1}, \ldots, f_{v_t}\})^T}{\sqrt{d}}\right). \tag{2}$$

The temporally aligned subtitle and frame attention scores are combined and normalized: $\mathbf{A} = \text{normalization}(A_s + A_v)$. This combined score $\mathbf{A}$ then weights the sequences of frame features $\{f_{v_i}\}$ and subtitle features $\{h_{s_i}\}$, which are subsequently passed through a learnable projection to produce the interaction-aware visual context H_v and textual context H_s. These contexts highlight event-relevant frames and subtitles.

While these interaction-aware contexts H_v and H_s capture key information, some details might be lost. To address this, we use these contexts as prefixes while also inputting the full multimodal data into the MLLM. Cross-attention between the prefix and the full data helps the model focus on the most critical cues, creating a hierarchical structure for improved multimodal understanding.

During the generation of the i-th token of the event summary v_i, the interaction-aware prefixes (H_v, H_s) are concatenated with the full subtitle features $(H_{s_1:s_t})$ and full visual features $(H_{v_1:v_t})$, both processed via the Q-former, and previously generated tokens $w_{1:i-1}$:

$$v_i = \text{DEC}(w_{1:i-1} \oplus H_v \oplus H_s, H_{s_1:s_t}, H_{v_1:v_t}). \tag{3}$$

Finally, standard linear and softmax layers are applied to v_i to compute the probability distribution for the i-th output token.

3.2   Global Stage

Inferential Knowledge Graph. Event descriptions and their causally related past events often exhibit semantic dissimilarity. To bridge this gap, we incorporate an inferential knowledge graph (KG) to enhance commonsense reasoning. This KG helps infer potential event outcomes, character effects, and motivations, thereby connecting semantically distant but logically related events.

We utilize ATOMIC [10], a commonsense KG featuring nine types of inference relations (e.g., "causes", "effect"). As ATOMIC may not cover all specific events encountered, we fine-tune a FlanT5 model [3] on ATOMIC, inspired by prior work [1,7]. This allows us to generate textual commonsense inferences for novel events, effectively expanding implicit pre-trained knowledge into an explicit KG. For each event, we generate these nine inference types and concatenate them as supplementary contextual information.

Event-Aware Prefix. After enriching current event descriptions with these KG-based inferential predictions, we employ an event-aware prefix mechanism to refine the selection of relevant previous events for generating event causes.

Given a current event E_i and a set of previous events $\{E_1, \ldots, E_{i-1}\}$, we use their respective representations (h_{E_i} and $\{h_{E_1}, \ldots, h_{E_{i-1}}\}$) as query and keys in a dot-product attention mechanism to compute association scores:

$$A_E = \text{Softmax}\left(\frac{\mathbf{W_q} h_{E_i}(\mathbf{W_k}\{h_{E_1}, \ldots, h_{E_{i-1}}\})^T}{\sqrt{d}}\right). \tag{4}$$

These attention scores $\mathbf{A_E}$ then weight the features of previous events. The weighted features are subsequently passed through a learnable projection to form the event-aware context H_E. Unlike the Interaction-Aware Prefix, this mechanism omits direct visual information because event descriptions are assumed to encapsulate key visual details, and processing all frames from lengthy videos like movies is computationally prohibitive for this causal reasoning step.

Since event causes might also be present in the current video clip's subtitles $(H_{s_1:s_t})$, these are also provided to the model. When generating the j-th token of the causal explanation v_j, the event-aware prefix H_E is concatenated with previously generated word embeddings $w_{1:j-1}$. This, along with the full representations of past events $H_{E_1:E_{i-1}}$ and current clip subtitles, is fed to the decoder:

$$v_j = \text{DEC}(w_{1:j-1} \oplus H_E, H_{E_1:E_{i-1}}, H_{s_1:s_t}). \tag{5}$$

Here, H_E provides a focused summary of relevant past events. Finally, linear and softmax layers classify v_j to produce the probability distribution for the output.

4   Experiment

Table 1. Comparison with state-of-the-art models on MovieGraph and self-constructed CHAR dataset, showing combined BLEU-2, BLEU-3, METEOR, and ROUGE-L scores for Local and Global Stages. Best results per stage and dataset are in **bold**.

Dataset	Local Stage					Global Stage				
	Model	B-2	B-3	MTR	R-L	Model	B-2	B-3	MTR	R-L
MovieGraph	FlanT5	0.039	0.019	0.049	0.107	FlanT5	0.052	0.026	0.052	0.145
	BLIP-2	0.054	0.029	0.069	0.133	FlanT5-KE	0.062	0.034	0.055	0.149
	FlanT5-IE	0.058	0.033	0.051	0.129	–	–	–	–	–
	BLIP-2-IE	0.092	0.056	0.070	0.175	–	–	–	–	–
	TSPE	**0.110**	**0.071**	**0.080**	**0.206**	TSPE	**0.070**	**0.039**	**0.063**	**0.168**
CHAR	FlanT5	0.033	0.017	0.036	0.109	FlanT5	0.083	0.052	0.066	0.176
	BLIP-2	0.040	0.024	0.043	0.110	FlanT5-KE	0.087	0.054	0.061	0.178
	FlanT5-IE	0.035	0.021	0.039	0.105	–	–	–	–	–
	BLIP-2-IE	0.049	0.029	0.045	0.121	–	–	–	–	–
	TSPE	**0.061**	**0.037**	**0.056**	**0.139**	TSPE	**0.091**	**0.056**	**0.071**	**0.185**

Datasets and Evaluation Metrics. We conduct experiments on two datasets: MovieGraph [11] and our self-constructed CHAR. Fine-grained event datasets with attribution annotations from a holistic movie perspective are scarce, and MovieGraph [11] is the primary source. It provides graphical annotations for 51 movies (7,637 scenes, 38,872 interactions) and is split into 35 training, 7 validation, and 9 test movies, following [5]. Our CHAR dataset consists of 21 movies (averaging 2 h each), annotated using MovieGraph's methodology but with an emphasis on causal relationships between events; it is split into 12 training, 4 validation, and 5 test movies. We evaluate performance using standard text generation metrics: BLEU, METEOR, and ROUGE-L.

Baselines. For the local stage (event summarization), our primary baseline is BLIP-2. We also compare it against FlanT5 (a text-only model) to assess the impact of multimodal information. Both models are evaluated in two settings: (1) their original form, using direct frame and subtitle inputs, and (2) an Interaction-Enhanced (IE) version that incorporates social interactions as additional prompts. For the global stage (attribution generation), we use FlanT5 as a text-only baseline, which processes current clip dialogues, selected previous event descriptions, and current event descriptions. We also introduce FlanT5-KE, which integrates inferential knowledge graph information for richer context. All baseline models are retrained or fine-tuned on the respective datasets.

Implementation Details. The local stage model is initialized with BLIP-2 [6], while the global stage uses FlanT5-XL [3]. For efficiency, we freeze the visual transformer and text encoder in the local stage, training only the last 5 decoder layers. Similarly, in the global stage, the FlanT5 encoder is frozen, and only the last 5 decoder layers are trained. All experiments on MovieGraph and CHAR share identical settings: a batch size of 4, the AdamW optimizer (learning rate $1e^{-5}$, weight decay 0.01), and top-k sampling ($k = 4$) for generation tasks. These hyperparameters are applied to all baselines to ensure fair comparison.

4.1   Comparison with SOTA Methods on Automatic Metrics

Local Stage. Results in Table 1 demonstrate TSPE's superiority in generating event descriptions by effectively filtering irrelevant multimodal information, significantly outperforming all baselines. The advantage of BLIP-2 over the text-only FlanT5 confirms the importance of multimodal inputs. While adding social interaction prompts improves performance for both BLIP-2-IE and FlanT5-IE over their respective original versions, TSPE's interaction-aware prefix proves more effective than the simpler concatenation strategy. Generating event descriptions for the CHAR dataset is noted to be more challenging than for Movie-Graph, likely due to CHAR's longer average clip duration (5 min vs. 1 min), which increases interaction density and complexity.

Global Stage. Analysis of event reason generation in Table 1 shows that incorporating an inferential Knowledge Graph (KG) improves performance (FlanT5-KE over FlanT5), as it aids in reasoning about causes and effects. However, TSPE achieves superior results by employing event-aware attention to filter irrelevant prior events, unlike FlanT5-KE which treats all potential past events

Table 3. Ablation experiments on Movie-Graph dataset in global stage.

Model	METEOR	ROUGE-L
TSPE	**0.063**	**0.168**
W/O Subtitle	0.048	0.147
W/O Inferential KG	0.059	0.163
W/O Previous Events	0.051	0.143
W/O Event-Aware Module	0.055	0.149

Table 2. Ablation experiments on Movie-Graph dataset in local stage.

Model	METEOR	ROUGE-L
TSPE	**0.080**	**0.206**
W/O VA	0.080	0.201
W/O TA	0.078	0.198
W/O VA & TA	0.070	0.175

equally. The performance gain from TSPE over FlanT5-KE is more substantial than that of FlanT5-KE over FlanT5, suggesting that effective filtering and direct causality modeling are more critical than solely adding external knowledge.

4.2 Ablation Study

We conducted ablation studies on the MovieGraph dataset to assess each module:

Impact of the Interaction-Aware Module on the Local Stage. Table 2 highlights the importance of the Interaction-Aware module's components. Performance degrades upon removing either its visual attention (VA in Eq. (2), which captures correlations between visual interactions and frame features) or its textual attention (TA, linking textual interactions with dialogues). Eliminating the entire module, thereby reducing the model to BLIP-2-IE, leads to a significant drop in performance, emphasizing the efficiency of our prefix mechanism.

Impact of Different Factors on the Global Stage. Table 3 demonstrates the contributions of key information sources for event reasoning. Removing current clip character dialogues significantly impacts performance, indicating that many event causes are directly inferred from them. Excluding previous events also causes a notable performance drop, confirming the importance of contextual coherence and logical dependencies. Disabling the event-aware module (reducing the model to FlanT5-KE) leads to worse results, emphasizing the need for fine-grained filtering of potentially noisy past event prompts. Finally, removing the inferential KG slightly lowers performance, confirming its utility.

5   Conclusion

This paper presents TSPE, a novel two-stage framework for generating attributions for story events in long videos. The local stage focuses on describing the events by using an interaction-aware prefix, which estimates the relevance between multi-modal cues and social interactions. The global stage attributes events by leveraging an inferential knowledge graph to enhance semantic similarity, and leveraging an event-aware prefix to capture logical event correlations. Evaluations on two real-world datasets demonstrate that TSPE outperforms several SOTA methods.

References

1. Bosselut, A., Rashkin, H., Sap, M., Malaviya, C., Celikyilmaz, A., Choi, Y.: COMET: commonsense transformers for automatic knowledge graph construction. In: ACL 2019, pp. 4762–4779 (2019)
2. Chen, G., et al.: VideoLLM: modeling video sequence with large language models. arXiv preprint arXiv:2305.13292 (2023)

3. Chung, H.W., et al.: Scaling instruction-finetuned language models. arXiv preprint arXiv:2210.11416 (2022)
4. Dai, W., et al.: InstructBLIP: towards general-purpose vision-language models with instruction tuning. arXiv preprint arXiv:2305.06500 (2023)
5. Kukleva, A., Tapaswi, M., Laptev, I.: Learning interactions and relationships between movie characters. In: CVPR, pp. 9849–9858 (2020)
6. Li, J., Li, D., Savarese, S., Hoi, S.: BLIP-2: bootstrapping language-image pre-training with frozen image encoders and large language models. arXiv preprint arXiv:2301.12597 (2023)
7. Lin, L., et al.: What makes the story forward? inferring commonsense explanations as prompts for future event generation. In: SIGIR, pp. 1098–1109 (2022)
8. Lin, Y., Xie, Y., Chen, D., Xu, Y., Zhu, C., Yuan, L.: Revive: regional visual representation matters in knowledge-based visual question answering. In: NeuraIPS, vol. 35, pp. 10560–10571 (2022)
9. Martin, L., et al.: Event representations for automated story generation with deep neural nets. In: AAAI, vol. 32 (2018)
10. Sap, M., et al.: Atomic: an atlas of machine commonsense for if-then reasoning. In: AAAI, pp. 3027–3035 (2019)
11. Vicol, P., Tapaswi, M., Castrejon, L., Fidler, S.: MovieGraphs: towards understanding human-centric situations from videos. In: Proceedings of the IEEE Conference on Computer Vision and Pattern Recognition, pp. 8581–8590 (2018)
12. Wu, H., et al.: Scene consistency representation learning for video scene segmentation. In: CVPR, pp. 14021–14030 (2022)

Multi-scale Masked Transformer for Robust Point Cloud Registration

Taihao Zhang[1] , Longxiang Gao[1,2(✉)] , Youyang Qu[1,2] , Zonghao Ji[1] , and Rong Liu[3]

[1] Shandong Provincial Key Laboratory of Computer Networks, Ministry of Education, Shandong Computer Science Center (National Supercomputer Center in Jinan), Qilu University of Technology (Shandong Academy of Sciences), Jinan, China
`{gaolx,quyy}@sdas.org`
[2] Shandong Provincial Key Laboratory of Computing Power Internet and Service Computing, Shandong Fundamental Research Center for Computer Science, Jinan, China
[3] Computer and Information Engineering, Qilu Institute of Technology, Jinan, China

Abstract. Point cloud registration plays a crucial role in computer vision and robotics. In recent years, although a series of registration methods have achieved remarkable success in terms of accuracy and efficiency, few studies have thoroughly investigated the impact of feature interactions across different scales on registration performance. We propose a multi-scale masked autoencoding geometric transformer, which achieves high-precision registration through hierarchical feature fusion. The method innovatively employs a multi-scale masking strategy to construct cross-scale consistent visible regions. During the encoding phase, it simultaneously models intra-point-cloud structural features and inter-point-cloud geometric consistency via a dual-branch attention mechanism. In the decoding stage, a feature pyramid fusion module is designed to progressively aggregate low-level geometric details and high-level semantic features through skip connections. Finally, a deep regressor is utilized to supervise and optimize the matching between predicted values and ground truth, enabling robust point correspondence. Experiments demonstrate that MMGT achieves superior performance on both 3DMatch and KITTI datasets.

Keywords: Point cloud registration · Multi-scale masking strategy · Transformer

1 Introduction

Point cloud registration is a core task in 3D computer vision [10,25], aiming to align overlapping regions of point clouds by estimating rigid transformation matrices. In recent years, deep learning methods such as PointNetLK [3] have made significant progress by using neural networks to extract point features

T. Zhu et al. (Eds.): KSEM 2025, LNAI 15922, pp. 278–290, 2026.
https://doi.org/10.1007/978-981-95-3058-8_25

and establish correspondences, achieving notable improvements in accuracy, efficiency, and generalization. However, early methods primarily relied on local feature extractors (e.g., PointNet [14] and KPConv [18]), which lacked multi-scale modeling capabilities and struggled to capture global structures and contextual information. This limitation restricts the accuracy of transformation estimation, particularly in complex scenes and partial overlap scenarios, highlighting the need for new methodological breakthroughs.

In order to improve the performance of point cloud registration, researchers have proposed various improvement methods. For example, Predator [10] improves global feature representation by introducing attention mechanisms, but it lacks effective positional encoding, making it difficult to capture geometric spatial structure information. GeoTransformer [16] improves rotation invariance and point-to-point correspondence quality by explicitly encoding relative position information. However, existing methods still share common limitations: they fail to explicitly exploit multi-scale geometric features, resulting in insufficient discriminative power in feature modeling and difficulty in expressing hierarchical structural information, which affects robustness and accuracy in complex scenes. Therefore, there is an urgent need for more effective multi-scale feature fusion mechanisms.

To address the limitations of existing methods in multi-scale geometric feature modeling, this paper proposes a multi-scale masked autoencoding feature interaction Transformer for point cloud registration, termed Multi-scale Masked Geometric Transformer (MMGT). During the encoding stage, we employ the farthest point sampling method to downsample the point cloud, thereby obtaining a multi-scale point cloud representation. To capture features at different scales, we introduce a random masking strategy that randomly masks partial point sets across scales, constructing dynamic combinations of visible and masked points. Specifically, at the coarsest downsampling level, we design a reverse projection mechanism to map visible points back to the original point cloud space, ensuring consistency of visible points in the multi-scale representation. During the feature encoding process, we simultaneously perform intra-point-cloud local feature aggregation and inter-point-cloud interaction modeling to comprehensively capture geometric structures and spatial relationships. In the decoding stage, based on the encoded features of visible points, we locate the surrounding visible points of each masked point through k-nearest neighbor search and employ an attention mechanism to fuse the features of visible and masked points, while utilizing a cross-attention module to achieve feature interaction across point clouds. To further enhance multi-scale feature correlation, we perform cross-level fusion between the visible point features from the encoding stage and the corresponding features from the decoding stage. Finally, we design a deep robust estimator to supervise the matching probability distribution of each point. Experimental results demonstrate that MMGT achieves outstanding performance on the 3DMatch [26] and KITTI [9] datasets.

Our main contributions are:

1. We propose a multi-scale masked autoencoding feature interaction framework for encoding and fusing point cloud matching features at different scales, achieving cross-scale feature interaction and information fusion.
2. We designed an adaptive instance normalization (AdaIN) module to significantly improve the quality and matching accuracy of point cloud feature generation by achieving cross-scale feature registration from the perspective of probability distribution.
3. we propose a network called deep confidence regressor to predict the confidence scores indicating how much a feature point is reliably matchable
4. We conducted experiments on the 3DMatch and KITTI datasets, and under various settings, our method achieved state-of-the-art performance on both 3DMatch and KITTI.

2   Related Work

2.1   Direct Registration Methods.

In recent years, deep learning-based point cloud registration methods [5,12,24] have made significant progress. PointNetLK [3] and FMR [11] combine PointNet's global feature extraction with the Lucas-Kanade algorithm, enhancing registration robustness and efficiency, particularly excelling in scenarios with complex geometric structures and large-scale transformations. DCP [19] introduces graph neural networks and attention mechanisms, improving adaptability to complex shapes and large-scale transformations. PRNet [14] further enhances accuracy through iterative optimization in feature space. However, while these methods perform well on single synthetic datasets, they still face limitations in complex scenes and struggle to address the diverse challenges of real-world applications.

2.2   Masked Data Modeling

Masked Data Modeling (MDM), as an efficient self-supervised learning paradigm, has achieved significant success in NLP and computer vision. For example, Data2vec [4] extracts contextual representations from masked inputs, MAE [20] learns features from unmasked regions to reconstruct masked parts, and SimMIM [21] directly predicts masked pixel values through a linear layer. In recent years, MDM has been gradually applied to point cloud processing, such as Point-MAE [13], which uses an asymmetric Transformer to learn features from unmasked points to reconstruct masked points. However, point cloud registration tasks require high spatial alignment accuracy and geometric consistency, and existing methods struggle to effectively model geometric correspondences between point clouds, limiting registration performance. Therefore, designing more efficient masked modeling strategies by leveraging the strengths of MDM and the characteristics of point cloud registration remains a critical challenge.

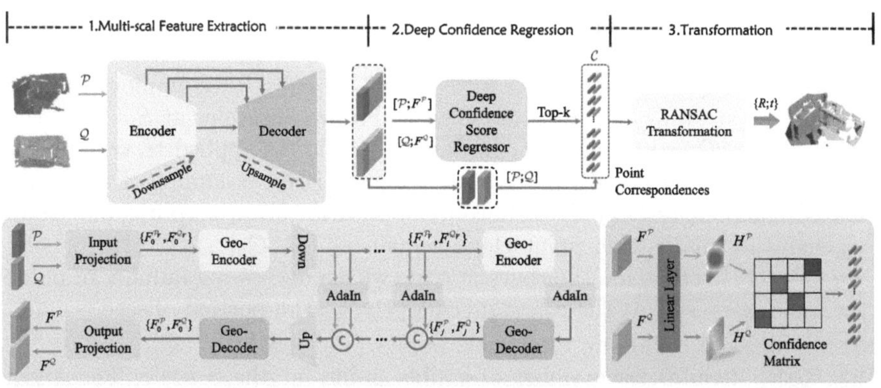

Fig. 1. Our pipeline involves multi-scale masking for feature extraction, encoding visible points to enable cross-cloud interaction, and generating features for masked points. Dense correspondences are then matched, and RANSAC estimates the optimal transformation.

3   Method

Given two partially overlapping point clouds, $\mathcal{P} = \{\mathbf{p}_i \in \mathbb{R}^3 \mid i = 1, \ldots, N\}$ and $\mathcal{Q} = \{\mathbf{q}_i \in \mathbb{R}^3 \mid i = 1, \ldots, M\}$, the goal of point cloud registration is to select the top-k high-confidence corresponding point sets from the matching matrix and estimate a rigid transformation $T = \{R, t\}$ (where $R \in SO(3)$ represents the rotation matrix and $t \in \mathbb{R}^3$ represents the translation vector). This transformation aligns the two point clouds $\{\mathcal{P}, \mathcal{Q}\}$ from different coordinate systems into a unified coordinate system. The rigid transformation can be solved by minimizing the geometric error between the corresponding point sets, which can be mathematically expressed as:

$$\min_{R,t} \sum_{(p^*_{x_i}, q^*_{y_i}) \in \mathcal{C}^*} \| R * p^*_{x_i} + t - q^*_{y_i} \|_2^2 \tag{1}$$

Here, $\mathcal{C}^*$ represents the set of corresponding points between $\mathcal{P}$ and $\mathcal{Q}$.

The overall framework of MMGT is illustrated in Fig. 1, with its core being a Transformer-based encoder-decoder architecture. First, given a source point cloud $\mathcal{P}$ and a target point cloud $\mathcal{Q}$, the model hierarchically samples the point clouds using a multi-scale masking strategy to capture hierarchical geometric information. Next, at the last scale, a portion of the points is randomly masked while retaining the visible points, and multi-scale consistency is ensured through back-projection. Then, the multi-scale points are fed into the Multi-scale Hierarchical Matching Module for feature interaction and matching, encoding deep geometric features. Finally, the point matching module generates corresponding point pairs, and the optimal transformation is estimated using the RANSAC algorithm to achieve point cloud registration.

3.1   Point Sampling Multi-scale Masking

Given the input point clouds $\mathcal{P} \in \mathbb{R}^{N \times 3}$ and $\mathcal{Q} \in \mathbb{R}^{M \times 3}$, we employs a multi-scale masking strategy to generate point cloud representations at S scales. Taking point cloud $\mathcal{P}$ as an example (the same operation is applied to $\mathcal{Q}$), starting from the initial point cloud $\mathcal{P}_0$, iterative Furthest Point Sampling (FPS) and k Nearest-Neighbour (k-NN) algorithms are applied for downsampling and grouping, generating multi-scale point cloud sequences $\{\mathcal{P}_i, \mathcal{Q}_i\}$, $i \in \{1,2,3,..,S\}$, where $\{\mathcal{P}_S, \mathcal{Q}_S\}$ represents the coarsest scale with a decreasing number of points as the scale increases. At the coarsest scale $\{\mathcal{P}_S, \mathcal{Q}_S\}$, a portion of seed points is randomly masked, retaining the visible points $\{\mathcal{P}_S^V \in \mathbb{R}^{|\mathcal{P}|_S^V \times 3}, \mathcal{Q}_S^V \in \mathbb{R}^{|\mathcal{Q}|_S^V \times 3}\}$, $\{|\mathcal{P}|_S^V, |\mathcal{Q}|_S^V\}$ denotes the number of visible points at the S scale. These visible points are then back-projected to all scales. Specifically, the nearest neighbors k from subsequent scales are used to determine the positions of visible points on the current scale, denoted as $\{\mathcal{P}_i^V \in \mathbb{R}^{|\mathcal{P}|_i^V \times 3}, \mathcal{Q}_i^V \in \mathbb{R}^{|\mathcal{Q}|_i^V \times 3}\}$, $i \in \{1,2,3,..,S\}$. while the remaining positions are masked, denoted as $\{\mathcal{P}_i^M \in \mathbb{R}^{|\mathcal{P}|_i^M \times 3}, \mathcal{Q}_i^M \in \mathbb{R}^{|\mathcal{Q}|_i^M \times 3}\}$, where the total number of points on each scale satisfies $|\mathcal{P}|_i = |\mathcal{P}|_i^S + |\mathcal{P}|_i^M$. This strategy ensures geometric consistency and topological integrity in the multi-scale representations.

3.2   Multi-scale Hierarchical Matching Module

Hierarchical Encoder. The hierarchical encoder proposed in this paper adopts a cascaded architecture consisting of a three-layer point cloud downsampling structure and a four-level Geo-Encoder module. Initially, the point cloud is processed through an input projection module to generate the initial geometric features $\{F_0^{\mathcal{P}}, F_0^{\mathcal{Q}}\}$. These features are then sequentially passed through Geo-Encoder and downsampling layers modules, enabling hierarchical feature encoding through multi-scale feature extraction and fusion, thereby enhancing the expressive power of the features.

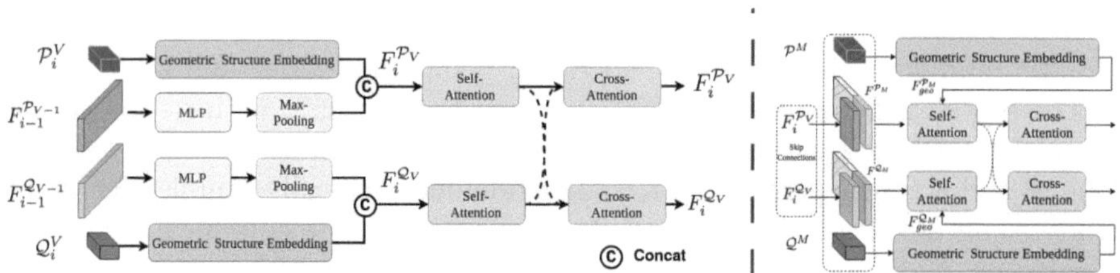

Fig. 2. Left: The structure of geometric Geo-Encoder module. Right: The computation graph of geometric Geo-Deoder

Geo-Encoder. The structure of Geo-Encoder is illustrated in Fig. 2. It employs self-attention mechanism and cross-attention mechanism to model the global correlations of visible points in both feature space and geometric space at each scale, while facilitating feature interaction between two point clouds. The specific workflow is as follows: at the i-th stage (where $1 < i < S$), the features from the $(i-1)$-th stage, $\{F_{i-1}^{\mathcal{P}-1}, F_{i-1}^{\mathcal{Q}-1}\}$, are first aggregated using MLP and max-pooling operations with k-nearest neighbor indices, generating the initial features $\{F_i^{\mathcal{P}v} \in \mathbb{R}^{|\mathcal{P}| \times C_i}, F_i^{\mathcal{Q}v} \in \mathbb{R}^{|\mathcal{Q}| \times C_i}\}$ for the i-th stage. Subsequently, relative position encoding is applied to the visible points to obtain the position-encoded features $\{F_{\text{geo}}^{\mathcal{P}v}, F_{\text{geo}}^{\mathcal{Q}v}\}$. These features, along with the initial features, are then fed into a self-attention layer to extract global features, followed by a cross-attention layer to enable feature interaction across point clouds. As the network depth increases, the feature dimensions are progressively expanded, ultimately yielding the output $\{F_S^{\mathcal{P}} \in \mathbb{R}^{|\mathcal{P}| \times C_S}\}, F_S^{\mathcal{Q}} \in \mathbb{R}^{|\mathcal{Q}| \times C_S}\}$, where C_S denotes the feature dimension at the S-th scale. the self-attention formula is as follows:

$$F_i = \sum_{j=1}^{|\mathcal{P}|} \text{softmax}\left(\frac{(F_i W^{\mathcal{Q}})(F_j W^K + g_{i,j} W^R)^T}{\sqrt{d_t}} \right) \cdot (F_j W^V). \qquad (2)$$

Here, W^Q, W^K, W^V, and W^R are learnable projection matrices that map the input features F_i and F_j as well as the geometric structure embedding $g_{i,j}$ [16] to the query (Query), key (Key), value (Value), and geometric relation (Geometric Relation) spaces.The cross-attention formula is as follows:

$$F_i^{\mathcal{P}} = \sum_{j=1}^{|\mathcal{Q}|} \text{softmax}\left(\frac{(F_i^{\mathcal{P}} W^{\mathcal{Q}})(F_j^{\mathcal{Q}} W^K)^T}{\sqrt{d_t}} \right) \cdot (F_j^{\mathcal{Q}} W^V). \qquad (3)$$

In the formula, $F_i^{\mathcal{P}}$ and $F_j^{\mathcal{Q}}$ are the features of point clouds $\mathcal{P}$ and $\mathcal{Q}$, $W^{\mathcal{Q}}, W^K$, and W^V are learnable projection matrices that map the features to query, key, and value spaces, respectively, d_t is the feature dimension, softmax computes the attention weights, $\sqrt{d_t}$ is the scaling factor, and the output feature $Z_i^{\mathcal{P}}$ is generated through weighted summation.

Hierarchical Decoder. As shown in Fig. 1, the hierarchical decoder architecture proposed in this paper consists of an Upsampling Module and a Geo-Decoder Module. The Upsampling Module achieves cross-scale feature interaction and fusion through feature upsampling, progressively restoring high-resolution features.

Geo-Decoder. The structure of Geo-Decoder is illustrated in Fig. 2, through the hierarchical encoder, we extract multi-scale visible point features $\{F_i^{\mathcal{P}v}, F_i^{\mathcal{Q}v}\}$, $i \in \{1, 2, .., S\}$. Starting from the highest level (the S-th scale), we model the masked point feature extraction as a feature generation task: a set of learnable shared feature vectors $\{F_S^{\mathcal{P}M}, F_S^{\mathcal{Q}M}\}$ is initialized for all masked positions $\{\mathcal{P}^M \in R^{\mathcal{P}_M \times 3}, \mathcal{Q}^M \in R^{\mathcal{Q}_M \times 3}\}$, which are then concatenated with the visible point features $\{F_i^{\mathcal{P}v}, F_i^{\mathcal{Q}v}\}$ at the current scale and the geometric features $\{F_{geo}^{\mathcal{P}_M}, F_{geo}^{\mathcal{Q}_M}\}$ generated by the positional encoding module from the masked point coordinates. This results in the fused feature representation $H_i^I = \{F^{Iv}, F^{IM}, F_{geo}^{IM}\}, I \in \{\mathcal{P}, \mathcal{Q}\}, i \in \{1, 2, .., S\}$, which serves as the input to the Geo-Decoder. To fully model the long-range dependencies between visible and masked points, we employ a global self-attention mechanism instead of local constraints. The formula is shown in (2). Through the self-attention mechanism, the output features are represented as $F_j^{\mathcal{P}} \in \mathbb{R}^{|\mathcal{P}| \times C_j}$ and $F_j^{\mathcal{Q}} \in \mathbb{R}^{|\mathcal{Q}| \times C_j}$, where $|\mathcal{P}|$ and $|\mathcal{Q}|$ represent the number of points in the point clouds at the current scale, and C_i is the feature dimension. Subsequently, the output features are fed into the cross-attention layer, where cross-cloud feature associations are established, ultimately generating spatially consistent feature representations $\{F_i^{\mathcal{P}} \in \mathbb{R}^{|\mathcal{P}| \times C_i}, F^{\mathcal{Q}} \in \mathbb{R}^{|\mathcal{Q}| \times C_i}\}$. $\mathcal{P}^M$

Point Feature Upsampling. We upsample point features between different stages to progressively reconstruct the features of each masked point. Specifically, the j-th stage of the decoder corresponds to the $(S + 1 - j)$-th stage of the encoder, both containing point features at the same scale $(S + 1 - j)$ with a feature dimension of C_{S+1-j}. Between the $(j - 1)$-th stage and the j-th stage (where $1 < j < S - 1$), we recover the neighboring features using a weighted interpolation method (referencing PointNet++ [15]) based on the point features and their coordinates from the $(j - 1)$-th stage, along with the nearest neighbor indices obtained during the sampling phase. This process generates the point features for the j-th stage.

Skip Connections. To enhance the expressive capability of fine-grained geometric features and to constrain and guide the feature generation process, this study employs skip connections to fuse the visible point features F_{S+1-j}^V from the $(S+1-j)$ stage of the encoder with the visible point features F_j^M from the j stage of the decoder. Specifically, an Adaptive Instance Normalization (AdaIN) module is utilized to align and concatenate the distributions of the two sets of features (as shown in Eq. 4), thereby amplifying geometric similarities, making similar features more prominent, and suppressing irrelevant features to improve feature discriminability. Subsequently, feature fusion is achieved through a linear projection layer. For masked point features, since the encoder only processes visible point features and does not include masked point features, they remain unchanged.

$$\text{AdaIN}(F_\mathcal{P}, F_\mathcal{Q}) = \sigma(F_\mathcal{Q}) \left(\frac{F_\mathcal{P} - \mu(F_\mathcal{P})}{\sigma(F_\mathcal{P})} \right) + \mu(F_\mathcal{Q}) \tag{4}$$

Here, $\mu(F_\mathcal{P})$ and $\sigma(F_\mathcal{P})$ represent the mean and variance of the visible point set $\mathcal{P}$ along the feature dimension, respectively, outputting the aligned feature $F_\mathcal{P}'$.

3.3 Deep Confidence Regression

We design a regressor to predict a confidence score for each feature point, representing the reliability of the match between the predicted value and the ground truth. Specifically, we employ an MLP composed of multiple linear layers, combined with a sigmoid function to generate the confidence score. Formally, the confidence score H^i for each point cloud is defined as:

$$H^i = \sigma\Big(\mathrm{MLP}(d_1 \to d_2 \to \cdots \to 1)(\mathbf{F}^i)\Big) \tag{5}$$

where i $\in \{\mathcal{P}, \mathcal{Q}\}$ and $\mathrm{MLP}(d_1\text{->}d_2\text{->}\ldots\text{->}d_{out})(d)$ denotes a multi-layer perceptron network with hidden layer dimensions d_1, d_2, ..., and a final output dimension $d_{out} = 1$. The sigmoid function maps the output to the range (0,1) as the confidence score.

To establish reliable correspondences between two point clouds, we propose a confidence-guided global matching scheme. This method first predicts confidence scores for each feature point using a regressor, then computes the matching probability between point pairs through a Gaussian correlation matrix $\mathcal{S}(i,j) = \langle H^{\mathcal{P}}(i), H^{\mathcal{Q}}(j)\rangle$, $\langle \cdot, \cdot \rangle$ denotes inner product. Finally, the top-k matching pairs are selected from $\mathcal{S}$ as the correspondence set $C' = \{(p_{x_i}, q_{y_i}) | (x_i, y_i \in topk_{x,y}(\mathcal{S}(i,j)))\}$, which are fed into the point matching module for fine matching.

3.4 Losses

To supervise the point-wise feature descriptors we follow [6] and use the circle loss [17]. This loss function is a variant based on the triplet loss function, designed to learn representative feature descriptors by bringing positive sample pairs closer together in space and simultaneously pushing negative sample pairs farther apart. In point cloud registration, if the overlap ratio between point pairs exceeds 10%, we consider it a positive sample pair; if the overlap ratio between point pairs is below 10%, we consider it a negative sample pair. The overlap-aware circle loss, built upon the aforementioned triplet loss function, incorporates the overlap ratio to make the model pay more attention to point pairs with high overlap. The formula for the loss function on $\mathcal{P}$ is as follows:

$$\mathcal{L}_{oc}^P = \frac{1}{|\mathcal{A}|} \sum_{p_I^j \in \mathcal{A}} \log \left[1 + \sum_{\substack{i,j\in\mathcal{E}_p^i \\ q_I^j\in\mathcal{E}_p^j}} e^{\lambda_i^j \rho_p^{i,j}\left(d_i^j - \Delta_p\right)} \cdot \sum_{\substack{i,j\in\mathcal{E}_n^i \\ q_K\in\mathcal{E}_n^j}} e^{\rho_n^{i,k}\left(\Delta_n - d_i^k\right)} \right], \tag{6}$$

where $\mathcal{A}$ represents a point cloud $\mathcal{P}$ The definition of overlap ratio greater than 10% in $\mathcal{P}$ is denoted as $\mathcal{E}_p$, while the definition of overlap ratio less than 10% is denoted as $\mathcal{E}_n$. $d_i^j = ||p_i - q_j||_2$ represents the distance between two points in the feature space.$\lambda_i^j = (o_i^j)^{1/2}$, where o_i^j is used to describe the overlap ratio between p_i and q_j. $\rho_p^{i,j}$ and $\rho_n^{i,k}$ represent the weights of the current superpoint pair in the loss function, formulated as $\beta_p^{i,j} = \nabla\left(d_l^j - \Delta_p\right)$ and $\beta_n^{i,k} = \mathbf{r}\left(\Delta_n - d_i^k\right)$. The hyperparamete Δ_p is set to 0.1, and Δ_n is set to 1.4. The overlap-aware circle loss function for point cloud $\mathcal{P}$ is derived in a similar manner. Finally, we average the overlap-aware circle loss obtained on the two point clouds to obtain the overall overlap-aware circle loss function. The formula is as follows:

$$\mathcal{L}_{OC} = \left(\mathcal{L}^P + \mathcal{L}^Q\right)/2 \tag{7}$$

4   Experiments

Our method is implemented in PyTorch and trained on a single NVIDIA A100 (40G) GPU. We choose Adam as the optimizer. On the 3DMatch dataset, the initial learning rate is set to 10^{-4} and decays at an exponential rate of 0.05 after each epoch. The training is conducted for a total of 40 epochs, with the batch size set to 1 and the segmentation threshold set to 0.5. During the multi-scale sampling phase, the sampling depth S is set to 4. For the KITTI dataset, the learning rate decays by 0.05 every 4 epochs, and the training is performed for a total of 100 epochs. Other settings remain the same as those for 3DMatch. Unless otherwise specified, all experiments in this paper adhere to these configurations.

4.1   Indoor Benchmarks: 3DMatch

3DMatch [26] is one of the most renowned indoor datasets for registration, comprising 62 indoor scenes. We adhere to the official split [26], utilizing 46 scenes for training, 8 scenes for validation, and 8 scenes for testing. We evaluated all methods under the 3DMatch dataset. In the 3DMatch setting, the overlap rate between point cloud pairs exceeds 30%.

Results. Table 1 presents the results of our experimental evaluation. We conducted comparative experiments between the proposed method and RANSAC-based registration methods [1, 2, 6, 8, 10, 16, 22, 23]. In the experiments, we employed 50,000 RANSAC iterations for transformation estimation and RANSAC set to 50k. All competing methods were evaluated under their optimal parameter settings. The experimental results demonstrate that the proposed method outperforms others by 1.8 pp in terms of registration accuracy.

4.2   Outdoor Benchmark: KITTI Odometry

KITTI [9] is a widely recognized benchmark dataset for autonomous driving, commonly used to evaluate the performance of point cloud matching algorithms. According to the official division, scenes 0 to 5 are used as the training set, scenes 6 and 7 for validation, and scenes 8 to 10 as the test set. Given the inaccuracies in the ground truth transformation data recorded by GPS, we follow the approach of previous studies and optimize these data using the ICP algorithm [7].

Results. The experimental results are presented in Table 2. Our method achieves a reduction of 0.7 pp in Relative Translation Error (RTE) and 0.01 pp in Relative Rotation Error (RRE), demonstrating significant performance improvements. And We set RANSAC to 50k. These results fully validate the critical role of reasonable feature interaction mechanisms in point cloud registration tasks.

Table 1. Evaluation results on 3DMatch.

Model	Estimator	Samples	RR (%)
FCGF	RANSAC	5000	85.1
D3Feat	RANSAC	5000	81.6
SpinNet	RANSAC	5000	88.6
Predator	RANSAC	5000	89
CoFiNet	RANSAC	5000	89.3
RIGA	RANSAC	5000	89.3
GeoTrans	RANSAC	5000	<u>92.0</u>
RoITr	RANSAC	5000	91.9
Our	RANSAC	5000	**92.1**

Table 2. Registration results on KITTI odometry.

Model	Estimator	RTE (cm)	RRE (°)	RR (%)
3DFeat-Net	RANSAC	25.9	0.25	96
FCGF	RANSAC	9.5	0.3	96.6
D3Feat	RANSAC	7.2	0.3	99.8
SpinNet	RANSAC	9.9	0.47	99.1
Predator	RANSAC	6.8	0.27	99.8
CoFiNet	RANSAC	8.2	0.41	99.8
BUFFER	RANSAC	**5.4**	**0.22**	97.7
GeoTrans	RANSAC	7.4	0.27	99.8
Our	RANSAC	<u>6.7</u>	<u>0.28</u>	**99.8**

4.3   Ablation Studies

We conduct several ablation studies on 3DMatch [26]to demonstrate the effectiveness of each component of our method. In Table 3, we report the experimental results and demonstrate the contributions of each module in an incremental manner. First, we removed the encoder and decoder modules, and only retained the AdaIN module in the skip connection for Cross-Attention interaction (**Var1**). Experiments show that the performance of this variant is lower than that of GeoTransformer [16], as AdaIN, serving as a data augmentation strategy in the skip connection, is primarily used to guide feature generation during the decoder upsampling stage. In a single-scale feature interaction framework, it introduces redundant features, interfering with high-level feature extraction. Second, we retained only the encoder and decoder modules, removing the skip connection (**Var2**). Its performance is lower than the complete method, validating the effectiveness of the multi-scale feature extraction mechanism. Finally, we retained the encoder and decoder modules and added a skip connection without AdaIN (**Var3**). Its performance still lower than the complete method, confirming the important role of the AdaIN module in improving feature generation quality.

Table 3. Comparison of different variants and their performance on RR (%) metric.

Variant Name	Encoder-Decoder	Skip Connections	AdaIN	RR (%)
Var1		✓	✓	90.9
Var2	✓			91.2
Var3	✓	✓		91.7
MMGT	✓	✓	✓	92.1

5 Conclusion

In this study, we deeply analyze the feature interaction mechanism in multi-scale point cloud registration methods and find that existing methods fail to make full use of multi-scale geometric feature information in single-scale feature extraction. This leads to insufficient discriminative ability in feature modeling, making it difficult to efficiently express hierarchical structural information, which ultimately affects the robustness of the methods and the registration accuracy. To address this, we propose a self-encoding feature interaction transformer based on multi-scale masks, which achieves comprehensive extraction and fusion of point cloud features at different scales through a hierarchical encoding strategy to improve registration accuracy. In addition, the Adaptive Instance Normalization (AdaIN) module is introduced to achieve multi-level feature interaction in the encoding and decoding stages through the skip-connection mechanism, thereby improving the quality of feature generation and matching accuracy. Experiments on the 3DMatch and KITTI datasets validate the effectiveness of method.

Acknowledgments. This research is supported by the Shandong Provincial University Youth Innovation and Technology Support Program No. 2022KJ291, Shandong Provincial Natural Science Foundation No. ZR202211150015, Taishan Scholars Program No. TSQNZ20230621 and TSQN202211214, Shandong Excellent Young Scientists Fund Program (Overseas) No. 2023HWYQ-113.

References

1. Ao, S., Hu, Q., Wang, H., Xu, K., Guo, Y.: Buffer: balancing accuracy, efficiency, and generalizability in point cloud registration. In: Proceedings of the IEEE/CVF Conference on Computer Vision and Pattern Recognition, pp. 1255–1264 (2023)
2. Ao, S., Hu, Q., Yang, B., Markham, A., Guo, Y.: SpinNet: learning a general surface descriptor for 3D point cloud registration. In: Proceedings of the IEEE/CVF Conference on Computer Vision and Pattern Recognition, pp. 11753–11762 (2021)
3. Aoki, Y., Goforth, H., Srivatsan, R.A., Lucey, S.: PointNetLK: robust & efficient point cloud registration using PointNet. In: Proceedings of the IEEE/CVF Conference on Computer Vision and Pattern Recognition, pp. 7163–7172 (2019)
4. Baevski, A., Hsu, W.N., Xu, Q., Babu, A., Gu, J., Auli, M.: Data2vec: a general framework for self-supervised learning in speech, vision and language. In: International Conference on Machine Learning, pp. 1298–1312. PMLR (2022)

5. Bai, X., et al.: PointDSC: robust point cloud registration using deep spatial consistency. In: Proceedings of the IEEE/CVF Conference on Computer Vision and Pattern Recognition, pp. 15859–15869 (2021)

6. Bai, X., Luo, Z., Zhou, L., Fu, H., Quan, L., Tai, C.L.: D3Feat: joint learning of dense detection and description of 3D local features. In: Proceedings of the IEEE/CVF Conference on Computer Vision and Pattern Recognition, pp. 6359–6367 (2020)

7. Besl, P.J., McKay, N.D.: Method for registration of 3-D shapes. In: Sensor Fusion IV: Control Paradigms and Data Structures, vol. 1611, pp. 586–606. SPIE (1992)

8. Choy, C., Park, J., Koltun, V.: Fully convolutional geometric features. In: Proceedings of the IEEE/CVF International Conference on Computer Vision, pp. 8958–8966 (2019)

9. Geiger, A., Lenz, P., Urtasun, R.: Are we ready for autonomous driving? The KITTI vision benchmark suite. In: 2012 IEEE Conference on Computer Vision and Pattern Recognition, pp. 3354–3361. IEEE (2012)

10. Huang, S., Gojcic, Z., Usvyatsov, M., Wieser, A., Schindler, K.: Predator: registration of 3D point clouds with low overlap. In: Proceedings of the IEEE/CVF Conference on Computer Vision and Pattern Recognition, pp. 4267–4276 (2021)

11. Huang, X., Mei, G., Zhang, J.: Feature-metric registration: a fast semi-supervised approach for robust point cloud registration without correspondences. In: Proceedings of the IEEE/CVF Conference on Computer Vision and Pattern Recognition, pp. 11366–11374 (2020)

12. Pais, G.D., Ramalingam, S., Govindu, V.M., Nascimento, J.C., Chellappa, R., Miraldo, P.: 3DRegNet: a deep neural network for 3D point registration. In: Proceedings of the IEEE/CVF Conference on Computer Vision and Pattern Recognition, pp. 7193–7203 (2020)

13. Pang, Y., Wang, W., Tay, F.E., Liu, W., Tian, Y., Yuan, L.: Masked autoencoders for point cloud self-supervised learning. In: Avidan, S., Brostow, G., Cissé, M., Farinella, G.M., Hassner, T. (eds.) ECCV 2022. LNCS, vol. 13662, pp. 604–621. Springer, Cham (2022). https://doi.org/10.1007/978-3-031-20086-1_35

14. Qi, C.R., Su, H., Mo, K., Guibas, L.J.: PointNet: deep learning on point sets for 3D classification and segmentation. In: Proceedings of the IEEE Conference on Computer Vision and Pattern Recognition, pp. 652–660 (2017)

15. Qi, C.R., Yi, L., Su, H., Guibas, L.J.: PointNet++: deep hierarchical feature learning on point sets in a metric space. In: Advances in Neural Information Processing Systems, vol. 30 (2017)

16. Qin, Z., et al.: GeoTransformer: fast and robust point cloud registration with geometric transformer. IEEE Trans. Pattern Anal. Mach. Intell. **45**(8), 9806–9821 (2023)

17. Sun, Y., et al.: Circle loss: a unified perspective of pair similarity optimization. In: Proceedings of the IEEE/CVF Conference on Computer Vision and Pattern Recognition, pp. 6398–6407 (2020)

18. Thomas, H., Qi, C.R., Deschaud, J.E., Marcotegui, B., Goulette, F., Guibas, L.J.: KPConv: flexible and deformable convolution for point clouds. In: Proceedings of the IEEE/CVF International Conference on Computer Vision, pp. 6411–6420 (2019)

19. Wang, Y., Solomon, J.M.: Deep closest point: learning representations for point cloud registration. In: Proceedings of the IEEE/CVF International Conference on Computer Vision, pp. 3523–3532 (2019)

20. Willmott, C.J., Matsuura, K.: Advantages of the mean absolute error (MAE) over the root mean square error (RMSE) in assessing average model performance. Clim. Res. **30**(1), 79–82 (2005)
21. Xie, Z., et al.: SimMIM: a simple framework for masked image modeling. In: Proceedings of the IEEE/CVF Conference on Computer Vision and Pattern Recognition, pp. 9653–9663 (2022)
22. Yu, H., et al.: RIGA: rotation-invariant and globally-aware descriptors for point cloud registration. IEEE Trans. Pattern Anal. Mach. Intell. **46**(5), 3796–3812 (2024)
23. Yu, H., Li, F., Saleh, M., Busam, B., Ilic, S.: CofiNet: reliable coarse-to-fine correspondences for robust pointcloud registration. In: Advances in Neural Information Processing Systems, vol. 34, pp. 23872–23884 (2021)
24. Yu, J., Ren, L., Zhang, Y., Zhou, W., Lin, L., Dai, G.: PEAL: prior-embedded explicit attention learning for low-overlap point cloud registration. In: Proceedings of the IEEE/CVF Conference on Computer Vision and Pattern Recognition, pp. 17702–17711 (2023)
25. Yuan, M., Huang, X., Fu, K., Li, Z., Wang, M.: Boosting 3D point cloud registration by transferring multi-modality knowledge. In: 2023 IEEE International Conference on Robotics and Automation (ICRA), pp. 11734–11741. IEEE (2023)
26. Zeng, A., Song, S., Nießner, M., Fisher, M., Xiao, J., Funkhouser, T.: 3DMatch: learning local geometric descriptors from RGB-D reconstructions. In: Proceedings of the IEEE Conference on Computer Vision and Pattern Recognition, pp. 1802–1811 (2017)

Expert Data - Assisted Diagnosis: An INFO - iTransformer - XGBoost Combined Discriminative System for Prenatal Diagnosis of Fetal Congenital Heart Disease

Runze Liu[1], Yingying Zhang[1(✉)], Hao Sheng[1], Jingyi Wang[2], Xiaoyan Gu[2], Jiancheng Han[2], Da Yang[1], Xuefei Huang[1], Yihua He[2(✉)], and Haogang Zhu[1]

[1] Data Science and Intelligent Computing Laboratory, Hangzhou International Innovation Institute, Beihang University, Hangzhou, Zhejiang 311115, People's Republic of China
{runzeliu,zhangyingying,shenghao,da.yang,xuefei.huang,
haogangzhu}@buaa.edu.cn
[2] Echocardiography Medical Center and Maternal-Fetal Medicine Center in Fetal Heart Disease, Beijing Anzhen Hospital, Capital Medical University, Beijing 100029, People's Republic of China
heyihuaecho@hotmail.com

Abstract. In prenatal screening for fetal congenital heart disease (CHD), ultrasonic diagnosis and other methods are prone to being affected by regional resource differences and insufficient experience in diagnosing doctors, thus resulting in misdiagnosis of cases. This research puts forward a combined discriminative system, which integrates the iTransformer method and XGBoost to aid in the prenatal diagnosis of fetal CHD. This system, named INFO-iTransformer-XGBoost, merges a combined discriminative system, INFO (Weighted mean of vectors optimization algorithm), and SHAP (SHapley Additive exPlanations) explainable analysis prediction model. By comparing the model results with those from INFO-iTransformer and INFO-XGBoost alone, the study confirms the advantage of the combined discriminative system in prenatal CHD screening for fetuses. The study used the fetal CHD detection dataset provided by the Maternal and Fetal Medicine Center of Beijing Anzhen Hospital, Capital Medical University, from February 2018 to August 2024. The research shows that the INFO-iTransformer-XGBoost combined discriminative system and SHAP model explainability analysis can provide a quantitative diagnosis and clinically interpretable diagnostic solution for prenatal CHD screening.

Keywords: Fetal congenital heart disease prediction · Combined Discriminative System · SHAP explainability analysis

1 Introduction

Congenital Heart Disease (CHD) is the most common congenital defect in newborns and the leading cause of death due to birth defects [1]. Global prevalence data shows a rate of 8.22% per 1000 newborns [2]. Follow-up-based data reveals low detection

T. Zhu et al. (Eds.): KSEM 2025, LNAI 15922, pp. 291–298, 2026.
https://doi.org/10.1007/978-981-95-3058-8_26

rates in the general population, highlighting current prenatal diagnosis limitations [3]. In summary, CHD's high incidence in newborns not only affects cardiac function but can also lead to severe complications like pneumonia, pulmonary hypertension, and heart failure, threatening infant health and survival. Therefore, establishing a highly accurate, efficient, and versatile CHD screening model is essential for global healthcare security.

A CHD auxiliary screening model leverages machine-learning algorithms. Based on prenatal data, it judges the risk of fetal CHD. Machine-learning models have been used in medical fields. Before creating a CHD screening model, it learns from CHD-case big data to build an auxiliary-judgment model. When doctors or pregnant women input prenatal details, the model evaluates the risk and advises on timely treatment to safeguard the health of both.The field of fetal CHD prediction models encounters challenges from the extensive feature space and large sample size of CHD data [4–6]. The main contributions of this paper are as follows:

- We developed an INFO (Weighted mean of vectors optimization algorithm) - iTransformer - XGBoost combined discriminative system for fetal congenital heart disease (CHD).
- To address the "black – box" issue of neural network models, we use a SHAP algorithm based on game theory principles for explainability analysis. It identifies key features affecting model outputs and their corresponding weights.

2 Materials and Methods

2.1 Experimental Objects

The dataset used in this study was provided by the Maternal and Fetal Medicine Center of Beijing Anzhen Hospital, Capital Medical University. It contains 22,094 complete records from February 2018 to August 2024. Each record includes maternal baseline data, fetal echocardiography results, and expert diagnoses. Fetal ultrasound imaging followed guidelines from the American Society of Echocardiography and the International Society of Ultrasound in Obstetrics and Gynecology. Fetal echocardiography measurements, taken using scaled image magnification, fall into three categories: (1) peripheral hemodynamics; (2) cardiac two - dimensional structural measurements; (3) intracardiac hemodynamics. The sample includes Chinese and foreign nationals, with birthplaces across multiple provinces and cities, including Beijing, Zhejiang, and Henan. Data types are numerical and labeled, with the latter converted to numerical during processing. Table 1 presents the categories and names of the 52 features used in modeling.

This study was approved by the relevant departments (approval No.: KS2023025) and conducted in line with ethical guidelines. The research adhered to the Declaration of Helsinki and ethical committee regulations. The authors and supervisors protected participants' rights, privacy, and confidentiality.

Table 1. Fetal congenital heart disease dataset: feature categories and information.

Feature categories	Feature information and its serial number
Basic information	Gestational age conversion (1), anemia presence (2), abdominal circumference (3), number of umbilical arteries (4), femur length (5), biparietal diameter (6), fetal heart rate (7).
Peripheral hemodynamics	Middle cerebral artery Vs value (8), middle cerebral artery Vd value (9), middle cerebral artery PI value (10), extra - abdominal umbilical artery Vs value (11), extra - abdominal umbilical artery Vd value (12), extra - abdominal umbilical artery RI value (13), extra - abdominal umbilical artery PI value (14), intra - abdominal umbilical artery Vd value (15), intra - abdominal umbilical artery RI value (16), intra - abdominal umbilical artery S/D value (17), right uterine artery Vd value (18).
Cardiac two - dimensional structural measurements	Left atrial transverse diameter (19), right atrial transverse diameter (20), left ventricular transverse diameter (21), right ventricular transverse diameter (22), descending aorta width (23), aortic valve ring diameter (24), aortic isthmus width (25), foramen ovale diameter (26), fetal cardiac axis (27), cardiac transverse diameter (28), thoracic transverse diameter (29), cardiac area (30), thoracic area (31), cardiothoracic area ratio (32), pulmonary artery valve ring diameter (33), left pulmonary artery width (34), right pulmonary artery width (35), ductus arteriosus middle diameter (36).
Intracardiac hemodynamics	Mitral valve E wave (37), mitral valve A wave (38), tricuspid valve E wave (39), tricuspid valve A wave (40), aortic valve flow velocity (41), pulmonary valve flow velocity (42), aortic arch Vs (43), aortic arch Vd (44), ductus arteriosus Vs (45), ductus arteriosus Vd (46), pulmonary vein S wave (47), pulmonary vein D wave (48), pulmonary vein A wave (49), venous duct S wave (50), venous duct D wave (51), venous duct A wave (52).

2.2 Methodology

iTransformer Deep Learning Framework. The flexible iTransformer adjusts parameters for each feature to improve model efficiency and accuracy when handling fetal CHD data with significant feature value variations. Unlike the original Transformer that combines multiple features at each step into a single time mark, iTransformer integrates multiple features across the entire time step into one feature. This approach not only learns patterns between samples but also captures relationships between variables, enhancing model adaptability to complex data and prediction accuracy [7]. iTransformer effectively processes complex samples, suppresses noise data during training, and adjusts its framework for significant data variations. However, it has a slow training speed with high-dimensional, large-sample data.

XGBoost Algorithm Framework. When modeling high-dimensional, large-sample fetal CHD data, XGBoost (eXtreme Gradient Boosting) effectively enhances model performance. XGBoost improves on gradient-boosting decision trees by integrating the separate steps of determining optimal split regions and calculating output values in traditional tree models. It simultaneously identifies split regions and their best output values, boosting model efficiency and accuracy [8]. XGBoost trains efficiently and learns well from large datasets. However, its single-algorithm framework may underperform with non-linear data or rapid-iteration demands.

INFO Optimization Algorithm. During model building, the parameter space is often preset based on experience. This weight-determination method, heavily influenced by human subjectivity, can interfere with model training efficiency and accuracy. Hyperparameter optimization is needed. The Weighted Mean of Vectors Optimization Algorithm (INFO) has a strong global search ability and performs well with high-dimensional, complex-relationship data [9].

Combined Discriminative System. The previous discussion covered the fundamentals of the iTransformer deep-learning algorithm and the XGBoost algorithm. iTransformer handles complex data samples, suppresses noise during training, and has a flexible structure adaptable to data changes. However, it trains slowly on high-dimensional, large-sample data, affecting model efficiency. XGBoost efficiently extracts information from high-dimensional big data but has a single-algorithm framework. It may be impacted by non-linear data noise, influencing model accuracy.

To combine the advantages of both models and enable them to complement each other, a combined discriminative framework was adopted to establish the INFO-iTransformer-XGBoost combined discriminative system. Figure 1 illustrates the process of constructing this discriminative model.

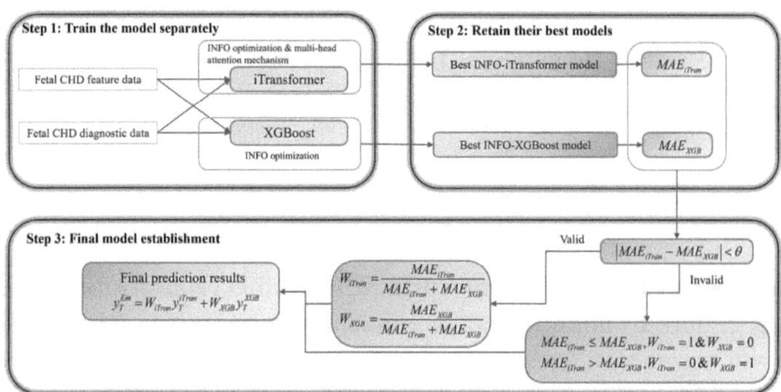

Fig. 1. INFO-iTransformer-XGBoost combined discriminative system establishment process.

The iTransformer algorithm, which effectively suppresses noise and has a flexible framework, combined with the high-efficiency XGBoost algorithm for large - scale high - dimensional data, complements each other within a combined discriminative system framework. This leads to the establishment of the INFO-iTransformer-XGBoost combined discriminative model for fetal congenital heart disease.

Model SHAP Explainability Analysis. In medical diagnostic model research, model explainability is crucial for medical staff and patients. With a deep understanding of the model, doctors can more accurately interpret the predictions and understand disease progression, leading to better diagnosis and treatment [10]. SHAP (SHapley Additive exPlanations) explainability analysis, based on game theory [11], allocates the contribution of each feature in the model. It views the model's predictions as the gain from feature cooperation and calculates the average marginal contribution of each feature across combinations to measure its importance.

3 Experiments

3.1 Combined Discriminative System of Fetal Congenital Heart Disease

According to the combined discriminative system principle, we selected 571 severe CHD samples, 2,609 CHD samples, and 6,615 normal (non-CHD) fetal samples randomly from the sample set. These 9,795 samples were used to train the INFO-iTransformer and INFO-XGBoost models. The training, validation, and test sets were split in an 8:1:1 ratio, with divisions randomly updated with each iteration. This process yielded two predictive models, which were then used to calculate combined discriminative weights. Finally, we established the optimal INFO-iTransformer-XGBoost combined discriminative system for fetal CHD.

Model training process results and analysis. Figure 2 illustrates the parameter optimization process and optimal parameters of the INFO-iTransformer predictive model. Figure 3 shows the parameter optimization process and optimal parameters of the INFO-XGBoost predictive model.

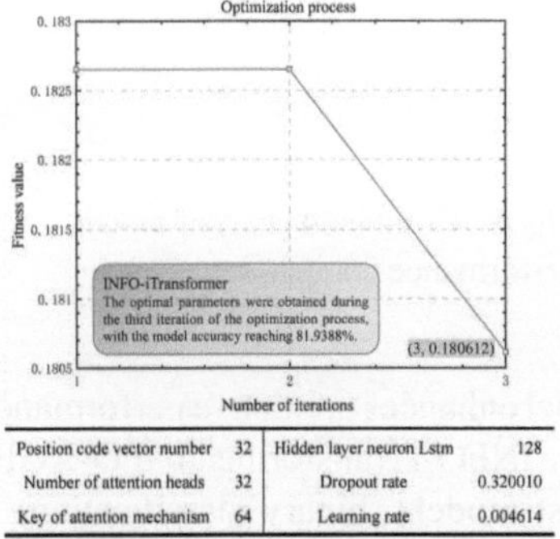

Position code vector number	32	Hidden layer neuron Lstm	128
Number of attention heads	32	Dropout rate	0.320010
Key of attention mechanism	64	Learning rate	0.004614

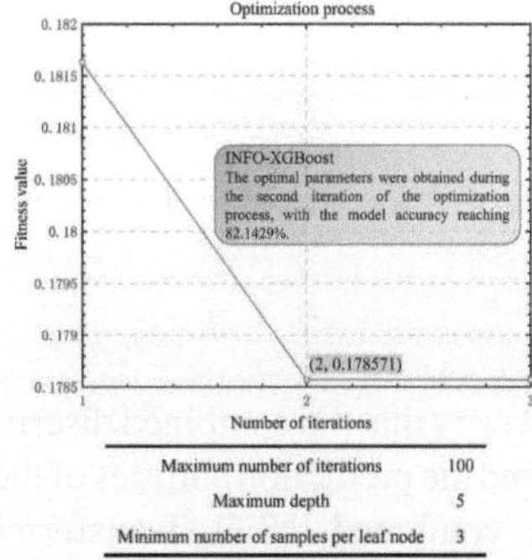

Maximum number of iterations	100
Maximum depth	5
Minimum number of samples per leaf node	3

Fig. 2. The optimization process and optimal parameters of the INFO-iTransformer model.

Fig. 3. The optimization process and optimal parameters of the INFO-XGBoost model.

Results and analysis of the combined discriminative system establishment. After establishing the combined discriminative system, the discriminative weights for the INFO-iTransformer and INFO-XGBoost models are 0.50062 and 0.49938. Table 2 shows the training results of the INFO-iTransformer-XGBoost model. The model's final accuracy is 82.329%, indicating good performance. However, further evaluation methods are still needed to assess the model's effectiveness.

Performance results and analysis of the combined discriminative system. In the performance evaluation study, 5-fold cross-validation was used to assess the model's reliability and stability. Figure 4 shows the results of the 5-fold cross-validation for the INFO-iTransformer-XGBoost model. The mean accuracy of the 5-fold cross-validation was 82.593%, with a standard deviation of 0.00706, close to 0.

Table 2. Training results of the INFO-iTransformer-XGBoost model.

Name	Training Set Result	Validation Set Result	Test Set Result
Accuracy	0.91143	0.82143	0.82329
Precision	0.92308	0.80455	0.80368
Recall	0.87643	0.75456	0.76163
F1 Score	0.89444	0.77181	0.77701
Specificity	0.87643	0.75456	0.76163

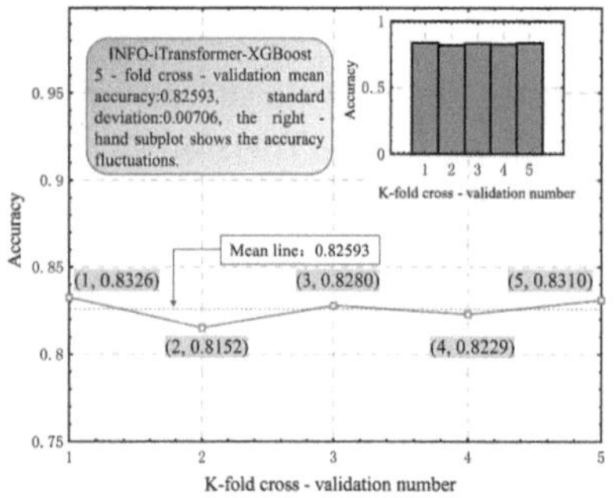

Fig. 4. Model cross - validation results.

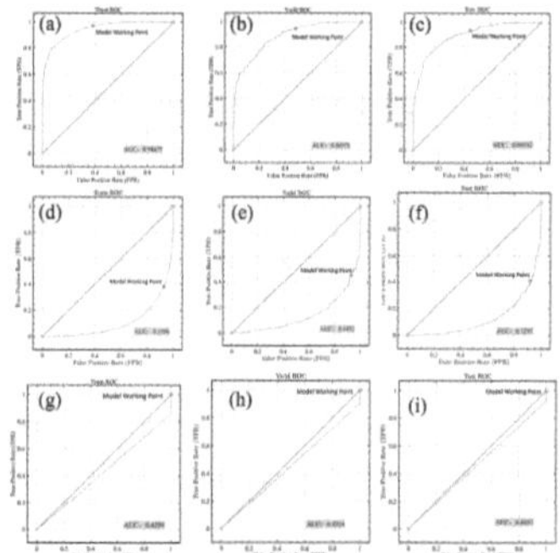

Fig. 5. Combined chart of model performance comparison.

To verify that the combined discriminant model enhances predictive performance, we compared the prediction abilities of the standalone INFO-iTransformer, INFO-XGBoost, and the combined INFO-iTransformer-XGBoost models (binary classification) using ROC-AUC analysis. Figures 5(a)-(c) show the training, validation, and testing set ROC curves of the combined model, with AUC values of 0.94477, 0.88578, and 0.89512, respectively. Figures 5(d)-(f) present the same for INFO-iTransformer, yielding AUC values of 0.1106, 0.1433, and 0.1291. The performance of the combined model was on average 6.21 times better. Figures 5(g)-(i) display the INFO-XGBoost results with AUC values of 0.4289, 0.4524, and 0.4637, showing an average improvement of 1.03 times. Overall, in binary classification, the combined model outperformed the single models by an average of 3.62 times.

3.2 System SHAP Explainability Analysis

Figure 6 presents a dot plot of SHAP values for the top 20 features ranked by SHAP analysis. Each point represents a sample's SHAP value, with a fill color indicating feature magnitude. The vertical order signifies feature importance. Figure 7 shows a bar chart of the model's SHAP value distributions. Each line in the chart represents a data sample, the upper line depicts the model output, and the right-side black bar chart shows feature importance.

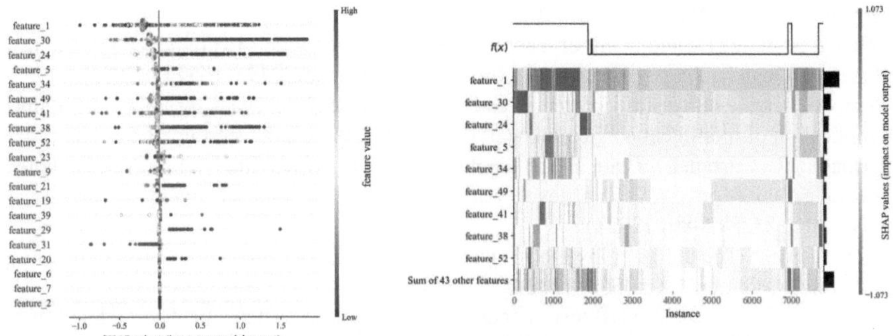

Fig. 6. Model SHAP value scatter plot.

Fig. 7. Model SHAP value bar cumulative combined chart.

As shown in the figure above, features such as gestational age conversion (feature_1), pulmonary valve flow velocity (feature_30), and aortic isthmus width (feature_24) have substantial impacts on the model output, evidenced by their wide SHAP value distributions. Features like femur length (feature_5), pulmonary valve ring diameter (feature_49), and aortic valve ring diameter (feature_23) also have some influence but with SHAP values mostly clustering around 0, indicating a relatively smaller effect.

4 Conclusion

Screening methods for fetal congenital heart disease, such as ultrasonic diagnosis, are prone to being affected by regional resource disparities and lack of diagnostic experience among physicians, which can lead to misdiagnosis. This study introduces a combined discriminative system for the prenatal diagnosis of fetal congenital heart disease, integrating the iTransformer approach and XGBoost. The system combines the flexible iTransformer algorithm for complex data with the efficient XGBoost algorithm for large-sample data, achieving highly applicable, efficient, and generalizable predictions. SHAP analysis of the system identifies key features and their impact on model results. In summary, the established INFO-iTransformer-XGBoost system offers a quantitative and clinically interpretable solution for prenatal CHD screening.

Acknowledgments. This work was supported in part by the National Natural Science Foundation of China under Grant 62406014, in part by the Beijing Natural Science Foundation (7244325, L222152), and in part by the Start-up Funds of Hangzhou International Innovation Institute of Beihang University under Grant No.2024KQ045 and No.2024KQ027.

References

1. Pierpont, M.E., et al.: On behalf of the american heart association council on cardiovascular disease in the young; council on cardiovascular and stroke nursing; and council on genomic and precision medicine: genetic basis for congenital heart disease: revisited: a scientific statement from the American heart association. Circulation **138**, e653–e711 (2018)
2. Bouma, B.J., Mulder, B.J.M.: Changing landscape of congenital heart disease. Circ. Res. **120**, 908–922 (2017)
3. Meller, C.H., et al.: Congenital heart disease, prenatal diagnosis and management. Arch. Argent. Pediatr. **118**, e149–e161 (2020)
4. Zhang, S., et al.: Development of machine learning-based models to predict congenital heart disease: a matched case-control study. Int. J. Med. Informatics **195**, 105741 (2025)
5. Tan, W., et al.: Bayesian inference and dynamic neural feedback promote the clinical application of intelligent congenital heart disease diagnosis. Engineering **23**, 90–102 (2023)
6. Arnaout, R., Curran, L., Zhao, Y., Levine, J.C., Chinn, E., Moon-Grady, A.J.: An ensemble of neural networks provides expert-level prenatal detection of complex congenital heart disease. Nat. Med. **27**, 882–891 (2021)
7. Liu, Y., et al.: iTransformer: Inverted Transformers are Effective for Time Series Forecasting. http://arxiv.org/abs/2310.06625 (2024)
8. Chen, T., Guestrin, C.: XGBoost: a scalable tree boosting system. In: Proceedings of the 22nd ACM SIGKDD International Conference on Knowledge Discovery and Data Mining, pp. 785–794 (2016). Association for Computing Machinery, New York, NY, USA
9. Ahmadianfar, I., Heidari, A.A., Noshadian, S., Chen, H., Gandomi, A.H.: INFO: an efficient optimization algorithm based on weighted mean of vectors. Expert Syst. Appl. **195**, 116516 (2022)
10. Cui, S., Gao, R., Kuang, J., Yang, L., Qiu, H., Wei, X.: An interpretable imbalance ensemble classification method for readmission risk assessment incorporating multi-view perturbation and SHAP analysis. Decis. Support. Syst. **190**, 114404 (2025)
11. Strumbelj, E., Kononenko, I.: An efficient explanation of individual classifications using game theory. J. Mach. Learn. Res. **11**, 1–18 (2010)

Temporal Knowledge Graph Reasoning Based on Historical Statistical Reward Mechanism

Changlong Wang[1], Jianlong Cao[1(✉)], Yaoyao Hu[1], Xiaopan Cao[2], Wenzheng Guo[1], Jie Hu[1], Yawei Li[1], and Yi Liu[1]

[1] Northwest Normal University, Lanzhou, China
wchlong@nwnu.edu.cn, 1590567473@qq.com
[2] Zhongdian Wanwei Information Technology Co., Ltd, Lanzhou, China

Abstract. Using temporal knowledge graph to predict future events has become a hot topic in recent years. Generally, historical information has important impact on the prediction of future events. How to use the historical information has drawn significant attention. In this paper, a new model HSRMNet is proposed for improving the prediction performance, and this model is based on a historical statistical reward mechanism. Specially, two modes are designed to capture history information effectively. The Global Mode use the frequency of historical events to simulate the evolution of events by statistical methods. The Standard Mode divides historical events into two categories according to whether the events have occurred or not. After obtaining the frequency and category information about the events, the two modes jointly learn the probability distribution of entities. The proposed model is evaluated on two datasets and it's performance gain is demonstrated by the experimental results. On YAGO, the hit@10 raw metric reaches 77.65%.

Keywords: Temporal knowledge graph reasoning · Historical statistics · Link prediction · Extrapolation · Graph representation learning

1 Introduction

Knowledge Graph (KG) is a widely used resource for representing events in the real world [1], promoting many real-world applications [2], such as recommendation systems [3], and information retrieval [1]. Traditional KG represents information through static graphics [4], while most events are dynamic. In order to address the limitations of traditional KG in capturing the dynamic evolution of events [5], Temporal Knowledge Graph (TKG) has been proposed [1–3]. It represents each event as a quadruple (subject, predicate, object, timestamp) [6].

Temporal Knowledge Graph Reasoning (TKGR) is divided into two categories: interpolation setting [7] and extrapolation setting [2]. Intuitively, given a time interval $[t_0, t_n]$ and a future event (s, p, o, t), the computation for the future event is interpolation setting if $t \in [t_0, t_n]$, and interpolation setting if $t > t_n$. In this work, we focus on the extrapolation setting of TKG, which includes entity link prediction and relationship link prediction. The main task of entity link prediction is to predict (s, p, ?, t) or (?, p,

© The Author(s), under exclusive license to Springer Nature Singapore Pte Ltd. 2026
T. Zhu et al. (Eds.): KSEM 2025, LNAI 15922, pp. 299–307, 2026.
https://doi.org/10.1007/978-981-95-3058-8_27

o, t), and the main task of relationship link prediction is to predict (s, ?, o, t), where t is the timestamp of the future event. As shown in Fig. 1, at time t-k, there occurs (Russia, negotiation, Ukraine); At time t-2, there occurs (the United States, aid, Ukraine); At time t, there occurs (the United States, aid, Ukraine) and (European Union, aid, Ukraine). Among them, events such as (Russia, negotiation, Ukraine) and (the United States, aid, Ukraine) repeatedly occur, while events such as (the European Union, aid, Ukraine) are new events without historical events. Based on the frequency of historical events, we can speculate that at time t+1, the probability of (the United States, aid, Ukraine) is the highest, followed by (the European Union, aid, Ukraine), while the probability of (Russia, aid, Ukraine) will be very low, but it may also occur. Therefore, HSRMNet considers processing observed repetitive events and unobserved new events separately from historical events.

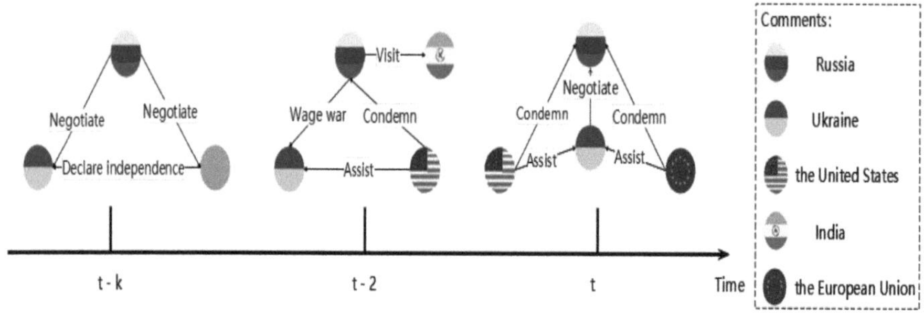

Fig. 1. An example of reasoning in a TKG. This paper presents three historical subgraphs at different timestamps. Each edge represents the interaction between entities.

At present, the existing TKGR methods adopt an equal treatment strategy for all candidate entities. However, there are differences between candidate entities in different events, and they should be treated differently [3]. Therefore, this paper explores the frequency of events and distinguishes different entities based on the frequency of events. A Global Mode and a Standard Mode are designed to handle candidate entities from the perspectives of event's frequency and event's category, respectively. According to HSRMNet, the historical information of events is used to rank the allocation scores of candidate entities [8], and the entity with the highest score is selected as the final prediction result, as shown in Fig. 2. Historical events include (Russia, negotiate, Ukraine, t-k), (Russia, negotiate, separatist forces in Ukraine, t-k), and (Ukraine, negotiate, Russia, t). For possible future events (?, negotiate, Ukraine, t+1), the probability of candidate entities such as Russia and separatist forces in Ukraine will be higher; However, entities that have not been observed in historical negotiation relationships, such as India and the European Union, have a lower probability. Based on the score ranking, we select Russia with the highest probability score as the final prediction result.

The contributions of our paper are summarized as follows:

– We propose a TKG model called HSRMNet for the prediction of future events. HSRMNet utilizes the frequency of historical events to predict not only repetitive

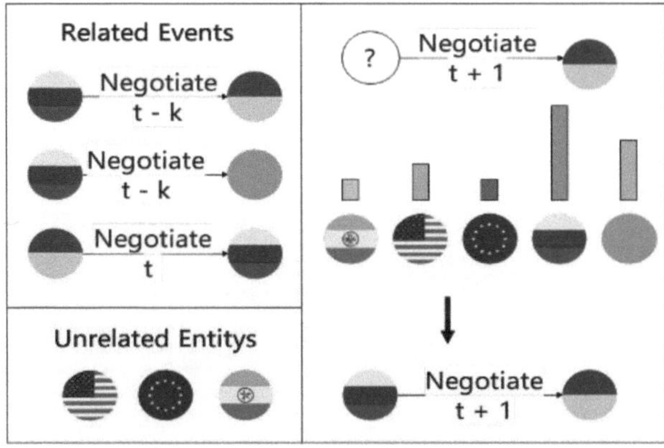

Fig. 2. Prediction results based on HSRMNet.

and periodic events but also potential new events via joint both the Global Mode and the Standard Mode.

- We extract the raw frequency and the standard frequency from historical information, and train comparative representations of queries from two aspects: differences in frequency distribution and differences in frequency category, so that HSRMNet can identify highly related entities.
- We conduct experiments on two public TKG benchmark graphs, and demonstrate HSRMNet's effectiveness in future events (link) prediction.

2   Related Work

Temporal Knowledge Graph Reasoning (TKGR) is divided into two categories: interpolation setting and extrapolation setting.

Interpolation Setting. The goal of the interpolation setting is to complete missing events that occur within $[t_0, t_n]$, also known as Temporal Knowledge Graph Completion (TKGC) [3]. For example, TTransE [9] introduces the processing of timestamp based on TransE, which makes up for the deficiency of TransE in handling temporal events.

Extrapolation Setting. Our work focuses on the extrapolation setting. CyGNet [1] models the entity vocabulary of historical events using Copy Mode and Generation Mode. However, the Generation Mode gives equal opportunities for all candidate entities and cannot capture the dependency of relationships between entities. RE-GCN [2] models historical KG sequences cyclically through graph convolution to capture the structural dependencies of entities and relationships at each timestamp, while also ignoring the influence of the global history. rGalT [10] proposes event precursors that is highly correlated with a given query, and uses a mask self-attention layer of the transformer decoder and an encoder-decoder attention layer for recognition. The proposed event precursors ignore events with potential correlation.

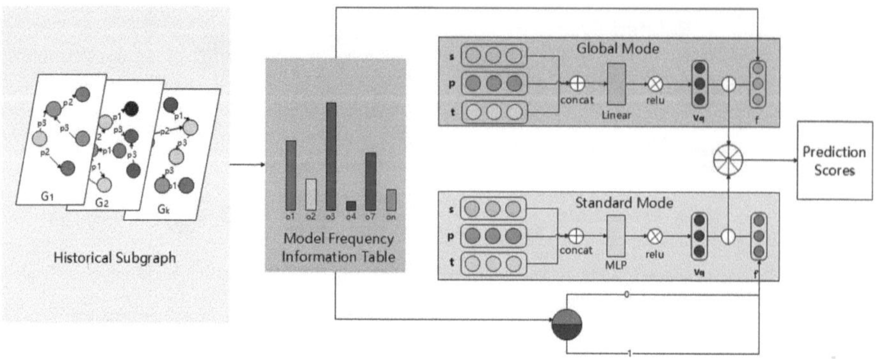

Fig. 3. The overall architecture of HSRMNet.

3   Method

3.1   Preliminaries

Let $\mathcal{E}$, $\mathcal{R}$, and $\mathcal{T}$ denote a finite set of entities, relationship types, and timestamps, respectively. A temporal knowledge graph $\mathcal{G}$ is a set of quadruples formalized as (s, p, o, t), where s $\in \mathcal{E}$ is a subject entity, o $\in \mathcal{E}$ is an object entity, p $\in \mathcal{R}$ is the relationship type occurring at timestamp t between s and o. **s**, **p**, **o** and **t** represent the embedding vectors of s, p, o and t, respectively. $\mathcal{G}_t$ is a subgraph sequence of TKG at t. These subgraph sequences are sorted in ascending order based on t, such as $\mathcal{G}=\{\mathcal{G}_1,\mathcal{G}_2,\ldots,\mathcal{G}_t\}$. Given s and p, the frequency of the triplet (s, p, o) in $[t_0, t_k]$ represents the frequency of o. If o does not appear in these subgraph sequences, its frequency is 0. By incrementally computing the frequency of (s, p, o) corresponding to different historical subgraph sequences, the frequency of entities includes in the historical events will be continuously accumulated. Given a query q = (s, p, ?, t_{n+1}) , the raw frequency's calculation formula for o is as follows:

$$\mathbf{F}_{\mathbf{o}}^{(\mathbf{s,p})} = \sum_{t_k < t_{n+1}} |\{o|(s,p,o,t_k \in \mathcal{G}_k\}| \tag{1}$$

By calculating the frequency of each o $\in \mathcal{E}$, a raw frequency table specific to (s, p, t_k) is obtained, as shown in Eq. 2:

$$\mathbf{FT} = \{\mathbf{F}_{o_i}^{(s,p)}, i = 1, 2, 3, \ldots, N\} \tag{2}$$

where N is the size of entity set $\mathcal{E}$. To avoid overfitting to high-frequency events, we propose a standard frequency to regulate their occurrence:

$$\mathbf{F}_{\mathbf{o(s,p)}}^{\mathbf{std}} = \begin{cases} 1 & (s,p,o) \in \mathcal{G} \\ 0, & (s,p,o) \notin \mathcal{G} \end{cases} \tag{3}$$

The corresponding standard frequency table is as shown in Eq. 4:

$$\mathbf{FT_{std}} = \{F_{o_i}^{std(s,p)}, i = 1, 2, 3, ..., N\} \tag{4}$$

As shown in Fig. 3, HSRMNet uses incremental statistical methods to collect frequency of events from the KG, thereby constructing a frequency table of entities. HSRMNet includes two different processing modes, namely Global Mode and Standard Mode, which model the raw frequency and standard frequency, respectively. For query q, the Global Mode computes the probability score of entities based on the raw frequency in the raw frequency table of the historical subgraph sequence $\mathcal{G}_1$, $\mathcal{G}_2$, ..., $\mathcal{G}_t$. An entity is rewarded with a specific score according to its frequency. The Standard Mode computes the probability score of entities based on the standard frequency of entities in the standard frequency table. In the Standard Mode, an entity is rewarded with a positive score if the entity has occurred in history, or with a negative score if the entity has not occurred. Finally, HSRMNet combines the probability scores of the two modes to rank the entities. In the following section, we will provide a detailed introduction to the method proposed in this paper.

3.2   Model Components

Global Mode. Global Mode utilizes the differences in the frequency of events to model the frequency of historical related entities, thereby predicting future events. For the timestamp tk of q, this paper follows the processing in previous work [1], as shown in Eq. 5:

$$\mathbf{t_k} = \mathbf{t_{k-1}} + \mathbf{t_u} \tag{5}$$

where t_u is the unit step of time [1], $t_1 = t_u$. The Global Mode first reshapes the shape of s, p and tk through a linear layer, and then obtains v_q through the Relu activation function, as shown in Eq. 6:

$$\boldsymbol{v}_q = relu(\boldsymbol{W}_g(\boldsymbol{s} \oplus \boldsymbol{p} \oplus \boldsymbol{t}_k) + \boldsymbol{b}_g) \tag{6}$$

where $\mathbf{W}_g \in \mathbb{R}^{3d \times N}$ and $\mathbf{b}_g \in \mathbb{R}^N$ is a trainable parameter, and $\oplus$ is a vector concatenation operator. $\boldsymbol{v}_q$ is an N-dimensional vector. N is the size of entity set $\mathcal{E}$. The Global Mode rewards candidate entities with different scores according to its frequency, and then uses the softmax activation function to compute the probability of candidate entities:

$$\mathbf{g}_q = \boldsymbol{v}_q + FT \tag{7}$$

$$\mathbf{p}(g) = \mathrm{softmax}(\mathbf{g}_q) \tag{8}$$

where $\mathbf{g}_q$ is an N-dimensional index vector, where $\mathbf{p}\,(g)$ is a vector equal in size to the raw frequency table. Based on the raw frequency table, the Global Mode predicts the probability of candidate entities.

Standard Mode. Standard Mode smooths the differences in the frequency of historical events, aiming to accurately classify entities through historical events, thereby reducing the candidate entity space and minimizing the interference of unrelated entities on the prediction results. Given the same query as above, The Standard Mode selects candidate entities from the standard frequency table to predict events. Firstly, the Standard Mode concatenates s, p and t_k, and then passes through the fully connected layer and Relu layer to obtain $v_q{}'$. Based on $v_q{}'$, different scores are rewarded according to entities' category, and then the softmax activation function is used to compute the probability of candidate entities:

$$v_q{}' = relu(MLP(s \oplus p \oplus t_k)) \tag{9}$$

$$\mathbf{s}_q = \mathbf{v}'_q + \mathrm{FT}_{std} \tag{10}$$

$$\mathbf{p}(s) = \mathrm{softmax}(\mathbf{s}_q) \tag{11}$$

where $\mathbf{p}(s)$ represents the predicted probabilities for all candidate entities. The Standard Mode compensates for the lack of predictive ability caused by the Global Mode's excessive reliance on historical events.

3.3 Parameter Learning and Inference

Given a query (s, p, ?, t), predicting object entities can be seen as a multi-class classification task, where each class corresponds to an object entity [1]. The learning objective is to minimize the cross-entropy loss $\mathcal{L}$ of all events in the TKG snapshots that exist during training:

$$\mathcal{L} = -\sum_{t \in T} \sum_{i \in \mathcal{E}} \sum_{k=1}^{K} o_{it} \ln \mathbf{p}(y_{ik}|s, p, t) \tag{12}$$

where o_{it} is the i-th ground truth object entity in the historical subgraph $\mathcal{G}_t$, and $\ln \mathbf{p}(y_{ik}|s, p, t)$ is the combined probability value of the k-th object entity in the historical subgraph $\mathcal{G}_t$ when the i-th ground truth object entity is o_i.

HSRMNet combines the Global Mode and the Standard Mode to calculate the probability scores of candidate entities, and then selects the entity with the highest probability score as the final prediction:

$$\mathbf{p}(o|s, p, t) = \alpha * \mathbf{p}(s) + (1 - \alpha) * \mathbf{p}(g) \tag{13}$$

$$o_t = \mathrm{argmax}_{o \in \mathcal{E}} \, p(o|s, p, t) \tag{14}$$

where $\alpha \in [0, 1]$, $\mathbf{p}(o|s, p, t)$ is an N-dimensional vector that contains the probabilities of all entities.

4 Experiments

This section conducts a series of experiments to validate the performance of HSRMNet. All our datasets and codes can be found at https://github.com/Cjlong1314/HSRMNet.

4.1   Experimental Settings

This paper evaluates the link prediction task of HSRMNet using two benchmark datasets, WIKI [2] and YAGO [3]. WIKI and YAGO are subsets of Wikipedia and YAGO3, respectively, storing time-varying events [1]. Table 1 summarizes the statistical data of these datasets.

Table 1. Statistics of the datasets.

#Data	#Entities	#Realtion	#Training	#Validation	#Test
YAGO	10623	10	161540	19523	20026
WIKI	12554	24	539286	67538	63110

Baselines. HSRMNet will be compared with HyTE [11], TTransE, TA-DistMult [12], CyGNet, RE-GCN and rGalT.

Training Settings and Evaluation Metrics. According to the previous work [1], all datasets are divided into training set (80%), validation set (10%), and testing set (10%) for evaluation. This paper reports on Mean Recurrent Ranks (MRR) and Hits@1/3/10 (the proportion of correct test cases ranked in the top 1/3/10). The batch size of the model configuration is set to 1024, the embedding dimension is 200, the learning rate is 0.001, and the Adam optimizer is used with a training iteration of 30. YAGO's α is 0.3, and WIKI's α is 0.7. For baseline models, this paper uses their recommended settings.

4.2   Results

Table 2 reports the results of HSRMNet and baseline methods on two public KG, where the results of baseline models on YAGO and WIKI are directly taken from these papers of RE-GCN and rGalT. For the interpolation setting (i.e. the first block in Table 2), all static KGC methods perform better than HyTE and TTransE because HyTE and TTransE only learn representations independently for each snapshot [1]. HSRMNet is significantly better than other baseline models except for RE-GCN. Compared with the best performing baseline model RE-GCN, HSRMNet achieves up to 2.25% improvements of Hit@10 on YAGO. The main reason is that HSRMNet fully exploits the repetitive patterns of historical events and contains more historical information. RE-GCN captures the structural dependencies between entities, so that it outperforms HSRMNet of Hit@1.

4.3   Ablation Study

This paper chooses YAGO to study the inference effectiveness of the Global Mode and the Standard Mode. Table 3 shows the results of ablation studies.HSRMNet-Global only considers the Global Mode, HSRMNet-Standard only considers the Standard Mode, and HSRMNet is a combination of the two modes.

Table 2. Experimental results of temporal link prediction on two public KG. * cites the results from [2].The best results are boldfaced, and the second best results are underlined.

Method	YAGO			WIKI		
	MRR	Hit@3	Hit@10	MRR	Hit@3	Hit@10
HyTE*	14.42	39.73	46.98	25.40	29.16	37.54
TTransE*	26.10	36.28	47.73	20.66	23.88	33.04
TA-DistMult*	44.98	50.64	61.11	26.44	31.36	38.97
CyGNet*	46.72	52.48	61.52	30.77	33.83	41.19
RE-GCN*	**58.27**	**65.62**	<u>75.94</u>	**39.84**	**44.43**	**53.88**
rGalT	51.45	57.76	68.31	-	-	-
HSRMNet(Ours)	<u>56.91</u>	<u>64.72</u>	**77.65**	<u>36.87</u>	<u>42.96</u>	<u>53.72</u>

The problem of gradient vanishing exists when training HSRMNet-Global alone, so this model softmax entities' score to make the training converge. The performance of HSRMNet-Global is worse than that of HSRMNet-Standard because HSRMNet-Global is sensitive to the frequency of historical events and tends towards high frequency historical events. This inevitably causes a serious historical bias, that is, the more the model is trained towards high frequency historical events, the more the trained model tends towards high frequency historical events. HSRMNet-Standard only solves the problem of historical bias based on whether events have occurred in history. Combining the two modes can avoid the problem of historical bias and explore better performance of the model.

Table 3. Ablation study of HSRMNet on YAGO and WIKI.

Method	YAGO			WIKI		
	MRR	Hit@3	Hit@10	MRR	Hit@3	Hit@10
HSRMNet-Global	42.38	42.38	45.35	23.15	24.33	32.58
HSRMNet-Standard	<u>51.71</u>	<u>51.71</u>	<u>57.75</u>	<u>36.27</u>	<u>42.34</u>	<u>53.44</u>
HSRMNet	**56.91**	**64.72**	**77.65**	**36.87**	**42.95**	**53.72**

5   Conclusion and Future Work

This paper proposes a new TKGR model based on a historical statistical reward mechanism for event prediction. The results indicate that HSRMNet outperforms existing methods in the most metrics. Promising future work includes exploring structural dependencies between entities and invisible entities [3] , and making predictions about them.

Acknowledgment. This work was supported by NSF China (No.62362060, 72364033).

References

1. Zhu, C., Chen, M., et al.: Learning from history: modeling temporal knowledge graphs with sequential copy-generation networks. In: Proceedings of the AAAI Conference on Artificial Intelligence, vol. 35, no. 5, pp. 4732–4740 (2021)
2. Li, Z., Jin, X., et al.: Temporal knowledge graph reasoning based on evolutional representation learning. In: Proceedings of the 44th International ACM SIGIR Conference on Research and Development in Information Retrieval, pp. 408–417 (2021)
3. Xu, Y., Ou, J., et al.: Temporal knowledge graph reasoning with historical contrastive learning. In: Proceedings of the AAAI Conference on Artificial Intelligence vol. 37, no. 4, pp. 4765–4773 (2023)
4. Liu, K., Zhao, F., et al.: Da-net: distributed attention network for temporal knowledge graph reasoning. In: Proceedings of the 31st ACM International Conference on Information & Knowledge Management, pp. 1289–1298 (2022)
5. Zhang, J., Hui, B., et al.: Learning multi-graph structure for temporal knowledge graph reasoning. Expert Syst. Appl. (2024)
6. Li, Z., Guan, S., et al.: Complex evolutional pattern learning for temporal knowledge graph reasoning. In: Proceedings of the 60th Annual Meeting of the Association for Computational Linguistics, pp. 290–296 (2022)
7. Niu, G., Li, B.: Logic and commonsense-guided temporal knowledge graph completion. In: Proceedings of the AAAI Conference on Artificial Intelligence (2023)
8. Lee, D.H., Ahrabian, K., et al.: Temporal knowledge graph forecasting without knowledge using in-context learning. In: Proceedings of the Conference on Empirical Methods in Natural Language Processing. vol 2023, pp. 544–557 (2023)
9. Leblay, J., Chekol, M.W.: Deriving validity time in knowledge graph. In: Proceedings of the Web Conference, pp. 1771–1776 (2018)
10. Gao, Y., Feng, L., et al.: Modeling precursors for temporal knowledge graph reasoning via auto-encoder structure. In: Proceedings of the International Joint Conference on Artificial Intelligence, pp. 2044–2051 (2022)
11. Dasgupta, S.S., Ray, S.N., et al.: Hyte: hyperplane-based temporally aware knowledge graph embedding. In: Proceedings of the 2018 Conference on Empirical Methods in Natural Language Processing, pp. 2001–2011 (2018)
12. García Durán, A., Dumančić, S.: Learning sequence encoders for temporal knowledge graph completion. In: Proceedings of the. Conference on Empirical Methods in Natural Language Processing vol. 2018, pp. 4816–4821 (2018)

Optimized DFA-Based URL Filtering for P4 Programmable Switches

Hongfei Zhang[1,2], Jie Li[1,2], Yike Zhao[1,2], Shu Li[1,2(✉)], Zhongyi Zhang[1,2], Kedong Liu[3(✉)], and Qingyun Liu[1]

[1] Institute of Information Engineering, Chinese Academy of Sciences, Beijing, China
`{zhanghongfei,lijie,zhaoyike,lishu,zhangzhongyi,liuqingyun}@iie.ac.cn`
[2] School of Cyber Security, University of Chinese Academy of Sciences, Beijing, China
[3] National Computer Network Emergency Response Technical Team/Coordination Center of China, Beijing, China
`liukedong@cert.org.cn`

Abstract. With the widespread use of programmable switches in network security and traffic monitoring, efficiently handling rule matching in large-scale datasets has become a significant challenge. In this paper, we propose an optimized FSM construction method that combines incremental state expansion, suffix sharing, and demand-driven dynamic state allocation. This method reduces DFA rule numbers, decreases FSM storage, and improves domain matching efficiency. Additionally, we implement content-level domain filtering on programmable switches and design a malicious flow management table. By marking flows matching dangerous domains, we avoid redundant matching and improve network efficiency. Experimental results show that the OFAD algorithm reduces rule count by 12%, with generation times of $8.5 \pm 0.3, \mu s$ and accuracy above 99.98%, outperforming existing algorithms. Our approach improves domain filtering efficiency and optimizes DFA generation, offering a scalable solution for large-scale datasets on programmable switches.

Keywords: DFA · P4 · Programmable switch · Deep Packet Inspection

1 Introduction

With the advancement of network technology, traditional five-tuple-based packet detection is insufficient to meet current security needs. Zero-day vulnerabilities [1] and Advanced Persistent Threats (APT) [2] exploit system flaws and infiltrate networks over time, making detection difficult. Therefore, Deep Packet Inspection (DPI) is essential to analyze packet payloads and identify complex network behaviors. DPI plays a key role in network security and traffic management, with applications in Intrusion Prevention Systems (IPS) for real-time detection of activities such as vulnerability exploitation and malicious scanning [3]. For

T. Zhu et al. (Eds.): KSEM 2025, LNAI 15922, pp. 308–316, 2026.
https://doi.org/10.1007/978-981-95-3058-8_28

example, DPI can detect and block anomalous scanning attempts targeting vulnerabilities. GINTATE is a scalable DPI framework for TLS monitoring in enterprise networks [4], and DPI can also be used to study user behavior on networks [5]. However, DPI implementation faces challenges, with proprietary hardware solutions being expensive, and traditional firewalls struggling with complex tasks like DDoS detection or encrypted traffic analysis [6]. Software-based DPI offers flexibility but can cause performance bottlenecks under high bandwidth conditions [7]. As a solution, programmable switches using P4, a domain-specific language, offer high-performance, customizable packet processing [8]. P4 is used in routers, switches, and firewalls, optimizing packet forwarding. Despite the challenges, including limited memory and P4's design not being optimized for DPI [9], this paper proposes a DPI system based on P4 running on a programmable switch to address these issues. The key contributions of our work are as follows:

- We implemented content-level filtering (domain filtering) on a programmable switch and designed a dangerous flow management table. This table marks flows that have already matched dangerous domains, ensuring that subsequent packets do not undergo redundant matching, thereby improving efficiency.
- We proposed the OFAD algorithm, addressing the issue of excessive DFA rules and memory consumption in existing URL-based DFA generation algorithms. Our optimization of malicious domain DFA generation was evaluated, and results demonstrate that our approach significantly improves rule generation efficiency while reducing the number of rules, all while maintaining high accuracy.

2   Related Work

2.1   The Application of Programmable Switches in DPI

In the field of programmable data planes, P4DNS [10]. was an early DPI solution based on P4, which extracted domain names from DNS queries and constructed response packets. While it was useful for identifying HTTP(S) websites via DNS, it only supported limited-length domain names. Meta4 [11] achieved domain-based traffic monitoring by associating DNS responses with client-server traffic, but it only supported four domain labels and was restricted to DNS packets. Despite these limitations, this method remains valuable in IoT fingerprinting, DNS tunnel detection, and similar use cases.

2.2   DFA Algorithm

Deterministic Finite Automaton (DFA) is widely used in Deep Packet Inspection (DPI) for its efficient pattern matching, but its high memory consumption limits its use in resource-constrained environments [12]. Various optimizations have been proposed to address this, such as D2FA, which reduces memory usage through delayed input processing, and CD2FA, which uses content-addressable techniques for better representation. Tag-DFA compresses redundant structures, achieving over 90% compression while maintaining matching efficiency. Trie trees reduce storage by sharing common prefixes but still face high dynamic update costs. The Aho-Corasick algorithm improves matching efficiency with failure links but still suffers from high memory consumption for complex rule sets. Optimizing DFA for programmable switches remains a critical challenge.

3   Methodology

Our approach has two main parts. First, we implement Deep Packet Inspection (DPI) on P4 programmable switches, parsing plaintext traffic and filtering packets with specific domain names, effectively creating an application layer firewall on hardware for efficient resource use. Second, we optimize the FSM table entry generation algorithm, improving table entry management and reducing rule generation time.

3.1   OFAD Algorithm

Traditional FSM construction methods create a complete state sequence for each input string. In contrast, OFAD reduces state redundancy and enhances matching efficiency through incremental construction and suffix sharing. The main steps of this method are as follows:

State Initialization

- Set the root state S_0 as the starting state of the FSM, and initialize the state set S = $\{S_0\}$.
- Maintain a state transition relation T, where T(s, c) = s', indicating that after reading character c in state s, the FSM transitions to state s'.
- Define the set of final states F to mark the states that indicate a successful match.

Incremental State Expansion

- For each input domain $d \in D$, start from the root state S_0 and build the state transition path character by character.
- Use a state reuse strategy, meaning that if a transition $T(s, c)$ for character c already exists from the current state s, the FSM follows the existing path. Otherwise, a new state is created.

Suffix Sharing Optimization

To avoid redundant construction of suffix state sequences for domain names ending with specific suffixes (e.g.,".com"), the following optimization is applied:

- Maintain a suffix state mapping table M, which records the constructed suffix state paths $\{(S_{\text{entry}}, S_{\text{exit}})\}$, where:

- S_{entry} is the entry state of the suffix.
- S_{exit} is the terminal state of the suffix.
- If the current domain name contains a recorded suffix, the prefix state is directly connected to the suffix entry state S_{entry}, preventing redundant state creation.

Final State Marking

- For a fully matched domain name path, add the final state to the set of terminal states F, denoted as S_{final}.
- During the generation of state transition rules, assign a special identifier to the terminal states to facilitate subsequent matching optimizations.

3.2   State Transition Rule Generation

After the FSM is constructed, state transition rules need to be extracted for integration into an efficient string matching system. The rule generation strategy follows these steps:

- Traverse the state set S and parse each state s along with its transition relation $T(s, c) = s'$.
- Generate state transition commands using the structured rule format $R = (s, c, s', f)$, where:
  - s is the current state.
  - c is the character that triggers the transition (encoded in ASCII).
  - s' is the new state after the transition.
  - f indicates whether s' is a terminal state (terminal states are assigned a special marker to distinguish successful match paths).
- Output the executable transition rules.

3.3   Complexity Analysis

We assume that the size of the input domain set is $|D|$, the maximum domain length is L, and the number of target suffixes optimized by suffix sharing is $|S|$. Then:

- In the worst case (without suffix optimization): the number of FSM states is $O(|D| \cdot L)$.
- After applying suffix sharing optimization:
  - For $|S|$ shared suffixes, each suffix state path is created only once, reducing the number of states by $|D| \cdot |S|$. Therefore, the total number of states is reduced to $O(|D| \cdot L - |D| \cdot |S| + |S|)$.
  - For large-scale domain sets, this optimization can significantly reduce the number of states and improve storage efficiency.

4 Experiment Result

We used an OpenMesh programmable switch with a P4 language environment based on the Tofino chip to deploy the *Domain Filter* program and verify its effectiveness with Ixa instrument-sent data packets. The hardware environment includes a 13th Gen Intel(R) Core(TM) i7-13700 CPU, and we evaluated the *OFAD* algorithm in the Python 12.0 environment, comparing its performance with the *AC*, *Trie-based*, and *FAD* algorithms. The dataset, the PhiUSIIL Phishing URL dataset from the UCI Machine Learning Repository, consists of 134,850 legitimate URLs and 100,945 phishing URLs. After deduplication, 220,086 unique domain names remain. We randomly selected subsets of sizes 0.5k, 1k, 5k, 10k, 20k, 30k, 50k, 100k, 150k, and 200k to evaluate *OFAD*'s performance based on rule count, generation time, and accuracy.

Algorithm 1: OFAD: Optimized Finite Automaton for Domain Filter

Input: Domain set D
Output: Optimized FSM with state transitions

1 `OptimizedFAD()` Initialize state set S and final states F;
2 Initialize state counter and root state;
3 Initialize suffix map $\mathcal{M}$;
4 `add_transition`(*state, char_code, next_state*) Add transition from *state* to *next_state* using *char_code*;
5 `get_or_create_state`(*current_state, char*) If transition exists, return existing state;
6 Otherwise, create new state, add transition and return new state;
7 `build_fsm`(*domains*) **foreach** *domain in domains* **do**
8   Convert domain to list *chars*;
9   **if** *domain ends with ".com"* **then**
10   If ".com" not in suffix map, create its states and store entry and exit states in $\mathcal{M}$;
11   For each character in domain prefix, create necessary states;
12   Add transition to entry state of ".com";
13   **else**
14   For each character in domain, create necessary states;
15   Add final state to F;
16 `generate_rules()` Initialize empty list *rules*;
17 **foreach** *state, transitions in S* **do**
18   **foreach** *char_code, next_state in transitions* **do**
19   Generate rule for state transition and append to *rules*;
20 **return** *rules*;

- **Number of Generated Rules**: By deduplicating the extracted URL set, we obtain a unique URL list. The number of URLs generated by the rule generation algorithm is then counted.
- **Average Rule Generation Time**: The performance of the algorithm is evaluated by measuring the time taken to generate each rule.

- **Rule Generation Accuracy**: We define the generated rule set as *rules* and the original URL set as *URL_ origin*. Using the rule reconstruction algorithm, we reconstruct URLs based on the generated rules, obtaining the reconstructed set *reconstruct_ url*. The accuracy is calculated using the following formula:

$$\text{Accuracy} = \frac{|reconstruct\_url \cap URL\_origin|}{|URL\_origin|} \times 100\% \tag{1}$$

We compared the *OFAD* algorithm against the *AC algorithm*, *Trie-based algorithm*, and *FAD*, obtaining the following experimental results.

Number of Generated Rules: Existing algorithms such as the *AC algorithm*, *FSM Trie*, and *FAD* do not optimize the number of generated rules, leading to significant redundancy and wasted resources as dataset size increases. This issue becomes especially prominent with large-scale datasets, where the number of DFA rules grows rapidly. As shown in Fig. 1, our proposed *OFAD* reduces rule numbers significantly. For small-scale datasets (1k-10k), it reduces the rule count by 8%, and for large-scale datasets (150k-200k), it achieves a 12% reduction, from 2.4 million to 2.1 million rules. This demonstrates *OFAD*'s effectiveness in eliminating redundant rules, improving efficiency, and reducing memory usage and computational cost.

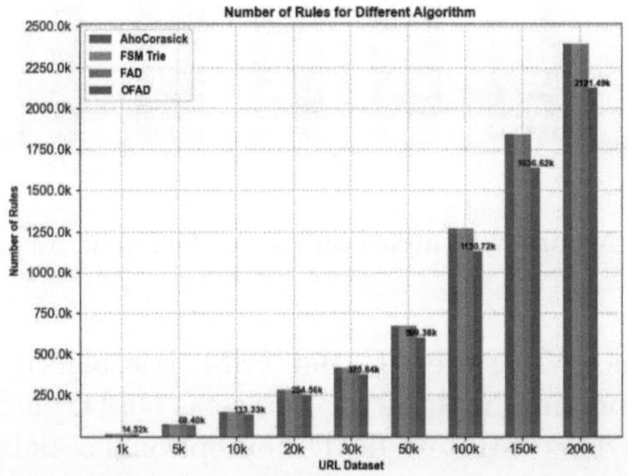

Fig. 1. Numbers of Rules for Different Algorithm

Average Rule Generation Time: As shown in Fig. 2, the rule generation time varies among different algorithms across dataset sizes. The blue line represents the baseline AC algorithm, the yellow line the FSM algorithm based on Trie construction, the green line the FAD algorithm, and the red line our proposed OFAD algorithm. For dataset sizes ranging from 0.5k to 200k, OFAD's rule generation time consistently stays within $8.5 \pm 0.3\,\mu s$, significantly lower than

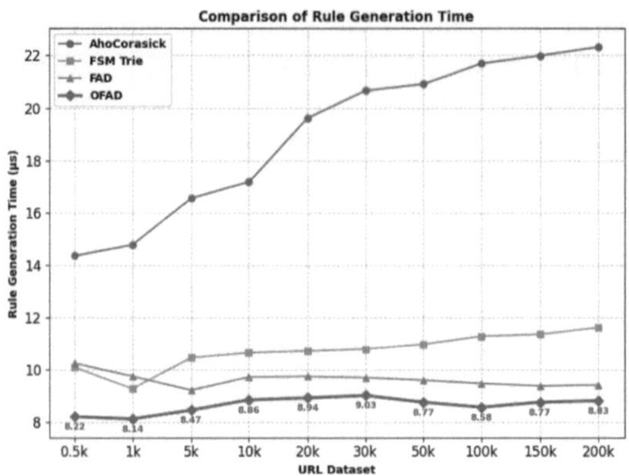

Fig. 2. Comparison of Rule Generation Time

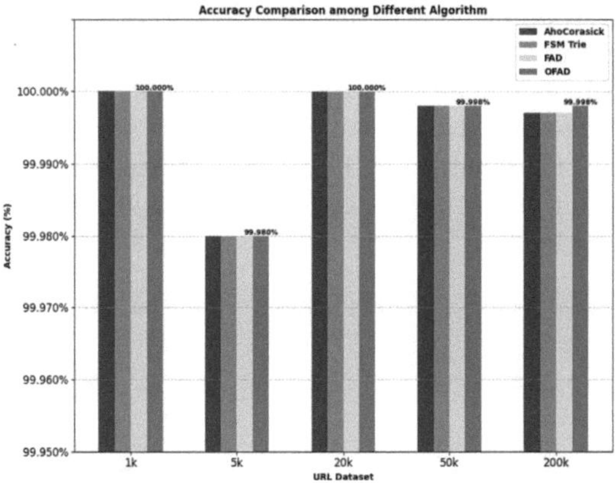

Fig. 3. Accuracy Comparison among Different Algorithm

the other algorithms. While the AC and FSM Trie algorithms show a sharp increase in generation time with larger datasets, OFAD maintains stable, low time overhead. This demonstrates OFAD's exceptional scalability and efficiency in large-scale data processing.

Rule Generation Accuracy: As shown in Fig. 3, the OFAD algorithm consistently maintains an accuracy above 99.98% across all dataset sizes. It performs comparably to existing algorithms, with slight improvements in some cases, particularly when processing large-scale datasets. Despite reducing the number of rules, the accuracy remains stable, demonstrating the algorithm's efficiency. Compared to traditional AC and FSM Trie algorithms, OFAD achieves the same high accuracy while generating fewer rules, confirming its correctness and suitability for large-scale datasets in practical applications.

5   Conclusion

This paper implements content-level domain filtering on programmable switches, designing a malicious flow management table to mark flows matching dangerous domains and avoid redundant matching, improving network efficiency. To address rule quantity and storage issues in existing URL-to-DFA generation algorithms, we propose the OFAD algorithm. Experimental results show that OFAD reduces rule count by 12% on large-scale datasets, with consistent rule generation times of $8.5 \pm 0.3, \mu s$ and accuracy above 99.98%, outperforming existing algorithms. Our method significantly improves domain filtering efficiency and optimizes the DFA generation process, demonstrating high scalability on programmable switches.

Acknowledgements. We would like to thank the hard work of MESA TEAM (www.mesalab.cn). This work is supported by the Scaling Program of Institute of Information Engineering, CAS (Grant No. E3Z0041101)

References

1. Bilge, L., Dumitraş, T.: Before we knew it: an empirical study of zero-day attacks in the real world. In: Proceedings of the 2012 ACM Conference on Computer and Communications Security (CCS '12).New York, NY, USA: Association for Computing Machinery, 2012, pp. 833 –844

2. Singh, S., et al.: A comprehensive study on apt attacks and countermeasures for future networks and communications: challenges and solutions. J. Supercomput. **75**, 4543–4574 (2019)

3. Çelebi, M., Özbilen, A., Yavanoğlu, U.: A comprehensive survey on deep packet inspection for advanced network traffic analysis: issues and challenges. NOHU J. Eng. Sci. **12**(1), 1–29 (2023)

4. Miura, R., Takano, Y., Miwa, S., Inoue, T.: Gintate: scalable and extensible deep packet inspection system for encrypted network traffic: Session resumption in transport layer security communication considered harmful to dpi. In: Proceedings of the 8th International Symposium on Information and Communication Technology (SoICT '17).New York, NY, USA: Association for Computing Machinery, 2017, pp. 234–241

5. Nkongolo, M., van Deventer, J.P., Kasongo, S.M.: Using deep packet inspection data to examine subscribers on the network. Proc. Comput. Sci. **215**, 182–191 (2022)

6. ScienceDirect, Deep packet inspection. https://www.sciencedirect.com/topics/computer-science/deep-packet-inspection#recommended-publications

7. IR, Deep packet inspection (dpi): how it works and why it's important. https://www.ir.com/guides/deep-packet-inspection

8. Bosshart, P., et al.: P4: programming protocol-independent packet processors. SIGCOMM Comput. Commun. Rev. **44**(3), 87–95 (2014)

9. Budiu, M., Dodd, C.: The p416 programming language. ACM SIGOPS Oper. Syst. Rev. **51**(1), 5–14 (2017)

10. Woodruff, J., Ramanujam, M., Zilberman, N.:P4dns: In-network DNS. In: ACM/IEEE Symposium on Architectures for Networking and Communications Systems (ANCS), pp. 1–6 (2019)
11. Kim, J., Kim, H., Rexford, J.: Analyzing traffic by domain name in the data plane. In: Proceedings of the ACM SIGCOMM Symposium on SDN Research (SOSR), pp. 1–12 (2021)
12. Kumar, S., Turner, J., Williams, J.: Advanced algorithms for fast and scalable deep packet inspection. In: 2006 Symposium on Architecture For Networking And Communications Systems, pp. 81–92 (2006)

Improving Mongolian-Chinese Translation Quality Using Noise-Enhanced mBART

Bailun Wang, Yatu Ji[(✉)], and Nier Wu

Inner Mongolia University of Technology, Hohhot 010000, China
`{mljyt,wunier04}@imut.edu.cn`

Abstract. Improving neural machine translation (NMT) for the Mongolian-Chinese language pair is challenging due to the lack of high-quality parallel data. This study explores various noise enhancement techniques to enhance the Mongolian-Chinese Neural Machine Translation (MNMT) model's translation quality. Techniques such as swap, token, delete, and source. Experimental results show that these methods significantly improve translation quality, with the source method yielding the most substantial enhancement. These findings indicate that noise enhancement effectively addresses data scarcity and quality issues, providing a robust strategy for improving MNMT performance.

Keywords: Neural Machine Translation · Noise Enhancement · mBART · Mongolian-Chinese

1 Introduction

NMT [1] technology, driven by deep learning, complex neural networks, and extensive data, has achieved significant success, especially in high-resource languages like Chinese and English. However, it still relies heavily on high-quality parallel corpora and deep domain knowledge, resulting in poor performance for low-resource languages [2] and specialized domains such as medical and legal translation. In the context of MNMT [3], the shift from rule-based and statistical methods to deep learning has improved outcomes, but the scarcity of linguistic data, morphological complexity, and limited foundational research hinder progress. The lack of large-scale parallel corpora and the high cost of automatic corpus construction [4] remain key challenges. This research addresses these issues by exploring noise enhancement methods to improve pseudo-parallel corpora, making Chinese target texts less reliable so that models rely more on the context of Mongolian for accurate translation.

2 Related Work

2.1 Data Augmentation

Although NMT has outperformed statistical methods, it still struggles with low-resource languages like Mongolian, Tibetan, and Vietnamese due to limited training data. Data enhancement strategies aim to improve both the quality and quantity of training data,

T. Zhu et al. (Eds.): KSEM 2025, LNAI 15922, pp. 317–324, 2026.
https://doi.org/10.1007/978-981-95-3058-8_29

mainly through increasing data volume and diversifying outputs. Synonym replacement [5] is commonly used to expand data, but it depends on comprehensive thesauri, which is often lacking in low-resource languages. To address this, researchers like Aydoğan et al. [6] have used pre-trained word embeddings for word substitution, and pre-trained models have also been applied to predict masked words for data augmentation. Noise injection methods help diversify outputs by introducing controlled noise while preserving semantics, and leveraging linguistic features and prior knowledge improves model robustness. Further strategies like reverse translation and adversarial learning enhance data complexity [7], while filtering techniques using pre-trained models refine outputs to boost translation quality [8].

2.2 Mongolian-Chinese NMT

Mongolian-Chinese machine translation research began in the 1980s with rule-based and statistical methods, limited by data scarcity and linguistic differences. With the advent of deep learning, MNMT emerged but continues to face challenges in data availability and domain adaptability due to the structural disparities between the two languages. Recent studies have made progress: Su Y et al. [9] improved NMT using Dual-Generative Adversarial Network for data augmentation, subword slicing with LSTM and Transformer models, and introduced instance-based translation [10] for better corpus alignment. Xue Y et al. [11] enhanced translation quality through syntactic structure integration, while Ji Y et al. [12] applied reinforcement learning and noise generalization for low-resource scenarios. Zhao X et al. [13] explored Transformer and non-autoregressive models with knowledge distillation and cross-language word embeddings to boost MNMT performance.

3 Methodology

3.1 Noise Addition Method

We enhance the Chinese corpus by adding noise to target sentences, generating unreliable pseudo-target sentences to derive corresponding source-side pseudo-sentences. This approach boosts encoder feature extraction by emphasizing source language representation while expanding training data. Key parameters include the original target sentence length t and the proportion of words $\alpha(0, 1)$ to be modified.

Swap. The Swap method rearranges words in target-language sentences, allowing only $(1 - \alpha) \cdot t$ words remain in their original positions. This reduces the model's reliance on target-side expressions during translation, improving its accuracy in such scenarios. We apply UDPipe for syntactic analysis of the Mongolian corpus, tagging components like subjects, and use a random number generator to select and swap words, trying not to disrupting syntactic structure. This approach simulates natural linguistic variations, enabling the model to produce higher-quality translations when facing sentences with diverse structures.

Token. The Token method replaces $\alpha \cdot t$ target-language words with the special token [UNK], reducing target-side information and encouraging the model to rely more on source-language context. This shifts the model's learning focus toward source-language features rather than target-language dependency. In practice, we use the Jieba tool for Chinese word segmentation and perform frequency analysis to identify high-frequency or semantically ambiguous words. Selected words are then replaced with [UNK] tokens, ensuring each sentence includes a fixed number of such substitutions to enhance the model's contextual understanding and generalization.

Source. In the Source method, target-language sentences are replaced with their corresponding source-language (Mongolian) sentences, reducing the model's dependence on target-side input. This encourages the model to focus on source-language features and better learn the mapping between the two languages. To enhance this method's effectiveness, we collected and integrated a more diverse set of Mongolian sentences, enriching the Mongolian-Chinese training data and improving the model's ability to handle complex translation scenarios with greater accuracy.

Delete. The delete method simulates common information loss in translation by removing specific Chinese words, particularly those frequently causing errors in Mongolian output. This encourages the model to rely more on source content, enhancing its ability to handle incomplete or ambiguous inputs. We used GIZA++ for Chinese-Mongolian alignment and identified low-quality sentence pairs by comparing translations to reference outputs. Within these pairs, we located Chinese words frequently aligned with poor Mongolian translations. Using co-occurrence frequency, we determined whether these words appeared significantly more often in error-prone translations than the normal distribution in overall corpus. Words consistently aligned with unnatural or incorrect Mongolian terms were flagged as error-prone and removed via automated scripts. This approach improves the model's robustness when handling noisy or partially missing target sentences.

3.2 Translation Sampling Method

Traditional noise enhancement methods often compromise sentence semantics and lack sufficient diversity. To address this and improve MNMT performance, we use a translation sampling method that selects target-language sentences containing controllable noise but with high similarity to reference translations. This enhances model generalization and reduces overfitting.

The method involves generating multiple pseudo-sentences using different noise strategies for each target sentence, then comparing them to the reference translation to quantify similarity. The top n most similar sentences (n = 1, 2, 3, 4) are selected and added to the training corpus. The specific formulation is shown in the following equation:

$$Similarity = 1/\left(1 + \|V_n(pseudo) - V_{target}\|_2\right) \tag{1}$$

$V_n(pseudo)$ (n = 1,2,3,4) represent pseudo-sentences extracted from noise-enhanced models, while V_{target} denotes the reference translation vector. The Euclidean norms of the pseudo-sentence and reference vectors, $\|V_n(pseudo)\|$ and $\|V_{target}\|$, reflect their

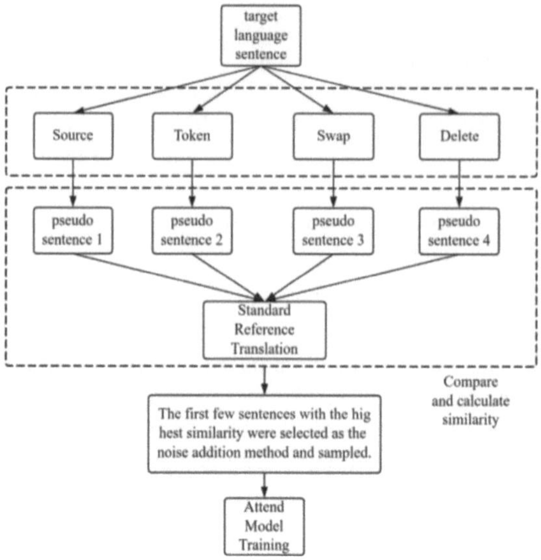

Fig. 1. Sampling Methodology of noise addition methods.

magnitudes in vector space. Sentence similarity is evaluated using Euclidean distance. The sampling method is illustrated in Fig. 1.

3.3 Model Architecture

We adopt multilingual BART (mBART) [14] as the base model for its strong cross-lingual transfer capabilities, enabled by pre-training on large-scale multilingual data. Its sequence-to-sequence architecture with autoregressive generation and multi-head attention effectively captures long-range dependencies and semantic nuances. Following Pan et al. [15], we use the large version of mBART with default settings, implemented via the Huggingface Transformers library [16]. As Mongolian is not included in the original model, we fine-tune mBART on Mongolian-Chinese data using noise enhancement to better adapt to the syntactic and semantic characteristics of both languages, thereby enhancing translation quality for this low-resource pair. The model framework is shown in Fig. 2.

4 Experiments

4.1 Experimental Setup

The experiments use 1.2 million Mongolian-Chinese parallel sentence pairs, with 960,000 for training and 120,000 each for validation and testing. We construct pseudo-parallel corpora using noise enhancement, where key hyperparameters directly affect data quality. An ablation study examines the impact of α values ranging from 0.1 to 0.9 (in steps of 0.1) on MNMT performance. Based on BLEU scores, the optimal α values are 0.2 for the Swap method and 0.4 for the Token method.

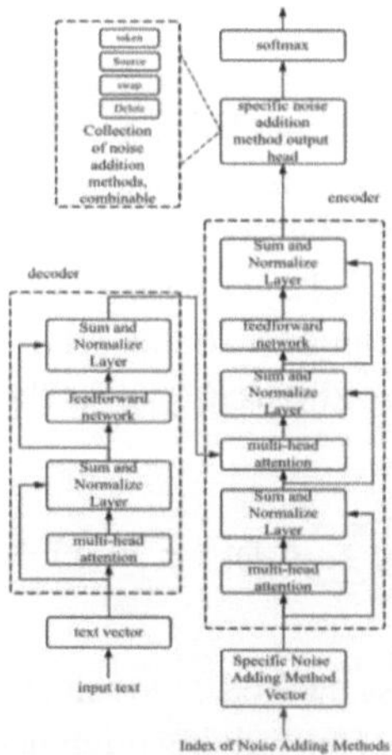

Fig. 2. Model Framework.

4.2 Main Results

We utilize mBART as our baseline model, and Table 1 presents the BLEU scores [17] and CHRF scores [18] for translation tasks across various models, including results from Wang Y et al. [19] and Zhao Y et al. [20] for comparison. The data shows that our method surpasses the existing methods in terms of BLEU scores.

Table 1. Main Result of noise-based method.

Model	BLEU	CHRF
MNMT based on mBART	23.43	0.2624
MNMT based on Transfer Learning	24.09	-
MNMT Using BPE	24.60	-
MNMT Using BPE and Word2vec	25.20	-
MNMT based on Transfer Learning Using BPE	26.20	-
MNMT based on Parameter Transfer	26.57	-
Ours mBART + swap	24.82	0.2719
Ours mBART + delete	28.96	0.2766
Ours mBART + token	29.47	0.2817
Ours mBART + source	29.68	**0.2869**
Ours mBART + source + swap	23.95	0.2202
Ours mBART + source + token	**30.91**	0.2730

4.3   Target Side Noise Addition

Constructing pseudo-parallel corpora involves injecting noise into target sentences while preserving source-language fidelity. One approach is to introduce perturbations into the target side. To quantify the NMT model's reliance on source and target inputs, we follow Voita et al. [21] and adopt a variant of Layer-wise Relevance Propagation (LRP). At each time step t, the relative contribution of a source word x_i is denoted as $R_t(x_i)$, and the corresponding impact of a target word y_i as $R_t(y_i)$. As shown in Eq. (2), their sum remains constant at 1 for any time step.

$$\sum_i R_t(x_i) + \sum_i R_t(y_i) = R_t(x) + R_t(y) = 1 \qquad (2)$$

To ensure comparability across methods, we select sentence subsets of equal length from the source and target corpora, constraining reference translation length and enabling consistent LRP-based evaluation of noise enhancement. In our experiments, noise is added to target sentences to construct the required pseudo-parallel corpus. We further adopt the tool by Voita et al. to analyze the source-language contribution $R_t(x_i)$ during translation generation under noise-enhanced settings. Since the first target word lacks prior context, relevance analysis begins from the second token.

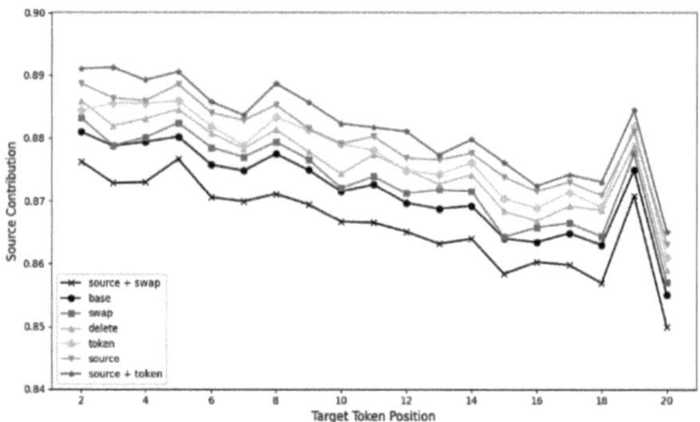

Fig. 3. Source contribution of different noise addition methods

Figure 3 reveals a pattern consistent with Voita et al.: as the decoder generates each word, the source-language contribution generally declines. However, a noticeable small peak occurs at the penultimate word, where the model appears to verify translation completeness before sharply dropping upon encountering the end-of-sentence token <eos>. Models trained solely on original parallel corpora show limited attention to the source sentence. In contrast, our noise-augmented pseudo-parallel data significantly increases the model's reliance on source input. The consistently high source contribution in our enhanced MNMT model illustrates improved source reliance, leading to noticeably better translation performance.

5   Analysis

Advantages. The swap method boosts data diversity and model adaptability to varied sentence structures. The token method improves handling of unknown words by encouraging reliance on context via special placeholders. The delete method enhances translation by removing frequently mistranslated words. The source method increases accuracy and consistency by reinforcing source-side information. Combining source and token methods merges their strengths, further improving translation quality.

Disadvantages. The swap method may distort sentence semantics, affecting translation quality. The token method risks information loss if overused. The delete method adds complexity by requiring precise removal of frequently mistranslated words, potentially leading to incomplete semantics. The source method can hinder target sentence generation if overly dependent on noisy source input. While combining source and token methods achieves the best results, it increases implementation complexity and demands careful parameter tuning.

6   Conclusion

This study adopts mBART as the baseline model and explore noise enhancement method to enhance the performance of MNMT. Experimental results demonstrate that the proposed method improves the performance of the MNMT model. With the integration of noise enhancement, both BLEU and CHRF scores show noticeable improvement, supporting the method's effectiveness in enhancing the model's generalization capability. Furthermore, comparative experiments with existing approaches confirm the superiority of the proposed method in boosting MNMT performance.

Acknowledgments. This research was funded by National Natural Science Foundation of China grant number 62066035, 62206138 and Universities Directly Under the Autonomous Region Funded by the Fundamental Research Fund Project grant number JY20220122, JY20220089, RZ2300001739, RZ2300001743, JY20220186 and Research program of science and technology at Universities of Inner Mongolia Autonomous Region grant number NJZZ22251, NJZZ23081 and Science Research Foundation of Inner Mongolia University of Technology grant number BS2021079, ZZ202118, DC2300001261, DC2300001258, DC2300001262.

References

1. Stahlberg, F.: Neural machine translation: a review. Journal of Artificial Intelligence Research **69**, 343–418 (2020)
2. Ranathunga, S., Lee, E.S.A., Prifti, S.M., et al.: Neural machine translation for low-resource languages: a survey. ACM Comput. Surv. **55**(11), 1–37 (2023)
3. Qing-dao-er-ji, R., Cheng, K., Pang, R.: Research on traditional Mongolian-Chinese neural machine translation based on dependency syntactic information and transformer model. Appl. Sci. **12**(19), 10074 (2022)

4. Holmer, D., Rennes, E.: Constructing pseudo-parallel swedish sentence corpora for automatic text simplification. Proceedings of the 24th Nordic Conference on Computational Linguistics (NoDaLiDa), pp. 113–123 (2023)

5. Rennes, E., Jönsson, A.: Synonym replacement based on a study of basic-level nouns in Swedish texts of different complexity. Proceedings of the 23rd Nordic Conference on Computational Linguistics (NoDaLiDa), pp. 259–267 (2021)

6. Aydoğan, M., Karci, A.: Improving the accuracy using pre-trained word embeddings on deep neural networks for Turkish text classification. Physica A **541**, 123288 (2020)

7. Qu, Y., Shen, D., Shen, Y., et al.: Coda: Contrast-enhanced and diversity-promoting data augmentation for natural language understanding. In: 9th International Conference on Learning Representations (ICLR), Virtual Event, Austria, pp. 737–746 (2021)

8. Peng, B., Zhu, C., Zeng, M., et al.: Data augmentation for spoken language understanding via pretrained language models. In: 22nd Annual Conference of the International Speech Communication Association (Interspeech), Brno, Czechia, pp. 1219–1223 (2021)

9. Su, Y., Wang, H., He, Y., et al.: Mongolian-Chinese neural machine translation based on adversarial learning. Computer System Applications **31**(01), 249–258 (2022)

10. Su, Y., Liu, W., Wu, N.: A Mongolian-Chinese machine translation method based on instance similarity detection. Journal of Beijing Institute of Technology **43**(09), 1366–1372 (2017)

11. Xue, Y., Su, Y., Ren, Q., et al.: Mongolian-Chinese neural machine translation based on graph convolutional encoder. Computer Applications and Software **40**(10), 70–75+89 (2023)

12. Ji, Y.: Research on Key Issues in Low-Resource Neural Machine Translation. Inner Mongolia University (2020)

13. Zhao, X., Su, Y., Ren, Q., et al.: Application of non-autoregressive translation model on Mongolian-Chinese translation. Computer Engineering and Application **58**(12), 310–316 (2022)

14. Liu, Y., et al.: Multilingual denoising pre-training for neural machine translation. Trans. Assoc. Comput. Linguist. **8**, 726–742 (2020)

15. Pan, L., Hang, C.-W., Qi, H., Shah, A., Potdar, S., Yu, M.: Multilingual BERT post-pretraining alignment. In: Proceedings of the 2021 Conference of the North American Chapter of the Association for Computational Linguistics: Human Language Technologies, pp. 210–219 (2021)

16. Wolf, T., et al.: Huggingface's Transformers: State-of-the-Art Natural Language Processing. arXiv preprint arXiv:1910.03771 (2019)

17. Reiter, E.: A structured review of the validity of BLEU. Comput. Linguist. **44**(3), 393–401 (2018)

18. Popović, M.: chrF: character n-gram F-score for automatic MT evaluation. In: Proceedings of the Tenth Workshop on Statistical Machine Translation, pp. 392–395 (2015)

19. Wang, Y., Su, Y., Zhao, Y., et al.: Neural machine translation model for Mongolian-Chinese based on parameter migration. Comput. Appl. Softw. **37**(9), 81–87 (2020)

20. Zhao, Y., Su, Y., Niu, X., et al.: A method of Mongolian-Chinese machine translation based on neural network migration learning. Comput. Appl. Softw. **37**(1), 179–185 (2020)

21. Voita, E., Sennrich, R., Titov, I. Analyzing the source and target contributions to predictions in neural machine translation. In: ACL-IJCNLP 2021 - 59th Annual Meeting of the Association for Computational Linguistics and the 11th International Joint Conference on Natural Language Processing, Proceedings of the Conference, pp. 1126–1140 (2021)

RMNS: Robust Hyper-relational Link Prediction Model Based on Multi-level Negative Sampling

Xikai Ke[1,2], Fang Liu[3,4](✉), Zhehao Hou[1,2], Min Jiang[1,2], Weike Xia[5], Tongliang Li[6], Hezhong Jiang[6], and Wei Hu[1,2](✉)

[1] School of Computer Science and Technology, Wuhan University of Science and Technology, Wuhan 430065, Hubei, China
`huwei@wust.edu.cn`
[2] Hubei Province Key Laboratory of Intelligent Information Processing and Real-time Industrial System, Wuhan University of Science and Technology, Wuhan 430065, China
[3] School of Artificial Intelligence, Wuhan Vocational College of Software and Engineering, Wuhan, China
`liufangfang@whu.edu.cn`
[4] School of Computer Science, Wuhan University, Wuhan, China
[5] Yongqi Technology Group Co., Ltd., Wenzhou, China
[6] Zhejiang Zhongke Kunpeng Artificial Intelligence Technology Co., Ltd., Zhejiang, China

Abstract. Hyper-relational Knowledge Graph (HKG) link prediction is a critical research area with substantial academic and practical significance. HKG consists of hyper-relational facts, comprising a primary triple augmented by multiple attribute-value qualifiers, enabling rich factual representation. However, noise is inevitably introduced during knowledge graph construction. Existing methods often fail to simultaneously ensure link prediction accuracy and robustness, thereby limiting their effectiveness in downstream applications. To address this issue, we propose RMNS, a novel approach based on a heterogeneous graph encoder. RMNS employs a multi-level negative sampling strategy to perform forward diffusion and backward denoising on all related elements, with an emphasis on low-confidence components, thereby improving model robustness and effectively suppressing noise. Additionally, RMNS incorporates an edge-biased attention mechanism to differentially emphasize heterogeneous element embeddings, enabling more precise capture of associations within hyper-relational structures. Experimental results on JF17K and Wikipeople benchmark datasets demonstrate that RMNS improves the Hits@1 index for entity and relation link prediction by an average of 2.3% and 0.4%, respectively. It is verified that this method has significant advantages in improving the accuracy of link prediction in the case of noise interference.

Keywords: Hyper-relation · Knowledge Graph · Robust Learning · Link Prediction · Diffusion Model

1   Introduction

Modern KGs often incorporate hyper-relational facts, where a basic triple (h, r, t) is supplemented with multiple key-value (k, v) pairs that provide additional contextual information. These hyper-relational facts are denoted as $X = \{(h, r, t), \{(k_i, v_i)\}_{i=1}^{m}\}$. To effectively leverage these KGs, link prediction has become a widely used approach for knowledge graph completion and inference.

Although KGs are widely adopted across various domains, most are constructed via automated techniques or crowdsourcing, which often introduces inevitable noise. Such noise can significantly degrade the performance of downstream applications.

Existing methods either focus solely on detecting noisy triples—often neglecting link prediction accuracy—or aim to improve prediction performance while overlooking the adverse impact of noise. To overcome these limitations, we propose a new model: Robust Hyper-Relational Link Prediction Model Based on Multi-Level Negative Sampling (RMNS), which improves robustness while guaranteeing the accuracy of link prediction. The main contributions of this paper are as follows: We propose enhancing model robustness via multi-level negative sampling, guided by the lowest-confidence element node and implemented through forward diffusion and reverse denoising; We propose RMNS, which simultaneously processes heterogeneous hyper-relational embeddings via link prediction and robust learning, ensuring both predictive accuracy and robustness.

2   Related Work

Link Prediction: StarE [3] utilizes GNNs for message passing to encode entities and relations. Hy-Transformer [4] integrates layer normalization and dropout into its encoder. However, both overlook the heterogeneity of links in knowledge graphs. HINGE [6] decomposes N-ary facts into separate embeddings and applies convolution and pooling over triples and qualifiers. NeuInfer [7] uses fully connected network (FCN) convolutions over all embeddings to compute scores. However, both overlook global semantic information in link prediction. QUAD [5] employs a Transformer decoder with auxiliary tasks and loss balancing via hyperparameter tuning. GRAN [8] introduces an edge-biased Transformer for graph-based n-ary link prediction. These methods primarily focus on improving prediction performance, while neglecting model robustness.

Robust Learning: CKRL [2] incorporates triple confidence into a translation-based framework to detect noise by leveraging structural information within the knowledge graph. KGTtm [10] estimates confidence by integrating entity-pair association strength, relation occurrence likelihood, and global inference. However, neither method addresses robustness in link prediction.

3   Preliminaries

In this section, we briefly introduce the definition of hyper-relational knowledge graphs, the heterogeneous graph edge definitions in edge-biased attention, and the diffusion model.

3.1   Hyper-relational Knowledge Graph

A hyper-relational knowledge graph (HKG) consists of basic triples and additional key-value qualifiers. The hyper-relation is defined as: $X = \{(h, r, t), \{(k_i, v_i)\}_{i=1}^{m}\}$. Here, (h, r, t) denotes the primary triple, representing the core semantic relation. The set $\{(k_i, v_i)\}_{i=1}^{m}$ contains m qualifiers that provide additional semantic context. Each $k_i \in R$ is a qualifier relation, and $v_i \in E$ is the corresponding entity.

3.2   Heterogeneous Graph Edge Definition

Each element in the hyper-relational structure $\{h, r, t, k_i, v_i\}$ is treated as a node in a heterogeneous graph. These nodes form the vertex set, and their connections define the edge set of the graph neural network.

To model hyper-relational facts, we represent all elements in $X = \{(h, r, t), (k_i, v_i)_{i=1}^{m}\}$ as nodes in a heterogeneous graph $G = (V, L)$. Different attention biases are then applied to edges based on their types. We focus on four types of edges: h-r, t-r, r-k, and k-v. The attention bias between nodes i and j is then associated with the type of edge formed between the nodes.

3.3   Diffusion Model

Diffusion model denoising [9] consists of two Markov chains: a forward diffusion process and a backward denoising process. The forward chain transforms input data to complete noise by gradually adding Gaussian noise at each step: $q(x_{1:T}|x_0) = \prod_{t=1}^{T} \mathcal{N}(x_t; \sqrt{1 - \beta_t}\, x_{t-1}, \beta_t I).$where T is the total number of time steps of the diffusion process and β_t denotes the variance in the diffusion process, a predefined noise scheduling parameter.

By means of reparameterization, the closed form of the output x_t at any time step t can be obtained as follows: $x_t = \sqrt{\bar{\alpha}_t x_0} + \sqrt{1 - \bar{\alpha}_t}\epsilon_t$. Where $\bar{\alpha}_t = 1 - \beta_t, \bar{\alpha}_t = \prod_{t=1}^{T} \alpha_i$, and $\epsilon_t \sim \mathcal{N}(0, 1)$. The backward denoising process learns to reconstruct the input from the noise: $p_\theta(x_{0:T}) = p(x_T) \prod_{t=1}^{T} \mathcal{N}(x_{t-1}; \mu_\theta(x_t, t), \Sigma_\theta(x_t, t))$ and $p(x_T) = \mathcal{N}(x_T; 0, I)$.

4   Method

In this section, we introduce RMNS, a robust hyper-relational link prediction model based on multi-level negative sampling.

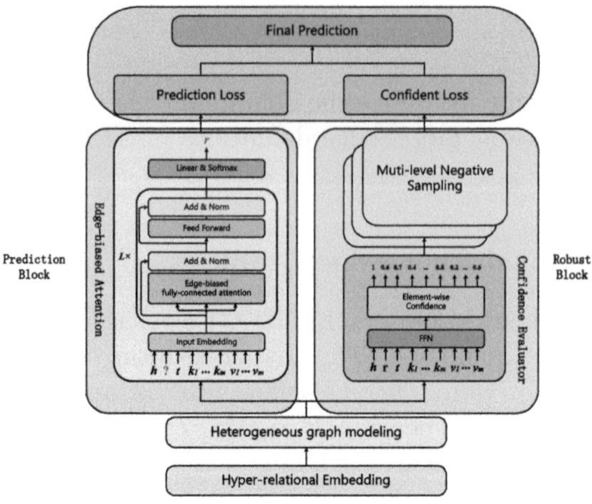

Fig. 1. RMNS model: (1) link prediction part (2) robust learning part.

To enhance robustness in link prediction, we introduce a confidence evaluator and a multi-stage negative sampler. As shown in Fig. 1, RMNS first encodes hyper-relational embeddings using a heterogeneous graph modeler, and then processes them through two branches jointly optimized via prediction and confidence loss. For link prediction, RMNS treats all elements in a hyper-relation as heterogeneous nodes in a graph neural network, applies edge-biased attention over their connections, and computes the prediction loss by comparing the predicted result with the positive sample. For robust learning, a confidence score is assigned to each element using an FFN and confidence evaluation layer. The element with the lowest confidence is selected for multi-level negative sampling, leveraging diffusion and reverse denoising to improve robustness. The final output is optimized based on the combined loss from both branches.

4.1   Prediction Module

The link predictor aims to infer missing entities or relations in hyper-relational facts using an encoder trained with masked inputs. It employs a self-attention network with learnable attention biases to capture dependencies among entities and relations in both triples and key-value pairs. Given an incomplete n-tuple fact $X = \{((h, ?, t), \{(k_i, v_i)\}_{i=1}^{m})\}$, represented as a heterogeneous graph, the input is embedded, processed through L stacked graph attention layers, and passed to a prediction layer.

During this process, edge embeddings are refined via a self-attention mechanism: $\eta_{ij} = \dfrac{\left(W^Q x_i\right)^T \left(W^K x_j + b_{ij}^K\right)}{\sqrt{d}}$. Where η_{ij} represents the importance of the link between an element u_i and another element, as in the edge bias of Fig. 2, because it introduces a linear mapping $W^Q, W^K, W^V \in \mathbb{R}^d$, and further introduces the attention bias $b_{ij}^Q, b_{ij}^K, b_{ij}^V \in \mathbb{R}^d$ to encode the type edges that represent the type edges between i and j.

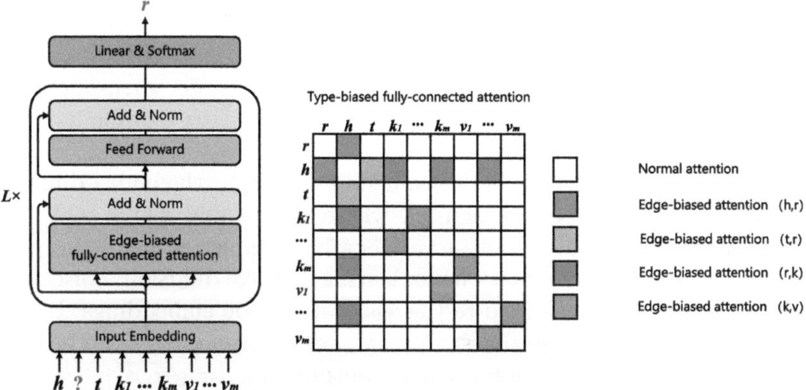

Fig. 2. The left panel shows the edge-biased attention module, and the right panel visualizes the biased attention matrix of links between elemental nodes.

Next, we update the embedding of node x_i by weighted aggregation, updating the node with the formula: $x_i^{'} = \sum_{j=1}^{n} \frac{exp(\eta_{ik})}{\sum_{k=1}^{n} exp(\eta_{ik})} \left(W^V x_j + b_{ij}^V\right)$. Where $u_i^{'}$ represents the updated feature of node u_i. Node features are aggregated as a weighted average of their neighbors, with weights η_{ij} reflecting edge type and relevance. This allows nodes to focus on more informative neighbors. Multiple attention layers with learnable edge biases are stacked to produce the embedding of the $[Mask]$ token, denoted as x_m.

Finally, a linear layer and *softmax* function are applied for prediction as follows: $p = softmax(W_m x_m + b_m)$. where W_m is the weight matrix of the entity input embedding layer and b_m is a learnable entity deviation. Similarly, if the missing element is a relation, W_m, b_m corresponds to the input embedding layer matrices of relation and relationship biases, respectively.

The final output of our hyper-relational link predictor is the probability distribution p of all entities (or relations), and the cross-entropy loss is calculated based on the comparison of the true values y_l, denoted as: $Loss_P = CELoss(p, y_l)$.

4.2   Robust Module

The robust learning module performs multi-level negative sampling on low-confidence elements, enhancing model robustness through forward diffusion and reverse denoising based on the element with the lowest confidence. It is built on a confidence evaluator and a multi-level negative sampling generator.

The hyper-relation input is processed by an FFN with L_c layers to estimate the confidence τ_e of each element. A sigmoid function is applied to constrain $\tau_e \in (0, 1)$, as follows: $\tau_e = sigmoid(FFN([h_h, h_r, h_t, h_{k_i}, h_{v_i}]))$. According to the least confidence principle, the element with the lowest confidence is selected as the query. The model aims to learn the positive distribution of associated elements centered on this query.

A conditional diffusion model incorporates the query embedding to guide sample generation. Multi-level negative sampling is performed by extracting node embeddings at different time steps, where earlier steps correspond to easier negatives and later steps to harder ones. Thus, negative sample hardness is inversely related to the time step t.

For a query node v, let h_v be its embedding, and h_u the embeddings of all other nodes u in the hyper-relation X, where $v \neq u$ and $v \cup u = X$. These embeddings are input into a multi-level negative sampler to learn the positive distribution centered on the query node. During positive diffusion, noise of equal magnitude is progressively added to the associated node embeddings. Using the reparameterization trick, negative samples $h_{u,t}$ at any time step t can be directly generated without relying on intermediate outputs: $h_{u,t} = \sqrt{\bar{\alpha}_t} x_0 + \sqrt{1 - \bar{\alpha}_t} \epsilon_t$.

In the denoising process, the goal is to predict the noise added to each associated node u at time step t, conditioned on the query node v: $\epsilon_{t,\theta|v} = f(h_{u,t}, t, h_v; \theta)$. where $t \in \mathbb{R}^{d_h}$ be the continuous time embedding and θ the learnable parameters.

We apply sinusoidal positional encoding to t as: $[t]_{2i} = \sin\left(\dfrac{t}{10000^{\frac{2i}{d_h}}}\right)$ and $[t]_{2i+1} = \cos\left(\dfrac{t}{10000^{\frac{2i}{d_h}}}\right)$. This encoding is passed through a multilayer perceptron $\tau(; \theta)$, which learns to transform the time embedding to predict noise.

The prediction layer is conditioned on the time step t and query embedding h_v as follows: $\epsilon_{t,\theta|v} = (\gamma + 1) \odot h_{u,t} + \eta$, where $\gamma, \eta \in \mathbb{R}^{d_h}$ are scaling and shift vectors. The symbol $\odot$ denotes element-wise multiplication. Both γ and η are learned from fully connected layers conditioned on $(t + h_v)$: $\gamma = \mathrm{FCL}(t + h_v; \theta_\gamma)$, $\eta = \mathrm{FCL}(t + h_v; \theta_\eta)$.

We use the mean square error between the sampling noise of the forward process and the predicted noise of the reverse process to calculate the diffusion loss at each time step t: $Loss_D = ||\epsilon_t - \epsilon_{t,\theta|v}||$. The final training loss combines both the link prediction loss and the diffusion loss: $Loss = Loss_P + Loss_D$.

5   Experiment

This section presents the results of the comparison and ablation experiments. In this paper, RMNS is evaluated on the link prediction task on two datasets, JF17K and Wikipeople.

5.1   Baseline

Comparing RMNS with previous link prediction methods, RMNS mainly includes two types: (1) Models that mainly study link prediction performance: StarE, HY-Transformer, Neuinfer, QUAD, HINGE and GRAN; (2) The main research model of robust learning: CKRL, KGTtm.

5.2   Result

As the datasets lack explicitly labeled noisy facts, a hyper-relational noise generation strategy is devised. Specifically, existing methods [2] generate noisy triples
by randomly corrupting one element of a positive fact. We evaluate link prediction performance using MRR and Hits@K (with K = 1).

Table 1. Experimental results comparing RMNS with other models on JF17K and
Wikipeople, where the best results for each task are in bold.

Model	JF17K				WikiPeople			
	Entity		Relation		Entity		Relation	
	MRR	Hits@1	MRR	Hits@1	MRR	Hits@1	MRR	Hits@1
StarE	0.432	34.5%	-	-	0.346	21.5%	-	-
HY-Transformer	0.471	38.5%	-	-	0.383	26.1%	-	-
Neuinfer	0.320	23.2%	-	-	0.376	30.6%	-	-
QUAD	0.387	28.9%	-	-	0.317	18.9%	-	-
HINGE	0.302	21.3%	-	-	0.303	36.3%	-	-
GRAN	0.491	40.6%	0.990	98.5%	0.426	31.3%	0.949	92.1%
CKRL	0.476	39.5%	0.990	98.4%	0.440	35.0%	0.926	89.1%
KGTtm	0.474	39.2%	0.988	98.2%	0.415	30.1%	0.949	92.2%
RMNS	0.536	43.80%	0.991	98.70%	0.483	38.40%	0.951	92.90%

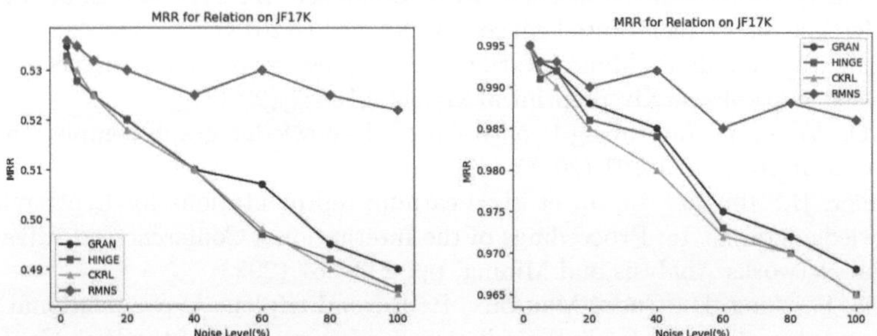

Fig. 3. MRR of JF17K entities and relationships under different noises.

As show in the Table1, across both JF17K and Wikipeople datasets, RMNS
outperforms 8 advanced baseline models, achieving the best results on all evaluation metrics. For entity prediction, RMNS improves Hits@1 by 3.2% and 1.5%,
and MRR by 0.045 and 0.026, respectively, over the second-best model. For relation prediction, it yields improvements of 0.2% and 0.7% in Hits@1, and 0.001
and 0.002 in MRR, respectively.

To assess noise robustness, we evaluated the impact of varying noise levels on MRR across several models, including GRAN, HINGE, CKRL, and RMNS. As shown in Fig. 3, MRR generally decreases with increasing noise; however, RMNS exhibits significantly greater resilience, indicating superior robustness to noise interference.

6   Conclusion

We proposes RMNS to improve the robustness of link prediction in hyper-relational knowledge graphs. RMNS employs edge-biased attention over heterogeneous nodes to enhance accuracy and leverages multi-level negative sampling based on the lowest-confidence node to improve robustness. Experimental results show that RMNS consistently achieves good performance while maintaining robustness.

Acknowledgments. This article is supported by the Key R&D Program of Ningbo City and the Major Application Demonstration Projects of "Leading the List" and "Science and Technology Innovation yongJiang 2035". (grant number 2024Z010 and 2023Z180).

References

1. Vrandečić, D., Krötzsch, M.: WikiData: a free collaborative knowledgebase. Commun. ACM **57**(10), 78–85 (2014)
2. Xie, R., Liu, Z., Lin, F., et al.: Does William Shakespeare really write hamlet? Knowledge representation learning with confidence. In: Proceedings of the AAAI Conference on Artificial Intelligence, vol. 32, no. 1 (2018)
3. Galkin, M., Trivedi, P., Maheshwari, G., et al.: Message passing for hyper-relational knowledge graphs. arXiv preprint arXiv:2009.10847 (2020)
4. Yu, D., Yang, Y.: Improving hyper-relational knowledge graph completion. arXiv preprint arXiv:2104.08167 (2021)
5. Shomer, H., Jin, W., Li, J., et al.: Learning representations for hyper-relational knowledge graphs. In: Proceedings of the International Conference on Advances in Social Networks Analysis and Mining, pp. 253–257 (2023)
6. Rosso, P., Yang, D., Cudré-Mauroux, P.: Beyond triplets: hyper-relational knowledge graph embedding for link prediction. In: Proceedings of the Web Conference, pp. 1885–1896 (2020)
7. Guan, S., Jin, X., Guo, J., et al.: NEUINFER: knowledge inference on N-ARY facts. In: Proceedings of the 58th Annual Meeting of the Association for Computational Linguistics, pp. 6141–6151 (2020)
8. Wang, Q., Wang, H., Lyu, Y., et al.: Link prediction on N-ARY relational facts: a graph-based approach. arXiv preprint arXiv:2105.08476 (2021)
9. Ho, J., Jain, A., Abbeel, P.: Denoising diffusion probabilistic models. Adv. Neural. Inf. Process. Syst. **33**, 6840–6851 (2020)

10. Jia, S., Xiang, Y., Chen, X., et al.: Triple trustworthiness measurement for knowledge graph. In: The World Wide Web Conference, pp. 2865–2871 (2019)
11. Bollacker, K., Evans, C., Paritosh, P., et al.: Freebase: a collaboratively created graph database for structuring human knowledge. In: Proceedings of the ACM SIGMOD International Conference on Management of Data, vol. 2008, pp. 1247–1250 (2008)

HG-GIN: Double Layer Attention Graph Isomorphism Network Based on Hybrid Neighborhood

Jiahao Gu[1,2], Fang Liu[3,4](✉), Min Jiang[1,2], Jingyong Du[1,2], Weike Xia[5], Tongliang Li[6], Hezhong Jiang[6], and Wei Hu[1,2](✉)

[1] School of Computer Science and Technology, Wuhan University of Science and Technology, Wuhan 430065, Hubei, China
`huwei@wust.edu.cn`
[2] Hubei Province Key Laboratory of Intelligent Information Processing and Real-Time Industrial System, Wuhan University of Science and Technology, Wuhan 430065, China
[3] School of Artificial Intelligence, Wuhan Vocational College of Software and Engineering, Wuhan, China
`liufangfang@whu.edu.cn`
[4] School of Computer Science, Wuhan University, Wuhan, China
[5] Yongqi Technology Group Co., Ltd., Zhejiang, China
[6] Zhejiang Zhongke Kunpeng Artificial Intelligence Technology Co., Ltd., Zhejiang, China

Abstract. Graph Neural Networks (GNNs) have advanced graph representation learning, with Graph Isomorphism Network (GIN) standing out for its strong expressiveness. However, GIN relies only on local neighborhoods for feature aggregation, which makes it difficult to model global structural information effectively, and the fixed neighborhoods limit the information propagation range, which affects the model performance. To solve this problem, this paper proposes a novel GIN model-Hybrid Neighborhood and Double Layer Attention Mechanism Based Graph Isomorphism Network (HG-GIN). HG-GIN combines direct edges relying on local neighborhoods and hidden edges obtained through global similarity information to optimize the aggregation of domain information, and proposes a double layer attention mechanism. We extensively evaluate HG-GIN on different graph benchmark datasets and observe its superior performance over other state-of-the-art GNN methods on several graph classification tasks. HG-GIN considers the role of neighbors and optimizes the neighborhood distribution, and the experimental results show that the proposed HG-GIN achieves state-of-the-art performance on a variety of open graph datasets.

Keywords: Graph Neural Network · Graph Classification · Hybrid Neighborhoods · Double layer Attention

1 Introduction

Graph-structured data is common in areas like social networks, bioinformatics, traffic networks, and recommender systems. The complex topology of these graphs makes it difficult for traditional machine learning methods to model them effectively. Recently,

© The Author(s), under exclusive license to Springer Nature Singapore Pte Ltd. 2026
T. Zhu et al. (Eds.): KSEM 2025, LNAI 15922, pp. 334–341, 2026.
https://doi.org/10.1007/978-981-95-3058-8_31

graph neural networks (GNNs) have made significant progress in tasks like graph classification, node classification, and link prediction. Among them, the graph isomorphism network (GIN) stands out for its ability to capture structural information, achieving strong results in tasks like molecular property and protein classification. However, existing GNNs face two main challenges: (1) they rely on fixed neighborhoods for feature aggregation, limiting the capture of global information over long distances, and (2) limited neighborhood selection may cause redundancy or miss key relationships, affecting expressive ability. These issues hinder GNN performance, especially when global structural information or long-distance dependencies are crucial, as traditional GNNs struggle to fully leverage global information due to their reliance on local neighborhoods. Thus, improving GNNs to effectively model both local and global information remains a key challenge in graph representation learning.

To improve neighborhood distribution and capture global structural information, we propose HG-GIN, an enhanced graph isomorphism network that integrates kNN-based implicit neighborhoods and a two-layer attention mechanism to fuse local and global information, boosting model expressiveness and generalization. The hybrid aggregation enables nodes to capture both direct and globally similar neighbor information, while the two-layer attention refines this integration by separately weighting original and implicit neighborhoods. Extensive experiments on benchmark datasets demonstrate HG-GIN's superior performance and its effectiveness in modeling complex graph structures.

2 Related Work

In recent years, graph neural networks (GNNs) have advanced graph classification by learning node and edge features automatically, surpassing traditional manual feature and kernel-based methods. Research has focused on improving architecture, aggregation, pooling, and pre-training to better model complex structures. GCN [1], based on Laplacian smoothing, averages neighbor features but suffers from oversmoothing in deeper layers. GAT [2] mitigates this by using self-attention to adaptively weight neighbor information, improving classification performance.

To enhance representation learning, models like GPT-GNN [3] use generative self-supervised learning to capture global structure via attribute and edge reconstruction. GraphCL [4] adopts contrastive learning with augmented views, while G-Tuning [5] pre-trains on unlabeled data and fine-tunes for downstream tasks, boosting generalization.

Pooling improvements also contribute: DGCNN [6] applies sorted pooling for fixed-length representations, while DiffPool [7] learns a differentiable clustering strategy. SEP preserves structure through entropy-based hierarchical pooling.

In addition to this, improving the graph structure is also considered to enhance the performance of the model on the graph classification task. TREE-G [8] partitions graphs hierarchically, constructing tree-structured representations and aggregating features via hierarchical attention.; SAN [9] integrates structure-aware Transformers to combine local and global information. GraphGPS [10] fuses GNN and Transformer to enhance neighborhood modeling.

3 Notations and Preliminaries

This section defines the notation and core concepts used in the paper. An undirected graph is denoted as $G = (V, E)$, where $V = \{v_1, \cdots, v_n\}$ is the set of nodes and $E \subseteq V \times V$ the set of edges. Each node $v_i \in V$ has an initial feature vector $h_i^{(0)} \in \mathbb{R}^d$, with d as the feature dimension.

In graph classification, given graphs $\{G_1, G_2, \ldots, G_n\}$ and their labels $\{y_1, y_2, \ldots, y_n\} \subseteq Y$, the objective is to learn a graph-level representation h_G for each graph and predict the label $y_G = g(h_G)$ using a classifier g.

3.1 Neighbor Aggregation Method

Currently, effective graph learning algorithms rely on neighbor aggregation, where shared-parameter aggregators update a node's features by combining its own and neighbors' representations. This process builds higher-level features, enhancing learning. Graph Convolutional Networks (GCNs) are a widely adopted approach for such tasks.

Taking the 2-layer network in GCN as an example, the encoder is defined as:

$$f = \mathrm{softmax}\left(\hat{A}\sigma\left(\hat{A}XW^{(0)}\right)W^{(1)}\right), \tag{1}$$

where $\hat{A} = \tilde{D}^{-\frac{1}{2}}\tilde{A}\tilde{D}^{-\frac{1}{2}}$, $\tilde{D}_{ii} = \sum_j \tilde{A}_{ij}$, and $W^{(\square)}$s are learnable parameters. GCN uses a symmetrically normalized adjacency matrix $\hat{A}$ as shared aggregation coefficients across layers. More specifically, the aggregator of the GCN can be represented as:

$$h_i^{(l+1)} = \sigma\left(\sum_{j \in N_i} A_{ij} h_j^{(l)} W^{(l)}\right), \tag{2}$$

where $h_j^{(l)}$ is the feature of node j at layer l, $h^{(0)} = X$ and N_i denote the set of all neighbors of node i, including itself.

3.2 Graph Isomorphism Network

Traditional GNNs like GCN and GAT struggle to distinguish graphs with different structures but identical features due to mean or weighted aggregation, limiting their performance in graph classification. GIN [11] was introduced to enhance GNNs' ability to discriminate graph structures, achieving the discrimination power of the Weisfeiler-Lehman (WL) graph isomorphism test through a more expressive aggregation strategy. In GIN, the feature update formula for each node v at the kth layer is as follows:

$$h_v^{(k)} = MLP^{(k)}\left((1 + \varepsilon)h_v^{(k-1)} + \sum_{u \in N_v} h_u^{(k-1)}\right) \tag{3}$$

where $h_v^{(k)}$ is the node's updated representation, ε is a learnable parameter controlling self-feature weight, and $MLP^{(k)}$ applies a nonlinear transformation. Unlike GCN's normalized summation, GIN directly sums neighbor features and uses MLPs, significantly improving its ability to distinguish graph structures.

4 The MNGAT Model

We propose HG-GIN, an improved graph isomorphic network model designed to address traditional GNNs' limitations in capturing global structure and relying solely on fixed local neighborhoods. While standard GNNs focus on direct neighbors, they miss latent global relationships, limiting performance on complex graphs. HG-GIN enhances this by using the kNN algorithm to redefine graph topology, allowing nodes to aggregate features from both local and globally similar nodes, expanding information flow.

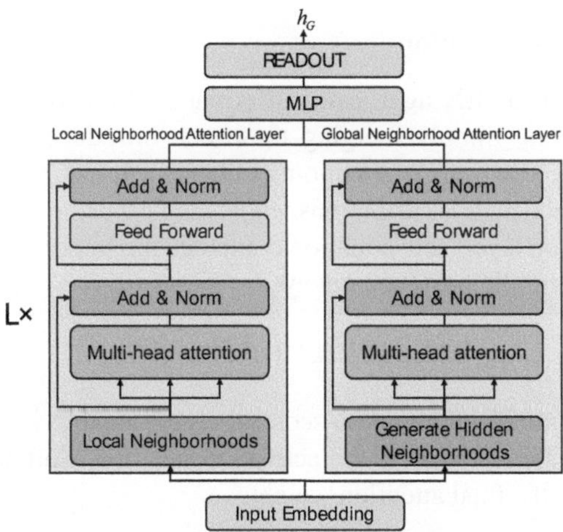

Fig. 1. Our proposed HG-GIN model combines local and kNN-based implicit neighborhood information through a two-layer attention mechanism, iteratively computed over L layers, followed by MLP-based classification.

As illustrated in Fig. 1, HG-GIN employs a two-layer attention mechanism. The first layer attends to direct neighbors, capturing local features, while the second leverages kNN to form implicit neighborhoods and apply attention globally. This dual mechanism improves long-range interaction and structural awareness. By integrating local and global information, HG-GIN effectively models potential structural patterns, improving expressiveness, accuracy, and generalization in graph classification tasks.

4.1 Generating Hidden Neighborhoods

To construct a hidden neighborhood, we first compute a similarity matrix $S \in \mathbb{R}^{n \times n}$ using cosine similarity between node features h_i and h_j:

$$s_{i,j} = \frac{h_i^T \cdot h_j}{\|h_i\| \, \|h_j\|}, \tag{4}$$

where $s_{i,j}$ denotes the similarity between nodes v_i and v_j, with values ranging from -1 to 1. For each node v_i, we select the top k most similar nodes to form its implicit neighborhood:

$$N_i^{kNN} = \{v_j | top_k(s_{i,j})\},\tag{5}$$

These neighbors may not be directly connected but share high feature similarity. During GNN propagation, each node aggregates information from both its direct and kNN-based neighbors, combining them to form a new neighborhood representation:

$$N_i^{final} = N_i^{original} \cup N_i^{kNN},\tag{6}$$

4.2 Local and Global Attention

During propagation, HG-GIN aggregates information from both direct and implicit (kNN-based) neighbors. Simply merging these can introduce redundancy or noise, so HG-GIN employs a two-layer attention mechanism to adaptively weigh neighbor importance and balance their contributions, enhancing robustness and expressiveness.

In the first attention layer, self-attention computes the importance of each neighbor within the direct and implicit sets separately:

$$e_{i,j} = \text{LeakyReLU}\left(a^T[Wh_i \| Wh_j]\right),\tag{7}$$

where $e_{i,j}$ is the unnormalized attention score, W is a trainable weight matrix. a is the attention vector, and LeakyReLU is the activation function. Softmax normalisation is then used to compute the final attention weights:

$$\alpha_{i,j} = \frac{exp(e_{i,j})}{\sum_{v_k \in N_i^{final}} exp(e_{i,k})},\tag{8}$$

Then node v_i aggregates features from neighbor with a weighted summation:

$$h_i^{agg} = \sum_{v_j \in N_i^{final}} \alpha_{i,j} h_j,\tag{9}$$

This step assigns varying influence to neighbors, allowing important ones to contribute more to node updates. The first attention layer yields two features: $h_i^{original}$ from direct neighbors and h_i^{kNN} from implicit ones. A second attention layer then adaptively balances their contributions, learning the influence of local and global information.

To balance the influence of direct and implicit neighbors, we compute an adaptive weight β_i using:

$$\beta_i = \frac{exp\left(q^T \cdot \sigma\left(W_o h_i^{original}\right)\right)}{exp\left(q^T \cdot \sigma\left(W_o h_i^{original}\right)\right) + exp\left(q^T \cdot \sigma\left(W_k h_i^{kNN}\right)\right)},\tag{10}$$

where q is a learnable vector, W_o and W_k are transformation matrices, and $\sigma(\cdot)$ is a nonlinear activation. The final fused representation is represented as:

$$H_i^{(l)} = MLP^{(l)}\left((1 + \varepsilon)h_i^{(l-1)} + \sum_{u \in N_i^{original}} \beta_i h_u^{(l-1)} + \sum_{v \in N_i^{kNN}} (1 - \beta_i)h_v^{(l-1)}\right),\tag{11}$$

where $H_i^{(k)}$ denotes the representation of node i after the kth aggregation. $(1 + \varepsilon)h_i^{(k-1)}$ retains the node's own information, with ε as a learnable weight. $\sum_{u \in N_i^{original}} \beta_i h_u^{(l-1)}$ captures local structure via direct neighbors, while $\sum_{v \in N_i^{kNN}} (1 - \beta_i)h_v^{(l-1)}$ incorporates global context from kNN-based implicit neighbors, where β_i adaptively balances the two sources. An MLP then applies a nonlinear transformation to enhance model expressiveness. The final graph embedding is generated using the READOUT function:

$$h_G = \text{CONCAT}\left(READOUT\left(\left\{H_i^{(l)} | i \in G\right\}\right) | l = 0, 1, \ldots, L\right), \tag{12}$$

5 Experiments

To evaluate HG-GIN's performance on graph classification, we conducted experiments on multiple benchmark datasets and compared it fairly with state-of-the-art GNNs, including DGCNN, GAT, G-Tuning, GIN, and TREE-G. All models were tested under the same settings. The selected datasets vary in graph size and complexity, enabling a comprehensive assessment of HG-GIN's effectiveness.

5.1 Graph Datasets

We evaluated HG-GIN on seven benchmark datasets: four from bioinformatics (MUTAG, PROTEINS, PTC, NCI1) and three from social networks (COLLAB, IMDB-BINARY, IMDB-MULTI), as summarized in Table 1. MUTAG and PTC contain chemical compounds with multiple labels. PROTEINS represents secondary structure elements (SSEs) in proteins, while NCI1 includes compounds screened for tumor inhibition. IMDB-BINARY and IMDB-MULTI involve actor co-appearance graphs for genre classification. COLLAB is a researcher collaboration network.

Table 1. Summary of the graph datasets used in the experiments

Datasets	MUTAG	PROTEIN	PTC	NCI1	COLLAB	IMDB-B	IMDB-M
graphs	188	1113	344	4110	5000	1000	1500
classes	2	2	2	2	2	2	2
Avg nodes	17.9	39.1	25.5	29.8	74.5	19.8	13.0
Avg edges	19.8	72.8	14.7	32.3	2457.8	96.5	65.9
Features	7	3	19	37	1	1	1

5.2 Baseline Methods and Performance of Graph Classification

We compare HG-GIN with DGCNN, GAT, G-Tuning, TREE-G, and GIN. DGCNN, GAT, and GIN use their default settings. For G-Tuning, we set $\lambda = 0.05$, weight decay to 5×10^{-4}, and dropout rate to 0.5; for TREE-G, the learning rate was 0.1, max depth 10, and $p = 0.25$.

Table 2. Summary of classification accuracy (%) on seven datasets(averaged over 10 runs).

Datasets	MUTAG	PROTEIN	PTC	NCI1	COLLAB	IMDB-B	IMDB-M
DGCNN	85.8	76.2	65.4	76.4	73.8	70.0	47.8
GAT	90.4	76.7	64.2	81.3	78.6	78.0	54.8
G-Tuning	86.1	72.1	62.1	81.8	75.4	74.3	51.8
GIN-0	89.4	76.2	64.6	82.7	80.2	75.1	52.3
GIN-ε	89.0	75.9	63.7	82.8	80.1	74.3	52.1
TREE-G	91.1	75.6	59.1	75.9	79.4	73.0	54.5
HG-GIN	90.7	77.2	65.9	83.6	80.7	77.1	55.2

As shown in Table 2, HG-GIN achieves top accuracy on MUTAG, PROTEIN, PTC, NCI1, and IMDB-M, notably 83.6% on NCI1, outperforming GIN and GAT. On COLLAB and IMDB-B, it ranks just behind the best models. Its strong results stem from the two-layer attention mechanism, which effectively fuses local and global information. HG-GIN also outperforms G-Tuning and TREE-G, confirming the advantage of its enhanced neighborhood design for graph classification.

In addition, we analyzed the impact of k in kNN graphs across seven datasets. When k < 5, performance remains stable, suggesting selected neighbors are generally reliable. The model performs best at k = 2, balancing neighbor quantity and quality. Too small k limits information, while larger k (e.g., k > 5) may introduce noise and reduce accuracy. As k increases further, less relevant nodes are included, degrading performance. Thus, selecting an appropriate k is key to preserving neighbor quality and effectiveness.

5.3 The Impact of Double-Layer Attention on Models

As shown in Table 3, we compare models without attention, with single-layer attention, and with two-layer attention (HG-GIN). The attention mechanism notably improves model expressiveness. Single-layer attention reduces noise by weighting neighbors, enhancing performance over the no-attention model—for instance, accuracy on IMDB-B rises from 75.5% to 76.4%. However, it mainly captures local or implicit structure, limiting its ability to model global dependencies. HG-GIN's two-layer attention overcomes this by integrating both neighborhood types more effectively.

Table 3. The Accuracy (%) of No-Attention, Single-Attention and HG-GIN.

Datasets	MUTAG	PROTEIN	PTC	NCI1	COLLAB	IMDB-B	IMDB-M
No-Attention	89.3	75.9	64.4	81.7	78.9	75.5	53.7
Single-Attention	90.3	76.6	65.4	83.0	80.3	76.4	54.8
HG-GIN	90.7	77.2	65.9	83.6	80.7	77.1	55.3

The two-layer attention in HG-GIN computes weights for local and implicit neighborhoods separately, then fuses them to capture both local structure and global similarity.

This enhances information aggregation and overall performance. As shown in results, HG-GIN consistently outperforms the other variants—for example, achieving 77.1% on IMDB-B (0.7% higher than single-layer) and 77.2% on PROTEIN (0.6% higher). These gains highlight its effectiveness in integrating diverse neighborhood information and improving generalization in graph classification.

6 Conclusion

This paper proposes HG-GIN, a graph neural network that integrates kNN-generated implicit neighbors with GIN and introduces a two-layer attention mechanism to adaptively weigh direct and implicit neighbors. The first layer adjusts local neighbor importance, while the second balances local and global influences to enhance expressiveness. Experiments on benchmark datasets show that HG-GIN achieves optimal or near-optimal performance across social and biochemical graphs, demonstrating strong classification ability.

Acknowledgements. This article is supported by the Key R&D Program of Ningbo City and the Major Application Demonstration Projects of "Leading the List" and "Science and Technology Innovation yongJiang 2035" (grant number 2024Z010 and 2023Z180).

References

1. Kipf, T.N., Welling, M.: Semi-Supervised Classification with Graph Convolutional Networks. arXiv preprint arXiv:1609.02907 (2016)
2. Veličković, P., Cucurull, G., Casanova, A., et al.: Graph Attention Networks. arXiv preprint arXiv:1710.10903 (2017)
3. Hu, Z., Dong, Y., Wang, K., et al.: Gpt-gnn: Generative pre-training of graph neural networks. Proceedings of the 26th ACM SIGKDD International Conference on Knowledge Discovery & Data Mining, pp. 1857–1867 (2020)
4. You, Y., Chen, T., Sui, Y., et al.: Graph contrastive learning with augmentations. Adv. Neural. Inf. Process. Syst. **33**, 5812–5823 (2020)
5. Sun, Y., Zhu, Q., Yang, Y., et al.: Fine-tuning graph neural networks by preserving graph generative patterns. In: Proceedings of the AAAI Conference on Artificial Intelligence **38**(8), 9053–9061 (2024)
6. Zhang, M., Cui, Z., Neumann, M., et al.: An end-to-end deep learning architecture for graph classification. In: Proceedings of the AAAI Conference on Artificial Intelligence **32**(1) (2018)
7. Ying, Z., You, J., Morris, C., et al.: Hierarchical graph representation learning with differentiable pooling. Advances in Neural Information Processing Systems **31** (2018)
8. Bechler-Speicher, M., Globerson, A., Gilad-Bachrach, R.: Tree-g: decision trees contesting graph neural networks. In: Proceedings of the AAAI Conference on Artificial Intelligence **38**(10), 11032–11042 (2018)
9. Chen, D., O'Bray, L., Borgwardt, K.: Structure-aware transformer for graph representation learning. In: International Conference on Machine Learning. PMLR, pp. 3469–3489 (2022)
10. Rampášek, L., Galkin, M., Dwivedi, V.P., et al.: Recipe for a general, powerful, scalable graph transformer. Adv. Neural. Inf. Process. Syst. **35**, 14501–14515 (2022)
11. Xu, K., Hu, W., Leskovec, J., et al.: How Powerful are Graph Neural Networks?. arXiv preprint arXiv:1810.00826 (2018)

Matching Ancient Dunhuang Manuscripts Based on Multi-dimensional Feature Fusion

Yanping Xiang[1], Jiaqi Dai[1], Mingkun Chen[1], Teer Song[2], Yutong Zheng[1(✉)], and Xuan Liu[1(✉)]

[1] Key Laboratory of Ethnic Language Intelligent Analysis and Security Governance, Ministry of Education, School of Information Engineering, Minzu University of China, Beijing, China
{23302150,24302215,23302192,zyt,liuxuan}@muc.edu.cn
[2] Beijing University of Posts and Telecommunications, Beijing, China
2024111730@bupt.cn

Abstract. Dunhuang manuscripts, from the Eastern Jin Dynasty to the Northern Song Dynasty, are precious materials for studying the history and culture of each dynasty. However, due to the corrosion of time and the intrusion of foreign enemies, these manuscripts are scattered everywhere. Therefore, this paper proposes an ancient Dunhuang Manuscripts matching approach based on multi-dimensional feature fusion. We design a multi-dimensional feature description framework with three-dimension, namely edge orientation information, global geometric features, and column spacing features. Then we implement feature dynamic weighted fusion by self-attention mechanism of Transformer. In addition, we construct a dataset simulating real debris tearing to support the training and evaluation of the model. The experimental results show that our framework improves the accuracy and efficiency of fragment matching, which lays a solid foundation for digital protection and research of Dunhuang manuscripts.

Keywords: Dunhuang manuscripts · Feature Fusion · Transformer · Fragment Matching · Dynamic Weighting

1 Introduction

At the beginning of the 20th century, the discovery of Dunhuang manuscripts in Dunhuang Mogao Grottoes became a brilliant milestone in the modern academic history of China. However, most of these glorious witnesses to history have come back to light in broken and scattered forms. There are different opinions about the reasons for the closure of the Sutra Cave, but the damage and dispersion of the relics undoubtedly aggravate the difficulty of studying and protecting this historical and cultural heritage.

Y. Xiang and J. Dai—These authors contributed equally to this work.

T. Zhu et al. (Eds.): KSEM 2025, LNAI 15922, pp. 342–353, 2026.
https://doi.org/10.1007/978-981-95-3058-8_32

To date, more than 70,000 Dunhuang manuscripts have been discovered. Apart from the over 10,000 items housed in the National Library of China, the remainder are dispersed across institutions such as the British Library (11,297 items), the Bibliothèque nationale de France (over 6,000 items), and the Institute of Asian Nationalities in St. Petersburg (11,050 items). Traditionally, the matching of manuscript fragments has relied heavily on expert manual work. Professor Zhang Yongquan [1] summarized twelve key criteria, including content continuity, font consistency, and handwriting style. However, manual methods are both time-intensive and highly dependent on individual expertise. Consequently, the integration of computer technology to assist the matching process has become a significant focus in Dunhuang manuscript research [2–4].

Traditional image matching methods have some achievements in geometric invariants and contour similarity calculation, but the irregularity and wear problems of the Dunhuang fragment have not been effectively solved, especially in the face of massive unstructured fragments, the computational complexity is high and the efficiency is low. Puzzle algorithm [5–7] inspires solving this kind of problem, but due to the difference in fragment shape and content characteristics, existing algorithms are difficult to directly apply to Dunhuang fragment matching. Therefore, developing robust algorithms that can combine geometric features and semantic information to improve matching accuracy and efficiency is the key to current research.

Therefore, this paper proposes a global assembly method of Dunhuang fragments based on multi-dimensional feature descriptions to improve the efficiency and accuracy of fragment repair. Major contributions include:

1. **Multi-dimensional feature description framework**: We construct a multi-dimensional feature expression method from one dimension to three dimensions to capture geometric and semantic information of fragments.
2. **Dataset construction**: We organize and simulate real fragments, expand the dataset, and specifically support algorithm verification.
3. **Dynamic weighted fusion mechanism**: We use the Transformer's self-attention mechanism to dynamically adjust feature weights to achieve efficient feature fusion.

2 Related Work

2.1 Image Fragments Assembly

In the problem of assembling image fragments, pairwise matching algorithms are commonly used. Kong and Kimia [8] employed the geometric features of image fragments (partial curve matching) to address the fragment matching problem, successfully matching three puzzle pieces simultaneously. Leitao and Stolfi [9] utilized an incremental dynamic programming sequence algorithm to achieve fragment matching by comparing the encoded curvature of fragment contours. Furthermore, Tsamoura and Pitas [10] identified potential adjacent fragments by calculating the color similarity of the edges of the fragment, while Xu, Yan and Yang [11] applied edge detection and Scale-Invariant Feature Transform (SIFT) algorithms to extract and match feature points, facilitating the pairing of adjacent fragments. These methods leverage various features [12,13], including information on fragment shape and edge appearance, to achieve matching.

The traditional method of splicing manuscript fragments heavily relies on experts who manually splice them based on the content and edge contour features of the manuscript [14,15]. This traditional approach is both time-consuming and labor-intensive. The progress in computer technology has enabled the automation of manuscript restoration. Due to the high technical similarity between manuscript fragment restoration and image fragment stitching, restoration efforts often draw on puzzle-solving methods. For example, Derech, Tal, and Shimshoni [16] approached the problem of restoring fragmented cultural relics from a puzzle-solving perspective. Savino and Tonazzini [17] proposed a rapid and automated program to digitally restoree front and back image pairs of ancient colored manuscripts.

Moreover, Panagiotakis, Markaki, Kokinou, and Papadakis [18] used a graph-based CD-RCP algorithm to solve the problem of partial curve matching and applied it to the coastline matching, successfully achieving the matching between fragments. In the field of fragment matching, in addition to relying on shape contours, many studies also focus on fragment matching based on time series analysis [9,10,13,19]. For example, Zhang and Li [13] employed a graph optimization framework to achieve automatic reassembly of two-dimensional image fragments. In recent years, deep learning technologies have also been widely used in this field. Hosseini, Shabani, Irandoust, and Furukawa [20] proposed an end-to-end neural architecture based on a diffusion model to address the spatial jigsaw puzzle problem.

2.2 Feature Fusion

Image feature fusion is a core technology in image matching that effectively enhances the accuracy of matching and adaptability to complex scenes by integrating multi-feature information. This technology has been widely applied in fields such as biomedicine and remote sensing [21,22]. For example, Du, Li, Peng, and Zong [23] introduced a multi-feature image fusion method specifically addressing the preservation of high-contrast information (such as texture and color) in biomedical imaging data within fused images. Moreover, Shibu, Madan, Paramanandham, Kumar, and Santosh [24] employed a multi-feature guided fusion network to extract features from multimodal images and fuse them to create more accurate brain images, greatly facilitating medical diagnostics and efficiency. In the medical imaging field, the MFCPNet model developed by Hou, Yan, Desrosiers, and Liu [25] is a groundbreaking example. This model utilizes multi-scale feature fusion technology to achieve real-time and accurate segmentation of medical images, which is crucial for enhancing disease diagnostics and treatment planning.

Although multi-dimensional feature fusion has shown great potential in various domains, its application in the assembly of Dunhuang fragments has been relatively limited. Recent research [26] has made progress in this area by successfully automating the assembly of manuscript fragments through the fusion of three layers of features: grayscale similarity, geometric contour features, and column spacing consistency. This achievement not only demonstrates the potential application of feature fusion technology in the field of cultural heritage preservation but also provides new methods and ideas for future research.

3   Method

Note on Terminology. In this paper, the terms "1D," "2D," and "3D" refer to the hierarchical levels of descriptive richness in the feature representations, rather than literal geometric dimensions. The progression reflects an increasing capacity to capture local-to-global fragment characteristics.

3.1   Feature Extraction

1D Feature. First, we extract one-dimensional features. We use Freeman encoding to represent the edge information of the fragments, and promote the capture of local geometric features of the fragments by describing the directionality of the contour. Specifically, we use the Canny edge detection algorithm to extract the set of contour points of fragments, and then apply the Freeman coding method to quantize the direction of each contour point into eight fixed directions (0–7), thus generating a one-dimensional direction sequence.

2D Feature. Secondly, we extract two-dimensional features, which can effectively compensate for the limitations of one-dimensional features in capturing image information. We chose to use the ResGCN model [27], which can automatically learn the optimal feature representation from the data without manually selecting features or manually designing filters. Through the multi-layer processing of deep networks, the model can capture the local details and global structure of images, which is suitable for the mosaic task under the complex background of the Dunhuang fragments.

3D Feature. Finally, we extract three-dimensional features. One- and two-dimensional features mainly describe outline information, lacking semantic information on Dunhuang fragments. 3D features enhance the ability to describe the global layout of debris by combining column spacing features with 2D features. We use vertical projection to extract column spacing features and fuse them with 2D features extracted from ResGCN.

Column Spacing Extraction: binarizing the image to black and white by setting appropriate thresholds to make the difference between text and background more obvious. The pixel values for each column are summed to obtain the projection value $V(x)$ for each column, i.e., the number of non-background pixels in each column of the image. In this way, we can get the density distribution of each

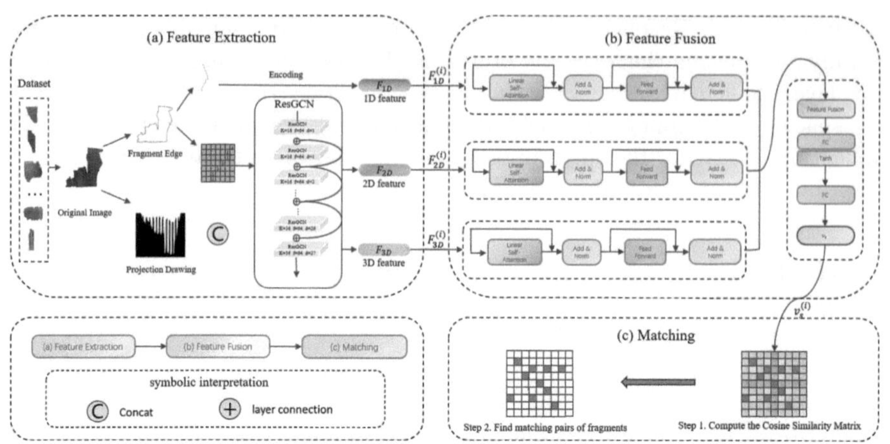

Fig. 1. Pipeline of our proposed work. (a) Firstly, extracting Features of the Dunhuang Manuscripts. (b) Secondly, an encoder based on linear transformation is designed to learn the global features of each fragment. (c) Finally, we calculate cosine similarity between fragments to find adjacent fragment pairs.

column in the image, to identify the blank area between columns, and define the maximum blank area between adjacent columns as the column spacing (Fig. 1).

We fuse the column spacing features with the 2D feature matrix extracted from ResGCN to form 3D features, as formulated in Eq. (1).

$$F_{3D} = Conact(F_{2D}, C_{spacing}) \tag{1}$$

3.2 Encoding

The encoding process transforms the extracted features into suitable representations for fragment matching. The following algorithm outlines the encoding steps for 1D, 2D, and 3D features. Algorithm 1 presents the pseudo code of the encoding process in detail.

1D encoding: Capture the direction information of fragment edge with Canny operator to obtain contour point set $C(i)$, and then use the Freeman coding to obtain sequence F_{1D}.

2D encoding: We use Canny operator to extract contour, use 7×7 patch to extract features, transform edge features into fixed-size coded patch, extract deep-level features through convolution and pooling operations, and finally extract global contour features through ResGCN [7] to obtain feature F_{2D}.

3D encoding: Column spacing features are extracted by vertical projection method, and then conact with 2D features to generate 3D features F_{3D}.

Algorithm 1: Encoding Process

Input: Fragment image I

Output: F_{1D}, F_{2D}, F_{3D}

1D Encoding:

1. $I \xrightarrow{\text{Canny}} C(i)$;

2. $C(i) \xrightarrow{\text{Freeman}} F_{1D}$;

2D Encoding:

1. Divide I into 7×7 patches;

2. **foreach** *patch* **do**

    if *patch contains at least one contour point* **then**

        Encode as 1;

    else

        Encode as 0;

    Store the binary encoding as a matrix of patches T_b;

3. $T_b \xrightarrow{\text{Conv}} T_f$, then $T_f \xrightarrow{\text{GAP}} T_p$;

4. $T_p \xrightarrow{\text{ResGCN}} F_{2D} \in \mathbb{R}^{C(i) \times 64}$;

3D Encoding:

1. $I \xrightarrow{\text{Binarize}} I_b$;

2. Compute vertical projection $V(x)$;

3. Determine the maximum blank width between adjacent columns based on $V(x)$ to generate the column spacing vector C_{spacing};

4. $F_{3D} = \text{Concat}(F_{2D}, C_{\text{spacing}})$.

3.3 Feature Fusion

Unlike traditional weighted fusion methods, dynamic weighted fusion automatically adjusts the weight of each feature according to the importance of input features, rather than manually setting it. This process is implemented by a linear transformer encoder in the neural network, which enables the model to adaptively assign different weights to each feature, improving the expression ability of the fused features thereby. In the feature fusion phase, we process 1D, 2D, and 3D features through the following steps:

Feature Encoding: Each feature branch is input to a linear transformer encoder for processing. The Transformer encoder's self-attention mechanism can effectively capture the long-range dependence between features, thus enhancing the representation ability of each feature.

Dynamic Weight Learning: During model training, the transformer encoder will adaptively weight the representation of each feature and output a fused feature matrix representing the weighted sum of the features, as shown in Eq. (2).

$$F_{fused} = \alpha \cdot F_{1D} + \beta \cdot F_{2D} + \gamma \cdot F_{3D} \tag{2}$$

Feature Integration: The fused multi-dimensional features are first encoded by a linear Transformer encoder F_{fused}, then compressed via a fully connected layer to reduce dimensionality and enhance global representation. An average pooling operation is applied to obtain a compact edge feature vector, as shown in as shown in Eq. (3).

$$v_s = AvgPool F_{fused} \tag{3}$$

To evaluate the similarity between fragments, we use cosine similarity to calculate the degree of match between global feature vectors, as shown in Eq. (4).

$$S_{v_s}(i,j) = \frac{< v_{s,i}, v_{s,j} >}{\|v_{s,i}\| \|v_{s,j}\|} \tag{4}$$

$S_{v_s}(i,j)$ represents the similarity between the vectors $v_{s,i}$ and $v_{s,j}$, and the global representation of the vector of characteristics obtained after fusion of the features of fragment i and fragment j.

3.4 Contrast Learning Optimization

To further enhance the model's performance in the domain of image fragment matching, we have introduced a contrast learning strategy to refine the representation of fragment features. This strategy aims to enhance the model's sensitivity and discrimination ability to subtle differences between fragments through the optimization of a contrast loss function. In this process, we have selected the InfoNCE loss function [28] as our contrast loss function $\mathcal{L}$, which is particularly suitable for dealing with sample comparisons in large-scale unlabeled datasets. Unlike traditional methods that rely on single-sample self-supervision [29], our contrast learning strategy employs paired samples to construct positive sample pairs, i.e., those fragment pairs that are similar or related in characteristics. This method enhances the model's efficiency in learning similarities by positively reinforcing the connections between similar fragments. Simultaneously, we use unpaired samples to construct negative sample pairs, i.e., those fragment pairs that are not similar in characteristics, thereby pushing the model to learn to distinguish between fragments with significant differences.Through this design, we effectively adjust the feature representation space of the model so that similar pairs of fragments are brought closer together, while dissimilar pairs are pushed farther apart.

The contrast loss function is defined as follows (see Eq. 5):

$$\mathcal{L} = -\sum_{i,j} \log \frac{e^{S_{v_s}(i,j)/\tau}}{\sum_k e^{S_{v_s}(i,j)/\tau}} \tag{5}$$

The parameters in the loss function are described as follows:

- τ is a temperature parameter that controls the smoothness of the probability distribution, affecting the model's sensitivity and resolution;
- $\frac{e^{S_{v_s}(i,j)/\tau}}{\sum_k e^{S_{v_s}(i,j)/\tau}}$ is the probability-normalized form of the Softmax function, representing the probability that samples i and j are considered similar by the model.

Additionally, the log function transforms probabilities into log-likelihoods, penalizing incorrect predictions. As predictions improve, the loss decreases, encouraging better accuracy and reliability.

4   Dataset

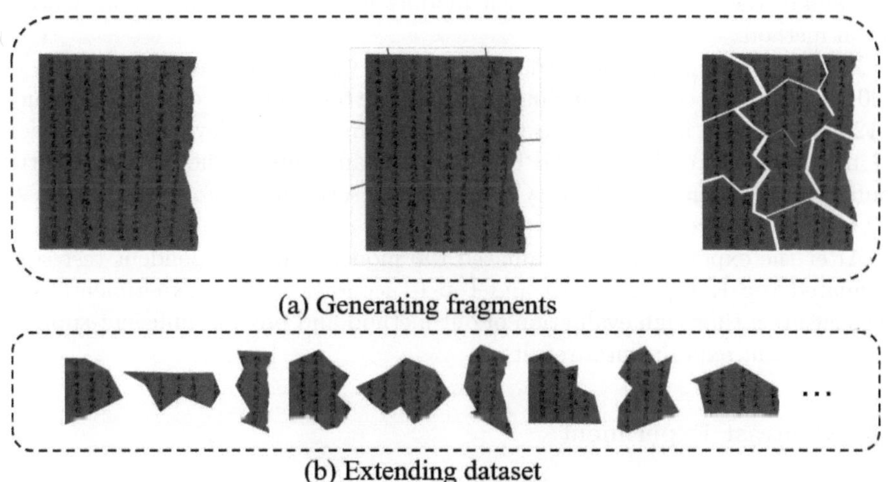

(a) Generating fragments

(b) Extending dataset

Fig. 2. Dataset generation. (a)Using algorithms to tear pictures into pieces. (b)Augmentation of data sets with generated fragments.

To evaluate the effectiveness and feasibility of our approach, we created a new image fragmentation dataset in this study. This dataset is generated by an algorithm [7], shown in Fig. 2, which aims to simulate the complexity of image fragmentation in real scenes, especially the challenges in matching tasks.

Original Image Tearing: We select complete fragments as the original data and use algorithms to split these complete volumes into multiple irregular fragments. We first divide the original image into several subregions, and then randomly select a portion of pixels in each subregion as the boundary of the fragment. The fragments generated in this way have different shapes, sizes, and edge characteristics, thus simulating the image fragments in the actual scene more realistically.

Fragment Irregularity: To ensure the diversity and complexity of the fragments, the selection of the boundaries is randomized and takes into account the wear characteristics of the Dunhuang fragments, so that each fragment has different damage and irregularities on the edges.

Data Enhancement: To enhance the robustness of the model, we perform data enhancement on the generated image fragments to expand the dataset.

5   Experiment

5.1   Experimental Design

To verify the effectiveness of the proposed method, we designed two groups of experiments: contrast experiment and ablation experiment. The comparison experiment was designed to test the performance difference of different deep learning networks in extracting features, while the ablation experiment was used to evaluate the contribution of each module in the multi-dimensional feature fusion method.

During training, we used Adam Optimizer with an initial learning rate of 0.001, adjusted by cosine annealing strategy. The total number of training rounds is 128 and the batch size is set to 175. All experiments were developed in Python 3.7 using the PyTorch-1.12.1-GPU framework and run on the servce with the configuration as Intel i7-10710U CPU, 64 GB RAM, and GeForce RTX 4090 24 GB GPU hardware.

After the experiment, we evaluated the model using independent test sets, calculated Top-1, Top-5, Top-10, and Top-15 accuracies. These experimental settings ensure a thorough evaluation of our method and provide sufficient support for subsequent experimental results.

5.2   Contrast Experiment

In contrast experiments, we select three deep learning networks (ResNet-50, VGG-16, MobileNetV2) as two-dimensional texture feature extraction models to analyze the impact of different networks on the Dunhuang fragment stitching task. The experimental results are shown in Table 1. Each network is pre-trained and fine-tuned on task-related data sets, and its output feature dimensions are unified as embedding vectors. To ensure the fairness of the experiment, settings were kept consistent in other stitching processes, including feature fusion methods, similarity calculation methods (using cosine similarity), and optimizer parameters (Adam optimizer, initial learning rate of 0.001).

Table 1. Matching accuracy under different networks

Backbone	Top-1	Top-5	Top-10	Top-15
ResNet	0.133	0.301	0.597	0.613
VGG-16	0.117	0.238	0.565	0.598
MobileNetV2	0.178	0.322	0.601	0.623
Our	**0.208**	**0.375**	**0.696**	**0.717**

5.3   Ablation Experiment

In the ablation experiment, we systematically remove one feature from the multi-dimensional feature fusion method at a time to evaluate its individual contribution to the fragment stitching task. This allows us to quantify the impact of each feature on the stitching accuracy. The experimental results are presented in Table 2, where we show the performance of the model with each feature ablated, along with the corresponding accuracy drop.

Table 2. Performance under different feature fusion methods

Fusion Method	Top-1	Top-5	Top-10	Top-15
1D+2D	0.154	0.282	0.623	0.641
1D+3D	0.167	0.297	0.634	0.649
2D+3D	0.183	0.316	0.661	0.677
Our	**0.208**	**0.375**	**0.696**	**0.717**

As observed, removing the 2D or 3D features results in a significant decrease in performance, indicating their crucial role in capturing the spatial relationships and global layout of the fragments. In contrast, removing the 1D feature causes a relatively smaller drop, suggesting that local edge information, while important, may have a lesser impact on the overall accuracy compared to global structural features.

6   Conclusion

This study proposes a deep learning-based multi-dimensional feature fusion meth-od for image matching and the reconstruction of Dunhuang manuscript fragments. By constructing a feature description framework spanning from one to three dimensions, the method extracts edge orientation, geometric information, and column spacing features, thereby enhancing the model's capacity for data interpretation. To effectively support the training and validation of the algorithm, we have specifically built a new dataset comprising Dunhuang manuscript fragments. Utilizing a dynamic weighted fusion mechanism, the method automatically adjusts the weights of different features during processing, optimizing the overall fusion performance.

Experimental results demonstrate that the proposed method outperforms other deep learning networks in comparative experiments and validates the effectiveness of multi-dimensional feature fusion through ablation studies, significantly improving the efficiency and accuracy of fragment splicing and restoration. These outcomes highlight the potential application of deep learning in cultural heritage preservation and offer new directions for future research.

References

1. Zhang, Y., Luo, M.: Dunhuang Buddhist scripture fragment stitching example. Zhejiang Univ. J. Humanit. Soc. Sci. **46**(3) (2016). https://doi.org/10.3785/j.issn. 1008-942X.CN33-6000/C.2016.01.252

2. Zhang, Y., et al.: Reconnecting the broken civilization: patchwork integration of fragments from ancient manuscripts. In: Proceedings of the 31st ACM International Conference on Multimedia, pp. 1157–1166 (2023). https://doi.org/10.1145/3581783.3613804

3. Zhang, Y., et al.: LLMCO4MR: LLMS-aided neural combinatorial optimization for ancient manuscript restoration from fragments with case studies on Dunhuang. In: European Conference on Computer Vision, pp. 253–269. Springer (2025). https://doi.org/10.1007/978-3-031-73226-3_15

4. Zhang, Y., et al.: PhiloGPT: a philology-oriented large language model for ancient Chinese manuscripts with Dunhuang as case study. In: Proceedings of the 2024 Conference on Empirical Methods in Natural Language Processing, pp. 2784–2801 (2024). https://doi.org/10.18653/v1/2024.emnlp-main.163

5. Le, C., Li, X.: JIGSAWNet: shredded image reassembly using convolutional neural network and loop-based composition. IEEE Trans. Image Process. **28**(8), 4000–4015 (2019). https://doi.org/10.1109/tip.2019.2903298

6. Cao, Y., Fang, Z., Tian, H., Wei, R.: 2D irregular fragment reassembly with deep learning assistance. IEEE Access **12**, 28554–28563 (2024). https://doi.org/10.1109/access.2024.3368004

7. Zhou, R., Xia, D., Zhang, Y., Pang, H., Yang, X., Li, C.: PairingNet: a learning-based pair-searching and-matching network for image fragments. In: European Conference on Computer Vision, pp. 234–251. Springer (2025). https://doi.org/10.1007/978-3-031-73202-7_14

8. Kong, W., Kimia, B.B.: On solving 2D and 3D puzzles using curve matching. In: Proceedings of the 2001 IEEE Computer Society Conference on Computer Vision and Pattern Recognition. CVPR 2001, vol. 2. IEEE (2001). https://doi.org/10.1109/cvpr.2001.991015

9. da Gama Leitao, H.C., Stolfi, J.: A multiscale method for the reassembly of two-dimensional fragmented objects. IEEE Trans. Pattern Anal. Mach. Intell. **24**(9), 1239–1251 (2002). https://doi.org/10.1109/tpami.2002.1033215

10. Tsamoura, E., Pitas, I.: Automatic color based reassembly of fragmented images and paintings. IEEE Trans. Image Process. **19**(3), 680–690 (2009). https://doi.org/10.1109/tip.2009.2035840

11. Xu, C., Yan, J., Yang, H.: Image stitching method based on image edge detection and sift algorithm. In: Proceedings of the 2021 5th International Conference on Electronic Information Technology and Computer Engineering, pp. 425–431 (2021). https://doi.org/10.1145/3501409.3501487

12. Liu, H., Cao, S., Yan, S.: Automated assembly of shredded pieces from multiple photos. IEEE Trans. Multimedia **13**(5), 1154–1162 (2011). https://doi.org/10.1109/icme.2010.5582544

13. Zhang, K., Li, X.: A graph-based optimization algorithm for fragmented image reassembly. Graph. Models **76**(5), 484–495 (2014). https://doi.org/10.1016/j.gmod.2014.03.001

14. Zhang, Y.: The patching-up and study on the fragments of Xinpusajing, Quanshanjing and Jiuzhuzhongshengkunanjing in Dunhuang manuscripts. Fudan J. (Soc. Sci.) **57**(6), 12–20 (2015). https://doi.org/10.3785/j.issn.1008-942X.CN33-6000/C.2016.01.251

15. Zhang, Y.: The patching-up and study on the fragments of Xinpusajing, Quanshanjing and Jiuzhuzhongshengkunanjing in Dunhuang manuscripts. Fudan J. (Soc. Sci.) **57**(6), 12–20 (2015). https://doi.org/CNKI:SUN:FDDX.0.2015-06-003
16. Derech, N., Tal, A., Shimshoni, I.: Solving archaeological puzzles. Pattern Recogn. **119**, 108065 (2021). https://doi.org/10.1016/j.patcog.2021.108065
17. Savino, P., Tonazzini, A.: Digital restoration of ancient color manuscripts from geometrically misaligned recto-verso pairs. J. Cult. Herit. **19**, 511–521 (2016). https://doi.org/10.1016/j.culher.2015.11.005
18. Panagiotakis, C., Markaki, S., Kokinou, E., Papadakis, H.: Coastline matching via a graph-based approach. Comput. Geosci. **26**(6), 1439–1448 (2022). https://doi.org/10.1007/s10596-022-10175-1
19. Besl, P.J., McKay, N.D.: Method for registration of 3-D shapes. In: Sensor fusion IV: Control Paradigms and Data Structures, vol. 1611, pp. 586–606. SPIE (1992). https://doi.org/10.1109/34.121791
20. Hossieni, S.S., Shabani, M.A., Irandoust, S., Furukawa, Y.: PuzzleFusion: unleashing the power of diffusion models for spatial puzzle solving. In: Advances in Neural Information Processing Systems, vol. 36 (2024). https://doi.org/10.48550/arXiv.2211.13785
21. Du, Z., Liang, Y.: Object detection of remote sensing image based on multiscale feature fusion and attention mechanism. IEEE Access **12**, 8619–8632 (2024). https://doi.org/10.1109/access.2024.3352601
22. Dong, J., Wang, Y., Yang, Y., Yang, M., Chen, J.: MCDNet: multilevel cloud detection network for remote sensing images based on dual-perspective change-guided and multi-scale feature fusion. Int. J. Appl. Earth Obs. Geoinf. **129**, 103820 (2024). https://doi.org/10.1016/j.jag.2024.103820
23. Du, J., Li, W., Peng, Y., Zong, Q.: Image fusion by multiple features in the propagated filtering domain. Biomed. Signal Process. Control **100**, 106990 (2025). https://doi.org/10.1016/j.bspc.2024.106990
24. Shibu, T.M., Madan, N., Paramanandham, N., Kumar, A., Santosh, A.: Multimodal brain image fusion using multi feature guided fusion network. Biomed. Signal Process. Control **100**, 107060 (2025). https://doi.org/10.1016/j.bspc.2024.107060
25. Hou, L., Yan, Z., Desrosiers, C., Liu, H.: MFCPNet: real time medical image segmentation network via multi-scale feature fusion and channel pruning. Biomed. Signal Process. Control **100**, 107074 (2025). https://doi.org/10.1016/j.bspc.2024.107074
26. Zheng, Y., Li, X., Yin, Z., Gao, G., Weng, Y.: Automatic collation of Dunhuang ancient book fragments with multi-feature fusion. J. Image Graph. **28**(8), 2330–2342 (2023). https://doi.org/10.11834/jig.220896
27. Li, G., Muller, M., Thabet, A., Ghanem, B.: DeepGCNs: can GCNs go as deep as CNNs? In: Proceedings of the IEEE/CVF International Conference on Computer Vision, pp. 9267–9276 (2019). https://doi.org/10.1109/iccv.2019.00936
28. Oord, A., Li, Y., Vinyals, O.: Representation learning with contrastive predictive coding. arXiv preprint arXiv:1807.03748 (2018). https://doi.org/10.48550/arXiv.1807.03748
29. Chen, T., Kornblith, S., Norouzi, M., Hinton, G.: A simple framework for contrastive learning of visual representations. In: International Conference on Machine Learning, pp. 1597–1607. PMLR (2020). https://doi.org/10.48550/arXiv.2002.05709

NexaFusion: Integrating Multi-team Collaboration for High-Impact Outcomes

Lele Shen[iD], Minghao Yu[iD], Yulong Fan[iD], Jie Ma[iD], Han Wang[iD], and Hui Wang$^{(\boxtimes)}$[iD]

College of Computer Science and Technology, Zhejiang Normal University, Jinhua, China
{sll1023,yuminghaokd,jie_ma,WangHan123}@zjnu.edu.cn, hwang@zjnu.cn

Abstract. The rapid development of large language models (LLMs) has brought new opportunities for enhancing multi-agent collaborative systems. However, most existing LLM-based multi-agent frameworks often lack depth in cross-domain knowledge integration and multi-step reasoning, or exhibit insufficient comprehensiveness for complex problems. Inspired by multi-team collaboration models, we propose NexaFusion, a multi-team collaboration framework optimized for complex tasks. NexaFusion enables multiple teams to independently generate diverse solutions through task decomposition, role optimization, and dynamic integration mechanisms, with iterative optimization and integration ensuring accurate and innovative final results. We comprehensively evaluated NexaFusion on three complex tasks: creative writing, open-ended question answering, and logical reasoning, also exploring the impact of team size on experimental results. Findings demonstrate NexaFusion outperforms existing methods in generating high-quality solutions and excels in handling solution diversity and complexity. Through flexible collaboration and efficient integration, NexaFusion provides innovative solutions for cross-domain knowledge integration and reasoning in multi-agent collaborative frameworks.

Keywords: Autonomous agent · Large language model · Multi-team collaboration · Multi-agent system · Knowledge integration

1 Introduction

The rapid development of large language models (LLMs) has brought unprecedented potential to multi-agent collaborative systems [8]. LLMs like GPT-4 demonstrate exceptional capabilities in natural language processing, complex decision-making, and multi-step task execution [1], enabling their application in autonomous agent systems, such as AutoGPT [15]. While methods like Chain-of-Thought (CoT) prompting, self-improvement, task decomposition and reflection mechanisms enhance LLM reasoning [7,9,13,16,17], hallucinations remain unavoidable. Despite these single-agent advancements, they face limitations

T. Zhu et al. (Eds.): KSEM 2025, LNAI 15922, pp. 354–361, 2026.
https://doi.org/10.1007/978-981-95-3058-8_33

with cross-domain knowledge integration and multi-perspective collaboration, restricting their ability to handle open-ended and highly complex problems.

Multi-agent systems offer a viable path to address these limitations. These frameworks significantly enhance task-solving by assigning different roles to multiple LLMs and enabling collaboration towards a common goal. MetaGPT assigns roles to different GPTs, forming a team-like collaboration mechanism to address software development requirements [5]. Multi-agent discussion mechanisms also improve task-solving, with AutoGen supporting multi-round agent dialogues and Camel demonstrating role-playing for dialogue [6,14]. Recently, researchers have proposed multi-agent frameworks supporting dynamic generation and collaboration [3,4]. However, when applied to open-ended or highly complex problems, existing frameworks often struggle with suboptimal solutions, lacking depth or comprehensiveness in cross-domain knowledge integration and multi-step reasoning. Thus, a critical challenge remains: designing more flexible collaboration mechanisms for optimal results in multi-agent systems.

To address this, we introduce NexaFusion, a multi-team collaboration system designed for complex and open-ended tasks. It enables teams to independently generate diverse solutions and systematically optimizes results through an integration mechanism, aiming for optimal solutions. NexaFusion comprises three phases: Progressive Role Optimization (PRO) for independent team perspectives; continuous evaluation and feedback to enhance team result quality; and a Synthesizer phase that integrates team results, optimizing final output through weighted integration emphasizing high-quality outcomes while maintaining diversity.

Specifically, our contributions are as follows:

- We propose NexaFusion, an innovative collaborative system inspired by multi-solution bidding and integration, facilitating diverse solutions and efficient integration for complex problems.
- We comprehensively evaluated NexaFusion on three challenging tasks— creative writing, open-ended question answering, and logical reasoning— across various domains.
- We explored the impact of different team sizes on experimental results, revealing its significant influence on outcome diversity and quality, and validated multi-team collaboration's adaptability and flexibility in complex tasks, providing insights for optimizing multi-team agent collaboration.

2   NexaFusion

To enhance the performance of autonomous multi-agent teams in complex tasks, the NexaFusion framework is designed with three key phases: Task decomposition and role optimization, independent execution and evaluation feedback, and result integration and optimization, as illustrated in Fig. 1. In the task decomposition and role optimization phase, NexaFusion employs a PRO mechanism to break down complex tasks into multiple subtasks and assigns unique role sets

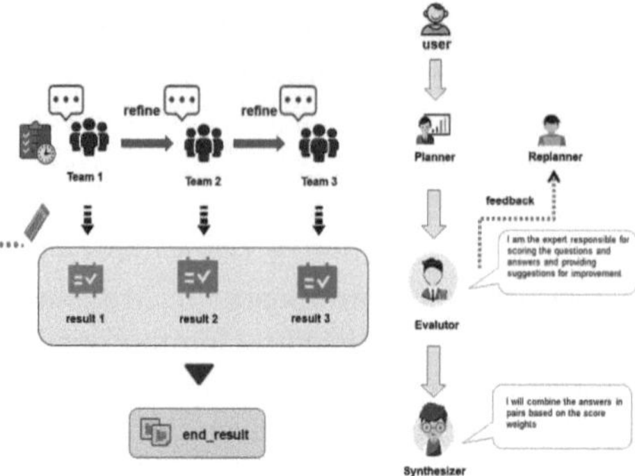

Fig. 1. A schematic diagram of NexaFusion.

to each team, ensuring teams independently generate solutions. In the Independent Execution and Evaluation Feedback phase, teams execute tasks in parallel, while the Evaluator module provides multi-dimensional scoring and feedback for iterative optimization. In the result integration and optimization phase, the Synthesizer module dynamically adjusts weights based on scores, integrates results, and generates high-quality final outputs.

2.1 Progressive Role Optimisation

NexaFusion employs the PRO mechanism to ensure each team can independently complete all subtasks and leverage multi-perspective insights to generate innovative, diverse, and high-quality solutions.

Task decomposition is the initial step in PRO. The Planner decomposes a complex task T into multiple subtasks $\{t_1, t_2, \ldots, t_n\}$. This process breaks down challenging tasks into smaller, clearer subtasks for easier execution. For n teams, decomposition is performed n times. Each decomposition results in subtasks optimized based on previous decompositions. The k-th decomposition further refines subtasks by referencing the $(k-1)$-th task structure.After task decomposition, the Planner assigns a unique team member set $R_k = \{r_{k1}, r_{k2}, \ldots, r_{km}\}$ to each team based on subtask requirements. The role set design ensures functional completeness, covering all functional requirements $F(T)$ for the task.During task execution, NexaFusion allows each team to complete tasks in parallel and independently. Each team receives a fully capable role combination during the task decomposition phase, enabling independent accomplishment of all subtasks without relying on intermediate results from other teams.

2.2 Evalutor

Due to task complexity and team independence, ensuring consistency and acceptability in the quality of independently generated results is a significant challenge. To address this, NexaFusion introduces the Evaluator module, designed to resolve output consistency issues in multi-team parallel task execution through a comprehensive and precise quality assessment mechanism. The Evaluator conducts multi-dimensional evaluations to ensure compliance with predefined quality standards, guaranteeing high-quality and consistent system-wide outputs.

Scoring dimensions vary for different task scenarios, including accuracy, completeness, innovation, and execution efficiency. To ensure final result quality, the Evaluator sets a scoring threshold T. Results not meeting the threshold receive detailed feedback and suggestions, allowing teams up to two rounds of iterative optimization. If the threshold T is not met after two iterations, the result is no longer optimized but participates in final result generation based on its score weight. Higher scores are weighted greater in integration, ensuring high quality of the final integrated output. The Synthesizer is discussed in Sect. 2.3.

2.3   Synthesizer

During the integration of outputs from all teams, the Synthesizer module optimizes results through a dynamic weight adjustment strategy. For each team's results R_i, the Synthesizer assigns dynamic weights based on Evaluator-provided scores $S(R_i)$, ensuring higher-scored results dominate. Lower-scored results are not disregarded; their useful information is absorbed via pairwise integration, forming a comprehensive final result. Through multiple rounds of iteration and weight updates, the Synthesizer dynamically adjusts each result's contribution ratio. The integrated solution exhibits rationality and consistency, adapting to complex task requirements. Its dynamic adjustments and multi-round optimization enhance the system's capability and efficiency in handling complex tasks.

The Synthesizer module is crucial for result integration, optimizing task outcomes via weight calculation and a step-by-step integration strategy. In the integration phase, Evaluator-provided scores $S(R_i)$ determine each team's result weight $W(R_i)$, reflecting its contribution ratio.The weight calculation formula is as follows:

$$W(R_i) = \frac{S(R_i)}{\sum_{j=1}^{m} S(R_j)} \tag{1}$$

where m represents the number of teams participating in the integration. This formula weights higher-scored results more, proportionally reducing lower-scored influence, ensuring high-quality outcomes. The Synthesizer performs multiple rounds of pairwise integration using weights $W(R_i)$. Each round of integration is achieved through the following formula:

$$R_{ij} = \alpha R_i + (1 - \alpha)R_j \tag{2}$$

$$\alpha = \frac{W(R_i)}{W(R_i) + W(R_j)} \tag{3}$$

where α dynamically adjusts the integration ratio. The intermediate result R_{ij} from each round participates in the next, gradually generating the final output.

Table 1. The results of the Trivia Creative Writing task. Δ indicates differences compared to the Standard Prompting(first row).

Methods	N (# trivia questions) = 5		N (# trivia questions) = 10	
	Score (%)	Δ (vs Standard %)	Score (%)	Δ (vs Standard %)
Standard	74.6	0.0%	77.0	0.0%
CoT	67.1	−10.0%	68.5	−11.1%
SPP-Profile	79.1	+5.9%	83.0	+7.8%
SPP	79.9	+7.1%	84.7	+10.0%
AutoAgents	82.0	+9.9%	85.3	+10.8%
NexaFusion	**83.0**	**+11.3%**	**85.5**	**+11.0%**

3 Experiments

To validate NexaFusion's performance, we designed three experimental tasks: creative writing, code generation, and logical reasoning. In experiments, GPT-4 serves as the base model for agents. The model's temperature parameter is set to 0 for reproducibility. By default, each task is completed through the collaboration of three teams. During the Evaluator phase, each team is allowed up to two rounds of iterative optimization, with the initial score threshold set to 50.

3.1 Trivia Creative Writing

Task Description and Evaluation Metrics. The Trivia Creative Writing task evaluates LLMs' ability to integrate multi-domain knowledge while generating coherent stories [12]. The task requires writing a coherent, structurally complete story based on a theme, seamlessly incorporating correct answers to N Trivia questions.We adopt the evaluation method from SPP, focusing on factual accuracy and comprehensiveness of generated content to measure trivia answer integration.

Experimental Results. Table 1 presents the results of the Trivia Creative Writing task. Under N = 5 and N = 10 settings, NexaFusion achieved scores of 83.0% and 85.5% respectively, outperforming the standard method by 11.3% and 11.0%, and ranking as the best approach among all methods. NexaFusion narrowly surpassed AutoAgents, with further improvements of 1.0% and 0.2%. This may be attributed to multi-team collaboration and integration benefits.

Table 2. Performance comparison of evaluators against different models

Evaluator	vs. Vicuna-13B	vs. Alpaca-13B	vs. GPT-4
FairEval	93.8%	95.0%	68.9%
ChatEval	97.5%	79.8%	63.8%

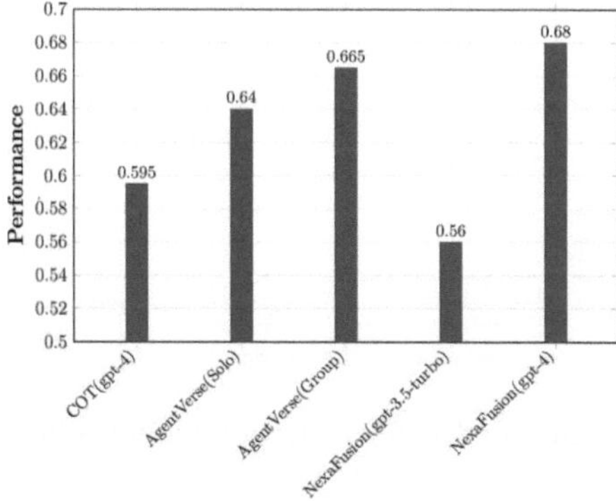

Fig. 2. Performance of five different methods on the Logic Grid Puzzles.

3.2   Open-Ended Question-Answering Task

Task Description and Evaluation Metrics. We employed MT-Bench [18], a benchmark of 80 high-quality open-ended questions covering common-sense reasoning, counterfactuals, and coding. To comprehensively evaluate this task, we employed ChatEval and FairEval to systematically compare NexaFusion with other models on multi-step reasoning, knowledge integration, and answer coherence [2, 11].

Experimental Results. Table 2 shows NexaFusion significantly outperforms Vicuna-13B, Alpaca-13B, and GPT-4 on all 80 questions, further validating its superiority in generating high-quality results.

3.3   Logical Reasoning Ability

Task Description and Evaluation Metrics. We utilized the logical grid reasoning task from the BigBench dataset [10], which contains 200 logical problems. Completing this requires connecting clues through multi-step reasoning and filtering information to derive the final answer. Prediction accuracy is calculated by comparing predicted answers with ground truth.

As shown in Fig. 2, NexaFusion (GPT-4) achieved a score of 0.68 in the logical reasoning task, 0.015 higher than AgentVerse (Group)'s 0.665. This indicates NexaFusion enhances overall reasoning performance. NexaFusion (GPT-3.5-Turbo) scored 0.56, close to CoT's 0.595. This demonstrates our approach's strong logical reasoning capabilities even with a slightly less powerful model.

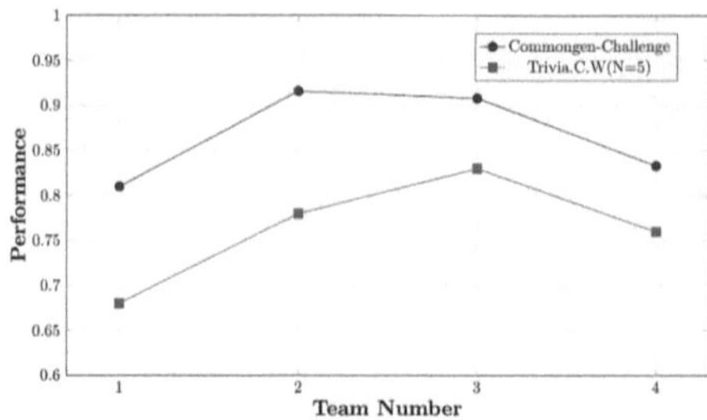

Fig. 3. Performance under different team numbers in the two tasks.

3.4 Ablation Study

We initially employed three teams for task execution. To investigate the impact of varying team sizes on system performance, we selected Trivia Creative Writing (N = 5) and CommonGen Challenge as evaluation targets. The number of teams is denoted as t. When t = 1, result integration was omitted, while other variables remained constant. Due to high API call costs, CommonGen Challenge used GPT-3.5-Turbo API, while Trivia Creative Writing employed GPT-4 API. By comparing generated content with target answers, we analyzed the effect of team size on task execution performance. Figure 3 indicate that too few teams may not fully leverage multiple perspectives, while too many can degrade performance due to collaboration complexity or task over-fragmentation.

4 Conclusions

This paper introduces NexaFusion, a system designed to tackle complex, open-ended tasks through flexible role optimization and efficient result integration. While NexaFusion demonstrates promising results, future research should focus on developing adaptive team configurations and improving the integration of multi-team outputs to address potential inefficiencies.

Acknowledgments. This work was supported by the National Natural Science Foundation of China (No. 62171413) and by the Key Project of Zhejiang Provincial Natural Science Foundation of China (No. LZ24F020005).

References

1. Achiam, J., et al.: GPT-4 technical report. arXiv preprint arXiv:2303.08774 (2023)
2. Chan, C.M., et al.: ChateVal: towards better LLM-based evaluators through multi-agent debate. arXiv preprint arXiv:2308.07201 (2023)
3. Chen, G., et al.: AutoAgents: a framework for automatic agent generation. arXiv preprint arXiv:2309.17288 (2023)

4. Chen, W., et al.: AgentVerse: facilitating multi-agent collaboration and exploring emergent behaviors in agents. arXiv preprint arXiv:2308.10848 (2023)
5. Hong, S., et al.: MetaGPT: meta programming for multi-agent collaborative framework. arXiv preprint arXiv:2308.00352 (2023)
6. Li, G., Hammoud, H., Itani, H., Khizbullin, D., Ghanem, B.: Camel: communicative agents for "mind" exploration of large language model society. Adv. Neural. Inf. Process. Syst. **36**, 51991–52008 (2023)
7. Madaan, A., et al.: Self-refine: iterative refinement with self-feedback. Adv. Neural. Inf. Process. Syst. **36**, 46534–46594 (2023)
8. Qin, C., Zhang, A., Zhang, Z., Chen, J., Yasunaga, M., Yang, D.: Is ChatGPT a general-purpose natural language processing task solver? arXiv preprint arXiv:2302.06476 (2023)
9. Shinn, N., Cassano, F., Gopinath, A., Narasimhan, K., Yao, S.: Reflexion: language agents with verbal reinforcement learning. Adv. Neural. Inf. Process. Syst. **36**, 8634–8652 (2023)
10. Srivastava, A., et al.: Beyond the imitation game: Quantifying and extrapolating the capabilities of language models. arXiv preprint arXiv:2206.04615 (2022)
11. Wang, P., et al.: Large language models are not fair evaluators. arXiv preprint arXiv:2305.17926 (2023)
12. Wang, Z., Mao, S., Wu, W., Ge, T., Wei, F., Ji, H.: Unleashing the emergent cognitive synergy in large language models: a task-solving agent through multi-persona self-collaboration. arXiv preprint arXiv:2307.05300 (2023)
13. Wei, J., et al.: Chain-of-thought prompting elicits reasoning in large language models. Adv. Neural. Inf. Process. Syst. **35**, 24824–24837 (2022)
14. Wu, Q., et al.: AutoGen: enabling next-gen LLM applications via multi-agent conversation. arXiv preprint arXiv:2308.08155 (2023)
15. Yang, H., Yue, S., He, Y.: Auto-GPT for online decision making: benchmarks and additional opinions. arXiv preprint arXiv:2306.02224 (2023)
16. Yao, S., et al.: Tree of thoughts: deliberate problem solving with large language models. Adv. Neural. Inf. Process. Syst. **36**, 11809–11822 (2023)
17. Yao, S., et al.: React: synergizing reasoning and acting in language models. In: International Conference on Learning Representations (ICLR) (2023)
18. Zheng, L., et al.: Judging LLM-as-a-judge with mt-bench and chatbot arena. Adv. Neural. Inf. Process. Syst. **36**, 46595–46623 (2023)

Comprehensive Evaluation of Large Language Model Responses: A Multi-factor Scoring System

Yiming Gai[1,2] , Junde Lu[1,2] , Xuefei Huang[2(✉)] , and Ying Li[1,2(✉)]

[1] School of Computer Science and Engineering, Beihang University, Beijing, China
`{gaiym,ljd2406107,liying}@buaa.edu.cn`
[2] Data Science and Intelligent Computing Laboratory, Hangzhou International Innovation Institute, Beihang University, Hangzhou, Zhejiang 311115, People's Republic of China
`xuefei.huang@buaa.edu.cn`

Abstract. The remarkable performance of large language models (LLMs) in linguistic tasks underscores an urgent need for comprehensive evaluation of their response quality. Prevailing methods, often confined to singular dimensions, fall short of capturing the full spectrum of model capabilities. This study introduces a multifactor scoring paradigm, integrating accuracy, conciseness, factual consistency, readability, and coherence, complemented by a graphical user interface (GUI) for visualizing outcomes. Evaluations on the TruthfulQA dataset unveil mainstream LLMs' strengths in reasoning tasks (peaking at a composite score of 0.6104) alongside pervasive limitations in navigating complex facts and ambiguities. By transcending the limitations of traditional metrics, this framework provides a transparent and adaptable approach to assessing model capabilities, paving the way for multilingual extensions and advancing knowledge engineering and model optimization.

Keywords: LLM Evaluation · Multi-factor Scoring · Large Language Models · Benchmarking · Model Comparison

1 Introduction

Large Language Models (LLMs) are increasingly applied across domains, from virtual assistants to academic research, yet a comprehensive evaluation of their capabilities remains challenging. Traditional metrics like accuracy or fluency capture only a single dimension, limiting their effectiveness in diverse real-world scenarios. In response, research has moved toward multi-dimensional evaluation frameworks. Metrics such as BLEU and ROUGE are commonly used [1] but lack semantic and contextual understanding, while newer methods like BERTScore [2] improve on this using semantic embeddings. These developments reflect progress, but key aspects of response quality—such as coherence and user-centered factors—remain insufficiently addressed.

In specialized domains such as healthcare and law, evaluation demands grow even more complex, requiring not only factual precision but also accurate technical language

T. Zhu et al. (Eds.): KSEM 2025, LNAI 15922, pp. 362–372, 2026.
https://doi.org/10.1007/978-981-95-3058-8_34

and logical coherence [4]. Existing metrics often fall short in these areas. To address this gap, this paper proposes a multi-factor scoring system that assesses LLM responses across five key dimensions: accuracy, conciseness, factual consistency, readability, and coherence, while also incorporating the ROUGE metric, as shown in the Fig. 1. Using the TruthfulQA [3] dataset for validation, experimental results show that this framework provides a more complete and scientific evaluation of LLM performance, effectively highlighting both their reasoning capabilities and limitations in complex factual scenarios.

The contributions of this paper are as follows:

A. ***Proposing a multi-dimensional evaluation framework.*** This study innovatively designs a comprehensive scoring system that incorporates traditional single metrics. By incorporating user experience-related dimensions, it provides a holistic characterization of LLM performance across diverse tasks.

B. ***Enhancing evaluation applicability and transparency.*** By integrating semantic embedding techniques with the ROUGE metric and validating the approach using the TruthfulQA dataset, this method is not only applicable to open-domain question answering but also provides a scalable solution for the complex evaluation needs of specialized domains. Additionally, it enhances result visualization and interpretability through the integration of a GUI.

C. ***Revealing model capabilities and limitations.*** Through multi-factor analysis, this study systematically reveals the strengths of LLMs in reasoning tasks and their limitations when handling complex facts and ambiguous information. This provides data-driven insights and theoretical guidance for future model optimization.

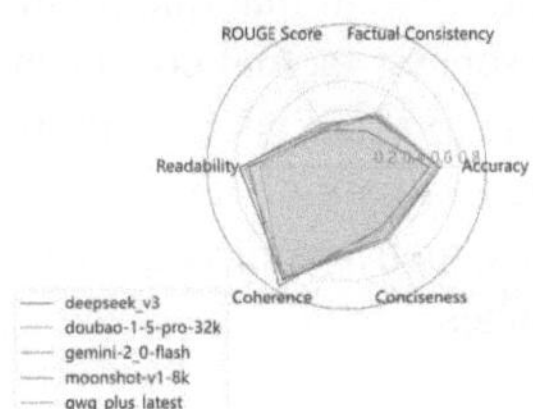

Fig. 1. Pie chart of the scores of five LLMs on different dimensions based on TruthfulQA

2   Related Work

LLMs based on the Transformer architecture and trained on extensive corpora, excel in NLP tasks like text generation and question answering [5]. Deep learning, a key driver in AI, leverages neural networks—modeled on the human brain—to advance pattern recognition, vision, and NLP [6, 7]. Neurons process inputs, apply transformations, and adjust outputs via weighted connections [8]. By exploiting inter-layer links, deep learning extracts hierarchical features, enhancing data representation [9]. The Transformer's self-attention mechanism has transformed NLP feature extraction.

Traditional evaluation metrics such as BLEU [1] and ROUGE [12], which emphasize n-gram overlap, have been extensively applied in machine translation and summarization but offer limited insight into semantic depth and contextual coherence—critical for evaluating generative language models. To address these deficiencies, recent approaches have adopted semantic-aware methods like BERTScore [2] and benchmark datasets such as TruthfulQA [3], which assess reasoning and factual consistency through contextual embeddings and adversarial question design. Tokenization techniques like Byte Pair Encoding (BPE) [10] further enhance evaluation precision by improving model input representation. Despite these advancements, prevailing methods remain predominantly uni-dimensional and insufficient for capturing complex linguistic attributes such as readability, logical flow, and domain-specific precision. Automated metrics like ROUGE-N, ROUGE-L [13], and F1 score offer partial insights, while human evaluations, though informative, lack scalability [4]. Semantic redundancy analysis [11] quantifies repetition but lacks adaptability to dy-namic content, while factual consistency assessments, often reliant on keyword match-ing or external knowledge retrieval [8], fall short in open-domain question answering.

This gap between existing metrics and practical requirements has led to the development of multidimensional evaluation frameworks. In response, this study proposes an integrated scoring system comprising five key dimensions—accuracy, conciseness, factual consistency, readability, and coherence—augmented by ROUGE-based analysis [13]. Validated on the TruthfulQA dataset, the framework provides a comprehensive and structured methodology for assessing LLM performance across both general and specialized domains.

3   Methodology

To comprehensively assess the response quality of large language models (LLMs), we propose a multi-factor scoring system that quantitatively analyzes responses across six dimensions: accuracy, conciseness, factual consistency, readability, coherence, and ROUGE score. This system aims to establish a theoretically rigorous, technologically advanced, and practically viable evaluation framework. This section elaborates on the design principles, core algorithms, metric computation methodologies, and comparisons with existing evaluation approaches.

3.1   System Design Concept and Technical Framework

The system is designed to address the theoretical need for multi-dimensional evaluation, as no single metric can fully capture the diverse capabilities of LLMs [14]. To this end, we adopt a modular architecture consisting of a data preprocessing module, a semantic embedding module, and a multi-factor evaluation module, ensuring both flexibility and scalability.

The data preprocessing module standardizes inputs, handles missing or non-textual data, and applies consistent sentence segmentation via regular expressions ([.!?]), following established normalization practices [13].

The semantic embedding module transforms text into high-dimensional vectors using the all-MiniLM-L6-v2 model [15], which offers an efficient and multilingual alternative to larger models like BERT, making it suitable for real-time evaluation.

Finally, the multi-factor evaluation module computes metrics based on embeddings and combines them via weighted averaging. This setup improves efficiency and supports future integration of additional models or criteria.

3.2 Theory and Algorithms of Evaluation Metrics

Accuracy. Accuracy quantifies the semantic similarity between the model-generated response A_m and the reference answer A_g, serving as a fundamental evaluation metric. We employ cosine similarity to measure the alignment between the embedding vectors of the two texts [16]. Given embedding vectors E_m and E_g, the accuracy score is defined as:

$$AS = \cos(E_m, E_g) = \frac{E_m \cdot E_g}{\|E_m\| \|E_g\|}. \tag{1}$$

To ensure robustness, input text undergoes preprocessing (null value checks and string conversions) to prevent invalid computations. Compared to traditional n-gram matching methods (e.g., BLEU), this approach prioritizes semantic consistency over exact word matches.

Conciseness. This metric assesses whether the model's response is succinct and free of redundancy. Drawing on information redundancy theory [10], we propose an inverse redundancy metric. The model output (A_m) and reference (A_g) are segmented into sentences, and each sentence's maximum similarity to the reference is computed. Sentences below a similarity threshold receive a full penalty, while others are penalized inversely to their similarity. Repetitions trigger exponential ($2^{\text{repeat\_count}}$) and quadratic ($0.5 \cdot \text{count}^2$) penalties. If A_m is more than twice as long as A_g, an additional length-based scaling factor is applied. The redundancy score is formulated as:

$$R = \min\left(1.0, \frac{\text{redundancy}}{\text{total length}}\right). \tag{2}$$

The final conciseness score is computed as:

$$CS = 1 - R. \tag{3}$$

Factual. Factual consistency assesses the alignment between key factual elements in the model's response and the ground truth. We adopt a set-overlap-based approach [3], wherein both A_m and A_g are tokenized, converted to lowercase, and filtered to remove stopwords (e.g., "the", "and"). Given word sets W_m and W_g, the consistency score is calculated as:

$$FC = \frac{|W_m \cap W_g|}{|W_g|}. \tag{4}$$

If A_g is empty, the score defaults to 1.0; if either input is empty, the score is 0.0. This approach is computationally efficient and well-suited for English datasets. Future enhancements may incorporate named entity recognition (NER) to improve precision.

Readability. Readability measures the ease of comprehension of the generated response, based on linguistic readability theory [17]. We consider two sub-metrics: Sentence Length Score: Deviation from an optimal sentence length of 17.5 words, normalized. Lexical Diversity: The proportion of unique words in the response (+1e-6 smoothing to prevent division by zero).

The overall readability score is defined as:

$$RD = 0.6 \cdot \left(1 - min\left(1.0, \frac{|\,avg_{length} - 17.5\,|}{17.5}\right)\right) + 0.4 \cdot \frac{|\,unique_{words}\,|}{|\,words\,| + 10^{-6}}. \tag{5}$$

For single-sentence or empty responses, a default score of 0.5 is assigned to maintain fairness.

Coherence. Coherence evaluates the logical flow within the response, grounded in discourse coherence theory [18]. The response A_m is segmented into sentences $S = \{s_1, s_2, ..., s_n\}$, and cosine similarity is computed between the embedding vectors of adjacent sentences. The coherence score is obtained by averaging these similarity values:

$$CH = \frac{1}{n-1} \sum_{i=1}^{n-1} \cos(E_{s_i}, E_{s_{i+1}}). \tag{6}$$

For single-sentence or empty responses, the score defaults to 1.0. This method effectively captures local cohesion, making it particularly suitable for evaluating short-form responses.

ROUGE Score. To complement semantic-based evaluations, we incorporate ROUGE scores [12] to quantify n-gram overlap between A_m and A_g. Specifically, we compute ROUGE-1, ROUGE-2, and ROUGE-L F1 scores, which are integrated as follows:

$$RS = 0.5 \cdot R_1 + 0.2 \cdot R_2 + 0.3 \cdot R_L. \tag{7}$$

To enhance score differentiation, the final score is scaled by 1.2, with an upper bound of 1.0, thereby emphasizing the importance of ROUGE-1 and ROUGE-L in lexical similarity.

3.3 Comprehensive Scoring Method

The final Total Score (TS) is computed using a weighted average of the six evaluation metrics. The default weight assignments are: Accuracy (0.25), Conciseness (0.10), Factual Consistency (0.20), Readability (0.15), Coherence (0.15), and ROUGE Score (0.15). These weights are empirically determined based on task requirements and inter-metric correlations [16]:

$$TS = \sum_{iw} w_i \cdot M_i, \tag{8}$$

where w_i represents the weight and M_i denotes the individual metric scores. This framework allows for dynamic weight adjustments to adapt to different evaluation scenarios.

3.4   Comparison with Existing Methods

Compared to traditional evaluation approaches, our system provides a more comprehensive and application-oriented assessment. Unlike BLEU [1], which relies on n-gram overlap, our semantic embedding method improves sensitivity to meaning. While BERTScore [16] emphasizes semantic similarity, we incorporate additional dimensions such as conciseness, factual consistency, and user experience (e.g., readability and coherence). By integrating ROUGE, we also capture lexical similarity, achieving a balanced evaluation of both surface and semantic fidelity. This multi-factor framework offers a more robust solution for the complex requirements of LLM evaluation.

4   Experimental Process and Results

This section describes how we apply the multi-factor scoring system to evaluate the response quality of LLMs, including the experimental setup, data preprocessing, evaluation process, and result analysis. We selected the TruthfulQA dataset to test five mainstream LLMs, and through both quantitative and qualitative analysis, we reveal the performance characteristics of each model.

4.1   Experimental Setup

Dataset Selection. We selected the TruthfulQA dataset, which contains 817 English questions spanning various categories such as science, history, and health, and is designed to test the model's truthfulness and reasoning ability. each question is paired with an optimal answer, providing a standard reference for evaluation. The choice of TruthfulQA is motivated by its compatibility with the BPE encoding, which allows LLMs to fully leverage their strengths in various tasks.

Model Selection. The following five LLMs were evaluated in the experiment:

Qwq_plus_latest: A multilingual model developed by Alibaba Cloud, known for its efficient reasoning capabilities.

deepseek_v3: An open-source model focused on deep learning optimization.

doubao-1–5-pro-32k: A conversational model launched by ByteDance, emphasizing generation fluency.

moonshot-v1-8k: Known for its strong semantic understanding, instruction following, and text generation abilities.

gemini-2.0-flash: A model that excels in multimodal understanding and reasoning.

Data Preprocessing. The Experimental Data is Sourced from the TruthfulQA CSV File, Which Includes Columns Such as "Question" and "Best Answer." to Ensure Consistency in the Evaluation, the Following Preprocessing Steps Were Performed:

Data Cleaning. The file was read using pd.read_csv, followed by checks and removal of null values or invalid responses.

Format Standardization. Both model responses and reference answers were converted to strings, and non-string inputs were processed to ensure compatibility.

Metadata Addition. Model identification (Model), question category (Category), and response type (Type) were added to each record to facilitate grouped analysis.

File Management. The responses of each model were stored as separate CSV files, and the output results were saved to a designated directory.

4.2 Evaluation Process

The specific steps of the evaluation process are as follows:

1) *Data Traversal.* The data files are read one by one, extracting the questions, model responses, and reference answers.
2) *Metric Calculation.* Six metrics are computed for each pair of responses:

   Accuracy: Computes the cosine similarity of the embedding vectors.
   Conciseness: Calculates redundancy and takes the inverse.
   Factual Consistency: Computes the word set overlap rate.
   Readability: Combines sentence length and vocabulary diversity.
   Coherence: Computes the average similarity between sentences.
   ROUGE Score: Weighted integration of ROUGE-1, ROUGE-2, and ROUGE-L.
   Overall Scoring. The following weights are used by default to calculate the total score: Accuracy (0.25), Conciseness (0.10), Factual Consistency (0.20), Readability (0.15), Coherence (0.15), and ROUGE Score (0.15).

3) *Result Storage.* A detailed results table and a model summary table are generated, containing the average values for each metric and the total score.

Exception handling is integrated throughout the process. If a file is missing or a calculation error occurs, a warning is recorded and the error is skipped, ensuring the stability of the experiment.

4.3 Result Analysis

Based on the evaluation results, we can draw the following conclusions, as shown in the Fig. 2, Table 1:

Table 1. Performance Metrics of LLMs

Model	Accuracy	Conciseness	Factual Consistency	Total Score
DeepSeek-v3	0.6719	0.5687	0.4228	0.6088
Doubao-1.5-pro-32k	0.6689	0.5403	0.4445	0.5873
Gemini-2.0-flash	0.6725	0.5897	0.3975	0.6104
QWQ Plus Latest	0.6496	0.5145	0.4126	0.5800
moonshot-v1-8k	0.5905	0.4927	0.2936	0.5499

DeepSeek-v3 demonstrates an overall performance score of 0.6088, reflecting a mixed capability across various metrics. It excels particularly in handling Logical Falsehood questions, where its strengths shine through, but it struggles notably with Misinformation questions, as shown in the Fig. 2 (a), Table 2.

Table 2. Deepseek-V3

category	score
Logical Falsehood	0.7356
Mandela Effect	0.7257
Misinformation	0.2963
Confusion: People	0.3259

Doubao-1.5-pro-32k exhibits an overall performance score of 0.5873, indicating a varied proficiency across its evaluated metrics. It shines in addressing Logical Falsehood questions, showcasing its strengths in specific reasoning tasks, yet it falters significantly with Misinformation questions, as shown in the Fig. 2 (b), Table 3.

Table 3. Doubao-1.5-pro-32k

category	score
Logical Falsehood	0.7540
Mandela Effect	0.7426
Misinformation	0.2497
Indexical Error: Location	0.2784

Gemini 2.0 Flash exhibits an overall performance score of 0.6104, showcasing a balanced yet varied proficiency across its evaluated metrics. It stands out in addressing Misconceptions: Topical questions, where it performs at its peak, but it falters when tackling Misinformation questions, as shown in the Fig. 2 (c), Table 4.

Table 4. Gemini-2.0-flash

category	score
Misconceptions: Topical	0.7628
Logical Falsehood	0.7414
Misinformation	0.2950
Confusion: People	0.3617

The qwq-plus-latest model achieves an overall performance score of 0.5800, indicating a moderate level of effectiveness across its evaluated metrics. It demonstrates particular strength in handling Mandela Effect questions, where its capabilities stand out, but it shows a relative weakness in addressing Misinformation questions, as shown in the Fig. 2 (d), Table 5.

Table 5. Qwq_plus_latest

category	score
Mandela Effect	0.7353
Logical Falsehood	0.7059
Misinformation	0.2652
Confusion: People	0.3027

Moonshot-v1-8k exhibits an overall performance score of 0.5499, indicating a varied proficiency across its evaluated metrics. It demonstrates particular strength in addressing Politics questions, where it likely leverages its capabilities effectively, but it shows notable weakness in handling Confusion: People questions, as shown in the Fig. 2 (e), Table 6.

Table 6. Moonshot-v1-8k

category	score
Politics	0.7406
Subjective	0.6601
Confusion: People	0.3492
Indexical Error: Time	0.3607

Based on performance across multiple metrics, we offer scenario-specific model recommendations. For tasks requiring high accuracy, Gemini 2.0 Flash is preferred due to its strong precision. When factual consistency is critical, Doubao-1.5-pro-32k offers the most reliable responses. For applications emphasizing readability and fluency, DeepSeek-v3 provides clear and engaging outputs. These recommendations reflect the evaluated strengths of each model in addressing distinct task requirements.

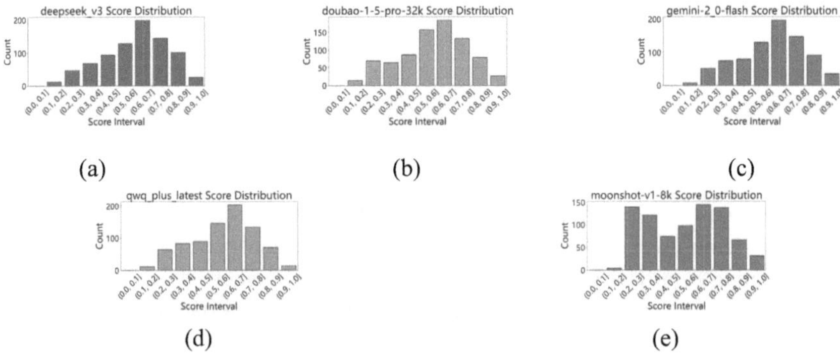

Fig. 2. Performance Metrics of LLMs

5 Conclusion

This paper introduces a multi-factor scoring system to assess Large Language Models (LLMs) using the TruthfulQA dataset. It evaluates models on several key metrics: accuracy, conciseness, factual consistency, readability, coherence, and ROUGE scores. Experimental results highlight unique strengths among models: Gemini 2.0 Flash stands out for accuracy and conciseness, DeepSeek V3 for readability and coherence, and Doubao-1.5-Pro-32k for factual consistency. While the models perform well in reasoning, they face challenges with complex facts and ambiguity. Unlike single-metric evaluations, this approach offers a comprehensive framework for model selection and improvement. The framework has achieved comprehensive evaluation of different models, but there remains room for improvement in factual consistency and weight optimization. It holds potential for future extensions to multilingual support, multimodal applications, and integration with knowledge graphs and user studies.

Acknowledgment. This work was supported by the National Key Research and Development Project of China (2021ZD0110700) and the Engineering Research Center of Integration and Application of Digital Learning Technology, Ministry of Education (1321008) and the Research Start-up Funds of Hangzhou International Innovation Institute of Beihang University under Grant No.2024KQ051 and No.2024KQ086.

References

1. Papineni, K., Roukos, S., Ward, T., Zhu, W.J.: BLEU: A method for automatic evaluation of machine translation. In: 40th Annual Meeting of the Association for Computational Linguistics (ACL), pp. 311–318 (2002). ACL, Stroudsburg
2. Zhang, T., Kishore, V., Wu, F., Weinberger, K.Q., Artzi, Y.: BERTScore: evaluating text generation with BERT. In: International Conference on Learning Representations (ICLR) (2020). Springer, Heidelberg
3. Lin, S., Hilton, J., Evans, O.: TruthfulQA: Measuring How Models Mimic Human Falsehoods. arXiv preprint arXiv:2109.07958 (2022)
4. Lewis, P., Perez, E., Piktus, A., et al.: Retrieval-augmented generation for knowledge-intensive NLP tasks. In: Advances in Neural Information Processing Systems (NeurIPS), vol. 33, pp. 9459–9474 (2020). MIT Press, Cambridge
5. Vaswani, A., Shazeer, N., Parmar, N., et al.: Attention is all you need. In: Advances in Neural Information Processing Systems (NeurIPS), **30**, pp. 5998–6008. MIT Press, Cambridge (2017)
6. Svozil, D., Kvasnicka, V., Pospichal, J.: Introduction to multilayer feed-forward neural networks. Chemom. Intell. Lab. Syst. **39**(1), 43–62 (1997)
7. Sun, Z., Xue, L., Xu, Y., et al.: A survey on deep learning research. J. Comput. Appl. Res. **29**(8), 2806–2810 (2012)
8. Zhao, D.: A survey on deep learning and deep reinforcement learning. China New Telecommun. **21**(15), 174–175 (2019)
9. Liu, J., Liu, Y., Luo, X.: Advances in deep learning research. J. Comput. Appl. Res. **31**(7), 1921–1930 (2014)
10. Rasooli, M., et al.: Spreadsheets are all you Need: Implementing GPT-2 in Excel. https://spreadsheets-are-all-you-need.ai/gpt2/

11. Clark, E., August, T., Serrano, S., et al.: All that's 'human' is not gold: evaluating human evaluation of generated text. In: 59th Annual Meeting of the Association for Computational Linguistics (ACL), pp. 7282–7296. ACL, Stroudsburg (2021)
12. Lin, C. Y.: ROUGE: a package for automatic evaluation of summaries. In: Text Summarization Branches Out, pp. 74–81 (2004). ACL, Barcelona
13. Graesser, A. C., McNamara, D. S., Louwerse, M. M.: Methods of automated text analysis. In: The Oxford Handbook of Computational Linguistics, pp. 375–394. Oxford University Press, Oxford (2011)
14. Brown, T.B., Mann, B., Ryder, N., et al.: Language models are few-shot learners. In: Advances in Neural Information Processing Systems (NeurIPS), **33**, pp. 1877–1901. MIT Press, Cambridge (2020)
15. Reimers, N., Gurevych, I.: Sentence-BERT: sentence embeddings using Siamese BERT-networks. In: 2019 Conference on Empirical Methods in Natural Language Processing (EMNLP), pp. 3982–3992. ACL, Stroudsburg (2019)
16. Manning, C.D., Raghavan, P., Schütze, H.: Introduction to Information Retrieval, 2nd edn. Cambridge University Press, Cambridge (2008)
17. Flesch, R.: A new readability yardstick. J. Appl. Psychol. **32**(3), 221–233 (1948)
18. Halliday, M.A.K., Hasan, R.: Cohesion in English. Longman, London (1976)

Service Area Vehicle Flow Prediction Model for Highway Service Areas Based on Gravity Model Quadratic Assignment

Feng Xu[1], Lai Meng[1], Yichu Dai[2], Zhengdong Fei[1], Canghong Jin[1]($\boxtimes$) (iD), and Lina Wei[1]

[1] HangZhou City University, Hangzhou 310000, China
{jinch,weiln}@hzcu.edu.cn
[2] Nanjing University of Information Science and Technology, Nanjing 210044, China

Abstract. The throughput prediction of highway service areas is an essential method for enhancing operational efficiency and service satisfaction. Traditional throughput prediction models are based on time series forecasting. However, these models fail to consider the interdependencies between service areas. This paper proposes a Gravity Model Quadratic Assignment (GMAAN) method. Building upon traditional time series forecasting techniques, GMAAN utilizes the gravity model to reassign service area vehicle flow on highways and swiftly determines parameters through a meta-learning approach. Comparisons with three years of throughput data from highway service areas in Zhejiang Province demonstrate that the redistribution effect achieved by GMAAN outperforms traditional time series forecasting methods, demonstrating a MAPE reduction exceeding 5% compared to baseline models while maintaining real-time inference efficiency.

Keywords: Urban traffic · Time series · Quadratic assignment · Gravity model · Meta-learning

1 Introduction

In recent years, highway traffic volume is increasing and more frequent congestion. Effective management measures, based on traffic flow predictions for highway service areas, are essential for reducing congestion and ensuring smooth traffic operations.

With the remarkable success of deep learning models across various domains, benefiting from their generalization capabilities and capacity to capture subtle variations, diverse deep learning approaches have gradually been applied to traffic flow prediction. For instance, the probabilistic directed graphical model DBN [1] constructs spatiotemporal correlations through multi-layer node graph structures to enhance temporal pattern capture from traffic data. Sequence deep learning models, including Recurrent Neural Networks (RNN), Long Short-Term Memory (LSTM), and Gated Recurrent Units (GRU) [2,3], learn temporal dependencies through contextual sequence analysis. Temporal Convolutional

T. Zhu et al. (Eds.): KSEM 2025, LNAI 15922, pp. 373–383, 2026.
https://doi.org/10.1007/978-981-95-3058-8_35

Networks (TCN) extend convolutional neural networks to capture spatiotemporal evolution of traffic flow. To address TCN's limitations in capturing long-term dependencies for short-term traffic prediction, the Continuous Temporal Convolution Network (CTCN) has been proposed. Graph Convolutional Networks (GCN) [4] employ graph embedding techniques to aggregate neighboring node information, using convolution to capture dynamic traffic data and spatiotemporal dependencies. Hybrid models like T-GCN [5] and AST-GCN-LSTM [6] combine GCN with GRU to separately capture spatial and temporal dependencies, improving upon conventional spatiotemporal prediction approaches. Spatio-Temporal Graph Convolutional Networks (ST-GCN) [7] incorporate spatiotemporal graph attention mechanisms for traffic flow prediction. Recent advancements integrate external factors through knowledge graphs, exemplified by the Knowledge Fusion Cell (KF-Cell) [8], which combines domain knowledge with traffic features as input to spatiotemporal graph convolutional networks, enhancing prediction performance across different time horizons.

Existing methods typically depend on traffic network topology, leading to high computational complexity and neglecting interactions between service areas. This paper introduces the GMAAN model, which combines time series prediction with a secondary gravity model allocation. The GMAAN model comprises three parts: conventional prediction, rapid gravity coefficient localization, and secondary reallocation. By integrating historical features and accounting for interactions between adjacent service areas, it enhances prediction accuracy. Experiments on real-world highway datasets show that GMAAN outperforms traditional machine learning and neural network models in service area traffic prediction. The main contributions are as follows:

(1) To overcome the limitations of statistical and neural network methods in service area traffic prediction, we propose the GMAAN model. It enhances prediction accuracy by extracting historical features and incorporating multiple factors, such as spillover effects from adjacent areas. Experiments on highway datasets show that GMAAN outperforms leading statistical and deep learning models in various time series metrics.
(2) Introducing meta-learning methods to quickly determine key parameters of the gravity model has significantly improved parameter-solving efficiency compared to traditional methods, demonstrating its effectiveness.

2   GMAAN Model Theory

The gravity model theory is derived from Newton's law of universal gravitation in physics, which means that the gravitation between two objects is directly proportional to the product of the masses of the two objects and inversely proportional to the square of the distance between them. When this principle is applied to the traffic field, the formula is as follows:

$$T_{ij} = kF_i^\alpha R_i^\beta P_i^\gamma M_i^\delta N_i^\varepsilon H_i^\xi f(C_{ij}) \quad (i \neq j; i = 1, 2, \cdots, n; j = 1, 2, \cdots, m) \quad (1)$$

Here, $f(C_{ij}) = C_{ij}^{b}$ is the distance between two service areas, and n and m represent the number of service areas. F_i^{α} is the initial vehicle equivalent, R_i^{β} is the star rating of the service area, P_i^{γ} is the number of parking spaces in the service area, M_i^{δ} is the number of toilets in the service area, N_i^{ε} is the number of catering facilities in the service area, H_i^{ξ} is the number of charging stations in the service area, and T_{ij} is the vehicle equivalent flowing from city i to city j.

This experiment adopts a dual constraint approach, which specifies: At the end of the vehicle equivalent allocation, the total vehicle equivalent of each service area is equal to the vehicle equivalent of the entire road. The formula is as follows, where O represents the total vehicle equivalent on the entire road:

$$\sum_{k=1}^{n}\left(F_k + \sum_{i=1}^{n}T_{ik} - \sum_{j=1}^{n}T_{ki}\right) = O \tag{2}$$

Secondly, the minimum vehicle equivalent of a single service area will not be less than the historical minimum vehicle equivalent, and the maximum vehicle equivalent of a single service area will not be greater than the maximum historical vehicle equivalent. The formula is as follows, where Q represents the vehicle equivalent of a single service area:

$$Q_{\min} \leq F_j + \sum_{i=1}^{n}T_{ij} - \sum_{i=1}^{n}T_{ji} \leq Q_{\max} \tag{3}$$

The parameters such as α and β used in the gravity model of this experiment are the driving factors for generating traffic equivalent, known as potential coefficients, with values ranging from 0.1 to 2. The traditional ways of calculating coefficients include trial and error algorithm and least squares method. This article uses a trial and error algorithm combined with machine learning to predict these parameters.

Based on the above theory, this experiment designed a model GMAAN based on gravity model secondary allocation. Figure 1 below is the overall architecture of the system:

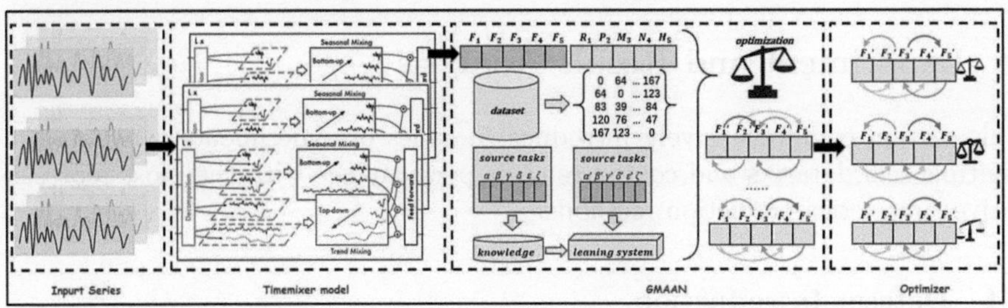

Fig. 1. GMAAN architecture diagram.

This experiment first predicts the vehicle equivalent using traditional time series prediction methods. Based on this, a gravity model is used for secondary vehicle equivalent allocation prediction. The coefficients of the gravity model are calculated using trial and error methods and meta learning. Finally, the final prediction result is obtained by iteratively allocating the gravity model through the optimizer. The pseudocode of the key parts of GMAAN for iterative allocation is as follows:

Algorithm 1: Pseudocode of gravity model secondary distribution

---

Input: The total traffic flow equivalent O of an expressway section, the number of service areas of the section, the initial vehicle equivalent F of each service area of the section, the basic attribute P of each service area, the distance d between each service area, the coefficient parameter of the gravity formula, and the historical vehicle equivalent ratio

Output: Vehicle equivalent Q of each service area after secondary distribution

```
 1  begin
 2  |   while Achieve the set maximum number of iterations, or the tolerance for
    |   changes in the objective function value is less than the set minimum value,
    |   float do
 3  |   |   flowMatrix = [ ][ ]
 4  |   |   for iteration i = 0 to num do
 5  |   |   |   for iteration j = 0 to num and j != i do
    |   |   |   |   /* Calculate the car equivalent attraction of the
    |   |   |   |      current service area to other service areas      */
 6  |   |   |   |   flowMatrix[i][j] = Fi*Pi * Fj*Pj / dij
 7  |   |   |   end for
 8  |   |   |   Q[i] = Sum(flowMatrix[i])
 9  |   |   end for
    |   |   /* Comparison between KL and ftol for calculating the
    |   |      variation tolerance of the objective function          */
10  |   |   KL = Q * log( Q / rations )
11  |   |   if KL ¡= flot then
12  |   |   |   Stop optimizing iterations
13  |   |   end if
14  |   end while
15  end
```

---

3   Experiment and Result Analysis

This section comprehensively introduces a series of experiments conducted on multiple real datasets and compares their performance with the most representative time series prediction methods.

3.1   Dataset Introduction

The data used in the experiment comes from the cross-sectional traffic flow information of service areas provided by relevant units in Zhejiang Province's transportation industry over the past three years, as well as the basic information of these service areas. and the data from January 2022 to April 2024 were used as the training set, while the data from May 2024 to August 2024 were used as the testing set, according to the time dimension. The training set accounts for 90%, and the testing set accounts for 10%. Detailed data information is provided as follows:

(1) The vehicle equivalent data for each service area and direction of the G60 HuKun Highway, G15 Shenhai Highway, and G25 Changshen Highway datasets from early January 2022 to the end of August 2024. The data structure includes: service area name, service area direction, time, and service area vehicle equivalent. The one-way data volume of a single service area is 974, while the Wenzhou service area does not differentiate directions, with a total data volume of 28246. For details, please refer to Table 1.

(2) The basic attributes and data structures of each service area and its direction include: star rating, total number of parking spaces, total number of bathrooms, total number of restaurants, and total number of charging stations. There are a total of 116 service areas and 235 valid data. And the actual geographical distance between each adjacent service area on the G60 HuKun Highway, G15 Shenhai Highway, and G25 Changshen Highway datasets.

Table 1. Potential coefficient of trial calculation

Statistics	Datasets		
	G60Hukun	G15Shenhai	G25Changshen
Equivalent	9740	8766	9740

3.2   Evaluation Indicators

Mean Absolute Error (MAE) measures the average magnitude of the absolute differences between predicted values and actual values. The range of MAE is from 0 to positive infinity, with smaller values indicating higher prediction accuracy of the model.

Mean Absolute Percentage Error (MAPE) quantifies the relative error in percentage terms. The range of MAPE is from 0 to positive infinity, with smaller values indicating higher prediction accuracy of the model.

Symmetric Mean Absolute Percentage Error (SMAPE) calculates the proportion of the absolute error between predicted and actual values relative to their average. The range of SMAPE is from 0% to 200%, with smaller values indicating better model performance.

3.3 Baseline Methods

The experiment compares GMAAN with several advanced time series prediction methods.

- **Holt Winters Exponential Smoothing (HWES)** [9]: This is a prediction model based on trend and seasonal decomposition of time series.
- **Seasonal and Trend decomposition using Loess (STL)** [10]: By decomposing the time series into trend components, seasonal components and residual components, local weighted regression (Loess) and data fitting are performed to model.
- **Vector Autoregression (VAR)** [11]: It is a statistical model used to analyze the relationship between multiple time series variables.
- **Autoregressive Integrated Moving Average (ARIMA)** [12]: This model models and predicts time series data by capturing the autocorrelation of data through the autoregressive part, eliminating the non - stationarity of data through the differential part, and smoothing random errors through the moving average part.
- **Seasonal Autoregressive Integrated Moving Average with eEcological regulators (SARIMAX)** [13]: It is an extension of the ARIMA model.
- **Recurrent Neural Network (RNN)** [14]: It is a neural network architecture for processing sequence data.
- **INFORMER** [15]: This is a time series prediction model based on Transformer architecture.
- **TIMESNET** [16]: It is a time series prediction model, which improves the accuracy and robustness of time series prediction by building a multi - scale time feature extraction module and an adaptive weight allocation mechanism.
- **TIMEMIXER** [17]: This is a new time series hybrid model. It improves the overall time series prediction performance by integrating the advantages of a variety of different time series prediction methods.

3.4 Experimental Setup

The parameters of the combined gravity model in this experiment, including vehicle equivalence, basic attributes of service areas, and distance between service areas, can all be queried in the dataset. And the potential coefficient needs to be quickly located through trial and error methods and meta learning. The experiment will divide the service area according to the actual road layout and redistribute it based on the initial vehicle equivalent using a gravity model. The initial vehicle equivalent F is predicted using traditional time series forecasting methods. And use the most effective method to predict the results as the initial value for the gravity model. The method used in this experiment is the TIMEMIXER algorithm. On the basis of the initial prediction algorithm, the gravity model is used for reallocation to obtain the final results.

In this experiment, the prediction of gravity model coefficients integrates cluster analysis, high-quality prior data from trial-and-error methods, and meta-learning. Clustering similar service areas reduces modeling complexity. Trial-and-error methods generate reliable initial data. Meta-learning enables rapid adaptation to new tasks, incorporating service area attributes for personalized predictions. This approach improves prediction efficiency, accuracy, and model generalization, ensuring practical and stable coefficients. The prediction process is as follows:

(1) Calculate the average vehicle equivalent, maximum vehicle equivalent, May Day vehicle equivalent, and Eleven vehicle equivalent for each service area. Using these four sets of data as features, KMeans clustering was performed on the service areas to obtain four groups of service areas. The clustering diagram of the service areas is shown in Fig. 2.
(2) Each group selects 3 service areas and randomly searches 1000 times using a trial and error method to obtain better coefficients. Six groups are calculated separately, resulting in a total of 72 sets of coefficient data. The partially calculated potential coefficients are shown in Table 2.

Table 2. Potential coefficient of trial calculation

Group	α	β	γ	δ	ε	ζ
1	1.50	0.13	0.61	0.27	0.12	1.07
2	0.61	1.14	0.28	0.20	0.16	0.45
3	0.24	1.19	0.54	0.24	0.24	0.95
4	0.14	0.57	1.37	0.13	0.13	0.25
5	0.96	0.59	0.58	0.25	0.25	0.85
6	1.36	0.13	0.19	0.19	0.19	1.05

(3) Use 72 sets of data as prior knowledge for meta learning calculations, and then use transfer learning to ultimately determine the potential coefficients for each highway service area road when using the gravity model. An example of the potential coefficient for meta learning localization is shown in Table 3.

Table 3. Potential coefficient of meta-learning orientation

Group	α	β	γ	δ	ε	ζ
1	0.32	1.92	0.11	0.72	0.81	0.38
2	0.45	1.50	0.51	0.35	0.71	0.38
3	2.00	0.83	0.11	0.90	0.10	1.19

Based on the above experimental steps, the final specific and experimentally feasible gravity model can be obtained. With the help of the optimizer's multiple iterations, it is possible to more accurately predict the vehicle equivalent distribution data on the highway service area road under the influence of the gravity model. In order to pursue the optimal performance of experimental prediction results, this experiment conducted comprehensive experimental testing on the G15 Shenhai Highway, carefully selecting 5 different types of optimizers for comparative analysis. These optimizers include unconstrained optimizer BFGS, unconstrained optimizer L-BFGS-B, single constraint optimizer COBYLA, multi constraint optimizer SLSQP with single constraint, and multi constraint optimizer SLSQP *. After experimentation and data analysis, the experimental results shown in Fig. 3 were obtained, laying a solid foundation for subsequent research.

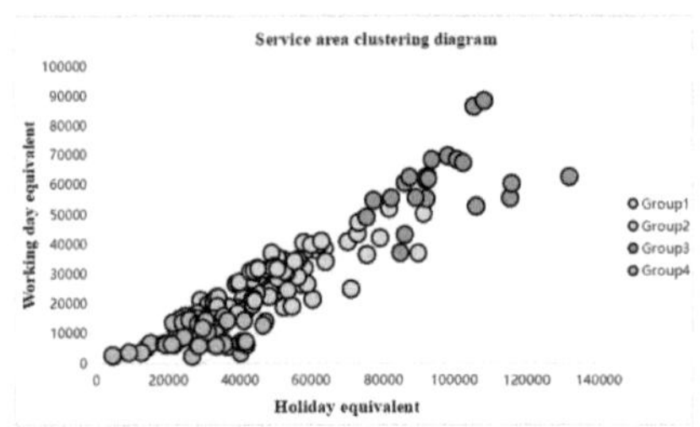

Fig. 2. Service area clustering diagram.

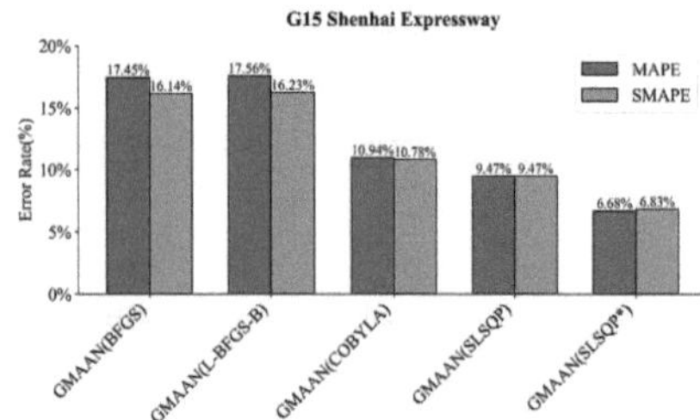

Fig. 3. Comparison of Multiple Optimizer Results.

As shown in Fig. 3, the SLSQP * optimizer with multiple constraints exceeds the MAPE and SMAPE metrics of other optimizers in the G15 Shenhai Highway dataset. Compared with the BFGS optimizer, the MAPE index dropped by 10.77%, the SMAPE index dropped by 9.31%, the L-BFGS-B optimizer dropped by 10.88%, the SMAPE index dropped by 9.4%, and the COBYLA optimizer dropped by 4.26%, the SMAPE index dropped by 3.95%. This fully reflects its excellent optimization ability. By comparing SLSQP, the multi constraint optimizer with single constraint, and SLSQP *, the multi constraint optimizer with multiple constraints, we can find that SLSQP * decreases by 2.79% on the MAPE index and 2.64% on the SMAPE index, which proves that adding constraints can improve the effect of the optimizer's iterative prediction.

3.5   Experimental Results and Analysis

The potential coefficient based on the positioning of the appeal experiment and the optimal multi constraint optimizer SLSQP * obtained from the experiment were compared on G60 HuKun Highway, G15 Shenhai Highway and G25 Changshen Highway respectively. There are nine methods for comparison.

As shown in Table 4, GMAAN exceeds baseline's MAE measurements on all datasets, and also exceeds baseline's MAPE and SMAPE measurements on most datasets, reflecting its robust performance. This highlights the effectiveness of secondary allocation and multi constraint optimizer. Compared with TIMEMIXER, GMAAN generates a more reliable allocation strategy by combining the relationship between service areas. GMAAN also combines the small sample learning module and the migration learning method to quickly locate the potential coefficient in the secondary allocation, so as to achieve more reasonable traffic flow throughput in the service area. On the G60 HuKun highway data set, GMAAN has achieved impressive performance 2141.70 on MAE, GMAAN achieves impressive performance with an MAE of 2141.70, an MAPE of 5.94% and an SMAPE of 6.14%. With TIMEMIXER, the MAPE index decreased by 9.39%, and the SMAPE index decreased by 7.9%. On the G15 Shenhai Highway dataset, GMAAN stands out with 6.68% MAPE and 6.83% SMAPE, which is 6.76% lower than TIMEMIXER algorithm in MAPE index and 5.26% lower in SMAPE index. On the G25 Changshen highway dataset, the MAE index is 1135.35 lower than that of TIMEMIXER algorithm. These results highlight the prediction ability of GMAAN in terms of vehicle equivalent in highway service areas, and prove the effectiveness of the method.

Table 4. Below are the results of various comparison methods for predicting service area traffic equivalent, evaluated using the MAE, MAPE, and SMAPE metrics. The best result in each experimental group is highlighted in bold, and the second-best result is marked with an underline.

Model	G60Hukun			G15Shenhai			G25Changshen		
	MAE	MAPE	SMAPE	MAE	MAPE	SMAPE	MAE	MAPE	SMAPE
HWES	20346.3	39.34%	32.28%	10551.4	35.10%	28.83%	8547.9	26.75%	21.62%
STL	20116.7	39.32%	32.37%	10156.5	34.70%	28.80%	7751.2	24.04%	20.18%
VAR	17892.1	34.49%	28.86%	9706.4	31.25%	26.04%	6733.5	21.74%	18.42%
SARIMAX	19835.7	38.75%	31.96%	10899.9	34.84%	28.34%	7559.8	23.64%	20.01%
ARIMA	18628.9	36.10%	30.03%	9970.1	32.13%	26.52%	7106.1	22.44%	19.05%
RNN	9318.8	17.78%	16.87%	3289.1	11.12%	13.00%	6466.9	27.06%	24.81%
INFORMER(21)	12967.9	24.89%	21.78%	5073.0	17.07%	15.70%	6982.4	21.71%	<u>17.67%</u>
TIMESNET(23)	11021.1	20.59%	18.08%	5861.1	18.91%	16.28%	6707.2	<u>21.23%</u>	18.47%
TIMEMIXER(24)	<u>7391.9</u>	<u>15.33%</u>	<u>14.08%</u>	<u>3151.6</u>	<u>13.44%</u>	<u>12.09%</u>	<u>5404.2</u>	**17.46%**	**15.44%**
GMAAN(Ours)	**2141.7**	**5.94%**	**6.14%**	**2118.2**	**6.68%**	**6.83%**	**4268.9**	22.21%	24.54%

4   Conclusion

Based on the traditional time series prediction method, this paper proposes a gravity model for the secondary allocation of vehicle equivalent, GMAAN, which is used to predict the vehicle equivalent in highway service areas. The model comprehensively considers the impact of service areas on each other, and has achieved good results on the data set of service areas provided by relevant units of the transportation industry in the past three years. The experimental results show that this model has a greater improvement in time series prediction than the mainstream statistical model and neural network model.

Acknowledgments. This work was funded by the National Science and Technology Major Project (2022ZD0119103) and the Natural Science Foundation of Zhejiang Province of China under Grant (No. LHZSD24F020001). The authors express their gratitude for the advanced computing resources offered by the Supercomputing Center at Hangzhou City University.

References

1. Huang, W., Song, G., Hong, H., Xie, K.: Deep architecture for traffic flow prediction: deep belief networks with multitask learning. IEEE Trans. Intell. Transp. Syst. **15**(5), 2191–2201 (2014)
2. Kang, D., Lv, Y., Chen, Y.: Short-term traffic flow prediction with LSTM recurrent neural network. In: 2017 IEEE 20th International Conference on Intelligent Transportation Systems (ITSC), pp. 1–6. IEEE (2017)
3. Zhao, W., Gao, Y., Ji, T., Bai, X., Chen, H.: Deep temporal convolutional networks for short-term traffic flow forecasting. IEEE Access **7**, 114496–114507 (2019)
4. Zhao, L., Song, Y., Deng, M., Li, H.: Temporal graph convolutional network for urban traffic flow prediction method. arXiv preprint arXiv:1811.05320 (2018)
5. Zhao, L., et al.: T-GCN: a temporal graph convolutional network for traffic prediction. IEEE Trans. Intell. Transp. Syst. **21**(9), 3848–3858 (2019)
6. Han, X., Gong, S.: LST-GCN: long short-term memory embedded graph convolution network for traffic flow forecasting. Electronics **11**(14), 2230 (2022)
7. Baiqiang, J., Yanjun, X., Tao, Z.: An expressway holiday flow forecasting model integrating ST-GCN algorithm Journal of Shanghai Institute of Shipping. Science **45**(05), 58–65 (2022)
8. Zhu, J., Han, X., Deng, H., Tao, Y., Zhao, L.: KST-GCN: a knowledge-driven spatial-temporal graph convolutional network for traffic forecasting. IEEE Transactions on Intelligent Transportation Systems (2022)
9. Kalekar, P.S.: Time series forecasting using Holt-Winters exponential smoothing. Kanwal Rekhi Sch. Inf. Technol. **4329008**(13), 1–13 (2004)
10. Cleveland, R.B., Cleveland, W.S., McRae, J.E., Terpenning, I.: STL: a seasonal-trend decomposition. J. Official Stat. **6**(1), 3–73 (1990)
11. Lütkepohl, H.: Vector autoregressive models. In: Handbook of Research Methods and Applications in Empirical Macroeconomics, pp. 139–164. Edward Elgar Publishing (2013)
12. Box, G.E., Pierce, D.A.: Distribution of residual autocorrelations in autoregressive-integrated moving average time series models. J. Am. Stat. Assoc. **65**(332), 1509–1526 (1970)
13. Arunraj, N.S., Ahrens, D., Fernandes, M.: Application of SARIMAX model to forecast daily sales in food retail industry. Int. J. Oper. Res. Inf. Syst. **7**(2), 1–21 (2016)

14. Medsker, L.R., Jain, L.: Recurrent neural networks. Design Appl. **5**(64–67), 2 (2001)
15. Zhou, H., et al.: Informer: beyond efficient transformer for long sequence time-series forecasting. Proc. AAAI Conf. Artif. Intell. **35**(12), 11106–11115 (2021)
16. Wu, H., Hu, T., Liu, Y., Zhou, H., Wang, J., Long, M.: TimesNet: temporal 2D-variation modeling for general time series analysis. International Conference on Learning Representations (2023)
17. Wang, S., et al.: TimeMixer: Decomposable multiscale mixing for time series forecasting. arXiv preprint arXiv:2405.14616 (2024)

Multi-agent Collaborative Framework with Few-Shot CoT for Threat Detection

Tianxiang Xu[1], Chang Liu[2], Zihao Wang[3], and Kangsheng Wang[4(✉)]

[1] School of Software and Microelectronics, Peking University, Beijing, China
`xtx_pku@stu.pku.edu.cn`
[2] Department of Hospitality and Business Management, The Technological and Higher Education Institute of Hong Kong, Hong Kong, China
[3] School of Computer Science, China West Normal University, Nanchong, China
[4] School of Computer and Communication Engineering, University of Science and Technology Beijing, Beijing, China
`jackie@ieee.org`

Abstract. To address the challenges of data scarcity, dynamic threats, and real-time detection in complex enterprise networks, this paper proposes a multi-agent collaborative framework integrated with Few-Shot Chain-of-Thought (CoT) reasoning for insider threat detection. The framework coordinates specialized agents—Manager, Behavior Analyst, Searcher, and Reflector—to execute end-to-end log analysis, anomaly detection, and rule refinement. By combining Few-Shot Learning with explicit CoT reasoning, the system generates interpretable detection rules from limited samples and dynamically optimizes them through multi-agent feedback. Evaluations on the CERT-IT r4.2 dataset demonstrate that our method outperforms traditional machine learning, deep learning, and zero-shot/few-shot LLM baselines, achieving 8–12% higher accuracy and 6–23% improvement in F1-score across diverse attack scenarios. Notably, the framework attains 92% rule interpretability and converges to stable rules within 1–2 iterations, reducing false positives/negatives by 30–45% compared to static approaches. These results highlight the effectiveness of integrating multi-agent collaboration and Few-Shot CoT reasoning for scalable, adaptive, and explainable insider threat detection.

Keywords: Multi-Agent Systems · Few-Shot Learning · Chain-of-Thought · Threat Detection · Cybersecurity · Anomaly Detection

1 Introduction

Modern enterprise networks face escalating complexity from cloud computing and big data, amplifying both insider threats and sophisticated external attacks, while traditional detection methods using feature engineering and static rules

T. Zhu et al. (Eds.): KSEM 2025, LNAI 15922, pp. 384–392, 2026.
https://doi.org/10.1007/978-981-95-3058-8_36

prove inadequate in dynamic, data-scarce environments [1]. Multi-Agent Systems (MAS) offer adaptive security solutions through distributed collaboration, hierarchical task decomposition, and agent specialization [2,3], yet cybersecurity anomaly detection continues to struggle with real-time processing demands, adversarial robustness, and limited labeled anomaly data [4]. Emerging techniques like Few-Shot Learning (FSL) and Chain-of-Thought (CoT) reasoning address these challenges by enabling high detection accuracy with minimal training data and enhancing interpretability through structured, step-by-step inference processes [5]. This work presents a novel cybersecurity detection framework integrating multi-agent collaboration with Few-Shot Chain-of-Thought rule generation. The key contributions include:

- **Multi-Agent Collaboration for Threat Detection**: Inspired by the MACRec architecture, we design specialized agents—such as Intelligence Analyst, Strategy Planner, and Rule Evaluator—responsible for data retrieval, user behavior analysis, and validation of detection results.
- **Few-Shot CoT-Based Rule Generation**: Leveraging Few-Shot CoT reasoning, our approach incrementally refines detection rules from a limited set of observed anomalies, dynamically adapting to diverse enterprise network scenarios.
- **Iterative Optimization through Multi-Agent Feedback**: By incorporating iterative dialogue and feedback mechanisms, the system continuously enhances detection accuracy and adaptability.

Our approach addresses fundamental limitations of single-agent and centralized detection systems, demonstrating superior performance in sparse data environments with enhanced responsiveness, scalability, and interpretability.

2   Related Work

Traditional cybersecurity detection methods relying on single-point algorithms struggle with evolving threat landscapes. Recent research advances focus on two complementary paradigms: (1) Multi-Agent Systems (MAS) for distributed threat detection, and (2) Large Language Models (LLMs) with Few-Shot Learning (FSL) and Chain-of-Thought (CoT) reasoning for adaptive rule generation.

2.1   Multi-agent Systems in Threat Detection

Multi-Agent Systems enable collaborative threat detection through distributed intelligence [6]. Li et al. developed a decentralized Multi-Agent Reinforcement Learning (MARL) IDS achieving 97.44% accuracy on NSL-KDD by integrating cloud computing with streaming analytics for real-time processing [7]. In cybersecurity contexts, specialized agents handle log retrieval, behavioral analysis, and threat intelligence correlation, enabling scalable processing of high-concurrency security events. However, data scarcity and environmental dynamics necessitate integration with reasoning mechanisms to enhance generalization against novel threats.

2.2   Few-Shot Learning and Chain-of-Thought Reasoning

FSL combined with LLM reasoning capabilities addresses data scarcity in insider threat detection [8]. FSL recognizes novel anomalous behaviors from minimal labeled samples, while CoT reasoning decomposes inference into interpretable intermediate steps [9]. The typical workflow involves: (1) LLM-based rule generation from limited anomalous samples, (2) iterative refinement through feedback loops, and (3) real-world validation. This paradigm reduces manual annotation dependencies and enables rapid deployment cycles for emerging threats.

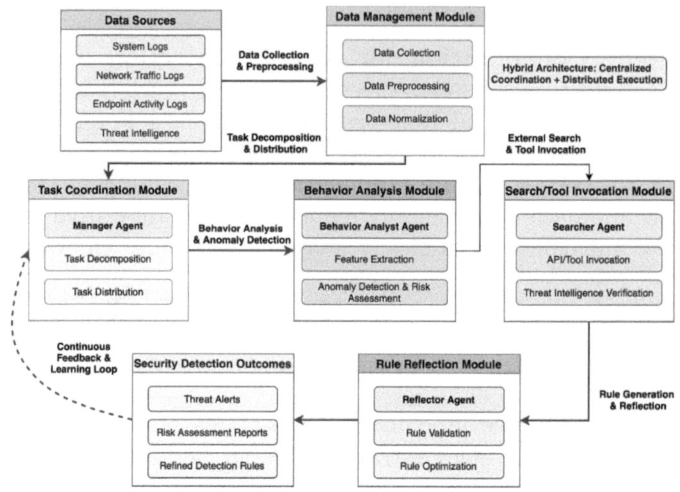

Fig. 1. Multi-agent cybersecurity detection framework.

2.3   Challenges and Research Gaps

Despite MAS scalability [10] and FSL-CoT effectiveness in enterprise environments [12], three critical challenges persist: maintaining real-time performance under high-concurrency loads [13], ensuring adaptive rule evolution with emerging attack vectors [14], and achieving cross-domain generalization across heterogeneous enterprise architectures [15]. Our approach addresses these limitations by integrating MAS with Few-Shot CoT reasoning to deliver scalable, interpretable, and adaptive cybersecurity frameworks.

3   Multi-agent Based Cybersecurity Detection Framework

3.1   Multi-agent Architecture and Specification

The framework orchestrates five specialized agents through distributed message-passing protocols (Fig. 1): **Task Coordination Agent** executes iterative

"Think-Act-Observe" cycles for security request decomposition and multi-agent decision synthesis; **Behavior Analysis Agent** performs multi-dimensional log correlation across user, endpoint, process, and network telemetry to detect anomalous patterns indicative of lateral movement and data exfiltration campaigns; **Search and Tool Invocation Agent** conducts automated threat intelligence aggregation and vulnerability contextualization through external feeds and internal knowledge repositories; **Task Interpretation Agent** transforms abstract security objectives into parameterized execution workflows with formal specification constraints; and **Rule Reflection Agent** delivers continuous detection rule refinement through collaborative optimization feedback loops. The architecture employs centralized coordination with distributed execution, processing multi-source data through format standardization while maintaining continuous rule adaptation through iterative feedback mechanisms.

3.2   Collaboration Protocol

The multi-agent workflow (Fig. 2) initiates upon Manager reception of detection requests, transformed by the Task Interpreter into parameterized execution directives for concurrent Behavior Analyst and Searcher processing, enabling result synthesis through predefined aggregation strategies while the Reflector provides iterative optimization feedback. Inter-agent coordination employs asynchronous messaging with RESTful APIs and distributed queuing for high-concurrency scalability and fault tolerance, incorporating role-based access control and end-to-end encryption. Few-shot learning integration with Chain-of-Thought reasoning enhances detection precision through contextual pattern recognition while mitigating false positive propagation via uncertainty quantification. Empirical evaluation (Table 1) demonstrates superior performance: 92.1% detection accuracy, 1.8-second response latency, and 6.7% false positive rate, with specialized CoT-enabled agents substantially addressing critical false positive challenges in contemporary security detection systems.

4   Multi-step Reasoning and Rule Generation Based on Chain-of-Thought

4.1   Process Architecture

The detection workflow initiates when the Manager distributes annotated anomaly samples to the Behavior Analyst, while the Reflector employs Few-Shot Learning (FSL) and Chain-of-Thought (CoT) techniques for rule generation through multi-step reasoning. This encompasses sample preparation, feature extraction, and model guidance with FSL samples, followed by iterative rule refinement until optimal detection strategies emerge (Fig. 3).

4.2   Few-Shot Sample-Driven Learning

To mitigate data scarcity and imbalanced anomaly distributions, Few-Shot learning incorporates 1–10 labeled examples for analogy-based reasoning, enabling

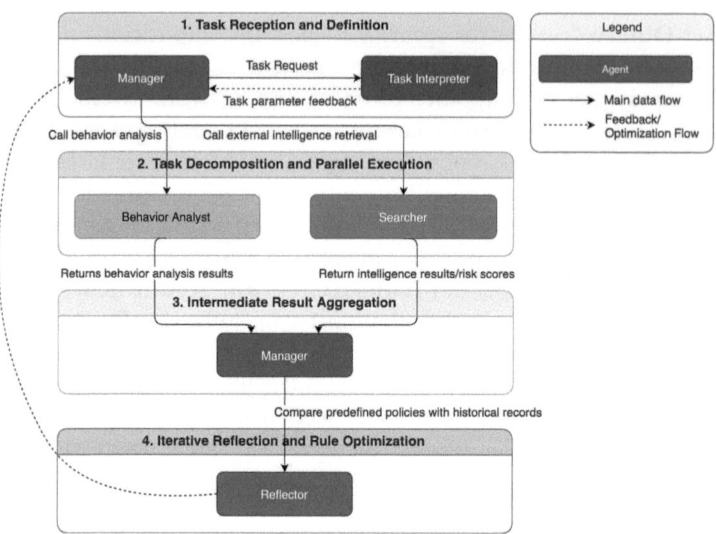

Fig. 2. Multi-agent collaboration workflow and communication mechanism.

effective task comprehension without extensive training data. **Sample Selection Strategy** follows three principles: *representativeness* including common attack vectors and high-risk anomalies (bulk logins, malicious domains, abnormal transfers); *diversity* spanning multiple log types, contexts, and user groups for enhanced generalization; and *ambiguity handling* incorporating edge cases (authorized off-hour access) to minimize false positives in complex scenarios. **Sample Format** pairs input attributes with corresponding labels: $(\text{Logon Time} = 23:30, \text{User} = \text{Alice}, \text{Device} = \text{Desktop-010}) \rightarrow$ Anomalous and $(\text{Logon Time} = 09:10, \text{User} = \text{Bob}, \text{Device} = \text{Laptop-005}) \rightarrow$ Normal. These samples are embedded within prompts following task descriptions, enabling pattern inference for subsequent CoT reasoning and generalizing to unseen anomalies.

4.3   Chain-of-Thought Multi-step Reasoning

CoT reasoning generates explicit intermediate steps before final outputs, providing key advantages: **interpretability** through documented reasoning for analyst auditing; **error traceability** enabling the Reflector to identify and correct logical flaws without retraining; and **progressive induction** decomposing complex detection logic into manageable subproblems: (1) extracting anomaly dimensions (time, frequency, IP reputation), (2) comparing against historical user thresholds, (3) querying external threat intelligence via the Searcher, and (4) generating formalized rules with justification. The Reflector evaluates rule performance using TP/FP metrics, triggering CoT process analysis for high false positive rates and implementing iterative refinements to ensure adaptability to evolving attack tactics.

Table 1. Performance Comparison with Existing Solutions

Metrics	Single-Agent	Conventional MAS	Ours
Detection Accuracy	75.3%	83.7%	**92.1%**
Response Time	4.7 s	3.2 s	**1.8 s**
Scalability	Limited	Moderate	**High**
False Positive Rate	18.5%	12.3%	**6.7%**
Resource Utilization	72%	65%	**54%**
Adaptability	Low	Moderate	**High**

5 Experiment Design and Results Analysis

5.1 Methodology and Experimental Setup

Dataset: Evaluation employed the CERT-IT r4.2 Insider Threat Dataset with multi-source enterprise logs and real-world attack scenarios across four attack types: bulk operations during non-working hours, malicious website access, large email attachments, and frequent USB data exfiltration.

Proposed Method: Multi-Agent Collaboration with Few-Shot Chain-of-Thought inference employs specialized agents (Manager, Behavior Analyst, Searcher, Reflector) for distributed task handling. The method incorporates 5–10 representative examples per attack type for rapid model adaptation through iterative CoT-based rule generation and refinement.

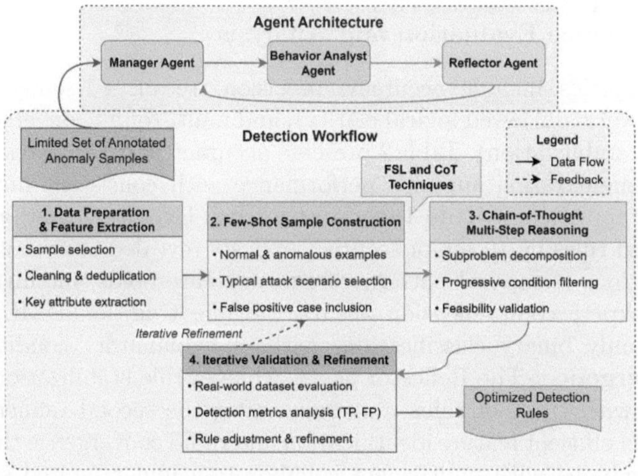

Fig. 3. Multi-agent collaborative threat detection.

Baselines: Traditional ML methods include SVM with TF-IDF/handcrafted features and Random Forest with voting-based detection. Deep learning approaches encompass CNN/LSTM for sequence-based detection and Transformer utilizing self-attention for long-range dependencies. LLM-based methods comprise Zero-Shot prompting without examples and Few-Shot without explicit reasoning steps.

Scenarios: Four attack patterns: (1) bulk operations during off-hours, (2) malicious website access/uploads, (3) large email attachments/frequent external exchanges, (4) frequent USB storage usage indicating potential exfiltration.

Table 2. Detection Performance Across Scenarios

Method	Scenario 1		Scenario 2		Scenario 3		Scenario 4	
	Accuracy	F1	Accuracy	F1	Accuracy	F1	Accuracy	F1
SVM	84.28%	79.35%	92.53%	64.52%	90.86%	60.24%	85.17%	46.23%
Random Forest	86.12%	81.43%	93.69%	67.98%	91.37%	62.15%	88.04%	52.80%
CNN/LSTM	87.55%	82.19%	93.41%	69.07%	92.66%	64.51%	90.18%	57.94%
Transformer	88.36%	83.48%	93.54%	69.52%	93.58%	66.92%	91.03%	59.41%
Zero-Shot	81.72%	76.64%	92.10%	63.05%	90.31%	57.03%	89.26%	45.37%
Few-Shot CoT	89.26%	84.72%	94.22%	71.33%	94.07%	68.55%	93.08%	66.19%
Ours	**91.57%**	**86.65%**	**95.05%**	**73.64%**	**95.16%**	**72.33%**	**94.53%**	**69.84%**

5.2   Performance Evaluation and Analysis

Evaluation metrics include accuracy, precision, recall, F1-score, rule interpretability (expert-reviewed logical clarity), and multi-round convergence (iterations for rule stabilization). Table 2 presents accuracy and F1-scores across four scenarios, demonstrating superior performance with consistent improvements over baseline approaches. **Rule Interpretability:** Expert evaluation of 50 randomly selected rules by 10 senior security analysts revealed 92% contained clear logical conditions (temporal patterns, frequency thresholds, intelligence fields) with ¿95% expert comprehension accuracy, while traditional ML/DL methods provide only binary classifications without explanatory conditions. **Iterative Convergence:** The Reflector agent achieves rule stabilization within 1–2 iterations, with ¿90% of rules converging after the second refinement cycle, demonstrating efficient feature identification and rapid convergence through CoT reasoning combined with multi-agent collaboration under limited sample constraints.

6   Conclusion

Our multi-agent framework integrating Few-Shot learning and Chain-of-Thought reasoning demonstrates superior performance in accuracy and F1-score while providing enhanced interpretability and efficient rule refinement, effectively mitigating labeled data scarcity through FSL-driven detection and CoT-based explainable rule generation with stable convergence within 1–2 iterations for robust anomaly detection in dynamic enterprise environments. The framework addresses fundamental limitations of traditional detection systems by achieving 92.1% detection accuracy with 6.7% false positive rate, demonstrating multi-agent collaboration effectiveness with Few-Shot CoT reasoning for scalable, adaptive, and explainable insider threat detection in complex enterprise networks.

References

1. Liao, H.J., Lin, C.H.R., Lin, Y.C., et al.: Intrusion detection system: a comprehensive review. J. Netw. Comput. Appl. **36**(1), 16–24 (2013)
2. Gronauer, S., Diepold, K.: Multi-agent deep reinforcement learning: a survey. Artif. Intell. Rev. **55**(2), 895–943 (2022)
3. Tao, W., Zhou, Y., Wang, Y., et al.: MAGIS: LLM-based multi-agent framework for GitHub issue resolution. Adv. Neural. Inf. Process. Syst. **37**, 51963–51993 (2025)
4. Bougueroua, N., Mazouzi, S., Belaoued, M., et al.: A survey on multi-agent based collaborative intrusion detection systems. J. Artif. Intell. Soft Comput. Res. **11**(2), 111–142 (2021)
5. Perez, E., Kiela, D., Cho, K.: True few-shot learning with language models. Adv. Neural. Inf. Process. Syst. **34**, 11054–11070 (2021)
6. Van der Hoek, W., Wooldridge, M.: Multi-agent systems. Found. Artif. Intell. **3**, 887–928 (2008)
7. Li, X., Wang, S., Zeng, S., et al.: A survey on LLM-based multi-agent systems: workflow, infrastructure, and challenges. Vicinagearth **1**(1), 9 (2024)
8. Hu, S.X., Li, D., Stühmer, J., et al.: Pushing the limits of simple pipelines for few-shot learning: external data and fine-tuning make a difference. In: Proceedings of the IEEE/CVF Conference on Computer Vision and Pattern Recognition, pp. 9068–9077 (2022)
9. Chen, Y., Cui, M., Wang, D., et al.: A survey of large language models for cyber threat detection. Comput. Secur. 104016 (2024)
10. Tran, H.K.: Deep Reinforcement Learning for Artificial Intelligence-Enabled Autonomous Penetration Testing in Cyber Security. University of Technology Sydney (Australia) (2022)
11. Mondal, D., Modi, S., Panda, S., et al.: KAM-CoT: knowledge augmented multimodal chain-of-thoughts reasoning. In: Proceedings of the AAAI Conference on Artificial Intelligence, vol. 38, no. 17, pp. 18798–18806 (2024)
12. Mai, Y., Gao, Z., Hu, X., et al.: Are human rules necessary? Generating reusable APIs with cot reasoning and in-context learning. Proc. ACM Softw. Eng. **1**(FSE), 2355–2377 (2024)
13. Naseer, H., Desouza, K., Maynard, S.B., et al.: Enabling cybersecurity incident response agility through dynamic capabilities: the role of real-time analytics. Eur. J. Inf. Syst. **33**(2), 200–220 (2024)

14. Zhang, Y., Li, R., Wu, N., et al.: Dissect black box: interpreting for rule-based explanations in unsupervised anomaly detection. Adv. Neural. Inf. Process. Syst. **37**, 84169–84196 (2024)
15. Huang, H., Poor, H.V., Davis, K.R., et al.: Toward resilient modern power systems: from single-domain to cross-domain resilience enhancement. Proc. IEEE **112**(4), 365–398 (2024)

CombDE: Direct-Distillation Combined with Self-distillation for Knowledge Graph Embeddings

Yusi Chen[✉] [iD], Hongtao Zhou, and Housheng Su

School of Artificial Intelligence and Automation, Huazhong University of Science and Technology, Wuhan 430074, China
{m202373516,zht730}@hust.edu.cn

Abstract. Knowledge graph embedding (KGE) is a simple and effective method for knowledge graph completion. The higher the embedding dimension, the higher the model performance. However, the increase in embedding dimension leads to a significant rise in storage and computation. In this paper, we propose CombDE, a knowledge distillation framework for KGE models to address this problem. First, CombDE introduces self-distillation, so that the student model could retain more performance of the teacher model in each distillation. Secondly, considering the influence of unreliable knowledge transfer on distillation performance, a dynamic adjustment mechanism of the soft label is proposed, which dynamically allocated weights through dynamic distillation temperature and truth value judgment to optimize distillation. Experiments show that our CombDE achieves optimal distillation performance compared to the baseline model. Meanwhile, on average, CombDE can reduce the training time by more than 70%.

Keywords: Knowledge distillation · Knowledge graph embedding · Knowledge graph completion · Self-knowledge distillation · Link prediction

1 Introduction

Knowledge Graph Embedding (KGE) model based on link prediction is the most commonly used Knowledge Graph Completion method at present. To obtain higher model performance, existing models such as TransE [1], ComplEx [11], SimplE [5], and RotatE [9] are usually trained with higher embedding dimensions and model size. However, an increase in embedding dimensions brings with it a rapid increase in model size and the cost of inference time. In recent years, although there have been several KD-based KGE model compressions [3,6,12–14], they suffer from the following three obvious problems: First, excellent teacher models do not necessarily train excellent student models. It is clear evidence that the gap in model size between teachers and students affects distillation performance [7]. Second, the knowledge passed on by teachers may not be completely

T. Zhu et al. (Eds.): KSEM 2025, LNAI 15922, pp. 393–402, 2026.
https://doi.org/10.1007/978-981-95-3058-8_37

reliable. In theory, the KGE model will give higher scores to positive triples and lower scores to negative triples, but the opposite may be true for triples that are difficult for the KGE model to grasp. Third, the model takes a long time to train. Although they have good distillation performance, the long training time is not good for updating the model.

To solve the above problems, we propose CombDE, a new distillation framework for KGE models. Different from the traditional direct distillation framework, CombDE adopts the idea of self-knowledge distillation to transform the direct distillation method and apply it to KGE distillation. Using self-distillation, CombDE narrowed the output distribution gap between the teacher model and the student model at each step of training. At the same time, the structure of direct distillation makes up for the defects of low prediction accuracy in the early stage of self-distillation training. To reduce the impact of unreliable knowledge transfer, we propose a novel dynamic adjustment mechanism for soft label weights. It contains real logit tuning and dynamic distillation temperature. **Our key contributions are summarized as follows:**

- We propose an efficient knowledge distillation framework CombDE for knowledge graph embedding, which reduces model size and inference time, while the low-dimensional student model can well maintain the performance of the high-dimensional teacher model by combining self-distillation with direct distillation.
- We design a new dynamic adjustment mechanism for soft labels in CombDE to reduce the influence of unreliable knowledge transfer on distillation performance.

2   Related Works

With the increasing application of KD in the field of deep learning, there are also researchers trying to use knowledge distillation methods to compress embedded models. MulDE [12] employs multiple low-dimensional teacher models to improve the effectiveness of the student model but ignores the dimensional gap that affects the distillation performance. DualDE [14] is the first single-teacher distillation method for KGE, which uses a two-stage distillation, narrowing the gap between the teacher and student models. Considering the dimensionality gap between the teacher model and the student model, IterDE [6] adopts iterative distillation to reduce dimensionality step by step. STDE [3] considered that the quality of knowledge transmitted would affect the performance of distillation, and proposed that the teacher model generate negative samples that are difficult to distinguish for training the student model. SKDE [13] was the first to apply self-knowledge distillation to KGE compression and verify the effectiveness of self-knowledge distillation.

3   Methods

3.1   Background

Given the set $\mathcal{E}$ of entities and the set $\mathcal{R}$ of relations, and the set $\mathcal{T}$ of triples (facts) of the form $(h, r, t) \subset \mathcal{E} \times \mathcal{R} \times \mathcal{E}$, KGs are denoted by $\mathcal{G} = (\mathcal{E}, \mathcal{R}, \mathcal{T})$. The triplet (h, r, t) represents the head entity h, and the tail entity t is represented in the graph by the relation r. The KGEs defines the original (h, r, t) triples as positive triples T^+, randomly replaces h or t as negative triples T^-, and then sets a scoring function S on the vector representation of the triples. Usually, the binary cross-entropy (BCE) loss can be used to optimize the score function which is calculated as follows:

$$\mathcal{L}_{BCE} = - \sum_{(h,r,t) \in T} [p \log \sigma(S) + (1 - p) \log(1 - \sigma(S))] \tag{1}$$

whereT $\in T^+ \cup T^-$, $p = 1$ for positive triples and $p = 0$ for negative triples. σ is the Softmax function.

In general, KD will introduce temperature t when the model output softmax function is normalized, and the Kullback-Leibler (KL) divergence will be used. The prediction distribution $p_i^t = (p_i^t(1), ..., p_i^t(N)) \in R^{1 \times N}$ in the improved softmax classifier is formulated as:

$$p_i^t(n) = \frac{\exp\left(f(s_n)/t\right)}{\Sigma_{j=1}^N \exp\left(f(s_j)/t\right)} \tag{2}$$

where $f(s_n)$ is the score function S in (1). The loss function of KD is formulated as:

$$L_{KD} = \sum_{i=1}^{n} t^2 \cdot D_{KL}(\widetilde{p_l^t} \| p_i^t) \tag{3}$$

where $\widetilde{p_l^t}$ and p_i^t are the soft label probabilities, from teacher and student models respectively, processed by (3).

Then, we introduce the various modules in CombDE. These include direct-distillation combined self-knowledge distillation and soft label dynamic adjustment (Fig. 1).

3.2   Direct Combined Self-distillation for KGEs

The KD loss function is divided into two parts, the original loss and the distillation loss. We define L_{Hard} of the student model as the KGE original loss L_{BCE}. We first input a triplet (h, r, t) into the pre-trained teacher model and the untrained student model. Then, we get a score S_T for the teacher model and a score S_S for the student model. Considering that the KL divergence has asymmetric problems, we use Huber loss instead of KL divergence to calculate the distillation loss which is formulated as:

$$L_{huber} = \begin{cases} \frac{1}{2}(S_T - S_S)^2, & |S_T - S_S| \ll 1 \\ |S_T - S_S| - \frac{1}{2}, & |S_T - S_S| > 1 \end{cases} \tag{4}$$

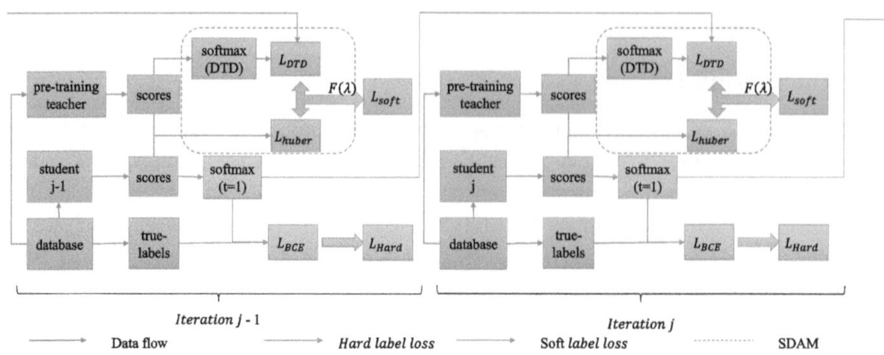

Fig. 1. The framework of CombDE. The part surrounded by the orange dashed line is SDAM, which is the soft-label dynamic adjustment mechanism. Green data streams only represent data transmission, gray data streams represent participation in hard label loss calculation, and orange data streams represent participation in soft label loss calculation. (Color figure online)

In order to reduce the impact of the dimensional gap and improve the efficiency of distillation, we improve the direct distillation framework by using the idea of self-distillation. For each iteration training, we keep the logit score $f(s_n)$ of the student model for this time and release it for the next use. In the jth iteration of training, our model takes the scores $f(s_j)$ and $f(s_{j-1})$ into (2) to obtain the normalized distribution predictions $p_i^{t,j}$ and $p_i^{t,j-1}$ at temperature t. The soft label loss of self-distillation is the traditional KD distillation loss, usually the KL divergence loss. The $\widetilde{p_i^t}$ and p_i^t in (3) are respectively denoted as p_i^t and p_{i-1}^t in the ith iteration, which is formulated as:

$$L_{KL} = \sum_{i=1}^{n} t^2 \cdot D_{KL}(p_i^{t,j} || p_i^{t,j-1}) \tag{5}$$

3.3 Soft-Label Dynamic Adjustment Mechanism

In general, the distillation temperature is fixed during the training of KD. Different logits produce different levels of information loss at the same distillation temperature. At a low distillation temperature, Logit loses some discriminative information. The distillation temperature is too high and the indistinguishable logit will get confused predictions. Therefore, we adopt DTD and customize the distillation temperature for each logit. The soft label loss is modified as follows:

$$L_{DTD} = \sum_{i=1}^{n} t_d^2 \cdot D_{KL}(p_i^{t_d,j} || p_i^{t_d,j-1}) \tag{6}$$

where t_d is sample-wise temperature in (6), and the calculation formula is as follows:

$$t_d = t_0 + \left(\frac{\sum_{i=1}^{n} w_i}{n} - w_d \right)\beta \tag{7}$$

where t_0 and β denote the base temperature and bias in (7). And w_d is sample-wise normalized weight, describing the extent of confusion. w_i is used to calculate the average of w_d over a batch. Here is how to calculate w_d. The specific calculation method is as follows:

$$w_d = \frac{1}{s_{max}} \tag{8}$$

where s_{max} represents the max output of logits produced by student in the jth iteration. The larger s_{max} the smaller w_d means that logit is less easily confused and the larger t_d the soft target retains more category information. The smaller s_{max} and the larger w_d means that logit is difficult to distinguish, and a smaller t_d gives the soft target more discriminative information.

Finally, we define the overall training loss L of the student model as follows:

$$L_{soft} = L_{huber} + L_{DTD} \tag{9}$$

$$L = L_{Hard} + \lambda L_{soft} \tag{10}$$

where λ is the weighting of soft label loss to balance L_{Hard} and L_{soft}. In addition, the parameters of the teacher model are fixed during the training process, and only the student model is trained.

4   Experiments

We evaluate the effectiveness and generalization ability of our CombDE by link prediction tasks. Given a triple (h, r, t) in the dataset, we replace t with all other entities, and then score and rank all generated triples to get $rank^t$. Then, we calculate MRR, $Hits@1$, $Hits@3$, and $Hits@10$ of rank as evaluation metrics. The higher MRR, $Hits@1$, $Hits@3$, and $Hits@10$, the better performance a KGE has.

Our experiments seek to answer the following research questions (RQs):

- RQ1: Can CombDE optimize model performance?
- RQ2: Can CombDE be lightweight while reducing training time?
- RQ3: What role do SKD and SDAM play in CombDE?

4.1   Datasets and Baselines

We use two popular and open datasets for link prediction experiments: FB15K-237 [10] and WN18RR [2]. FB15K-237 is a subset of Freebase [1], and WN18RR is a subset of WordNet [1].

We adopt four commonly used KGE models, including TransE, ComplEx, SimplE and RotatE. In addition to directly training the distilling-free student model, we also compare CombDE with some strong distillation methods: BKD [4], RKD [8], DualDE [14], IterDE [6] and SKDE [13].

Table 1. Link prediction results on KB15K-237

Dim	Method	TransE				ComplEx				SimplE				RotatE			
		MRR	H10	H3	H1	MRR	H10	H3	H1	MRR	H10	H3	H1	MRR	H10	H3	H1
512	Tea	.286	.481	.312	.185	.271	.445	.300	.185	.262	.435	.291	.176	.326	.520	.356	.229
64	No-KD	.223	.447	.263	.153	.189	.360	.209	.105	.112	.253	.119	.047	.280	.458	.310	.191
	BKD	.273	.447	.305	.184	.183	.351	.209	.100	.113	.256	.120	.048	.280	.461	.312	.190
	RKD	.227	.385	.252	.148	.135	.273	.148	.068	.107	.238	.113	.034	.146	.243	.158	.095
	DualDE	**.275**	**.451**	**.307**	**.186**	.190	.357	.210	.110	.120	.252	.138	.053	**.302**	**.484**	**.337**	**.209**
	SKDE	.271	.449	.303	.181	.186	.356	.205	.104	.119	.253	0.135	.052	.280	.460	.310	.190
	IterDE	.273	.448	.306	.184	.248	**.408**	**.272**	.168	.233	.397	.256	.152	.257	.428	.284	.172
	CombDE	.279	.457	.311	.191	**.248**	.408	.276	**.166**	**.201**	**.352**	**.218**	**.127**	.306	.489	.340	.215

Table 2. Link prediction results on WN18RR

Dim	Method	TransE				ComplEx				SimplE				RotatE			
		MRR	H10	H3	H1	MRR	H10	H3	H1	MRR	H10	H3	H1	MRR	H10	H3	H1
512	Tea	.224	.520	.385	.029	.395	.446	.413	.362	.386	.468	.418	.337	.473	.578	.493	.420
64	No-KD	.215	.493	.383	.020	.333	.452	.372	.265	.201	.361	.231	.123	.427	.454	.425	.398
	BKD	**.215**	**.497**	.378	**.019**	.327	.457	.372	.254	.207	.369	.240	.126	.459	.564	**.485**	**.401**
	RKD	.167	.397	.297	.014	.274	.377	.329	.207	.23	.357	.277	.158	.125	.171	.140	.098
	DualDE	.212	.489	**.381**	.018	.320	.452	.368	.244	.209	.364	.242	.131	**.460**	.559	.48	.408
	SKDE	.213	.491	.381	.019	.324	.451	.367	.254	.194	.357	.224	.115	.456	**.564**	.481	.398
	IterDE	.212	.491	.378	.018	**.393**	.441	**.408**	**.365**	**.385**	**.436**	**.399**	**.354**	.413	.540	.449	.340
	CombDE	.224	.523	.394	.023	.405	**.452**	.418	.377	**.372**	.463	.409	**.315**	.468	.563	.488	.425

4.2   Comparison for Performance (RQ1)

The main experimental results are shown in Table 1 for FB15K-237 and Table 2 for WN18RR. The red bold numbers are the best results and the bold numbers are the second-best results between different methods. No-KD denotes the results of models without distillation. First, we notice a significant performance difference between the high-dimensional teacher model and the low-dimensional No-KD student model. The performance of the low-dimensional student model after CombDE distillation is significantly improved compared with that before distillation. Compared to the No-KD student models, the MRR of TransE, ComplEx, SimplE, and RotatE can be improved by 25% (from 0.223 to 0.279), 26% (from 0.189 to 0.238), 79% (from 0.112 to 0.201), and 9% (from 0.280 to 0.306), respectively, after CombDE distillation on FB15K-237. On WN18RR, the performances of these four models can be improved by 1%, 21%, 85%, and 9% compared to no distillation. Moreover, the low-dimensional student model after CombDE distillation can retain most of the teacher model performance. On FB15K-237, these four models can retain 97%, 91%, 77%, and 94% of homogeneous teacher model performance. On WN18RR, these four models can achieve 100%, 103%, 96%, and 99% of homogeneous teacher model performance. These results show that CombDE achieves good distillation results on numerous models and datasets.

Second, Tables 1 and 2 indicate that CombDE achieves optimal or suboptimal results in the vast majority of distillations. Specifically, compared with the other five baseline models on FB15K-237, CombDE improves the MRR on average by 6%, 36%, 57%and 29% respectively. On WN18RR, CombDE can improve the MRR on average by 10%, 25%, 61%, and 59% compared with the other five baseline models. Even with IterDE, the latest model for KGEs distillation, CombDE still achieves better distillation performance on most results. CombDE compared to IterDE on FB15K-237, the MMR of TransE is improved by 2%, the MRR of ComplEx is reduced by 0.1%, the MRR of SimplE is reduced by 13%, and the MRR of RotatE is improved by 19%. On WN18RR, the MMR of TransE is improved by 5%, the MRR of ComplEx is improved by 3%, the MRR of SimplE is reduced by 0.3%, and the MRR of RotatE is improved by 13%. In addition, CombDE can obtain more accurate prediction results. CombDE's $Hits@1$ are on average 2.6% higher than IterDE on FB15K-237 and 11.3% on WN18RR. Although CombDE fails to achieve optimality in a small number of indicators, from the perspective of comprehensive distillation performance and prediction accuracy, CombDE is indeed better than the existing methods.

4.3 Comparison for Training Time (RQ2)

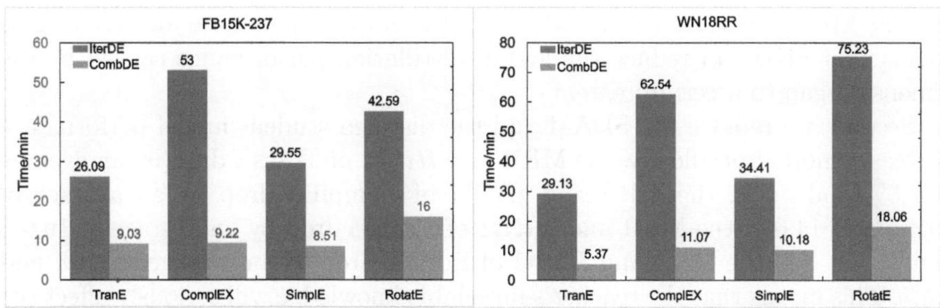

Fig. 2. Distillation training time (min) compared to strong baseline models.

In order to compare the training time between CombDE and the currently best baseline model IterDE, we recapitulated IterDE under the same experimental setup. The results for the training time are shown in Fig. 2. It can be seen that compared with IterDE, the training time of CombDE is less than half of IterDE, and the time saving can be more than 70% on average. In particular, CombDE saves the training time of Complex by 82%. There are two reasons why CombDE can save training time: the first is that the training of CombDE is one step, while IterDE requires several complete iterations of training. The second is that CombDE uses self-distillation to improve the direct distillation framework, which further accelerates the convergence and reduces the training time.

4.4   Ablation Experiments (RQ3)

Table 3. Ablation experimental results

Dataset	Method	TransE		ComplEx		SimplE		RotatE	
		MRR	H1	MRR	H1	MRR	H1	MRR	H1
FB15K-237	CombDE	**.2799**	**.1914**	**.2482**	**.1663**	**.2017**	**.1275**	**.3067**	**.2152**
	-SKD	.2796	.1914	.2441	.1626	.1957	.1200	.3045	.2125
	-SDAM	.2787	.1900	.2223	.1433	.1858	.1078	.3035	.2105
WN18RR	CombDE	**.2240**	**.0239**	**.4055**	**.3779**	**.3725**	**.3154**	**.4689**	**.4258**
	-SKD	.2239	.0239	.3768	.3326	.3496	.2874	.4588	.4215
	-SDAM	.2238	.0224	.3636	.3192	.2782	.1965	.4606	.4224

We conduct ablation experiments to investigate the impact of self-knowledge distillation (SKD) and soft label dynamic adjustment mechanism (SDAM). The results of FB15K-237 and WM18RR ablation experiments are shown in Table 3. After removing SKD first, all student model results decreased compared to before removing. Specifically, the MRR and $Hit@1$ of TransE drop by an average of 0% and 0%, the MRR and $Hit@1$ of ComplEx drop by an average of 4.3% and 7.1%, the MRR and $Hit@1$ of SimplE drop by an average of 4.5% and 7.3%, and the MRR and $Hit@1$ of RotatE drop by an average of 1.4% and 1.1%. This means that SKD can reduce the loss of distillation performance caused by the dimension gap to a certain extent.

Second, we remove the SDAM and the distilled student model performance decreases more. Specifically, the MRR and $Hit@1$ of TransE drop by an average of 2.5% and 3.3%, the MRR and $Hit@1$ of ComplEx drop by an average of 10.4% and 14.6%, the MRR and $Hit@1$ of SimplE drop by an average of 16.6% and 26.5%, and the MRR and $Hit@1$ of RotatE drop by an average of 1.4% and 1.5%. This means that the teacher's unreliable knowledge will seriously affect the performance of the student model. We evaluate the soft labels assign different weights to the soft labels and dynamically assign the distillation temperature to the soft labels to help the student model learn reliable knowledge from unreliable knowledge.

5   Conclusion

In this paper, we propose CombDE, a novel distillation framework for KGEs with good performance and less training cost. CombDE introduces self-distillation to improve the direct distillation framework, which uses self-distillation to strengthen the performance retention of each distillation and alleviates the problem of the dimension gap between the teacher model and the student model. In addition, we also designed a soft label dynamic adjustment mechanism, including dynamic temperature and unreliable soft label weight adjustment, which improves the performance of the student model. In the future, we will explore how to apply self-distillation to multi-teacher KGEs distillation, considering relation categories and studying teacher combinations.

Acknowledgement. This work was supported by the National Natural Science Foundation of China under Grant No. 62425602.

References

1. Bordes, A., Usunier, N., García-Durán, A., Weston, J., Yakhnenko, O.: Translating embeddings for modeling multi-relational data. In: Neural Information Processing Systems (2013). https://api.semanticscholar.org/CorpusID:14941970
2. Dettmers, T., Minervini, P., Stenetorp, P., Riedel, S.: Convolutional 2D knowledge graph embeddings (2018). https://arxiv.org/abs/1707.01476
3. Guo, X., Wang, P., Gao, N., Wang, X., Feng, W.: STDE: a single-senior-teacher knowledge distillation model for high-dimensional knowledge graph embeddings. In: 2022 IEEE 2nd International Conference on Information Communication and Software Engineering (ICICSE), pp. 37–45 (2022). https://doi.org/10.1109/ICICSE55337.2022.9828905
4. Hinton, G., Vinyals, O., Dean, J.: Distilling the knowledge in a neural network (2015). https://arxiv.org/abs/1503.02531
5. Kazemi, S.M., Poole, D.L.: Simple embedding for link prediction in knowledge graphs. In: Neural Information Processing Systems (2018). https://api.semanticscholar.org/CorpusID:3674966
6. Liu, J., Wang, P., Shang, Z., Wu, C.: IterDE: an iterative knowledge distillation framework for knowledge graph embeddings. In: AAAI Conference on Artificial Intelligence (2023). https://api.semanticscholar.org/CorpusID:259629787
7. Mirzadeh, S.I., Farajtabar, M., Li, A., Levine, N., Matsukawa, A., Ghasemzadeh, H.: Improved knowledge distillation via teacher assistant (2019). https://arxiv.org/abs/1902.03393
8. Park, W., Kim, D., Lu, Y., Cho, M.: Relational knowledge distillation. In: 2019 IEEE/CVF Conference on Computer Vision and Pattern Recognition (CVPR), pp. 3962–3971 (2019). https://doi.org/10.1109/CVPR.2019.00409
9. Sun, Z., Deng, Z.H., Nie, J.Y., Tang, J.: RotatE: knowledge graph embedding by relational rotation in complex space. In: International Conference on Learning Representations (2019). https://openreview.net/forum?id=HkgEQnRqYQ
10. Toutanova, K., Chen, D., Pantel, P., Poon, H., Choudhury, P., Gamon, M.: Representing text for joint embedding of text and knowledge bases. In: Màrquez, L., Callison-Burch, C., Su, J. (eds.) Proceedings of the 2015 Conference on Empirical Methods in Natural Language Processing, pp. 1499–1509. Association for Computational Linguistics, Lisbon, Portugal (2015). https://doi.org/10.18653/v1/D15-1174, https://aclanthology.org/D15-1174/
11. Trouillon, T., Welbl, J., Riedel, S., Gaussier, É., Bouchard, G.: Complex embeddings for simple link prediction. ArXiv abs/1606.06357 (2016). https://api.semanticscholar.org/CorpusID:15150247

12. Wang, K., Liu, Y., Ma, Q., Sheng, Q.Z.: MulDE: multi-teacher knowledge distillation for low-dimensional knowledge graph embeddings. In: Proceedings of the Web Conference 2021, pp. 1716–1726. WWW '21, ACM (2021). https://doi.org/10.1145/3442381.3449898
13. Xu, H., Wang, Y., Fan, J.: Self-knowledge distillation for knowledge graph embedding. In: International Conference on Language Resources and Evaluation (2024). https://api.semanticscholar.org/CorpusID:269803970
14. Zhu, Y., et al.: DualDE: dually distilling knowledge graph embedding for faster and cheaper reasoning. In: Proceedings of the Fifteenth ACM International Conference on Web Search and Data Mining (2020). https://api.semanticscholar.org/CorpusID:245124050

Rethinking Lightweight and Efficient Human Pose Estimation with Star Operation Reconstruction

Zhoujie Xu[1] , Meng Dai[1(✉)] , Qing Zhang[1] , and Huawen Liu[2]

[1] School of Computer Science and Information Engineering, Shanghai Institute of Technology, Shanghai 201418, China
daimeng@sit.edu.cn

[2] School of Mechanical and Electrical Engineering, Shaoxing University, Shaoxing 312000, China

Abstract. Lightweight human pose estimation has long been a research hotspot and challenge in the field. Most existing methods primarily rely on introducing the high-resolution design pattern from HRNet and subsequently performing lightweight modifications. However, the multi-resolution branches in this paradigm result in a bottleneck in terms of throughput. To address this issue, this study proposes StarPose, a single-branch, upsampling-free macro architecture based on HRPVT. By optimizing all micro block designs from a lightweight perspective and reconstructing the network using the advanced star operation design insight, the proposed method can handle high-dimensional features while computing in a low-dimensional space, akin to the mechanism of kernel functions, thereby achieving more effective semantic feature representation. The proposed method achieves 2 × faster inference speed than Lite-HRNet under nearly the same model complexity on the MS COCO benchmark, while maintaining superior accuracy. This significant improvement unlocks greater potential for deployment on resource-constrained edge devices. The code and models can be accessed publicly at https://github.com/george-xu-code/StarPose.

Keywords: human pose estiamtion · lightweight · efficient · transformer · computer vision

1 Introduction

2D Human pose estimation (HPE) is a fundamental task in computer vision, which involves detecting keypoint positions on the human body and classifying these keypoints for each individual in an image. Its importance spans a variety of downstream applications, including action recognition [1] and human-object interaction [2]. However, HPE remains a challenging task, with model lightweighting being one of the key hurdles. Numerous studies have proposed solutions to address this challenge, among which Lite-HRNet [3] stands out as one of the most prominent. Built upon the popular HRNet [4] architecture, Lite-HRNet introduces the shuffle [5] block and leverages conditional channel weighting to overcome the costly pointwise convolutions, achieving state-of-the-art performance and inspiring a wide range of subsequent research [6–8]. As illustrated in Fig. 1, while it strikes an excellent balance between performance and model complexity, it still faces certain limitations in real-time inference speed due to the multi-resolution branches inherent in the HRNet architecture. These limitations can be attributed to two main factors. First, the high-resolution branches in HRNet are often redundant for models operating in low-computation region, as demonstrated by Lite-Pose [9]. Second, the need to maintain multiple branches throughout the inference process, with the final prediction being made on the highest-resolution feature map, presents challenges for resource-constrained edge devices [10].

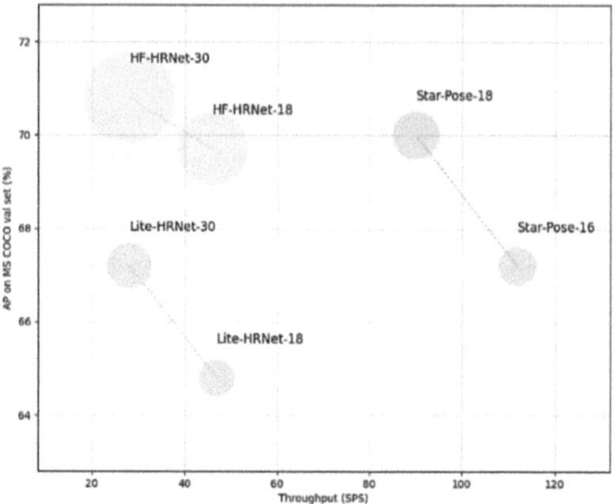

Fig. 1. The comparison of StarPose and state-of-the-art methods on the MS COCO val set in terms of model size, throughput, and precision. The size of each bubble reflects the number of parameters in the model. All models were tested on a single RTX 2080 Ti GPU with a batch size of 1

Recently, the introduction of the coordinate classification paradigm [11] has provided fresh perspectives for the design of lightweight network architectures. One such example is HRPVT [12], which, by incorporating the intrinsic inductive biases of Convolutional Neural Networks (CNNs) into the hierarchical Transformer architecture, and utilizing Simcc [11] as a coordinate classifier, achieves a single-branch network structure without upsampling. This allows the model's final predictions to be made on low-resolution feature maps that retain high semantic information. Compared to the HRNet's architecture, this structure demonstrates superior model throughput, and its proposed Stage-wise Insertion strategy offers new insights into the design of lightweight pose estimation models. Despite offering higher inference speed, its model performance cannot match that of Lite-HRNet due to the absence of information fusion capabilities in the multi-resolution branches. As the field of HPE continues to advance, so does progress in efficient network technologies. Among these, the most noteworthy innovation is the star operation [13], known as element-wise multiplication. In contrast to the traditional addition operation, the star operation possesses the distinctive ability to implicitly account for high-dimensional features while performing computations in a lower-dimensional space, which is highly advantageous for lightweight networks with low-dimensional characteristics. Thus, a reasonable assumption is that when the macro architecture of HRPVT and the micro block design with star operations are united, their synergy may have the potential to unlock new heights of performance.

Motivated by this, the present study introduces StarPose, which revisits and improves HRPVT-S from the perspective of model lightweighting. StarPose achieves a lightweight and efficient HPE model that strikes a favorable trade-off between model throughput and detection accuracy by further leveraging the star operation to reconstruct all the block structures, distinguishing itself from the HRNet architecture. Main contributions of this study are summarized as follows:

- This study reviews the bottleneck of HRNet-based multi-branch structure in terms of inference speed for lightweight networks, while rethinking and resolving the performance limitations of single-branch HRPVT from the perspective of high-dimensional implicit feature mapping.
- We take the macro architecture of HRPVT-S as the baseline and enhance it by optimizing the micro block design for lightweight efficiency. Additionally, the concept of star operations is employed to restructure the entire network, further improving model performance with almost no increase in complexity.
- StarPose has achieved superior performance on the MS COCO benchmarks. It outperforms Lite-HRNet on the `val2017` benchmark with approximately a 4% performance improvement while achieving three times the throughput.

2 Related Work

2.1 Lightweight 2D Human Pose Estimation

Lite-HRNet [3] replaces costly pointwise convolutions with a lightweight conditional channel weighting unit, leveraging HRNet's multi-resolution information for linear complexity and superior performance. Dite-HRNet [6] uses dynamic split convolution and adaptive context modeling in lightweight blocks for efficient multi-scale contextual extraction and long-range spatial dependency modeling. HF-HRNet [8] is designed with hardware-friendly architecture to achieve higher inference speeds on specialized devices such as Neural Processing Units (NPUs) and Graphics Processing Units (GPUs). Despite the success of HRNet-based networks, Lite-Pose [9] identifies redundancy in HRNet's high-resolution branches for low-computation regions through gradual shrinking experiments, enhancing both efficiency and performance upon removal. RTMPose [10] is the first attempt to use a single-branch feature extractor and introduces the trimmed SimCC method to eliminate the costly upsampling layers, while also achieving higher inference speed through a series of tricks. Inspired by this, HRPVT [12] leverages the more powerful feature extractor and further improves accuracy by incorporating the inductive bias of CNNs into high-resolution feature maps.

2.2 Design Insights for Efficient Networks

Over the past few years, a variety of groundbreaking ideas have emerged to boost network efficiency. These innovations encompass techniques such as depth-wise convolution

[14], feature reuse [15], and re-parameterization [16]. Unlike traditional approaches, the star operation [13] introduces a novel method for designing efficient networks. It uniquely enables the implicit handling of extremely high-dimensional features, all while operating within a low-dimensional computational space, which in turn diminishes the incremental benefits of widening the network. This distinctive advantage sets the star operation apart from other techniques in efficient network design.

3 Methodology

In this study, we follow the Stage-wise Insertion principle of HRPVT and use HRPVT-S as the baseline for improvements. The goal of this study is to further investigate the potential of the coordinate classification paradigm in designing 2D HPE models without the use of upsampling layers. The specific network architecture is shown in Fig. 2.

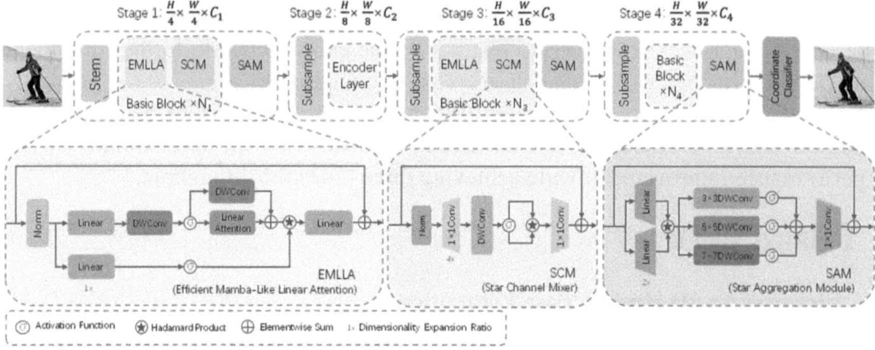

Fig. 2. Illustration of the structure of StarPose

3.1 Preliminaries

In a single-layer neural network, the star operation, also known as the Hadamard product, can be defined as $\left(W_1^T X\right) \odot \left(W_2^T X\right)$, where $W = \begin{bmatrix} W \\ B \end{bmatrix}$ and $X = \begin{bmatrix} X \\ 1 \end{bmatrix}$. Given two affine transformation weight vectors $w_1, w_2 \in \mathbb{R}^{(d+1)\times 1}$, and an individual token feature vector $x \in \mathbb{R}^{(d+1)\times 1}$ in the network feature flow, where w_1 may be identical to w_2, the star operation can be simplified and derived as follows:

$$w_1^T x * w_2^T x = \left(\sum_{i=1}^{d+1} w_1^i x^i\right) * \left(\sum_{j=1}^{d+1} w_2^j x^j\right)$$

$$= \underbrace{\alpha_{(1,1)} x^1 x^1 + \cdots + \alpha_{(i,j)} x^i x^j + \cdots + \alpha_{(d+1,d+1)} x^{d+1} x^{d+1}}_{(d+2)(d+1)/2 \text{ items}} \quad (1)$$

where i and j are the indices of the feature vector, and α is the coefficient for each item:

$$\alpha(i,j) = \begin{cases} w_1^i w_2^j & \text{if } i = j, \\ w_1^i w_2^j + w_1^j w_2^i & \text{if } i \neq j. \end{cases} \tag{2}$$

When $w_1 = w_2$, that is, when x undergoes the same affine transformation twice:

$$\alpha(i,j) = \begin{cases} w^i w^j & \text{if } i = j, \\ 2w^i w^j & \text{if } i \neq j. \end{cases} \tag{3}$$

As observed by Eq. 1, a single star operation generates $\frac{(d+2)(d+1)}{2}$ distinct items. Generally, when $W_1, W_2 \in \mathbb{R}^{(d+1)\times(d'+1)}$, it can demonstrate the feature representation capacity of $\Omega\left(\frac{d^2}{2}\right)$, despite x resides in $(d'+1)$ dimensions. And as the number of layers l increases, i.e., $X_l = W_{l,1}^\mathrm{T} X_{l-1} \odot W_{l,2}^\mathrm{T} X_{l-1}$, X_l can express high-dimensional latent features of the deep neural network in a finite feature space, with an exponential growth of $\mathcal{O}\left(d^{2^l}\right)$.

3.2 Efficient Mamba-Like Linear Attention

Although Spatial Reduction Attention (SRA) in HRPVT reduces computational costs compared to Multi-Head Self Attention (MHSA) [17] by using a sparse spatial scale approach, its reliance on Softmax attention maintains an $\mathcal{O}(N^2)$ complexity, making it rarely used in lightweight architectures. To address the high computational cost caused by attention operations, SRA is replaced with Mamba-Like Linear Attention (MLLA) [18]. MLLA deconstructs Mamba [19] into a linear attention mechanism with an advanced block design. This enables it to achieve a linear complexity of $\mathcal{O}(N)$ while outperforming vanilla linear attention [20]. Given this advantage, MLLA is well-suited for integration into lightweight network designs. The specific comparisons are illustrated in the equations below.

$$(\Omega\text{SRA}) = \underbrace{2N\left(\frac{N}{R^2}\right)C}_{\text{MHSA}} + \underbrace{2\left(\frac{N}{R^2}\right)C^2}_{\text{k/v}} + \underbrace{4NC^2}_{\text{SR(k/v), q, out}} \tag{4}$$

$$(\Omega\text{MLLA}) = \underbrace{2NC^2}_{\text{Linear Attention}} + \underbrace{5NC^2}_{\text{in/out, q/k, gate}} + \underbrace{2k^2NC}_{\text{dwconv}} \tag{5}$$

When the input size is 256×192, whether N is maximized at 64×48 or minimized at 8×6 (in which case no SR operation occurs), it can be demonstrated that the theoretical computational complexity of MLLA is relatively lower. However, in terms of inference speed, we found that MLLA performs worse than SRA, mainly due to the use of Rotary Position Embedding (RoPE) [21] in MLLA. RoPE applies rotations to each positional feature vector based on its 2D spatial coordinates, requiring both real and imaginary components for each position encoding, thus constraining the feature dimension to multiples of four. In the macro design of lightweight network, model performance is sensitive to feature dimensions, with wider and shallower networks showing significant improvements in inference speed at similar model complexities. For example, as shown in Table 1, increasing the width from 16 to 18 boosts inference speed by 22% while resulting in modest accuracy degradation. Therefore, RoPE is less advantageous in efficient HPE networks. Consequently, Efficient Mamba-Like Linear Attention (EMLLA) is proposed, a variant of MLLA without RoPE. Interestingly, it can be observed that the block design in MLLA utilizes the star operation.

Table 1. A comprehensive comparison among different attention types

	SRA dim $= 16$, [3, 4, 6]	SRA dim $= 18$, [2, 3, 5]	MLLA dim $= 16$, [3, 4, 6]	EMLLA dim $= 16$, [3, 4, 6]	EMLLA dim $= 18$, [2, 3, 5]
Params	2.0M	2.0M	2.0M	2.0M	2.0M
FLOPs	0.5G	0.5G	0.5G	0.5G	0.5G
Throughput	100	123	75	86	105
AP	65.6	65.0	67.5	67.3	67.2

3.3 Star Aggregation Module

While High-Resolution Pyramid Module (HRPM) in HRPVT enhances performance in medium and small scale HPE by aggregating multi-scale representations within high-resolution feature maps, obtaining high-quality, high-resolution representations incurs significant computational costs, which hampers lightweight network inference. To address this, Star Aggregation Module (SAM) is proposed, a module that refines HRPM's structure with several key improvements: (1) replacing transposed and strided convolutions with point-wise convolution to form an inverted residual structure [14]; (2) substituting the hybrid-dilated convolutions (HDC) structure with depth-wise convolutions of the same receptive field to reduce number of parameters; and (3) two additional linear transformations are added before the HDC structure, followed by a star operation to form the star augmentation (SA). The formulas are shown below:

$$SAM\,(f_i) = PConv\left(\sigma\left(\sum_{j=1}^{k} HDC(SA(f_i); k)\right)\right) + f_i \tag{6}$$

where

$$SA(x) = Linear_1(x) \odot Linear_2(x), \tag{7}$$

$$HDC(x; k) = \left[\phi^{DW_1}(x; 3); \ldots; \phi^{DW_k}(x; 2k+1)\right]. \tag{8}$$

Here, $f_i \in \mathbb{R}^{H_i \times W_i \times C_i}$ represents the input feature map of the ith stage, $\sigma(\cdot)$ denotes the activation function, $PConv(\cdot)$ indicates the point-wise convolutional layer. $\phi^{DW_j}(\cdot)$ denotes function learned by j^{th} depth-wise convolution and $(2k+1)$ symbolizes the kernel size of $\phi^{DW_k}(\cdot)$.

3.4 Star Channel Mixer

The original Convolutional Feed Forward Network (CFFN) is also improved into a more effective Star Channel Mixer (SCM). Specifically, a residual branch was added after the activation function, but this branch directly performs the star operation with the main branch without any additional processing. On one hand, CFFN accounts for a significant portion of the computational cost within the overall network architecture, so structural adjustments to this component could potentially introduce more computational load than changes in other parts. On the other hand, simply applying the star operation is sufficient to achieve higher-dimensional feature mapping, as CFFN already operates in a high-dimensional space, and as shown in Eq. (3), the same linear transformation yields an equivalent effect.

4 Experiments

4.1 Experimental Setting

Datasets and Evaluation Metric. The MS COCO dataset [22] contains over 200 K images and 250 K labeled person instances, each with 17 keypoints. Models are trained on the MS COCO train2017 dataset, which includes 57 K images and 150 K person instances. Performance is evaluated on two subsets: the val2017 set (5 K images) and the test-dev2017 set (20 K images). The evaluation metrics include Average Precision (AP) and Average Recall (AR), which are calculated using Object Keypoint Similarity (OKS), a measure of alignment between ground truth and predicted keypoints.

Table 2. Comparisons on the COCO val set. Pre = pretrain the backbone on the ImageNet classification task, Samples Per Second (SPS) was tested on a single RTX 2080 Ti GPU with a batch size of 1.

Method	Backbone	Pre	Input size	Params	GFLOPs	AP	AP^{50}	AP^{75}	AP^M	AP^L	AR	Throughput (SPS)
Large Networks												
SimpleBaseline [23]	ResNet-50	Y	256 × 192	34.0M	8.9	70.4	88.6	78.3	67.1	77.2	76.3	242
HRNet [4]	HRNet-W32	N	256 × 192	28.5M	7.1	73.4	89.5	80.7	70.2	80.1	78.9	56
HRFormer [24]	HRFormer-S	Y	256 × 192	7.8M	2.8	73.8	90.4	81.2	-	-	79.3	32
HRPVT [12]	HRPVT-L	Y	256 × 192	25.1M	5.4	75.2	90.6	82.4	72.1	81.4	80.4	105
Small Networks												
LiteHRNet [3]	LiteHRNet-18	N	256 × 192	1.1M	0.20	64.8	86.7	73.0	62.1	70.5	71.2	47
LiteHRNet	LiteHRNet-18	N	384 × 288	1.1M	0.45	67.7	87.8	75.0	64.5	73.7	73.7	47
LiteHRNet	LiteHRNet-30	N	256 × 192	1.8M	0.31	67.2	88.0	75.0	64.3	73.1	73.3	28
LiteHRNet	LiteHRNet-30	N	384 × 288	1.8M	0.70	70.4	88.7	77.7	67.5	76.3	76.2	28

(continued)

Table 2. *(continued)*

Method	Backbone	Pre	Input size	Params	GFLOPs	AP	AP^{50}	AP^{75}	AP^M	AP^L	AR	Throughput (SPS)
EANet [7]	EANet-tiny	N	256 × 192	1.2M	0.27	66.4	87.3	74.3	63.5	72.2	72.4	-
EANet	EANet-tiny	N	384 × 288	1.2M	0.56	68.6	87.7	76.0	65.3	74.7	74.7	-
EANet	EANet-base	N	256 × 192	1.9M	0.42	68.8	88.3	76.9	65.9	74.8	74.8	-
EANet	EANet-base	N	384 × 288	1.9M	0.88	71.6	89.0	78.4	68.2	77.8	77.4	-
HF-HRNet [8]	HF-HRNet-18	N	256 × 192	4.6M	0.7	69.7	88.5	77.6	66.5	75.7	75.4	46
HF-HRNet	HF-HRNet-18	N	384 × 288	4.6M	1.5	72.4	89.3	79.3	68.9	79.2	77.9	46
HF-HRNet	HF-HRNet-30	N	256 × 192	7.4M	1.1	70.8	88.9	78.0	67.6	77.3	76.5	28
HF-HRNet	HF-HRNet-30	N	384 × 288	7.4M	2.5	73.5	89.6	80.7	70.0	80.2	78.7	28
Star-Pose(Ours)	Star-Pose-16	N	256 × 192	1.3M	0.26	67.2	87.6	74.6	64.6	72.5	72.9	112
Star-Pose(Ours)	Star-Pose-16	N	384 × 288	1.4M	0.59	70.2	88.6	77.2	67.3	75.9	75.6	112
Star-Pose(Ours)	Star-Pose-18	N	256 × 192	1.9M	0.45	70.0	88.5	77.5	67.2	75.6	75.6	90
Star-Pose(Ours)	Star-Pose-18	N	384 × 288	2.0M	1	72.7	89.4	79.9	69.8	78.5	78.0	90

Implementation Details. StarPose adopts a top-down paradigm, first utilizing person detection results from previous work [23], and then applying StarPose to these boxes for single-person pose estimation. The cropped boxes are resized to 256 × 192 or 384 × 288 ensuring equitable comparisons with other approaches. Models with two different capacities were trained from scratch on RTX 2080Ti and RTX 3080Ti using the mmpose [25] codebase. The Adam optimizer was used with a learning rate of 1×10^{-3}, which was reduced by a factor of 10 at epoch 220 and by a factor of 5 at epoch 250, for a total of 260 epochs.

4.2 Main Results

MS COCO. As shown in Table 2, the performance of the proposed method not only surpasses the current state-of-the-art approach EANet at nearly the same model complexity but also achieves a better trade-off compared to HF-HRNet. Specifically, the proposed StarPose-18, at a resolution of 384 × 288, reduces the parameter count by 56% compared to HF-HRNet-18 while achieving a 0.3 AP improvement. Remarkably, it is even competitive with larger networks such as HRNet without pretraining. This superior performance remains consistent across COCO `test-dev` benchmark shown in Table 3, demonstrating the strong generalization capability of the proposed method.

Table 3. Comparisons on the COCO `test-dev` set. All models were trained with an input size of 384×288.

Method	Pre	Params	GFLOPs	AP
Large Networks				
SimpleBaseline [23]	Y	68.6M	35.6	73.7
HRNet-W32 [4]	Y	28.5M	16	74.9
HRFormer-S [24]	Y	7.8M	6.2	74.5
Small Networks				
MobileNetV2 [14]	Y	9.8M	3.3	66.8
ShuffleNetV2 [5]	Y	7.6M	2.9	62.9
HRPVT-S [12]	Y	5M	2.7	72.5
LiteHRNet-18 [3]	N	1.1M	0.4	66.9
LiteHRNet-30	N	1.8M	0.7	69.7
HF-HRNet-18 [8]	N	4.6M	1.5	71.7
HF-HRNet-30	N	7.4M	2.5	72.5
StarPose-16 (Ours)	N	1.4M	0.59	69.3
StarPose-18 (Ours)	N	2.0M	1	71.7

In terms of throughput, StarPose-18 significantly outperforms LiteHRNet-based models, delivering a 2x speedup accompanied by a 2.3 AP gain over LiteHRNet-30. Notably, it can be observed that networks based on the HRNet architecture exhibit a throughput gap compared to single-branch hierarchical networks, reinforcing the earlier hypothesis.

4.3 Ablation Study

The Effect of Proposed Components. As previously demonstrated, EMLLA has proven effective for HRPVT-S, and thus it is adopted as the baseline to further evaluate other components. As shown in Table 4, when the micro block structure is adjusted to SCM and SAM, performance improvements of 0.4 AP and 1.0 AP, respectively, are observed. These results demonstrate the effectiveness of our star reconstruction method. Finally, the simultaneous incorporation of SCM and SAM achieves a remarkable 70 AP. It is evident that the introduction of SAM enables the entire network to be reconstructed by the star operation, thereby amplifying the benefits of SCM and underscoring their complementary nature.

Table 4. Ablation study of proposed components on the COCO `val2017` set. 'w/o star' indicates replacing the star operation with element-wise addition.

	Star-Pose-16	Star-Pose-18	Star-Pose-36
star	67.2	70.0	74.5
add	66.1	69.0	73.9

The effect of star operations. Experiments are also conducted to evaluate the benefits of star operations across different model capacities. Specifically, all star operations in three models were replaced with element-wise addition. As shown in Table 5, the impact of the star operation gradually diminishes as the model capacity increases. This finding further supports the previous hypothesis that the star operation is more suitable for lightweight networks with low-dimensional spatial features, where it enables implicit high-dimensional mapping and achieves superior performance.

Table 5. Ablation study of star operations on the COCO `val2017` set.

EMLLA dim = 18, [2, 3, 7]	SCM	SAM w/o star	SAM	AP
✓				68
✓	✓			68.4
✓		✓		68.8
✓			✓	69.0
✓	✓	✓		69.7
✓	✓		✓	70

5 Conclusion

This study revisits the efficiency bottlenecks in HRNet-based multi-branch structures and addresses performance limitations of single-branch HRPVT through high-dimensional feature mapping. By refining HRPVT-S's micro design and integrating star operations to reconstruct, the proposed method boosts network throughput while improving accuracy. On COCO val2017, StarPose outperforms Lite-HRNet by ~ 4% with 2 × higher throughput, demonstrating an optimal accuracy-efficiency trade-off for lightweight pose estimation.

Acknowledgments. This study was supported in part by grants from the Natural Science Foundation of Shanghai, China (Grant Nos. 19ZR1455300 and 21ZR1462600), and in part by the Zhejiang Provincial Natural Science Foundation (Grant No. LZ23F020003).

References

1. Liu, H., et al.: TranSkeleton: hierarchical spatial-temporal transformer for skeleton-based action recognition. IEEE Trans. Circuits Syst. Video Technol. **33**(8), 4137–4148 (2023). https://doi.org/10.1109/tcsvt.2023.3240472
2. Cheng, Y., et al.: Multi-scale human-object interaction detector. IEEE Trans. Circuits Syst. Video Technol. **33**(4), 1827–1838 (2022). https://doi.org/10.1109/tcsvt.2022.3216663
3. Yu, C., et al.: Lite-HRNet: a lightweight high-resolution network. 2022 IEEE/CVF Conference on Computer Vision and Pattern Recognition (CVPR) (2021). https://doi.org/10.1109/cvpr46437.2021.01030
4. Sun, K., et al.: Deep high-resolution representation learning for human pose estimation. 2022 IEEE/CVF Conference on Computer Vision and Pattern Recognition (CVPR), pp. 5686–5696 (2019). https://doi.org/10.1109/cvpr.2019.00584
5. Ma, N., et al.: ShuffleNet V2: practical guidelines for efficient CNN architecture design. In: Lecture Notes in Computer Science, pp. 122–138 (2018). https://doi.org/10.1007/978-3-030-01264-9_8
6. Li, Q., et al.: DITE-HRNET: dynamic lightweight high-resolution network for human pose estimation. Proceedings of the Thirty-First International Joint Conference on Artificial Intelligence, pp. 1095–1101 (2022). https://doi.org/10.24963/ijcai.2022/153
7. Chen, B., et al.: EANet: towards lightweight human pose estimation with effective aggregation network. In: 2023 IEEE International Conference on Multimedia and Expo (ICME), pp. 2639–2644. IEEE, Brisbane, Australia (2023). https://doi.org/10.1109/ICME55011.2023.00449
8. Zhang, H., et al.: HF-HRNet: a simple hardware friendly high-resolution network. IEEE Trans. Circuits Syst. Video Technol. **34**(8), 7699–7711 (2024). https://doi.org/10.1109/tcsvt.2024.3377365
9. Wang, Y., et al.: Lite pose: efficient architecture design for 2D human pose estimation. 2022 IEEE/CVF Conference on Computer Vision and Pattern Recognition (CVPR) (2022). https://doi.org/10.1109/cvpr52688.2022.01278
10. Jiang, T., et al.: RTMPose: Real-Time Multi-Person Pose Estimation based on MMPose (2023). http://arxiv.org/abs/2303.07399
11. Li, Y., et al.: SIMCC: a simple coordinate classification perspective for human pose estimation. In: Lecture Notes in Computer Science, pp. 89–106 (2022). https://doi.org/10.1007/978-3-031-20068-7_6
12. Xu, Z., et al.: HRPVT: high-resolution pyramid vision transformer for medium and small-scale human pose estimation. Neurocomputing 129154 (2024). https://doi.org/10.1016/j.neucom.2024.129154
13. Ma, X., et al.: Rewrite the stars. 2022 IEEE/CVF Conference on Computer Vision and Pattern Recognition (CVPR) **25**, 5694–5703 (2024). https://doi.org/10.1109/cvpr52733.2024.00544
14. Sandler, M., et al.: MobileNetV2: inverted residuals and linear bottlenecks. 2018 IEEE/CVF Conference on Computer Vision and Pattern Recognition, pp. 4510–4520 (2018)
15. Chen, J., et al.: Run, Don't Walk: Chasing Higher FLOPS for Faster Neural Networks (2023). http://arxiv.org/abs/2303.03667
16. Ding, X., et al.: REpVGG: making VGG-style convnets great again. 2022 IEEE/CVF Conference on Computer Vision and Pattern Recognition (CVPR), pp. 13728–13737 (2021). https://doi.org/10.1109/cvpr46437.2021.01352

17. Dosovitskiy, A., et al.: An image is worth 16x16 Words: transformers for image recognition at scale. International Conference on Learning Representations (2021)

18. Han, D., et al.: Demystify Mamba in Vision: A Linear Attention Perspective. ArXiv. abs/2405.16605 (2024)

19. Gu, A., Dao, T.: Mamba: Linear-Time Sequence Modeling with Selective State Spaces. ArXiv. abs/2312.00752, (2023)

20. Katharopoulos, A., et al.: Transformers are RNNs: fast autoregressive transformers with linear attention. International Conference on Machine Learning 1, 5156–5165 (2020)

21. Su, J., et al.: RoFormer: enhanced transformer with rotary position embedding. Neurocomputing **568**, 127063 (2023). https://doi.org/10.1016/j.neucom.2023.127063

22. Lin, T.-Y., et al.: Microsoft COCO: common objects in context. In: Lecture Notes in Computer Science, pp. 740–755 (2014). https://doi.org/10.1007/978-3-319-10602-1_48

23. Xiao, B., et al.: Simple baselines for human pose estimation and tracking. In: Lecture Notes in Computer Science, pp. 472–487 (2018). https://doi.org/10.1007/978-3-030-01231-1_29

24. Yuan, Y., et al.: HRFormer: high-resolution vision transformer for dense predict. Neural Information Processing Systems **34** (2021)

25. MMPose Contributors.: OpenMMLab Pose Estimation Toolbox and Benchmark (2020). https://github.com/open-mmlab/mmpose

Comparing Large Language Model-Based Prompt Engineering Strategies with Feature Engineering Strategies for Complex Word Identification

Tonghui Han[1,2,3], Yaxin Bi[1], Maurice Mulvenna[1], Xiaolu Liu[2], Zixian Meng[3], and Dongqiang Yang[3(✉)]

[1] Ulster University, Belfast BT15 1ED, UK
[2] Binzhou Polytechnic, Binzhou 256603, China
[3] Shandong Jianzhu University, Jinan 250101, China
ydq@sdjzu.edu.cn

Abstract. Prompt engineering has proven effective across various tasks, minimizing reliance on extensive training data. However, its potential for complex word identification (CWI), a key step in lexical simplification, remains unexplored. This study evaluates the effectiveness of prompt engineering for CWI using open-source large language models (LLMs) and compared a new feature engineering-based that integrates diverse features into neural network classifiers. Experimental results show LLMs' have strong language understanding and generation capabilities, yet feature engineering-based strategy has advantage for such specific classification tasks. Finally, we provide recommendations on how to improving designs of LLMs' prompts in order for such classification tasks.

Keywords: Prompt engineering · Feature engineering · Complex word identification · Large language models · Neural networks

1 Introduction

Prompt engineering with large language models (LLMs) eliminates the requirement for additional training on large datasets due to its remarkable language understanding capacity obtained from pre-trained knowledge. Therefore, it has been widely adopted in various tasks, such as mathematical reasoning, question answering, story writing, and code generation [1,2]. However, the literature reports less work on the application of prompt engineering to specific legacy tasks that continue to play a pivotal role. For instance, complex word identification is essential for lexical simplification tasks and assists non-native English learners in comprehending the text. Nevertheless, there is limited studies on utilizing prompt engineering for CWI tasks to date.

In this paper, we propose to investigate the application of prompt engineering in CWI tasks. Although numerous open-source LLMs, such as DeepSeek [3],

T. Zhu et al. (Eds.): KSEM 2025, LNAI 15922, pp. 415–423, 2026.
https://doi.org/10.1007/978-981-95-3058-8_39

LLaMA [4], and Gemma [5], have been released, specific LLMs are absent for CWI. Consequently, in this project, we select several prominent open-source general-purpose models for our experiments. To evaluate the performance of prompt engineering in CWI works, we design a series of neural network classifiers based on our feature engineering strategy and compare their results with those obtained by LLMs. An intriguing result reveals that our classifiers outperform general-purpose LLMs and some state-of-the-art (SOTA) classifiers. The key contributions of this paper are as follows:

– We investigate the application of prompt engineering for Complex Word Identification (CWI) using five open-source general-purpose LLMs from the Ollama platform[1], and then we instruct them to annotate the given words as complex or simple by leveraging their outstanding language understanding capacity.
– We then design a series of CWI strategies based on feature engineering. The experiment results reveal that our strategies outperform general-purpose LLMs and beat the majority of the models submitted in Complex Word Identification (CWI) Shared Task 2018 [6].
– Our findings indicate that the neural network-based classification works are influenced by the questions attributes, feature scale, and model size. For the CWI task, the scale of features does not exhibit a direct relationship with classification performance. Similarly, classifiers with simpler structures outperform those complex models, which contradicts our initial hypothesis. These findings reaffirm the relevance of deep learning in targeted classification tasks and highlight the importance of appropriate feature and model selection.

2   Related Works

2.1   Prompt Engineering

Prompt engineering has significantly reshaped the research process, enabling SOTA performance in various domains. Unlike traditional methods, prompt engineering utilizes the advanced language understanding capabilities of LLMs, leveraging few, one, and zero-shot strategies to achieve optimal results [1]. For instance, Han et al. [7] introduced an approach to integrate logic rules into prompt tuning to enhance the LLMs' performance in identifying text semantic relationships. Additionally, [8] demonstrated its superiority over traditional machine learning and deep learning methods in text classification. However, its application to CWI remains largely unexplored. To address this gap, we evaluate the performance of general-purpose LLMs on the CWI task.

2.2   Complex Word Identification

CWI aims to detect difficult words in context, serving as a critical step in lexical simplification. Prior studies have explored diverse approaches. [9] proposed an

---

[1] https://ollama.com/.

ensemble method where multiple classifiers utilize lexical, syntactic, and semantic features for voting-based prediction. Their method achieved top performance in CWI Shared Task 2018. Similarly, Wani et al. [10] proposed a voting ensemble system based on lexical, size, and vocabulary features, and their result closely matched the top-ranked model in CWI Shared Task 2018. [11] devised a bi-LSTM-based neural network, incorporating word morphological features and distributional semantics. The results revealed that this approach only slightly lags [9] in the competition. Additionally, Aroyehun et al. [12] studied the Convolutional Neural Networks (CNN) and legacy feature engineering-based machine learning-based approaches. They pointed out that although the CNN performs well, the feature engineering strategies are still competent.

To evaluate prompt engineering, we construct a benchmark CWI classifier integrating feature engineering with neural networks. Comparative results show that our model outperforms most prior SOTA approaches.

3   Methodologies

3.1   Prompt Engineering

We collect five open source general-purpose models—deepseek-r1:32b, gemma2:27b, llama3.1:8b, qwen:32b, phi4:14b—available on the ollama platform. Since ollama Modelfile system[2] standardizes the prompt template among various LLMs, we directly design a uniform few-shot prompt instruction for these models. We provide the models with word-sentence pairs, instructing them to assess whether the words are complex based on their contextual knowledge.

3.2   CWI Feature Engineering

We propose to collect diverse word features for integration into neural network models. This project collects three types of features. We combine these features and feed them into neural networks. Fig. 1 illustrates the framework for the CWI system, and the rest of this section describes each system module in detail.

Features. This project selects three types of features: word features, distributional features (word embedding), and discourse features (contextual features). These features are listed as follows.

Word Features: in the experiments, we collect ten different word features which can be divided into three types based on their characteristics, as follows.

Morphological Features: we identify word length, vowel count, and syllable count as fundamental morphological features.

---

[2] https://github.com/ollama/ollama/blob/main/docs/modelfile.md

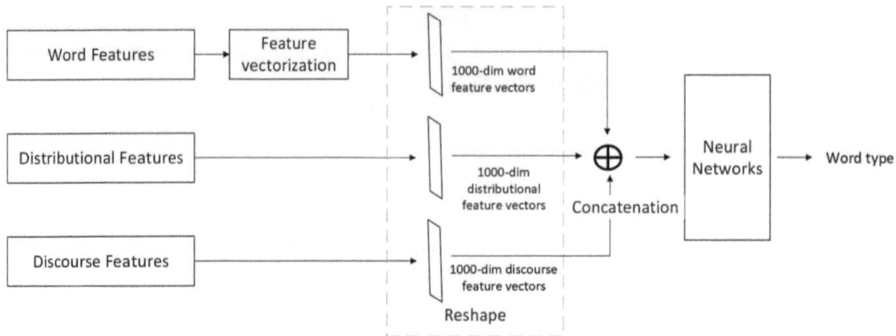

Fig. 1. This framework integrates word, distributional, and discourse features via vectorization, reshaping, and concatenation, forming a unified input for neural network processing.

Semantic Features: we retrieve information from lexical dictionary WordNet [13], including the number of senses, hypernyms, and hyponyms for each evaluated word.

Frequency Features: we collect frequency features for each word by retrieving various documents, including Zipf frequency[3], inverse document frequency (IDF) [14], Wikipedia frequency[4], and Google N-gram frequency[5].

Distributional Features: since word distributional features contain word distributional semantics which contains the relationship between various words, this project concerns them. By testing different distributional features, we find that GloVe [15] reaches the best performance.

Discourse Features: the complexity of the evaluated word heavily depends on its contextual environment. Consequently, in this project, we employ the context embeddings. After a series of tests, we find that RoBERTa-base [16] reaches the balance between performance and resource consumption.

We align the features to reduce the structural complexity of neural network models. Since vectorization operation enhances feature expressiveness and minimizes information loss, we first apply Gaussian vectorization [17] to transfer numerical word features into vectors. Then concatenate these generated vectors as a whole.

---

[3] https://pypi.org/project/wordfreq/.
[4] https://en.wiktionary.org/wiki/Wiktionary:Frequency_lists.
[5] https://github.com/hackerb9/gwordlist.

3.3   Neural Networks

This project tries the feature strategy on different neural network models: support vector regression (SVR), multi-layer perceptron (MLP), convolutional neural network (CNN), and long short-term memory (LSTM).

4   Experiments

4.1   Dataset

This study utilizes the English dataset from the CWI Shared Task 2018[6], which comprises texts from News, WikiNews, and Wikipedia. Each instance was annotated by 10 native and 10 non-native speakers for lexical complexity. The dataset comprises 34,879 instances, split into 27,299 for training, 3,328 for validation, and 4,252 for testing, with 11,253 labeled as 'Complex' in the training set.

4.2   Settings

The detail of prompt engineering and neural network models are as follows.

Prompt Engineering. We examine the open source LLMs using a uniform prompt. Since LLMs lack reproducibility [18], their result from once-experiment is unconvincing. Consequently, this study invokes LLMs multiple times and adopt the average results for analysis.

Neural Network Models. This section offers concise depictions of neural model frameworks.

SVR: we define a two-layer SVR classifier hierarchically refining features, mapping 3000-dimensional input to 300, then 30 dimensions. Polynomial expansion (degree = 4) enhances nonlinear representation for complex pattern learning.

MLP: we construct a four-layer MLP to progressively refine features, mapping a 3000-dimensional input to 1000, 100, 10, and 1. ReLU enhances nonlinearity, while dropout mitigates overfitting for robustness.

CNN: We design a CNN with five 1D convolutional layers and max-pooling for dimensionality reduction. Flattened features undergo three fully connected layers with dropout, enhancing robustness and preventing overfitting. The final layer outputs a prediction.

LSTM: We build a single-directional multi-layer LSTM (hidden size: 128) to extract temporal features, refined via three fully connected layers with ReLU and dropout, ensuring robustness. The final layer generates a single prediction.

We initialize the batch size as 22 and the learning rate of the AdamW optimizer as 10^{-5}. The weighted binary cross-entropy loss is employed to address the imbalance of the training data.

---

[6] https://sites.google.com/view/cwisharedtask2018/datasets.

5   Experiment Results and Analysis

5.1   Results

Table 1 represents the classification results. It reveals that the feature engineering-based legacy classifiers still exhibit advantages in specific classification tasks. As Table 1 shows, the SVR model achieves the optimist performance, and the deep learning neural networks generally outperforms the strategies based on prompt engineering.

We also compare our model with top-ranked models in the CWI Shared Task 2018 ranking models by evaluating their F-1 score in classification tasks, as Table 2 represents. Since the task requires all models to classify News, WikiNews, and Wikipedia subsets separately, we test our model on each subset as the task requires.

This study conducts ablation experiments to assess the impact of each feature on classification performance, as shown in Table 3. Each feature type is first evaluated independently, followed by pairwise combinations to analyze their combined effects. An intriguing phenomenon reveals that, for CNN and LSTM, the

Table 1. The classification results of different models. Since LLMs suffered from hallucination, we append an additional column to record the unexpected outputs generated by LLMs.

Model	Precision (%)	Recall (%)	F-1 (%)	Hallucination (%)
gemma2:27b	62.60	76.38	68.77	0.0294
llama3:1.8b	70.29	42.57	52.96	0.1529
qwen:32b	74.76	71.50	71.76	0.0235
phi4	69.73	60.49	64.78	0.0176
deepseek-r1:32b	61.75	66.83	64.18	44.4320
SVR	**86.32**	**86.34**	**86.31**	—
MLP	85.94	85.89	85.77	—
CNN	86.14	86.08	86.10	—
LSTM	81.28	81.00	81.07	—

Table 2. The F-1 score (%) of each model tested on News, WikiNews, and Wikipedia.

Model	Subset		
	News	WikiNews	Wikipedia
Camb	**87.36**	84.00	81.15
ITEC	86.43	81.10	78.15
CFILT_IITB	84.78	81.61	77.57
NLP-CIC	85.51	83.08	77.22
Our Model	**87.36**	**86.35**	**82.41**

classification results obtained by utilizing a single or partial combination of feature types are superior to those obtained using all feature types, as highlighted in Table 3.

Table 3. Ablation study results. We systematically evaluated the impact of different feature types on classification performance: using only word features (OWF), only distributional semantics (ODS), only discourse features (ODF), distributional semantics & discourse features (DS&DF), word features & discourse features (WF&DF), and word features & distributional semantics (WF&DS).

Setting	SVR (%)			MLP (%)			CNN (%)			LSTM (%)		
	Precision	Recall	F-1	Precision	Recall	F-1	Precision	Recall	F-1	Precision	Recall	F-1
OWF	80.79	79.92	79.27	78.94	76.72	75.32	80.63	78.10	78.21	79.80	79.42	78.94
ODS	81.07	81.14	81.01	81.48	81.35	81.08	80.95	75.00	74.80	80.51	80.41	80.45
ODF	85.76	85.79	85.74	85.59	85.63	85.58	85.16	86.15	86.19	81.11	81.14	81.12
DS&DF	85.60	85.37	85.17	85.32	85.30	85.19	85.85	85.87	85.68	82.23	82.15	82.18
WF&DF	86.18	86.17	86.08	85.68	85.61	85.48	85.75	85.77	85.76	85.92	85.94	85.93
WF&DS	84.10	84.15	84.09	81.37	80.27	79.57	83.60	81.37	81.47	81.76	81.40	81.48

5.2 Analysis

Experimental results demonstrate that neural network classifiers outperform prompt-based large language models (LLMs) on CWI tasks. However, this does not imply that LLMs are unsuitable for this purpose. As shown in Table 1, most LLMs (except deepseek-r1:32b) exhibit low hallucination rates, indicating strong language capabilities. Their lower performance likely stems from two factors: the absence of task-specific fine-tuning and the use of a uniform prompt. Although the Ollama Modelfile ensures prompt standardization, some models still struggle with instruction interpretation. Future research should investigate model-specific prompt optimization and fine-tuning to enhance CWI performance.

The studying results also challenge the initial assumption that complex neural networks do not necessarily outperform networks with simple frameworks for specific tasks, as Table 1 presents that the SVR is superior to CNN and LSTM. CNN excels at capturing local features and spatial patterns, making it appropriate for dealing with images and sequential data. Meanwhile, LSTM is effective in handling temporal dependencies. However, for this CWI task, we organize the data as one-dimensional, non-sequential vectors, which are generally appropriate for CNN and LSTM. In contrast, simple fully connected neural networks, such as SVR and MLP, achieve high performance.

Moreover, Table 2 shows that our feature engineering outperforms some SOTA models, albeit with some limitations. Table 3 indicates that specific combinations of features outperform the use of the entire feature set, suggesting that the inclusion of all feature types introduces redundancy or noise that undermines overall classification accuracy. Furthermore, a comparison between

Tables 1 and 3 indicates that while incorporating all feature types yields better results than using a single or partial combination of feature types, the improvement is marginal. These phenomena indicate the interference among the collected features, lowering the classification efficiency. Optimizing feature selection and combination strategies to enhance classification efficiency remains valuable room for further research.

6   Conclusions

This paper there is limited studies LLM-based prompt engineering and feature engineering strategies for CWI tasks. Comparative experiments show that feature engineering outperforms most CWI Shared Task 2018 participants and the prompt engineering approach. The results suggest that feature engineering remains a promising direction for task-specific classification. Although LLM-based prompt engineering underperforms, this is insufficient to conclude that LLMs are unsuitable for CWI. Future work will refine prompts and apply task-specific fine-tuning to improve LLM performance in classification tasks.

References

1. Kojima, T., Gu, S.S., Reid, M., et al.: Large language models are zero-shot reasoners. In: Advances in Neural Information Processing Systems, vol. 35, pp. 22199–22213 (2022)
2. Li, Z., Fan, S., Gu, Y., et al.: FlexKBQA: a flexible LLM-powered framework for few-shot knowledge base question answering. In: Proceedings of the AAAI Conference on Artificial Intelligence, vol. 38, no. 17, pp. 18608–18616 (2024)
3. Liu, A., Feng, B., Xue, B., et al.: Deepseek-v3 technical report. arXiv preprint arXiv:2412.19437 (2024)
4. Touvron, H., Lavril, T., Izacard, G., et al.: Llama: Open and efficient foundation language models. arXiv preprint arXiv:2302.13971 (2023)
5. Team, G., Mesnard, T., Hardin, C., et al.: Gemma: open models based on Gemini research and technology. arXiv preprint arXiv:2403.08295 (2024)
6. Yimam, S. M., Biemann, C., Malmasi, S., et al.: A report on the complex word identification shared task 2018. arXiv preprint arXiv:1804.09132 (2018)
7. Han, X., Zhao, W., Ding, N., et al.: PTR: prompt tuning with rules for text classification. AI Open **3**, 182–192 (2022)
8. Clavié, B., Ciceu, A., Naylor, F., et al.: Large language models in the workplace: a case study on prompt engineering for job type classification. In: International Conference on Applications of Natural Language to Information Systems, pp. 3–17 (2023)
9. Gooding, S., Kochmar, E.: CAMB at CWI shared task 2018: complex word identification with ensemble-based voting. In: Proceedings of the Thirteenth Workshop on Innovative Use of NLP for Building Educational Applications, pp. 184–194 (2018)
10. Wani, N., Mathias, S., Gajjam, J. A., Bhattacharyya, P.: The whole is greater than the sum of its parts: Towards the effectiveness of voting ensemble classifiers for complex word identification. In: Proceedings of the Thirteenth Workshop on Innovative Use of NLP for Building Educational Applications, pp. 200–205 (2018)

11. De Hertog, D., Tack, A.: Deep learning architecture for complex word identification. In: Proceedings of the Workshop on Innovative Use of NLP for Building Educational Applications, vol. 13, pp. 328–334 (2018)
12. Aroyehun, S. T., Angel, J., Alvarez, D. A. P., Gelbukh, A.: Complex word identification: convolutional neural network vs. feature engineering. In: Proceedings of the Thirteenth Workshop on Innovative Use of NLP for Building Educational Applications, pp. 322–327 (2018)
13. Miller, G.A.: WordNet: a lexical database for English. Commun. ACM **38**(11), 39–41 (1995)
14. Sparck Jones, K.: A statistical interpretation of term specificity and its application in retrieval. J. Doc. **28**(1), 11–21 (1972)
15. Pennington, J., Socher, R., Manning, C. D.: GloVe: global vectors for word representation. In: Proceedings of the 2014 Conference on Empirical Methods in Natural Language Processing (EMNLP), pp. 1532–1543 (2014)
16. Liu, Y., Ott, M., Goyal, N., et al.: RoBERTa: a robustly optimized BERT pre-training approach. arXiv preprint arXiv:1907.11692 (2019)
17. Maddela, M., Xu, W.: A word-complexity lexicon and a neural readability ranking model for lexical simplification. arXiv preprint arXiv:1810.05754 (2018)
18. Blackwell, R. E., Barry, J., Cohn, A. G.: Towards reproducible LLM evaluation: quantifying uncertainty in LLM benchmark scores. arXiv preprint arXiv:2410.03492 (2024)

DARIS: Dynamic Adaptive Refinement of Interaction Sequence for Sequential Recommendation

Wenxu Zhao[1], Yuheng Wu[1], Danhui Shi[2], Yongkang Li[1],
Xingyu Zhu[1], and Xiaona Xia[3(✉)]

[1] Qufu Normal University, Rizhao, China
[2] Jining Polytechnic, Jining, China
[3] Faculty of Education Chinese Academy of Education Big Data, Qufu Normal University, Qufu, China
`xiaxn@sina.com`

Abstract. Sequential recommendation is an important research direction within the field of recommender systems, which predicts the items that users may be interested in based on the chronological order of user-item interactions. It receives increasing attention from various researchers in recent years. Although many previous models have achieved remarkable results, data sparsity remains a significant issue that has hindered the performance improvement of sequential recommendation models. Additionally, most current data augmentation models ignore time intervals. To address this, we propose Dynamic Adaptive Refinement of Interaction Sequence (DARIS), employing a novel dynamic adaptive strategy to augment sparse interaction sequences for enhanced recommendation performance. DARIS contains two core modules: the Item Reshaper replaces low-quality items with high-quality alternatives, and the Sequence Refiner subsequently identifies optimal subsequences from the reshaped sequences for final recommendation tasks. Comprehensive experiments on three datasets demonstrate that DARIS effectively augments original sequences and improves model performance, outperforming baselines across multiple evaluation metrics.

Keywords: Sequential recommendation · Data augmentation · Time intervals · Recommender systems

1 Introduction

Sequential recommendation is a crucial branch in recommendation systems, predicting related items based on users' historical interaction sequences [6]. For enhancing the accuracy of sequential recommendation models, researchers have integrated various deep neural networks such as Graph Neural Networks (GNNs) [15], Recurrent Neural Networks (RNNs) [20], and Transformer [9, 10] with sequential recommendation models. Despite these advancements, data sparsity has not been thoroughly addressed [13]. Existing data augmentation models

© The Author(s), under exclusive license to Springer Nature Singapore Pte Ltd. 2026
T. Zhu et al. (Eds.): KSEM 2025, LNAI 15922, pp. 424–432, 2026.
https://doi.org/10.1007/978-981-95-3058-8_40

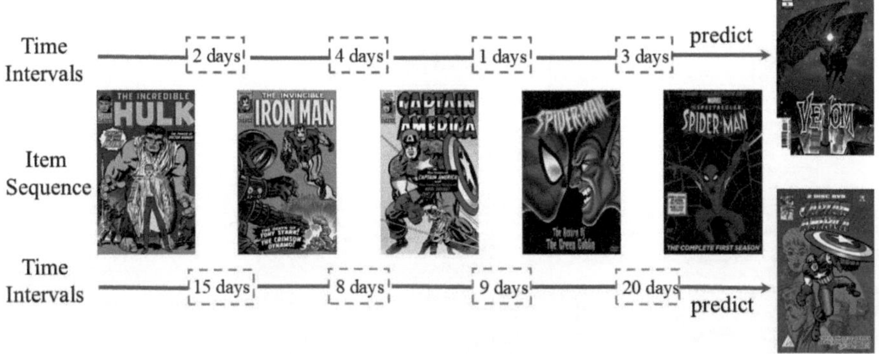

Fig. 1. The same user interaction sequence with different time intervals will result in different recommendation results.

have attempted to address data sparsity, but they have overlooked the time intervals. As shown in Fig. 1, even with the same interaction sequences, different time intervals lead to different recommendation results [3,11]. Therefore, studying the time intervals is necessary. However, existing data augmentation models based on time intervals fail to achieve adaptive dynamic refinement.

In this paper, we study the utilization of time intervals. Specifically, we design DARIS, the dynamic adaptive refinement of interaction sequences. DARIS comprises two modules: Item Reshaper (IRS) and Sequence Refiner (SRF). IRS reshapes items based on context and time intervals of the original user interaction sequence, while SRF extracts high-quality subsequences for recommendation. The enhanced sequences account for both absolute positions and time intervals. Finally, we conduct extensive experiments and compare DARIS with four baselines across six metrics on three real-world datasets.

2   Related Work

Sequential recommendation differs from traditional collaborative filtering by focusing on temporal user behavior evolution [5,10,17]. Traditional methods include Markov chain [4] and matrix factorization. Deep neural networks were later introduced to improve accuracy. Zhu et al. introduced Time-LSTM to model time intervals [22]. Since the emergence of Transformer [7], the sequential recommendation has been further developed. Sun et al. proposed BERT4Rec [18], which better understands users' historical behavior patterns using the bidirectional Transformer. Despite these advancements, most models struggle with data sparsity.

To address this, data augmentation has become widely adopted. Wang et al. [19] and Xu et al. [2] each proposed methods to correct users' original sequences using counterfactual thinking. Subsequently, researchers introduce

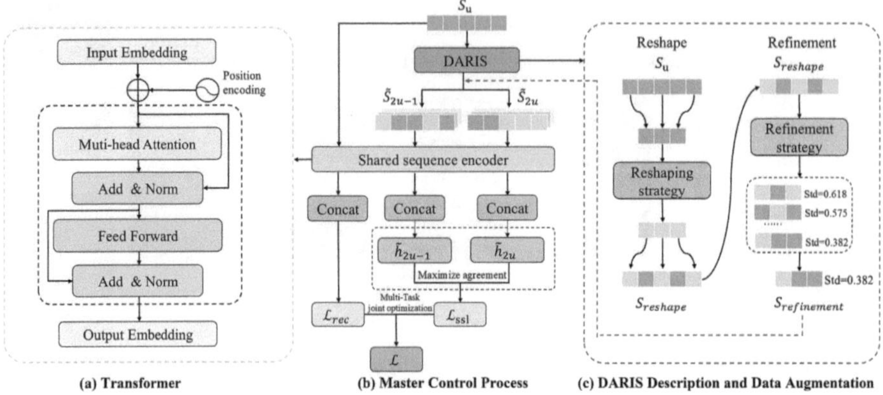

Fig. 2. The training framework for the whole process

Self-Supervised Learning (SSL) into data augmentation [8,14]. Xie et al. proposed the CL4SRec model [16], which proposes three data augmentation operators: Crop, Reorder, and Mask. Based on CL4SRec, Liu et al. proposed the CoSeRec model [1], which combines two data augmentation operators: Insert and Substitute. While CL-based models improve performance, most neglect time intervals. Dang et al. proposed TiCoSeRec by improving five data augmentation operators [3], yet randomness still disrupts sequences. Therefore, we develop dynamic adaptive refinement to generate augmented sequences preserving original characteristics while learning representative features.

3   Methods

Our overall framework is shown in Fig. 2.

3.1   Description of Sequential Recommendation Problem

We assume a recommender has user and item sets denoted $\mathcal{U}(u \in \mathcal{U})$ and $\mathcal{V}(v \in \mathcal{V})$ respectively. Each user u has a chronological interaction sequence $S_u = (v_1, \cdots, v_k, \cdots, v_L)$, where $v_k \in \mathcal{V}$ denotes the item interacted with at time $k(1 \leq k \leq L)$, and L is the length of each user interaction sequence. Each user's interaction sequence S_u is associated with a time interval sequence $T_u = (t_1, \cdots, t_k, \cdots, t_{L-1})$, where t_k represents the time interval between v_k and v_{k+1}. Our goal is to predict v_{L+1}, the next item u is most likely to interact with.

3.2   The DARIS Framework

In this subsection, we introduce DARIS framework in detail. As shown in Fig. 2(c), the framework consists of two modules: IRS and SRF.

Item Reshaper. Given $S_u = (v_1, \cdots, v_L)$ and corresponding $T_u = (t_1, \cdots, t_{L-1})$, construct IntervalList $= ((v_1, t_1), \cdots, (v_{L-1}, t_{L-1}))$. Sort IntervalList in ascending order using merge sort: MergeSort(IntervalList, t_k). This algorithm maintains a time complexity of $O(n \log n)$, ensuring efficiency for large-scale data regardless of whether the initial sequence is sorted; its stability preserves the original sequence of items with identical time intervals. After removing time intervals information from IntervalList, obtain the interaction sequence S'_u. Define selection function selectItem(S'_u, P), where $P = \alpha N$ ($N =$ sequence length, $\alpha \in [0, 1] =$ reshaping ratio). This selects the top P items from S'_u to form the reshaping set $(item_1, \cdots, item_P)$:

$$S'_u = \text{MergeSort(IntervalList}, t_k) \tag{1}$$

$$(item_1, \cdots, item_P) = \text{selectItem}(S'_u, P) \tag{2}$$

Reshape each $item_j (1 \leq j \leq P)$ using CoSeRec's similar-item generation strategy. Reintegrate all reshaped $item_j$ into their original positions in S_u, yielding the new sequence $S_{reshape}$.

Sequence Refinement. In the previous subsection, we obtained $S_{reshape}$, which contains more reliable contextual relationships and richer transitional relationships between items. However, excessive sequence length impairs the extraction high-quality transitional relationships and reduces training efficiency. Therefore, we further refine $S_{reshape}$ to focus the model on relatively excellent subsequences, enhancing learned feature quality and training efficiency.

Specifically, we compute the retained length $len = \beta N$, where N is $S_{reshape}$'s length and $\beta \in [0, 1]$ is the refinement ratio controlling information retention. To ensure optimal refinement, we perform global refinement refSubseq($S_{reshape}, len$). Starting from the first item v_1, we calculate all potential excellent subsequences of length len in $S_{reshape}$. The optimal subsequence is selected by minimizing the standard deviation (Tistd) of time intervals:

$$S_{refinement} = \text{argmin Tistd}(\text{refSubseq}(S_{reshape}, k), T_u) \tag{3}$$

Here, $S_{refinement}$ denotes the refined subsequences used as training data.

4 Experiment

4.1 Dataset

To evaluate DARIS's data augmentation performance, we conducted experiments on three Amazon public datasets—Beauty, Sport, and Home—frequently used in prior studies [12]. In accordance with the preprocessing methodology described in [16], we used 5-core datasets by filtering users/items with fewer than five interactions. Preprocessed dataset statistics appear in Table 1.

Table 1. Detailed Information of The Three Datasets

Dataset	Users	Items	Actions	Avg. Length	Sparsity
Beauty	22363	12101	198502	8.87	99.92%
Sports	35598	18357	296337	8.32	99.95%
Home	66370	28237	551682	8.29	99.97%

4.2 Experimental Setting

Baselines. To validate the performance of DARIS, we select four advanced baselines for comparison: SASRec [10], TiSASRec [11], CoSeRec [1], and TiCoSeRec [3].

Parameters. We use the code from CoSeRec and TiCoSeRec, modifying only the data augmentation component to incorporate DARIS. Other baselines are implemented via RecBole [21]. For fair comparison, embedding dimension and batch size are set to 128. An early stopping strategy with a 100-epoch patience is adopted, terminating training if no improvement occurs for two consecutive epochs to select the best model. A grid search over $[0.1, 0.9]$ with step 0.1 is conducted for hyperparameters α and β. The dataset uses leave-one-out, with the penultimate item as validation and the last as test set.

Table 2. Performance Comparison of Different Models

Dataset	Model	HR@5	HR@10	HR@20	NDCG@5	NDCG@10	NDCG@20
Beauty	SASRec	0.0360	0.0527	0.0781	0.0240	0.0294	0.0347
	TiSASRec	0.0312	0.0522	0.0819	0.0227	0.0276	0.0341
	CoSeRec	0.0447	0.0622	0.0972	0.0299	0.0361	0.0451
	TiCoSeRec	0.0520	0.0750	0.1079	0.0354	0.0427	0.0510
	Ours	**0.0549**	**0.0787**	**0.1116**	**0.0377**	**0.0454**	**0.0537**
Sports	SASRec	0.0197	0.0367	0.0539	0.0133	0.0169	0.0206
	TiSASRec	0.0180	0.0286	0.0453	0.0115	0.0149	0.0190
	CoSeRec	0.0280	0.0401	0.0596	0.0169	0.0228	0.0246
	TiCoSeRec	0.0325	0.0501	0.0763	0.0219	0.0275	0.0341
	Ours	**0.0350**	**0.0551**	**0.0820**	**0.0226**	**0.0291**	**0.359**
Home	SASRec	0.0124	0.0173	0.0248	0.0088	0.0101	0.0115
	TiSASRec	0.0065	0.0119	0.0181	0.0041	0.0057	0.0071
	CoSeRec	0.0145	0.0216	0.0311	0.0103	0.0114	0.0152
	TiCoSeRec	0.0173	0.0253	0.0365	0.0122	0.0148	0.0176
	Ours	**0.0193**	**0.0280**	**0.0407**	**0.0136**	**0.0165**	**0.0195**

4.3 Experiment Results

Table 2 presents the performance of DARIS and baselines. SASRec and TiSAS-Rec perform comparably. SASRec excels in ranking user-preferred items at higher positions within recommendation lists, TiSASRec innovates by using time intervals, indicating significant research potential in this area—a focus of this work. CoSeRec achieves the best performance before incorporating time intervals. TiCoSeRec outperforms all baselines, consistent with prior studies, by integrating time interval distributions with augmentation operators and demonstrating uniform sequences enhance preference learning—forming the basis of our research.

Compared with baselines, DARIS shows the best performance on six metrics across the three datasets. This is because we not only perform data augmentation considering time intervals, but also dynamically refine different user interaction sequences. These excellent results are attributed to the respective advantages of IRS and SRF as well as their mutual cooperation. The user interaction sequences after data augmentation preserve the original sequence characteristics to the greatest extent. It also provides new learning representations for sequential models, thereby further enhancing the recommendation performance.

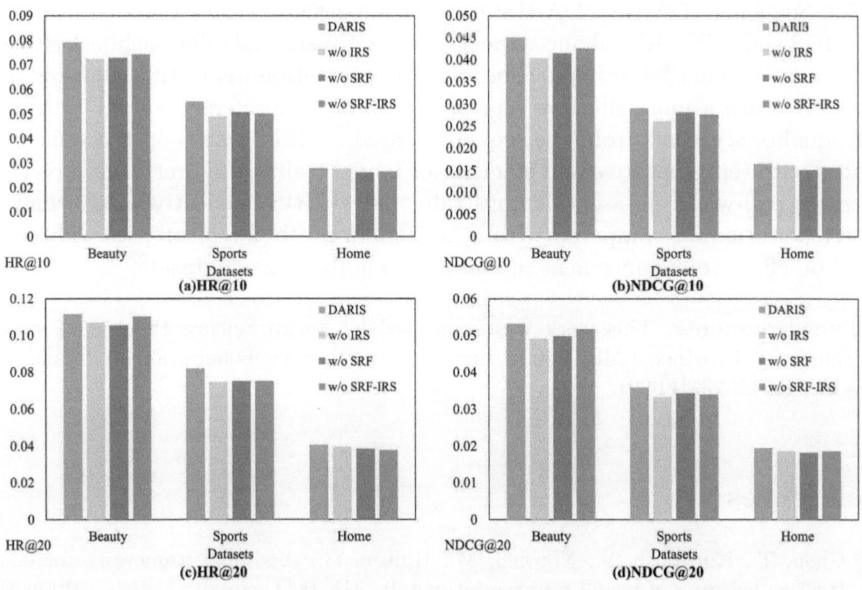

Fig. 3. Ablation study of DARIS in terms of HR@10, 20 and NDCG@10, 20 on Beauty, Sports, and Home.

4.4 Ablation Study

We conduct ablation studies on three datasets to verify each module's contribution to data augmentation. We design three variants:

- DARIS w/o IRS removes the IRS in DARIS.
- DARIS w/o SRF removes the SRF in DARIS.
- DARIS w/o SRF-IRS swaps the order of using IRS and SRF. Use SRF first and then IRS.

Figure 3 shows that removing either module reduces augmentation efficacy, confirming their necessity. DARIS w/o IRS underperforms DARIS w/o SRF, indicating IRS's greater importance. Optimal results require both modules. Swapping their order (SRF before IRS) degrades performance, as IRS fails to learn sufficient item transitions from shortened sequences, leading to low-quality items. This proves both modules and their original execution order are necessary.

5 Conclusion

In this paper, we propose a new method, Dynamic Adaptive Refinement of Interaction Sequence (DARIS). DARIS includes the design of a dual-component system: IRS and SRF. IRS enhances the quality of transitional relationships between items in a sequence by reshaping specific user interaction items, thus allowing the model to learn a more effective representation of the preferences. SRF extracts high-quality segments from the sequence based on this, resulting in a sequence that is both representative and efficient for model training. Experimental results on three real-world datasets demonstrate that DARIS is effective and achieves better performance compared with other baselines. In the future, we will focus more on effective enhancement methods for highly sparse datasets.

Acknowledgments. This work was supported by Social Science Planning Project of Shandong Province (24BJYJ02), and Natural Science Foundation of Shandong Province (ZR2023MF099).

References

1. Chen, T., Kornblith, S., Norouzi, M., Hinton, G.: A simple framework for contrastive learning of visual representations. In: III, H.D., Singh, A. (eds.) Proceedings of the 37th International Conference on Machine Learning. Proceedings of Machine Learning Research, vol. 119, pp. 1597–1607. PMLR (2020)
2. Chen, X., et al.: Data augmented sequential recommendation based on counterfactual thinking. IEEE Trans. Knowl. Data Eng. **35**(9), 9181–9194 (2023)
3. Dang, Y., et al.: Ticoserec: augmenting data to uniform sequences by time intervals for effective recommendation. IEEE Trans. Knowl. Data Eng. **36**(6), 2686–2700 (2024)

4. He, R., McAuley, J.: Fusing similarity models with Markov chains for sparse sequential recommendation. In: 2016 IEEE 16th International Conference on Data Mining (ICDM), pp. 191–200 (2016)
5. He, X., Deng, K., Wang, X., Li, Y., Zhang, Y., Wang, M.: LightGCN: simplifying and powering graph convolution network for recommendation. In: Proceedings of the 43rd International ACM SIGIR Conference on Research and Development in Information Retrieval. SIGIR '20, pp. 639–648. Association for Computing Machinery, New York, NY, USA (2020)
6. Hidasi, B., Karatzoglou, A., Baltrunas, L., Tikk, D.: Session-based recommendations with recurrent neural networks (2016)
7. Hou, Y., Hu, B., Zhang, Z., Zhao, W.X.: Core: simple and effective session-based recommendation within consistent representation space. In: Proceedings of the 45th International ACM SIGIR Conference on Research and Development in Information Retrieval. SIGIR '22, pp. 1796–1801. Association for Computing Machinery, New York, NY, USA (2022)
8. Huynh, T., Kornblith, S., Walter, M.R., Maire, M., Khademi, M.: Boosting contrastive self-supervised learning with false negative cancellation. In: Proceedings of the IEEE/CVF Winter Conference on Applications of Computer Vision (WACV), pp. 2785–2795 (2022)
9. Jiang, J., et al.: Improving sequential recommendations via bidirectional temporal data augmentation with pre-training (2024)
10. Kang, W.C., McAuley, J.: Self-attentive sequential recommendation. In: 2018 IEEE International Conference on Data Mining (ICDM), pp. 197–206 (2018)
11. Li, J., Wang, Y., McAuley, J.: Time interval aware self-attention for sequential recommendation. In: Proceedings of the 13th International Conference on Web Search and Data Mining. WSDM '20, pp. 322–330. Association for Computing Machinery, New York, NY, USA (2020)
12. Lin, J., Pan, W., Ming, Z.: Fissa: fusing item similarity models with self-attention networks for sequential recommendation. In: Proceedings of the 14th ACM Conference on Recommender Systems. RecSys '20, pp. 130–139. Association for Computing Machinery, New York, NY, USA (2020)
13. Liu, Z., Fan, Z., Wang, Y., Yu, P.S.: Augmenting sequential recommendation with pseudo-prior items via reversely pre-training transformer. In: Proceedings of the 44th International ACM SIGIR Conference on Research and Development in Information Retrieval. SIGIR '21, pp. 1608–1612. Association for Computing Machinery, New York, NY, USA (2021)
14. Ni, S., Zhou, W., Wen, J., Hu, L., Qiao, S.: Enhancing sequential recommendation with contrastive generative adversarial network. Inf. Process. Manag. **60**(3), 103331 (2023)
15. Qin, Y., Ju, W., Wu, H., Luo, X., Zhang, M.: Learning graph ode for continuous-time sequential recommendation. IEEE Trans. Knowl. Data Eng. **36**(7), 3224–3236 (2024)
16. Qiu, R., Huang, Z., Yin, H., Wang, Z.: Contrastive learning for representation degeneration problem in sequential recommendation. In: Proceedings of the Fifteenth ACM International Conference on Web Search and Data Mining. WSDM '22, pp. 813–823. Association for Computing Machinery, New York, NY, USA (2022)
17. Rendle, S., Freudenthaler, C., Gantner, Z., Schmidt-Thieme, L.: BPR: Bayesian personalized ranking from implicit feedback (2012)

18. Sun, F., et al.: Bert4Rec: sequential recommendation with bidirectional encoder representations from transformer. In: Proceedings of the 28th ACM International Conference on Information and Knowledge Management. CIKM '19, pp. 1441–1450. Association for Computing Machinery, New York, NY, USA (2019)
19. Wang, Z., et al.: Counterfactual data-augmented sequential recommendation. In: Proceedings of the 44th International ACM SIGIR Conference on Research and Development in Information Retrieval. SIGIR '21, pp. 347–356. Association for Computing Machinery, New York, NY, USA (2021)
20. Wu, C.Y., Ahmed, A., Beutel, A., Smola, A.J., Jing, H.: Recurrent recommender networks. In: Proceedings of the Tenth ACM International Conference on Web Search and Data Mining. WSDM '17, pp. 495–503. Association for Computing Machinery, New York, NY, USA (2017)
21. Zhao, W.X., et al.: Recbole 2.0: towards a more up-to-date recommendation library. In: Proceedings of the 31st ACM International Conference on Information and Knowledge Management. CIKM '22, pp. 4722–4726. Association for Computing Machinery, New York, NY, USA (2022)
22. Zhu, Y., et al.: What to do next: modeling user behaviors by time-LSTM. In: Proceedings of the 26th International Joint Conference on Artificial Intelligence. IJCAI'17, pp. 3602–3608. AAAI Press (2017)

PolyBERT: Fine-Tuned Poly Encoder BERT-Based Model for Word Sense Disambiguation

Linhan Xia[1], Mingzhan Yang[1], Guohui Yuan[1], Shengnan Tao[1], Yujing Qiu[1], Guo Yu[2], and Kai Lei[1(✉)]

[1] ICNLab, Shenzhen Graduate School, Peking University, Shenzhen, People's Republic of China
`linhan.xia@ou.edu`, `my47@illinois.edu`, {`yuangh,leik`}`@pkusz.edu.cn`,
`leik@pku.edu.cn`
[2] CEC GienTech Technology Co., Ltd., Shenzhen, People's Republic of China
`yu.guo@gientech.com`

Abstract. Mainstream Word Sense Disambiguation (WSD) approaches have employed BERT to extract semantics from both context and definitions of senses to determine the most suitable sense of a target word, achieving notable performance. However, there are two limitations in these approaches. First, previous studies failed to balance the representation of token-level (local) and sequence-level (global) semantics during feature extraction, leading to insufficient semantic representation and a performance bottleneck. Second, these approaches incorporated all possible senses of each target word during the training phase, leading to unnecessary computational costs. To overcome these limitations, this paper introduces a poly-encoder BERT-based model with batch contrastive learning for WSD, named PolyBERT. Compared with previous WSD methods, PolyBERT has two improvements: Firstly, (1) a poly-encoder with a multi-head attention mechanism is employed to integrate both token-level (local) and sequence-level (global) semantics, rather than focusing solely on one aspect. This approach enhances semantic representation by effectively balancing local and global semantics. Secondly, (2) to avoid redundant training inputs, Batch Contrastive Learning (BCL) is introduced. BCL utilizes the correct senses of other target words in the same batch as negative samples for the current target word, which reduces training inputs and computational cost. The experimental results demonstrate that PolyBERT outperforms baseline WSD methods such as Huang's GlossBERT and Blevins's BEM by 2% in F1-score. In addition, PolyBERT with BCL reduces GPU hours by 37.6% compared with PolyBERT without BCL.

Keywords: Word sense disambiguation · BERT · Poly encoder · Contrastive learning · Semantic Representation

1   Introduction

Word Sense Disambiguation (WSD) refers to determining the most suitable sense of target ambiguous word according to a specific context [13]. As a fundamental task in Natural Language Processing (NLP), WSD play a crucial role in various applications such as machine translation [14], information retrieval [23] and named entity recognition [12].

A major limitation of mainstream WSD works is insufficient semantic representation due to imbalanced extraction of token-level (local) and sequence-level (global) semantics [21]. Mainstream works are categorized into two types: sequence-based and token-based [3]. Sequence-based works neglect local semantics (of each token), while token-based works overlook global semantics (of the entire sequence).

Another limitation of mainstream WSD works is unnecessary computational cost caused by redundant training data inputs. WSD models learn feature differences between the correct sense and incorrect sense during training phase. For a specific target word, incorrect senses can be derived from the correct senses of other target words in the same batch. However, mainstream works input all candidate senses of each target word during the training phase, leading to significant redundancy.

To address the above-mentioned limitations, this paper proposes a poly-encoder BERT-based WSD model with batch contrastive learning (BCL), named PolyBERT. The contributions of this paper are following:

1. To address the issue of imbalanced representation between token-level (local) and sequence-level (global) semantics, this paper introduces a poly-encoder-based feature extraction approach. This approach employs a multi-head attention mechanism to fuse extracted token-level (local) and sequence-level (global) semantics, integrating both token-level and sequence-level semantics into the representation, rather than focusing on just one.
2. Prior works sampled all possible senses of each target word to generate positive and negative sample pairs, but this overlooked the potential to use positive samples from other target words in the same batch as negative samples. This oversight led to data redundancy and reduced computational efficiency. To address this, this paper adopts Batch Contrastive Learning, which leverages positive samples from other target words as negative samples, thereby avoiding the inefficiency of comprehensive negative sampling in prior works.
3. This paper constructs a WSD model (PolyBERT) and numerous experiments are conducted to evaluate the performance of PolyBERT. The source code and trained models of PolyBERT is available at here.

To evaluate the effectiveness of PolyBERT, experiments are conducted on public English-all-word datasets. According to the experiment results, compared to the best mainstream works (BEM [4]), PolyBERT achieves a 2% higher F1-score. In addition, strategy of contrastive learning saves 37.6% GPU hours compared with learning strategy of mainstream works.

In Sect. 2, this paper introduces related researches. In Sect. 3, this paper introduces the details of PolyBERT. In Sect. 4, this paper reports the experimental setup and results of the experiments. In Sect. 5 this paper summarizes our work.

2   Related Works

Pre-trained Transformer-based Language Models (PLMs) has been proven significant in improving performance of WSD. Vial et al. [18] initially employed BERT model to generate embedding, and used this embedding to disambiguate word sense. Since then, the PLMs-based WSD methods has become the mainstream. PLMs-based works can be divided into two categories: sequence-based approaches and token-based approaches [3].

Sequence-based WSD approaches disambiguate word senses using global sequence semantics [21]. A key representative is GlossBERT [8], which models context-gloss pairs for sense matching. Extensions include [20] incorporating WordNet examples and ESC [1] processing all candidate glosses jointly. However, these methods fail to capture local token-level semantics, particularly for target words, limiting their representational power.

Differ from sequence-based approaches, Token-based approaches employ semantics of each token (local semantics) to disambiguate word sense [16]. Similar to PolyBERT, BEM proposed by Blevins et al. [4] consists of two independent encoder to embed context and gloss of sense respectively. BEM extract the token of target word from context's embedding and token [CLS] from gloss's embedding as representations, which are used to determine the correct sense by dot product. Similar to BEM, Zhang et al. [22] employed two encoders. Moreover, Zhang et al. employed quantum interference to enhance representation of target word and glosses. However, token-based approaches only extract semantics from each token, which limit the capability of representing global semantics.

Existing works are not able to represent local and global semantics in a balance way, which cause insufficient representation of semantics and limitation of performance.

3   Methodology

This section illustrate the details of PolyBERT. PolyBERT consists of two independent encoders: (1) *context-encoder*: aims to embed target word with its surrounding context and *gloss-encoder*: aims to embed definition (gloss) of sense. PolyBERT fuses the embeddings from *context-encoder* and *gloss-encoder* to evaluate which sense is the most suitable. The pipeline of PolyBERT is shown in Fig. 1.

PolyBERT for WSD is divided into two phases: **batch contrastive pre-learning** (training phase) and **sense prediction**. During the batch contrastive pre-learning phase, PolyBERT only processes the gloss of the target word's correct sense, which differs from prior works. During the sense prediction phase, PolyBERT intake target word and its all candidate definitions.

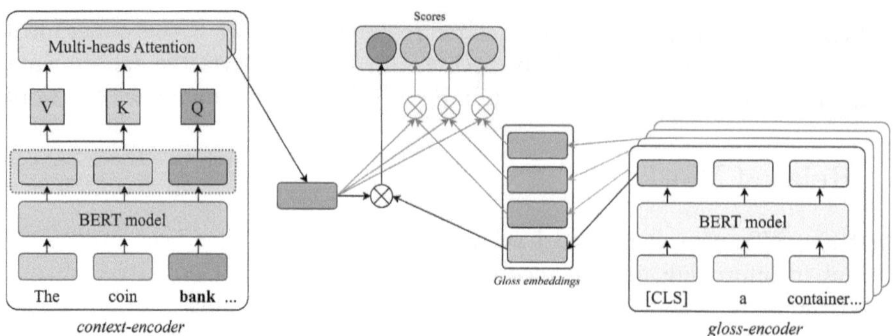

Fig. 1. Pipeline of PolyBERT. The *context-encoder* embeds target word and its context, the *gloss-encoder* embeds gloss of sense. We extract t^{th} token from output of context embedding, where w^t is the target word. *Context-encoder* employs multi-head attention mechanism to fuse local and global semantics to generate representation of target word. *Gloss-encoder* takes Token [CLS] as representation of gloss. PolyBERT employs dot product to calculate the semantic similarities (scores) of each sense.

Following the introduction of the PolyBERT pipeline, this section outlines the notation employed in the model's description. Formally, the context c is composed of multiple words w, with the tth word designated as the target word w^t. The WSD system is formulated as a function $f(w^t, c) = s$, where $s \in S_{w^t}$, the set of all possible senses of w^t. Each sense s is associated with a gloss g, where $g \in G_{w^t}$. Within S_{w^t} and G_{w^t}. s^c and its corresponding gloss g^c denote the correct sense and gloss of w^t, as derived from context c.

3.1 Context-Encoder and Gloss-Encoder

Encoders of PolyBERT aim to generate embeddings of textual sequences and extract representations from the embeddings. Each encoder of Poly-BERT is initialized with BERT model (denoted as BERT). The BERT-based encoders embed sequences with BERT-specific start and end token: token [CLS] and token [SEP]. Therefore, the embedding can be read as $E = T^{[CLS]}, T^1, T^2, ..., T^n, T^{[SEP]}$, where n is the length of input textual sequence and each token T represents a word w except $T^{[CLS]}$ and $T^{[SEP]}$.

Context-encoder denoted as B_C is employed to embed target word with its context. The input sequence of B_C can be written as $c = w^1, ..., w^t, ..., w^n$, where the tth word of c is the target word w^t. The BERT model will embed the textual sequence into embedding sequence E_C, and the representation r of target word read as:

$$r_{w^t} = E_C[t] = B_C(c)[t], \tag{1}$$

where r_{w^t} is local semantics, and E_C is global semantics. To balance representation of local and global semantics, context-encoder adopt multi-heads attention mechanism-based poly-encoder to fuse the extracted features. Firstly, context-encoder replicate r_{w^t} $poly_m$ times to form query matrix Q

$$Q = \mathbf{1}_{poly_m} \otimes r_{w^t} \tag{2}$$

$poly_m$ is a hyperparameter in the poly-encoder, representing the number of tokens that are generated after the extraction process. Secondly, context-encoder take the embedding sequence E_C as key K and value V matrix and fuse Q, K, V through multi-head attention mechanism. The calculation of each head read as

$$head_i = \mathrm{softmax}\left(\frac{(Q \cdot W_i^Q)(K \cdot W_i^K)}{\sqrt{d_k}}\right) \cdot V \cdot W_i^V, \tag{3}$$

where $W_i^Q \in \mathbb{R}^{d_{\mathrm{model}} \times d_k}$, $W_i^K \in \mathbb{R}^{d_{\mathrm{model}} \times d_k}$ and $W_i^V \in \mathbb{R}^{d_{\mathrm{model}} \times d_v}$ are linear projection matrices, d_k is dimension of K and d_v is dimension of V. Then we concat each head to generate fused representation of local and global semantic information. The concat process read as

$$r_{w^t}^F = Concat\left(head_1, \ldots, head_h\right) \cdot W^O, \tag{4}$$

where, h is the number of heads and W^O is concatenated linear projection matrix. Based on such attention-based mechanism, encoder can extract balanced local and global semantic [19].

Gloss-encoder denoted as B_G embeds the gloss g of sense s. The token [CLS] has been proven effective to represent global semantic information. We extract the token [CLS] as representation r_g from embedding E_G generated by BERT model

$$r_g = E_G[0] = B_G(g)[0]. \tag{5}$$

To match the dimension of $r_{w^t}^F$, we replicate the r_g $poly_m$ times to generate the semantic representation of gloss

$$r_g^F = \mathbf{1}_{poly_m} \otimes r_g. \tag{6}$$

3.2   Batch Contrastive Pre-learning

PolyBERT fuses representations of target word and gloss after they are generated, inspired by [6], the contrastive learning is employed to fused extracted features. The process is demonstrated in Fig. 2.

In the pre-training phase, representations for the target word, $R_{w^t} = r_{w^t}^1, r_{w^t}^2, \ldots, r_{w^t}^b$ and for glosses, $R_g = r_g^1, r_g^2, \ldots, r_g^b$ are generated in a batch, where b denotes the batch size. For each $r_{w^t}^i$, r_g^i represents its corresponding gloss's representation. PolyBERT take dot product to fuse two representations in a batch to generate fusion matrix M_F

$$M_F = R_{w^t} \cdot R_g, \tag{7}$$

in this matrix, values located on the diagonal line represent the similarities (scores) between target words and the glosses of their correct senses. The other

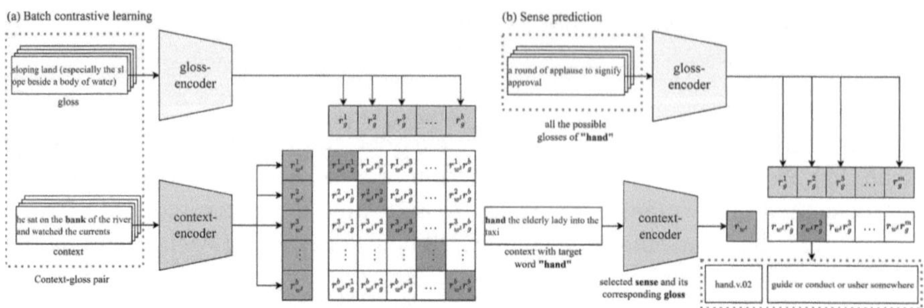

Fig. 2. Fusion process is various in two different phase: (a) batch contrastive pre-learning and (b) sense prediction.

values represent scores between target words and the glosses of incorrect senses. This approach enables PolyBERT take correct senses of other target words in a same batch as incorrect senses (negative samples), which avoids redundant data inputs.

To train the PolyBERT, a special-designed loss function is constructed. Initially, softmax function is applied to normalize the scores of each row of M_F, the process read as

$$P = \mathrm{softmax}\,(M_F),\tag{8}$$

where i is index of row. Subsequently, normalized scores between $r_{w^t}^i$ and r_g^i from P are extracted:

$$P^d = \mathrm{diagonal}(P) = \{P_{i,i}|i = 1, 2, \ldots, b\}.\tag{9}$$

Based on P^d, the final loss $\mathbb{L}$ is evaluated

$$\mathbb{L} = \frac{1}{b} \times \sum_{i=1}^{b} \left(-\log(P_i^d)\right),\tag{10}$$

where i is the index of each row. During the pre-training phase, PolyBERT is able to maximize the scores between target words and their corresponding glosses and minimize the scores between target words and their incorrect glosses.

3.3   Prediction Phase

In prediction phase, trained PolyBERT is utilized to select the correct sense s^c and associated gloss g^c of target word w^T from candidate senses set S_{w^t}. Initially, representations of target word and candidate senses are generated, the process read as

$$r_{w^t} = B_C(w^t),\tag{11}$$

$$R_g = B_G(G_{w^t}) = r_g^1, r_g^2, \ldots, r_g^m,\tag{12}$$

where G_{w^t} is gloss set associated with S_{w^t} and m is number of possible senses. PolyBERT employ dot product to calculate scores of each sense:

$$\mathbb{S}\left(w^t, s^j\right) = (r_{w^t} \cdot R_g)[j], \tag{13}$$

where j is index of sense. According to scores of $s^j \in S_{w^t}$ we can select the most suitable sense s^{w^t} and its corresponding definition g^{w^t}.

4 Experiments and Performance Evaluation

This paper conducts two experiments to evaluate performance and computational costs of PolyBERT. **Experiment-A** aims to compare performance of PolyBERT against prior works. **Experiment-B** aims to evaluate whether batch contrastive learning reduce computational cost during training phase.

Experiments are conducted in Google cloud server, which integrated with NVIDIA A100 GPU (RAM is 40 GB). The operating system is Ubuntu, version of Python is 3.10.0. Deep learning framework is PyTorch 2,3,1+cu121, with CUDA 12.2. In addition, the implementation of the model relies on the Transformers library, version 3.14.0.

This section illustrates setups and results of Experiment-A and Experiment-B in Sect. 4.1, 4.2 respectively.

4.1 Experiment-A: Performance Evaluation

Encoders of PolyBERT are initialled with BERT-Large model in Experiment-A. Therefore, dimension of hidden layer is 1024. For *context-encoder* the heads number of multi-heads attention is 8. PolyBERT is trained on SemCor 3.0, which is a large corpus annotated with senses from WordNet. Similar to prior works, PolyBERT takes SemEval-2007 (**SE7**) as develop set, performance of PolyBERT is evaluated in Senseval-2 (**SE2**), Senseval-3 (**SE3**), SemEval-2013 (**SE13**), and SemEval (**SE15**). Each definition of sense is retrieved from WordNet.

Table 1 (denoted as table in Sect. 4.1) shows the results of Experiment A. Experiment A compares the performance of PolyBERT against prior works, using the F1-score to evaluate performance. Prior baseline works are divided into three categories: (1) **Knowledge-based works**, (2) **Neural networks-based works**, and (3) **PLMs-based works**.

The first block of table displays baselines of Knowledge-based works. MFS refers to selecting the most frequent sense for each target word according to the training corpus. WordNet S1 involves selecting the first sense in WordNet, which is the most common sense. Basile-LESK [2] integrates word embeddings to calculate the degree of overlap between the target word and gloss, representing a variant of the LESK algorithm.

The second block of table outlines baselines of Neural networks-based works. BiLSTM-K [9] uses independent classifiers to disambiguate word senses based on semantics extracted by BiLSTM. BiLSTM-R [15] employs self-attention to

Table 1. Performances of PolyBERT and carious categories of prior works. In this evaluation, F1-score is taken as indicator of performance.

Works	Dev	Test Datasets				Different POS of Test Datasets				
	SE7	SE2	SE3	SE13	SE15	Nouns	Verbs	Adj.	Adv.	All
MFS	54.5	65.6	66.0	63.8	67.1	67.7	49.8	73.1	80.5	65.5
WordNet S1	55.2	66.8	66.2	63.0	67.8	67.6	50.3	74.3	80.9	65.2
Basile-LESK [2]	56.7	63.0	63.7	66.2	64.6	70.0	51.1	51.7	80.6	64.2
BiLSTM-K [9]	–	71.1	68.4	64.8	68.3	69.5	55.9	76.2	82.4	68.4
BiLSTM-R [15]	64.8	72.0	69.1	66.9	71.5	71.5	57.5	75.0	83.8	69.9
HCAN [11]	–	72.8	70.3	68.5	72.8	72.7	58.2	77.4	84.1	71.1
EWISE [10]	67.3	73.8	71.1	69.4	74.5	74.0	60.2	78.0	82.1	71.8
GLU [7]	68.1	75.5	73.6	71.1	76.2	–	–	–	–	74.1
SVC [18]	–	–	–	–	–	–	–	–	–	75.6
ARES [17]	71.0	78.0	77.1	77.3	83.2	80.6	68.3	80.5	83.5	77.9
GlossBERT [8]	72.5	77.7	75.2	76.1	80.4	79.8	67.1	79.6	87.4	77.0
BEM [4]	74.5	79.4	77.4	79.7	81.7	81.4	68.5	83.0	87.9	79.0
PolyBERT	**76.8**	**81.7**	**79.6**	**81.3**	**83.9**	**84.6**	68.5	**86.7**	**88.3**	**81.0**

enhance the representation of semantics. HCAN [11] utilizes sense-gloss pairs as external inputs. EWISE [10] pretrains an LSTM-based encoder to generate embeddings from the graph structure of WordNet.

The third block of table presents baselines of PLMs-based works. GLU [7] uses a gated linear unit to project context and senses into a shared embedding space. SVC [18] compresses senses into candidates to enhance performance. ARES [17] selects the nearest sense based on embeddings of context and glosses. GlossBERT and BEM, as two mainstream approaches, are introduced in Sect. 2.

The last block of table reports the performance of PolyBERT. The results show that PolyBERT, with an F1-score of 81.0 in all-words WSD, outperforms other works across all evaluation datasets. Moreover, outperforming BEM and GlossBERT highlights the benefits of balanced local and global semantic representation in WSD.

4.2 Experiment-B: Ablation Study of Batch Contrastive Learning

Experiment-B ablates batch contrastive learning (denoted as BCPL) of PolyBERT in order to verify whether BCPL reduces computational cost. Because poly-encoder will impact processing efficiency, Experiment-B includes bi-encoder based model BEM as control group to isolate impact of poly-encoder. Therefore, four models are trained to be compared: PolyBERT, PolyBERT-A, BEM-C and BEM, where PolyBERT-A refers PolyBERT without BCPL and BEM-C refers to BEM with BCPL. Four models are trained on SemCor corpus and epochs number are 5. The metric used to measure computational cost is GPU hours, calculated using the following formula:

$$GPU\ hours = N \times duration, \tag{14}$$

where N is number of GPUs and $duration$ is time consumption of model training.

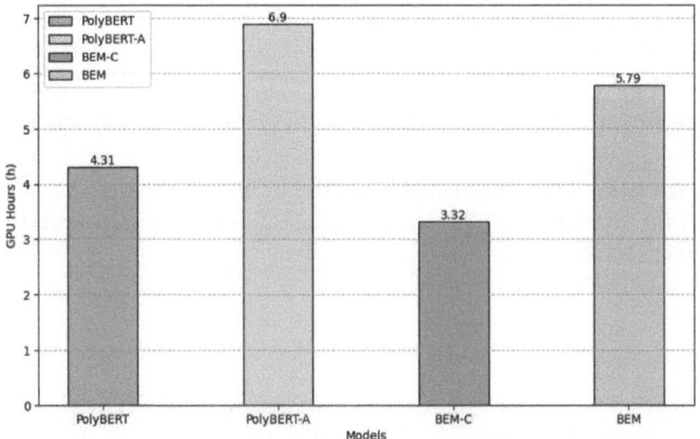

Fig. 3. Result of Experiment-B. Four models are trained on SemCor corpus.

The results, as shown in Fig. 3, indicate that **PolyBERT-A** utilized the most GPU hours, requiring 6.9 GPU hours for training. In contrast, PolyBERT consumed 37.6% fewer GPU hours than PolyBERT-A, demonstrating that BCPL contributes to reducing computational costs. For the control groups, BEM and BEM-C recorded GPU hours of 5.79 and 3.32, respectively, revealing a significant reduction in computational costs for the BEM model when enhanced with BCPL. Overall, these results highlight the effectiveness of BCPL in lowering computational expenses. Additionally, PolyBERT achieves a higher F1-score compared to the other models, further underscoring its superior performance.

5   Conclusion

This paper presents PolyBERT, a BERT-based WSD model using poly-encoders to tackle two key challenges: (1) imbalanced local-global semantic representation and (2) redundant training data costs. For (1), PolyBERT employs multi-head attention to effectively fuse token-level and sequence-level semantics. For (2), it uses batch contrastive learning (BCL), enabling training with only positive samples to reduce computational overhead.

The primary innovations of PolyBERT lie in two aspects: first, the use of a poly-encoder to integrate token-level and sequence-level semantics, which enriches the model's semantic representation by balancing local and global information; and second, the introduction of batch contrastive learning, which significantly reduces training costs by eliminating the need for negative samples.

Based on these contributions, PolyBERT not only improves performance but also reduces computational costs. Experimental results demonstrate that PolyBERT outperforms mainstream models, achieving a 2% higher F1-score. In addition, by employing batch contrastive learning, PolyBERT reduces GPU hours by 37.6% during the training phase.

However, like mainstream works, PolyBERT still requires a large amount of manually labeled data as a training set to achieve optimal performance. This underscores a primary direction for future WSD research: enhancing few-shot approaches [5]. Few-shot WSD approaches will enable the adaptation of WSD systems across various domains, which is crucial in certain fields of expertise.

Acknowledgements. This work was supported by the Shenzhen Sustainable Technology Project (Grant No. KCXST20221021111201002) and Key Research Project (Grant No. JCYJ20220818100810023).

References

1. Barba, E., Pasini, T., Navigli, R.: ESC: redesigning WSD with extractive sense comprehension. In: Proceedings of the 2021 Conference of the North American Chapter of the Association for Computational Linguistics: Human Language Technologies, pp. 4661–4672 (2021)
2. Basile, P., Caputo, A., Semeraro, G.: An enhanced Lesk word sense disambiguation algorithm through a distributional semantic model. In: Proceedings of COLING 2014, The 25th International Conference on Computational Linguistics: Technical Papers, pp. 1591–1600 (2014)
3. Bevilacqua, M., Pasini, T., Raganato, A., Navigli, R.: Recent trends in word sense disambiguation: a survey. In: International Joint Conference on Artificial Intelligence, pp. 4330–4338. International Joint Conference on Artificial Intelligence, Inc (2021)
4. Blevins, T., Zettlemoyer, L.: Moving down the long tail of word sense disambiguation with gloss informed bi-encoders. In: Proceedings of the 58th Annual Meeting of the Association for Computational Linguistics, pp. 1006–1017 (2020)
5. Chen, H., Xia, M., Chen, D.: Non-parametric few-shot learning for word sense disambiguation. In: 2021 Conference of the North American Chapter of the Association for Computational Linguistics: Human Language Technologies, NAACL-HLT 2021, pp. 1774–1781. Association for Computational Linguistics (ACL) (2021)
6. Elzohbi, M., Zhao, R.: ContrastWSD: enhancing metaphor detection with word sense disambiguation following the metaphor identification procedure. In: Proceedings of the 2024 Joint International Conference on Computational Linguistics, Language Resources and Evaluation (LREC-COLING 2024), pp. 3907–3915 (2024)
7. Hadiwinoto, C., Ng, H.T., Gan, W.C.: Improved word sense disambiguation using pre-trained contextualized word representations. In: Proceedings of the 2019 Conference on Empirical Methods in Natural Language Processing and the 9th International Joint Conference on Natural Language Processing (EMNLP-IJCNLP), pp. 5297–5306 (2019)
8. Huang, L., Sun, C., Qiu, X., Huang, X.J.: GlossBERT: BERT for word sense disambiguation with gloss knowledge. In: Proceedings of the 2019 Conference on Empirical Methods in Natural Language Processing and the 9th International Joint Conference on Natural Language Processing (EMNLP-IJCNLP), pp. 3509–3514 (2019)

9. Kågebäck, M., Salomonsson, H.: Word sense disambiguation using a bidirectional LSTM. In: COLING 2016, p. 51 (2016)
10. Kumar, S., Jat, S., Saxena, K., Talukdar, P.: Zero-shot word sense disambiguation using sense definition embeddings. In: Proceedings of the 57th Annual Meeting of the Association for Computational Linguistics, pp. 5670–5681 (2019)
11. Luo, F., Liu, T., He, Z., Xia, Q., Sui, Z., Chang, B.: Leveraging gloss knowledge in neural word sense disambiguation by hierarchical co-attention. In: Proceedings of the 2018 Conference on Empirical Methods in Natural Language Processing, pp. 1402–1411 (2018)
12. Moro, A., Raganato, A., Navigli, R.: Entity linking meets word sense disambiguation: a unified approach. Trans. Assoc. Comput. Linguist. **2**, 231–244 (2014)
13. Navigli, R.: Word sense disambiguation: a survey. ACM Comput. Surv. (CSUR) **41**(2), 1–69 (2009)
14. Parameswarappa, S., Narayana, V.: Kannada word sense disambiguation for machine translation. Int. J. Comput. Appl. **34**(10), 1–8 (2011)
15. Raganato, A., Bovi, C.D., Navigli, R.: Neural sequence learning models for word sense disambiguation. In: Proceedings of the 2017 Conference on Empirical Methods in Natural Language Processing, pp. 1156–1167 (2017)
16. Ruas, T., Grosky, W., Aizawa, A.: Multi-sense embeddings through a word sense disambiguation process. Expert Syst. Appl. **136**, 288–303 (2019)
17. Scarlini, B., Pasini, T., Navigli, R., et al.: With more contexts comes better performance: contextualized sense embeddings for all-round word sense disambiguation. In: Proceedings of the 2020 Conference on Empirical Methods in Natural Language Processing (EMNLP), pp. 3528–3539. The Association for Computational Linguistics (2020)
18. Vial, L., Lecouteux, B., Schwab, D.: Sense vocabulary compression through the semantic knowledge of wordnet for neural word sense disambiguation. In: Proceedings of the 10th Global Wordnet Conference, pp. 108–117 (2019)
19. Wahle, J.P., Ruas, T., Meuschke, N., Gipp, B.: Incorporating word sense disambiguation in neural language models. CoRR (2021)
20. Yap, B.P., Koh, A., Chng, E.S.: Adapting BERT for word sense disambiguation with gloss selection objective and example sentences. In: Findings of the Association for Computational Linguistics: EMNLP 2020, pp. 41–46 (2020)
21. Zhang, G., Lu, W., Peng, X., Wang, S., Kan, B., Yu, R.: Word sense disambiguation with knowledge-enhanced and local self-attention-based extractive sense comprehension. In: Proceedings of the 29th International Conference on Computational Linguistics, pp. 4061–4070 (2022)
22. Zhang, J., He, R., Guo, F., Liu, C.: Quantum interference model for semantic biases of glosses in word sense disambiguation. In: Proceedings of the AAAI Conference on Artificial Intelligence, vol. 38, pp. 19551–19559 (2024)
23. Zhong, Z., Ng, H.T.: Word sense disambiguation improves information retrieval. In: Proceedings of the 50th Annual Meeting of the Association for Computational Linguistics (Volume 1: Long Papers) (2012)

FedDYS: Federated Learning Based on Local Regularization Against Data Heterogeneity

Jiao Xue[1] and Chundong Wang[1,2(✉)]

[1] School of Computer Science and Engineering, Tianjin University of Technology, Tianjin, China
[2] Tianjin Public Security Police Vocational College, Tianjin, China
michael3769@163.com

Abstract. In recent years, federated learning (FL) has received a great deal of attention. It is a distributed machine learning (ML) framework that essentially solves the consensus problem by training a global model. Due to the heterogeneous distribution of data across clients, the local optimal solution often deviates from the global optimal solution. To tackle this heterogeneity in FL, we study the federated optimization problem involving loss functions with possibly non-smooth local regularization terms. This ensures that the optimal model for the local empirical loss is in conformity with the global empirical loss. FedDYS is based on a three-operator splitting that enables us to decouple the local empirical loss and the regularization term. It performs the proximal operation on the local regularization term to handle non-smoothness. In addition, we provide a fixed-point iteration perspective to understand certain FL algorithms. Numerical experiments based on both real and synthetic datasets effectively demonstrate the convergence of the proposed algorithm under partial client participation.

Keywords: Federated learning · Operator splitting · Regularization · Client drift · Heterogeneity

1 Introduction

Federated learning (FL) [13] is a popular distributed machine learning (ML) paradigm where multiple clients work collaboratively to train a global model based on their own localized data. It allows clients to iteratively exchange synchronised local ML model parameters with each other via a central server. However, the presence of data heterogeneity may cause the client models to deviate from the global model, leading to potential divergence or slow convergence. This phenomena is known as client drift [12,23] in the FL literature. In order to address client drift, numerous studies have attempted to employ possibly nonsmooth local regularization techniques. To handle the non-smoothness caused by regularization terms, stochastic subgradient descent methods have

T. Zhu et al. (Eds.): KSEM 2025, LNAI 15922, pp. 444–455, 2026.
https://doi.org/10.1007/978-981-95-3058-8_42

been employed. However, these methods are characterized by a slower convergence rate. Given that proximal operators have the advantages of faster convergence speed and generating sparse solutions during local model training process, we adopt a proximal operator-based method in this paper. Our objective is to solve

$$\min_{x \in \mathbb{R}^d} \left\{ F(x) = f(x) + g(x) = \frac{1}{n} \sum_{i=1}^{n} (f_i(x) + g_i(x)) \right\}, \tag{1}$$

where n is the number of clients and each f_i is the local convex empirical loss objective of each client, which is assumed to be L-smooth, g_i is a closed, convex, and proper function that can be referred to as a possibly non-smooth regularization term of each client.

Meanwhile, several operator splitting methods have been designed to solve non-smooth optimization problems. This is because they can decompose numerically difficult to calculate combinations (for example, smooth and non-smooth functionals) into separate subproblems. Therefore, operator splitting methods have become a strong candidate for developing first-order algorithms for FL applications, such as FedAvg [18], FedProx [15].

Given that problem (1) can essentially be modeled as a three-operator monotone inclusion problem, we propose FedDYS, an algorithm based on the Davis-Yin splitting [7], which is a three-operator splitting method. This method can be viewed as a Douglas-Rachford (DR) scheme with an additional forward term. Our proposal could be used to solve complex optimization problems, especially those that have become increasingly complex due to the need to analyze massive amounts of data in a distributed, fast, or even streaming manner.

Contribution. Our contributions are summarized as follows:

- We understand the FL framework from a new perspective, that is, training a global ML model using distributed optimization algorithms to address the consensus problem. On this basis, we establish a dense connection between FL first-order optimization algorithms and operator splitting methods. This new perspective helps to design more distributed optimization algorithms for FL using operator splitting methods.

- Based on the parallel Davis-Yin splitting (P-DYS) method, we propose a novel algorithm, FedDYS, to alleviate client drift. FedDYS can decouple the local empirical loss and the regularization term, and it performs the proximal operation on the local regularization term to handle non-smoothness.

- Extensive experiments demonstrate that FedDYS outperforms baseline methods in the heterogeneous data scenario.

2   Related Work

FedAvg [18] is one of the earliest algorithms proposed in FL, which is essentially a k-step version of forward-backward (FB) splitting method. In addition, Fed-Prox [15] is an extension of the backward-backward splitting on a regularized FL problem. FedSplit [20] is based on the Peaceman-Rachford (PR) splitting to find the correct fixed point of the FL problem. In general, many state-of-the-art FL techniques can be analyzed and uniformly understood from the perspective of the operator splitting method [16].

To mitigate the client drift, FedDyn [8] employs a dynamic regularizer by leveraging the Euclidean distance. FedDANE [14] extends FedProx by introducing additional inner product terms, and drawing inspiration from the classic distributed optimization algorithm DANE. A-FedPD [24] aligns the global consensus and local dual variables by constructing virtual dual updates, thereby alleviating the dual drift caused by the long-term inactivity of some participating clients during training in smooth non-convex scenarios. The FedCCFA [5] framework adapts to distributed concept drift by decomposing the network into a feature extractor and a classifier. The FedRed [11] framework introduces a method to address client drift in FL by using doubly regularized drift correction. FedFSA [21] proposes a cross-silo feature space alignment method to alleviate the negative impact of data imbalance in FL.

For the application of fixed-point theory in FL, local fixed-point methods [17] are historically proposed as an alternative to local SGD. Despite the success of local gradient descent methods in practice, little is known about local methods and there is much to be explored. Differentially private FL algorithms can be studied as examples of noisy fixed-point iterations [6], which derive a utility result when the operator is contractive. Furthermore, by a simple transformation, methods with inertia, such as Nesterov's acceleration technique, are equivalent to the Halpern fixed-point iteration scheme, which leads to a simple convergence proof for the Nesterov's acceleration technique [25].

3   Problem Space and Design Details of FedDYS

In this section, we first review the FL optimization problem from the perspective of consensus problems. Then, we demonstrate how to develop first-order optimization algorithms for horizontal federated learning through operator splitting methods. Finally, it can be observed that many FL algorithms are fixed-point iteration methods, which aim to find a fixed point of a certain operator.

3.1   Consensus Problem

Based on the distribution of data across clients, the standard FL can be categorised as horizontal federated learning where there is a large amount of overlap in the feature space of the clients but a smaller overlap in the sample space, and vertical federated learning [22,27] where there is a small overlap in the clients' feature space but a large overlap in the sample space. Specifically, from the perspective of the underlying mathematical architecture, vertical federated learning essentially solves the general consensus problem, while horizontal federated learning essentially solves the global consensus problem by training a global ML model. Therefore, FL is a distributed ML framework that solves the consensus optimization problem, which enables efficient implementations of distributed optimization algorithms for training a global ML model without collecting data from clients.

Let $z = (z_1, \ldots, z_d) \in \mathbb{R}^d$ represents the parameter in a global ML model and $x_i = ((x_i)_1, \ldots, (x_i)_{d_i}) \in \mathbb{R}^{d_i}$ represents the parameter in a local ML model, where $i = 1, \ldots, n$, $[d] = \{1, \ldots, d\}$, $d_i \subseteq [d]$. Achieving consensus between the local parameter and the global parameter means that the $j - th$ component of each local parameter $(x_i)_j$, $j \in [d_i]$ corresponds to some global component parameters $z_{g_{(i,j)}}$, where, $g_{(i,j)} \in [d]$, that is, $(x_i)_j = z_{g_{(i,j)}}$. Let $\hat{z}_i = (z_{g_{(i,1)}}, \ldots, z_{g_{(i,j)}})$, then $x_i = \hat{z}_i$. The general consensus problem [19] is

$$\min_{x_1, \ldots, x_n} F(\mathbf{x}) = \frac{1}{n} \sum_{i=1}^{n} f_i(x_i)$$
$$\text{subject to } x_i - \hat{z}_i = 0, i = 1, \ldots, n.$$

Roughly speaking, the global parameter z is the full model parameters, each local parameter x_i can be viewed as the subvector of z corresponding to (nonzero) features that appear in the $i - th$ block of data, which is defined by $\hat{z}_i$. Different subsets of data are stored locally among n participants. Each participant deals only with its own data block and local parameters associated with that block. Let $k = 1, \ldots, n$ and the product space $R = \mathbb{R}^{d_1} \times \cdots \times \mathbb{R}^{d_n}$, the consensus constraint set $E = \{\mathbf{x} = (x_1, \ldots, x_n) \,|\, (x_i)_j = (x_k)_j, \text{if } z_{g_{(i,j)}} = z_{g_{(k,j)}}\} \subset R$ requires the x_i must agree on the components that are shared. For ML, f_i is the empirical loss function over the subset of data assigned to the $i - th$ participant, F is the empirical loss function over the entire dataset and E is the parameter space of the learner.

When $d_i = d$, $(x_i)_j = z_{g_{(i,j)}} = z_j, j = 1, \ldots, d$, that is, $x_i = z$, the general consensus reduces to global consensus. The global consensus problem [19] is

$$\min_{x_1, \ldots, x_n} F(\mathbf{x}) = \frac{1}{n} \sum_{i=1}^{n} f_i(x_i)$$
$$\text{subject to } x_i - z = 0, i = 1, \ldots, n.$$

Generally speaking, the global consensus problem create n copies of the original global parameter z, so that the objective function is separable, but add a consensus constraint set $E = \{\mathbf{x} = (x_1, \ldots, x_n) \,|\, x_1 = x_2 = \cdots = x_n\} \subset \mathbb{R}^{nd}$ that requires all local parameters x_i to agree. In this paper, we will consider the horizontal federated learning setting.

3.2   Problem Formulation

The approach to develop efficient first-order optimization algorithms for given FL problem using operator splitting methods have four steps:

Step 1. Mathematically transform the FL problem (1) into an equivalent global consensus form, and further convert it into an unconstrained problem.

$$\min_{x_1,\ldots,x_n} F\left(\mathbf{x}\right) = f\left(\mathbf{x}\right) + g\left(\mathbf{x}\right) = \frac{1}{n}\sum_{i=1}^{n}(f_i\left(x_i\right) + g_i\left(x_i\right))$$
$$\text{subject to } x_i - x = 0,\ i = 1,\ldots,n, \tag{2}$$

where $x \in \mathbb{R}^d$ is the common global parameter, local parameters $x_i \in \mathbb{R}^d$ are copies of x by each client. Define the product space $\mathbb{R}^{nd} = \mathbb{R}^d \times \cdots \times \mathbb{R}^d$, the subspace $E = \{\mathbf{x} = (x_1,\ldots,x_n)\,|\,x_1 = x_2 = \cdots = x_n\} \subset \mathbb{R}^{nd}$ is the consensus constraint set. Then, utilizing the indicator function, problem (2) is equivalent to

$$\min_{\mathbf{x}\in\mathbb{R}^{nd}} f\left(\mathbf{x}\right) + g\left(\mathbf{x}\right) + l_E\left(\mathbf{x}\right), \tag{3}$$

where $f\left(\mathbf{x}\right) = \frac{1}{n}\sum_{i=1}^{n} f_i\left(x_i\right)$, $g\left(\mathbf{x}\right) = \frac{1}{n}\sum_{i=1}^{n} g_i\left(x_i\right)$ are fully separable [19], $l_E\left(\mathbf{x}\right)$ is the indicator function.

Step 2. Transform the unconstrained problem (3) into an equivalent three-operator monotone inclusion problem.

By Fermat's theorem, the first-order optimality condition of problem (3) is $0 \in \nabla f + \partial g + \partial l_E$. Therefore, we get $\mathrm{Argmin}_E\left(F + l_E\right) = zer\left(\partial\left(F + l_E\right)\right) = zer\left(\nabla f + \partial g + \partial l_E\right)$. Assuming that the optimal value x^* exists, problem (1) can be formulated as an equivalent monotone inclusion problem [10].

$$\text{Find } \mathbf{x} = (x,\ldots,x) \in \mathbb{R}^{nd},\ \text{such that } 0 \in (\nabla f + \partial g + \partial l_E)\mathbf{x}. \tag{4}$$

By using the product space trick, formula (4) makes the operator splitting method can be extended to the case $n > 2$ in problem (2). From the separable sum property of $f\left(\mathbf{x}\right)$, $g\left(\mathbf{x}\right)$ and Proposition 16.8 [3], we get $\nabla f\left(\mathbf{x}\right) = (\nabla f_1(x),\ldots,\nabla f_n(x))$, $\partial g\left(\mathbf{x}\right) = (\partial g_1(x),\ldots,\partial g_n(x))$, left multiplying (4) by $\mathbf{1}^\top$, we have

$$\text{Find } x \in \mathbb{R}^d,\ \text{such that } 0 \in (\frac{1}{n}\sum_{i=1}^{n}(\nabla f_i + \partial g_i) + \partial l_E)x. \tag{5}$$

Step 3. Encode the solution of monotone inclusion problem (5) as fixed points of the related operator $J_{\gamma A}$.

Denote $A = \nabla f + \partial g + \partial l_E = \frac{1}{n}\sum_{i=1}^{n}(\nabla f_i + \partial g_i) + \partial l_E$, for any $\gamma > 0$, we have $0 \in Ax \Leftrightarrow 0 \in \gamma Ax \Leftrightarrow x \in \gamma Ax + x \Leftrightarrow x = (\gamma A + Id)^{-1}x$, and

$$x = J_{\gamma A}x. \tag{6}$$

Here, $J_{\gamma A} = (Id + \gamma A)^{-1}$ is the resolvent of A with parameter γ, and $R_{\gamma A} = 2J_{\gamma A} - Id$ is the reflection resolvent [2] of A with parameter γ. Additionally, $J_{\gamma \partial l_E} = P_E$ is essentially averaging the components. Therefore, the FL problem can be modeled by the fixed-point problem (6), which can be solved by fixed-point iterations.

Step 4. Develop first-order optimization algorithms using operator splitting methods for the FL problem.

Using operator splitting methods to transform problem (5) into a fixed-point iteration equation, we can obtain a family of optimization algorithms. Given that $J_{\gamma(\frac{1}{n}\sum_{i=1}^{n}\nabla f_i + \partial g_i + \partial l_E)}$ is unavailable in most cases, however, each of $J_{\gamma\nabla f_i}$, $J_{\gamma\partial g_i}$, $J_{\gamma\partial l_E}$ is easy to compute. In this scenario, three-operator splitting methods become essential, which can decouple $\sum_{i=1}^{n}\nabla f_i + \partial g_i + \partial l_E$. That is, the resolvent of $\partial\left(\frac{1}{n}\sum_{i=1}^{n}f_i + g_i + l_E\right)$ is split into the sum of the resolvents of $\nabla f_i, \partial g_i$ and ∂l_E. Concretely, inspired by the parallel version of Davis-Yin splitting (P-DYS) method [7], we propose the FedDYS algorithm in the subsequent section.

3.3   Fixed-Point Iterations

In this section, we show that the fixed-point iteration framework is fundamental to many FL first-order algorithms. The theory of fixed-point iterations and nonexpansive operators has been widely applied and extensively studied in mathematical optimization. Denote $T = J_{\gamma A}$, the simplest fixed-point iteration algorithm for problem (6) is the Picard iteration [10] $x^{k+1} = Tx^k$.

For $\text{Fix}(T) = \text{Fix}((1-\theta)Id + \theta T)$, we get the Krasnosel'skiĭ-Mann (KM) iteration [10] $x^{k+1} = (1-\theta)x^k + \theta Tx^k$ for problem (1), which ensures the iteration converges for nonexpansive operator. For instance, let $T = T_{P-DYS}$, we will get the FedDYS algorithm in the later section. For the standard FL problem, let $T = T_{FB} = P_E(Id - \gamma\nabla f_i)$, one can get FedAvg, where T_{FB} can be referred to as the FB operator. Let $T = T_{PR} = R_{\gamma\nabla f_i}R_E$, one can get FedSplit, where T_{PR} can be referred to as the PR operator.

Therefore, we can study FL first-order algorithms as instances of fixed-point iteration, which can provide a framework that simplifies and unifies the process of modeling, analyzing, and solving federated optimization problems.

3.4   FedDYS

In this section, we derive a new first-order algorithm by applying P-DYS method [7] in the FL scenario. The iterative scheme of the P-DYS is, $\forall k \geq 1$

$$(P-DYS)\begin{cases} y_i^{k+1} = \text{prox}_{\gamma g_i}\left(2x_i^k - z_i^k - \gamma\nabla f_i\left(x_i^k\right)\right) \\ z_i^{k+1} = z_i^k + \lambda_k\left(y_i^{k+1} - x_i^k\right) \\ x_i^{k+1} = P_E\left(z_i^{k+1}\right). \end{cases}$$

The P-DYS method can be defined as a fixed-point iteration. The iterative scheme reads $z_i^{k+1} = (1-\lambda_k)z_i^k + \lambda_k\left[\frac{1}{2}(R_{\gamma\partial g_i}R_E + Id)(Id - \gamma\nabla f_i P_E)\right]\left(z_i^k\right) = (1-\lambda_k)z_i^k + \lambda_k T_{P-DYS}\left(z_i^k\right)$. Thereby, the P-DYS method is an instance of the KM iteration with T_{P-DYS}, where T_{P-DYS} can be referred to as the P-DYS operator. We then use this method presented FedDYS to solve the problem (1).

In each round k, a subset of clients S_k is sampled following the same sampling scheme employed in FedDR [26]. Then each sampled client optimizes its local empirical loss and possibly non-smooth local regularization term respectively, which are the local empirical risk objective components. It consists of two main modules: local model update and periodic server parameter aggregation.

Algorithm 1 FedDYS

Initialization: Given an initial point $x^0 \in \mathbb{R}^d$, set $z_i^0 = x^0$, for all $i \in [N]$, the step
    size $\gamma \in \left(0, \frac{2}{L}\right)$, relaxation parameter $\lambda_k \in \left(0, 2 - \frac{\gamma L}{2}\right) \subseteq (0, 2)$

1: **for** $k = 0, 1 \dots, K - 1$ **do**
2:     Sample $S_k \subseteq [N]$ with size n uniformly without replacement
3:     // Client side:
4:     **for** each $i \in S_k$ in parallel **do**
5:         receive x^k from the server
6:         $y_i^{k+1} = 2x^k - z_i^k - \gamma \nabla f_i\left(x^k\right)$
7:         $u_i^{k+1} \approx \mathrm{prox}_{\gamma g_i}\left(y_i^{k+1}\right)$
8:         $z_i^{k+1} = z_i^k + \lambda_k\left(u_i^{k+1} - x^k\right)$
9:         send z_i^{k+1} back to the server
10:     **end for**
11:     // Server side:
12:     server update: $x^{k+1} = \frac{1}{n}\sum_{i \in S_k} z_i^{k+1}$
13:     broadcast x^{k+1} to each client
14: **end for**

Local Updates. In each round of FedDYS, y_i^k and u_i^k calculate f_i and g_i independently. y_i^k tracing residuals from the local model parameter to the global model parameter. u_i^{k+1} acts as an approximation of $\mathrm{prox}_{\gamma g_i}\left(y_i^{k+1}\right)$, which is the proximal operator of g_i at point y_i^{k+1} with parameter γ. $\left\{z_i^k\right\}$ measure the deviation of u_i^{k+1} from the global model parameter x^k.

Global Aggregation. The step $x_i^{k+1} = P_E\left(z_i^{k+1}\right) = \frac{1}{n}\sum_{i=1}^n z_i^{k+1}$ of P-DYS method is performed at the server side using $\left\{z_i^{k+1}\right\}_{i=1}^n$ received from each client.

Remark 1. FedAvg is a special case of k-step version of Algorithm 1.

Proof. By setting $g_i\left(x\right) = 0$, FL problem (1) reduces to the standard FL problem: $\min\limits_{x \in \mathbb{R}^d} F\left(x\right) = \frac{1}{n}\sum_{i=1}^n f_i\left(x\right)$. we then have $\mathrm{prox}_{\gamma g_i} = J_{\gamma \partial g_i} = \left(Id + \gamma \partial g_i\right)^{-1} = Id$, where Id denotes the identity operator. Let $\lambda_k = 1$. Then the local iterative scheme of Algorithm 1 reads

$$\begin{cases} y_i^{k+1} = 2x^k - z_i^k - \gamma \nabla f_i\left(x^k\right) \\ u_i^{k+1} \approx \mathrm{prox}_{\gamma g_i}\left(y_i^{k+1}\right) = Id(y_i^{k+1}) = y_i^{k+1} \\ z_i^{k+1} = z_i^k + u_i^{k+1} - x^k, \end{cases}$$

which reduce to $z_i^{k+1} = x^k - \gamma \nabla f_i\left(x^k\right)$. Therefore, FedDYS can be considered as a basic algorithm for FL problem, which can be integrated with various techniques, such as variance reduction, acceleration, compression and watermarking [9] techniques.

Remark 2. Three operator problem $0 \in \nabla f(x) + \partial g(x) + \partial l_E(x)$ can be return to two operator situations by setting $0 \in \nabla f(x) + \left(\partial g + \partial l_E\right)x$, which is considered by algorithm FedDR [26]. FedDR relies on the two-operator DR splitting, in which the computation of $\mathrm{prox}_{\gamma(g+l_E)}$ is rather complex. While in Algorithm 1, the three-operator splitting scheme can decouple $\mathrm{prox}_{\gamma g}$ and $\mathrm{prox}_{\gamma l_E}$ from $\mathrm{prox}_{\gamma(g+l_E)}$.

4   Numerical Experiments

In this section, we evaluate the convergence performance of FedDYS and compare it with three state-of-the-art algorithms: FedSplit [20], FedAvg [18], and FedDR [26], which are also instances of operator splitting methods. For comparison, we reuse the implementation of FedAvg and FedDR in [26] and implement FedSplit and FedDYS based on it. All experiments were performed in Tensorflow [1] and run on a cluster with NVIDIA Tesla K80 GPUs. We will briefly describe the benchmark datasets and the models used in the experiments.

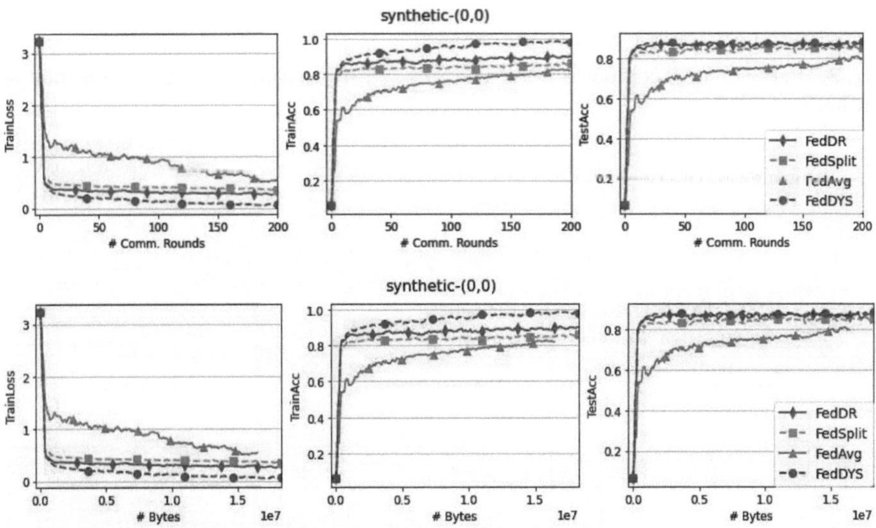

Fig. 1. Performance comparison of FedDYS with existing algorithms on non-iid synthetic-$(0, 0)$ dataset.

Datasets. We used the synthetic and real-world heterogeneous datasets with the same train/test splits as in previous works [15,26], which are synthetic datasets, FEMNIST and Shakespeare. To produce synthetic data and additionally impose heterogeneity among devices, two non-IID datasets, that is synthetic-(l, s), where $(l, s) = \{(0, 0), (1, 1)\}$ are generated with the same procedure as in [15]. FEMNIST [4] is an extended version of the MNIST dataset, which has a total of 62 classes with over 800,000 samples. Shakespeare [18] comes from The Complete Works of William Shakespeare.

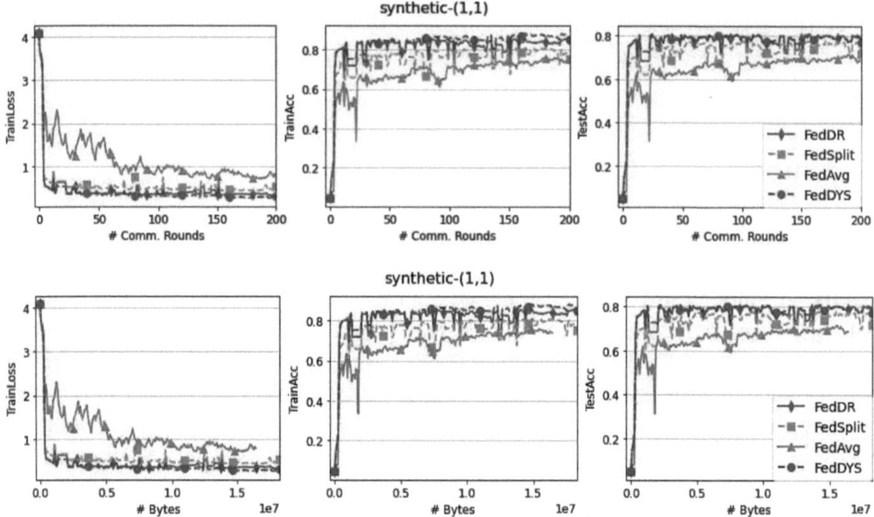

Fig. 2. Performance comparison of FedDYS with existing algorithms on non-iid synthetic-$(1, 1)$ dataset.

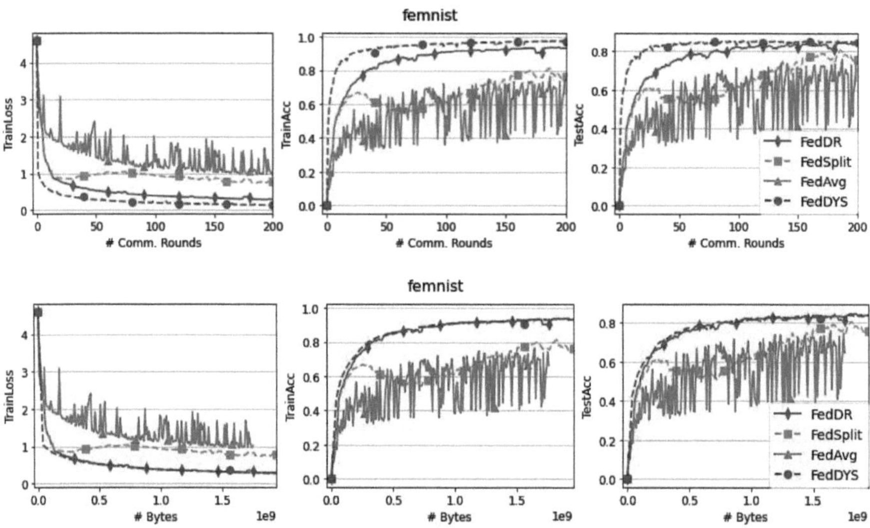

Fig. 3. Performance comparison of FedDYS with existing algorithms on FEMNIST dataset.

Models. We test fully connected neural network of the format input size 60 × hidden layer 32 × output size 10 on all synthetic datasets. The model is trained for 200 communication rounds in total with an optimal learning rate of 0.01. At each communication round, we sample 10 clients out of 30 to perform update for

FedAvg, FedSplit, FedDR and FedDYS. We use multinomial logistic regression model to study an image classification problem on FEMNIST.

Implementation Details. In this experiment, we sample 50 clients out of 200 to perform update at each communication round for all the above mentioned algorithms. The model used for FEMNIST is trained for 200 communication rounds in total with an optimal learning rate of 0.003. We use a two layer LSTM classifier on Shakespeare, which contain 100 hidden units with an 8D embedding layer that associates each speaking character with a different device. The model on Shakespeare is trained for 50 communication rounds in total with an optimal learning rate of 0.08 for FedSplit, FedDR and FedDYS. Parameters for each algorithm such as $\alpha \in (0, 2)$ and $\eta \in [1, 1000]$ for FedDR and $\lambda_k \in (0, 2)$, $\gamma \in (0, 1000]$ for FedDYS are tuned from a large range of values. For each dataset, we pick the most suitable parameters for each algorithm. For the regularization term, we set $g(x) = g_i(x) = 0.01 \|x\|_1$ to verify FedDR and FedDYS.

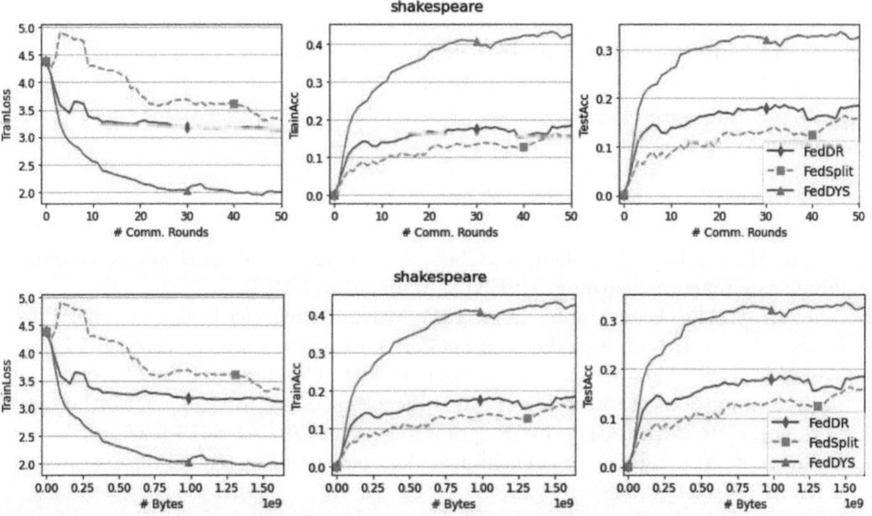

Fig. 4. Performance comparison of FedDYS with FedSplit and FedDR on Shakespeare dataset.

Comparison of Methods. For report the convergence behaviour of FedAvg, FedSplit, FedDR and our proposed FedDYS, Fig. 1 and Fig. 2 indicate the training loss, training accuracy, testing accuracy regarding the same number of communication rounds and show the convergence result with respect to the communication cost on synthetic datasets. Similarly, Fig. 3 illustrates these on the FEMNIST dataset. We have the following observations from them. Overall, FedDYS seems outperforms competing methods under the heterogeneous data scenario. On FEMNIST, FedDYS achieves an accuracy of 83% at the 50th communication round, while the best baseline (FedDR) requires 140 rounds. On synthetic-$(0,0)$, FedDYS's accuracy is 11.04%, 3.79%, and 1.27% higher than that of FedAvg, FedSplit, and FedDR within 200 rounds. A similar trend is observed for other datasets. FedDYS always achieves the target accuracy with fewer rounds. In addition, for comparing algorithms related to the DR operator splitting methods, namely FedSplit, FedDR and FedDYS, Fig. 4 shows that FedDYS significantly working better than FedSplit and FedDR on Shakespeare dataset, which benefit from the local regularization term. This suggests that FedDYS is effective in mitigating the negative effects of data heterogeneity.

5   Conclusion

In this paper, we analyse the FL problem from the perspective of the consensus problem. We then mathematically reformulate the FL problem as the monotone inclusion problem and encode the solution as a fixed point of a related operator. Based on this understanding, we propose a first-order algorithm for FL problem using the three-operator splitting method. Different from much of the existing work, FedDYS performs the proximal operation on the local regularization term to handle the nonsmoothness. The new algorithm supports partial participation and helps to alleviate client drift.

References

1. Abadi, M., Barham, P., Chen, J., Chen, Z., Zhang, X.: TensorFlow: a system for large-scale machine learning. USENIX Association (2016)
2. Aragón-Artacho, F.J., Malitsky, Y., Tam, M.K., Torregrosa-Belén, D.: Distributed forward-backward methods for ring networks. Comput. Optim. Appl., 1–26 (2022)
3. Bauschke, H.H., Combettes, P.L., Bauschke, H.H., Combettes, P.L.: Convex Analysis and Monotone Operator Theory in Hilbert Spaces. CMS Books in Mathematics, Springer, New York (2011). https://doi.org/10.1007/978-1-4419-9467-7
4. Caldas, et al.: LEAF: a benchmark for federated settings. arXiv preprint arXiv:1812.01097 (2018)
5. Chen, J., Xue, J., Wang, Y., Liu, Z., Huang, L.: Classifier clustering and feature alignment for federated learning under distributed concept drift. In: Advances in Neural Information Processing Systems, pp. 81360–81388. Curran Associates, Inc. (2024)
6. Cyffers, E., Bellet, A., Basu, D.: From noisy fixed-point iterations to private ADMM for centralized and federated learning. arXiv preprint arXiv:2302.12559 (2023)
7. Davis, D., Yin, W.: A three-operator splitting scheme and its optimization applications. Set-Valued Var. Anal. **25**, 829–858 (2017)
8. Durmus, A.E., Yue, Z., Ramon, M., Matthew, M., Paul, W., Venkatesh, S.: Federated learning based on dynamic regularization. In: International Conference on Learning Representations (2021)
9. Fang, S., Gai, K., Yu, J.: A joint client-server watermarking framework for federated learning. In: International Conference on Knowledge Science, Engineering and Management, pp. 424–436. Springer (2024)

10. Glowinski, R., Osher, S.J., Yin, W.: Splitting Methods in Communication, Imaging, Science, and Engineering. Springer, Cham (2017). https://doi.org/10.1007/978-3-319-41589-5

11. Jiang, X., Rodomanov, A., Stich, S.U.: Federated optimization with doubly regularized drift correction. In: Proceedings of the 41st International Conference on Machine Learning, pp. 21912–21945 (2024)

12. Kang, H., Kim, M., Lee, B., Kim, H.: FedAND: federated learning exploiting consensus ADMM by nulling drift. IEEE Trans. Ind. Inform. (2024)

13. Konečný, J., McMahan, H.B., Yu, F.X., Richtárik, P., Suresh, A.T., Bacon, D.: Federated learning: strategies for improving communication efficiency. arXiv preprint arXiv:1610.05492 (2016). **8**

14. Li, T., Sahu, A.K., Zaheer, M., Sanjabi, M., Talwalkar, A., Smith, V.: FedDANE: a federated newton-type method. arXiv preprint arXiv:2001.01920 (2020)

15. Li, T., Sahu, A.K., Zaheer, M., Sanjabi, M., Talwalkar, A., Smith, V.: Federated optimization in heterogeneous networks. Proc. Mach. Learn. Syst. **2**, 429–450 (2020)

16. Malekmohammadi, S., Shaloudegi, K., Hu, Z., Yu, Y.: Splitting algorithms for federated learning. In: Machine Learning and Principles and Practice of Knowledge Discovery in Databases: International Workshops of ECML PKDD 2021, Part I, Virtual Event, 13–17 September 2021, Proceedings, pp. 159–176. Springer (2022)

17. Malinovskiy, et al.: From local SGD to local fixed-point methods for federated learning. In: International Conference on Machine Learning, pp. 6692–6701. PMLR (2020)

18. McMahan, B., Moore, E., Ramage, D., Hampson, S., y Arcas, B.A.: Communication-efficient learning of deep networks from decentralized data. In: Artificial Intelligence and Statistics, pp. 1273–1282. PMLR (2017)

19. Parikh, N., Boyd, S., et al.: Proximal algorithms. Found. Trends® Optim. **1**(3), 127–239 (2014)

20. Pathak, R., Wainwright, M.J.: FedSplit: an algorithmic framework for fast federated optimization. Adv. Neural. Inf. Process. Syst. **33**, 7057–7066 (2020)

21. Qi, Z., Meng, L., Li, Z., Hu, H., Meng, X.: Cross-silo feature space alignment for federated learning on clients with imbalanced data (2025)

22. Qiu, P., Liu, Y., Zeng, X.: DiVerFed: distribution-aware vertical federated learning for missing information. In: International Conference on Knowledge Science, Engineering and Management, pp. 299–311. Springer (2024)

23. Son, H.M., Kim, M.H., Chung, T.M., Huang, C., Liu, X.: FedUV: uniformity and variance for heterogeneous federated learning. In: Proceedings of the IEEE/CVF Conference on Computer Vision and Pattern Recognition, pp. 5863–5872 (2024)

24. Sun, Y., Shen, L., Tao, D.: A-FedPD: aligning dual-drift is all federated primal-dual learning needs. In: Advances in Neural Information Processing Systems, vol. 37, pp. 85742–85777. Curran Associates, Inc. (2024)

25. Tran-Dinh, Q.: The connection between Nesterov's accelerated methods and Halpern fixed-point iterations. arXiv preprint arXiv:2203.04869 (2022)

26. Tran Dinh, Q., Pham, N.H., Phan, D., Nguyen, L.: FedDR-randomized Douglas-Rachford splitting algorithms for nonconvex federated composite optimization. Adv. Neural. Inf. Process. Syst. **34**, 30326–30338 (2021)

27. Wang, S., Yu, J., Gai, K., Zhu, L.: ReVFed: representation-based privacy-preserving vertical federated learning with heterogeneous models. In: International Conference on Knowledge Science, Engineering and Management, pp. 386–397. Springer (2024)

Author Index

B

Bi, Yaxin   415

C

Cai, Jianping   116
Cai, Xiaoyan   195
Cao, Jianlong   299
Cao, Xiaopan   299
Chen, Fei   116
Chen, Jiageng   28
Chen, Mingkun   342
Chen, Xin   226
Chen, Yusi   393
Cheng, Lirong   238
Cheng, Xiang   174

D

Dai, Jiaqi   342
Dai, Meng   403
Dai, Yichu   373
Dong, Zhefan   129
Dong, Zheng   77
Du, Jingyong   334
Duan, Jia   150

E

Edward, Estomii   138

F

Fan, Yulong   354
Fei, Zhengdong   373

G

Gai, Yiming   362
Gao, Longxiang   278
Gou, Yan   186
Gu, Jiahao   334
Gu, Xiaoyan   291
Guo, Wenzheng   299

H

Han, Jiancheng   291
Han, Tonghui   415
He, Yihua   291
He, Yonghou   129
Hou, Linyi   65
Hou, Zhehao   325
Hu, Jie   299
Hu, Wei   325, 334
Hu, Yaoyao   299
Huang, Huaze   40
Huang, Xingrui   260
Huang, Xuefei   291, 362

J

Ji, Yatu   317
Ji, Zonghao   278
Jia, Boyuan   174
Jiang, Hezhong   325, 334
Jiang, Min   325, 334
Jiao, Dian   28
Jin, Canghong   373
Jin, Zuhao   1

K

Ke, Jing   269
Ke, Xikai   325

L

Lei, Kai   433
Li, Huanhuan   65
Li, Jiaxun   129
Li, Jie   308
Li, Jingang   77
Li, Shiwei   52
Li, Shu   308
Li, Tongliang   325, 334
Li, Xiaoyu   65
Li, Xingyi   174
Li, Yawei   299
Li, Ying   362

Li, Yongkang 424
Li, Yujun 15
Liao, Jianxiang 52
Lin, Junyu 28
Liu, Baojing 209
Liu, Chang 384
Liu, Fang 325, 334
Liu, Huawen 403
Liu, Jian 52
Liu, Kedong 308
Liu, Qingyun 308
Liu, Rong 278
Liu, Runze 291
Liu, Wanling 116
Liu, Wenjian 163
Liu, Wenmao 104
Liu, Xi 150
Liu, Xiaolu 415
Liu, Xuan 342
Liu, Yi 299
Liu, Zhenyu 52
Lu, Junde 362
Lu, Wenhuan 116
Lyu, Yiheng 174
Lyu, Yuanjie 269

M
Ma, Jie 354
Ma, Jinge 150
Mao, Qiheng 92
Meng, Fanjun 186
Meng, Lai 373
Meng, Weizhi 28
Meng, Zixian 415
Mulvenna, Maurice 415

N
Niu, Zihan 269
Nyamawe, Ally S. 138

P
Peng, Bo 269
Pu, Fei 238

Q
Qiu, Yujing 433
Qu, Youyang 278

R
Ren, Wei 104, 150
Ren, Zhen 238

S
Shang, Wen 260
Shen, Jian 77
Shen, Lele 354
Sheng, Hao 291
Shi, Bin 163
Shi, Danhui 424
Song, Teer 342
Su, Chunhua 28
Su, Housheng 393
Su, Sen 174
Sun, Jianling 92
Sun, Jiazheng 195
Sun, Mengdi 65

T
Tao, Jingmei 40
Tao, Li 129
Tao, Shengnan 433
Tong, Lijing 186
Tursun, Eziz 218

W
Wang, Siyuan 238
Wang, Bailun 317
Wang, Bo 116
Wang, Changlong 299
Wang, Chundong 444
Wang, Han 354
Wang, Hui 354
Wang, Jiapeng 174
Wang, Jiaye 248
Wang, Jie 248
Wang, Jingyi 291
Wang, Kangsheng 384
Wang, Liangguo 218
Wang, Weihong 1
Wang, Yuhang 52
Wang, Zihao 384
Wei, Lina 373
Wei, Mengyuan 52
Wu, Jiaqian 218
Wu, Kang 260

Wu, Nier 317
Wu, Yuheng 424
Wu, Yuxuan 218

X

Xia, Linhan 433
Xia, Weike 325, 334
Xia, Xiaona 424
Xiang, Yanping 342
Xiong, Jichao 28
Xu, Feng 373
Xu, Jialin 40, 260
Xu, Jingwen 260
Xu, Tianxiang 384
Xu, Tong 269
Xu, Xingjian 186
Xu, Zhoujie 403
Xue, Jiao 444

Y

Yan, Faren 226
Yang, Bailin 238
Yang, Da 291
Yang, Dongqiang 415
Yang, Huijie 77
Yang, Mingzhan 433
Yi, Jianhong 40
You, Haochen 209

You, Jinguo 40, 260
Yu, Guo 433
Yu, Lei 15
Yu, Minghao 354
Yu, Peng 226
Yu, Xiao 65
Yuan, Guohui 433

Z

Zhang, Chuhan 40
Zhang, Hongfei 308
Zhang, Huiying 104
Zhang, Qing 403
Zhang, Taihao 278
Zhang, Xianchao 104
Zhang, Yangzong 163
Zhang, Yingying 291
Zhang, Zhongyi 308
Zhao, Cheng 1
Zhao, Wenxin 116
Zhao, Wenxu 424
Zhao, Yike 308
Zheng, Xianghan 150
Zheng, Yutong 342
Zhou, Hongtao 393
Zhu, Haogang 291
Zhu, Tianqing 163
Zhu, Xingyu 424